THE PUNCHDRUNK ENCYCLOPAEDIA
FIRST EDITION

Written and prepared by
Josephine Machon with Punchdrunk

Cover design and layout by
Stephen Dobbie

Routledge
Taylor & Francis Group

LONDON AND NEW YORK

First published 2019
by Routledge
2 Park Square, Milton Park, Abingdon, Oxon OX14 4RN

and by Routledge
52 Vanderbilt Avenue, New York, NY 10017

Routledge is an imprint of the Taylor & Francis Group, an informa business

British Library Cataloguing-in-Publication Data
A catalogue record for this book is available from the British Library

Library of Congress Cataloging-in-Publication Data
A catalog record has been requested for this book

ISBN: 978-1-138-55678-2 (hbk)
ISBN: 978-1-138-55679-9 (pbk)
ISBN: 978-1-315-15035-2 (ebk)

Typeset in Garamond
by Swales & Willis Ltd, Exeter, Devon, UK
Printed by Ashford Colour Press Ltd

THE PUNCHDRUNK ENCYCLOPAEDIA

FIRST EDITION

The Punchdrunk Encyclopaedia is the definitive book on the company's work to date, marking eighteen years of Punchdrunk's existence. It provides the first full-scale, historical account of one of the world's foremost immersive theatre companies, drawn from unrivalled access to the collective memory and archives of their core creative team.

The playful encyclopaedic format, much like a Punchdrunk masked show, invites readers to create their own journey through the ideas, aesthetics, contexts and practices that underpin Punchdrunk's work. Interjections from Felix Barrett, Stephen Dobbie, Maxine Doyle, Peter Higgin, Beatrice Minns, Colin Nightingale and Livi Vaughan, among others, fill out the picture with in-depth reflections.

Charting Punchdrunk's rise from the fringe to the mainstream, this encyclopaedia records the founding principles and mission of the company, documenting its evolving creative process and operational structures. It has been compiled to be useful to scholars and students from a variety of backgrounds and disciplines, from secondary level through to doctoral research, and is intended for those with a fascination for theatre in general and immersive work in particular. Ultimately it is written for those who have dared to come play with Punchdrunk across the years. It is also offered to the curious; those adventurers ready and waiting to be immersed in Punchdrunk worlds.

JOSEPHINE MACHON is Associate Professor in Contemporary Performance at Middlesex University, London. She is the author of *Immersive Theatres: Intimacy and Immediacy in Contemporary Performance* (2013) and *(Syn)aesthetics: Redefining Visceral Performance* (2009, 2011), and has published widely on Punchdrunk's work and other experiential performance practice.

CONTENTS

ACKNOWLEDGEMENTS

This encyclopaedia would not have been possible without the support of the full Punchdrunk team. In particular, I am indebted to Felix Barrett, Peter Higgin, Colin Nightingale, Stephen Dobbie, Rebecca Dawson, Maxine Doyle and Livi Vaughan. Their generosity of time, thought and spirit has made this book what it is.

For vital support across the process an important mention is due to Sophie Mak-Schram, Charley Sargant and Despina Tsatsas. Many thanks also to Laura Soppelsa and Ben Piggott at Routledge for advice and flexibility in bringing this encyclopaedia to publication.

Sincere thanks to Tina Bicât, Elizabeth Booth, Adam Curtis, Codie and Kyle Entwistle, Lyn Gardner, Matthew Grant, Stephen Hodge, Nicholas Hytner, David Jubb, Sharon Lynch, Arne Maynard, Tom Morris, Connie Oppong, Maria Oshodi, Alex Poots, Jonathan Reekie and Joana Seguro for their valuable time and input, with acknowledgement to Camilla Gibbs and Jennie Spears, Jodie Gilliam, Emma Hall, Maggie McTiernan and Sian Weeding for assisting with scheduling certain interviews.

Deepest gratitude is due to Margaret and Simon Barrett. Their incidence throughout this encyclopaedia is testament to their presence and constant support across Punchdrunk's history. Thanks to Margaret in particular for last-minute information retrieval from her extensive Punchdrunk archive.

My thanks to Nicola Stammers at Middlesex University for ongoing support during the writing process. For time, insight and constant reassurance, my unreserved appreciation to Janet Free. For exacting comments, always shared with encouragement and humour, my wholehearted thanks to Sam Beale. And my love to Glenda Cooper and Jessica Cornish, Andrew and Rufus, for bearing the brunt.

INTRODUCTION

The publication of this encyclopaedia marks eighteen years of Punchdrunk's existence and provides a definitive record of its wide-ranging and award-winning practice at this point in its history. It documents in one source for the first time the founding principles that underpin the evolution and mission of the company.

Like a Punchdrunk masked show, there are multifarious journeys that you might choose to take and many paths you can opt to follow in navigating this book. Following encyclopaedic convention, entries are alphabetised and refer to terms that define, illustrate or examine Punchdrunk's approach to practice. In style and content, these intentionally fall between anecdote, reflection and critical analysis. It is formatted in a manner that enables the reader to identify the depths and details that exist in the overall subject matter via the cross-referencing system encouraged by the 'see also' guide, parenthesised at the head of each entry. The compilation works on the assumption that the reader is willing to be curious and find various routes through to enjoy piecing together Punchdrunk's narrative and iterative process, as it evolves and returns along the way. The encyclopaedia's scope necessitates broad strokes while aiming to clarify the advanced ideas that underpin past and present work and motivate future practice. Reference to wider sources has been kept to a minimum although further reading suggested in some entries indicates where critical and contextual debate may be sourced.

Students, teachers and practitioners should note that exercises are offered along the way, set within related topics rather than compiled as a separate entry. As the 'exercises' entry explains, practical activities suggested are not always a Punchdrunk exercise, unless introduced as such, but a route into practices of this kind and a way into examining Punchdrunk's work. Ideas and approaches to practice also nestle quietly within entries for readers to notice, be inspired by and reinvent as they choose. In this regard, note such entries as 'boxes, chest and drawers', 'corridors', 'darkness' or 'mazes' as much as any explicit ideas for practice. Any techniques or exercises shared are intended to be applicable to a teaching environment and can be modified for the reader's own needs.

Productions, by entry, record learnings pertinent to Punchdrunk's evolving philosophy and practice alongside historically significant detail, often providing as yet unrecorded information on these works. References to productions as illustration are also scattered throughout the encyclopaedia. Production entries are not intended as extensive accounts or in-depth critique and, rather than being uniform, the length of each relates to said learnings alongside stories that came to the fore in the compiling of this text. Additional projects are included on the Timeline and Punchdrunk's full works with relevant credits can be sourced via Punchdrunk's website, listed in the References. Websites for referenced artists, artworks or organisations are also provided in this list.

Individual contributions from past and present personnel, alongside entries from external collaborators, offer insight into the company's evolution, process and practice across the three Acts. Each of these has been generated and shaped from conversations between myself and the contributor. Guest entries and personal recollections, whether short citations or longer reflections, have been transcribed from original interviews and edited to enable the voice of each contributor to remain present on the page. For this reason, they intentionally retain an informality of expression and are relaxed in regard to grammatical rules, in order to capture the conversational tone and remain true to that individual's perspective on the work of Felix Barrett and Punchdrunk.

Direct quotations from Punchdrunk core members or collaborators within entries, unless otherwise indicated, have been sourced from original interviews and correspondence conducted by myself in compiling this encyclopaedia, and should be cited to this text accordingly. References to productions within these direct quotations, on the whole and where obvious from which work reference is being drawn (*Firebird*, for *The Firebird Ball*, or *Masque*, for *The Masque of the Red Death*, for example), have been left in the more concise form that the contributor chooses to use. This is further intended to capture the colloquial tone and ensure a fluid reading experience, which acronyms might prevent. In keeping with this, within entries where productions are first introduced in full, abbreviations continue by key word rather than acronym in this manner.

If you choose to navigate this encyclopaedia by alphabetical entry, take your time, working from Aardvark to Zeus, meandering back and forth between 'see also' suggestions as you do, while making use of the index to assist you on your way. To follow a relatively linear route, start at 'Barrett, Felix', move to 'Exeter Experiments' then 'Acts 1–3', and continue in a manner that is steered by the 'see also' entries and productions from there. Cross-referencing the Timeline as you navigate this course may help you on your way. Alternatively, you could forge a path according to a particular discipline or interest beginning with the relevant entry, such as 'costume', 'design', 'dance' or 'lighting', 'in-show-world' or 'space'. Chart a trajectory from there that supports your particular specialism or area of study. If following a subject-specific route, be mindful of Punchdrunk's philosophy that different disciplines work synergistically, as analysis and anecdote will show.

As you read you will notice shared stories from differing perspectives, thematic threads and repeated words that describe both the intention and impact of the work, from practitioner and audience alike. Whatever the path you choose to follow, the reading experience is intended to become one of your own making and one to which, we hope, you will choose to return.

Josephine Machon, May 2018

ABBREVIATIONS

ACE	Arts Council of England
AHRC	Arts and Humanities Research Council
aka	also known as
ART	American Repertory Theater
BAC	Battersea Arts Centre
BBC	British Broadcasting Corporation
BFI	British Film Institute
CCE	continuous comprehensive evaluation
CCTV	closed-circuit television
CEO	Chief Executive Officer
CPD	continuing professional development
DCMS	Department of Digital, Culture, Media and Sport
DJ	disc jockey
ENO	English National Opera
GDF	Greenwich & Docklands Festivals
HQ	headquarters
JFK	John F. Kennedy Airport, New York
KS1	Key Stage 1 in primary education in England, Wales and Northern Ireland
KS2	Key Stage 2 in primary education in England, Wales and Northern Ireland
KS3	Key Stage 3 in secondary education in England, Wales and Northern Ireland
LED	light-emitting diode
LIFT	London International Festival of Theatre
L–R	left to right
MIF	Manchester International Festival
MIT	Massachusetts Institute of Technology
MITE	Multiplatform Immersive Theatrical Experience
NESTA	National Endowment for Science, Technology and the Arts
NT	National Theatre
NYC	New York City
PHF	Paul Hamlyn Foundation
R&D	research and development
RADA	Royal Academy of Dramatic Art
RFO	regularly funded organisation
RSC	Royal Shakespeare Company
SATs	Standard Assessment Tests
SM	stage manager
UK	United Kingdom
US	United States
VR	virtual reality

FIGURES AND TABLES

TIMELINE

Act 1
2000–2008

— *Woyzeck*. Exeter, UK. 2000.

— *The Cherry Orchard*. Exeter, UK. 2000.

— *The Moon Slave*. Exeter, UK. 2000.

— *The House of Oedipus*. Devon, UK. 2000.

— *Jonny Formidable: Mystery at the Pink Flamingo*. Exeter, UK. 2001.

— *The Tempest*. Dartmoor, UK. 2001.

— *Chair*. London, UK. 2002.

— *A Midsummer Night's Dream*. Norfolk, UK. 2002.

— *Sleep No More*. London, UK. 2003.

— *The Tempest*. London, UK. 2003.

— *Woyzeck*. The Big Chill Festival. Ledbury, UK. 2004.

— *Marat/Sade*. The Big Chill Festival. Eastnor Castle, Ledbury. 2005.

— *The Yellow Wallpaper*. Battersea Arts Centre. 2005.

— *The Firebird Ball*. London. 2005.

— *Faust*. London. 2006–2007.

— *The Masque of the Red Death*. London, UK. 2007–2008.

— *Under the Eiderdown*. Primary School Project. UK. 2008.

Act 2
2008–2015

— *The Bunker*. Suffolk, UK. 2008.

— *Holland Park Halloween Fair*. London, UK. 2009.

— *The West Wind*. Kent, UK. 2009.

— *It Felt Like a Kiss*. Manchester, UK. 2009.

— *Tunnel 228*. London, UK. 2009.

— *Sleep No More*. Boston, USA. 2009.

— *Brixton Market*. London, UK. 2010.

— *The Night Chauffeur*. London, UK. 2010.

— *The Duchess of Malfi*. London, UK. 2010.

— *Apricot Project*. London, UK. 2010.

— *Space Invaders Agency*. London, UK. 2011.

— *The Uncommercial Traveller*. London, UK. 2011.

— *Sleep No More*. New York City, USA. 2011.

— *The Crash of the Elysium*. Manchester, UK. 2011.

— *The Black Diamond*. London, UK. 2011.

— *The Séance*. New York City, USA. 2011.

— *And Darkness Descended*. London, UK. 2011.

Timeline

Grey's Printing Press. Primary School Project, UK. 2012.

Up, Up and Away. Primary School Project, UK. 2012.

The Lambeth Walk. Primary School Project, UK. 2012.

Goldwell. Kent, UK. 2012.

The House Where Winter Lives. London, UK. 2013.

The Travelling Museum Society. Primary School Project, UK. 2013.

The Borough. Suffolk, UK. 2013.

The Drowned Man: A Hollywood Fable. London, UK. 2013.

Searching for Stories. Primary School Project, UK. 2013.

The Lost Lending Library. Primary School Project, UK. 2014.

The Invisible College. Primary School Project, UK. 2014.

The Lost Toy Depository. Primary School Project, UK. 2014.

St Ethelburga's Hallowtide Fair. London, UK. 2014.

Prospero's Island. Secondary School Project, UK. 2014.

Beneath the Streets. Cardiff, Wales. 2014.

Against Captain's Orders. London, UK. 2014.

Beneath the Streets. Cardiff, Wales. 2015.

Silverpoint. London, UK. 2015.

Act 3
2015–Present

Greenhive Green. London, UK. 2016.

Sleep No More. Shanghai, China. 2016.

Punchdrunk Enrichment: Imagination, Engagement and Education. London, UK. 2016.

A Small Tale. Primary School Project, UK. 2016.

The Oracles. Primary School Project, UK. 2017.

Kabeiroi. London, UK. 2017.

The Miniature Museum. Primary School Project, UK. 2018.

Small Wonders. London, UK. 2018.

A

aardvark (see also: **awe and wonder**; boxes, chests and drawers; **curiosity**; **discovery**; doors; dreams; haze; Hide-and-Seek; *House of Oedipus, The*; interaction; letters; Moonjuice; one-on-one; portals; text; wardrobes; **Zeus**): An insectivorous quadruped, the aardvark is a medium-sized African mammal. Nocturnal and elusive creatures, they usually wait until dark before emerging from burrows to feed. Previously recorded as one of the Edentata (*Orycteropus capensis*) and 'an intermediate between armadillos and anteaters' in the Shorter Oxford English Dictionary, Vol. 1 (1932, 1973, 1983), this has since been redacted in later editions. Armadillos and anteaters are native to Peru rather than South Africa. Despite sharing the features of names that begin with the letter 'a' and having long snouts, **these** mammals are altogether different species.

Abloy (see also: Bow; **keyholders**; Valet; Zeiss): Abloy keys were designed to fit Abloy locks, invented by the Finnish mechanic and inventor Emil Henriksson in 1907 and first manufactured under the Abloy brand in 1918. Abloy locks are formed from slotted rotating discs, their keys cut from a metal half-cylinder with the indentations in the blade made at different angles so that when the key is turned in the lock it rotates each disk to varying degrees. Abloy locks are among the most secure and thought to be almost impossible to pick. Abloy keyholders are Punchdrunk's highest-level supporters, each of whom choose to remain anonymous.

abstract/abstraction (see also: atmosphere; cinematic; dance; **design**; **dreams**; durational; forests; masked shows; mass production; **multiples**; ritual; **scale**; *unheimlich*): Abstract and abstraction are terms that relate primarily to Punchdrunk's conceptualisation of design. The verb 'to abstract' and thus 'abstraction' names the technique of refining and distilling to the essence of an idea, theme or form to capture and communicate an experience.

Abstraction does not imitate 'the real', but instead suggests what lies beneath the imitative. Through this, abstraction can access an expression of 'the lived', through shape, tempo, tone and a not-quite-ness that taps into perception on a subconscious level. This enables the receiver of that image, action or sound to comprehend a quality of experience and understand the essence of a situation directly. Since his A Level projects, this has been central to Felix Barrett's designs, where hints of the real are made strange via abstraction. The minimalist set-dressing of all early productions up until *Faust*, for Barrett, established a 'purity' of abstracted design, necessitated by a sparsity of props and materials available to create imagined worlds. In terms of Punchdrunk's aesthetic, abstraction and the creation of the uncanny, the dreamlike, via its juxtaposition with and within the touch-real authenticity of the installations, is a key way to tap directly into atmosphere, to throw the logic of the real world out of kilter. As Barrett puts it, 'what do we want the audience to feel? It has to resonate with the senses, the stomach, not the head'. Themes, or symbolic references to narratives and character psychologies, are structured into the layout of floors and embedded in the composition within installations, repeated in symbolic and physical ways across spaces. Livi Vaughan clarifies:

We play with scale as a method of abstraction – the audience is the camera cutting together its own film. Felix refers to the wide, panoramic opening shot zooming to close-up; choosing the long shots and details. As a designer, if you set yourself that exercise, think of yourself as a camera, it's a really different way to experience the work and equally an interesting way to view and create it. But there's no abstraction for the sake of it; all design experiences are in response to the source text, its ideas, characters, moods, in equal measure, all narratively and thematically driven.

Spaces that are wholly abstracted in a masked show, such as the room

filled entirely with prosthetics in *The Drowned Man*, create an *unheimlich* feeling, setting the dream-bordering-nightmare quality of the world. As Vaughan describes, these rooms also have a practical function in that they provide 'zero space' to distinguish the cinematic detail of the more naturalistic installations they accompany, operating like a 'palate cleanser' or photographic negative, a contrast that invites the audience to be ready to absorb the counterpoint.

Abstraction often involves a repetition of mundane items in unusual settings or touch-real objects that have an otherworldly quality, placed to subvert expectation. Such was the case with the series of identical Blessed Virgin Mary statues placed at entrances to every floor of 21 Wapping Lane, for *Faust*. The repetition of these statues across an already linear layout was wholly intended to disorientate the audience, underscoring a sense of the uncanny while simultaneously making audience members question which floor they might be entering. For Barrett, multiples and the blurring of the touch-real with the abstracted 'is all about shifting audience expectation, subverting logic' as much as 'visual and tactile impact'.

Abstraction as a technique and style also resonates with the choreographic approach taken by Maxine Doyle and the company of dancers on any large-scale masked show. In Doyle's choreographic approach the dance language moves away from narrative codes and conventions that solely communicate a story and denote character in favour of more open, figurative movement vocabulary that is inspired as much by the space, surfaces, fixtures and temperature as it is by textual narrative and character psychology; in fact, the former feeds the latter. Movement and gesture in Punchdrunk worlds become multilayered and expressionistic in regard to the themes, situations and moods they convey. High-impact choreography is contrasted with intensely ritualised, abstracted durational performances. Maxine Doyle notes below how the rhythms of these 'places of stillness' establish quiet movements that 'balance out the chaos' from beyond, resonating with Vaughan's idea of the designed 'palate cleanser' that 'changes the pace' of the world. This layering of abstracted aesthetics upon a hyper-realistic setting requires a piecing-together in individual interpretation to collage an overall impression of the world from the combined whole.

access (see also: **Enrichment**; Fallow Cross; **Oshodi, Maria**; Seguro, Joana; stewarding; touch; **touch-real**): Access and inclusivity are important factors for consideration in interactive and immersive theatre practice. Punchdrunk continually seek out and learn lessons in regard to this with every new project. Peter Higgin explains:

Punchdrunk is audience-centred and we consider how our productions will work for all who experience them, ensuring disability or impairment doesn't impact or dilute from the original intent. The sensory nature of the work, and especially the installations, engages and activates the senses holistically. Narrative is important but experience and personal response is equal, if not more important. The work is always created to be accessible and if there are barriers structurally or otherwise, we have a commitment to addressing that.

Colin Nightingale pinpoints the run of *Faust* as a corner of 'major progress in developing an approach to accessibility for masked shows':

Accessibility was a growing area of interest for me as I'd been working on the Mayor of London's Liberty, Disability Rights Festival for a number of years. Initially, due to the free roaming audience that we were encouraging, it felt daunting to take on this challenge, but we had an elevator across all floors of the building that meant that audience with restricted mobility or wheelchair users were catered for on this occasion. Although we allocated them

an access steward to assist their journey in the building we were keen to ensure these individuals were free to explore as they chose. The stewards avoided acting like guides, generally lurking in the shadows unless assistance was requested. Visits to *Faust* by wheelchair users became a regular occurrence, which meant that we could analyse and refine our procedures.

Nearing the end of the run we were informed by the National Theatre Box Office that an audience member with visual impairment was very keen to attend. Initially this seemed a particularly challenging request, but we were keen to facilitate. The audience member, Maria Oshodi, was asked to bring a partner who could act as a guide and they entered the show with the rest of the audience, leaving Maria's guide dog at the box office. We shadowed their journey around the space to ensure their safety and so that we could step in should we need to steer them away from unexpectedly getting caught in the middle of any intense choreography. As it turned out Maria was more drawn to exploring the installations, filled with sound and smells, and it was truly enlightening watching her 'read' the space with her hands. It reinforced the companywide desire; to create multisensory worlds where objects are touch-real as touch is a strong sense for all audiences and a vital method of engagement for visually impaired audiences. Our experiences with audiences with specific access needs during *Faust* really started to give the company confidence in the ways in which accessibility could be prioritised; approached in the right way, our masked shows could be extremely accessible and, on the flipside, there was lots that we could learn about our process from being as inclusive as possible.

Oshodi, in her contribution below, identifies *The Masque of the Red Death* as a seminal example of inclusive practice, 'a stand-out theatrical access

experience' due to Punchdrunk's signature 'inventiveness' being 'worked in absolutely the right way'. Access and inclusivity are central to Enrichment projects and any workshops conducted on site at Fallow Cross. More broadly Punchdrunk continues to explore approaches to access and inclusive practice in its audition procedures for its ensemble of performers, as much as for audience members in masked shows and all other public works.

Joana Seguro, in her entry below, offers an interesting perspective within the broader debate related to immersive practice, access and *exclusivity*. Her argument addresses criticism levelled at Punchdrunk in this regard, especially in relation to the elusiveness of one-on-ones, cameos, one-off events or *Kabeiroi*'s limited tickets and their lottery allocation. Similarly, Barrett muses on Punchdrunk's artistic drive and commitment to creating exclusive moments that reward patience, curiosity and synchronicity in the entry below for 'awe and wonder'.

accidents (see also: building; curiosity; **design**; discovery; **failure**; Fallow Cross; process; R&D; **synchronicity**): A shorthand term for the 'accidents' that occur, by chance, during creative explorations and production. A respect for creative accidents partly defines the Punchdrunk process and relates to the manner in which Felix Barrett and Livi Vaughan respond to the idiosyncrasies of architecture, 'without which the show wouldn't have its personality'. Equally they both recount how enforced 'limitations' and accidents of necessity, as prescribed by the building, discipline the design process for masked shows and offer solutions, influencing both aesthetic and narrative as the show evolves. The creative accidents enforced by the strictures of a building resonate with Punchdrunk's 'scavenging mentality' enforced in the early days of Act 1. Lack of budget and time demanded a 'working with the hand you're dealt', as Barrett puts it, ensuring design was dictated by materials and objects left discarded on site, as much as any existing architectural peculiarities: 'Livi and I might find a hundred folders in the building, so we'd use them in the design, or a room filled with coat-hangers, so we'd retrofit the story to work with that'. Consequently, for Barrett, 'nothing is an accident, it's process. If there's no space for accidents, if everything is premeditated, it's in danger of becoming bland or saccharine'.

'Accidents' also corresponds to the pleasure and delight to be taken in serendipitous discoveries, both artistic and organisational, made as a consequence of getting it wrong as much as through happenchance during the process of devising a project or putting on a production. Maxine Doyle elaborates, demonstrating affinities with Merce Cunningham's chance procedures (see Copeland 2004; Cunningham 1985):

> Much of our creative process is driven by chance. A rehearsal process without creative accidents is a dull one. We search for those accidental moments of surprise not only in the dancing but in light, sound and design. Committing to the 'accidental' in art suggests an openness towards an organic creation and invites us to play in a chaotic world. Accident and imagination are a formidable duo.

Peter Higgin adds as an aside,

> I can think of plenty of actual accidents and injuries to performers and crew, which highlights both the dynamic nature of this performance environment and, in early productions, the process of audiences finding areas of danger that we hadn't foreseen.

Correspondingly, Colin Nightingale shares memories of breaking both feet during the build of *The Bunker*, forging on despite the pain, and recuperating once diagnosed. An 'actual accident' which led him to 'daydream in ways that working life had not permitted for a few years', and so, fittingly, by chance and synchronicity, led to the creation of *Clod & Pebble*.

Act 1 (**2000–2008**, see also: **accidents**; adrenalin; **audience**; atmosphere; Balfour, Katy; **Barrett, Felix**; Barrett, Margaret and Simon; Bicât, Tina; Big Chill, The; ***Chair***; ***Cherry Orchard, The***; collaboration; community: '**company building**'; crescendo; darkness; decay; Dobbie, Stephen; Doyle, Maxine; durational; Entwistle, Codie and Kyle; **Exeter Experiments**; **failure**; *Faust*; *Firebird Ball, The*; Gardner, Lyn; Gideon Reeling; Higgin, Peter; Hodge, Stephen; ***House of Oedipus, The***; Hytner, Nicholas; *Jonny Formidable: Mystery at the Pink Flamingo*; **journeying**; Jubb, David; lighting; **loops**; *Marat/Sade*; Marsh, Colin; masked shows; **masks**; *Masque of the Red Death, The*; Maynard, Arne; McDermott, Laura; *Midsummer Night's Dream, A*; Minnigin, Aaron; Minns, Beatrice; ***Moon Slave, The***; Morris, Tom; music; Nightingale, Colin; **one-on-one**; Oshodi, Maria; **process**: '**punch-drunk**'; *Quest of a Wave*; Red Death Lates; reveal; Seguro, Joana; ***Sleep No More*, London**; synchronicity; Taylor, Jennifer; ***Tempest, The*, 2001**; ***Tempest, The*, 2003**; text; timeline; ***Tunnel 228***; Vaughan, Livi; ***Woyzeck*, 2000**; ***Woyzeck*, 2004**; *Yellow Wallpaper, The*): For Felix Barrett, Punchdrunk's Act 1 'is a lifetime's worth of work'. The first three years in particular, 2000–2003, were a condensed and concentrated period of experimentation and discovery, which Barrett describes as 'the blueprint' for all the work that followed through Act 2, and for certain concepts and forms that are only now being realised in the early stages of Act 3, such as Punchdrunk Travel. The cross-references provided above hint at the breadth of areas that were covered across this period and provide a guide for the reader in going on this journey, by entry, with Punchdrunk in order to locate the details and depths of the discoveries that were made.

Barrett summarises in regard to masked shows, 'in the first few years, up until *Firebird* the blueprint for everything we were going to do had already been drawn up', setting 'the purity of the idea' as a foundation for

practice. *Woyzeck*, 2000, as the production that originated this format, thus marks the beginning of Act 1. Barrett recalls that it was around graduation that Sally Gibson (since Scott) and Joel Scott (who would go on to form their own company, Goat & Monkey, in 2002) suggested that they join together to start a theatre company, 'because we were all trying to do something similar' with the intention of taking turns 'to do our own different styles of work' (Barrett 2012). Punchdrunk Theatrical Experiences, named by Barrett, initially comprised a collective of like-minded Drama graduates. In addition to Gibson and Scott, it included Peter Higgin, Euan Maybank and Becky Smith. Higgin notes, 'the support of tutors, including Jon Primrose, Jane Milling and Stephen Hodge, cannot be underestimated in our early practice', adding:

> During our final term at Exeter I had unassumingly, and by merit of having some practical nous, positioned myself as a production manager of sorts. Summer jobs had often been manual in nature and, as an assistant in a boat yard, I understood how to lift and store things. Felix saw the practical in me and that was going to be needed if Punchdrunk was going to get off the ground. I was completely entranced by Felix's third-year work; it was innovative and had a real sense of adventure. I knew that the work was going to be ground-breaking and I wanted to be a part of making that happen.

Barrett describes the 'first year of Punchdrunk, the first four shows' as being committed to experimentation, composed of 'different forms and shapes' (2013). It was driven by the mantra of 'don't talk about it, do it'; focus on a shared goal and rather than discussing it endlessly, put it swiftly into practice to achieve the objectives. *The Cherry Orchard*, in 2000, was the first project to execute this. Barrett describes this project as 'having another go at doing a masked show, this time with real-world intervention' (2013).

Attracting an audience of approximately thirty-five, it was a durational piece that took place across four hours:

The Cherry Orchard was the same as *Woyzeck*, using the mask again to probe that but still using speech and a more conventional but filmic performing style. It was so intimate, it was in a domestic town house, so the scale was fine, performers could whisper sections of speech. Chekhov's language is so sparse anyway, all the action happens between the lines, it was perfect. That felt good, solid. We played with the idea of intervention. The audience picked up their mask in one house, had to walk down the road to another but unbeknownst to them we had a plant on the street, a 'real' person walking past who asked for money, partly as a device to destabilise the audience. For most of the audience it didn't work because they knew he was an actor, a friend, but for some American tourists who were in town thinking they were booking to see *The Cherry Orchard* in the Northcote Theatre, it worked amazingly. It was seeing that 'real' audience response, as opposed to my friends and fellow graduates, that gave me confidence.

(2013)

The Cherry Orchard employed new Punchdrunk devices and flagged important learning for Barrett. It was the first point at which there was a fusion of film within the narrative and aesthetic, the first use of intervention to blur the boundaries of the real and imagined world and a critical learning curve in regard to the use of masks, due to some unexpected audience responses within the world, as detailed in *The Cherry Orchard* entry below. This factor also demonstrated to Barrett the need for clear instructions, alongside a curation of sound, to guide the audience and establish rules for engagement within the world.

Barrett secured Poltimore House for the next project, *The House of Oedipus*, in the late summer of 2000, a project that was important for the many useful lessons it taught as a consequence of its 'failings'. It proved the loop format was now perfected; however, 'the mask was wrong, cumbersome, uncomfortable'. Secondly, putting duration to the test by running a performance across 'six hours rather than three' proved vital in teaching Barrett about logistics for site-based, durational work, 'where the audience is allowed to follow your every move and there's no backstage', highlighting basic problems: 'some performers didn't even get a loo break'. Yet the pivotal learning for Barrett related to lighting, speech and 'the reveal':

Outdoors, daytime, six-hour durational, masks. Didn't work. Because of the natural light... Punchdrunk is about curiosity, exploration and discovery of those beats of wonder. If you can see in the distance what you're going to discover in five minutes time, once you actually get there, it invalidates it; there's no reveal. You need the reveal. The reveal is crucial. Planning any new show now, we start from the end, that final image. There have been two eureka moments for me. I remember them because the adrenalin is so incredible and then the euphoria you get from it all clicking into place. The first eureka moment was the mask and the second one was about the reveal. The reveal is key.

(2013)

Stage-crafted as opposed to natural lighting was 'imperative, because without it you can't control the audience'. In regard to creating work outdoors: 'if you can't control the environment the atmosphere bleeds out the sides. Outside there are always holes that are sucking atmosphere away . . . you need an atmosphere to be thick with the crackle of distant magic' (Barrett 2013).

It was now the end of the summer and the mainstay of the collective were drifting back to family homes, jobs, travel, all leaving Exeter. Barrett had to plan the next projects around holiday periods, times where he could galvanise forces to produce the work. Undaunted and eager to test new approaches that addressed the lessons learned, Barrett incubated the concept for his next project and set about securing Poltimore House again to make it happen. The problem of the reveal and lighting when outside continued to bother him. Autumn was approaching so Barrett knew he wanted to harness the potency of Halloween; he also knew that it needed to be a 'mini-project'. He devoured short ghost stories to find a source that would be stimulus for and support a one-on-one so he could further investigate this form, 'distil it down to a show for one audience member at a time'. The form matched the uncanny atmosphere that he wanted to tap into: 'I'd been reading about Marina Abramović and I knew that, theatrically, the form would *feel* more dangerous if you're by yourself' (2013). Barrett believed this was an alternative solution to the problem of audience-getting-in-the-way-of-audience. With the mask, audiences are cast as anonymous, passive ghosts, an absent-presence, becoming part of the aesthetic for other audience members while also enabling them to 'get close to the performer', share the secrets of the same playing space. With the one-on-one it is the 'opposite end of the spectrum' in that audience is cast as protagonist, '*so* present, you're the lead character'. When clear on this concept, it was an orchestrated film soundtrack combined with alighting on the perfect source text that unlocked the problem of the reveal in daylight for Barrett. The music 'had this surge to it, a huge crescendo, and I knew that had such theatrical power when I listened to it that there was a show inside it'. At the same time Barrett had read Barry Pain's 1901 gothic story, *The Moon-slave*, with an ominous italicised sentence, '*and she was no longer dancing alone*' (Pain 1901, 57). For Barrett, this sentence implied 'raw, theatrical crescendo'. With these factors combined, Barrett's second 'eureka moment' was born. If Poltimore House 'didn't work in the daytime', what if 'we took it at night-time and controlled the environment with this story and this bit of music'. Darkness, gothic source that was pure one-on-one material, a musical crescendo and a crumbling site charged with its own narrative and atmosphere: 'that was *The Moon Slave*' (Barrett 2013).

The Moon Slave was planned to be performed in the twilight hours of autumn, the spell of decay all around, where magic and macabre hung in the ether. The purest of Punchdrunk forms; a one-on-one journey, across Exeter countryside, employing a rendezvous for the lone audience member that set the adrenalin going, a masked, silent chauffeur, a soundscore played out between a car stereo and then wholly via headphones, a crumbling mansion, evocative installations, pyrotechnics and a powerful reveal, with audience members gradually realising they have become the protagonist. It also incorporated a momentary beat of intervention that could easily be missed if on the wrong side of the car for the journey back; a role for which Joel Scott briefly returned.

Furthering the techniques of a one-on-one encounter, an experiment for Barrett was the audience member wearing a headset on which much of the narrative and soundscore played out. As Barrett puts it, 'it was a way of controlling the environment, between the ears, in the imagination' (2013). This was a time before iPods and smart phones, so a basic Walkman was used, the same piece of equipment for each audience member. Barrett recalls seeking the expertise of technical tutor, Jon Primrose, to find out how to 'make a track fire at the right point on a journey':

> We had to get a car battery and a radio transmitter and to follow the audience member at a distance, transmitting a signal to the headset while changing the tracks manually. It was really lo-fi but it worked. It meant that when the protagonist was reaching a gate in the story, the audience was meeting a gate at the same time.
>
> (Barrett 2013)

Higgin remembers Barrett and Becky Smith 'creeping ten metres behind the audience member' as this was all the range permitted, while he 'hid in a bush waiting for a phone call to let off a flare'. Higgin adds, across the four-day run, 'Felix burnt a hole in his trousers because the battery acid leaked'.

The Moon Slave provides illustration of achieving an ambitious vision 'with no money at all'. Barrett notes the pleasures of gaining the technical knowledge required 'to transmit radio signals and cue a marine flare in time with a remote soundtrack'; details that would nowadays make use of advanced technologies and expensive resources. Barrett financed these early productions, collaborators funding themselves:

> I worked in a coffee shop, at the restaurant in the evening and then did bits of lighting, technician stuff, for the university. We built and rehearsed *The Moon Slave* over five days and then performed it for one night. That was it. It only cost £200 because so much of the resource was given via the university. I'm also very lucky that my parents loaned me their car.
>
> (Barrett 2013)

Higgin adds, 'It was just us, no volunteers, minimal infrastructure. Brutal'. After *The Moon Slave* Higgin recalls a Christmas experience created 'for a select few influencers in the South West of England', invited to meet at a location in Exeter and 'to look to the east':

> Approximately five miles due East we were frantically wrapping a tree in tin foil and attempting to make a generator work to illuminate it, a star in the distance, a nod to the journey of the Magi. My chief responsibility was to fire a marine flare high into the night sky. Our intention was, audiences would have been treated to a brief moment of magic, a light on the horizon. In execution things didn't quite go to plan, visibility was poor and light

pollution hampered our efforts. Yet we learned about communications, audience care, and the problems and potentials of technical effects.

Punchdrunk went on to experiment with *Jonny Formidable: Mystery at the Pink Flamingo* in early spring 2001. By deploying the principle of the headset as used in *The Moon Slave*, but in a studio environment with multiple audience members, as opposed to one at a time, the project failed 'because the audience read it as a theatrical experience rather than an event that was invading real life' (Barrett 2013). Undeterred, keeping up the momentum and despite the problems of the Magi event, Punchdrunk was commissioned by the National Trust to create a piece for Buckland Abbey in Exeter. *The Tempest*, 2001 resulted. This was to be the last of Punchdrunk's Exeter projects and would offer further lessons in performing style. Buckland Abbey and its grounds were reimagined as Prospero's Island. Excited by the increased scale of the event, Barrett blended internal and external environments of the site effectively, making use of twilight to good effect, rather than being hampered by daylight as with *House of Oedipus*. Despite the setting of Buckland Abbey being more at one with the language of Shakespeare, Barrett still noted that speech itself was incongruent with the experiential form. Summarising this period, Barrett 'loved the Exeter shows because there was no barometer for success. It wasn't good or bad, it was just amazing to be doing something'. Higgin adds, 'they experimented with form and scale and created a shared experience and a dialogue amongst us'.

Armed with this knowledge, Barrett took the decision to return to London. The London projects produced during 2002–2004 saw the formation of new creative relationships with individuals who would become and remain members of Punchdrunk's core creative team. Higgin remained in contact with Barrett while training and working as a teacher on the Isle of Wight and continued to collaborate in any way needed on projects during his holidays. Similarly, Maybank offered support as needed while pursuing a career in technical theatre. Stephen Dobbie was introduced to Barrett and Higgin through a mutual friend which resulted in him designing the poster and flyer for *Chair*. Dobbie would then go on to design the publicity material and audience bar-cum-waiting-area for *The Tempest*, 2003. It was as a consequence of *Chair* that Barrett met Colin Nightingale who became an integral member of the core creative team.

For Barrett, 'so much thinking had been worked through in the early shows', between 2000 and 2002. The learning at each stage of Act 1, from the perfunctory and prosaic to the virtuoso, continued to be embedded in the questions being asked, as much as the strategies being put in place in each project from then on. In simple terms, 'doing anything that's outside of a three-hour show on a stage is complicated'. Underpinning the practice, and a fundamental principle for Punchdrunk's process during the early experiments of Act 1, was how each new form or technique trialled could only ever prove effective or otherwise when 'putting an audience through the world'. Across the London projects of 2002, Barrett continued to explore a gestural and durational language in the performing style, first uncovered with the Miranda moment, as described in *The Tempest*, 2001 entry, below. The Exeter projects had proven that naturalistic speech, within the performance style he was evolving, was fundamentally flawed, failing to work within the installation-led, site-sympathetic experience on a practical level as much as in terms of it jarring with the aesthetic. Whether a landscape that stretches beyond one's line of vision as was the case with *The House of Oedipus* at Poltimore House and *The Tempest* at Buckland Abbey, or a vast, cavernous space such as Deptford's Old Seager Distillery for *The Tempest*, 2003, there was the problem of volume. Where the event requires intimacy, whispering would not work across an expanse, as it did within the confines of the domestic

setting for *The Cherry Orchard*. Barrett by now was certain that his work required a capacious physical language that had the potential to match the immensity of the space and equally pull focus, to create closeness. *The Tempest*, 2003 had incorporated a dancer as a sprite who improvised around the space. Barrett remembers how, at the time, he focused more on how this dancer might disappear into darkness so the audience were unable to locate her, yet equally he knew that dance might provide a key to a more gestural language that he was searching for, to fill the space physically and remove the need for speech. With this in mind, the events that led to *Sleep No More* proved crucial.

Barrett made contact with the organisation Independance as he had noted they had produced a site-based piece by a choreographer, which he had been keen to see, being 'desperate to meet others making site-based work'. The performance was sold out but, as a consequence of his phone conversation, he was made aware of the Independance Prize for producing support the closing day for applications within that same week. Barrett knew that exploring dance would offer him a way to test a new, physical performance language in space. Given the limitation in time and the consideration of a new discipline within the known format, *Sleep No More* was 'an entirely spontaneous idea'. In the middle of *The Tempest* run, alongside the fact that Barrett had been listening to 'a new, sumptuous score for *Vertigo*', his idea for the application 'came together very quickly':

Femme fatale, power, lust, ambition, vengeance. Film noir *Macbeth*. As it's a dance application, let's go all out and do everything physically. I was aware that I was so late to the party and had no track record in the dance world so was a bit of an anomaly. I attempted to demonstrate the aesthetic, what *the experience* would be. Rather than sending an email, I delivered a suitcase. Open the suitcase and there's a man's belongings,

a suit jacket, other objects, his life-story packed up. It's only if you hunt for it that you find the application as a letter in the breast pocket of the jacket – drafted on an old-fashioned typewriter.

This suitcase was a portent, a tangible indication of the experience that would follow if the proposal were accepted. By presenting the written proposal as a letter in the style and era of the world and, further still, *hiding* this in the breast pocket of the suit so it had to be discovered by a curious recipient, Barrett's intention was that the suitcase would become a 'living' illustration, a preview, to tantalise and communicate 'the sense of mystery and discovery' that would exist in the world, and to make tangible in the hands of the reader of the proposal that it was about *the journey* to the letter, as much as what was uncovered once located and read. It was designed on the principle of 'don't tell the audience everything, give them as little information as possible' but with as much atmosphere as can be manufactured, 'to allow their imagination to fill in the gaps', to encourage the recipient to *work at*, and so work out, what the event might become. For Barrett, the suitcase was a physical means of expressing 'the experience of exploring a Punchdrunk space and showing that the deeper you go the more that you'll discover'. It was the last hour of the deadline for all applications to the Independance Prize when Barrett arrived with this suitcase, dropped it off and waited. Luckily for him, it ended up in the hands of Colin Marsh, who proved to be that inquisitive adventurer. A couple of days later Marsh called and told him that Independance wanted to go with his proposal. Marsh himself agreed to take it on and made a point of visiting *The Tempest* to experience Barrett's work. It was Marsh who suggested Barrett meet with Maxine Doyle. They did and immediately clicked. Doyle recalls:

Felix and I agreed to collaborate with no real knowledge of each other's work. During our first meeting, in The Prince Albert, a pub in Brixton, we talked about David Lynch, Robert Wilson and live art. We shared similar tastes, which is always a useful indicator of successful collaborations. I was intrigued and inspired by the vision, confidence, ambition and fun of Felix. I trusted Colin Marsh as both a friend and a mentor. That was the beginning.

Marsh wrote a successful Arts Council application, awarding Punchdrunk £30,000, the maximum for project funding at the time. Barrett adds, 'without a doubt I depended on Colin Marsh then. I remember thinking that he's the person who knew how the industry worked':

Up until the success of the Indepen*dance* application and being introduced to Max, no-one had offered anything, I'd always driven and pushed for it, I extended the request to others. That was the first time someone extended an offer to me, which meant the project had a different emphasis from the off. Prior to that my experience of making stuff happen was like being at a standstill, with no motion unless you physically take a step. But if someone extends an arm towards you to help pull you, that feels very different.

With Doyle now also in the mix, an exploration of dance as the embodied language that could match the scale of the space and equally create a direct intimacy that Barrett had been searching for in large-scale events was, literally, set in motion. *Sleep No More*, presented for the first time in a dilapidated Victorian school building, saw dance become a key element in the masked show aesthetic, merging perfectly with site and installation as affective modes of storytelling. In so doing, it brought core performers into the fold including Sarah Dowling, Hector Harkness, Geir Hytten and Robert McNeill. For Barrett:

That first *Sleep No More* was exciting because we were growing up.

It still had the threat and danger of early shows where the police would come, and no heating in the building, so it was endurance for us getting it on, endurance for the performers every night, but it had a purity. It still felt within the realms of performance art; the sense of suffering, with bodies steaming in that cold space as they moved. It wasn't a sustainable process but, my gosh it had a power.

Higgin, now working as a teacher on the Isle of Wight, took his A Level Theatre students to visit *Sleep No More* as a field trip. The manner in which it inspired them, as Codie Entwistle eloquently describes below, demonstrated to Higgin the potency of the work and the immersive form as a model of pedagogical as much as artistic practice. Lyn Gardner reviewed the production which brought the company wider acclaim. The Big Chill projects, *The Firebird Ball* and *Faust* saw a further galvanising of Punchdrunk's collaborators, including Livi Vaughan and Beatrice Minns as well as Katy Balfour, Sam Booth, Kate Hargreaves and Kathryn McGarr.

From *Sleep No More* onwards Punchdrunk's creative process, operational structures and the company itself expanded. *Sleep No More* and *The Firebird Ball* were the first productions where there were funds, albeit limited, to pay people. With success and growth, setting the company up as a charity plus funding bids, there was a need for a board which meant that the complexities of professionalising a collective that was nomadic and project-driven to its bones were slowly uncovered and addressed. Key figures such as Sally Scott, Laura McDermott, Tom Morris, Nicholas Hytner, David Jubb and Lyn Gardner played important roles in supporting Punchdrunk's practice and thereby assisting its rise to prominence, to which their individual entries bear testament. The support of the National Theatre saw what would be Punchdrunk's grandest production to that point, *Faust*. Across *Faust* Punchdrunk's ensemble of performers

grew, welcoming Conor Doyle, Fernanda Prata and Vinicius Salles, with stalwarts such as Matthew Blake and Kath Duggan joining for *Masque of the Red Death*.

Each of the Act 1 projects through to *The Masque of the Red Death* cemented working processes and, for Barrett, felt like 'seismic steps'. As Barrett summarises, much of the innovation acknowledged as the Punchdrunk method occurred in the first three years of the company's practice: 'in terms of the ground covered conceptually, practically, physically'. Those early years were also vital in terms of the core creative team coming together, 'sharing a mindset and plotting for the future'. From Barrett's A Level work, through his Exeter experiments, to the early Punchdrunk London explorations there are notable themes that pervade; the doggedness and determination that made projects happen; a desire to learn from mistakes in order to hone formulae and form; synchronicity and connectivity in creating work *and* building workforce; respect for creative collaboration underpinned by an acceptance of the long, hard slog to make it happen; pulled together by Barrett's approach and ability to inspire others in that team effort.

Act 1's collaborative practice produced a shared shorthand among Punchdrunk's core members; a vocabulary for making the work. With each new masked show across Act 1, for Barrett, Punchdrunk was moving forward with form and approach 'in leaps and bounds':

We were resourceful. Creating narratives and themes from materials that could be scavenged in order to achieve scale. Our approach as makers is that you have to make the best of the hand that you're dealt. An equivalent exercise nowadays, if there's nothing already available on site, would be to go to the local pound shop and use whatever bulk item's available as your basic material to make a show.

Act 1

It is a principle that was exposed across Act 1, exploring what could be achieved with as little resource as possible but with as big an imagination as could be mustered, sharing that with the audience: 'how can you manipulate the audience imagination to fill in the gaps?'. In this way, reflecting on 'the creative leg work' that got Punchdrunk to Act 3, for Barrett:

The hard graft occurred in Act 1. The hunger to break new ground was matched by Colin Nightingale, Pete and me loading, unloading and driving vans full of stuff, spending hours sewing, putting up fabric, packing, repeat, learn, learn, learn. If we hadn't had that time we'd be doing different jobs now. We were so responsive – it's quite a strange place to be now where we're imagining future shows and we have the potential to get a certain amount of financial support to spend on building something from scratch. It's almost the opposite approach to the work we made in those first seven years which relied on what we could scavenge to turn those ingredients into a show. It was blissful, artistically, those first seven years because you had to make the best of what was around you, a very different process to now.

If Punchdrunk's ideology, forged through hard work and practical application, was birthed during Barrett's Exeter experiments and nurtured across the first two years of Punchdrunk productions ('testing ideas as a means of plotting a process for the future'), first steps towards professionalising would follow suit. With the scale of *The Masque of the Red Death* and the collaboration with BAC, the need for operational structures to support working processes became clear. Barrett recalls:

I remember being astounded because BAC would have meetings about the next meeting. At that point we had a complete and utter lack of structure, and the idea of a meeting was alien. We were just making work – there was no

point in having a meeting to talk about it because we were doing it. I didn't even see the point in having an office, but Colin Marsh secured us one in Clapham and Jennie [Taylor] was our single employee.

Barrett, Dobbie, Doyle, Higgin, Marsh and Nightingale, during March 2008 while *The Masque of the Red Death* was enjoying a successful run, took a trip to the East Sussex seashore, Camber Sands, for time and space to reflect, and be inspired by Derek Jarman's Garden in neighbouring Dungeness. This time of reflection was of great significance to Higgin, setting in motion plans for Enrichment:

It was the first time the core team had ever left a show, to a capable production team that we trusted. That, in itself, felt like a serious step, the first time that none of us were present on site. Punchdrunk's work had always been project-based and, although there was a sense of a core company, beyond project work there wasn't a mechanism for regular communication or gathering everybody together to talk about company business. It was the first time we'd spent any time together outside the context of 'making work'. It's remarkable to think that, despite Punchdrunk existing strongly in the public consciousness, its infrastructure was still incredibly fragile and undeveloped. Occurring around the time we first received PHF and RFO Arts Council funding, which enabled and required us to make space for imagining how the future might look, it was a chance to dream and aspire.

For Barrett it allowed time for 'the imagining of a laboratory, a space for designers, performers, community – everything that Fallow Cross now is'. On the cusp of what was to become Act 2, he firmly believed Punchdrunk should continue the experimentation of Act 1 and explore practice beyond the masked shows for which it had become renowned.

Act 2 (**2008–2015**, see also: *Against Captain's Orders*; *And Darkness Descended. . .*; *ANTIdiaRy*; *Apricot Orchard, The*; *Beneath the Streets I & II*; Booth, Elizabeth; *Borough, The*; Boyd, Carrie; *Brixton Market*; *Bunker, The*; *Clod & Pebble*: 'company building'; *Crash of the Elysium, The*; Curtis, Adam; *Drowned Man, The*; *Duchess of Malfi, The*; **Enrichment**; ensemble; *Greenhive Green*; *Grey's Printing Press*; *House Where Winter Lives, The*; *It Felt Like a Kiss*; keyholders; *Lambeth Walk, The*; *Lost Lending Library, The*; *Lost Toy Depository*; Lynch, Sharon; notation; Oppong, Connie; Poots, Alex; production management; *Prospero's Island*; **R&D**; Reekie Jonathan; Reynoso, David Israel; *Séance, The*; *Searching for Stories*; *Silverpoint*; *Sleep No More*, Boston; *Sleep No More*, NYC; *Space Invaders Agency*; stage management; Thomas, Jen; timeline; *Travelling Museum Society, The*; *Uncommercial Traveller, The*; *Under the Eiderdown*; *Up, Up and Away*): With a turning point that can be dated from *The Masque of the Red Death* and the team's visit to Camber Sands to take stock and imagine the future of the company, Act 2 is the phase that saw to Punchdrunk's professionalisation and the implementation of much-needed operational and organisational structures. Having gained valuable knowledge and honed an approach to large-scale projects, Act 2 saw Punchdrunk enter a time that was, as Felix Barrett puts it, less about innovation and more about 'making better what we knew'. For Maxine Doyle, from *Masque* through *Malfi* to *The Drowned Man*, 'Act 2 was about digging deeper into the form' of the masked shows. Although intent on refining Punchdrunk's approach, for Barrett, this resulted in the core team becoming 'stuck on not doing something if it couldn't be perfect', a prioritisation of perfection that 'wouldn't have bothered' Barrett across the experiments in Exeter and early London productions of Act 1. Where Act 1 had been, as Barrett puts it, 'so hand to mouth', and operated out of homes or offices set up in masked show buildings, Punchdrunk set up its first permanent office in Shoreditch, London, in 2008. Making use of Colin Nightingale's foresight and skills, Punchdrunk developed a production management formula to meet the demands of the increasing size of masked shows. Act 2, as Barrett summarises, was a 'great learning curve', albeit often partnered by some creative frustrations:

We were almost crazily unprofessional in Act 1, so nomadic and nobody had any interest in having an infrastructure. None of us knew what the conventions of theatre were and what running a company was supposed to be like. None of us had followed the usual track where you work in a theatre of some scale and you learn how it all functions. We had technical skills but no knowledge of how to run theatre as a business.

Barrett recalls being 'intimidated by having a Board because everyone was theatrical professionals', which underscored Punchdrunk's previous position; a relishing of the freedoms and 'safety to be had' afforded by 'being the outsider', which allows for risk-taking and rule-breaking. Reflecting on the position of Punchdrunk back in 2013, Barrett identified the positives of expanding and professionalising: 'we're now in a place where we can implement ideas. Before they've always been these ephemeral floaty things you can't quite get a grip on and suddenly now we're ticking them off, we're working out ways to do them' (2013). Where Barrett and collaborators had relied on the support of Exeter University and Barrett's parents to realise ambitions in the early phase of Act 1, Act 2 garnered internal support from evolving, workable company structures and external backing from organisations such as Aldeburgh Festival, American Repertory Theater in Boston, English National Opera, The National Theatre and Manchester International Festival. As Barrett put it, the ability to tick ambitious ideas off directly related to having access to professional know-how and connections,

'working with people who, rather than say no, look and it and say, well how might we achieve that' (2013). As the entries by production evidence, the public attention and increasing audience numbers that Punchdrunk attracted across Act 2 meant that large-scale projects were realised, yet, for Barrett, at a much slower pace than Act 1, partly due to this feeling that the work could only be presented to the public when it was perfected. Consequently, partnering with brands enabled the creative team to undertake small-scale R&D projects for smaller audiences to investigate technique and technologies, while providing a budget that supported associates and ensemble. Connie Harrison was engaged to represent Punchdrunk as Brand Partnerships Director in March 2011, to ensure Punchdrunk remained in control of these collaborations and the artistic integrity of any project. Harrison's position was illustrative at that time of Punchdrunk's desire to make this responsibility an artistically driven, rather than commercially led, role. Hector Harkness, a member of the original ensemble for *Sleep No More*, London, took on an Associate Director role and responsibility for focusing and evaluating the R&D aims of each project.

Transnational relationships were also fostered. With the success of *Faust* and *The Masque of the Red Death* came *Sleep No More*, Boston, followed by a partnership with Emursive and the creation of Punchdrunk's longest-running masked show to date, *Sleep No More*, NYC, and the growth of Punchdrunk's international ensemble of performers. These vast and intricately installed productions owe their form and delivery to the smaller scale and shorter running projects produced across Act 1. As Nightingale notes,

if the core team hadn't had the learning experiences of Act 1 we wouldn't have been able to make *Sleep No More*, NYC. Ten years' worth of work and experiences meant that we knew what to do, the right choices to make.

Following the successful mounting of *Sleep No More*, NYC, Colin Marsh stepped down and, in 2011, Griselda Yorke took the position of Executive Producer. Yorke strengthened the management of the office; supporting Jennie Taylor's promotion, bringing in extra support for Barrett in Stephanie Allen as his assistant, taking on Judith Glynne as Finance Manager and Sarah Davies to lead fundraising activity and successfully implement the important 'keyholder' scheme. The producing and negotiation required for the scale of *The Drowned Man* was lengthy and extensive and was the first time the charity had raised independent commercial investment to finance a production. In 2013, Yorke secured the building which would become Temple Studios, and got the production off the ground. Before leaving to join the RSC, Yorke initiated the process that eventually led to the formation of Punchdrunk International.

Outside of the glare of public attention, quietly, productively and driven by Peter Higgin, Act 2 saw the growth and prominence of Punchdrunk Enrichment's work within the company and across communities. It is this legacy, perhaps lesser known because less in the spotlight during the period itself, that Barrett, Higgin and the core team celebrate as the overriding achievement of Act 2. Jen Thomas joined the Enrichment team in 2009 and was vital to the development of pilot, now flagship, projects. *Under the Eiderdown* and *The Lost Lending Library* were tested and perfected in schools in London during this period and are now lauded as exemplary of immersive practice as a tool for raising academic standards and all-round engagement in rich and multilayered ways in schools. *The Uncommercial Traveller*, a small Enrichment project devised by a group of amateur performers from Arcola 50+, achieved national recognition, reviewed alongside professional performance practice by Lyn Gardner in *The Guardian* as 'a little bit of a beautiful thing' (2011). Elin Moore Williams joined as Enrichment Projects Manager in 2013 to oversee Punchdrunk's first full programme of professional development, masterclasses and school workshops on site during *The Drowned Man*. As Act 2 drew to a close, Jen Thomas left Enrichment to pursue freelance projects while continuing to collaborate with Punchdrunk on R&D. Alex Rowse stepped into the Enrichment Producer role in 2014 and straight into the largest-scale Enrichment production to date, *Against Captain's Orders* in collaboration with the National Maritime Museum, with a UK-wide audience.

Barrett concludes of Act 2, 'up until Fallow Cross the last ten years has been about refining process and professionalising', establishing effective operational strategies. For Barrett, Act 2 seemed to set the masked shows as 'what Punchdrunk did', whereas the forms and formats of the full range of productions across Acts 1 and 2, including *Tunnel 228*, *Crash of the Elysium* and *The Borough*, were for Barrett equally valid, despite being considered as alternative to that for which the company had become known. The masked shows were one form that had been tried, tested and evolved to a degree that 'had profile and scale' whereas these other formats 'were in their infancy'. These early incarnations held rich scope within them, which Punchdrunk is now looking to test further in Act 3.

Act 3 (**2015–Present**, see also: *Believe Your Eyes*; collaboration; **digital technologies**; Enrichment Symposium; failure; **Fallow Cross**; *Greenhive Green*; *Kabeiroi*; *Miniature Museum*; *Oracles, The*; producing; Punchdrunk Travel; *Sleep No More*, Shanghai; *Small Tale, A*; *Small Wonders*): Act 2 prioritised 'making a company' and finding appropriate operational structures and strategies that supported, while being shaped by, the artistic work. It honed the form of the masked shows and built an international reputation. For Felix Barrett:

If Act 1 and 2 broke the fourth wall, Act 3 is about finding ways to

remove, literally, the other walls of the space, of site-sympathetic practice. In the early years we were so agile. We'd say we were going to do a show and three months later it would happen. You get to a certain scale and that's just not possible any more. Act 2 felt like we suddenly became too big too quickly which prevented us from being nimble. We needed and wanted to return to smaller interventions, but it was difficult to do that.

For Barrett, Act 3 is a return to founding principles, 'doing it, not just talking about it, to experimenting', and a return to early working processes, embracing play and proactivity. Given that Punchdrunk would 'never do any advance planning' for a source text until the right site arose ('we can't fully imagine a production until we're in the space'), during Act 2 this resulted in a number of projects being jettisoned if the site fell through. Now in Act 3, with an attitude of forging forward with experimentation despite knowing the results are unlikely to produce the original intention or ambition when a site falls through, Barrett is committed to the return to the desire to 'do it, even if it means failing, as long as clear aims are in place so that lessons can be learned'. Sitting in his parents' dining room, surrounded by the piles of documents, flyers and memorabilia that archive his very early Act 1 projects, Barrett reflects:

We had booklets made purely as a means to look professional, so people would trust us and give us a shot at doing what we thought we could do. The early days, 2000–2002, were about trying to get people to have enough confidence to let us have a go, and it feels a little bit like that again now. Masked shows are fine, they're proven, but not so new forms.

Across Act 2, the masked shows received greater attention while other forms and formats conceived in Act 1 lay dormant, awaiting complex producing structures behind them to

make them deliverable and 'to give them a longer run'. In this spirit and marking the end of Act 2, Punchdrunk International – a commercial production entity – was formed in 2016. Run alongside Punchdrunk the charity, it prioritises the delivery of large-scale works for an international audience and delivers a financial return to the charity for the use of its name and the origination of any work re-produced internationally. The distinction this permits to aspects of the organisational structure and the creation of certain projects provided a practical solution to how Punchdrunk might evolve in relation to global reach and production scale (and accordingly to financial risk). For Barrett, it marks a return to 'building something again', this time reaching out globally:

The fun of it is that creation, that building, trying to achieve the impossible because no one believes it can happen. Making the future form happen. It's about me having a sense of what that could be and trying to convince other people to achieve it with me.

Work produced by Punchdrunk International respects the remit set by the public funding of the charitable arm, which is to produce innovative work within the UK, for a UK-based audience, and simultaneously removes the charity from any financial risk or commercial imperative. As Barrett explains:

The scale of what we want to do, breaking down the experiential and durational barriers, it's big, it's weighty and involves different disciplines. There are crossovers between the work of the charity and the practice behind Punchdrunk International. The charity is there to innovate, to do the raw, cutting-edge breaking of new ground. We simply want a wider audience to experience that. The only way to achieve that scale is potentially risky, and we would never want to put the charity at risk or to compromise its mission. In hindsight,

I probably would have called the international arm 'Punchdrunk Studios' as the work we're exploring globally would actually come closer to how Thomas Heatherwick is working, the variety and cross section that such design studios are embracing.

In addition to changes in the structure of the company, the start of Act 3 also saw personnel shifts. These underpinned the skills required to deliver the new business model and maintained the culture of collaboration, guiding the way in which Punchdrunk and Punchdrunk International would work together. Despina Tsatsas joined in late 2015 to steer the separation of the original charity from the commercial entity, and to take up the Executive Producer role in Punchdrunk International before leaving in 2018 to join the Young Vic. A new set of producers joined Punchdrunk International to model and midwife the development of creatively and commercially complex projects: Gareth Collins, Stephen Makin and Lucy Whitby along with International General Manager Andrew Morgan and Finance Director Lauren van Zyl. Rebecca Dawson took up the position of Punchdrunk's Executive Director in 2016 while Tara Boland joined as Enrichment's Associate Director, demonstrating the growth of Enrichment's work. After a nine-year journey with Punchdrunk, during which time she rose from Administrative Assistant to Punchdrunk International's General Manager, Jennifer Taylor left the team. Katy Balfour also stepped away from her Punchdrunk roles to pursue a career in children's immersive literature.

Expansion in operational structures saw Andrea Salazar and Ben Hosford bringing new skills, contacts and knowledge to the ever-increasing technical challenges company-wide, alongside bolstering the production capacity for Punchdrunk's work at Fallow Cross and internationally. Jim Bending contributed vital skills and virtual worlds in the development of Punchdrunk's digital experimentation before leaving in 2018. With

Connie Harrison's departure in 2016 a new role of Creative Partnerships Lead was established for Punchdrunk International and filled by Sandy McKay, while Stephanie Allen was promoted to R&D Projects Manager, indicating the focus on this work across Act 3 and her long relationship realising Punchdrunk's ideas. Where in Act 1 Punchdrunk had relished the underground and word-of-mouth growth of an audience, in Act 3 JoJo Tyhurst was appointed to the role of Communications Manager, demonstrating the need to manage and maintain a quality of secrecy and adventure while also respecting Punchdrunk's need for a public-facing presence in the media. Adam Driscoll stepped down from Punchdrunk's Board of Trustees and with his knowledge of the mission of the charity, took up an Executive role with Punchdrunk International, bringing vital expertise into its management, underpinned by the Punchdrunk ethos.

Punchdrunk today comprises a workforce who operate collaboratively in an open-plan office at Fallow Cross. Administration, Enrichment, technical and digital personnel, producers and core creatives work together, physically and philosophically side-by-side, which is indicative of the collaborative attitude at the heart of the creative work produced. For Peter Higgin:

Approaching Punchdrunk's eighteenth birthday offers an opportunity to reflect on how far we've come and to celebrate the work of the company. Punchdrunk's reorganisation acknowledges the need to create a structure that best suits the wide-ranging nature of our practice and also ensures that we're able to take advantage of all of the opportunities that are on our slate. Over the course of Act 2 we pushed the limits of the scale of work that can be sustainably produced within a charitable structure and it became clear that a new model needed to be devised to help realise Felix's ambition, while supporting Punchdrunk's Enrichment work,

which has a clear charitable mission and public benefit. Although on paper the restructure looks like a split, it's strengthened Punchdrunk, brought us closer together.

Act 3's opening has seen *The Oracles*, *A Small Tale, Small Wonders* and *Miniature Museum* reinvent the tools and techniques of Enrichment's work and the team are busily developing approaches to a regional programme, working closely with partners across the UK. Fallow Cross has become an industrious hub for a wide range of Punchdrunk's immersive investigations, while *Sleep No More*, Shanghai forcefully kicked off Punchdrunk International's projects and firmly placed long-time ensemble member Conor Doyle as Associate Artist and Kath Duggan as Creative Associate. Shifts in organisational structures and the opportunities this creates for international collaboration are driven by a desire to return to Punchdrunk's core principles and its founding mission; to unearth ideas seeded in Act 1, tilling these to find the best forms and formats to share with an audience. The naming of Fallow Cross was in recognition of this period of incubation and sustainable regeneration, and, as Higgin explains, 'about taking root and making home':

A significant aspect of the Camber Sands discussion in 2008 was the imagining of 'The Lab'; a space to nurture creativity and form; to initiate and investigate new ideas. For many years this idea lay dormant. Only now, in Act 3 with Fallow Cross, do we begin to understand the potential that a permanent home affords. Fallow Cross has been an experiment into what a home feels like; it feels good and productive. Act 3 is about growing up, getting older, as a company and as people. Finding a permanent home will help to uncover the future of Punchdrunk's work. That will inevitably lead onto the next act.

Projects exploring new forms, such as *The Oracles*, investigated at Fallow

Cross and delivered in the schools for which they are designed, are simultaneously testing Punchdrunk's wider ideas for employing technologies on their most exacting audience: children. Barrett adds:

From *Sleep No More*, London it felt like the experimentation began to stretch and slow, which is why those formative years prior to that were crucial in terms of Punchdrunk's process. In the past seven years we've talked about it rather than doing it, not undertaken a project if it wasn't going to work perfectly. Now in Act 3 we've returned to the Act 1 mantra and taken on projects even though we knew they couldn't be perfect. *Kabeiroi* was fraught with difficulty and flawed but thank goodness we did it because of what it will grow into.

As the core team's ideas have morphed with time, so too has technology moved on, and in a way that serves the needs of Barrett's original ambitions for Act 1. Act 3 involves the investigation of 'deeper immersion', where an audience can 'be inside the world for longer', by enabling 'that world to spill out beyond the confines of the building so the experience is no longer held within the architectural footprint of a space':

Kabeiroi has been the first attempt since Act 2 to do something quickly, to test some ideas. It's been a perfect project for Fallow Cross to allow us to experiment and make discoveries through failing. Build and logistics worked but, experientially, it wasn't the show it was meant to be. With masked shows, the show goes up and its loops run efficiently according to their own time and logic, regardless of which part of the building the audience is in and what moments they're finding. Projects like *Moon Slave*, *The Borough* or *Kabeiroi*, on the other hand, are so reliant on a precise and relatively specific audience flow; if the audience stop they can't

progress. If we'd tested *Kabeiroi* on two participants each performance it would have worked perfectly but as soon as you scale-up audience numbers, the ways in which you're able to create a coherent arc become more difficult. Much of that first test required a lot of 'sticking plasters' as we went. The whole placement of performers was predicated by logistics, not narrative or experiential arc, which of course impacts on what the outcome is.

As this suggests, for Barrett the lineage of what the one-on-one has been and might become is a primary focus for Act 3. Charting its trajectory from the Exeter experiments into *The Moon Slave* identified as its paradigm in Act 1, through *The Borough* in Act 2, and to *Kabeiroi* and the aims with Punchdrunk Travel, Act 3 will home in on 'finding the vocabulary and best format to explore and define that palette'. Barrett is quick to acknowledge, with the focus here on audience engagement via digital devices,

theatre without performers is too simplistic a description, but there's something in it in relation to how we achieve scale; which technology can support. Some of these ideas could only happen if we achieve a certain scale in order to make a project cost-neutral.

For Punchdrunk, Act 3 is full of promise. Ideas germinated in the early years of Act 1 are finally coming to fruition. Interpretations of sources that Barrett 'was interested in back then, that have been dormant for ten years, are now underway'; partly because Punchdrunk has the resources and expertise more readily available, and partly because of technological progress. As for those experiments to come, a handwritten note in one of Barrett's early Act 1 journals reads:

Future shows:

Rocky Horror

Woyzeck

Masque of the Red Death

Bluebeard

Steppenwolf

Metropolis

Blood Wedding

Interactive opera

Theatre without performers, audience become protagonist

Barrett concludes, 'the future was set back at the start of Act 1, 2002–2003. Those existing ideas now just need to be realised'. He adds that to realise his original ideas, vast projects residing in his head or in notebooks for so long, would take one to two years of work per project, which looks ahead to many more Punchdrunk Acts to come. As Barrett summarises:

Act 1 was the seeding, the experimentation and discovery.

Act 2 was the bedding in.

Act 3 has barely begun.

adrenalin (see also: audience; awe and wonder; crescendo; intervention; lens; **senses**; visceral): The hormone produced in the human body when a person is angry, scared or excited. It makes the heart beat faster than when in its resting state in order to make the body alert and reactive and provides it with more energy in order to deal with any potential threat or pleasure. 'Adrenalin' is a shorthand, for Felix Barrett, for the heightened state of reception that Punchdrunk's work seeks to induce, so the audience member 'experiences the world through an entirely theatrical lens':

In raw, scientific terms, Punchdrunk's work intends to flood the body with adrenalin. We want to get the audience to that flight or fright place, not to create shock or panic, but because if you're in a state of distress the blood rushes to the skin, your synapses are firing, so that you're ready to receive any hint of a call to arms that you can perceive, as sensorially aware as possible. That's what we want: our audience to be going into our worlds. Whether you like or hate it, it doesn't matter, it's that you're going to *feel* it. In traditional theatre set-ups you're usually calm and at one with the world around you and we're actively trying to do the opposite, through lighting, sound, punctuation, perceived threat, audience context, intervention, all of these things are triggers to flood the body with adrenalin. We balance that, provide time for calm, contemplation. You can't be in a perpetual state of heightened emotion, you need the peaks and troughs.

These moments of balance are designed and 'plotted' within each show, especially those that are driven by adrenalin, such as *It Felt Like a Kiss, Crash of the Elysium* or *Kabeiroi*.

aesthetics (see also: **audience; immersive; senses; visceral**): This term in Punchdrunk's practice is threefold and relates firstly to form; that is, the ways in which the work is created and presented. Secondly, it relates to the dramaturgies and processes by which the form is originated and realised and, thirdly, to the audience appreciation of those forms and processes. In Punchdrunk's practice form and process are multisensory and intertextual which moves an audience appreciation of aesthetics beyond 'the look' of the event, to incorporate the smell, touch and so *feel* (both haptic and emotional) of the work, typically involving some kind of interaction within the piece. In this way, the audience is directly implicated in the aesthetics of immersive work, from concept through to production. Furthermore, the sensually participatory forms correlate to subsequent embodied appreciation.

afterbeat (see also: **coda;** crescendo; **music;** narrative; **soundscore**): Each large-scale masked show has a dramatic crescendo which involves an equivalent climax in the soundscore. The afterbeat is a contrasting piece of music, usually a song of the era, to punctuate the

time-plane of the world and inspire a certain 'nostalgia' for its passing. Intended to serve as the first step into decompression, this piece of music will act as a friend to accompany the audience member to the bar. Similar to coda.

Against Captain's Orders (**2015,** see also: Act 3; Enrichment; **objects**. Further reading: Bennett 2012; Tims 2016): For a good while, museums have been at the forefront of producing immersive experiences to redefine what an interactive exhibition can be. Punchdrunk regularly receives interest from cultural institutions that would like to create innovative and dynamic approaches to public expositions. *Against Captain's Orders* took families on an adventure through the National Maritime Museum's incredible wealth of maritime history and artefacts. It was to be Punchdrunk's biggest children's show to date, well reviewed, with a national audience of around 33,000. For Enrichment Producer, Alex Rowse, who joined Punchdrunk just as the project was announced, taking the helm involved diving in at the deep end:

I received a crash course in Punchdrunk principles and processes as we were already making the thing; from 'make the experience fully accessible' to 'no natural light, bring the lights right down, and, haze. Lots of haze'. I had to take these on board while simultaneously trying to get my head around the environment and organisation of a museum. We had lots of challenges, discovering: how not to ruin the floor and walls of the exhibition space; how to be able to use haze without setting off the fire alarms across the site; how to use old props and furniture without infesting the museum with bugs. Thanks to the long lead-in time with our host partners, a great creative team and production manager, Andrea Salazar, it was a smooth build.

Aimed at six- to twelve-year-olds, audiences donned lifejackets, joined the crew of the HMS Adventure and stepped

into the heart of the action, *into* maritime history, as Peter Higgin elaborates:

The National Maritime Museum wanted to present a piece to kick-off its new 'special exhibition' structure; winter for adults, summer for families. We were given access to a swathe of museum staff and carte blanche to create whatever excited us. We toured exhibitions, departments and storage areas. It was the storage areas that excited us most; vast warehouses full of maritime treasures, from obscure 1930s radar instruments to a bureau used by Nelson, old ship engines, skidoos from artic exhibitions, draws full of swords; objects potent with the most amazing stories. I was interested in heroism and expeditions, pushing the limits of our knowledge and forcing people to come up with new inventions, exploring new territories and shifting paradigms. Increasingly it seemed almost all significant voyages were doing what couldn't be done or what was deemed impossible. They were breaking rules and reaping the benefits. We wanted to embody this spirit of rule breaking, of being brave and going into the uncharted. The production demonstrated how you could play around with the core ethos of a museum and create a fantastical adventure without degrading or belittling historical fact. The show took place in the museum so had to feel possible within the museum. That's what drew us to the stores, this magical place that actually exists; it's very believable for an audience.

The show took a group of forty on a journey that started as a somewhat run-of-the-mill interactive museum exhibition, getting into nautical teams of Ship Watch, Navigation, Midshipmen and Salvage, taken down to be sat in wooden rowing boats, surrounded by haze. Audiences met two curators who would guide them on their journey, Glan, carefree and spirited and Arthur, curmudgeonly

△
FIGURE 1 *Against Captain's Orders*, 2015.

Photo credit: Stephen Dobbie

and risk averse, who introduce four key objects, all of which represent the spirit of going against orders, of rebelling. Things quickly take a wrong turn when the audience spots that there is a letter in a bottle which wasn't there before. As a major historical find, they decide they must open the bottle and find out what the letter says. As soon as the object is touched an alarm sounds and the objects disappear. Our curators take the audience on a journey into the clandestine and fantastical world of the museum stores to retrieve the four objects. Once inside the stores, its quickly realised that an archaic security protocol has been challenged and it becomes a race against time to retrieve the objects and prevent a total lockdown of the stores. The audience become the heroes of the hour, solving riddles, finding objects; using their newly acquired knowledge of objects. The objects are all retrieved in the nick of time and order is fully restored.

agency (see also: **audience**; digital technologies; **Enrichment**; Exeter Experiments; Fallow Cross: 'Mantle of the Expert'; R&D; text. Further reading: Carlson 2012; Heathcote and Bolton 1995): In general terms, agency defines the manner in which individuals, on their own or as part of a collective, act autonomously, or are acted upon, in any given circumstance. In terms of a live performance experience, creating opportunities for different types and level of agency for any audience, according to the specific objectives and artistic concerns of the work in question, is an overriding aim for Punchdrunk. A basic degree of creative agency in decision-making exists in an audience's control of their own narrative journey and artistic experience within masked Punchdrunk events, despite this being wholly manipulated by Punchdrunk. Levels of imaginative agency exist in the varied ways audience members take decisions around which route they wish to forge, which narratives to construct and which themes to uncover. All of the Exeter experiments, and experimental works such as *The Borough* or *The Crash of the Elysium*, as well as any collaborative R&D project and current investigations at Fallow Cross, set out to test new approaches to, and mechanisms for, types of creative agency that might be shaped for the audience in Punchdrunk immersive experiences that do not follow the format and workings of large-scale masked events. Current investigations at Fallow Cross with digital technologies and certain concepts for Punchdrunk Travel, as explored through *Kabeiroi*, are seeking to advance Punchdrunk's approach to the creative agency of the audience.

Punchdrunk Enrichment works hard to ensure active and productive agency is generated by the work for any individuals who participate in projects in schools and with communities. These projects require that all participants are co-creators in the work and place young people and school pupils in the role of expert in scenarios, following Dorothy Heathcote's pedagogic practices. The creative agency of the host community in Enrichment projects is fundamental to the planning, design, delivery and evaluation of all aspects of the work. Pilot projects such as the original *Under the Eiderdown* or *Against Captain's Orders*, *Greenhive Green*, *Prospero's Island* and *The Oracles* are examples of projects that have proactively explored and evaluated mechanisms for educational agency that might be shaped for individuals within, and alongside, their communities.

And Darkness Descended. . . (**2011**; see also: **Act 2**; **adrenalin**; *Crash of the Elysium, The*; **digital technologies**; **gaming**; intervention; *Oracles, The*; R&D; site-sympathetic. Further reading: Biggin 2017; Klich 2016; Montola, Stenros and Waern 2009): *And Darkness Descended. . .* was an R&D project in collaboration with Sony PlayStation, resulting in an underground gaming performance, presented at what are now known as The Vaults in Waterloo, London. It was an important project for Felix Barrett and the Punchdrunk team as it offered them the first opportunity to test the intersections between theatre, gaming and 'real life' and an early investigation into the experience of the audience member as 'player'. The audience were invited to the work via online correspondence, and then, arriving at designated times, set off in groups to undertake a mission to get to a computer hidden in the depths of this underground space, where they were required to upload a file. In advance of entering the space and what each group perceived to be the performance/play beginning, they were told by front-of-house staff that if they were tagged at any point in the performance by a performer then this would indicate they had been destroyed and would be escorted immediately off the premises. Each audience member had to sign a waiver to agree that they understood the show may only last a matter of minutes if this were the case. This cunning ruse was, however, a method of intervention, similar to that first employed during *The Cherry Orchard*. Although led to believe this could happen, and thus on high alert to prevent it, in this prototype 'survival-theatre'-cum-'game-of-tag' the truth was that at no point did or would any performer tag any audience member. It was a ploy, before entering the site, to destabilise and serve as a trigger for the adrenalin and accentuate the collective fight-or-flight required to fulfil the mission. *And Darkness Descended. . .* followed processual rules of play, borrowed from games design, similar to those employed later in *The Crash of the Elysium*. As Barrett recalls of the 'gamifying of experience', the dynamic amongst audience members, and creative agency involved, shifts when the 'audience is only aware of objective':

It's a raw, binary response. It was exploring how you can tell a story when the audience is working at an adrenalin-fuelled tempo. It was entirely different to a masked show in that it followed a linear journey, one set route, with the audience on a mission and the performers talking and improvising directly with each group. It totally gamified the experience for them. What was noticeable was the audience coming out drenched in sweat.

Techniques tested with this project were further explored with *The Crash of the Elysium*. They have since been expertly crafted to underpin the design and delivery of *The Oracles*, supported by developments in digital technology and the on-site physical world of Fallow Cross.

ANTIdiaRy (**2015**, see also: Act 2; building; digital technologies; **gaming**; **R&D**; scale; scalability): A cross-platform experience, created by Punchdrunk International and Samsung North America, to lead up to the launch of Barbadian music artist Rihanna's eighth album. Punchdrunk's challenge was to come up with a concept that could tie together a large-scale campaign that took in television adverts, social media and 360-degree digital and live experiences. Associate Director Hector Harkness summarises:

We wanted to create a compelling experience that was led by narrative, all the elements together adding up to a cohesive, while mysterious, whole. We started by creating a conceptual building, much like we always start with a physical building, a series of eight rooms, each one containing a secret that would be unlocked. Like one of our characters in a masked show, we imagined Rihanna travelling through these rooms and eventually finding the eighth room, which contained *Anti*, Rihanna's album. The content for the rooms became like a physical diary – the seven rooms from the past, based around the 'versions' of Rihanna that were represented with each of her previous albums. It was important to have a solid conceptual centre from which all collaborators could work.

The live experiences appeared and disappeared in an elusive manner; a series of black boxes on beaches, industrial estates and islands. The challenge

became who could reach them before they disappeared. With a hugely dedicated audience of Rihanna fans they were swiftly sought out, yet only by a small number of people. For Harkness, 'the project played with scale, ranging from huge audience numbers for the narrative of the television advertisement to approximately 100 individuals who were curious enough to discover the live experiences'.

Apricot Orchard (**2010**, see also: **Act 2**; **Duchess of Malfi, The**; **Enrichment**; **forests**; mass production; music): With a full title of *The Duchess of Malfi Apricot Orchard*, this was an early Enrichment production, created, as with all Enrichment projects, in a bespoke fashion for Brittania Village Primary School. Staged at school and on the set of *The Duchess of Malfi*, this project re-imagined the apricot orchard as an orchard of phonic trees that grew songs. Worried about the health of his trees, the orchard owner runs a tree-planting workshop at a local school. The trees seeds thrive, not only on water but also on an original song composed by pupils, which must be sung to it daily to help it grow. Each class at Britannia Village nurtured the unusual seedlings and watching them grow daily, until they had reached such a height that they sprouted an invitation for the class to visit the site of the Malfi orchard to plant them. As pupils planted each sapling, the orchard magically played back an orchestral reworking of their song.

architecture (see also: **building**; **dance**; **design**; ensemble; **found space**; **framing**; Hide-and-Seek; **lighting**: **'listening to the building'**; site-sympathetic. Further reading: Pallasmaa 2005): The style and structure of any building, specifically its internal spaces and fixtures, lay the foundations of a Punchdrunk world. Felix Barrett explains:

Architecture is the canvas on which we paint. It dictates flow, narrative, crescendo. It's the basis for the script, the loop structure. In terms of how we notate any masked show,

the architectural blueprint is the first layer. Upon that we layer spaces and character. If anyone asked for a script it's that that we'd show them. We have a source play but alongside that we need the architectural blueprint to unlock, unpick and unpack that text across the space.

Architecture, as a shorthand, differs from 'building' and both are fundamental. The building provides the emotional resonance and is solidly impressionistic, whereas the architecture provides a structural frame. As Barrett puts it, 'The building has atmosphere, holds ghosts of the past; the architecture is fixed, provides the hard lines on which you build. The architecture we can change if we must, but the building, the atmosphere, we only ever accentuate'. Architecture wholly influences the design and atmosphere of a Punchdrunk world and is key to the generation of material by the performers . . .

Maxine Doyle

On architecture and dance . . .

Dance and architecture . . .

Choreographic process

Space and performance . . .

The creation of a new work begins with the dancers off-site. It's important that we begin our journey as an ensemble in a 'safe' space – a space free of drama, narrative emotion and tension. A space with soft floors and natural light, where the dancers can take physical and emotional risks. It is here we discover the essence of the performance language – where we work out how we can take the words away from a Shakespearean soliloquy and transpose them into a choreographic dance and movement form. It's vital before the cast begin developing material and character on-site that a strong physical and visual performance aesthetic has been explored and established.

The building is the most formidable character in a Punchdrunk work. It can be a daunting challenge for the dancer to match the architectural prowess of a grand staircase or the vastness of concrete basement. Creating choreography for such spaces involves a constant interrogation of the body in relation to architectural frames, planes and vistas. The space becomes an improvisational playground – dancers searching for spaces to climb, suspend, hover, disappear, push, slip and slide. We ask the dancers to find frames – like doorways, windows, corners, mirrors, and to create images in the frames – a nurse hovering through a doorway, a woman looking out of a window, a man with his face to the corner, a fleetingly ghostly reflection in the mirror.

In improvisations and movement tasks we describe the body as an architectural form, using terms like surfaces and edges. Dancers may perch on their partner's shoulders as if it were a window ledge or lie or climb up a wall as if running up a spine. In the first *Sleep No More*, 2003, I remember giving Sarah Dowling, as Lady Macbeth in the sleepwalking scene, the task to 'find places to sleep'. I followed her through a freezing building (she was wearing a silk dressing gown and oversized men's slippers), stopping randomly as she would try and lie on a series of narrow ledges.

We are always practising a multidimensional awareness – the space above you, behind you, under your feet or armpit, around the corner, the lift shaft above your head. We ask characters to frame themselves in light – sometimes the whole body, sometimes just the palm of the hand, body parts often fragmented. 'Find your light' is a constant Punchdrunk direction, which evolved from both artistry and need – performers literally having to find light for their scene. Lighting the building *always* comes before lighting the action. It is this delicate duet of dance and light, dancing in and out of frame and light, which supports the audience's journey through dark spaces.

The choreography emerges as an organic dance between skin, muscle, bone and surface, edge and frame. It is when the cast truly begin to dance with the building that body, character and story come alive.

archiving

archiving (see also: Barrett, Margaret and Simon; *Drowned Man, The*; durational; experiential; Hide-and-Seek; **legacy; notation**; senses; visceral. Further reading: Punchdrunk and Abrams 2015): Archives are a collection of images, historical documents or artefacts that record and bear testament to the activity and passing of events. Punchdrunk has deliberately chosen not to document shows in video or film format, partly due to the problems of attempting to archive this work and partly because the ephemerality of the work is a fundamental element to the dreamlike quality of an experience. Written documentation of Punchdrunk projects are rare although a notation method for stage management of masked shows has been followed since *Sleep No More*, Boston. Regulations and pro forma for Punchdrunk one-on-ones and Enrichment projects are formalised in writing due to the specific, ethical requirements of the practice involved. Felix Barrett and Maxine Doyle keep journals as written documentation for each production. These record ideas and document process as well as reflecting on outcomes, both in general and in relation to specific projects. Barrett has kept all of his journals, from the undergraduate documentation of his practical investigations to his journals for each Punchdrunk production and project planning. Since *The Drowned Man* these have been leather-bound notebooks, the spines of which Barrett has embossed with the title of the production once this is finalised. There are a number bought ready and awaiting embossment for Act 3.

Approaches to sketching concepts, notating process, and documenting and evaluating outcomes are continually discussed and explored by the company. Various reflective, image-led and infographic formatted diagrams and documents exist that are testament to an evolving approach to communicating and recording practice. Barrett recalls of his first collaboration with Stephen Dobbie how, prior to *Chair*, and other than his undergraduate portfolio for his final-year projects at Exeter, he had never documented any of his work through photography or video because he 'didn't believe you could capture through image the feeling of what it was like to be inside an event'. With *Chair's* poster Dobbie 'contained the atmosphere that we were striving for in the work within an image'. Dobbie identifies that he and Barrett shared an aesthetic and approach in terms of capturing image which served to support Punchdrunk's work as both publicity and record of the otherworldly and ephemeral quality of the event. For Barrett, the flyer that Dobbie went on to create for *The Tempest*, 2003 was 'immediately the atmosphere, the right level of teasing without overselling, alluding to rather than dictating what the audience would get so the mystery was preserved' (see Figure 24).

In terms of archiving, Punchdrunk regularly questions the significance of, and best approach to, the ways in which the company might archive any production for posterity and future creative and critical reference. Images and reflective writings have proven to be a useful form of documentation. London-based photographer Julian Abrams, inspired by his experience of *The Drowned Man*, collaborated with Punchdrunk during the run in 2014 to document the production through images, which resulted in Punchdrunk independently publishing the limited-edition book in 2015. A more recent acknowledgement of the need to archive and capture work in a more immersive photographic form has been explored through 360-degree panoramic image capture. Colin Nightingale expands:

Charles Mansfield-Osborne, a Punchdrunk fan and specialist in 360-degree digital experiences, approached us about photographing Temple Studios to produce a virtual tour. His equipment could capture the in-show lighting so we swiftly got him to document the whole set before we tore it down. Under Dobbie's guidance we encouraged him to do a special treatment on the 800-plus panoramic images captured, to make the images feel more like computer game graphics, give them an otherworldly feel. We eventually released a virtual tour of part of Temple Studios as a treat for keyholders to mark Christmas 2016.

Punchdrunk is most concerned with archiving masked events in a manner that captures the atmosphere, the essence of the moment, in order to, as Peter Higgin puts it, 'invoke feeling and arouse a sensation of being there'. In terms of archiving the choreography for past masked shows, much of this has been digitally recorded for reference and to ensure a rigour of form, although, as Maxine Doyle explains:

The issue is time and money. Ideally the choreography would be re-imagined for camera and lit like a feature film. We embrace the photographic form – but the life of the work is definitely lost when a show closes. There's a great tension surrounding archiving.

This tension is due to the fact that video archiving of masked shows can never capture the multidimensional and sensual quality of the work. It undermines the transient nature of the work, which is an important feature of its experiential potency. A vital, though somewhat more ineffable, mode of archiving productions exists in the bodies of the ensemble members. Doyle urges caution in this regard: 'of course the body remembers, but movement memory fades and with it the nuances of choreographic language'. With this in mind, contributions from ensemble members draw explicit or passing attention to the manner in which they create, evolve, store and pass on the choreography of large-scale productions within and through their bodies, highlighting a sensitivity to, and respect for, a range of modes of archiving that meet, and articulate, the work itself. Conor Doyle, long-time Punchdrunk performer, eloquently notes the manner in which experience is archived in the body, from Barrett's first Hide-and-Seek game through owning the choreography to remembering past performances . . .

Conor Doyle

On addiction, awareness and archiving

M ax and Felix are a good jigsaw. They facilitate each other's ideas and make those happen on performers. With something that could be quite flat, like a scene where we're exploring the seven deadly sins, Felix has found the right bit of music and Maxine has found the right choreographic language to discuss how we're going to take a word and put it into our bodies, while both of them are talking about the structure of the scene and how it will crescendo. It all fits really well and they've carefully considered how to communicate that, as well as the research required to make it happen. I remember during early rehearsals for *Faust* that Max and Felix sent Meline Danielewicz and I, both of us Witches, off to the zoo to look at the meerkats, because meerkats are referenced in the original *Faust*, and they wanted us to have that same quality in our movement.

You hear about the building when you're in the studios but it's a really big moment in the process when you eventually visit it; you're never quite ready for the building. With *Faust*, we were given the Wapping address but they kept everything else secret in order that it had maximum impact on us. I'd been walking around Wapping for ages because the building wasn't what I was expecting so kept walking past it. Eventually I saw other members of the company going in there. We all got changed and warmed up in the car park and then were led into the building one by one, with Felix like a little Pied Piper, really excited, sending us in different directions. It was very dark with very little theatrical lighting at that point. There were smart candles around, different music playing in different rooms, with tasks left around for us: 'sing a lullaby to the child who's in the corner': 'be invisible': 'tell a story': 'tell a secret'. The point of the exercise is about you and the space, responding to what the space creates in you, and these tasks help facilitate that. It's never about interacting with the other performers, it's very much a solo exploration of the building and how the building moves you. We call it Hide-and-Seek; you're trying not to be seen by other people, whether that's by being still, turning your inner light off, or whether it's hiding under a desk while you watch someone else explore the room. If you find a good hiding spot it gives a great sense of what it is to be a voyeur, the excitement that the audience must get when they pop that mask on and watch you through the window.

I remember being quite scared, in a heightened state of awareness. My skin was on fire, my hearing was acute, I could feel everything with a readiness to move in quite a primitive way. There was a sense of my body being not at all casual, of being alive in my body and being aware of the possibilities for that as a performance mode. Imagination-wise that exercise feeds you and it opens up your own fantasy world. It makes you connect to something instinctive, innate, something very pure.

The space is such a strong frame that you're always needing to have your outside camera on yourself to see how you fit into the space, more than you do when you're on a stage. With *Faust*, we'd been working so much with the Edward Hopper images in advance that the Wapping building, already partly designed, really did have that feeling of walking into a painting. Where you position yourself in the spaces of a building becomes really important. The possibilities that you get choreographically open up. There's such a duet with the building, its fixtures, whether you're dancing on the bar, or a table, it's a duet with the space. You're not ice-skating on top of it, you're in an active conversation with it, as you would be if you were dancing with a person. Each space has its own unique choreographic potentials. It's like a playground; you have to try out loads of different things, fall over, get the most you can out of each room and its spaces.

The one-on-ones in *Faust* were powerful. I had two. I'd been given a piece of paper that had six out of my twelve scenes detailed on there, which allowed for this wonderful dialogue with Max and Felix about what they already had fixed in their minds and what was open and possible for me to discover in the space. The space led to a lot of interesting abstract work. For me there was definitely less of a narrative drive than there was in *The Drowned Man*. With *Faust* it was so much about trying to find how space could unlock those new scenes that weren't already fixed. The one-on-ones emerged from that. I found a safe in the building and discovered you could walk down the side of it, a really tiny corridor. I remember rehearsing it with other cast members and it was so exciting to be the person leading someone, establishing a one-on-one relationship to an audience member; being able to touch them, to look at them, or not; to blow on their neck and feel your breath rebound; to play a game with the audience member and make them feel like your only child because they have all your attention. Felix talks a lot about that relationship being a gift and it really is; this amazing play that just the two of you enter into together. Being able to scare, to charm. To have that close impact on the audience in theatre is quite difficult but in a Punchdrunk show it's much easier because the audience member's energy level is, usually, already really high.

An intention behind Hide-and-Seek is that performers experience the show as an audience member. When we start performing it's really important for us to remember that experience, to understand the experience that the people in front of you in the white masks are having; to remember that it can be a scary or stressful environment. To know that we should be looking after the audience is set from that first game with the building. You don't get very many written documents at Punchdrunk, but the rules of a one-on-one are very clearly written down. There are very clear boundaries for performer and audience safety. We always make sure any experience undergone or emotion created is always done in good taste, to ensure that we're not veering off into Haunted House schlock. We want the audience to feel like everything is done with good reason, relates to the world, so we always keep our taste-eye on anything that might be on the edge of that. One-on-ones for the dancers are always highly choreographed, from where you place your hand to where you're looking when you're not looking at them, to the distance between you and them to how you're manipulating them around the space. There's such rehearsal in that and it gives you a massive amount of confidence so you can safely look after that person and remain in charge. We're always instructed that we're in charge of the one-on-one for our safety as much as the audience member's safety. Despite being extremely choreographed, there is still room for modulation. For example, if someone is coming into the one-on-one already petrified, it's possible to change the intention of actions, from 'to create unease', into being 'to soothe', to ensure that there's still a sense of journey through the one-on-one for that person. If audiences enter a one-on-one that's supposed to finish with a scary conclusion, and they're already really scared, then there's no journey for them to go on. For one-on-ones to have a distinct beginning, middle and end you have to be able to manipulate the audience member's feelings to give them that journey.

Things come up that are new all the time for us as an ensemble. There's constantly a dialogue about how to do a show where the audience is free roaming and immersive, where it has a degree of interactivity but with unspoken rules around that. There are many things for us performers to talk about in relation to that; from a safety point of view, an artistic point of view and a human point of view, as a person who is having that experience. The Punchdrunk ensemble has grown from being a single cast performing five shows a week to, in NYC, doing ten shows seven days a week with three casts, or in Shanghai, six shows a week with two casts. With *Faust*, over six months it recast only three people, whereas now every six months we do a large recast of people. The infrastructure to maintain these shows has certainly changed. NYC has been running since 2011, so we've evolved a way to maintain high production values, running a show for that length, while maintaining a cast who are doing the same show for three nights a week, three loops a night for, potentially, years on end. We have an ensemble who are happy and healthy – injury and sanity wise – supported by that infrastructure and artistically satisfied by the work. These are areas that we continue to work on.

We also question how we document these shows, how we remount them in a new place. Documenting the work is really difficult; it might end up being a video of rehearsal with a really detailed written document. There's so much that you wouldn't get from the video, which is necessary to pass on. The work is documented in our bodies. We're very fortunate that the old cast teach the new cast the roles. All the work they have in their bodies gets passed on, goes into a new body and morphs slightly. If organising rehearsal directors, I might put myself forward for particular scenes if I know I have information absorbed from doing it or from watching it for a long time. The same would be the case for other rehearsal directors. The roles that I physically know are archived in my body somewhere.

One of the things that makes Punchdrunk unique is that the work's always been about an equality between the performers, the sound, the lights, the set and the audience. That mentality has meant that there's a strong family bond between the people who work for Punchdrunk and between us and our audience. Punchdrunk is also a 'yes' company. There's never a sense of not being able to do something. It's such a crazy idea from the outset that everyone who works on it has to be a bit nuts. It's such a hard job as well that you have to be really passionate about it. Pied Piper Felix takes you on these amazing journeys, whether he's enthusing about the next show as a friend or talking about your performance as your director. He's a bit like a magician with this magical perfume that's intoxicating. As a dancer the work is really addictive. Going back to the stage after working with Punchdrunk can feel less exciting, less engaging. There's something so powerful about that relationship with the audience.

arsenic (see also: decay; **design**; in-show-world; nature; **senses**; *Duchess of Malfi, The*): The smell of almonds was employed in various rooms in *The Duchess of Malfi* as olfactory manipulation to denote arsenic. This is illustrative of the way in which smell is hugely significant to installations in Punchdrunk worlds, specifically smells that hint at underlying themes or denote character narratives; bottles of scent in bedrooms, lipstick and powder in dressing rooms, opiates and medicines in old laboratories or doctors' cabinets, pine trees in forests. Sam Booth, below, illustrates how incense and Dettol created atmosphere and narrative for *The Firebird Ball*. Smell emphasises the importance of activating the whole human sensorium when designing and experiencing these worlds. It contributes to the logic and unity of the in-show world and is often a key element in any audience recall of a Punchdrunk event.

atmosphere (see also: adrenalin; aesthetics; building; darkness; design; experiential; **lighting**; **soundscore**; visceral): Felix Barrett neatly sums up Punchdrunk's practice as being most concerned with 'atmosphere and audience'. In Punchdrunk works, atmosphere is created via multiple theatrical elements. Soundscore, a key element in the Punchdrunk aesthetic, drives creative inspiration and consequent atmosphere. Lighting, darkness and shadows are vital to establishing atmosphere in masked shows and slowing down the rhythm and tempo of a situation, charging it with a sense of potential threat, of the uncanny, or with a spell of enchantment, 'thick with the crackle of distant magic' (Barrett 2013). Prior to entering the world, a readiness to receive the charged atmosphere is manipulated via the journey to the site, the encounter with the external façade of the building, perhaps even clues or information received prior to the event; all intended to get the adrenalin pulsing. As Barrett puts it, 'it's the crackle of tension. The electrical charge. A feeling that the audience experience ambiently. It's threat. It's being able to feel particles collide'. As regards the manner in which the performers influence the atmosphere, for the masked shows, prior to entering the building the performers have honed their skill in creating and shifting atmospheres in a bare studio, before working with light, sound and installation on-site. The ability to make and break dramatic tensions through movement language and presence alone is vital and feeds into the idiosyncratic atmospheres established in masked shows.

audience (see also: **agency**; atmosphere; **awe and wonder**; flow; immersive; legacy; loops; masked shows; **one-on-ones**. Further reading: Bennett 2003; Biggin 2017; Flaherty 2014; Freshwater 2009; Morgenstern 2012; White 2013): Punchdrunk employs the term 'audience' as shorthand to encompass the participant who is offered the role of adventurer, comrade, collaborator or player, according to the audience/performance relationship set up for each specific project. For Punchdrunk, it is audience and the audience experience that is the fundamental concern and driving force for making work. Developing his analogy of the concept that drives the work as the 'blueprint' for any project, Felix Barrett is emphatic that the 'audience is the cornerstone':

If the blueprint is the method for creating the work, it exists only when we fold it up and post it to the audience, the joy of them opening it up for the first time and receiving this gift that we've built for them. When you crack a show, the wash of euphoria that pours through your body is a thing to live for, and that's what you want to give to the audience. It's the act of sharing and the only way you can do that is if someone else experiences it, feels that same sensation. Audience is the reason we set out to make any project, the springboard for action. They're creative comrades. The biggest thrill that I have is when I see a building for the first time, I respond to it at a purely visceral and immediate level. It's exciting, the whole gamut of emotions. The intention is that audience gets to experience that too but once we've tinkered with the space, accentuated those emotions, harnessed the power. In that way I'm a little jealous of them because they get to do it for the first time over again but with a narrative layering. There's nothing more satisfying than when an audience member repeats an anecdote back to me about something they encountered within the show, as though I'm just a friend and nothing to do with the making of the show. For them it was entirely unique, pure and spontaneous, so they felt it was chance, accident, and that they were the only person to experience it. I would never let on that it was completely choreographed, that it happened to someone half-an-hour before, and someone else half-an-hour later. The purity of what they're feeling is entirely what we're trying to create.

It is the audience that proves how far the worlds created are effective in both artistic and practical terms. The manner in which an audience, whether individual or collective, will find and become present in an event underpins the concept, the testing for and thus the eventual success of any Punchdrunk project, as Barrett explains:

We only learn if it works by putting an audience through the world, to stress-test an idea. The audience is our reason for being, but they're also sometimes a direct threat. We need them to expose the weaknesses that exist.

Audience is conceived as part of the rhythm and fabric of each performance and it is important that they understand the context in which they are invited into the show. With any new concept for a Punchdrunk event, the experience is always discussed by the creative team first and foremost from the audience's perspective. Barrett explains:

Context is vital; audiences must have a clear understanding of their position within the work. What are the rules set? Why is the audience there? This is a crucial question that Punchdrunk asks when creating the work. The mask provides the audience member with a spectral and aesthetic context as well as the opportunity to become voyeur, witness, presence. With non-masked performances the audience is given a role.

If cast in role, even where this emerges for the audience-participant during the event, as with *The Moon Slave* or *Kabeiroi*, the audience are charged with being present, responsive and integral to the development of the work in form and content. The role of the audience always has clear parameters defined within the design of each project; ranging from anonymous and spectral masked voyeurs to a collective of comrades on a mission.

Enrichment audiences vary from community to community and the approach to mechanisms for immersion is shifted accordingly. Creative Associate Kath Duggan asserts that it is the commitment to exploring audience experience in community contexts as much as in large-scale public events that makes Punchdrunk's practice so distinctive:

Seeing first-hand the impact of projects like *The Lost Lending Library* on the children that experience it, watching the children's responses, and witnessing the effect it has on individuals in the classroom and corridors afterwards, is infectious. To me, it makes complete sense of Punchdrunk's need to put the audience at the heart of every project.

Peter Higgin notes that the Enrichment team often employ the term participants for various projects:

What is challenged is the performer/performance and audience relationship. For Enrichment productions, broadly speaking, we only ever cast the audience as themselves. Expecting them to take a role

becomes more complex in terms of 'character' and can feel alienating. Audience members can play themselves, and the key is that the experience has the potential to be transformative and cast them as a version of themselves that they didn't know existed. Interestingly, this is a feature that can be identified in the large-scale masked shows as well; *Sleep No More* audiences defined themselves as ghosts and from *The Drowned Man* a group emerged from the audience who created their own club, 'The Red Ribbon Club' in a reference to Erin Morgenstern's novel *The Night Circus*. As I understand it, they were imitating the '*rêveurs*', from the novel, who were a collective of hardcore audience members that followed the circus on its travels. In the novel they identified themselves by wearing a red scarf. With *The Drowned Man*, The Red Ribbon Club identified themselves in the manner that the club moniker suggests and made repeat visits to the production together, becoming heightened versions of themselves once inside the world in order to work as one to piece together the experience.

Morgenstern visited *Sleep No More*, Boston and makes reference to its influence in her novel *The Night Circus*, expressing gratitude for 'the immersive experience of Punchdrunk, which I was lucky enough to fall into' within the acknowledgements (Morgenstern 2012, 495; see also Flaherty 2014). The Red Ribbon Club, imitating the identification method of Morgenstern's *rêveurs*, may also be referencing the red ribbon in the narrative loop(s) of *The Drowned Man*, which makes its way via the character of Studio Executive Alice Estee from The Gatekeeper's breast pocket to Mr Stanford, Temple Studio's omnipresent boss, to be briefly shared with The Seamstress. Stanford then later knots it around Romola Martin's neck, from where she 'finally' ties it to the wrecked Studebaker where it is discovered by The Gatekeeper, and so 'begins' each loop again.

In regard to masked shows, Maxine Doyle notes, for her choreographic practice, the audience becomes a living element within the building that brings the world to life:

I witness it become a white-faced beast, crashing and cascading through the building, devouring both set and cast. During previews I watch the audience obsessively noting where it travels, how it watches, how bold it dares to be and how fast (or slowly) it moves. As the show develops and the cast begins, deftly, to negotiate the audience dynamic, a subtle duet between both sides emerges. The dance between audience and performer moves between a myriad of states; from frantic to friendly, sympathetic to sensual and tense to timid.

awe and wonder (see also: **audience**; crescendo; cross-fade; Enrichment; **epic**: '**punch drunk**'; **synchronicity**; **transportation and transformation**): For Punchdrunk, awe and wonder are not related to grand, frivolous spectacle, but that which is personal, precious, possibly profound. The climatic finales of Punchdrunk projects aim to be impactful; to provide a collective and fitting end to the literally sensational experience that the audience has undergone. Yet it is the carefully planned and intimately executed crescendo moments, intended to be encountered by one person, or small numbers, that fully illustrate the aim and outcome for which Punchdrunk strives. A strong example of this is from Punchdrunk's first production of *The Tempest* in Exeter, 2001; precisely choreographed to the swell of Debussy's *La Mer*, Miranda gently raises her hand to touch the pane of a window in a room on the topmost floor of Buckland Abbey, her gaze focusing across the grounds to the middle distance where a lone firework is set off. A profound and intimate moment that conveys the complex layers of Miranda's longing, designed for those audience members who chose to follow her at that point, which perhaps only one person, standing closest to her and following her gaze, would have witnessed, while experiencing the crescendo of the music. Underscored by the sense of the clandestine, led by individual curiosity, rewarded by discovery. The experience of that audience member's chance finding and following of Miranda, the accident of gazing in the same way at the same time, illustrates the designed moment *intended* to create an experience of awe and wonder, thereby marking that feeling in subsequent recall and interpretation of the event. Important to this is the sense of mystery and discovery that underscores these glimpses of wonder. For Barrett, it is vital that individuals feel they have found these moments for themselves, rather than having them overtly signalled, so they are imbued with a sensation of '**things** not to be explained' . . .

Felix Barrett and Peter Higgin

On awe and wonder

Pete: This is the core feeling we aim to inspire in the audience, whether a primary school pupil or an adult audience member, the wow factor; stepping over the threshold and taking in a vast installation. The audience losing themselves in the unexpectedness of the world, or its sheer scale. It's gifting them something which they take away – the unexpected, the wide-eyed childlike feeling.

Felix: We've always been conscious of trying to trigger that effect; identifying that moment, that beat where it's exemplified. For *The Tempest* at Buckland Abbey, we drove all the way to Birmingham to buy the biggest fireworks we could afford so that at the zenith of the crescendo to Debussy's *La Mer*, as Miranda looks out of the window, the one audience member that followed her and her gaze would see that lone firework popping at the peak of the orchestral crescendo. It takes so much effort for that one beat of awe and wonder.

Pete: In more recent works, it's a case of making sure that there's an opportunity for every audience member to have that moment, whether it's in a smaller space or in the biggest, collective finale; it's a case of being in the right place at the right time, the combination of lighting, sound, all of the stagecraft coming together.

Felix: It's synchronicity, those moments where in one beat everything comes together and then separates again. Unfortunately, it's the nature of the work to have audience members who may feel they've missed out on that one moment. There's arguably a degree to which it would dilute the work if that didn't happen. The need to feel that there's something special, individual, a personal anecdote, a gift within the work.

Pete: You have to construct that experience for Enrichment work to greater or lesser degrees according to the group and audience with which you're working. When promenading there are moments that are crafted to create that sense of awe and wonder; in some respects it can mean it's less a sense of individual discovery of that moment. The questions that we ask through the experience are always related to achieving moments of awe and wonder, making them feel genuine, surprising. With *The Lost Lending Library*, how will we put the library in the right place to spark curiosity? How will the teacher deliver the emergency assembly? There's as many variables as there are with the large-scale Punchdrunk work. *The Oracles* has seen a further development for this practice. All school projects must start in the classroom. The work has to begin in the 'everyday' for a class, a place that is safe and known by the pupils. Always the start must be plausible. A games designer visits the school, wants to test a game on the pupils, plausible and 'on point' in terms of pupil interests, plus it's exciting and realistic to model this as a potential career path for pupils. The game they test introduces a world, the replica 'physical' world that they will go on to visit on-site at Fallow Cross. This is new for Punchdrunk; usually you wouldn't show where you're about to go and give away the surprise. However, because it's via a different medium, it serves as a great way to 'upskill' the pupils in the world of the production, to give them an induction of sorts. Additionally, the point that the physical village is revealed to them is a moment of pure awe and wonder, Punchdrunk at its best. Pupils, believing they're looking at a big digital display, at the transition, the stepping across into the physical space, are genuinely amazed, saying things like 'The village is real!' or 'I've always wanted to step inside a game'. With our school projects wherever it is that we end up, however imaginative, it always begins in their reality and we slowly take pupils to the fantastical.

Often our work is described as site-sympathetic; with the bigger work you're looking at fabricating the work within a vast, empty space or taking an existing space and responding to the ways in which it helps to interpret source. With Enrichment projects where we're working in, say, a school or a care home, we're asking how we merge the Punchdrunk world into the day-to-day running and organisation of that site in a way that will feel meaningful, authentic and awe-inspiring while not disrupting that organisation's working day. It's site-sympathetic but responding to a different set of parameters. In a school you could be working with the day's timetable and set breaks and four sets of staircases and the fact that not everyone can fit into the hall at one time for assembly, or where you have two separate sites in one school, so we had to set up two separate but connected departments of the same library. In terms of the awe and wonder, the delivery of that is often less individual and less personalised, but that's not to say that each individual audience member won't have their own individual response or chance encounters with the performer. You witness pupils returning to installations to try to get in, the school feels transformed.

Felix: There can be awe and wonder in a tear forming in the eye of a performer as they're holding an audience member. It doesn't always need to infer scale, but synchronicity, attuning to the rhythm of the performance; the rhythm of a performer or the building and realising that suddenly the soundtrack is heard all the way through the space. The audience has to discover these moments for itself. If we told them where to find them, it would remove all sense of awe and wonder.

B

'Bad Bar' (see also: *Faust*; **influences**): An audition exercise first used when casting for *Faust*, now 'Bad Bar' has become a seminal movement score for the company and is still used in auditions for masked shows. A scene from David Lynch's *Twin Peaks: Fire Walk With Me* serves as the inspiration for Punchdrunk's 'bad bar' sequence. Among the first ensemble members to participate in this exercise were Conor Doyle, Geir Hytten and Vinicius Salles. Conor Doyle recollects 'a long improvisation', where each was given a deadly sin: 'I was given "Lust" and Geir and Vinicius were given "Wrath". We began the improvisation, told to grow our word over ten minutes. Vinicius – who's always at 100 percent – just one minute in was 100 percent Wrath'. Maxine Doyle elaborates,

'Bad Bar' was born in a dance studio in East London but multiple iterations of it exist throughout the masked shows. Felix and I set up the context for the improvisation as a 'bar at the end of the world'. It's the kind of place that simultaneously excites and terrifies you. Each performer is given a trigger word on a piece of paper – based on one of the seven deadly sins. They are asked to keep this a secret from the group. Each person then enters the space one at a time – in a slow, slightly underwater tempo. The movement direction to begin with is a slow and sustained flow through the body. This creates a dramatic tension between bodies in space as well as specific attention to detail. Small gestures and shifts of focus become loaded with meaning and intimate moments charged with electricity. We slow the pace down so the observer can see the storytelling unfold. As the movement score progresses we offer the direction to performers to turn up the intensity of 'wrath', 'pride', gradually until the tension explodes and the movement languages erupt. It is this connection between

dance and imagination that surprisingly is a kind of epiphany for dancers; they are given permission to connect their technique with their humanity. This process is a challenge for actors as they have to channel their physicality and play against the urge to mime or speak. We play a droning soundscape to set the atmosphere and help the performers lose themselves. After playing the 'bad bar' improvisation performers often describe feeling as if they've been in another world. That's really what we try and do with audiences – take them to a different world. There are layers of otherworldly dimensions that coexist in this work.

In the original 'Bad Bar' scene in Punchdrunk's *Faust*, Sarah Labigne and Raquel Messeguar created the solo material for Gretchen's downfall, intertextualising Goethe's depiction of Gretchen's demise with the imagery and sensations of Lynch's bar. 'Bad Bar' palpably evoked 'Goethe's conceit of the devil existing in dangerous desire . . . a moral vacuum of a place where corruption wins over purity, lust over love' (Machon 2015, 274).

Balfour, Katy (see also: *Borough, The*; community; **Enrichment**; ensemble; letters; **one-on-one**): Formerly Associate Director, Associate Artist and Performer, Katy Balfour was a significant contributor to Punchdrunk's history and practice up until 2017 when she left to pursue a career as a Story Producer for Wonderbly, a publisher of interactive children's books. Her first experience of Punchdrunk was as an audience member at *Sleep No More*, 2003. So captivated was she by this that she was keen to be part of the creative team:

I volunteered as a performer at the 2004 Big Chill, working with others on a production of *Woyzeck*. My overwhelming memory of this experience was the sense of community that surrounded it. As a performer, I was also building set, painting signs, digging holes,

cooking communal meals. Everyone mucked in. That ethos has served us well. The people who have stayed and thrived at Punchdrunk tend to wear lots of 'hats'.

Balfour went on to perform again in *Marat/Sade* in 2005 and created one-on-one roles in *Faust*, *Masque of the Red Death* and *The Drowned Man*. She played the first Mrs Weevil in *Under the Eiderdown* and has contributed to many Enrichment projects and workshops since. Balfour quickly progressed from performer to Associate Director and, working closely with Felix Barrett, Colin Nightingale and Stephen Dobbie, she was responsible for driving the concept and direction of *The Borough*. She has worked as Associate Director on many Enrichment projects including *Against Captain's Orders* as well as for *Sleep No More*, NYC and as a co-director with Hector Harkness for *Black Diamond*. As writer and deviser-performer she helped create several Enrichment projects including *Grey's Printing Press* and *Prospero's Island*. Balfour has been central to the company's development of one-on-ones in masked shows and, consequently, helped define Punchdrunk's signature intimate performing style.

bar (see also: caretaking; crescendo; **masked show**; **narrative**; *Sleep No More*, NYC): This is a crucial, communal space for audience debrief and deconstruction enabling a collective curation of the show. The bar in any large-scale masked production is a liminal space where the audience end up (and can visit as they choose during the evening's run) to share experiences, piece together different fragments and create a collective interpretation. Following the crescendo of the masked event, it is the bar to which the audience as a whole is led and becomes the space that concludes the show and encourages the transportation of the event from a solitary to a shared experience. This is the space in which audience members can address frustrations they may have encountered in interpreting events or journeying through the space by piecing together clues and anecdotal narratives from the experience of others. The Manderley Bar in *Sleep No More*, NYC has become a rendezvous for members of the audience needing to reflect on the experience of the world of The McKittrick Hotel during and immediately following the event. It is also a destination for late-night revellers, with its post-show DJ sets or, more frequently, late-night performances from live bands.

Felix Barrett notes how *The Drowned Man* and *Kabeiroi* provide a useful illustration of the problems of not incorporating a bar into a project which requires a place to support shared conversation and provide a transitional space before re-entering the everyday world. The licence to serve alcohol was delayed for the first month of *The Drowned Man* which meant, despite serving water in dressed space, the audience were choosing not to stay in favour of heading to pubs or straight back onto public transport, back to normality, so as Barrett puts it:

No decompression, no chance to find friends, stop and talk about it and process the evening collectively. As a result it didn't work because it was too singular, too abstract, because a satisfaction comes from understanding how other people have interpreted it. It allows you to make sense of what you've seen. You need the time to process, you need that conversation.

Integral to a Punchdrunk 'formula' is the setting up of routes to acclimatise to the world before being inserted into it, with space and time to decompress before leaving it: 'you need a space to be eased back in and to be given a chance to evaluate'. Virtual versions of this liminal space exist on fan wikis, blogs and Facebook groups, sharing clues and experiences. As Barrett summarises:

Within the masked-show model approximately a third of the audience will have an agenda, find a lead character, follow them, and work hard to find the narrative; a third are adventurers, will explore the space, be led by the environment, stumble across themes in a non-linear manner; while a third are more *laissez faire*, might be more bewildered by the larger space and so enjoy the sanctuary of the bar, entering its cosiness, because for them it feels like the centre of the space. They appreciate the musical variety of the band, the power of the singer, the relationship with the performers who only operate in the bar. That third will stay in the bar and appreciate being in that realm for much of their time.

Kathryn McGarr provides illustration below of the manner in which the performers interact and create a world within the world in the bar environment, noting how, in *The Drowned Man*, it required a sensitivity to and tacit understanding of 'what that moment needed to be for people within their wider experience of the show'. For Barrett, 'all of those experiences need to have equal weight, an equal pay-off', with the bar space remaining 'experientially safe', while clearly within the mood, tempo and logic of the wider world of the event.

Barrett, Felix (see also: **Act 1**; **Act 2**; **Act 3**; adrenalin; atmosphere; **audience**; **Barrett, Margaret and Simon**; boxes, chests and drawers; **corridors**; **dens**; **Exeter Experiments**; **eyes**; Grant, Matthew; *H.G.*: **Hide-and-Seek**; **influences**: **'listening to the building'**; **music**; **one-on-one**; **process**: **'punch-drunk'**; Tonkin, Geoff; visceral): Founder and Artistic Director of Punchdrunk, Felix Barrett acknowledges that it is only relatively recently that he began to refer to himself as a director. For Barrett, from first pitch to final outcome, directing 'is about taking an audience by the hand and guiding them through a story, an environment, a narrative, an experience':

Directing is about purity and clarity of vision *and* enabling everyone else you're working with to see it so that you can all work together to get there. That vision is about the impact on the audience. What I try to maintain, whatever the project, is the focus on a distilled hit of an emotion to an audience. With the team, my role is about how best I ensure that it delivers. And it doesn't matter in what medium or platform, in the twenty-first century it could be anything, and often it's a fusion of different disciplines.

Barrett's directorial vision for practice was formed early on in his childhood. The eldest son of Margaret and Simon Barrett, Barrett grew up with his younger brother, Nathaniel, in a large Victorian house in the London Borough of Bromley. It was a household that actively encouraged Barrett's imagination and curiosity. The look and feel of the family home was his first artistic inspiration and design landscape. A living room that was piled high with books and music in all formats; an upright piano that Margaret would regularly play; a dining room with a log-burning fire, paintings, photographs and heirlooms; a kitchen with an uneven floor and cabinets full of crockery and curios; an attic full of ephemera. Alphonse Mucha prints, hung along the upstairs corridor, ethereal faces clothed in diaphanous shifts that Barrett believed 'would watch' him when he ran to his parents' bedroom, woken from bad dreams; spectre-like eyes observing him from the shadows. Barrett has vivid memories of playing within the architectural features of the house, identifying those he found ominous and those that were 'pockets of absolute safety'; a game that would later evolve into a distinctive and recurrent exercise in Punchdrunk's creative process. Vinyl and CDs, played constantly, instilled an appreciation of music of all varieties, from the crooning of The Ink Spots to the eerily atmospheric vocals of Kate Bush to the swell of orchestral scores and much more in-between. The Ink Spots, an American group of the 1930s and 40s and distinctive precursor to 'doo-wop', provided background music for Barrett and Nathaniel from a very young age. Margaret recollects, 'they had a cassette player in the back of the car and the two of them sat there playing The Ink Spots over and over again'.

A crucial aspect of Barrett's childhood, in relation to the theatre he would go on to create, relates to how he spent much of his time during his primary school years, building dens in his bedroom and the attic space. Barrett would transform his bedroom into dens with fake entrances, making good use of his mosquito net arranged around the bed and changing the bulbs from natural light to various colours in order to modify the lighting states and play with the atmosphere in the room. He scaled the dens up when at the age of twelve or thirteen, with his best friend and neighbour, Alex, they moved into the narrow attic space and then onto the Greenbelt woods of Beckenham.

It was the attic that held the most potential for play. It was full of boxes and drawers containing generations of objects and memories, kept by parents who were hoarders, alongside that which came with the house, inherited from his grandfather. Margaret recalls how she had tidied the attic up as a repository for the memorabilia, with a neat set of shelves that she had established as 'a museum', only for 'Felix and Alex' to unmake this in the construction of 'yet another of their camps'. For Barrett and his active imagination, this attic was a place of fear, mystery and curiosity, a physical space that allowed his imagination to run wild: 'so much shadow, it wasn't open-plan, you couldn't just flick a light on and see everything. It was so filled with detritus, strange objects that were from a foreign time, a mythical time' (Barrett 2012). Barrett recalls hearing stories of how his father was once a magician but had a car crash and from that day never performed again, with only drawers 'literally filled with magic' as a reminder of this past, archived in the museum in the roof. It turned out it was simply the tale of a thirteen-year-old boy whose box of tricks had smashed during a minor collision; a box of tricks which still resides in that small space in the eaves to this day. Barrett identifies how this

illustrates the power of the imagination, triggered by the possibility and the potency of the boxes and chests of found objects, 'in my mind's eye it became vast, I'd pictured my father in Victorian theatres'. That box of broken tricks took on a mythical magic where the box itself 'felt really charged, on the left as you came into the attic as if guarding the entrance' (Barrett 2012).

These recollections highlight how Barrett's childhood inventiveness spawned an attitude of curiosity and an aesthetic appreciation of architectural corners and domestic curios; a delight in the puzzles and play afforded by dens and labyrinths; an understanding of the mystery and threat cast by gloomy corridors and spectral eyes that watch from the darkness; and the power of the imagination in building stories from the triggers and trinkets hidden in boxes, chests and drawers.

The Barretts would make regular family trips to the cinema, galleries and the theatre. Of these there were four formative experiences that remain with Barrett in terms of how theatre became experiential and overturned the norms of engagement with an audience. The first was Andrew Lloyd Webber's *Cats*. Barrett recollects, visiting the production, aged seven, for a friend's birthday: 'in my mind's eye it was Care Bears on the stage, for children, and I didn't like stuff "for children" because even at that point I knew it was spoon-feeding us' (Barrett 2012). On arrival, however, 'the set spilled out into the audience', followed by a blackout and the orchestra striking up; 'it makes me tingle now to think about it. I felt it was out of control because it was so far away from what my perception of theatre was'. What remains with Barrett most is the manner in which members of the cast began their performance in the auditorium, directly behind him, one of whom 'brushed my shoulders, looked me in the eye', all of which happened 'in a moment' (Barrett 2012). So overwhelmed was he by the production that Barrett wished for, and received, the soundtrack as a Christmas gift: 'we put it on and as soon as it started playing

I cried, because the experience came back again, was utterly visible'. The potency of that experiential recall would remain with Barrett, 'that beat of tactile intimacy where among all these people, and that big production, there was one moment that only two of us shared and no one else had' (Barrett 2012).

A second defining theatrical experience came about by mistake, as Barrett, with both parents, reminisces:

Felix: I was taken to *The Rocky Horror Show* when I was nine. We turned up at the theatre and it was instantly noticeable that everyone was adult yet in fancy dress, which I'd never seen before. It wasn't funny at all, it was terrifying. It felt like one of those dreams where people are possessed.

Margaret: I'd seen a poster for *The Rocky Horror Show*, was vaguely aware of the title and I thought, 'ah, this contains two elements that my son likes' –

Simon: rock and horror –

Margaret: – 'perfect for my nine-year-old!'

Felix: Dad always opted for seats in the front row. We got to our seats and everything was immediately out of control. It was like all the laws of society had broken down. Everyone was heckling, swearing and talking. Everything was traumatic.

Margaret: These people were rising up and shouting over my little boy.

Felix: And that's before it started. I was thinking, you're supposed to be quiet in the theatre and to behave in a certain way. I assumed when the show started it would all settle down but then it just got worse, the call and response and everyone breaking the rules. The audience were saying the lines before the characters and the performers would be heckling back to them. And then they singled Dad out. In my memory it was scary, like a zombie film, the end of the world, it was so out of control.

Simon: We left after ten minutes.

Felix: It felt apocalyptic, to see my parents panic to the extent that we had to evacuate emergency-style. And then I discover I've left my coat, so Dad has to go back in and I hear the whole theatre roar at his re-entry, jeering at him, onstage and in the audience, like some Hogarthian excess.

It was the sense of being out of control, as much as the dressing up, the gothic party aesthetic and direct participation that was impactful for Barrett:

Talk about breaking the rules of theatre; they absolutely decimated then. It was the experience of a total rug-pull by those rules being broken. To be in a theatre and for it to feel so dangerous, enough for your parents to pull you out. It felt more like being in a football match with the crowds rising up. When I was thirteen, I became obsessed with the film because I understood what was going on by then. I wish I'd been old enough to see the original version at The Royal Court.

Following this, Barrett was taken by his parents to *Return to the Forbidden Planet*, 'a musical reworking of *The Tempest* on a spaceship'. Barrett notes that the concert-level volume of the music was thrilling to him but, 'most exciting was, when you sat down in the auditorium, the performers were already there, walking around in the stalls, talking to you in character'. Barrett was fascinated by the manner in which this enabled the audience to connect with the characters which then heightened the subsequent experience of their performance on the stage. However, on a demanded repeat

visit for his birthday, where Barrett requested the family get there even earlier to experience the pre-performance interaction:

They didn't speak to us. I feigned an asthma attack and we had to leave because I was so devastated that hadn't happened. Without that high, the one-on-one connection that I'd had previously, the show suddenly felt much thinner and pointless.

The fourth formative experience, shared with Margaret when he was nineteen, was De La Guarda's *Villa! Villa!*, performed in the vast space of Camden's Roundhouse. The audience stood amidst the performance space as the event fused theatre, dance, carnival, gig and clubbing:

There was a point where the ceiling came off and it turned into a massive club night, which felt crazy. A performer was moving through the crowd, making eye contact and she settled on me. She took one end of the chewing-gum in her mouth, stretched it and put the other end in my mouth. Everyone was watching me, so I felt absolutely mortified. I was made a performer and felt absolutely exposed, I hated it. I didn't want to be the 'performer' that backs down. She started biting in, pulling us together with that chewing-gum string and it was doubly weird as Mum was watching. I felt the anticipation and pressure to deliver, not let the performer down, but in the end I was the one that broke it. The amazing part of that experience was that I could feel the fluctuation between being audience, performer and somewhere in-between. It was the power of eye contact and being singled out, the shift in relationship, in the power dynamic from performer to audience to two people locked in a one-on-one. But with people watching it was mixed with humiliation, no sense of being protected. The watching was emphasised by the fact that it was Mum watching.

I don't know what I would have done had no one else been there, but the rules-set was unclear, so I felt they'd crossed a line. It was respectful, but I didn't like *my* reaction because I was so self-aware. I felt that I'd curtailed a scene prematurely because I hadn't been able to continue.

This memory highlights Barrett's realisation of a need for clear, even if unspoken, rules of engagement to set individuals at ease and provide opt-outs when tacitly negotiating any interaction. It also indicated a need for crescendo and a sense of closure, carefully controlled by tempo and duration as much as interaction; for the performer to provide some acknowledgement that the audience-participant's contribution had been resolved, whatever the outcome of that intimate moment. It initiated in Barrett a desire to create that same quality of experience but with readable safety-nets for the audience-participant, where exposure is reduced, as is the case in Punchdrunk's work via the wearing of the mask or the exclusion of a wider audience.

Barrett's secondary school years were vital to his vision for theatre, nurturing in him a skills-set, resources and critical attitude supported by influential ideas and methodologies for practice. Barrett won a scholarship to attend Alleyn's School in Dulwich, renowned for its arts education. The award can be attributed to Barrett's eleven-year-old theatrical imagination; he spent the majority of his interview talking about a musical he wanted to create based on The Beatles' *Octopus's Garden*. Barrett recalls how his study of Theatre through to A Level, facilitated by two inspiring teachers, Matthew Grant and Geoff Tonkin, focused 'on the outer reaches of theatrical practice'. In addition to Edward Gordon Craig and Antonin Artaud, he was introduced to the breath-taking scenographic practice of Czech scenographer, Josef Svoboda, and the nightmarishly imagistic theatre of Romanian director Silviu Purcărete. Barrett was particularly inspired by the retelling of rehearsal techniques that

Purcărete employed for his 1996 production of Aeschylus's *The Suppliant Women*, adapted by Purcărete as *Les Danaïdes*. Purcărete met his company in an old aircraft hangar, pairing them, giving each couple a candle and instructing them to find a space in which to improvise the murderous wedding night of Hypermnestra and Lynceus. Barrett was particularly taken by the description of how, in this unusual and potentially perilous rehearsal location, the improvised scene could only reach its conclusion when the last candle had burnt to the ground. This story fed Barrett's imagination in regard to how space could both unlock and underscore psychologies, themes and narratives. It highlighted the significance of light and the importance of duration, captured in the flickering and sputtering of a candle flame. It illustrated an approach that established theatre as *experience* and clarified the notion of experiential time, where duration becomes tangible in action and aesthetic with narrative 'woven into the flicker of a flame'.

Barrett recalls a practical session, facilitated by Grant, that fused Craig's theories around the delivery of text 'on the edge of the breath' and Purcărete's rehearsal techniques, where the class hunkered under chairs in a blacked-out studio, with only the flicker of candlelight glowing as they whispered snatches of *The Cherry Orchard* across the space; powerful and ritualised, it is an exercise that remains in Barrett's visceral recall to this day. He also remembers that he was especially inspired by Grant's obsession with 'light as a solid entity, his enthusiasm and passion for sculptural shards of light as tangible elements in the space. I remember him showing me black and white pictures of Craig's work and Svoboda's opera sets from the 1950s'. These images and Grant's ability to communicate his enthusiasm proved deeply influential to Barrett.

Practical workshops would test these theories. Unusual for many A Level students at the time was Grant's support of investigating lighting as a means of theatrical expression. For Barrett, these 'continued the conversation' around lighting in technical terms and gave him the opportunity to sculpt light in darkness, to play with illuminated shards that cut through the blackout and watch how these states enabled performers to appear and disappear as if conjured from thin air. Barrett was later to test this effect further with more rudimentary lighting sources during his Deptford reworking of *The Tempest* in 2003, exploring the manner in which a dancer could move around the space, appearing from and disappearing into the gloom as if by magic.

Barrett was also heavily influenced by visits that he made during the mid-1990s with the school's Music Department to the English National Opera for revivals of Benjamin Britten's *Peter Grimes* and Béla Bartók's *Bluebeard's Castle*. *Peter Grimes*, directed by Tim Albery, proved inspirational because of its powerfully visceral staging; atmospheric, rainy, windy scenarios created by the evocative score and the 'sheer force of the chorus far downstage singing at the audience' (2012). With *Bluebeard's Castle*, alongside Bartók's score, it was David Alden's design that Barrett was especially taken by, how it could subvert expectation:

The perspective of the set was skewed, nothing was as it seemed. The seventh door, a skewed panel, had wallpaper which started to slip so its formation broke, as if whoever was wallpapering had lost control. It was left unfinished; that unfinished motif *felt* so dangerous.
(Barrett 2012)

These experiences remained with Barrett as visceral recall: 'elements I can replay in real-time in my memory, that I'd never seen anything like before'. From these formative experiences, Barrett knew that he 'wanted to create theatre with an operatic sensibility', which led later to him, observing, volunteering and eventually working as a Revival Director and General Manager on two operas with the English Touring Opera.

It was during his Upper Sixth year that Barrett was transformed by a defining theatrical experience. His class were taken by Grant to see Robert Wilson and Hans Peter Kuhn's immersive installation, *H.G.*, after which, for Barrett, 'everything changed' (2012). For Barrett, this was a point at which he palpably felt the potency of light as a performance language:

There was a simple room with a body lying on the floor which would fill with dense smoke and then slowly a beam would appear above the body, so solid that when I put my hand in it, I couldn't understand why it wasn't possible to take hold of it. It wasn't that it was a revelation, that I'd never thought of it before, but that it was using haze in a way that wasn't trashy. Back then there was an implication of dry ice as a naff effect, whereas this was giving validity to haze as a lighting tool.

Where Barrett had assumed such techniques would be rubbished by an audience, candles being viewed 'as hippie things you had at home' and haze merely a gimmicky 'haunted house effect', this exposure to artists using these techniques 'with integrity opened up a whole chasm of possibility', for the young practitioner.

The interweaving of all of these innovative practices made a great impression on Barrett's vision for theatre. These influences combined underpinned Barrett's own practical experimentation, giving him methods and vocabulary for exploring abstraction and experiential aesthetics in his approach to theatrical design and performance. It led him further on the path to questioning the manner in which the audience might experience the work from within. It served to foster Barrett's own idiosyncratic inventiveness as well as giving him the language and techniques to realise his vision, and a theatrical legacy to build on. Spurred on by this, and greatly inspired by *H.G.*, Barrett took Directing as a specialist option.

For Barrett this skill was not simply 'directing bodies' but concerned with driving a concept and its corresponding aesthetic. Directing meant shaping the experiential form of the playing space, designing the scenography and, crucially, sourcing music that established an atmosphere and drove the narrative in an abstract manner. Barrett's final project involved him mixing a cacophonous orchestral crescendo, the peak of which 'dropped into a dance track', written by a fellow student studying music. Barrett recalls that, beyond the aesthetic, he was wholly concerned with creating 'a whole experience for the audience. I'd written it, which I realised I was no good at, didn't enjoy, I found it difficult, but to be able to get the corners I wanted to put in I had to write it myself'. The piece had a post-apocalyptic narrative, conveyed primarily through sound and scenography and performed by Sam Booth, classmate of Barrett's younger brother, who would go on to become a longstanding Punchdrunk performer. Grant describes Barrett's installation, assembled in the school's nineteenth-century gymnasium, as 'a massive junk-sculpture, a giant horseshoe of discarded white goods and car components' with discarded television sets embedded in it displaying deconstructed loops of Fritz Lang's *Metropolis*. Using a material that would be redeployed on a mountainous scale for *The Drowned Man*, Barrett covered the gymnasium floor with sand on which the audience sat.

With his A Level success, a pivotal and final detail to which Barrett remains indebted was that:

Geoff Tonkin knew which university was right for me. I went to Loughborough and before the interview started the interviewee said, 'a little bird has told me that you should go to Exeter'.

These stories from his childhood, through his time at Alleyn's School and on to Exeter University, map the route to the practice for which Punchdrunk

is now renowned. While sifting through the archives that Margaret has steadfastly kept, the gathering of recollections and personal effects revealed to Barrett that he was committed to site-sympathetic practice, to adventuring and journeying, from an early age, before he even had the vocabulary to define it: 'I stubbornly refused to consider a different way of working':

I knew what I wanted to be from an early age, but I never had the language to think or talk of it. I didn't have a word for it. I knew I wanted to build worlds, and the world surrounding an event, and the term director didn't fit that. From the off I knew it was something other and that it had the word theatre in it, but then I got distracted by film, for six months. I thought it was film that answered what it was. For much of my year out, between school and university, I attempted to make a film, while still exploring the idea of installation. I was slightly scared to create an installation because I felt it might be perceived as trivial, that it wasn't substantial art. So instead, as part of the film, I remember taking rooms in my Granny's house and trying to abstract and stylise it to use as a location for the film. In my head I couldn't be an artist because I wasn't allowed to do Art at GCSE and there was also no way I equated the word 'artist' with what it was I wanted to do. Whereas 'director' meant talking to actors on a stage, and I knew it wasn't that either. It kind of was theatre but related to experience and adventure. What I felt when I went into different spaces, the sensation, adrenalin and euphoria, I knew I wanted to try and give that to audiences. It was always about audience and always about *feeling*. At no point did I want to direct a show on a stage, I never had that desire.

Barrett also notes that his father's regular aside that he should become a taxi driver was not solely a get-a-trade-behind-you quip but tapped into

the practice to which he was drawn: 'because I liked night, a bit of adventure, and people. There would always be a story to tell'.

Barrett's indefatigable curiosity and desire for adventure, alongside his predisposition to tell stories through work which makes its audience think through *feeling*, has been present since those early den days and underpins Punchdrunk's concept and vision for theatre. Architecture, landscape, site serving as inspiration for creative exploration. The adventure and puzzle-breaking play that exists in the folds of labyrinthine structures. The power of magic, mystery and curiosity that resides in hidden spaces with the at once intimate and mythical stories that might be told through found objects. The power of eye contact, eyes that watch you, that send you running or draw you in. The thinking through of the audience experience, the power of the one-on-one, the importance of sound that crescendos, the potency of a multidimensional image which invites you in to explore rather than preventing you from entering. All present. Here. All ready to be tested further, strengthened and supported, in Barrett's 'Exeter Experiments' undertaken across his undergraduate years.

Barrett, Margaret and Simon (see also: **Act 1**; Act 2; Act 3; **archiving**; **Barrett, Felix**; design; Exeter Experiments; **influences**; masked shows; **music**): Parents to Felix Barrett and unstinting supporters of Punchdrunk, Margaret and Simon, according to Barrett, 'lived and breathed' Punchdrunk across Act 1. Barrett's parents were the first and foremost influences on his outlook and practice. For most of the early projects they provided familial support and a London base, and allowed the family home to be raided of furniture; a grandfather clock (which, according to Margaret, 'is lost and gone forever'), the piano, crockery, ornaments, tools and sundries in order that Felix might create his installations in the design of those early worlds. Simon, as well as assisting with the transportation of these household items, provided vital musical influences for Barrett and allowed him to plunder the contents of his record collection to seek out tracks from which he could create his soundscores. Barrett recalls, while sitting on his parents' living room floor amid stacks of vinyl and books, 'there was a point when all of the design for Punchdrunk projects relied solely on this house'. Margaret concurs, illustrating this through *The Tempest*, 2003, 'our neighbours went to this show, came back and thought it was hysterically funny because they'd seen all the contents of our house used as the set'.

Punchdrunk also, for a long time, was dependent on the willingness of Barrett's parents to do, as Margaret puts it, 'anything that was required', including using the family home as the Punchdrunk business address, culminating in Margaret taking on the hard work of single-handedly running the box office from the family dining room for *The Firebird Ball*. Margaret remembers:

Felix bought us an answerphone and we had to have another landline put in. I had to take a note of people's number and then phone the full list on to Colin Marsh on a daily basis so that he could deal directly with the ticket sales. A very peculiar arrangement. As it got into the run I was returning from work at lunchtime to deal with it and there would be thirty calls and requests. Eventually we had to set another message to say there were no longer tickets available. Simon and I would be woken up by constant calls, hearing that message echo out on repeat.

Margaret notes a reward was that 'those were the days when Punchdrunk always let me be the first person in to the show. I'd have this wonderful experience where there would be nobody else but me'. Modestly referring to herself at that time as 'the odd-jobs' person, Margaret notes how, by *Faust*,

she and Simon were no longer needed to help run the productions (although certain items of furniture and various housewares may still have been lent) and could enjoy the work solely from the perspective of the audience member; stating simply, 'it got much bigger once The National got involved'. For Margaret, it was from Barrett's final-year project at Exeter University, *Woyzeck* in 2000, that she knew he had found a unique theatrical approach:

Felix had forewarned us that we were probably going to be in there for a twenty-minute loop, and then we'd most likely come out. I, along with everyone else I saw, was there to the bitter end. The first thing I saw was this flotilla of people wearing masks, trotting after somebody across the courtyard of the barracks, exploring different rooms. It had all the elements, the masks, the candles. The fact that everybody stayed in made me realise that he had something, that this was completely different; nobody wanted it to end. It made me realise his idea was worth pursuing.

Simon adds 'the only shame of it was that those early runs were so short', with relatively few people making up the audience during the run, in comparison with today's standards.

In addition to being a source of unparalleled memories and anecdotes of the emerging artist and his early work, Margaret is solely responsible for having garnered an extensive archive of Punchdrunk's history and practice, including every review and newspaper feature since Barrett's first production at Alleyn's School.

Believe Your Eyes (2016; see also: cinematic; **digital technologies**; **dreams**; in-show-world; R&D; reveal; senses; vanishing): Originated as a commission from Samsung to appear at Cannes Lions Festival, 2016, this was Punchdrunk's first public experiment with Virtual Reality (VR), created by Kath Duggan and Hector Harkness. The creative development

began with a discussion about the possibilities of VR and what it can do that cannot be achieved in a live experience. Punchdrunk imagined a character duplicating around the audience-player, able to engage in a tactile manner from multiple directions simultaneously. Research for the project's narrative alighted on shapeshifting spirits, mythical creatures and dream stories about the bogeyman. Investigating theories of sleep paralysis helped shape a one-on-one scene in which the audience is told a story by a character via both live-action and film.

In a prologue, a female performer met an audience member in the bustle of the space, and led him or her away from the hubbub into the bowels of the building, hinting at a story to come. They enter an otherworldly room installed in meticulous Punchdrunk detail and she places the VR goggles over the eyes, and her replicated, virtual counterpart comes into view. The story continues, involving gentle physical interaction that matches the visuals. She multiplies, five different versions of her, the soundscore crescendo builds, she looks up, horrified by what she sees; the bogeyman walking towards her. This old man in the virtual realm reaches down to take off your goggles and, the reveal, she has vanished and he now stands as a physical presence in her place. With a wicked grin, he sends you away from the room, the waking dream, and back into the bustle of the everyday.

The design process was much like a masked show; touch-real, 360-degree and precisely lit for the protagonist to vanish into the shadows. Great attention was given to matching the VR camera to a human sitting in chair, and the subsequent rehearsal with the live performers so that any live contact entirely matched what the audience was seeing on their headsets. The shape and crescendo of the event came from a build in the intensity of convincing, physical touch that matched the virtual interaction. The piece was subsequently performed at Art Basel in Miami, Phi

Centre Montreal and had an extended run at Samsung 837, NYC.

Beneath the Streets *I* and *II* (2014, 2015, see also: **access**; Act 2; found space; journeying. Further reading: Tims 2016):

Hidden in Cardiff is a world of lost things. In the shadows, behind closed doors, we await you. We invite you on a tour of Fo[U]nd Corp, a chance to explore behind the scenes of the premiere manufacturer of remembrance and immersive realities. Publicly, memories are harvested ethically and consensually. Beneath the streets, it's another story . . .

The full title of the project is *Beneath the Streets: Lost and Found* and was written and directed by Matthew Blake for Punchdrunk Enrichment, in collaboration with Hijinx Theatre. Hijinx approached Punchdrunk to work with their Academy on its theatre programme, assisting a group of adults with learning disabilities on routes to employability via a two-week residency, working alongside local professional performers in found space. This was a residential opportunity for Enrichment to work outside of London with a group who would help the team develop approaches to participatory practice. A piece was devised using a café and hairdressing salon in one of Cardiff's busy shopping arcades, which led to an underground service tunnel. The first half of the experience was devised to sit in the reality of the shop worlds, but the piece took an unexpected turn when audiences were led into the subterranean tunnel where, beneath the streets, a more sinister and fantastical world was revealed.

Matthew Blake led as the director and writer while Julie Landau, freelance designer and regular Enrichment collaborator, reinvented the spaces as the premises of 'Fo[U]nd Corps'. Following the success of this, the project was remounted as *Beneath the Streets II*, commissioned for Hijinx's Unity festival in Cardiff, 2015.

Installed this time in Jacob's Antiques Market emporium, the original concept was developed to feature a larger cast of actors, with and without disabilities, with many of the original cast returning to perform in it. The narrative developed the Fo[U]nd Corp brand; a new age corporation promising happiness and synthetic memories. The reality behind the corporation was much darker, with the mistreatment of workers, held captive and having their thoughts feelings and experiences harvested to further the advancement of the corporation emerging as the piece played out. Peter Higgin notes, 'it was great to see a project of this nature develop into a fully fledged work and receive critical acclaim'. It was nominated for 'Best Production in English' at the Wales Theatre Awards 2015, with Blake nominated in the Best Director category.

Bicât, Tina (see also: Act 1; Act 2; **costume**; design; *Duchess of Malfi, The*; *Faust*; *Masque of the Red Death, The*; mass production; *Night Chauffeur, The*; research; scenography; **senses**; touch; visceral): Theatre designer, inventor, consultant and maker, Bicât's design and realisation of costume, set, puppets, mask and installation often produce transformations or illusions. Bicât has written seven books on practical aspects of theatre practice. She is Costume Designer and Technician for the theatre programmes at St. Mary's University College in Strawberry Hill, which is where she first collaborated with Maxine Doyle, on student productions. Doyle introduced Felix Barrett to Bicât and invited her to create the costumes for *Faust* because 'I knew she was the only woman I had worked with who could do a high-quality job on a very low budget'. Bicât continues to collaborate with Punchdrunk on small-scale projects and was Costume Designer for *The Night Chauffeur*, *The Duchess of Malfi* and *The Masque of the Red Death* . . .

△
FIGURE 2 *Beneath the Streets.*

Photo credit: Simon Gough

Tina Bicât

On costuming decadence, death and dancers

*M*asque of the Red Death had all that feeling of decadence, the European nature of storytelling that you find in *fin-de-siècle* Paris. It mooches into that thick, dark, sensual area of time, so Punchdrunk, and absolutely appropriate for that wonderful building. *Masque* had a much clearer structure than anything else I'd worked on with Punchdrunk. I know that I would always go and watch the morning class because of getting to know the bodies; bodies that I was quite used to by then and so I knew how I wanted to work with them. I knew also that they'd let me. It was having the confidence of knowing that I could do what Punchdrunk wanted me to because they wouldn't think it was weird to work in such an untraditional way.

Working in a traditional theatre setup, you present your costume design concept at a meeting, talk about it with the director first and then show it to the actors and, that's it, it's set. Working with Punchdrunk is a completely different process and because I'd worked with them before, I could see how I would work best, how I could invent best; there would be a need for me to invent as much as a desire to invent. I had the most wonderful, happy and, remarkably for Punchdrunk, comfortable workroom. It was in the most perfect place, on the right as you entered, past the box office before the café. Everyone passed the door every time they walked up the stairs or had a coffee, so I could look out and see them and get them to try things on. That was what was so good about being by the stairs because I could dress someone and ask them to run up and down again, slide down the bannisters; it was a ready-made playground for them to try everything on my workroom doorstep. It gave perspective; you could check it from a distance, stand at the bottom and look up and get them to cross the balustrade at the back or come out of various adjoining rooms so you could see what the audience would see from a long way away, while also seeing what they look like right up close.

I built this *Masque* heap from a mixture of fabric shops and carboot sales, clothes and fabric, all of which were in the language of the piece, the texture, because I knew once we started there wouldn't be much time for shopping. The shopping can be a lengthy process because a lot of the time you're looking for items in the language of the world, the stories and the characters, rather than for a specific thing. The *Masque* world was doubled too because it involved both the Music Hall and the Poe world. I had a team of two or three people. It was where I met Kate Rigby for the first time. She'd come in to do a few days' work experience and I knew she had it, that intuition and instinct and imagination and she was frank.

Felix came up with this terrific idea in the beginning of having everybody in cloaks, but the cost of it was huge, we needed 500 or so. I emailed David Jubb and said, 'what would you say if I asked everybody in the building who worked in *any* department at all, to cut five cloaks with me?', because it was the cutting that was so difficult and time consuming. And with the most wonderful faith in his company he said, 'yes, go for it'. So that's what we did, every morning. There were sign-up slots, I laid the fabric out on the table and everyone, administration, cafeteria, performers, absolutely everyone, came in in pairs. A member of the local Battersea community who had taken a look into the workroom – I think she was a curtain maker with no theatrical leanings but she had a sewing machine at home and was keen to earn some money – came in every day, collected a pile, took them home, whipped up the fastenings and put a collar on them.

The steeping of the atmosphere was very powerful in *Masque*, partly because Poe is so Punchdrunky, and partly because the vision of the journey was very strong and the building lent itself so well to the era and the narrative, to its episodic nature. Each room had its own feeling and the performers were very strong in their space, like the boudoir with Fernanda [Prata] and Rob [McNeill], where the audience see her preparing for her wedding, putting on her dress and petticoats. Because corset lacing is a right pain and takes so long, I knew if I gave it to Maxine with the dancers they would make it into something beautiful. After making it, I laid the costume on the bed; it was a wonderful feeling of giving Maxine, Fernanda and Rob something to play with.

When you see Fernanda and Rob working, the ratio of each separate part of their bodies is so perfectly matched plus, watching them, you're conscious of a lightness in their bodies, a lightness of mood. In contrast, watching Vini [Salles] working, you're conscious of a heaviness and power. Fernanda and Rob can make you hold your breath, they're otherworldly, a bit like when you observe children immersed in an activity, an unexpected quality. I wanted to keep that in what they were wearing. I'd seen when they were warming up that, for Rob, it was very important that what he wore was very light so that it didn't affect his movement at all. I remember making him five delicate shirts, because when he sweated it stuck to him, you could almost see through it. There was something about that and the innocence in their bodies, that combination of that sensuality and innocence is very strong in the two of them. With Fernanda I used a lot of silk. I was very careful with her underclothes. Obviously it was difficult, because they were upside down a lot of the time, to make them decent while also looking as if they were nothing but film, diaphanous. The whole feeling of it and the way they threw themselves about the bed and the ceiling, merging with the design of the room.

△ FIGURE 3 'Costuming decadence, death and dancers' – *The Masque of the Red Death*. 2008. Robert McNeill, Fernanda Prata.

Photo credit: Stephen Dobbie

One of the things that made the job such fun was that it played with opposites and differences. There was a dancer called Jane (Leaney), who had a massive skirt, she was extremely statuesque, dark, very beautiful and she was exactly the opposite of Fernanda. Her body was strong, tall and powerful and I remember making her a skirt with so much material in it, like a waterfall down the stairs because she had this naturally very upright yet bendy body and because of that I was able to make this amount of skirt, a golden colour, that could fill space and trail down steps.

There were a lot of sweat difficulties in *Masque* because they were all wearing nineteenth-century costume, which is thick and heavy, coats and waistcoats, which they all really enjoyed wearing. Vini and Kath [Duggan] contrasted with Fernanda and Rob; stocky and they sit squarely on their hips, not ethereal at all, very go-gettery, they'll chuck themselves at anything. Vini really wanted to feel heavy, so I ended up boiling up some pure wool tweed so that it became almost like board and making him a jacket out of that so that under his arms he had these wrunkles of thick cloth. You wouldn't think that anyone would have wanted to work in it, wrunkly and itchy, but he loved it. It was short, so his waist was free but to bend your elbow you had to get past all this thick fabric and he had a thick shirt underneath it, bundled up, thick trousers and braces, the sort of costume that you'd put someone in in a film where they were labouring down a coalmine. Similarly, Kath didn't want to feel quite so heavy but she wanted to look it, so I remember putting her in lots of layers, things that looked heavy but were actually cotton. And of course, all the time you have to think about how to manage the washing, because they sweat a lot, and the mending, which was a huge task, because of course they rip things through. There was a single washing machine on site and someone came in and did that as a job.

There was the whole Music Hall section, which was almost like a different performance, a world within the world and it was much more like designing for a play. Old-fashioned variety technicalities were required like hiding cards and flying. Fernanda flew and Conor [Doyle] did the best quick change I've ever managed, where he just walked round a statue and changed from Pierrot to Policeman. It was a recreation of the scene in the film *Les Enfants du Paradis*, very complex, and he practised for ages to get it right. Conor's very neat, the sort of person who never tears his costume. He had a lovely sweep of his body, could make shapes with such elegance and grace. When you're designing for him you want to use that sweep, accentuate those curved limbs.

The audience of course influence the design practically all the time because you never know how close they're going to be. They might be close enough to see the stitching on a strap so attention to detail is vital, you can't fudge stuff like you can on stage. The work has to be really strong, so the thinnest spaghetti strap would require hidden strengthening, almost like para-cord, invisible to the eye and hidden inside the strap that would go under the arm and out the other side to make sure that it didn't rip off, unless of course you wanted it to. The design is full of those types of tricks. If you're trying to make clothes look like real clothes, they have to be reinforced. It's a mixture of hiding all the tricks that you need to keep costumes practical while also making big pictures, like a film a lot of the time. You have to think about the audience but you haven't got an angle for them. On stage you know what angle they're going to be looking at it from and you know the lighting is going to be telling them to look in a certain way. In Punchdrunk worlds they're right in front of you or behind you or they also might be seeing you as part of a wider picture with twenty-five other people all moving, so they might be seeing you as a whirling pattern of colour. It's knowing that that's what it needs. And knowing that it's not just visual, tactility and texture are important; if they touched Vini's jacket they'd feel the coarseness. I'm sensitive to what fabrics *feel* like visually and viscerally, in the character, the mix of the person, the performer and the character they're playing. In this work, it's not about silhouette on a stage, it's very much to do with the person mixed with the character they're playing mixed with the way that they're moving mixed with the weight and the colour and the feeling of everything that they're wearing.

I remember the wild mayhem of the final sequence. Felix had wanted ash to fall but they couldn't make it happen. It was a beautiful idea, that the whole thing would became covered in ash as they were dancing amidst this wild party; gradually becoming grey. You can imagine the picture. I remember being really surprised that people were so astonished by the vanishing because, when you've worked on a conjuring trick, all the technicalities of it are so complex that you're only aware of how it's achieved, where fastenings are and so on, so I forgot that it was going to be astonishing for the audience. I remember being very pleased with the colours because there was a lot of whirling around the edge, then whirling in the middle, and the colours, lots of waistcoats and bodices, stained-glassy yet without the blues.

I could see how Punchdrunk evolved across those early productions. In *Malfi*, they already seemed to be more in control of separate departments rather than everybody doing multiple things, with a clearer sense of a hierarchy, which was actually a more convenient way to work. From the Artistic Directors down across departments, if you were in charge of your department you could be trusted to do the right thing. Individuals had responsibilities and it was easier to know where to go to check, say, what tone of colour a room would be painted, get a swatch of colour; so the whole process became more cohesive while still holding moments of total mayhem.

There was a very nice feeling of sharing the process with the community. There was this lovely Battersea couple who were there every day, very untheatrical, salt-of-the-earth types. I remember them saying how they'd never had such a good time in their life. In one of the rooms there was a real, coal fire, and a theatre cat, and they were happy to come in every day to light it, look after it and sweep the ashes. They felt really valued and part of it. It was real community work.

Big Chill, The (see also: **Act 1**; **audience**; *Marat/Sade*; **R&D**; *Woyzeck,* **2004**): Founded in 1994 by Peter Lawrence and Katrina Larkin, The Big Chill began as a series of DJ nights and party events at the Union Chapel in Islington, London. It developed into an outdoor music festival in 1995 and established itself, annually, at Eastnor Castle from 2002. The most recent Big Chill Festival was held in August 2011. During its time at Eastnor Castle, the organisers invited contributions from emerging and high-profile artists and arts bodies, including two from Punchdrunk; *Woyzeck* in 2004 and *Marat/Sade* in 2005. These productions proved vital in positioning Punchdrunk's work, literally and figuratively, outside of theatre conventions, thereby expanding Punchdrunk's early audience and fan-base from non-theatre backgrounds. They also enabled the team to test approaches to enticing and interacting with that audience.

Black Diamond (2011; see also: **Act 2**; cinematic; journeying; *Night Chauffeur, The*; R&D; scalability): An R&D project in collaboration with Stella Black and Mother, developed from the learning, narrative and French film noir aesthetic of *The Night Chauffeur*. A site-specific production partnered by a series of journeying events, learning from which fed into *Kabeiroi*. *Black Diamond* began at a party in an open-plan flat in Shoreditch, East London, where characters mingled with audience, all guests together, all witnesses to events that led to the stealing of the eponymous diamond. For those who took up the invitation, the narrative concluded across separate nights in the following weeks as a series of intimate performances for audiences of two at a time. Instructed to arrive at a phone box in Old Street Station at a given time, on approach it would ring until answered, the denouement playing out in cars, phone booths and locations across the streets of Shoreditch. The R&D focus of *Black Diamond* tested approaches to mobile and online engagement, sharing invitations, clues and a series of films that augmented the narrative. Live interactions investigated the interweaving of durational narrative from different perspectives while journeying by car. Co-director and writer, Hector Harkness, elaborates:

As a sequel to *The Night Chauffeur*, we'd established a solid narrative world, augmenting it with episodic stories that created multiple conclusions. Our desire to produce a complex, longer-form experience for two at a time, with dual perspectives for each pair, was challenging. One person might be spying on a crime taking place in a garage while the other was complicit in that crime; or one would be behind the scenes in a jazz club while the other sits alone in the audience, watching the show. The really satisfying thing about the project was tying together disparate locations into a narrative whole, in a manner that felt cinematic. It was bookended by a payphone; the first call giving you instructions to begin the journey, and the last containing a little note in the coin slot that said 'FIN', ending the 'real-world' movie for which you'd been the star.

blackout (see also: **atmosphere**; **darkness**; design; **lighting**): Crucial to any work in buildings, in particular the large-scale masked shows. The first technical exercise undertaken in any found space is to create a full blackout in order to rid the building of natural light and the outside world.

Booth, Elizabeth (see also: Act 1; Act 2; Act 3; **awe and wonder**; **Enrichment**; *Firebird Ball, The*; Grey's Printing Press; *Lost Lending Library, The*; **Lynch, Sharon**; *Under the Eiderdown*; *Up, Up and Away*): Booth has served as Headteacher for eighteen years at Dalmain Primary School, Lewisham. Dalmain was the first school to collaborate with Punchdrunk Enrichment, at Booth's instigation, as part of a collaborative of partner primary schools. Since then Dalmain has experienced all of Punchdrunk Enrichment's projects for primary schools. Mother to longstanding Punchdrunk performer, Sam Booth, Elizabeth first discovered Punchdrunk's work as an audience member for *The Firebird Ball*.

Borough, The (2013, see also: **Act 2**; digital technology; journeying; *Kabeiroi*; *Moon Slave, The*; **music**; **Reekie, Jonathan**; synchronicity; *Uncommercial Traveller: Living Cities, The*; vanishing; wardrobes): Felix Barrett vividly remembers a school-trip to Benjamin Britten's *Peter Grimes*, directed by Tim Albery. Britten's score made a lasting impression, as did Albery's staging of the final act, with the sheer force of the chorus far downstage singing directly at the audience, overwhelming, like the crashing Aldeburgh sea it conveyed. Barrett remained inspired by the interludes in *Peter Grimes*, viscerally recalling how it first held him in its grip. In 2009, when Jonathan Reekie asked him if he wanted to create a *Peter Grimes*, Barrett's response was, 'yes I do'. The result was Punchdrunk's *The Borough*, for the Britten Centenary Aldeburgh Festival, 2013, which reimagined Britten's opera through its original source, George Crabbe's poem of the same title. Following Reekie's invitation, Barrett recalls 'a four-year process' working out 'what that production might look like':

Initially I'd imagined a masked show opera, predating *Malfi*, but what became clear was that for Reekie the defining, full-scale production would be on the beach at Aldeburgh on a stage. So, instead, it became an opportunity to build on what we'd learned with *Moon Slave*; how to create the epic and emotionally operatic in the most intimate scenario. As with any project, the site defined and crafted the show. We were working with daylight so had to thinking about what the crescendo could be, how it might be built. The sequence of *Peter Grimes* that lived with me from that school-trip to the ENO coliseum, was the huge choral number where Grimes is singled out, singing his name over and over again, where the entire chorus walked to the edge of the stage, hanging over the pit and at maximum volume were singing out his name. It chilled me. Imagine if that was happening to you, you were Peter Grimes, what would that feel like? That was what *The Borough* became. How could we shift the audience from safe spectator to realising that they are Grimes? To feeling like it's mistaken identity, that they're being singled out and ousted by a community for something they may or may not have done. It culminates in the full sonic impact of that piece of music, with you at the root of it all.

Aldeburgh, the home of Britten before his death, is the original inspiration and setting for Crabbe's *The Borough* and thus Britten's *Peter Grimes*. Punchdrunk, collaborating with writer Jack Thorne, created a fifty-minute, audio-led experience for one individual at a time, set off in staggered fashion across a day. Audience members would head to Aldeburgh's seashore lookout at an allotted time, receive their headsets and from there be directed towards an empty deckchair on the shingle beach, where the headphones would be checked, turned on. The composed soundscore of the waves on shore blurred with the panorama of the beachfront before your eyes as the narration, and the journey, began. Interweaving Crabbe's poem with Montagu Slater's libretto and the wider history of Aldeburgh, drawn through Britten's score as the emotional compass of the experience, the piece was not linear but took the audience 'into the crevices and cracks of the work to feel beyond the page, to exist within the score, to breathe within the inspiration for the composition' (Machon 2013b, 61). For the audience, the lines between performer and spectator blurred as the unfolding story followed Grimes' footsteps around the town; beginning as voyeur, spying on Ellen Orford from a wardrobe in her lodgings above a tavern, hiding in a cluttered fishing cabin, observing scenes from Grimes' life playing out, before realising you are Grimes, trapped in the narrative just as you are trapped at the end in the cabin with the young boy before being hurled out in front of an accusatory mob at the peak of Britten's crescendo, pointing the finger at you, then vanishing.

For Barrett, *The Borough* 'pre-empted' the agenda of Act 3. It returned to the format of *The Moon Slave*, 'theatre spilling out of the confines of a building, across fields and woodlands'. *The Borough*, similarly, 'was firmly in the real world', picking up the baton of a one-on-one audio experience, supported by technologies that had caught up with Barrett's ideas. Stephen Dobbie adds, the 'headphone experience offers so much more than large-scale shows. The craft that goes into it needs to be so much more precise and refined, because the sound is right in-between the ears . . . transforming the world the participant is in' (2013). Here sound accompanies the participants in an immediate, intimate fashion, enabling them to attune to the environment and their place within it. This extended to volunteers from the local community in Aldeburgh becoming plants on the street, who stopped and stared, as Barrett puts it, 'the townsfolk literally watching you'. Some with ear-pieces would lip-synch to what the audience member was hearing in real-time. For audiences that caught these moments, it chillingly underscored the libretto. As Barrett explains, 'you were under accusation and everybody was in on it'. The intention for Barrett was, as much as 'you know you're not Peter Grimes', the audience becomes palpably aware of the essence of the narrative, 'the ultimate conflict':

You're in a room with a child, with no witnesses, so whose story will be believed. You know that you're innocent and musically we had chosen the warmth, the protection and support, yet you get pushed out of the cabin and the town see you and accuse you.

The Borough benefitted from lessons learned with *The Moon Slave* and the international Enrichment project *The Uncommercial Traveller: Living Cities*. The mechanisms for journeying have since been tested further in *Kabeiroi*. *The Borough* ran for fifteen days with an audience of forty per day, totalling 600 overall. It was in stark contrast to *The Drowned Man* which opened in London a couple of weeks later and had nightly audiences of the same number. And, with Punchdrunkean synchronicity, Tim Albery, whose production had proved so inspirational to Barrett, directed the full-scale version of *Peter Grimes* on Aldeburgh beach for that same centenary festival.

Bow (see also: Abloy; boxes, chests and drawers; **keyholders**; Valet; Zeiss): The design of a typical key consists of two conjoined parts, the blade and the bow, the whole piece cut from a strong metal such as iron or brass. The blade of a key is the length that slides into the keyhole of the lock. It is cut in a unique shape to distinguish it between different key types and different locks, so that it can only be used in one door or lockable device, such as a box, chest or drawer. The bow is usually round or 'bowed' in shape and forms the section of the metal that is left protruding once the blade has been inserted into the lock. Its design is such that the user might gain leverage in order to turn the blade of the key in the lock. A bow key can describe any key where the bow is accentuated, strengthened, enlarged or made ornate. Bow is the name given to keyholders who are significant benefactors of Punchdrunk. At time of writing, these are:

Jack Attridge • Aaron Badaime • Michael Badelt • Paola Barbarino & James Kitchen • Stuart Barker • Colin Barlow • Magali & Julien Barraux • Nicola Berger • David Birks • Darren Bourget • Lee Braybrooke • Dave Brittain • Tamara Brummer • Kay Buxton • Simon Carmichael • James Cavanaugh • Kate Chandler • Samantha Chisnall • Charles Clarke • Blaine Cook • Anne Corlett • Garry Davenport & Michael Walker • Alistair Davie • Janet Davies • Paul Davies • Mike

Duggan • Raymond Dunthorne • Rebecca Eaves • Cameron Eeles • Carol Ellinas • Chloe Emmerson • Jane Ensell • Marja Flipse • Brandon Fox • Miles Franklin • Antony Freelove • David Gabbe • Jane Gill • Somil Goyal • Paul Graham • Paul Graves • Alke Groppel-Wegener • Richard Hall • Gareth Hazzelby • Christiane Hirt • Alison Hooper • Isabella Howarth • Alexis Huang • Kate Hughes • Dr Samuel Hugueny • Rebecca Hurn • Fiona Hutchinson • Damien Hyland • Tristan Jakob-Hoff • In memory of Antonia King • Josh Klausner • Laura Leslie • Sophie Mackenzie • Alex Mahon • Andrew Mansi • Melina Masci • Rhiannon McClintock • Fiona McLaren • Andrew McManus • Colin McQueen & Tina Kotrotsis • Tamsyn Manson • Louise Meney • Damian Mitchell • Marcus Moresby • Simon & Annabel Morley • Tarek Mouganie • Katherine Naylor • Evan Neidan • James O'Brien • Shad Ohayon • David Remfry & Caroline Hansberry • Patricia Ryan • Eva Sanchez-Ampudia • Peter Scott • Hopi Sen • Eugene Sepulveda & Steven Tomlinson • Mike Servent • Peter Sheil • Ksenia Sheveleva • Graham Sleight • Peter Sykes • Helen Taylor • Stephanie Thompson • KT Tunstall • William Turtle & Vassilena Karadakova • Sanjay Vijayanathan • Wenyin • Gary Westfallen • Daniel & Hayley White • Stuart White • Peter Williams • Veronika Wilson • Alexander Woolfson • Su Yuen Ho • Lain Zhong

Boyd, Carrie (see also: **Act 2**: 'Rebecca the Bird'; *Sleep No More, Boston*; *Sleep No More, NYC*; **stage management**): Boyd was the first, professionally trained stage manager Punchdrunk worked with on a masked show, appointed by ART for *Sleep No More*, Boston. Significantly, it was Boyd who helped the core creative team refine a notation system, begun during *The Masque of the Red Death*, in order to keep a production book for large-scale masked events. She has

been working on *Sleep No More*, NYC, since opening:

While touring the Boston space before rehearsals started Felix loosely explained what the structure of the show was. I distinctly remember my shock when I realised how many scenes and events were happening simultaneously and that I was going to have to create a methodology for managing this. I knew it would be different from anything else I had ever done. During that rehearsal process I spent most of my time trying to triage, create a priority list for the factors in the show that would need to be tracked and documented and those which I needed to let go and allow to happen without management, for which I would abandon my traditional stage manager mentality and allow a freer approach to overseeing. I remember going into rehearsals for individual scenes and noting everything I saw the performers touch or interact with in order to create a props and pre-set list. I timed all their arrivals and exits to make a master map of journeys through the building. The performers were kind, but a bit confused about why the lady with the notebook was being so nosy about what they were making.

I watched the 'stumble through' run of *Sleep No More*, without an audience, with only work lights and music playing in half of the spaces, with most of the cast in rehearsal clothes, but I was still mesmerised by it. I remember bumping into Felix in the De Winter boudoir, as we both went in to check in on that performer, and just grinning from ear to ear at him, suddenly understanding how amazing this beast was when put together and in awe that I was going to be at its helm. At the close of the Boston run I was intent on working on another Punchdrunk show, with my new-found knowledge of how these worked and with the methodology for notating these that I had evolved

with the team. *Sleep No More*, NYC came to fruition about a year later and we were able to expand upon our practices to make the show happen as seamlessly as possible while also accepting the flexibility and unexpected that is inherent to each and every performance. Ultimately this style of work and the stage management it requires has led to creating one exceptional 'hive mind' in the building, with incredible teamwork between the various departments running the show, to a degree you wouldn't really see on a traditional production where everyone has their job and responsibilities and doesn't migrate far out of those boundaries.

When I work on traditional shows now I'm always initially a bit thrown by how regimented and insulated team members can be within their jobs, and it always makes me appreciate the unique nature of the show-run and the camaraderie that we've established as the *Sleep No More* way of being. I've had the privilege of working for Punchdrunk from its first endeavour in the United States, and in these last eight years I've been able to watch the evolution of immersive theatre making its way from niche, 'back-alley' work, to the forefront of game changing, mainstream theatre. Dozens of immersive shows have cropped up in NYC alone since Punchdrunk made its stamp here in 2011 and it's a form that is now part of the vernacular of both locals and tourists. It's been surreal to watch the evolution of how we view and participate in theatre around me while at the centre of the most influential and groundbreaking piece of them of all.

boxes, chests and drawers (see also: abstract/abstraction; characters; **curiosity**; **discovery**; design; doors; influences; keyholders; letters; *Miniature Museum*; portals; **wardrobes**. Further reading: Bachelard 1994, 74–89): Always open them, if you can, to discover their secrets. What clues **are** offered on opening? What stories do they hold?

Brixton Market (**2010**, see also: **Act 2**; community; design; **Enrichment**; immersive; **installation**; **Space Invaders Agency**): A Level students from five schools in Lambeth and Wandsworth worked alongside Punchdrunk Enrichment to transform a market unit in the Granville Arcade, Brixton. The project aimed to raise the aspirations of these young artists and to develop the standard of their work. Using Brixton as their starting point, students developed the content, narrative and aesthetic of the space. The final piece created a study owned by a man called Jeeves, a direct reference to Jeeves from P.G. Wodehouse's *Jeeves & Wooster* books, as research had revealed that the character hailed from Brixton. Jeeves' study contained articles, stories, sounds and smells of Brixton throughout the ages. This project was also the stimulus for a CCE Teacher Training day in which teachers were able to explore the transformation of space and use of immersive work in school settings. The project was part of a regeneration initiative by Space Makers. The focus on installation as the method and outcome for participatory arts practice within a community became a means of testing an approach that would be reworked in *Space Invaders Agency* in 2011.

building (see also: **architecture**; lifts: **'listening to the building'**; process; **site**; **site-sympathetic: 'space-hunting'**. Further reading: ABTT 2016; Pallasmaa 2005): A shorthand, often affectionate, term for the site in which a large-scale production is housed, used by creative team, crew and ensemble alike. The building is fundamental to the process and is the instigator of what any Punchdrunk event will become. It is the building which influences which source will be unpacked and inspire the lens through which it will be reimagined. Felix Barrett identifies how the dark, claustrophobic desolation of 21 Wapping Lane immediately lent itself to *Faust*, whereas it took the faded

fin-de-siècle glory of the BAC building to find a home for his long-held fascination with the clandestine decadence of masked balls, made manifest in *The Masque of the Red Death*. With any masked show, as Maxine Doyle succinctly puts it, 'the building is the most formidable character':

> I know how much of a player the building is; it becomes a battle to try and match it. That's what marks Punchdrunk out amongst other companies that do site work; so often the site or building dominate and the show doesn't do anything in it.
>
> (Doyle 2013)

Buildings are often leased to Punchdrunk by councils or leaseholders not only for the artistic legacy that a Punchdrunk work provides, but also on an understanding that a mutually beneficial relationship exists where Punchdrunk make what are often decrepit sites into safe and habitable venues. Nowadays, given the nature of such refurbishment, and the year-long or lengthier duration of the run, certain buildings become known by the name conferred by the work they house, such as is the case with The McKittrick Hotel with *Sleep No More*, NYC, or its Shanghai counterpart, The McKinnon Hotel, or *The Drowned Man*'s Temple Studios. Colin Nightingale acknowledges, 'I learned most things about the process of making projects in disused buildings on the job. When we were starting out it was hard to get guidance as Punchdrunk was doing something quite different from the norm'. Because of the popularity of site-based work in performance practice, the Association of British Theatre Technicians brought out a guide, which Nightingale recommends as a useful starting point for anyone attempting a project in a building or an unconventional site for the first time. This guide identifies such 'non-conventional' practice as 'Experiential/Pop-Up/Site Specific/Site Located/Found Space/ Immersive/ Promenade/Experimental/ Transformative/Game Playing/Secret and other Non-Traditional forms of

theatre' (ABTT 2016). In terms of Punchdrunk's approach, which covers all of these descriptions, Nightingale has outlined the key factors and questions the team consider in gauging the suitability of a building for a project, whether large or small . . .

Colin Nightingale

On assessing a building's potential

Visiting a potential site for the first time is a key moment in the development of the concept and creative ideas for any Punchdrunk production. There are a number of practical considerations that can have a big impact on whether a building is suitable, how it might be used and, ultimately, if those creative ideas can be achieved.

Table 1 shows a list of questions that can be used as a starting point to progress the conversation that must occur between creative and practical considerations. Ideally there should be an ongoing dialogue between these two, potentially competing, areas and their influence on the decision-making process. This ongoing dialogue will help identify realistic and satisfying solutions to ways in which the building can be used. If the concept and its creative exploration is developed in isolation, then you can run the risk of the ideas being undeliverable in the space for practical or budget reasons. At the same time, while you have to ensure that everything is safe and legal, it is also important to avoid practical considerations leading the creative thinking as this can be too constraining.

I have provided some questions and thoughts below on areas that need to be addressed but please do not use this as an exhaustive list. As your experience with creating site-based works expands then you will eventually learn to quickly 'read' a space and process its creative possibilities:

Table 1 Assessing a building's potential

What is the audience capacity of the whole building and what are the individual spaces within the layout?	This will obviously determine the potential audience sizes which could have a huge impact on the budget available if ticket revenue from ticket sales is important. It will also influence any creative aims.
What are the entry points to the building?	Is the way an audience enter important to the overall creative aims? When we made *Faust* we purposefully chose an entrance point furthest away from the site entry as we want the audience to have to search for it and question if they were in the right place as we wanted to unnerve the audience before they entered the building.
	Is there potential for a separate stage door entrance? Important to consider if there is a need for staff to enter the building during the show without being visible to the audience
	The size of the entrance points needs to be considered when thinking about set and props that you might want to use.
How does the building flow? – e.g. where are staircases and corridors? How do they link up spaces? How wide are they are? Is there a lift?	This is a massively important consideration for Punchdrunk especially when creating a masked show. The possible routes around a building that both audiences and performers take are important for us to think about when assessing a building's suitability for a masked show and what layout changes might need to be made.
	If you are working on multi levels and there isn't a lift then you need to think about how this will impact on the accessibility of the show.
What are the ceiling heights?	Needs to be considered when thinking about sightlines if dealing with large audience numbers.
	The ceiling height will affect the 'feeling' of a room to an audience. It is difficult to create a feeling of grandeur with very low ceilings.
What are the floors like?	Are they level and safe?
	If you are considering bringing in any heavy equipment or set then you need to consider the weight loading on the floors.

Where is the building located, and who are the neighbours?	If it is an isolated location, then consideration needs to be given to how crew and audiences will travel to the site.
	Does this journey evoke any emotional responses relevant to the narrative themes in the creative?
	If it is in a residential area there may be noise restrictions enforced by local authorities. This could be connected to the sound coming from the building and also from audiences entering and exiting the space.
Is there an existing fire alarm and emergency lighting?	Fire safety and the ability to evacuate safely is a major area of risk assessment. Try to establish immediately what existing infrastructure is working as it could have a big impact on your budget.
	If you plan to use theatrical haze then the impact of the type of fire detection (e.g. smoke, practical or heat) needs to be considered.
	Where is the fire alarm panel? This will need to be accessible during performances and its location will need to be in a 'backstage' area.
Does the building have historic listing?	This is important to establish as it may restrict what physical changes can be made, so this needs to be considered before the design ideas are extensively developed.
When and for what was the building last used?	Is there anything relevant in its previous usage for the narrative or the design?
	If it has been left empty for a long period, then lots of infrastructure (plumbing, power, lighting, internet, alarms etc.) might need lots of attention and budget to get them back into good working order.
	What is the current planning consent? This may impact on whether it can be used for the performance.
Where are the windows?	Is blackout important for the performance? If so are there a lot of windows? If yes, then budget and time will be required to block out light.
How long will you need access to the building?	You must consider how long you want to run the project and how much time you need for the installation of the design and rehearsals.
What is the power distribution and supply?	Is enough power available and in the right location for the tech (lighting, sound etc.) that will be required for the performance?

Bunker, The (**2008**, see also: **Act 2**; curiosity; durational; **found space**; journeying; *Lost Persons*; music; Reekie, Jonathan; **Seguro, Joana**): As part of the experimental music festival Faster Than Sound at Bentwaters Air Base, Suffolk, a balaclava-clad man drove audience members to a decommissioned nuclear bunker containing an unexpected sound-based experience. Presented on one night only, audiences were invited to explore the space and discovered the durational performance by composer, multi-instrumentalist and performer, Seaming To and composer, cellist and performance artist, Semay Wu at the centre of the installation. Colin Nightingale recalls how the event, once the space was chosen and the concept agreed, was put together in thirty-six hours:

Following our collaboration with Joana Seguro on Red Death Lates and spurred on by Felix's enthusiasm for the *Faster Than Sound* Festival, I pursued Joana's offer to us to get involved in 2008. I was really excited about the idea of us doing something small, secret and one-off after the extensive exposure that Punchdrunk had started to receive in the wake of *Faust* and *Masque*. Press support by now was overwhelmingly positive but it felt like we were being pigeon-holed before we'd really got started. The masked shows were always only one part of the overall vision for the company. Joana's offer opened up the opportunity for Punchdrunk to make a sound-led installation, which Felix and I were keen to revisit following *Lost Persons*. It was also a good opportunity for core members to reconnect through making something after dealing with the pressure of two major shows and running large teams of people. It felt important to remember the fun that we could have making something small together. It was going to be very 'early Act 1' in approach, with limited time and budget, and would need us to be extremely creative in our solutions, as had previously felt easy and immensely

satisfying. Felix and I, after visiting the site, had chosen a Cold War era command-control centre. Built to withstand a major chemical attack, it came complete with oppressive-looking exterior concrete blast walls and eerie decontamination entrance chambers, with showers and airlocks. It was ripe with potential that wouldn't require much design budget.

We had a very loose concept for the project and sourced key props and equipment, including a vintage army Land Rover. Joana had programmed us to work with Seaming To and Semay Wu. The first time we met them was when we all arrived on site. Felix, Pete, Stephen, Euan Maybank and I went to the pub with them and it came as a bit of surprise when we explained that they'd need to play for a duration of five hours continuously, but they took it in their stride. Their buy-in to the idea was important as we'd decided that we wanted the audience exploring the bunker to hear deconstructed elements of their live performance, eventually reaching the end room where they would discover the source of the sound and hear the complete picture.

Our initial intention was for one person at a time to be taken in the Land Rover to the bunker but it quickly became apparent that we needed to increase the capacity. The Land Rover became the means by which we transported groups, lining up for an unknown event at the main festival site to the bunker, where they were then ordered to enter one at a time via a corridor through an old training centre with dilapidated, leaking ceilings. At the end of this block they entered the main bunker through decontamination shower air locks.

Our presence at the festival was kept fairly secret. Because of the one-off nature and the fact that we were simultaneously building and

rehearsing the installation, it was hard for us to take a step back and fully understand what we created. Jim Bending was one of the limited audience that went through the experience and, years later when he joined Punchdrunk, explained to us how impactful it had been. It had a big impact for me as, in a moment of stupidity during some downtime, I managed to break both my feet. This forced me to take some rest after years of intense physical work building and running shows which allowed me the headspace to work on the creative concepts that eventually turned into *Clod & Pebble* and *Tunnel 228*.

C

Cake Friday (see also: **community**; People; **Piggott, Greg**; ritual): During production builds, Cake Fridays are established as a community-building ritual to nurture a sense of company among the core creatives, new members of Punchdrunk and volunteers. This was an initiative instigated by Greg Piggott, the Production Manager at BAC during the run of *The Masque of the Red Death*. Peter Higgin recalls, 'we had a major work force on *Masque*, with people working all over the building. We designed various activities to bring people together, but Greg suggested that a good way was to gather around cake on a Friday. We have continued this communal ritual with many of our productions since'.

cameos (see also: Act 2; *Drowned Man, The*; *Sleep No More*, NYC): When *Sleep No More*, NYC opened it quickly attracted a celebrity audience. A number of high-profile actors who had been captivated by the show expressed interest in getting involved. Punchdrunk was asked by Emursive to consider ways in which it might incorporate guest performances. Felix Barrett and Colin Nightingale proposed that Punchdrunk teach these guest performers a one-on-one. The first secret cameo was performed by Alan Cummings, who played a doctor in the hospital. Cummings' performance was followed shortly afterwards by Neil Patrick Harris delivering The Porter's one-on-one. As well as creating intense and surprising experiences for that night's audience, the cameos also boosted the show's notoriety in the press and across social media. Since then, other guests have included Evan Rachel Wood, Aaron Paul and Dita Von Teese. Subsequently, with this Punchdrunk format for facilitating cameos, during *The Drowned Man*, Andrew Garfield and the singer Florence Welch become residents of Temple Studios for one night only.

caretaking (see also: **audience**; **cross-fade**; ethics; **mask**; notation; process; **restraint**; **safe-words**. Further reading: Frieze 2017, 135–192; Gardner 2018a; White 2013; Zerihan et al. 2009): This term, although not originally Punchdrunk terminology, incorporates both the impetus behind, and the implementation of, the mechanisms for participation put in place for an audience. It relates in operational terms to safeguarding procedures that are put in place for any project, yet also refers to the more creative approach and expertise in understanding how to enable safe, while still exciting or even frightening, participation in an event. Caretaking comprises the explicit rules of engagement shared prior to entering a Punchdrunk world and the implicit codes of conduct that become clear when within the world of the event (do not enter areas that are staffed by black-masked doorkeepers; follow the music that echoes in the distance; follow the direction of lights). These rules and codes of conduct ensure the safekeeping of participants and artists alike. These align themselves to the Punchdrunk mission to place the audience, as a collective and as individuals, at the centre of the work. Felix Barrett strongly believes that audience members are able to take more risks if they know those risks are going to be supported:

We pride ourselves on caretaking. Feeling like the rug's been pulled from beneath you is only exhilarating if you know, and can forget, that it's a theatrical conceit. So much of what we do is about caretaking. On practical terms alone, it's hugely important. If you're creating a dreamworld then you want nothing to break from the dream. You have to make sure it's as secure as possible. Anything that's off, anything that's outside of that world will break it. The caretaking is as much about that dreamworld not being broken for audiences as it is about their health and safety. That places a lot of responsibility on the part of the performers, especially in one-on-ones, which are built on intimacy, and all about the filmic close-up, trying to establish a live-action insight into a character's soul.

With all one-on-ones, different levels of exit strategies are devised, enabling the world to be as secure as possible for both performer and audience member. Caretaking in these instances extends to performers not making ill-judged decisions in the spirit of the scenario, or panic moves if they feel unsafe. No content or actions can be improvised if they have not been carefully agreed, witnessed and signed off by a director. Chaperones are positioned close by for performer and audience alike and, from years of honing what is required for a one-on-one, the Punchdrunk performer will have been trained and had a safeguarding sign-off which ensures that safe ways to end scenes prematurely are designed into the narrative and execution of a one-on-one. Sam Booth provides illustration of this above, as does Katy Balfour in the entry on one-on-ones below. Punchdrunk remains aware of the manner in which proximity can be irresponsibly manipulated by artists and dangerously abused by audience members, which emphasises the need for respect and responsibility on both sides with the perceived freedoms and intimacies associated with immersive practice in general and one-on-ones in

particular. Clear guidelines for practice are provided for all performers, as Risa Steinberg mentions in her contribution below. From years of designing one-on-one encounters to be experienced in close-up and from afar, Barrett is highly attuned to how 'proximity has connotations and that's why caretaking is so vital'. Equally, where work is designed to be exciting, full of trepidation and adrenalin fuelled, it must be carefully disciplined by form. Barrett notes:

Four-fifths of the time and half the budget is spent on safeguarding and risk assessments and stewarding. Once a space is secure then you can layer in the theatrical adrenalin. It's vital that it's not 'real' adrenalin, and also not kitsch, but that its entirely and carefully *theatricalised* adrenalin.

Caretaking, in practice and procedure, underpins Enrichment projects, requiring lengthy planning to ensure all protocols, both artistic and administrative, are in place. Punchdrunk has also devised careful approaches to in-show, in-character, caretaking-enabling access and support where it is needed. Maria Oshodi describes her experience of the in-show approach to access and safety for *The Masque of the Red Death* below. Similarly, for *The Crash of the Elysium*, the safety net was that there was a chaperone inside the show in costume, embedded in role as a Medic, called Ripley (a nod to Ridley Scott's *Alien*), who was primarily a steward, only there to assist people who needed it. Barrett adds, always, in terms of safeguarding and support of the audience:

We try and make it work for everyone so if anyone requires help, it's there, but for those that don't, the flow of the show isn't disturbed. And for those that might need it and then want to return to the show, it enables their smooth passage back into that world.

Colin Nightingale adds, 'performer and audience safety need constant

caretaking

attention. As our audience becomes more mainstream, ways of communicating the rules need to be reevaluated'. Caretaking is thus a fundamental and ongoing process for artistic and production team alike, taking into consideration performer and audience and evidenced in the free workshops around making and caretaking established in Act 3 for early-career immersive practitioners.

A way into . . . caretaking, audience interaction and establishing trust

Punchdrunk's practice requires performers to care for fellow performers, themselves and their audience. The work can often place audiences in a place of vulnerability and heighten feelings of fear, anxiety and loneliness. All performers have a duty of care towards their audience and company members. For audiences especially, it is important for performers to be able to build a rapport quickly and gain their trust and confidence. It is also useful to understand techniques and strategies that communicate specific emotions or make an audience feel a certain way. The following exercises explore aspects of performance and audience caretaking.

Before beginning either exercise check the needs of the group; everyone will have differing abilities and the exercise should be adapted accordingly.

The 'blindfolded' partners should note when they feel safe, secure, buoyant and when they feel anxious, timid, unsure or unsafe. You can choose to do this as the exercise progresses or at its end during collective reflection.

Take a journey with a partner . . .

Establish pairs. Together take a journey around the space, noticing its surfaces and features, sharing anything of interest as you notice it. Return to your original starting point.

In the same pair, one should remain sighted and the other now becomes the blindfolded partner. The sighted should lead the blindfolded around the room by holding their arm; their left hand held gently in your left hand, as they feel comfortable, with your right hand gently supporting and guiding their right elbow in such a way that you will be walking closely alongside them with access to their whole arm in both of your hands, steering with your upper body. As you lead and guide them be sure to talk with them – you can describe the space, have a conversation or tell them a story.

This time, lead your blindfolded partner around the room by only holding their arm, finding the nuances of that hold, ways to gently support and guide without forcing, instead encouraging. Experiment with direction and intention only by communicating through pressure of touch, no words or sounds.

Can you lead a blindfolded partner around a room using only sound? How might this work?

What happens when both partners are blindfolded? What happens when all but one of the group are blindfolded? What strategies might work to journey safely across the space?

Make them feel . . .

The aim of this exercise is to try to invoke a specific feeling in a single audience member. It should be carefully handled by the facilitator and the group. This audience member is automatically put in a place of vulnerability because they know nothing and they need to be guided and cared for, whatever the mood or emotion you intend to establish and especially if you're trying to scare them or make them feel anxious (you might want to think about the use of 'safe-words' here). A starting point is to take care in choosing and thinking through the emotions you wish to generate in the space. Using source material will help to guide this – in turn, it may also help you to discover alternative ways to interpret that source material. What are the strategies you will put in place to support that member of the group, to bring them back to a neutral or safe emotional state? Audience care is paramount. This work should highlight the benefits of carefully thinking through and crafting an experience. It can also demonstrate how easy it is to go to a place of extremities, and the importance of subtlety.

Ask one volunteer to leave the room. This person will become the visitor.

caretaking

Choose the emotion as a group or pull an emotion from a hat. The group then work together to create an experience that they think best communicates this. A more advanced approach is to create a situation that will produce the intended emotion in the visitor.

The visitor then returns and experiences the group's response. A discussion should follow for the outsider to share how they felt, for the group to respond and for choices and actions to be explained and analysed, with the success or otherwise, of the actions discussed.

This exercise can be adapted and extended in many ways. The visitor could be blindfolded or props, textures and smells introduced. Source materials could be explored. Music, light and darkness could be incorporated to add to the impact. It is interesting to attempt this in a realistic scenario, as well as in a more abstract fashion. The exercises can be adapted for any group size and can be done in pairs as well as in larger groups. If possible, all members of the group should take the role of the visitor so a shared understanding of that position is facilitated.

chainsaw (see also: Act 2; **adrenal-in**; Curtis, Adam; *It Felt Like a Kiss*; mazes; Poots, Alex): The use of chain-saws was a device employed in 1950s dark rides. Consequently, a masked, chainsaw-wielding figure was used to terrorise the audience in the final stages of a journey through the building that housed *It Felt Like a Kiss*. As the audience reached the end of a maze of metal cages, The Crystals' song, *He Hit Me (It Felt Like a Kiss)*, swelled to a crescendo and a chainsaw suddenly started up behind the, already on tenterhooks, audience members, closely followed by its operator who appeared out of the dark. Colin Nightingale adds:

We had major logistical issues to overcome around the safety of using a petrol chainsaw inside due to the potential of carbon monoxide poisoning. Performers had to wear personal monitors and take regular breaks. It was the sound alone as the motor was disengaged. A worth-while effort as the sound instantly unsettled people and sent them fleeing for the exit. Certain audiences tried to defend themselves, such as one older gentleman who picked up a fork off the table of the domestic kitchen, through which the audience found themselves running. Another group overturned the table and hid behind it.

Responses to the chainsaw finale were varied from audiences and critics alike. Dominic Cavendish described it as 'thrill-a-minute visceral excitement . . . raising adrenalin levels and setting pulses racing' with a 'playfulness' that makes 'profound, thought-provoking points' (2009), whereas for Michael Billington it was 'infantile . . . fairground shock-tactics' (2009). From either perspective, the chainsaw left its mark.

Chair (**2002**; see also: **Act 1**; Barrett, Felix; Barrett, Margaret and Simon; Dobbie, Stephen; **durational**; **installation**; mass production; **mazes**; Nightingale, Colin; **smart candles**; **wardrobes**): An adaptation of *The Chairs* by Eugene Ionesco, commissioned by The Deptford X Festival of Contemporary Art and created within the Old Seager Distillery in Deptford, London. A production composed of installation and an intimate durational performance that came about through Felix Barrett's tenacious desire to keep making work. Barrett recalls meeting festival producer Reuben Thornhill: 'I was trying to find any venue to make a show and he gave me the room'. A limited number of flyers, designed by Stephen Dobbie, to whom Barrett had been introduced by mutual friends, enticed an audience to the work by capturing, as Barrett remarks, 'tone through image, in keeping with the Punchdrunk aesthetic'. Relying on word-of-mouth, the show attracted a steady, albeit relatively small, audience. They entered the former distillery, through a maze of suspended pages from the text and then through to a further labyrinth of fabric corridors and rooms which housed the installations, painstakingly constructed, from the sewing to the hanging, by Barrett. The act of construction alone added to the durational underpinning of the production. Barrett elaborates:

There was about a week where I was in my parents' dining room, with piles of sail cloth up to the ceiling, bought from Torquay at twenty pence a metre. I spent twelve hours a day sewing a curtain rail on hundreds of metres of this fabric to create that maze. I was happy doing that, it was nice, that process, knowing you've got to sew a thousand metres of fabric and just getting on with it, knowing the impact at the end will make it worthwhile. We had a big, empty space and we turned it into a maze of twenty-four rooms.

As a durational installation it was open to the audience across eight hours, for which two performers, playing the husband and wife, inhabited their designated spaces, directed by Barrett to 'ignore the audience and just be. They had tasks they would be doing but they would also just potter. It was much more live art in approach than straight theatre'. Various people took on the roles each night, 'because it was quite a tough gig', having to perform across the full eight hours. Barrett remembers how one, Miles Latimer-Gregory, 'would get into the bed and just sleep for eight hours' while Bob Cappocci would knit for hours on end, 'proper durational activity'. Barrett also notes that *Chair* was the first masked production for which he used smart candles rather than lit tea-lights, for expediency related to health and safety, simply because he 'couldn't afford the flame-proofing of the fabric'. These design limitations exercised his artistic resourcefulness, rather than forestalling ambition, and helped establish a minimalist aesthetic:

I had no money, so could only buy cheap sailing cloth, only rent scaffolding mere days to hang it. I deconstructed the idea of a house into each room. I literally reconfigured what was in Mum and Dad's kitchen. In one I had a fish-tank with Rover, my fish, in it, with an old typewriter from the attic submerged, which Rover swam around. That was particularly effective because of the way the lighting caught it. Importantly, every room had the *presence* of a chair in it, but one that had been removed. There were no chairs at all in any of those rooms.

Barrett's father, Simon, recalls knowing, as he entered an installation with a roll-top bath, that was the point that his son was 'an artist', creating installations that *felt* animated, held their own presence and being. *Chair* explored the themes underpinning Ionesco's original play, by indicating the suggestion of chairs through sound or their implied partnership with other items of furniture, or marks on the floor, until eventually the audience exited 'through a tunnel that was a sculpted mass of piled-up chairs'.

Chair was Colin Nightingale's first introduction to Barrett's work as an audience member and consequently saw to his joining the team:

My experience of *Chair* was so pure. I was about to leave the

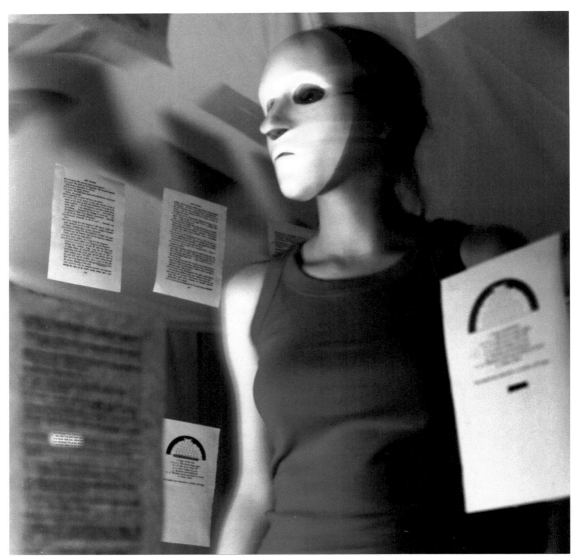

△ FIGURE 4 *Chair*. 2002. 'Mask and text'.

Photo credit: Stephen Dobbie

site of the festival when someone stopped me and asked if I'd experienced the Punchdrunk piece. I headed up a staircase, was given a mask and sent through the door. I had zero expectation, no-one had explained what it was. I ended up in the first sub-maze that was made from pages and pages torn from the play and candles; instantly edgy. I ended up in a fabric maze and realised that I could just keep going. It was a while before I came across any other audience members, and when they did appear, wearing the masks, all the other pieces of installation art I'd seen up until that point paled into insignificance. I was always so frustrated by how I'd be returned to reality whenever I came across someone else and this fixed that. Masked audience members became part of the installation. I also remember the power of the moment when I was standing in the bedroom and someone suddenly came out of the wardrobe and I realised that I could go through it too. Embryonically, everything that now makes up the masked shows was there in *Chair*. It was so progressed, the artistic work had been done. Still now it gives me chills when I think about it, because I'd been searching so hard for something that was transformative and here it was.

Chair propagated a sense of camaraderie, bringing into the fold key team members, galvanised by their response to the event. It illustrates Barrett's approach to making work at that time where those who 'got it' became part of projects that evolved from it: 'it felt like a collective coming together, everyone sharing in the making of it'.

'chairs' (see also: caretaking; **close-up**; **exercises**; framing; **long shot**; masked shows; **one-on-one**; restraint; **scale**. Further reading: Lecoq 2002): Not to be confused with, and bearing no relation to, Felix Barrett's production of *Chair*, this is an exercise devised by Maxine Doyle for dancers as a way of building character and narratives for masked shows during studio rehearsal. It modifies Jacques Lecoq's 'levels of acting', which establish and communicate varying levels of physical tension. In Lecoq's teaching and terminology this scale is:

1. Catatonic/'Corpse'
2. Relaxed/'Californian' or 'Laid back'
3. Neutral/'Economic'
4. Alert/'Curious'
5. Suspense/'Melodrama'
6. Passionate/'Opera'
7. Tragic/'Shakespearean'

Doyle's 'chairs' illustrate how everyday terminology, emotional and physical states, accord with these levels of tension, becoming stimuli for movement. This encourages dancers to explore the notion of close-up and long shots in their choreographic vocabulary. The nuances of these states in terms of close-up and long shot in design have since been adopted and adapted by Livi Vaughan and Beatrice Minns. The main focus of Doyle's exercise is to encourage dancers to incorporate facial expression in performance; as Doyle puts it, 'to connect to emotion, albeit imagined, and harness the life behind the eyes' . . .

Maxine Doyle

On 'chairs'

Set a horizontal line of four to eight chairs, depending on the size of the group.

Each person takes a chair and the rest of the group becomes a conventional end-on audience to watch the exercise.

Ask each person to sit in a neutral position with feet parallel and hands resting on thighs.

Give the performer a trigger to respond to or 'play'

– grief / anger / fear / drunk / waiting –

There is intentionally no backstory or context offered. I'm interested in the performer's approach to this. The performer is then asked to explore the trigger on a scale from 1–7, where 1 is the least intense and 7 is the most intense. 7 – allows the performer to really go over the top and commit to extremes and melodrama.

1–2 is very subtle but should ignite some sparks behind the eyes.

3–5 should feel familiar and readable.

6 begins to tip over.

The rule is to try and stay, where possible, in the frame established within the chair and only move beyond it when the need is strongest.

Use this exercise to introduce the 'close-up'. For '1' the camera shot is just the eyes. As the imaginary camera pulls back across the numbers, the shot widens; more of the face and body come into play.

It can be fun to transition between states and move from grief to joy, for example. It can become really embodied as the intensity grows on those higher numbers. However, it's a sensitive business and you must take care of the people in the room as this exercise can unlock emotion. I always try and finish on a more humorous or light trigger like 'laughter'.

It's a fascinating exercise and provokes discussion around atmosphere. Often the 'audience' in this exercise feel affected by the performers, so we talk about the possibility to effect a change in your audience – and the power of that. This then links back into the work in relation to proximity and specifically in relation to the one-on-one.

characters (see also: **dance**; **design**; **durational**; ensemble; in-show-world; installation; **lens**; letters; **loops**; **masked shows**; **narrative**; **one-on-ones**; **text**): Character is often explored and exposed first and foremost through the design and installation, which plunders the source material for information. As Felix Barrett describes:

When we're crafting the space, we go through the text looking for visual signifiers, motifs, portents, such as Woyzeck's obsession with the moon, and these are then folded into the space. Sometimes it's location specific, because we know the character will travel through that space, otherwise it's allowing that essence of a character to envelop or be embedded in the space more generally. It's initially wholly explored through setting, we deliberately don't think about the performer in the space at that point. What we're building is an environment, a world that has echoes of these characters, regardless of whether they actually end up in the show or not. They infuse the space so the empty space is pregnant with their trace, their possibility. Once you've got a living, breathing, albeit dormant environment then, only then do you start to populate it. The period during which the performers are rehearsing on space, the character detail hits into the design; myriad props and adjustments and reimagining to make the ideas fit. It's almost like a slightly impractical two-phased process that gives it the depth and layers so that the audience can keep on excavating, ad infinitum.

In masked shows, characters that are portrayed by performers are either 'travelling' or 'resident'. All travelling characters are instrumental to the main narrative of the action. Whether a central role, providing the narrative backbone, or a supporting role, all of these characters are responsible for progressing the overarching narrative and communicating themes, layering both through their interactions with other characters and various locations. Character-led narratives are guided by storyboarding or treatment, assigned to a particular space, worked out in a preparatory period by Barrett and Maxine Doyle, 'in a little room together planning the show' which, for Doyle,

is the most intense part of our collaboration because it's about the thinking behind it, we commit to these characters, we create their arcs and their stories, we're looking at the space, the site, trying to work out how the building needs to work, where people need to be so that the building is animated and alive and places don't die unless we want them to, to become quiet. We do a lot of that work so that when we enter the building each character has a strong sense of where they're going, who they're going to meet, what their arc is, what that scene is about. The performer's job is then to create a language to tell those stories and, of course, in the studio we've already created a concentrate of that language; the studio process is very much about equipping the performers to go into the building with the right material.

(Doyle 2013)

Travelling characters will traverse the building, entering, interacting with and leaving different spaces across the run of the loop and the full duration of the event. Residents have clear objectives within a narrative, although without a significant dramatic arc in comparison with the travelling characters. They tend to dwell in one space and perform durational activities, making lockets, folding sheets, creating origami, scraping animal bones, polishing glasses, writing on walls. Resident characters sometimes communicate the secrets of their narratives via one-on-one encounters with audience members. These one-on-one scenarios remain in specific locations, throughout the three-hour run of the masked show at timed points during each loop. Consequently, resident characters may perform a structured one-on-one to different individuals up to fifteen times for the duration of the whole event. When not performing these one-on-ones, resident characters silently go about their business in their space, indifferent to the audience that might come and go. Doyle and Risa Steinberg, in their discussion of *Sleep No More*, NYC, note how some roles (in this instance, Danvers) may be conceived originally as less rounded 'residents' but evolve during long-running shows to become more significant travelling characters. Steinberg draws attention to the experiences of the playing out of such roles; those that 'circle' the main narrative arcs and those that 'intersect'.

Katy Balfour, Sarah Dowling, Conor Doyle, Kathryn McGarr, Rob McNeill and Fernanda Prata all provide direct or oblique reflections on building a character and the passing on of roles, which lend further insight to performer approaches to generating and evolving characters. Beatrice Minns and Livi Vaughan take meticulous care over the manner in which character is revealed through the design alone. Often it is through the installations in characters rooms that the audience is most able to piece together the histories and emotional states of the characters who may inhabit those spaces . . .

A way into . . . designing place and space as character, characters from place and space

Much of Punchdrunk's work depends on our ability to make places that belong to characters and characters that belong to spaces. This is an exercise developed by Livi Vaughan and Beatrice Minns as a way of getting designers to think about reading and designing space and character. It works equally well with performers as a way to generate ideas for character in space.

Faces and places

Gather a collection of images of spaces, places and 'faces'. It works best if the places are devoid of people. These can be sourced from image banks online, magazines, old photo albums. Variety is key and nostalgia, intrigue, mystery are words that must help lead your choice. Images that cause a strong emotional response or take time to absorb and understand, that require close attention and are difficult to take in fully with a quick glance, are best.

Places: 'empty space'

Individually or in small groups, from your selection of images choose a space that is without detailed design or furnishing.

How does it make you feel? What is interesting about the architecture?

What are the key points that you notice in the space?

How could you accentuate these points:

- in terms of structure?
- if you added a single object?

How could you make this place look loved?

How could you make it a secret place?

What character might inhabit it?

Places: 'Furnished space'

What can you see?

Is it public or private?

How would you feel if you entered that space?

Where would you sit? What would you do?

To whom does it belong? What do they love? Of what are they ashamed? Of what are they scared?

Describe their dreams . . .

Are the clues to these questions revealed through that which is present or that which is absent?

Faces

Choose an image – a painting or a photograph and think about the person that you see.

Who are they, and what is their name?

What do they do? What do they like and dislike?

Who or what do they love?

Of what are they ashamed? Of what are they scared?

Of what do they dream?

Where do they dwell? In which room do they choose to reside?

After each of these exercises or at the end of all three, share your thoughts and ideas in discussion.

Working individually, in pairs or more, the group could then develop these explorations in a range of ways:

Create a collaged image, adding to the original image according to the response.

Add textures, colour sketches, create a mood board to represent the response.

Embellish the original image through collage and drawing to indicate the response.

Fit the faces to the places . . . through mood boards, collage, and create letters or diary entries in their handwriting.

Cherry Orchard, The (2000, see also: **Act 1**; installation; **intervention**; journeying; **masks**; Punchdrunk Travel: 'space-hunting'; **text**): An early Punchdrunk project, led by Felix Barrett, conceived as a radical reworking of Anton Chekhov's play. As was the case during this initial period of Act 1, Barrett was constantly noting where empty buildings existed and gaining the trust of local residential agencies in order to 'borrow' sites; in this case, an empty and deteriorating geographical survey building on Hillsborough Avenue, Exeter, for three days: 'I remember drawing a line around the key in my hand because it meant a show was going to happen. It felt crazy that there was only one key for the whole building'. Once a town mansion house that had been converted to offices and sat emptied, it comprised 'twenty rooms, three storeys that would have been a grand, residential property in its day' with the servants' quarters in the roof. The design was 'abstraction heavy'; Barrett and collaborators brought in furniture and installed it carefully; a lone chair was placed in the middle of the room with candles around it, deliberate and stylised; Trofimov's room contained only a desk surrounded by a sea of paper; the bedroom was filled with borrowed mattresses, combined to make one complete bed, distended, to indicate the characters' way of living was unreal, exorbitant as the building crumbled around them. 'It was cheaply realised, involving nothing complex, but created an impact'. The performing style was similarly minimalist and subtle, a consequence of the 'sparse and dreamy' source material, which Barrett had 'hacked to stylise it' further; a deconstruction of the text to get to its essence, which 'worked' because the writing permitted it. In turn, the hushed delivery of this version of Chekov's text was effective 'because it was intimate, a cast of ten and only twenty-five audience in the house at any one time which meant speech could be whispered, film acting, all about restraint, yet it could still be heard'.

The experience began at Barrett's own rented house, a domestic setting employed as a waiting room as guests arrived. It spotlighted a cinematic impulse behind the performance by having Nick Roeg's *Don't Look Now* playing on the television as a theatrical prologue, which the audience watched the first seven minutes where the daughter is drowned, referencing the death and constant presence of Ranevskaya's son. As the audience left this antechamber, intervention was employed to destabilise the situation, which Barrett describes 'less as a narrative device and more thematic, to charge the audience', as punctuation in the tempo and narrative to trigger adrenalin so that the audience were 'put in flight or fright mode'. A plant on the street asked the group for money as they walked along the avenue, from the domestic home to the decaying mansion. In addition to the rug-pull this was also intended to suggest a class differential, obliquely referencing an economic hierarchy. Once in the building, the intention was 'you felt like you were back with your own', yet the mansion itself was crumbling around its inhabitants who haunted the space, as the audience looked on, exposing the themes of Chekhov's doomed aristocracy as the performance played out.

The production ran for two nights with no dress rehearsal, as was standard practice with those early, time-restricted projects:

I remember two Americans, in the days before we began with the audience 'briefing', thought they were attending *The Cherry Orchard*, had watched a drowning, been hassled for money by a stranger, been given a mask and left at the door of a huge house. They wouldn't move from the porch. I'd wrongly assumed the power of the mask would trigger exploration but I realised then that to make it accessible, if it's too confusing it's alienating, it needs to be just solvable enough. That was my learning there.

Barrett also recalls how a group from the Phoenix Arts Centre, people who worked professionally in theatre, visited the show but arrived drunk and unruly, finding it 'strange how people could disrespect the experience'. There was 'an interesting beat', where a couple from this group, who had taken their masks off, began to canoodle in the room with the beds. Audience members who discovered them assumed they were part of the experience and started watching them, setting an interesting and 'beautiful shift' in the world and making Barrett aware for the first time of how the mask 'delineated between performer and audience almost as clearly as an auditorium stage does. The simple action of taking the mask off elevated your status'. Additionally, the problematic unruliness made Barrett aware of a need for devices in place as a control method to protect audience and performers alike, while respecting the parameters of the world. It was here that Barrett learned, given that *The Cherry Orchard* employed 'no sound at all' other than the whispers of speech and natural sounds created by the audience wandering through the building, that a composed soundtrack may provide the means to guide the audience through the building and to action, serving as a device for control and supporting narratives within the world of the event. This production flagged the need for introductory instructions to the audience in a manner that was appropriate to the world, as part of the preparation and acclimatisation for the audience. It also highlighted a need for stewards. From here on stewards would be in place, comprising anyone working behind the scenes, and positioned within and alongside audience members in white masks watching the action: 'we couldn't allow that chaos, because it was neither safe nor theatrically satisfying'.

For Barrett, *The Cherry Orchard* is illustrative of many of the early projects of Act 1 in that it was 'joyous' for its impromptu industriousness: 'we had a space and created a show. It was a live, spontaneous response to space and opportunity'. In retrospect he notes how the principles and practice it

△ FIGURE 5 *Cherry Orchard*. 2000. Simon Davies as Trofimov.

Photo credit: Sam Holden

explored 'fused Punchdrunk Travel and a masked show in one'.

cinematic (see also: close-up; cross-fade: 'framing'; lens; lighting; long shot; restraint; Reverse Dolly Zoom; tracking shot. Further reading: Machon 2018): Cinematic in Punchdrunk terms describes both aesthetic influences, made manifest in particular in masked shows, alongside a quality of experience to be had in appreciation. Felix Barrett has been an avid appreciator of cinema since childhood, initially intending to study the artform, believing that he would 'do a Drama degree as a stepping stone to a postgrad in Film'. Barrett recalls how, following his response to Robert Wilson and Hans Peter Kuhn's *H.G.*, he 'became more interested in installation yet film seemed to have scale, I couldn't see how theatre would have that scale'. A Level influences such as Edward Gordon Craig or Josef Svoboda, renowned for creating cinematic scale in theatre, fed his theatrical tastes, but Barrett's access to these practitioners was only via archives, slide projections and book references of the work. Consequently, the idea of the theatrical experience on stage:

> felt removed from me, dislocated. Film felt more immersive, to use that word. There was also a sense at that time that theatre was largely text-driven, more about language and the head. Whereas film could be *textural* rather than textual, more of a collage.

Punchdrunk's aesthetic response to any source material when creating public works 'is always of a film persuasion' (Barrett in Barrett and Machon 2007) as all masked shows, *The Borough*, *The Bunker* or *Tunnel 228*, illustrate. *It Felt Like a Kiss*, in collaboration with Adam Curtis, was a hybrid of film-theatre-installation. The online reviews, profiles, blogs and academic critiques that abound are testament to the manner in which audiences immediately identify the cinematic scale and blurring between film and theatre in Punchdrunk's work, as illustrated by Codie and Kyle Entwistle, Peter

Higgin's former students and early audience members, both of whom went on to work in film. It is notable that external collaborators also refer to Barrett's vision as cinematic. Tina Bicât highlights how *Malfi* achieved feats of 'filmic imagination', while Tom Morris reflects that Barrett conceived ideas 'like a film-maker' to the extent that, just as Barrett had once aspired, Morris believed he 'would almost certainly end up making films'.

Punchdrunk's design approach absorbs and executes cinematic techniques, indicated primarily through the team's use of technical terms, such as 'lens' and 'long shot', in defining process, as scattered across this encyclopaedia. The performing style equally responds to these techniques, as Maxine Doyle's and various performers' references to 'close-ups' and 'framing' evidence. Longstanding Punchdrunk performer, Sarah Dowling, who also works as a movement director for films, with credits including *Tarzan*, *Fantastic Beasts and Where to Find Them* (both directed by David Yates) and *Mary Queen of Scots* (written by Beau Willimon and directed by Josie Rourke), draws astute and detailed comparison with Punchdrunk's style and film in regard to the development of a role and the delivery of that performance . . .

Sarah Dowling

On cinematic characters, light, image, action

My first experience with Punchdrunk, despite being 'only' an audition, went deep into playing seriously in a creative environment so expertly crafted by Max and Felix. I remember Felix's first talk with the company on day one of the rehearsals. I got this ridiculously excited feeling about this 'thing' he was explaining that we were about to do, for which we had no reference points. I'd never before experienced or seen anything like that which he was describing. I was unlocked by that Punchdrunk process, by the looped performance, the proximity to audience, the sound, design, space, all wrapping around the work, making it feel anchored and wild all at once. Punchdrunk shows are thrilling to perform and your experience of them, whether as audience or performer, live in that special dreamlike space inside your mind. I still dream of that first production of *Sleep No More*, and I revisit the lights, the sound, the corridors, the smells and the encounters I had with the most charismatic and enchanting fellow performers. No other company has ever matched Punchdrunk for the experience of being a performer and being involved in the devising process. The vitality and the importance of the role of the performer with Punchdrunk is wholly fulfilling for me and I maintain a desire to keep that pure, rather than taking on any additional directorial roles. It is a very collaborative creative process. The overarching vision for Punchdrunk, the company and its work, is so singular and so clear. That vision is very specifically from Felix and filtered through the core creative team, who all help to define what the vision is. It's closely related to a commitment to the audience being at the heart of everything that Punchdrunk create.

There's a huge commitment in the Punchdrunk process, on the performer's part, to make the work and build the character and narratives. If we were to imagine the character as a building, Maxine and Felix give you the scaffolding and the walls of that building and then the performer is responsible for creating the internal features, the partitions, the decorating, the furniture, fixtures and fittings. You create the content of that character and then that content is viewed and experienced by Max and Felix. Discussion and editing and questions arise from that which feed into your independent character development, creating the stuff of the role; the physical language, the interaction with the space and the soundtrack – all of that is self-generated. Felix and Max give you your character and your twelve scenes and your space. Most of those scenes have titles, for instance, 'The Persuasion Duet', between Lady Macbeth and Macbeth; titles designed to help the performer find a movement language for that action and objective. Those titles and scenes give you a starting point to initiate the creation of content and are an anchor for that material. They always originate from the source text, from our reading of the scene, extracting and interpreting the essence of it from our perspective.

With *The Drowned Man* and the double cast in place from the outset, there was a slight adjustment to that in that there was a degree of shared development of roles. Jane Leaney and I created the role of Diva together. Our end results were extremely different, but the material was exactly the same that we generated. Where that process works well is in giving you an extra 'you'. We might begin by exploring ideas on our own and then show Maxine and each other. We'd then accumulate or reject or take on the other's material, completely creating that role together in a physical dialogue. Day by day, hour by hour we would show, assimilate, put it into our own body and shape it like that.

I passed on the role of Lady Macbeth to Tori Sparks in Boston, which was a really interesting process. Max would be present at a lot of those passing on rehearsals. She would keep reminding me not to talk about the psychology or feeling of the material, as I saw it, instead to talk only about action, refining it down to the purity of the physical language in order to pass on that material. That's really difficult to do as this is the kind of work where the performer has necessarily attached psychology to action, back-story, history. I really enjoyed that discipline as it was interesting to question and note how the physical vocabulary alone holds the essence of that work. I was interested to view photographs of *Sleep No More*, NYC and video footage of the Lady Macbeth and Macbeth duets some years on, to see the choreography was almost exactly the same. The choreography remained intact as it was passed on pair to pair, year by year, but each pairing and each performer would fill that – which takes us back to the scaffolding and the walls – would fill that series of actions, those patterns and motifs, with their own view of the character, their own body history and life experiences. There were lots of different bodies playing these roles and each of those has a story in and of itself that adds a layer on top of the mechanics of the movement. The performer's body functions as an archive of all that material in that something fundamental is passed down over the years, an essence of the character and relationships, yet it is also always an ever changing, morphing essence dependent on who's playing it.

For that reason, the audience's experience of these characters is so changed by the specifics of each performer and each performer's interpretation of that role. I'm sure that embedded in me as a performer, because I've worked with Punchdrunk for so many years, is something that people outside of the company would identify as a Punchdrunk style and way of being; I've practised it for so long that these characters, this physical language, that style is in my body.

There's a unique balancing act that we explore as performers in Punchdrunk between emotional investment and dance vocabulary. I do feel that I'm both acting and dancing. As I've continued performing in Punchdrunk's work I've tried to act less and see what the physical can communicate all by itself. This moves more into the realm of immersion in a role, where you wouldn't call it acting anymore, particularly when you're in your twelfth month of an eighteen-month run. I no longer correlate that with what I think of as acting because through the repetition of these movements in that scenography with that soundtrack, I don't feel like I'm acting, I feel like I'm *being* it, doing it. I guess that corresponds to theatrical practices that are trying to access that zone where you move into a state of not performing but just doing and being.

I've always thought of Punchdrunk's style as incredibly filmic. I've just movement directed for a film and I really was struck by the similarities with Punchdrunk's approach and film acting and what the camera requires from film actors. It's related to proximity of audience, because they can be in that close-up, that intimate proximity where you can't push anything out in your performance. Pretending, the kind of acting that you might be able to get away with when you've got a proscenium arch and a metre or more between you and the audience, all that's done away with when your audience is close to you, smelling you. It requires an internalisation of emotion, a restraining of it, holding it back and down and in, in the way that we often do in real life. It's very similar to filmic actors and how they perform with the same restraint. I've worked with the film director David Yates and he often gave advice to the actors to hold back and just tell the story in the eyes. It's about containing the idea or emotion, and subtly letting it leak out instead; the leakage rather than overt presentation of an emotional state is the way I would describe how Punchdrunk performers often need to operate. Another filmic connection relates to the power of image and the relationship with lighting associated with Punchdrunk's style. Again, that resonates with the film world where one third of the set-up time is spent on acting rehearsals and two thirds on lighting the space. The darkness and the shafts of light that Felix lets us have and, more importantly, *find*, come close to that.

The lighting, the space, the touch-real locations, all of that is helping you to lose yourself in that world as a performer; to lose self-consciousness, lose inhibition and to go into another landscape and world that is not reality, not your own. The lack of an enforced scrutinising frame of the proscenium arch or the camera lens makes performing in Punchdrunk worlds a very different experience. It's not a mechanical lens that's in your face but these breathing, ghostly presences that help you to lose yourself in that otherworldliness, which in turn, hopefully, helps them, the audience, to lose themselves in it too. Everything is in place for you to lose yourself; I've experienced so many iterations of that, feeling that I'm in a dream, or that it's blurring with my reality, that I'm suspended or transformed, transfigured into someone or something else. At the same time, because of the extreme liveness of each moment, the unrepeatability of each performance, where the audience could be in any relationship to you, could be doing something completely different to what it had done before, you have to be alert, to be able to switch back into pragmatic decision-making, to shift and change things – don't move there because that group of people look as if they won't shift out of the way – all of those quick-witted judgements have to be possible at the same time as losing yourself. The best way to describe it is that it's like a two-year-old playing; they're completely and utterly in their imaginative world but at any moment they can pop back out and want some milk or ask a banal question. We continually practise keeping those channels of deep, serious play open, going deep into the realm of the subconscious and places of rich creative playing, in our rehearsal process while equally ensuring we can snap back, be safe and back in the space, back to ourselves and making practical decisions.

Images provide an important palette of shared starting points among the ensemble and the designers. The first thing we'll have is a table of materials, which will include the text and loads of visual stimuli, photographs, artwork, that help us build a shared movement vocabulary across the departments. For *Sleep No More*, Michelangelo's 'Last Supper' image became the way we created that entire scene. The shared aesthetic across the visual imagery and films and soundtrack certainly influences the movement vocabulary. It's something to do with the power of the iconic image and the situation we're in as Punchdrunk performers where our audience is mobile and choosing when to stay and when to leave. Strategies you start employing to hold your audience's attention directly relate to that power of the image. Within those iconic Michelangelo, Edward Hopper, old Hollywood images, the distillation of character and psychology and aesthetic, they're extremely powerful because they're so dense. Each Punchdrunk performer has carved for themselves an equivalent dense, thick image version of their character so that when an audience member comes across you after wandering the building for the last forty-five minutes, they could, in an instant, get a flavour of what you are, who you are, where you're going and what's come before. I remember Felix talking to us about it being important that within the first three seconds of an audience finding you they can detect your whole story in that moment. Each moment of action, to a degree, holds your whole story and character within it. You're looking for that density, using your body in space, partnering that very carefully with light, and attaching action to sound to help create these anchored, strong images.

Key techniques that we return to that define the Punchdrunk approach to creating character are:

- Find your frame – within every space there's a frame so in a way you are finding your own little proscenium arch or screen, to provide a frame within which the audience's eye can be focused. That frame might be a window frame or it might be light.
- Find your light.
- Find your clarity of intention – know who you are, what you're doing there, what you want to do and what your over-arching objective is. All of that has to be super clear for your audience.
- Find the reveal, surprise, the change-the-room moment, the nothing-is-what-you-thought-it-was feeling. That's an important part of every little scene. You have to be open to that as a performer and you have to create that for the audience.

Clod & Pebble (**2008**, see also: **curiosity**; **doors**; journeying; **keyholders**; **one-on-one**; portals; **R&D**): Themed around the William Blake poem from which it took its name, this was an intimate one-on-one piece produced for the Christmas period. It was a test piece for exploring alternative approaches to establishing what are commonly known in theatre and venue-funding streams as 'Friends' schemes, which later evolved into the Punchdrunk keyholders. *Clod & Pebble* was inspired by Hermann Hesse's *Steppenwolf* idea of creating a magical door into another world only for those people adventurous and curious enough to notice the unusual façade of a shop, which Colins Nightingale and Marsh had secured from Shaftesbury Estates, quirkily nestled among the chain-stores and retail outlets of London's Carnaby Street. The tags on each item in this shop all had 'not for sale' written on them. Nightingale recalls:

After I broke both of my feet during *The Bunker*, I found myself with a lot of time on my hands and able to daydream in ways that working life hadn't permitted for a few years. Colin Marsh had mentioned that we needed to create an event for Punchdrunk's expanding 'Friends' scheme. It was important that this first formal event wasn't the standard drink and canapes evening. These initial supporters had fallen for our unconventional approach to theatre so we should give them more and it also felt important to try to maintain some kind of mystery and magic around Punchdrunk. I'd shaped up the basic idea of an odd little shop that didn't actually have anything for sale. We knew we wanted to have a one-on-one in the basement. In his research Hector Harkness discovered the location of the shop was very close to the site of the house in which William Blake was born, on Broadwick Street, now a block of flats visible from the front of the shop, called William Blake Tower, so we put a telescope in the window pointing

towards this building. He also discovered that William had a beloved younger brother called Robert who had died. Hector set about creating a one-on-one about his ghost searching for William. During our continual search for props to dress the shows, and also in my years of hunting for old records, I'd ended up in a lot of bizarre thrift stores, charity shops, antique shops and markets. I thought it would be fun and cheap if we took some of the crazy contents of our prop store to make our own emporium complete with an eccentric shopkeeper. Not long after I'd met Felix I'd been told by a friend of his to read *Steppenwolf*. Felix and I had talked a lot about making a project that was unpublicised and then waiting to see who would choose to wander in, like the door in the book with the sign, 'Magic theatre, For madmen only'. For me, *Clod & Pebble* was finally a real opportunity to do this, a chance to create a doorway that only the most curious, observant, bravest – or 'mad' – would enter. We set about installing the shop in secret and it opened in December 2008 during the run-up to Christmas. We worked hard to make the shopfront feel real, if slightly out of place and maybe from another time. We wanted people who had regularly walked the street to wonder whether they had just never noticed it before or to question its sudden appearance.

Shared as a free event, supporters were provided with an allotted timeslot and the directions to arrive at a 'The Clod and Pebble', a nineteenth-century shop, otherworldly in its countenance and design, offset by the more commercial shops of Carnaby Street's Newburgh Quarter. It was equally available for those members of the general public driven by curiosity. The unsuspecting audience member would stumble in to a fully realised, antiquated world sitting behind the shop door. As they entered they were met by a man, quietly reading, towards the rear of the shop. On gaining their trust,

they were eventually led down to the basement to be told a tragic tale of the love and loss of a brother only to be surprised by a happy twist on exit, sent on your way with a sprig of holly as a 'Merry Christmas from Punchdrunk'. Nightingale continues:

Random members of the public did stumble through this portal into the odd retail environment, where every price tag revealed nothing in the shop was actually for sale. Some found 'Robert' and were taken down into the basement to experience the intense performance that had been skilfully crafted by Hector to a specially designed soundtrack that Stephen Dobbie had created. The intensity of its crescendo was very powerful and still to this day we often return to using this sound design when creating one-on-ones. Even the 'Friends' who were invited to come to the experience were not given the address, only the rough area, a riddle to solve to find it and an instruction to ask for Robert. They had to be brave to make the choice to enter the shop and then navigate the narrow path through the stacks of antique furniture, and then braver still to venture behind the shop counter to find 'Robert'. Livi had worked hard with Hector and the assistant designers to fill these back areas with detail hinting at this character's restless search for something he'd lost. Some of the invited guests never made it this far with some not even being confident enough to push the front door open. At least one person ended up in the office above the shop in a strange conversation with someone who, coincidently, was also called Robert.

Blurring lines between the real and the imagined in this way, there was a different quality of experience noted, following the event, by those supporters who had been invited to the event via secret online means and the experience of inquisitive members of the general public who just happened to stumble into the piece by chance.

Nightingale recalls receiving a letter from a member of the general public, rather than a keyholder, after having stumbled upon *Clod & Pebble*, which asserted she was 'never going to look at the world the same way again'. Felix Barrett summarises:

Clod and Pebble was following in the footsteps of the Exeter experiments, and *The Yellow Wallpaper*. It was an excuse to do something, when the pace of the output had started to slow down. What was exciting about it was the blurring of the real world and the fictional. I would link it to Punchdrunk Travel and *Kabeiroi*, where you can't quite tell the point at which the show has begun.

close-up (see also: **'chairs'**; **cinematic**; dance; design; framing; **long shot**; **touch-real**): This is an example of how film terminology is often employed by Punchdrunk, more so than theatre vocabulary, when creating a project. In film, a close-up defines an image shot at close range and in intimate detail, tightly framing an object or subject. 'Close-up' in Punchdrunk masked shows describes the cinematic detail of the design. It also describes the manner in which the dancers are trained to consider their choreography and performance. Maxine Doyle clarifies:

Close-up and long shot are terms we employ regularly to bring focus to choreographic detail and perspective. I may ask the dancer in an improvisation to play the close-up and pay attention to small details or adversely, play the long shot and thus take in the shape and image of the whole form, in isolation or in relation to a spatial frame. We have an exercise called 'chairs' which is great for developing the performers' attention to possibilities of proximity and emotional expression. 'Chairs' is all about the close-up.

In response to this focus on design and dance and the resultant way in which the audience is invited to interact with a Punchdrunk masked show, close-up is a term that describes the manner in which the audience views and interacts with the world of the event.

Club Shelter (see also: **Act 2**; contact improvisation; cross-fade; **ritual**; Seguro, Joana; 'space-hunting'): An infamous NYC party and club night during the 2000s that opened its doors at midnight on a Saturday and ran until early afternoon on the Sunday. During a space-hunting trip to NYC in 2008, Colin Nightingale made a slightly reluctant Felix Barrett go to bed early on a Saturday night so that he could take him to Shelter at seven in the morning to witness the club at its peak time with a rested mind. From the deserted early morning Tribeca streets, Nightingale and Barrett headed into an old warehouse building and walked into a highly charged atmosphere. Other club-goers were also just arriving, entering as if in attendance at a church or sacred space, ready to be spiritually uplifted, as they joined the dancing, jamming with each other much like contact improvisation. Nightingale recollects the experience having quite an impact on Barrett: 'I'm not sure if was the unexpected nature of what I showed him or whether he'd ever seen that type of energy in a club before'. Barrett's memory of the experience, in retrospect, underscores the power of how an individual audience member might 'discover something':

The show is as much the journey as what you discover when you get there. Waking up and seeing a New York City that I'd never seen before at 6am, cold and empty and dormant. Travelling to what seemed like the middle of nowhere to walk into something that was in full swing. It was bizarre at that time of day, and yet there was a purity to it because everyone had come solely for the music. It wasn't about hedonism but movement and allowing your body to be led by the sound. It was so pure, so distilled, so otherworldly. Going to a nightclub at breakfast time was like an experience of displacement.

For Barrett the Club Shelter anecdote emphasises how the quality of any

encounter with an experiential form is made possible, certainly intensified, by an equivalent lead-in to that encounter. When crafted to be so, that lead-in increases the quality of ritual that comes to bear: 'it's about creating context for the audience; something out of time, out of place, out of shape becomes completely magical'.

coda (see also: **afterbeat**; dreams; immersive; letters; synchronicity): In music this is a cadence or passage that brings a movement or piece to a close. In Punchdrunk's practice it is shorthand for an otherworldly occurrence that happens after an event. It may be a moment created in the bar at the end, or a phone call received to close an online interaction. It may be a text message received the next day or a letter received months later.

collaboration (see also: Act 1; Act 2; Act 3; **audience**; building; caretaking; community; compromise; design; **ensemble**; process): A layered understanding of what defines collaboration exists within Punchdrunk's practice. Collaborative investigation is at the heart of Punchdrunk's mission; a commitment to the creative possibilities inherent to an interdisciplinary company make-up. Colin Nightingale observes that Punchdrunk has evolved a method of collaborating for large-scale productions since *Sleep No More*, London. This requires clearly defined, while mutually attuned, organisational and artistic structures in order to function successfully, thus creating mechanisms for safe and playful engagement within the work. Nightingale summarises:

Collaboration acknowledges interrelated practices from the outset; that decisions are not made in isolation and there's a blur between all of the departments – creative and organisational. That interconnectedness is vital. The framework has to be right on an organisational level which, for Punchdrunk, involves an acceptance that things can't always be planned and budgeted at the start, so we plan for that! Best practice involves a degree of being open to discovery and issues that will arise – good and bad – at any stage during the process. That is a significant approach to practice that we've learned over the years, with each production – the interrelatedness of creative and organisational structures. Bridging the gap between the creative ambition and the organisational and financial constraints in addition to any physical constraints of the building. We've learnt from experience to question and address the overall artistic ambition of any project in order to troubleshoot organisationally as the process evolves. Leaving space for the troubleshooting is an important part of the process.

In terms of artistic practice there is always a degree to which collaboration extends to the audience. Creating any event involves a respect for the audience and possible audience journeys within the work, while offering opportunities to push at comfort zones.

communal (see also: **audience**; **bar**; community; immersive; **masked shows**; Red Death Lates. Further reading: Flaherty 2014; Ritter 2016): Punchdrunk experiences are designed with a focus on individual journeying and experience, influenced by the presence of others but not necessarily reliant on that, which then opens out to a communal sharing, of narrative, theme or drink at the end. Maxine Doyle asserts:

> The form of the masked shows draws on the oppositions of individual (make your own story) and shared (ensemble sections and finale) experience. We aim to harness the power of a shared experience by reuniting the audience to watch some grand denouement or spectacle. The banquet scene in *Sleep No More*, London, was the first manifestation of this, and an innovation to the existing form.

Unlike conventional theatre experiences, it is notable that with immersive work in general and Punchdrunk work in particular, strangers will often talk with each other following an event. There is a compulsion to share, often to piece together experience, with other audience members following the event in person or via social media networks.

community (see also: **Cake Friday**; collaboration; **Enrichment**): Establishing a strong sense of community is important to the Punchdrunk process when working on projects. In early projects community was established through a shared and non-hierarchical collaboration, supported by the fact the group were living, perhaps camping and eating together, as recalled by Sam Booth, Arne Maynard and Kathryn McGarr in their separate contributions. Sitting down to share food together as a whole company, once a week, is a legacy attributable to Griselda Yorke that remains an important feature of a Punchdrunk's working structure. The act of sharing food as a whole company on-site during large-scale projects continues to the present; a feature commented on by David Jubb in his recollections of *The Masque of the Red Death*. More broadly, understanding and remaining committed to the needs of a host community, whether a school, a cultural organisation, a care home or a wider social and geographical community, is vital to the work of Enrichment. The social and geographical histories of a local community provided not only the site but also the foundations for the research and eventual aesthetics of a number of projects including *Beneath the Streets*, *Brixton Market*, *The Borough*, *The Lambeth Walk* and *The Uncommercial Traveller* projects. In turn an intended legacy of such projects is the fostering of the very spirit of community.

'company building' (see also: **Act 1**; Act 2; Act 3; curiosity; ensemble; in-show-world; **process**; **synchronicity**; touch-real): Across Act 1 the core team came together not simply through a shared aesthetic sensibility and ambition for each project, but through the resolve to, as they all put it, 'make the work happen' despite difficult, sometimes grim, circumstances (especially when it came to clearing 21 Wapping Lane). Even with the less brutal builds, for the core design and production team, as Felix Barrett succinctly puts it, 'so much of life was about loading and unloading a van'.

Barrett identifies how the coming together of the original team, and especially those that have remained as its core creatives, occurred via an 'organic absorption of people who shared a goal, an ambition, interests and an aesthetic'. As Act 1 chronicles, during the early years, the initial and longest-standing members of the core creative team conjoined, by chance or design, as a consequence of being drawn to the work. A Punchdrunk sensibility for Barrett is defined by a commitment to 'the audience experience always coming first' supported by shared instinct, imagination, and responsiveness to sources. It is this focus that drives the concept and outcome and nuances 'an understanding that the passage through something, as much as what you experience when you get there' is of equal importance:

> It's shaped by an innate awareness that theatre doesn't start and stop when the lights go down. It's an understanding that how you find out about the event, who you take and why you take them with you is important; that when the show ends at ten o'clock and you then go and talk about it is as critical an ingredient and just as crucial in terms of your memory of the event, the material you've experienced and the rooms you've just walked through. It's about appealing to the eternal adventurer. It's the whole gamut.

In addition to Peter Higgin, this sensibility was identifiable to Barrett in core Punchdrunk members, the likes of Stephen Dobbie, Colin Nightingale or Livi Vaughan. In simple terms, as Barrett summarises, after their first experience of Barrett's work:

> The way they would talk about their experience was exactly what I

was trying to do. Immediately they understood at a profound, base level and could *feel* it, we could feel the same thing. It wasn't about a cerebral response, they felt it because they stepped outside of their comfort zone to experience it.

It was focused by Barrett's cinematic vision which inspired and corresponded to a collective instinct for what the concept was and what the project could become. Dobbie notes the serendipitous fortune in the formation of the core creative team:

It's rather wonderful that so many people have come together with a shared instinct which has allowed Punchdrunk, and so the worlds we create, to evolve organically. And it's important to note that that shared instinct has been nurtured across the company and has grown with the scale and nature of the work. It means that we're fortunate in having the luxury of not having to worry about second-guessing people's decisions. Generally, we're all going in the right and instinctive direction, so the process becomes about tweaking and editing and it's rarely about noticing where something is *really* wrong.

For Barrett, the reason that Punchdrunk has 'grown organically' is because 'individuals have *found* themselves as artists and practitioners here. It's not like we did a recruitment drive. In fact, whenever we do recruit now it's often difficult because our process is idiosyncratic'. Of the early projects, from *The Tempest*, 2003 to *Marat/Sade*, Barrett describes how Punchdrunk functioned as 'a collective, with no hierarchy'. In this set-up, 'people would contribute an idea', including guest or ad interim collaborators, 'and if it felt right for the project the collective would go with it'. Reflecting on the core principles involved in pulling a team and an ensemble of performers together in the formation of a theatre company, Barrett elaborates in conversation with Dobbie and Higgin:

Felix: We were a ramshackle bunch of people none of whom really identified as theatre makers. Nowadays where we might do a recruitment drive to find a Production Manager, at that time, Colin Nightingale walked in, got what we were doing and just took on that role. Similarly, Dobbie was a photographer and hip-hop music producer, who got the aesthetic and created our first posters.

Stephen: Many of our anecdotes actually relate to building a company –

Felix: – and our sense of adventure. It's because we were living it, living in those spaces, working seven-day weeks, that we can reminisce about the time, at 3 a.m. when we put some big tunes on the sound system and claimed the space as our own. If we hadn't done that, because of the amount of work it took, it would have broken us. We needed to burn off steam, dance in the space, duel with polystyrene buffers.

Stephen: Felix and I staying in the motel in *Faust* was us claiming that world, living within the world, right up until it opened.

Pete: It relates to company building and finding a process, finding ways to work through and continue to have fun, despite the toil, despite being knee deep in mud. Of course, that's a pace that we've not been able to maintain. As it grows, Punchdrunk's not able to work in that way. It's one chapter, the first act, that set a shared attitude and approach among our core members. Punchdrunk has grown out of a core of people who lived and breathed it, with blood, sweat and tears, not taking holidays, working for nothing or very little to make it succeed. The reality of that succeeding is that we've been able to establish a much bigger, professional company but that means that those core members often wrangle with the tension of having to work within those professional

parameters, 'what do you mean we can't be in the building twenty-four hours?!', born out of a period where we could and did do that. Now the operations are so much bigger and we all have wider responsibilities and families. That said, none of those early productions could have happened had there not been that commitment to make the work happen, with the compulsion to do it solely coming from that, not from remuneration. It was never about money. Put it this way, nobody submitted an invoice to claim for overtime.

Felix: It was more like, you did your day job to pay for your 'Punchdrunk holiday', which would leave you absolutely broken but creatively restored.

Barrett is quick to point out, 'the final stages in the making of the shows was a slither of the work' that marks out Punchdrunk's practice and history. Instead, 'it was the gristle between the shows going up' that saw to the evolution of the company. He emphasises how the shared 'muscle memory' for making work was underpinned by the collective 'living, eating and breathing in the world that the team was creating, sleeping in the space as the build of that world took place'. For Barrett, across Act 1, 'the basic rules of company building' related to 'getting collaborators to a place of shared ethos, a way of working and breathing together'. Higgin reiterates this idea of the core team 'living and breathing the work'. It is notable that Tina Bicât, an external collaborator, describes the shared sensibility that has led to the Punchdrunk 'stamp' as 'breath . . . much more than style or brand. If you think about the key people and the way they all breathe into something you'd find a pretty clear circle of connection'.

compromise (see also: building; **collaboration**; **design**; *Sleep No More*, Boston; *Sleep No More*, NYC; synchronicity): Any collaboration involves some degree of compromise. As Punchdrunk became more critically acclaimed, the company became aware of the tension between the need to support the operational structures required to fulfil creative ambitions and the financial constraints of supporting this from funding bodies and trusts. Concurrent with Punchdrunk's critical acclaim, and a defining feature of Act 2, arts organisations, national and international producing companies and commercial brands have been keen to partner with Punchdrunk. Always mindful of the need to partner on projects where Punchdrunk's artistic integrity can remain at the forefront, the team is constantly aware of the impact of needing to produce work that is a box office success, in commercial terms, in order to run and to support ongoing innovation and Enrichment projects, while training up artists and practitioners of the future. Any production that involves collaboration with another artist or arts company involves a degree of compromise in the creative process, especially where disparate needs need to be addressed; such as the comfort of a sixty-piece symphony orchestra being at odds with the need for a roaming performing style, as was the case with *The Duchess of Malfi*. International productions, beginning with *Sleep No More*, Boston, through NYC and Shanghai, also involve a degree of compromise related to creative process and producing models where the commercial interests of the partner companies necessitate negotiations, sometimes concessions, while maintaining high production values and artistic integrity. As Felix Barrett and Livi Vaughan illustrate in the entry for design, compromise and working with limitations always help rather than hinder creativity.

contact improvisation (see also: **dance**; *Sleep No More*, London; **touch**. Further reading: Pallant 2006; Tufnell and Crickmay 2001, 2004): A dance form that underpins much of Maxine Doyle's choreographic practice and a method used when generating work in the studio and on-site with any Punchdrunk dance ensemble. Pioneered in America in 1972 by Steve Paxton with his colleagues and students, the technique is concerned with physical contact with another in a duet form and the spontaneous movement that occurs when interacting with that partner, giving and taking weight improvisationally. As the improvisation develops, the contact may extend to multiple partners within a group. Sensitivity to others' bodies and an allowance of any movement that evolves is of prime importance. The basic principles of the form are: transference of weight; balance and off balance; leaning, lifting and carrying. The improvisation follows the flow of energy and momentum between partners – falling, rolling, spiralling, lifting and supporting. It emphasises the centre of the body, the weight and momentum or energy flow of the body, and explores loss of balance and shifting away from the vertical. There is no predetermined dance vocabulary and the movement is generally focused internally and within the group rather than towards an audience. Given that it follows no prescribed codification beyond its basic principles, it is widely regarded among practitioners as requiring no formal training. It embodies the egalitarian values and highlights individualism within a group. Felix Barrett provides illustration of the significance of this form to *Sleep No More*, London and all masked events from then on, encapsulating how Rob McNeill demonstrated his expertise in extending contact partnerships to objects and architecture.

corner (see also: **discovery**; **loops**; narrative; **synchronicity**): A Punchdrunk term that indicates a turning point in the narrative. This can also refer to an experiential corner for the audience member where the chance happening across a key moment for that individual, at any point during the event, might hold a moment of discovery as well as leading to the next significant scenario in the loop. The term thus holds the idea of dwelling in a corner as 'a chamber of being' (Bachelard 1994, 138) as much as it indicates the turning of a corner in character narrative and knowledge of the world under scrutiny.

cornfield (see also: community; design; *Faust*; forests; Harvey, Robin; **mass production**; **multiples**; nature; **volunteers**): A cornfield in *Faust* occupied much of the third floor of 21 Wapping Lane, flanked by two large rooms filled with a maze of shelves. It was created by a combined effort of all members of the design team, cast and crew for *Faust*, including a number of volunteers. The prototype for a single corn plant was made by Robin Harvey from pages of scientific formula related to the growing of corn, as a reference to the scientific papers and formulae in *Faust*'s laboratory. Other members of Punchdrunk were then instructed in how to make these stems and, through a collective build, thus the cornfield grew. Tina Bicât, touring the building with Colin Nightingale, recalls entering 'a room with a designer creating, with a crowd of volunteers, masses and masses of ears of corn for the cornfield; it was a surreal feeling as we breezed through that as if it were a perfectly ordinary thing to be happening and back into this dark cavern'. Peter Higgin reminisces:

In the days when Punchdrunk's production operation was much smaller, every piece of the production jigsaw was hard to achieve. Rarely were we able to match the scale of ambition with a paid production team, so any area that required mass production of a specific item, or intensive labour, was usually approached in a communal way. One person took on the process of building the prototype, in this instance a single corn stem was made from bamboo, wire, paper and glue. Although simple materials, the making process was intricate and required the assembly of many different elements. With all its different construction processes it would take an individual a long time to create just one piece of corn. Once the making of an item was refined and the process understood we became speedier at it. As a production team, we became very good at breaking down the process and, gathering a team of volunteers, production crew or friends and family, to break the back of the job. Often the operation would become like a factory line. I remember we hosted a few evenings of corn making for *Faust*, asking performers to join in.

corridors (see also: abstract/abstraction; aesthetics; building; corner; curiosity; influences; journeying; loops; **mazes**; multiples; *Shining, The*; **tunnels**): A recurring motif in Punchdrunk's work. Corridors and corners are employed within the build and detailed design of an event. They are used to good effect to choreograph the flow of the audience, evident in all journeys across levels in any buildings of masked shows. Corridors also provide the route for characters on their journey through their looped narrative. In Punchdrunk worlds, corridors offer a practical aesthetic and establish potent imagery as well as producing threatening and disorientating journeys within the geography of a building, as was the case with *It Felt Like a Kiss*.

costume (see also: abstract/abstraction; **Act 1**; **Barrett, Felix**; Bicât, Tina; *Chair*; **close-up**; crescendo; curiosity; dance; darkness; **design**; **durational**; Exeter Experiments; **long shot**; mazes; Reynoso, David; **scenography**; *Sleep No More*, London): Costume is not considered as separate to but deeply embedded in the aesthetic of Punchdrunk worlds. For Felix Barrett, costume is an extension of space and performer, darkness and light. It functions as signifier in relation to all of the other elements of the experience: 'in a Punchdrunk landscape costume is either an extension of design or an extension of performer'. Costume partners in the design concept, rather than leads: 'I studied it at university and strongly believe in it as a form', gauged in relation to it being an extension of the space, the landscape, the scenography or in its augmentation of a performer.

In the early Punchdrunk worlds created in Act 1, costume had a more abstracted, sensual presence, offering what Barrett refers to as 'snapshots' of colour, sensation and stories. With the first *Woyzeck*, in 2000, 'the decision to dress characters in black or white related purely to darkness' assisting the performer's ability to be visible or to disappear in the gloom'. Conversely, in all of the projects that preceded *Faust*, primarily due to the building of an aesthetic from 'scavenged' objects and materials, the costumes came from second-hand shops or Barrett's parents' attic and were configured within the work to accentuate the very quality, the look, feel and smell of time passed, regularly sticking with a standard, evening wear that was always of 'another time'. As Barrett explains, 'it was us making do with what was around us, that was the art of putting together costume in those early projects, as opposed to us designing and making something new'. Barrett found the effectiveness of those borrowed vintage clothes added an eerie authenticity, rather than a distracting 'theatricality', or staginess, that may have diluted the experience. They lent themselves to the Punchdrunk principle of creating an idiosyncratic world from the resources available, rather than deciding immovably what the world would be in advance. Moreover, being purloined from his parents' attic ensured that those early costumes 'were part of the same design world, from the same source, with the same smell of mothballs':

The fact that they didn't fit properly didn't matter because it was more important that it was black-tie from the thirties. The reason why those shows were all set in the past was because that was all we had.

For Barrett, costume is at its most powerful as a signifier when it resonates within the continuum of design, over and above any clues about a character or the era in which a world is set. Barrett cites the influence of Edward Gordon Craig in this respect, and the images from Craig's production of *Hamlet* where Gertrude and Claudius wear a cloak that spans the court and all of the courtiers, to illustrate his interest in 'costume that was also the set, that was also the building that was also a crescendo':

Costume is as much installation as anything else and should always be about what it makes the audience feel. It might be camouflage, or it's there to highlight the performer or make them disappear. It has to accentuate the desired impact they need to have on an audience. If you need to lurk in the shadows, appear from out of the darkness, then you'll be costumed in dark colours. If you need to tantalise in the distance, then it's a flash of white, Miranda in her slip or Viola from *Moon Slave*, figures you'll never get close to. The simpler they are, the purer. Where costume becomes logical and narrative, it becomes a problem.

As this suggests, Barrett is intrigued by the mystery that costume as a signifier might conjure and the various ways that this can be achieved. The suitcase that ended up in the hands of Colin Marsh, as Barrett's application for an Indepen*dance* award in 2002, is an important illustration of this. As the sole means by which Barrett shared his proposal for the first production of *Sleep No More*, it contained clothing as set, character, narrative. It established a mystery and suggested itself as a clue, a key to unlocking the experience. It held a secret to be found by the curious in that the letter that outlined the proposal had to be discovered in the breast pocket of this anonymous suit jacket. It implied a psychological story that needed to be, literally, unpacked. It was anonymous in shape and style, yet with a smell of mothballs that suggested it came from a long-gone person and a forgotten time. The suit jacket encapsulated the form; it led the recipient into another world, was a thing of curiosity because of the very absence of information about the character. It required interaction and rewarded curiosity with discovery. Barrett adds:

I often find if a costume *tells* you what to think it spoon-feeds the audience. I'm far more interested in the live art approach to costume where it's durational, it gets dirty, it falls apart or is cut to pieces, and is transformed over the course of so many hours. The Witch in *Sleep No More*, NYC, gets her hair wet once a loop by plunging her head into water. By the end of the three loops her dress is sodden and stained with blood.

Barrett's interest in the way in which costume might respond to, or be impacted upon by, space, time and external forces and how, in and of itself, it can establish a mood and movement vocabulary was first tested as one of his Exeter Experiments. While studying costume in his second year at university, he explored the way in which it could create the unexpected, imply magic and mystery, as well as conveying a feeling of immensity. He was concerned with designing and constructing pieces with the express intention of them working with, while simultaneously transforming, the world in which they were presented. He made a huge grey cloak, which 'billowed impossibly' when the wearer moved in it, becoming both gestural and transformational. It had the ability to transfigure the performer that wore it through its movement quality. Its astonishing capaciousness also had a transformative relationship with and to space. Barrett took this experimentation with the way in which costume could 'trigger a change in the landscape', by modifying an oversized, full-length coat, 'sewing hundreds of five-metre lengths of fabric to it' to create a piece that 'looked like a rock and was more like a sculptural object. I took it out to Dartmoor, stood it on top of a real boulder and when the wind hit, it would *really* billow'. With this piece he was examining 'costume as crescendo, as punctuation' where the costume has a purpose beyond the narrative, creates an impact that is at once awe inspiring, durational and experiential. The outcomes of these experiments were later reinforced by the vast amounts of heavy-duty sewing he undertook for the early Punchdrunk projects; creating scenography to dress space, as opposed to costumes that dressed characters. This deepened Barrett's interest

in costume being invested with a durational quality at every stage of its life, from the act of construction, through installation and presentation to its storing and reusing. Equally, Barrett is drawn to the durational quality of costume as it is both worn and worn out by the performers through the run of a masked show; the manner in which the sweat, the soiling and tearing, adds to that quality of duration and the life it lives within the event.

For Barrett and the team designing Punchdrunk worlds, costume is at its most effective when it creates mystery by going against the literal and logical, whether that be through its abstracted and sculptural form or because it presents a clash of era, the vintage of the costume implying a blurring of time and temperament, through shape and scent. Colin Nightingale notes how a shift away from the early approach to 'scavenged' costume occurred from *Faust* onwards, towards a respect for collaborating with similarly inventive, costume designers, such as Tina Bicât or David Reynoso, who were 'excellent makers' and wardrobe technicians: 'because we're working with dancers, the need to remake and maintain costume is *so* important in the masked shows'. Great skill and hard work are required to design and maintain costumes for athletic bodies that are performing on a dynamic, durational loop, across the course of an evening's performance as much as a year's, or longer, run. Bicât's eloquence on the interrelationship between design and dance is recorded in her recollections of *Masque of the Red Death*. For every Punchdrunk collaboration Bicât would closely observe early warm-ups on-site for what these revealed regarding how dancers would 'work and wear costumes. You can see how their bodies work, how much some sweat, or not, you get a feeling for the way their bodies move with each other'.

Collaborating designers need to understand the Punchdrunk principle of subverting expectation, as Barrett illustrates through Reynoso's costume design for *Sleep No More*, Shanghai:

He's good at using archetypes and signifiers, but with subtle tweaks. Boy Witch has got a nice dinner jacket but if you look closely, it has black raven feathers just around the outside of the lapel. If you blinked, you'd miss them. It's about the close-up, it needs to have a modicum of restraint in the same way that the action does, so that you don't get it all on first glance.

As this illustrates, costume adds to the cinematic detail, the touch-real narratives and the dreamlike states intertwined in a Punchdrunk world. Livi Vaughan explains that it serves to 'elevate the performers in a fundamental way, highlights them, you notice them when they enter a room. And it tells a story'. In whatever way it might be employed, costume in a Punchdrunk world taps into the manner in which the audience is charged with noticing. Costume adds to the beat of the unusual, the uncanny. As Barrett puts it, 'it's about looking twice'. Costume, like the nuances and subtleties of the installation or the layered loops of the performance, rewards curiosity and offers a chance for discovery. Pay attention, in close-up or from afar, and you will notice clues, identify why that something 'is not quite as it seems'.

Crash of the Elysium, The (2011–2012; see also: **Act 2**; Poots, Alex. Further reading: Biggin 2017, 113–133): Commissioned by Alex Poots for MIF, *The Crash of the Elysium* was the first large-scale Punchdrunk event that was created especially for children aged between six and twelve, and their families. This one-hour show, a live *Doctor Who* theatre adventure, was conceived in close collaboration with members of *Doctor Who*'s creative team at the BBC, including Stephen Moffat and Tom McRae. With the input of Peter Higgin and Katy Balfour, the production developed out of Punchdrunk Enrichment's work with primary schools and has gone on to inform adventure-driven projects since, such as *Against Captain's Orders*. Designed for a transferable, temporary site, in 2012 the piece was reworked for the Ipswich Arts Festival. Once again it was made in collaboration with the BBC and co-produced and presented by MIF, London 2012 Festival, the New Wolsey Theatre and Ipswich Borough Council, supported by Suffolk County Council and Arts Council England. The project played to an audience of nearly 7,000 across both runs.

crescendo (see also: **awe and wonder**; cinematic; **corner**; **'Grandmother's Room'**; masked shows; **one-on-one**; process; pyrotechnics; reveal): The crescendo is a culminating point, as Felix Barrett puts it: 'The Reveal. The "woah" moment'. It is a vital element of any Punchdrunk experience, often being part of the early concept for a production, as Barratt explains, 'when creating any project we always work back from its emotional peak, the zenith of the crescendo. Knowing what that will be early on enables us to form the show'. For *Moon Slave* it was the marine flare shedding light on 200 scarecrows across a vast stretch of land at Poltimore House, in Devon. For *Faust*, the crescendo grew on the journey to the ominous underground basement, and was heightened by a spine-tingling soprano solo, a dynamic aerial display and a powerful duet between a vicious Mephistopheles and a vulnerable *Faust*. The crescendo is always triggered by a key musical corner; for Barrett, 'the music controls everything coming together'. In early works, because of a limitation in resources and performers, the powerful image created for a crescendo would often be achieved via impressive design installations, which usually involved a clever use of multiple humanoid effects created to be experienced alongside the climax in the soundscore and, often, a lighting or pyrotechnic effect. The reveal of the field of scarecrows in *The Moon Slave* is a clear example of this. For *Malfi*, an extraordinary reveal was where hundreds of hanging figures were uncovered, as smoking incense balls swung and Ferdinand, literally, pulled the walls – transformed into his cloak – with him on his murderous procession across the stage. Statues

were similarly deployed in *The Firebird Ball* to populate the space and make up for a lack of live performers. Barrett expands:

For *Firebird Ball* we spent so much of our design budget, a thousand pounds, getting a specialist to create them, stone like statues out of polystyrene, in order to populate the space with statues so that when audience members saw a humanoid figure out of the corner of their eye, they would assume it was a performer. Because it was quite a linear show we deliberately positioned them to create the crescendo. The statues thickened the space and meant that the audience were on tenterhooks because they were placed at precise points so that when the audience turned the corner they suddenly discovered the performers and the final sequence.

It was with *The Masque of the Red Death* that a formal finale was created to ensure the whole audience were brought together to experience the crescendo as a collective, the zenith of which was the firing of a full-sized cannon, showering red, swirling confetti (originally conceived by Barrett, in reference to Poe's imagery, as falling ash). Prior to *Masque*, the building was slowly closed down and the audience ushered out, with the intention of creating an impression for audience members that the world being left continues without them. With *Faust*, audience members were partly led or enticed, down to the basement, which helped with clearing the building, although, given that certain scenes elsewhere in the building continued as the crescendo played out, it did mean that an audience member could potentially miss this moment while enjoying the conclusion of those other sequences. In experimenting with a pulling together of the entire audience for the finale, *The Masque of the Red Death* thus established a masked-show convention. Barrett emphasises that, beyond the finale of a masked show, a crescendo is a Punchdrunk compositional device in and of itself, that is echoed

in the detail of the one-on-one experiences. Although only lasting minutes (whereas the outside crescendo marks the climactic end to the third and final hour-long loop), in terms of tempo, narrative structure and the experiential quality at its core, the one-on-ones have an equal approach to crescendo, as illustrated by the original and repeatedly reinvented 'Grandmother's Room' encounter. Barrett adds, Punchdrunk performers are trained in understanding that any interaction with an audience member must result in some sense of completion, some turning of a corner: 'you never want a beat to be left unfinished or to miss resolution. To tease and not deliver is the absolute worst. Never begin an encounter that cannot be finished in some way', even where those moments involve a degree of improvisation. In that respect, 'some sense of crescendo is implicit in any encounter; there needs to be a zenith reached and then a release for the audience member. If you're given a note which tells you to do something, if you do it, it needs to give you a route to a one-on-one or some other kind of payoff that bears its own crescendo'.

cross-fade (see also: agency; audience; bar; caretaking; **cinematic**; Club Shelter; *Greenhive Green*; *Grey's Printing Press*; lifts; *Lost Lending Library*; 'Mantle of the Expert'; mazes; **objects**; **portals**; **transportation**; tunnels): A term employed by Punchdrunk as shorthand for the mechanisms to enable immersion and encourage the audience-participant to cross, physically and imaginatively, from the everyday world into the world of the event. Whatever form it may take, the 'cross-fade' is the mode of transportation into that world. In cinematic terms, specifically in sound or film editing, this is a technical effect where a picture appears, or sound is heard and builds, gradually, as the previous image or sound disappears or becomes silent. For Punchdrunk, the cross-fade is the point at which the participants are invited to cross the threshold into the world established; this may occur immediately on entering the building as a physical journey, as with the large-scale productions, following a short maze from the box office where everyday business is stilled and external noise is replaced by quiet before entering the antechamber (often a lift) that takes you to a level of the world into which you are thrust; or over hours or days with Enrichment projects in schools. This mechanism establishes the physical and imaginative journey taken to get the participant into the world of the event and interweaves various elements according to the particular world created. For Punchdrunk masked events, this involves the acceptance of the mask, the sharing of the rules and regulations, delivered by a character who straddles the peripheral world of the event (entrance rooms or tunnels, lifts and bar).

Punchdrunk Enrichment applies cross-fade techniques in diverse contexts, finding the most appropriate methods to work for a community, according to the specific needs of a given project. For Enrichment projects, the cross-fade for a group of primary school students will be nuanced differently to that required for a group of residents in a care home. Objects are often employed by Enrichment to assist this; items that travel between the world of the event and the edges of that world where project activity blurs with daily activity. The interaction with the object, by performers and audience-participants alike, provides an initial mechanism for crossing the border between the everyday world of the host site and the magical world of the project. In Enrichment projects this initial activity can also extend to the taking on of a role (detectives, journalists, scientists, writers) which is facilitated by a performer in role who guides them through this, consistently with the participants from an initial workshop and through the journey of the event, such as Petra in *Lost Lending Library*. The type of world created, driven by its underlying concept and/or R&D needs, in tandem with the amount of time spent with the audience on that production, from small-scale Enrichment projects through journeying experiences to long-running

masked shows, influences the duration of that work and the type of cross-fade required. Whatever the activity and tools deployed, the cross-fade is a component act of caretaking by Punchdrunk and is an important mechanism for participation that sets up the codes of conduct and levels of creative agency on offer for engaging in the world of the event.

curiosity (see also: agency; **audience**; awe and wonder; boxes, chests and drawers; coda; **discovery**; **doors**; *Miniature Museum*; objects; research; wardrobes): The fourfold dictionary definition of this word is relatable to all aspects of Punchdrunk's practice: An eager or strong desire to know or learn something; inquisitiveness, the quality of being curious, eager to learn; something strange or fascinating; a rare or strange object, curio.

The quality of being curious, of being called towards the mysterious, drives Punchdrunk's practice. It is embraced in practice as well as being an attribute shared among core creative team members. Core or long-standing members of the team and erstwhile collaborators, such as Katy Balfour, Matthew Blake, Kate Hargreaves, Kathryn McGarr, Beatrice Minns, Colin Nightingale and Livi Vaughan, describe in the contributions to this encyclopaedia how they discovered Punchdrunk's work before it had entered the mainstream, and, in the spirit of adventure, resolutely knew that this was work with which they wanted to be involved. Felix Barrett and Nightingale bonded during a discussion following Nightingale's visit to *Chair*, where they shared a deep interest in giving great attention to the manner in which an event could be shrouded in mystery, where the journey to it activated the adventure an audience might have upon reaching the destination. Nightingale at the time was organising party nights by leaving invitations along a convoluted path to the venue, each with only the destination noted, as an 'x marks the spot' detail, to entice the curious few who would choose to follow the path and find the event. Barrett and

Nightingale instantly understood that there was a shared ideology in the separate events they were creating, with an interest beyond a single discipline and art form being presented to the audience. Both realised that the work that they were keen to put on was as much about a belief in the adventure, in shifting the perception of the audience in advance of the event, as it was about the theatre of the event on arrival. As Barrett puts it, 'we both instinctually know that the way you approach something is as important as what you find when you get there. It gives you the base plate from which you're ready to absorb'. Nightingale recalls that at that point in time he was wholly drawn to that which was hidden, had to be discovered, as illustrated by his following of an early piece of Banksy street-art; a trail of paint that took those with a keen and curious eye on a walk around Shoreditch in London.

Punchdrunk's approach to creating opportunities for discovery has had to shift, partly due to its success, and increasingly to a wider enthusiasm for immersive experiences that has seen a more knowing audience, actively seeking out such events. Barrett continues:

Now we have to create antechambers and mazes almost to cheat that sense of discovery, firstly because so many more people are creating this kind of experiential work and secondly because of the scale of our audience. That's why *Woyzeck* at The Big Chill was so crucially important in learning about setting up the approach and mystery. We spent two thirds of the budget on disguising the space, not on the show and the set, but hiding what we were doing with Heras Fencing and camouflage netting. There was always some sense of mystery and discovery in those early projects. It was the layering of the journey. First you discover the entrance, then a maze to another maze, then you discover a wardrobe that you can enter. It's the motion through – it's not static. That's core Punchdrunk. We're all fascinated by that.

Barrett emphasises that it is important that curiosity is satisfied. The success of the work does not rely solely on the excitement of discovering a portal, finding a clue, 'but ultimately finding out that there's something at the end which provides further pleasure in working out what it means'. It is the experience of the journey and the pleasure of the artistry revealed at the end, combined, that add a transformative edge to the work. In Punchdrunk productions the curious audience member delights in the **mysteries** and secrets the world offers, is eager to chance upon unexpected entrances, to open doors, rifle through drawers, seek out hidden clues as she plots her narrative through the performance and connects the themes from the layers of the world in which she dwells. This has been invited by the level of detail offered by the design, itself underpinned by a natural curiosity in the research terms of Beatrice Minns and Vaughan. An audience member who takes up these opportunities and invitations to be curious is usually rewarded, whether that be with a letter or a phone call or perhaps a one-on-one or a curio silently proffered at a point in the show or, simply, with a more layered experience and appreciation of the world during and subsequent to the event.

Curtis, Adam (see also: Act 2; chainsaw; corridors; darkness; immersive; *It Felt Like a Kiss*; **narrative**; **Poots, Alex**): The British documentary artist with a unique approach to investigative journalism. Curtis creates films that collage newsreel and historical footage with images and songs from popular culture, succinctly described by critic Charlie Brooker as 'complex ideological arguments and emotional tone poems in one' (2009). Curtis first met Felix Barrett at a meeting both attended at the former BBC Television Centre, White City and ended up showing a curious Barrett, fascinated by the building, around the warren-like space. Following discussion with Alex Poots about creating a potential project for MIF 2009, and visiting *The Masque of the Red Death*, discussion ensued which resulted in Curtis and Punchdrunk collaborating on *It Felt Like a Kiss* in an immersive realisation of Curtis's film of the same title: 'a psycho-political theme experience . . . A walk of enchantment and menace' (Curtis in Brooker 2009) . . .

Adam Curtis

On immersive theatre and political stories

We live in an age where the individual is the central concern; what the individual wants and what the individual feels is the central dynamic. What all immersive theatre does is say, you come here and explore it your own way, you're not going to be told what to do by the old elites. That's welcomed by people, it connects with how they feel and in that sense it's very good. It allows them to go into a space which is magical, explore wherever they want and create their own story of that evening. The downside is – and this is the limitation of immersive theatre and why it's a product of its time – because they're going where they want to go, you can't tell them something they don't already know, they'll only follow their own narrative. There are two functions to art; one is to magicalise, but the other is to take people to places they don't yet know and I'm not sure if immersive theatre can ever do that. It has established something that traditional theatre cannot do, which is to allow the audience to create its own story and experience. People have got bored with sitting in conventional theatre, with actors declaiming and people like David Hare writing scripts that tell them what's what in the world. In that sense, immersive theatre is a complete liberation. However, it's never going to be a revolutionary art form because the revolution is placed within the individual, so it can't bring people together and tell a collective something new. That said, Felix is the best practitioner of it that I've seen because he very cleverly pulls people together at moments and when he does that you glimpse something beyond. He did it with *The Duchess of Malfi*. His problem with it was that no one knew the story, it was too complicated, despite it being beautiful. But the conclusion, with the curtains, was an extraordinary work of art and transported people as well as bringing everyone together. It was a glimpse of something else, born of spectacle.

Immersive theatre works when it tells a myth or fable that people know, whereas when you've got a complicated story it can't work. With what we were doing, Felix originally wanted to split the film up into sections, each being relevant to the environment through which people walked. We found, only the day before it opened, that that didn't work. We had to reconstitute the film, let people explore the world and come upon the film, which then explains to them the world that they've already experienced. That was the solution; let people have a fragmentary experience, then watch the film together in a big ballroom to make sense of those fragments; the film being me saying this is my version of events. Then you split them up again and send them on a walk of terror. A problem is, if you're trying to tell political stories, you can't tell people very much when they're going all over the place. Immersive theatre is like squealing piglets running everywhere. The piglets love it and it's really exciting, but you then can't pull them together and say listen to this.

It Felt Like a Kiss was not typical Punchdrunk because it was having to deal with me and I was wanting to tell people stuff because I'm a journalist, that's what I do. It was a hybrid and very good for me because I had to find more emotional ways of saying things. I wanted to suggest that the rise of individualism is fantastic in some ways, very liberating, but it's also quite frightening because when things go wrong in society and you find you're on your own, you're not empowered. At the end, each individual was left alone in total darkness, and a caption come up on a monitor above their heads which read, 'you're on your own. It's what you wanted isn't it?', at which point they realised there was someone else in the darkness there with them and they ran out screaming. I was trying to make a political point, and I don't think that's normally what Punchdrunk does. Punchdrunk allows people to experience things in their own way. That's liberating, it's part of the democracy of our age. But that is a democracy that only works when you *can* let people go where they choose and make their own stories. If you have a growing fear in society, as with America and post-Brexit here, people are actually yearning for new stories, for a coming together to feel strong. You get that in Nationalism, but the Left haven't found it yet because they're still being squealing piglets.

What Punchdrunk is trying to do is to bring people together in a democratic way, where they can explore things yet at the same time take them out of themselves and give them a new kind of experience. That's problematic because it doesn't allow you to then say to everyone, listen to me, I'm going to tell you a story. With the Punchdrunk bar, where people are brought together, what you're getting there is still people coming together and telling each other their version of the story. It's a very nice idea, again liberating, there isn't anyone telling them what it's about, it's them working it out for themselves. But to make that work you have to have an original story that people already get the framework of; myth. So, you're still stuck with stuff they already know. *It Felt Like a Kiss* didn't have a bar, which was my decision. Felix was dubious about that, but I was trying to make a point about how being on your own might be liberating yet showing, in an immersive way, the downside of that. It some ways it was immersive theatre critiquing itself. The immersive world is a fantastic world if you're feeling secure, just like in the bigger society, but when things go really badly wrong, you feel lonely and separate.

It Felt Like a Kiss was a different approach for Felix, and for me, which is why it was interesting. It was a political work rather than, simply, an experiential work. Felix and I are also very similar in that we both understand mood. I understand that a way to get over what I'm saying is by creating a mood in the film that transports you, invites you into my world. Most documentary makers don't get that, disapprove of it because they think its manipulative and propagandistic, but it's not, it's more than that. It's saying I want to tell you something in a way that shows to you why I believe in it; the emotional aspect as much as the facts. *It Felt Like a Kiss* was good in that sense because it created a powerful mood. I understood that approach, to create this mood that you lose people in. I was trying to make it more dynamic in order to take people somewhere. This is part of the individualism of our age and that may be diminishing, people are seeking something else now. I sense that in Felix's way of seeing the world, there's something more waiting to be discovered and he's got the ability to pull people together. A lot of immersive theatre has a limited idea, 'we're going to do refugees, so we're going to make you feel like a refugee'; that's so literal and slightly dictatorial whereas Punchdrunk will create that world and allow you to explore it, make of it what you will. I want to take that further, so that it lets you work out what the world means in a social and political way. People are fed up of being kept in their separate social media bubbles, they're fed up with that and they want a sense of coming together and sharing a bigger story. I reckon Felix could be the person to give them that.

D

dance (see also: Act 1; archiving; **audience**; **building**; **characters**; **collaboration**; contact improvisation; corner; crescendo; **dance phrase**; **design**; **Doyle, Maxine**; **ensemble**; **flow**; **immersive**; **loops**; lighting; **masked shows**; multiples; *Sleep No More*, NYC; site): Since *Sleep No More*, 2003, dance has been a significant element of Punchdrunk's masked shows. As Felix Barrett explains, all of the signature languages of a masked show were in place and refined in the first two years of Act 1:

The only way we changed the masked shows following that was to find a way, once you finally discovered action, to ensure the physical language of the piece matched the experience of finding it.

For choreographer Maxine Doyle, dance is 'the heartbeat of a Punchdrunk masked show'. Barrett's mother, Margaret, an appreciator of Punchdrunk's practice in its many forms, notes how, following her first experience of *Sleep No More* in 2003, 'the dance gave the work another life, another dimension. The movement the speed, the fact that the music incorporated so well with the dance' added to the impact of the overall experience. The dance vocabulary provided an answer to Barrett's concerns regarding the problem of speech, especially with weighty, albeit beautiful, classical sources. Dance freed the audience from needing to wait to find out the narrative, to let the speech play out in order to understand a scene. Instead, the dance language offered a constant and abstracted revealing of the moment, thereby ensuring a fluid experience for the audience member to support individual journeys through the event; no need to hang around and wait for speeches to play out in order to get its gist. For an audience member, pleasure can be gained from observing the cycle repeat itself, altered each time by the effects of the dancers' ongoing toil, alongside different responses and

positioning of new audience members. Music, movement, emotion, narrative scores and composition, combined in the dance language, allow access to something deeper and meet the building and the design to communicate on a more open level. The language of the dance in Punchdrunk worlds works symbiotically as both narrative and character driven *and* abstract and open in terms of the nuances of what it is communicating. For Doyle, in a Punchdrunk masked show:

You *notice* the choreography, you *notice* the performers and that's an intention. In contemporary dance theatre the ego of the choreographer and the choreographic language is *really* what's being presented; you see shape, form, composition in a very particular way. In a Punchdrunk masked show in a building, if you see that composition too obviously then you've lost the connection with a character, so it breaks the illusion of 'reality' that you're constructing between the performer and the audience. It's important that the audience see the performers as characters not dancers. It's an interesting conundrum. We couldn't do these shows with a cast of actors; we wouldn't have found the language. In the US it's viewed more as dance, because of the dancers that have come through the show. It's dancers and dance, in relationship with design, which has allowed the masked shows and Punchdrunk masked shows to become so successful.

The characterisation through dance in masked shows is powerful and the signature approach to character portrayal is unique to the style of these large-scale productions. It owes much to the training, skill and artistry of the performers who make up the Punchdrunk ensemble and their intuitive expertise in performing in Punchdrunk immersive worlds. Notably, this is also because Punchdrunk masked shows are usually reviewed in the theatre listings of any online or print publication as opposed to the dance section; evidence

of the problems of categorisation in the analysis of immersive performance in general and Punchdrunk's work in particular. It highlights the need for attention to the language that is used to describe, understand and critique this work.

The choreographic process for any masked show has been honed by Doyle since 2003, supported latterly by rehearsal directors, stalwarts of the ensemble themselves, such as Conor Doyle and Fernanda Prata. Doyle and the dancers develop material in a studio, only entering the building once it has been made safe and after much of the design, installation, lighting and sound has been finalised. For Doyle time spent in the studios is 'workshop time, playtime', where 'the movement language can be really abstract' and explored in a safe and warm environment, 'where the floors are soft' and she can give personal attention to nurturing the dancers (2013). Doyle and Barrett, with the latter in and out of studio in a constant process of consultation, 'bombard' performers with information, visuals, sound and literature, offering 'stimulus and starting points', ensuring 'everyone is on the same page for the creative frame'; that studio time produces 'a concentrate' of the movement language that will be transposed and translated to communicate in the space (Doyle 2013). The studio devising process is about working with instinct, through long improvisations which are carefully structured to begin with and then guided by Doyle as the dancers develop their roles. These improvisations 'can last for hours' with Doyle shifting music, adding props, developing the phrases created by the dancers. Prata refers to Doyle's process as being like 'a DJ', sampling the material generated and combining it in new ways. For Doyle this process is like 'going on a journey where you don't know your destination, driving on a long road and following the sunshine', intuitively building the work with the support of Barrett: 'Felix understands how important time is and how long things take . . . to get good work you need to give people the time and space to find those solutions' (Doyle 2013), establishing the skills to create a movement vocabulary and dynamic that is responsive to and effective in the space.

When the dancers eventually enter the building, Barrett facilitates Hide-and-Seek, which 'offers the performers the opportunity to engage with the space, to pick up on its atmospheres, to be excited by it, challenged by it, frightened by it' (Doyle 2013). The choreographic language then goes through a combination of facilitating, editing and creating, with Doyle, Barrett, performers and designers reworking the multilayered material in the space. Doyle's particular focus turns to the lead narratives, the backbone for every other character's story; if these narratives can be made 'exciting and dynamic and clear, everything else develops in reaction to that' (Doyle 2013).

Doyle notes that there is something special about the choreography produced for the masked shows as a consequence of her collaboration with Barrett: 'we can nail it together' (2013). Where Barrett, Nightingale, Higgin and Vaughan refer to a shorthand and shared language, intuitively being able to achieve the same goals, Doyle is striving for her own choreographic stamp within each production and 'Felix helps me realise that':

> Sometimes we clash and go in wildly different directions and we have to make a decision about which one is right. Felix has such a crystal-clear idea of what's right, which makes him quite remarkable as an artist and I don't have that always, I could go in any direction and make it work. But together, we're going to get the best thing, which is right for both of us.
>
> (2013)

Prata, a Punchdrunk performer-deviser, rehearsal director and workshop facilitator since 2006, has performed in all masked shows since *Faust*. She used her experiences as a dancer and rehearsal director on *The Drowned Man* as a case study for her master's dissertation, examining the role of the director-choreographer and dancer within the devising process. Inspired by the dance theorist, Helena Katz, who refers to the choreographer as a DJ (Katz 1997), Prata closely examined the processes involved in the development of the choreographic language in Punchdrunk's work, and reflected on this across her experiences since *Faust*.

Fernanda Prata

On dancing, devising and directing

Maxine as a choreographer is very much like a DJ. She won't arrive with steps, or the dance already constructed in her head, but instead will use a variety of exercises and give a lot of ideas for the performer to play with in order to generate movement. She'll then play with the material that's originated, like a DJ mixing it together, choreographing it so that with each phrase that the performer created, she makes something new. Jo Butterworth [see Butterworth 2011] set up a framework that pinpoints the role of choreographers and performers in five different types of process; from the more dictatorial choreographer as expert and the dancer being an instrument, then the choreographer as author and dancer as interpreter; through the choreographer as pilot and dancer as contributor, or choreographer as facilitator and dancer as creator; to the choreographer as collaborator and dancer as co-owner. I was interested in how that framework applied to Punchdrunk's process, how the choreographer, director, performer roles transit. As a performer in Punchdrunk's work you can range across the spectrum; dancer as interpreter, where the choreographer has control of the style and content, or being a creator, a contributor, even co-owner, especially in the solos, where decisions are taken in a very collaborative way between Maxine and the performers. The solos are devised by individual dancers, which makes the movement unique. That's the beauty of the company, Maxine and Felix will step in and shape the work but it's an amazing strength and power in directors who allow you to create and be part of the process and project.

As a performer and rehearsal director I understand the process from both sides; the need and the reasoning for adaptations to a scene and equally the frustrations of this for performers who may not see the wider practical or artistic need for the change. At Punchdrunk the rehearsal director evolved with the creative process of productions and involves taking warm-ups for the company, working on choreography, organising the rota for the dancers, sometimes even taking on roles. *The Drowned Man* had a vast cast of forty-two or so, a lot of people to coordinate. The role required taking artistic decisions when Max and Felix weren't around and, mostly, practical organisation, such as setting up physio treatment for dancers, making sure they were always ready for the show. Importantly it was ensuring the performers had constant a feedback process in terms of how they're feeling artistically and health-wise in relation to the show – because it's very intense, those three-hour runs, sometimes seven days a week. It required intuition, having eyes open and feeling where a person might really need a break, so finding a cover-performer for them. Equally, noticing where performers might be skipping warm-ups, or their activities outside of the show, and being injured as a result. It is a bit of a devil and angel role but always it's about the cast being top priority.

Conor Doyle, Hector Harkness and I were the rehearsal directors for *The Drowned Man*, and so each of us had to share the role of observing each performance, taking notes in pairs and feeding back each night, and deciding how to run rehearsals in light of that the next day. We have to rehearse almost every day, even when the performance is running, to find solutions for various problems that might arise, or reworking roles on different cast members where a recasting might be needed because of injury. It's about adapting a new body with a different shape and quality to an existing role. It's almost like a whole separate performance each night 'behind' the show; we're constantly on radio-mics, dealing with any problems, especially where injuries require back-up performers to take over. The building was so large, and stewards had such distance to cover, that if an injury had occurred and a switch to the understudy had taken place, a performer would arrive for their moment and only then discover the different performer in place. Recasting roles is not easy in a devising process because very specific people are selected for the process which might have something to do with the look and the demeanour as much as their movement quality and style. Different bodies and different movement styles shift the way roles are choreographed and performed, how those stories are told. Hector, Conor and I try not to change very much in terms of the choreography when recasting or selecting covers, but there always has to be some flexibility in respecting individual qualities.

In terms of the original creation of character stories, performers receive a loop of twelve scenes, each around five minutes, some of which are detailed, some of which are blank for you to explore and come up with ideas and material with Max and Felix. Sometimes they're only worked out once you're in the space. Within the twelve scenes you'll also have the in-between scenes; micro-scenes, transition scenes. For example, between scene one and two a character might have to cross the building to encounter another character which is itself a different scene. As much as it's twelve set scenes across the building, there's the potential for more than that as you journey from one to the other, which sometimes evolve intuitively during previews or across the run. This becomes complex when recasting and finding covers for performers. Learning those roles involves choreographing the twelve scenes within the loop *and* finding your way through those transitional scenes. That's why it's a loop; it's one constant, moving circle. It's not a case of blocking a scene and then walking to the next, it's a whole choreographic journey, constantly living across the space. Once you have your loop in place you become obsessed by detail. The detail of every single movement you perform is extremely important, even how you grab a glass of water or shift your gaze from one place to another. The set helps the performers with this precision. Livi Vaughan and Bea Minns are the queens of detail and this helps when you're building your character and loop, giving you information and nuances towards your scenes.

The Drowned Man was the first time in the UK that we had two casts from the beginning, which allowed many ways of telling the story to emerge. It also created complexity in deciding which versions to go with and how to put performers together as couples. In earlier shows there was only ever one cast and if you were ill you just had to get on with it. That said, *Faust* was so electric and dangerous, matched by that powerful space. The process was completely different from anything I'd experienced up until that point; everything was a surprise, magical. Punchdrunk performers get a bit addicted to the work; it's amazing being so close to the audience. There's something beautiful about being part of that early work and seeing how far it's moved on. It was rough and raw, which injected it with danger, excitement and charm. It's very special being part of the old generation of Punchdrunk.

dance phrase (see also: abstract/abstraction; **dance**): A short sequence in a dance improvisation, or set choreography, composed of a series of connecting movements. A dance phrase can be broken down into its component parts and learned in order to set the choreography. The construction of the sequence through these component parts is similar to the way in which connecting words are put together to create a sentence as a spoken or written 'phrase'.

darkness (see also: **adrenalin; atmosphere;** Barrett, Felix; **blackout;** dreams; failure; Grant, Matthew; **haze; lighting;** masked shows; reveal; smart candles; **tempo; vanishing.** Further reading: Alston and Welton 2017): Darkness is a core ingredient in Punchdrunk events, simultaneously an aesthetic quality and a dramaturgical device. In a stage/auditorium set-up darkness is an indicator of a show beginning; it delineates the world of the performance by removing the audience from this world, removing it from view, to establish a safe space for spectatorship. In Punchdrunk's practice darkness is employed to heighten awareness of the audience member's presence in the world and to activate the imagination; as Felix Barrett describes, darkness embraces 'the space where the imagination lies'. Darkness is also vital as a compositional tool to slow an audience down so that their experience of journeying through a space and following a narrative becomes more fluid. Barrett learned important lessons regarding darkness during Act 1:

We put on *House of Oedipus* without darkness and the show failed. Darkness, first and foremost, controls the rhythm and the tempo of the audience and thus the show. Darkness enables discovery. What we learned with *House of Oedipus* is that, if you can see the scene in the distance, by the time you've got there, there's nothing to discover, all you get is a sense of anticlimax. Then, with *Sleep No More*, Boston, before the first night, the

Fire Officer inspected the show and told us it was too dark, and we had to put the lights up. We did it and the show failed completely because the audience were treating it like a safe, secure art gallery, no threat or menace. The soundtrack didn't work without the darkness, the pace and flow of the audience was completely different to our usual shows. Very few watched the action, they walked past characters. Nothing could pull focus, so you didn't know where to look nor what was being prioritised. It was a disaster. The ART team and Fire Officer immediately realised it was flawed so set the lighting back and the next day it worked a treat, because the audience were moving at half the tempo. It was wholly to do with the darkness.

Colin Nightingale adds, 'the Fire Officer also got it and was on board with that decision. He ended up getting more involved in the project and helped us get all the haze levels we needed', noting as an aside, 'he'd lived through the 60s and loved *Blade Runner*, so got why the lighting was important'.

In masked shows, light is usually set at twenty per cent to eighty per cent pure darkness. This establishes a state and mood within the world that allows for a 'teasing out' of the experience and the narrative for the audience member, where the instinctual body responds. Barrett elaborates:

Darkness immediately intensifies an event, amplifies its impact. Darkness establishes a sense of threat. It reawakens that childlike fear of the dark. The mythic, the folkloric, exists in the dark because your imagination fills in the gaps. A large part of it is about adrenalin, flight or fright; that's a base state in terms of charging an audience. They need to be in a heightened state of awareness and darkness is the best trigger for that, it's immediate. Switch the lights off and suddenly the space transforms, it moves from the familiar

to the unknown in one second. *The Borough* and *Kabeiroi* move from daylight to darkness, but it's taken a while for us to get there and find what works. It's about different ways of shifting the context for the audience, making sure that we've created enough threat so that at a base, biological level there's enough adrenalin pumping around the body for them to be fully present, fully aware. Masked shows couldn't work in daylight, whereas *The Borough* and *Kabeiroi* are a different form, the audience don't require a mask because *they* are the lead character, it's happening to them. If you actively know your role and you're implicit within the action, that maintains attention and heightens awareness.

Punchdrunk's approach to qualities of darkness and the manner in which it requires a tuning-in to the world has influenced Maxine Doyle's choreographic practice:

Dancing in the darkness helps to develop the 360-degree body and sensitises the performer to moving in a multi-dimensional space. The performers are comfortable with the low light levels in a masked show, thus giving them an advantage over the audience. It's important as an audience that you feel the performers inhabit the darkness.

Barrett has been investigating this relationship between performer and darkness since his Exeter Experiments. It was *The Tempest*, 2003, collaborating with a dancer, Adrienne, playing Prospero's Sprite, that first tested the way in which a performer could emerge from and disappear into the darkness, as if by magic, using mainly domestic lighting. The vast space of the Old Seager Distillery was recast as Prospero's enchanted island through darkness and shadow via the flicker of smart candles and the ambient glow of domestic lamps:

Giant space, dark concrete walls, one light source. You just get pools of gloom and if you have one small light source in the room it will cast shadow that moves into pitch black, as opposed to moody black created by theatrical lighting.

These short-range lighting sources threw lengths of moving shadows, their reach absorbed by the thickness of the dark which supported the, now standard, Punchdrunk principle for the performer finding a light source, dancing a duet with it, darting in and out of light. Working with darkness, haze and light in this way is an important technique for the Punchdrunk performer. Given that the lighting is set to the soundscore and the space, performers are required to learn the tempo, shifts and *feel* of the sound and light score; performers must respond to these, as opposed to technical cues being set to the performers. In the early projects, domestic lamps and candles animated the darkness and created a playground of light for performers to improvise within. Nowadays in masked shows, alongside domestic sources, haze blends light and darkness to set chiaroscuro states and performers become adept at finding light while harnessing the power of the darkness as a partner in their performance. Barrett notes:

Performers don't immediately know how to do it. It takes great skill to find your light. A key skill for any Punchdrunk performer, whatever the type of project, not just the masked shows, is that they need to know when and how to disappear, to evaporate, or when to come out forcefully from the darkness. It's about flow and crescendo and controlling that, surfing the darkness. They have to know when their scene is going to warrant pure focus; when they have to take the light, rear up out of, and then return to, an ocean of obsidian gloom. That's a craft that we rehearse with them. Once you know what you're doing with the darkness, it's an amazing tool.

decay (see also: abstract/abstraction; **durational**; forests; **multiples**; **nature**): Usually established through repetition in design, multiples and replicas. Establishing an aesthetic of decay adds to the sensation of the space having history, of events having occurred in that room and emphasising the suggestion of time passing, drawing attention to the audience dwelling in space and time. The suggestion of decay in an installation illustrates how, in Punchdrunk worlds, designed space alone tells stories, plays with duration and holds energy.

dens (see also: **Barrett, Felix**; **installation**): As a child Felix Barrett spent much of his time buildings dens to create labyrinthine worlds. The skill of building these translated to the early entrance mazes, suspended by Barrett, constructed from reams of sewn-together sail fabric. The concept and aesthetic of the den remains a clear reference point in Punchdrunk's practice. Peter Higgin acknowledges:

Like Felix, I have very clear childhood memories of building dens, of small-world play, creating dioramas out of found wild spaces. I grew up in a rural setting and was surrounded by woodland, old industrial buildings and the odd rundown ramshackle cottage. I vividly remember many occasions when I built or found something to repurpose as a den. I think this instinct is within all children. My son loves dens and even using our bodies and a blanket we quickly create our own little world. Enrichment work resonates with this because it taps into a primal instinct to make camp, make home. We referenced den-building when we were creating *Under the Eiderdown*; partly due to the small rooms we worked in, partly the number of props hanging in your path. We also improvised the design as we went. We enjoyed them as such, more so the handing over for the enjoyment of a school community. Many of the core team have a 'den sensibility', can each remember moments from childhood when we created or found the ultimate den. The masked shows are a very large expression of den-building, albeit extremely elaborate. The den is a liminal space, a transformative space with a world of imaginative possibilities. Punchdrunk's practice, for creatives and audiences alike, taps into this instinct and our natural excitement at the prospect of making and stepping into the otherworldly realm that a den affords.

design (see also: **abstract/abstraction**; accidents; architecture; atmosphere; bar; **Barrett, Felix**; blackout; **building**; characters; close-up; compromise; corridors; **costume**; crescendo; dance; darkness; dreams; experiential; flow; Harvey, Robin; intervention; in-show-world; **installation**; **lens**; **lighting**; **'listening to the building'**; long shot; mazes; **Minns, Beatrice**; **multiples**; narrative; **process**; **research**; scale; **scenography**; site; **site-sympathetic**; **space**; text; **touch-real**; *unheimlich*; **Vaughan, Livi**): Shorthand for every element of design in concept, research, build and installation for any Punchdrunk project. In Punchdrunk's process, spatial design is the force behind a project, inspired, led and underpinned by the building. As Felix Barrett summarises, 'the design *always* comes first. Once you've done that the performers can play within the space'. For masked shows, 'design' covers all aspects of Barrett, Beatrice Minns and Livi Vaughan's collaborative practice encompassing set-design, interior design and installation art. It is a practice and process that is driven by the necessity and limitations enforced by working through a site-sympathetic process. It relishes the discipline and solutions that might come by being limited in options and materials, whether through budget or as a consequence of the space, its features and flaws, or any foraged materials already available on that site. Barrett asserts that it is through the design process that 'the emotional analysis of the text' is manifested, while the show is 'already half designed by the building'. Responding first and foremost to the 'emotional blueprint of the building', and the manner in which rooms, corridors and the natural flow through the site, unlocks themes and narratives present in the source material; the subsequent installations and performance loops are set 'retroactively', layering that world upon the existing spaces and architectural features.

Barrett's immediate response to a building's spaces, scents, shadows and atmosphere sets the emotional and narrative blueprint for how the source material will be interpreted. In this way, the existing design of a building and the ways in which rooms, corridors and integral features open up ways to interpret the source serves as both the code that cracks the concept as well as the space that realises any textual interpretation. Vaughan summarises, 'The building *is* the design concept, the set construction, installation and sound is then at the heart of that design, and costume and lighting are then detailed layers on top of that'. Barrett adds that Punchdrunk's process prioritises 'experiential design, not visual design' which demands an audience '*enable* it', not simply look at it, but move through it, interact with it.

Punchdrunk design includes the large-scale layout for each floor and the contiguous spaces of the building, alongside the more intricate design and dressing of the interior rooms. Design grounds audiences in era and environment. Design not only locates the audience temporally and geographically, it also activates the space and helps to communicate character, narrative and theme on a more abstract level. The design of a space influences the manner in which the performers interact with it and, ultimately, with the audience. Barrett illustrates, through *Faust*:

The design of the space opens up the way in which Mephistopheles can take you by the hand and run with you, lead you somewhere only to drop you and leave you in its abyss. The design has to be the launch pad; if we'd started with Mephistopheles' action we would never have got to that idea. We have to be able to imagine the audience in the space first, only then is character overlaid.

Design is also rooted in practicality, for performers and audience, according to the technicalities of the performance that will occur in that space and possible positioning of the onlooker. Installations pay forensic attention to detail, filtered through the lens of the source material. The dressing of each of the spaces combines 'the business side', as Vaughan puts it, that the rooms and its objects require for the purposes of the choreography and audience flow, in partnership with the interpretative qualities layered into those locations:

A really solid bed for Lady Macbeth to fling herself around on also creates a platform for the audience to see her. It defines the space where the audience will be situated as well as instantly conveying the details of era, geography, narrative and theme through an artistic lens.

Barrett begins with 'a bird's-eye view' of the full canopy of the world, which swoops in from above, like a cinematic tracking shot, to the detail of the narratives in the space in close-up . . .

Felix Barrett and Livi Vaughan

On design

Felix: The design process with any Punchdrunk project is very different to creating work for a stage, where you'd most likely begin with a script and one focal point from which you create a design concept. We have eighty stages in a building and they all have to be viewed from 360 degrees. There are so many limitations imposed by working with a building, which defines the process.

Livi: Working creatively with those parameters is how we approach the work. Audiences, or even collaborating designers, often assume that our shows must cost so much money and are impossibly complex, when in fact it's often created thriftily by necessity and through shortcuts. Once you have your formula and start cutting things down, shaping within the limitations, the solution becomes incredibly simple. There often aren't many solutions, only ever a few things possible.

Felix: The design process drives our process overall, starting with architecture, which dictates what the narrative will be through aesthetic and atmosphere. It dictates whether there will be height, scale, sight-lines, expanse or closeness, claustrophobia and oppression.

Livi: Felix will change what the show will be depending on the building, as was the case with Boston *Sleep No More*. We intended to take *Faust* to America but Felix immediately changed his idea because of the linear corridor and adjacent rooms; the flow didn't work for *Faust*. Felix decides the show based entirely on his reaction to the space. It's then a case of knowing when to work with what the building's offering and when to work against it. When we've had the opportunity to build spaces, we've found that harder, because we're not reacting to something. It's more difficult to make decisions when the answer could be anything, not disciplined by existing limitations. Our initial palette is drawn from building, text and soundscore. We don't analyse the text in the way that I was taught at design school, as the first and foremost approach. The text is a third of the preliminary input. The building is equivalent to the text as a source in that early design work.

Felix: We mine the text for various things later, but the building offers an important emotional analysis prior to that. We analyse what it *feels* like to go around the space. In the same way that you would break down a play line-by-line, we break the building down room-by-room, wall-by-wall, ceiling-by-ceiling, crack-by-crack. Those early walks through the building, then, are the equivalent for us of first, then painstaking, read-throughs of the text.

Livi: You have to walk the route repeatedly and understand all the different iterations of the journey through to know what it feels like and make the right decisions about the way to set different journeys for the audience.

Felix: You can't do that hypothetically; not from a plan of the building, nor from your desk in an office. You can do as much research as possible, read the source material multiple times, do this planning and that planning, but that's all moot until you stand in the space and *feel* the experience, feel how it makes you respond. It's only by being in the space, in the moment, being spontaneous and responsive, that works it all out. Our job is to accentuate that sensation, guaranteeing that impact on the audience. Colin [Nightingale], Livi and I then spend months planning the show and breaking the idea, through the building and the design concept, before the other elements are layered in. The mainstay of the design is the building, that *is* the show. Performers, light and sound then lead you around.

Livi: It's the building that cracks it. How the building breathes. The relationship between production, design and direction at the beginning, between the three of us, is complex. We have to think of the limitations of the space in a practical way; where the bar is, where the audience entrance is, yet that can also frustrate us, limit the ideas, or if we reach a conclusion too quickly we discover problems with original decisions. That fixing and unfixing is an important part of the early process. The idea is worked out by going backwards and forwards with it, moving from production, to a bit of hypothetical blue-sky thinking ignoring production constraints, and then returning to the practical.

Felix: Once we know the building's safe, that there are the necessary stairwells and that the basic flow will work –

Livi: – and we've had Colin's advice and know how it will work logistically, Felix and I can then forget that to work out the other details, confident that the production side is supporting that. For masked shows, we like the building to be less obvious on the outside, for the audience not to know exactly what they're going into. The ideal would be, even if we had a really huge building, that there would be a really tiny entrance door, non-descript, so you wouldn't be able to work out the size of the space you're entering. Whereas if you have a site that's a known building by the majority of your audience –

Felix: – you can't fight it, that becomes your frame. You can't control it nor pre-empt it.

design

Livi: That's why, for most projects, Felix thinks about the journey of the audience to the door, from the tube station or the various ways they would approach the building. It's a significant detail of when the experience begins.

Felix: What unifies the core team, makes us inherently 'Punchdrunk', is the fact that we think about the whole journey, about the fact that the way in which you get there *is* the show, not simply what you see when you get there. How you build that initial impact on arrival at the entrance, such as the danger sign with *Faust*. Once you work out how the audience will approach it then it's easier to imagine it with their eyes.

Livi: We start the shows by deciding what entrance the audience will use. Then you work out what the bar is, how it links to the wider space, whether it's present-day or 'of the world'.

Felix: How we design the shift from present-day world outside to in-show-world. We might create the decompression before the bar, sometimes afterwards, it all depends what that bar space is. You have to have the context for the audience. They need to know who they are, what the frame is, before they enter.

Livi: In that respect, any 'set design' that follows is the easy bit.

Felix: Design cracks the concept so that's where 'design' for us is more than scenography, something overlaid. It's intrinsic – it *is* the show. It's only then that the detail of the installations, how spaces are dressed, follows more conventional rules of scenography.

Livi: That's the next phase. Bea and I get on with that without Felix.

Felix: To give an idea of the process, with Boston, we cracked the flow, divided up different environments. We knew that the basement was the darkest, most foreboding space, so we decided to blackout and accentuate that.

Livi: In terms of limitations, we knew we could only afford to blackout one area –

Felix: And it's easier to blackout a basement rather than a top floor where there's natural light everywhere; decisions led by basic practicalities.

Livi: The bar was perfectly situated, off an alleyway. We needed to replicate the bar within the world, so we had to ensure there was a partner space big enough for that.

Felix: Those elements are always preordained. Bar, finale and entrance –

Livi: – plus making sure there are spaces that are big enough to hold an ensemble scene –

Felix: – knowing, and understanding the transitions as we go.

Livi: It's like drawing a picture. The first phase is drawing the outline of it and then the colouring-in involves a more conventional design process, because the parameters have been set. Then the consideration is how far each space will be designed as naturalistic, stylised or completely abstract, or experiential. For example, we always have a wilderness, a focused area where the narrative will be strongest, and the opposite end of the building is where it's as empty and forgotten as possible so that the audience can get lost in it. With *Sleep No More*, NYC, we focused on Macbeth's loop being on a couple of floors in the middle of the building. Performers can't be running from the sixth floor down to the basement all the time. It's logistics. The heart of the show will usually occur in the middle of the building, and the outer reaches will often be the wildernesses, while the basement often holds the more abstracted spaces. The performance itself works logistically in that way so the design team knows what's required to stretch out in each direction across the building, how the specifics of each loop work within that. Within the rooms that set scenes with performers we would have worked out Lady Macbeth's loop and the fact that she needs three rooms because she's a high-status character. The loop directs the division of rooms among characters, which would then leave around ten rooms open to interpretation. That's important because we know that we'll want to include abstracted rooms, but we're not yet ready in the process to decide what they are.

Felix: Resident characters come about *because* of the design process. For example, we have a town area and want to incorporate a tailor or an undertaker because it fits the town, the themes or narrative. A performer is then invited to inhabit that space.

Livi: We also have rooms unpopulated by performers, to make the world feel authentic. For example, if the town has a diner and a toy shop, we would create additional shops that support the story and that world, but only some have residents in, because the world is bigger than just those rooms that are required. There are rooms where the priority is the performance, which have strong furniture, space for audience, appropriate sightlines and allow full-on dance. Then there are character rooms, where you may observe a hushed conversation or duet, a story told through performers but more intimate, not spacious or requiring sturdy furniture. Then there are rooms that need to stand alone and tell the story with no performance in it; the room is the character.

Felix: The abstracted rooms at the outer reaches, like the basement prosthetic store in *The Drowned Man*, establish the uncanny; spaces we have to fill, despite running out of time. Working on a stage, if you'd run out of ideas and time, it might be easier to scrap a scene. When you have an empty room in an otherwise full building, you have to do something with it. By that point we're often having to scour our creative brains for ideas, which is why the abstraction distends.

Livi: That relates to another important point about audience and their input to the design in concept. Because it's not on the stage, you need enough matter for the audience to discover, to make it full. If you had a percentage graph it would denote the balance between performer interaction, design and style of installation. The best Punchdrunk shows are where the building is the show, and the performance is only one layer that's highlighting that. Similarly, there's a tiered approach to the lighting; you light the room itself and, only then, any performance sequence that might occur in that room. You could spend your whole time across a loop in one room and feel the states change, the light move, even with no performers in there.

Felix: You *feel* the space as character. We spend more time lighting spaces without performers than those with. The *Faust* cornfield had the most lighting states *because* it wasn't populated by any performers. We're trying to haunt those spaces through light. Those are the experiential spaces, the forests, cornfield, deserts. We always have forests, because they're disorientating, and spaces that are pitch black.

Livi: You need the negative spaces, rooms that are wholly experiential or just darkness, perhaps filled with one repeated item – suspended spoons – because if everything was intricately detailed, you wouldn't be able to *see* that detail. We use abstraction to change the pace in that respect. It functions like a palate cleanser between courses. Knowing the rules-set around the logic of the story-world allows us to go on that design journey, and helps us know when we need to alter the journey.

Felix: The negative or abstracted spaces create the experience of the rules changing via a visual language; audiences get a handle on the world and then it suddenly shifts. A lot of that follows our instinctive, design 'hunch', *feeling* the point that it needs to shift. If the audience can predict what they're going to see when they go around a corner –

Livi: – then there's no point in them going around the corner in the first place.

Felix: The idea of the palate cleanser is key. It's achieved via a change in visual language or shifting the logic of the space, you're suddenly in a domestic room when you've just been in an office. It establishes the sensation of the dream world –

Livi: – shifts in logic, detail or abstraction. It's like a breath that the audience is allowed to take. An illustration of that shift of logic would be Mrs De Winter's room in *Sleep No More*, taking you into the morgue through a cupboard.

Felix: That's a combination of negative and experiential space. The wardrobe opens up and if you walk through it, it keeps on going, feeling your way through in darkness. It's a tactile transitional experience and then you come out in the morgue. It's similar to the space through the fireplace in *Masque of the Red Death* that leads you between two distinct rooms. The absence of detail means that when you're smacked by detail you really absorb it. There are so many practical decisions to be made, there's not that much space for premeditated, creative mulling. It's much more a case of quick, clear creative decision-making. What do the spaces need to do and what do we want it to feel like? It's fascinating how much we worry about floor and ceiling. It's not about naturalistic aesthetics, but about how it needs to feel. If you're creating a town, walking on Astroturf or wooden boards will feel fake. To make it *feel* like a town the one thing we can do is put a road in, or wood chips and soil underfoot in a forest; if you're walking on a real surface you suspend your disbelief experientially. Even if it's subconsciously working it *feels* touch-real. Whatever we do subsequently, no matter how stylised it is, audiences won't enter into it as if it's a set. We always design for a feeling rather than a visual aesthetic.

Livi: The sound the space makes, the sound materials make underfoot, makes you feel differently. The lighting levels are low, so other senses are heightened. It's like a bat, it's sonar.

Felix: With ceilings its equally about atmosphere bleeding out. Creating a space that's just the right level of enclosed so that your sonar stays in. Walls and ceilings are important in preserving atmosphere.

Livi: It's Felix's idea of editing together your own film, using light and sound within space to enable the audience to home in on what the shot is. Whether a still or an energetic space, it's designed from all those elements.

Felix: So much of our work is 'experience design' as opposed to 'visual design'. The impression of the ceiling, the quality of the feeling underfoot. Ultimately the shows would still work if the floor and ceiling were right. Say you needed a dining room for narrative, you could establish that with one table and a single plate on it, while the floor and the ceiling are creating the *experience* around that.

Livi: We never had a formula when we started. It's been a learned language, a learned sensibility. It's grown up over the last ten years where we've developed it collectively, between Felix, Colin and me.

Felix: Together we crack the concept, then Livi cracks all the spaces, then Bea comes in with Livi and layers the narrative, cracks the detail. The process is much like zooming in on the detail, a letter on a table, first established from a tracking shot of the full expanse from above. It's a useful exercise to think of it in that way. We use that language as a tool for design; the opening shot, the world that you'd see from above, then the specific town, where you zoom in and see its structures, then you end up going inside the hotel, inside Lady Macbeth's bedroom, into the bathroom, zoom into the bath, to see a letter floating, from Macbeth. The detail is there but initially it's a bird's-eye view that then becomes micro.

Livi: Knowing that that's the way Felix's eye is approaching it means that that's how Bea and I filter the focus within the design of the rooms. We always know that we're working with a 360-design but we prioritise a certain shot, focus an impact within the space. We put the smart candles just out of sight in order to curate the experience of that space, focusing through the main space, through to the room and a specific way of viewing something once inside.

design

Felix: Much of the domestic lighting is thought through by Livi and Bea. There's so much crossover between elements.

Livi: The fine-tuning of the design also comes from the way in which we work collaboratively with production and performance. We might need to adjust a space to add height for something to be seen, lock a door to change the flow. It's a series of practical problem-solving from day one. It's only in the preview period where we will work out exactly where doorways should be and how the flow works. Sometimes people assume with more planning the problems wouldn't exist but, in fact, this is why we always have a contingency plan and budget entitled, 'New Ideas', because we know there will always be an unknown; we need to be able to react and adapt once everything is in, including production management, design and performers. Even if we model-boxed it in advance it would never be the same –

Felix: – because you can't *see* what it *feels* like. Model boxes work perfectly for a wholly visual medium with limited sightlines. When it's wholly experiential and multiple sightlines, it's another matter.

digital technologies (see also: access; Act 3; *And Darkness Descended. . .*; *Believe Your Eyes*; *Black Diamond*; Enrichment; Fallow Cross; **gaming**; *Kabeiroi*; *Last Will*; lighting; **Oracles, The**; *Séance, The*; senses; *Silverpoint.* Further reading: Dixon, Rogers and Egglestone 2013; Bending and McKay 2017; Biggin 2017; Klich 2016; Reid et al. 2010): Punchdrunk is interested in exploring how digital technology can extend the possibilities for whole-world immersion, taking the audience into the sensual experience rather than distancing them from it. Digital technologies are an important area of investigation for Enrichment in terms of form, reach and legacy. Punchdrunk has in the past collaborated with MIT to create *The Séance*, supported by a Nesta and ACE Digital R&D award, which investigated the blurred 'in-world' relationship between a transatlantic, online audience and those physically within the in-show-world of *Sleep No More*, NYC. Following lessons learned from R&D projects, including *Believe Your Eyes* and *Last Will*, more recent investigations such as *Silverpoint*, *Kabeiroi* and *The Oracles* have advanced Punchdrunk's interplay between visceral and virtual worlds. With increasing developments in haptic and digital technologies Punchdrunk is now, in Act 3, testing the possibilities of how technologies might support the present and sensory experience for an audience, taking them further into the sensual rather than removing them from it, as well as advancing modes of access and inclusive practice. Felix Barrett, aware of the tension between the virtual and visceral, how technology can remove an audience from the emotional fabric or feeling of the performance, recapitulates, 'fundamental to the Punchdrunk ethos is that the body is active, present and, before now, being in front of a computer invalidated all that' (2013). Now technologies have advanced to augment imaginative worlds, to alter perception and enhance, or certainly help manipulate, the ways in which the human body is active and present.

A current focus of R&D at Fallow Cross is haptic technologies, in an ongoing desire to find new ways to influence audience experience. Haptic technologies that are worn or held and employ movement or vibration, such as a smart watch or hand-held devices, can be used to guide audiences where sight has been removed, and are just beginning to be investigated by the team. Sonic and spatial experiments have advanced, primarily via a room at Fallow Cross that contains a waterbed rigged with speakers to test sub-bass manipulation through water to create a whole-body experience for one audience member. The first testing of similar ideas can be dated back to the sensory experience underpinning Rob McNeill's one-on-one during *The Masque of the Red Death*, as described below. The Fallow Cross waterbed experiments further explore the tactile quality of sound, as Barrett explains:

Medieval cathedral organs have got a 'God Note' which is the bottom key, sourced from a special pipe that runs the length of the body of the church, rather than up into the rafters. It creates a note that is inaudible because it's so low, so evokes the presence of God in the room through vibration, you *feel* God. We've tried to recreate sound as a physical force to unsteady and suggest a character in the space. Another focus on haptics is how they might accentuate the sensation of music. With crescendo and its shape, how do you put a button on the sonic world to guarantee the impact of the sound is as great as it can be? The Japanese are amazing at this, the use of low-bass frequencies, finding the note that's the same pitch as the room and playing a bass note with it so the sound makes the room reverberate. Using industrial vibrators strapped to the bottom of the floor or chairs to literally shake the room. We're using these tools along with a water bed; water conducts base frequency which goes straight into the person lying on it. We're playing with these ideas to find ways of physically punctuating the sound.

discovery (see also: **agency**; audience; boxes, chests and drawers; **curiosity**; **darkness**; doors; **lighting**; **portals**; **reveal**; wardrobes): Crucial to Punchdrunk's practice, the audience member is offered creative agency, partly by having to solve the riddle of how any show works. Deciding navigation, which rooms to seek out and in which to dwell, which characters one might choose to follow, or **not**, the possibility of discovery underpins any Punchdrunk world in form, theme and narrative. Peter Higgin asserts:

Discovery is key to the success of any Punchdrunk project, really you want the audience to feel like they are discovering things alone and for the first time. Discovery can be hard won, or a chance encounter. In truth nothing is left to chance in most of Punchdrunk's work; instances are highly engineered and made purposefully with an audience in mind. A single audience may find a secret embedded within the set and they may be the only one ever to do so. We engineer a state of discovery, giving audiences the thrill of finding a clue or making a narrative connection. Often in Enrichment work the performance is guided and the performers have to gently nudge audiences, helping them to make discoveries that drive the narrative forward, ensuring they feel like they're in the driving seat.

Dobbie, Stephen (see also: **Act 1**; Act 2; Act 3; archiving; *Chair*; music; **soundscore**): Creative Director for Punchdrunk International, Dobbie's first experience of Punchdrunk was as an audience member at *Chair* at the Deptford X festival, describing this as 'a classic example of your first fix'. *Chair* was also Dobbie's first time as a collaborator. Having studied photography at university, he offered his graphic design skills to create the poster and flyers and has since been responsible for Punchdrunk's visual materials, all of which display the shared aesthetic and a sensitivity to how images capture Punchdrunk's worlds.

△
FIGURE 6 'Doors'. *The Lost Lending Library*, at The Mulberry Primary School, London. 2018.
Photo credit: Stephen Dobbie

Dobbie is perhaps better known for designing Punchdrunk's soundscores. His skills in sound composition evolved prior to his collaboration with Punchdrunk, from early experimentations creating sample-based scores and DJing by the name DJ Ethics. A particularly effective sound composition that addresses a challenge or need in the world under construction is referred to by the creative team as an 'Ethics Special'. Felix Barrett explains:

> With every show Dobbie pulls an Ethics Special out of the bag. With a twinkle in his eye, he'll say, 'come and listen to this'. Intuitively, he's crafted something perfect; a snatch of a soundscore pulled through four other different tracks to create the best crescendo, a narrative whole.

Sleep No More, London in 2003 marked the first time Dobbie designed the sound for Punchdrunk events. He has designed the sound for many Punchdrunk projects since:

> I have a broad range of musical interests but the work I've created for Punchdrunk is inspired by my early influences, such as James Lavelle, DJ shadow, lots of the producers coming out of the 1990s bedroom DJ scene, for want of a better name, digging through crates and finding these gems. The attitude wasn't just about finding a good soul or funk loop but instead, sound could come from anything; something rhythmic, or atonal, something textural, a vocal, a field recording of, literally, a field. It was drawing inspiration and appropriating sound from anywhere, any style, from what felt right. It was a combination of the visceral, the instinctive and the intellectual. It may not come from a logical fit but once it's part of the mix it makes sense in the world.

doors (see also: boxes, chests and drawers; **curiosity**; discovery; **one-on-ones**; portals; **wardrobes**): If you see a door, be curious and open it. Access will either be denied, or it will be a portal **to** another world, a further layer of the story.

Doyle, Maxine (see also: **Act 1**; Act 2; Act 3; collaboration; crescendo; **dance**; ensemble; **masked shows**): An independent choreographer and director, Doyle was Artistic Director of First Person Dance Company from 1996–2003. She is Punchdrunk's choreographer and has been co-director for all masked shows since *Sleep No More*, 2003. Doyle also co-directed *The Yellow Wallpaper*, *Tunnel 228* and *The House Where Winter Lives*. Her dance-theatre piece, *After Lethe*, premiered at Staastheater Kassel in May 2016 followed by an international workshop series, *Tension State: Amplifications of the Human Condition*, during autumn 2016. As a principal artist at Springboard Danse Montreal she began the first part of a new work, *Electric Sheep*. Doyle has been integral to the expansion of Punchdrunk's international ensemble:

> My agenda was to build up a company of amazing artists, so when we come to do a project like *The Drowned Man* where we have thirty-seven cast, thirty of them dancers of the highest quality and calibre, and we're making huge, large-scale work which thousands will see and experience, lots of them experiencing choreography for the first time, then I feel like I've realised my ambition (2013) . . .

Maxine Doyle

On the choreographer-director

I consider myself to be a choreographer-director or director-choreographer – I merge both those processes. It's a combination of changing hats and wearing both hats at the same time. For me, the director's head is about examining the sources, *understanding* the sources, storyboarding the show, writing the treatments for each of the characters, writing scenes. For *The Drowned Man* working out the finale in my head, what that would look like, I wrote it as a story, like a treatment for a film to visualise it. When there is text, directing that, through a process of actioning and intention, which I did for the first time with *The Drowned Man*. The choreographer, which is definitely the dominant hat, is that search for physicality and movement language. My personal interest is the relationship between dancing and acting, acting and dancing. I feel there's a misconception of the role; in theatre, you have the director and then the person who does the movement is the movement director, whereas co-direction in Punchdrunk work is such a different role.

Masked Punchdrunk shows are defined by the relationship between dance, design and site; there's an equality between those elements. There's a process of investigation and an investment in the performer that only exists in the masked shows. It's a core principle in one genre of our work. In other Punchdrunk work the performer is the facilitator, which is a different emphasis. What's fundamental in the masked shows is the equality between the dance language and other performance languages, the performer as creator and collaborator, the dancer as a charismatic force that pulls an audience through a space.

Where the work shifts more towards the audience as the epicentre of the work, such as with a travel project or a digital project, where the audience essentially becomes the performer, then the role of the performer and the content shifts. This encyclopaedia teases out the difference between all those processes and the variety in the portfolio of Punchdrunk work. Where the emphasis is on the audience becoming performer and the status of the performer is lessened, and the content is less intricate, then my interest is lessened. I'm always going to be inspired by the people that I'm working with, in front of me; the dancers that I'm in the room with. That's where my drive is going to be and the space and the architecture is going to support that and fuel it.

dreams (see also: **abstract/abstrac-tion**; decay; design; doors; haze; **immersive**; **influences**; in-show-world; lens; mazes; multiples; text; *unheimlich*; vanishing; **visceral**; wardrobes): The play with the illogical and imaginative in the immersive aesthetic of any Punchdrunk project establishes an otherworldly, dream-like state. Textual sources chosen are often directly dreamlike, magical or abstracted and experiential, such as *The Tempest*, *Macbeth* or *Woyzeck*. Similarly, influential references usually have dreamworlds at their heart. The dance and design are both familiar and representational while simultaneously abstracted and expressionistic, so defamiliarised. Livi Vaughan and Felix Barrett are emphatic that the overriding rule in the Punchdrunk 'rules-set' for creating a production is to 'break the rules as soon as they become comfortable or too familiar', thereby pulling the aesthetic and narrative rug from beneath the audience's feet. In design terms this is key in setting a non-linear dream logic where objects and rooms repeat themselves, becoming different with each iteration. Abstraction foregrounds the uncanny; nothing is quite as it seems and yet everything makes sense within the logic of that world. Liminal spaces are hidden across the building; wardrobes that are portals, corridors and mazes that lead the audience episodically, yet fluidly, between one realm and another within the world. Here abstraction and repetition hint at subconscious imagery that exists in the source texts and produces a sensation of rooms that blur. Lighting establishes hazy states from which characters appear, vanish. Another world is created; an otherworld. The otherworldly feeling that is evoked pertains to an *unheimlich* experience. Audience members are invited to immerse themselves in a Punchdrunk dreamworld where everyday objects and actions are recast and shimmer in the haze with a subconscious hue. The experience within this aesthetic state may **be** pleasurable or disquieting or both in equal measure.

Sam Booth

On dream logic and dynamos

The first Punchdrunk show I saw was *Sleep No More*, 2003. I'd run into Felix at our old school when we were both attending a production of *Antigone*, directed and designed by our beloved drama teachers, Geoff Tonkin and Matthew Grant. Both had helped to shape our sensibilities by taking us to see all sorts of extraordinary theatre, and their own productions were outstanding, which is why Felix and I were back at the school years after leaving. I'd been hearing about what Felix had been up to at Exeter University and was very curious, so in the pub afterwards, when he told me he needed masked stewards, I volunteered to help for a couple of nights.

Experiencing the show as an audience member, I was deeply impressed. The masks, the pervasive sound design, the wordless storytelling through stylised movement, the heavy sense of fatalism expressed by the looping repetition of the story. Roaming freely and piecing together the fractured narrative was thrilling to me, intellectually and sensually. I remember trying to figure out the practicalities: How are they synchronising all this? Where are the cues enabling the performers to arrive together on time from different parts of the building? How did they devise and rehearse it? The ambition and complexity of the format was exciting. Whenever I've worked with Punchdrunk since, I've tried to give audiences a feeling similar to the experience I had then. I aim for a high degree of precision in timing, to make the coordination of the performers' intersecting loops seem unlikely, and our complicity with each other seem magical; using symbolism and repeated motifs, ambiguity and dream-logic to intrigue and invite the audience's analytical faculties to interpret and make sense of these worlds.

The production design in 2003 was sparse, nothing like the detailed aesthetic of later shows, but this light touch had the power to engage your imagination and draw you in to this weird world. It was a rough magic and so potent. They used the space, a disused Victorian school building, brilliantly, without transforming it all that much. I remember the rooms so well, particularly what had been the caretaker's domestic area; a zone with a 1970s vibe that was quietly terrifying in its dreary mundanity, reminding everybody of the Overlook Hotel, from the film *The Shining*. This was now the Witches' domain, where you might find a solo in a bathtub, with a living room where Duncan, played by Gerard Bell, went to sit after his murder – a strangely banal afterlife – singing a lullaby to a Witch. It was the most atmospheric theatre I'd seen that wasn't from Eastern Europe. It was one of those shows you feel compelled to describe in detail to people for weeks afterwards.

The first time I worked for Punchdrunk was on *Woyzeck* at The Big Chill, 2004. Felix invited me on board when we met again at a house party. Making it sound like he was forming a commune, Felix said we would all live together on-site for a week prior to the festival, and feed on soup while building the set and getting everything ready. We made a village using military tents for Woyzeck and Marie's home, the Doctor's surgery, the Captain's barracks, and fabricated a forest, 'trees' individually planted in holes that we drilled into the ground. There was a fairground with attractions including a dark maze where lurked a figure in a knitted woollen head-mask, referred to as 'Peruvian Michael', different people taking turns in the role. We created a hidden world behind a camouflaged fence at the top of a field; you entered through a wardrobe in the middle of the fence and then a tunnel you had to crawl through. We opened after dark and performed nonstop for hours each night. It was wild, scary and great fun. After word got around about what was going on, big queues formed at the wardrobe and it became difficult to get in.

I played the Doctor. When I wasn't performing a scene with Tommy Lawrence as Woyzeck – who was the only character moving around on a set loop – I was holding consultations with individual audience members. I was well prepared, having been worried I wouldn't be good at improvisation. Sitting behind a desk, I invited the visitor to be seated on a tiny stool. In a Bavarian accent, learned from Werner Herzog commentaries, I would ask, 'What seems to be the problem?'. If they didn't improvise a medical complaint then I would immediately eject them with a reprimand for wasting my time: 'Please, I am a busy man'. Depending on the nature of their ailment there were a number of absurd roads we could go down. If I suspected they were under the influence, as many festivalgoers clearly were, I could perform a cranial examination that segued into a head massage. I sometimes laid them on a couch and employed the use of an electromagnetic dynamo machine, a genuine antique medical appliance that I brought from home. I held one metal cylinder, the patient held another, and while turning the handle I would complete the circuit by applying my hand to the afflicted area of their body. There was a wide variety of responses to the sensation of the electrical current. I had learned Dmitri Shostakovich's 'Jazz Waltz' on the accordion so

I could play while they were on the other side of a folding screen. Of course, nobody was harmed or irresponsibly treated in the playing out of our interactions. As always has to be the case in a one-on-one, there was no coercion; the audience has to be free to leave at any time if they wish, and it is our artistic responsibility to ensure that alternative endings still feel rounded, so nobody feels as though they've done wrong. If somebody refused to go along with any of the Doctor's requests, it made for an equally satisfactory scene, as I could then go into a speech about how their unwillingness to cooperate might jeopardise the future progress of medical science and describe for them the imminent revolution in human knowledge that my research projects were going to bring about.

I remember defusing a potentially dangerous situation by baffling an aggressively drunk audience member. Out of control, sweeping objects off my desk, messing about with my props, he refused to leave, outraged by my repeatedly insisting for this. Maybe he was having trouble distinguishing what was real from what wasn't, in which case he must have been quite intoxicated, because although we were doing a good job at blurring that boundary, for him to get that offended in so obviously a fictional situation was alarming. I had to deal instinctively with his bizarre, drunken behaviour; bizarre, given that he was in somebody else's tent, and that somebody was clearly pretending to be a German doctor in a totally incongruous context. Technically not a one-on-one, as the tent wasn't closed and there was no one guarding the entrance so audience members were at liberty to come and go as they pleased, he had some friends with him, who I recall were more willing to move on than he was. I was definitely the one in the vulnerable position in this case, trying to clear the tent of this unruly gang, while remaining in character. I saw his jaw and his fist clench as if he was about to punch me, so I locked eyes with him and quietly but intently launched into some particularly obscure lines from Büchner's play. Very soon I saw his eyes glaze over with incomprehension and then, chaperoned by friends, he walked away shaking his head. The incident was a crash course in how to handle tricky one-on-ones.

A few months later, in 2005, *The Firebird Ball* became my first collaboration with the classic format: Shakespeare's *Romeo and Juliet* combined with the Firebird myth and beautiful music from Sergei Prokofiev and Igor Stravinsky's respective ballet suites. I played Friar Lawrence and I felt quite insecure at being one of the only cast members who wasn't a dancer. I don't have performance training, so being surrounded by such a lot of highly trained individuals made me nervous about my lack of technique. I've always aimed to complement the dancers by being as judicious and deliberate as I can in the way I move my body and by blending naturalism and stylisation in my performances, as they do. Maxine and Felix also wanted me to provide a contrasting element to the predominant mode of dance; for example, I would declaim from the book of common prayer for the secret marriage ceremony and for Juliet's funeral procession, or whisper fragments of Shakespeare's text to the audience through the grille of a confessional booth. Back then, the performers took on more design responsibility than we tend to nowadays. I remember going with Felix to woods near Nunhead cemetery to get a carload of fresh foliage for me to crawl into when Friar Lawrence has a crisis of faith following the lovers' deaths, before being led back to the light by the Nurse. I also recall buying incense at Westminster Cathedral – burning it on charcoal on my altar – and Dettol antiseptic liquid to sprinkle throughout the Nurse's area before each show for the aroma.

Felix and his collaborators share an unpretentious dedication to provoking sensation with their productions. Theatre should aspire to move us strongly, whether it's to laughter, tears or goosebumps. I remember hearing that when he was on a school trip to see Robert Wilson's installation piece *H.G.*, Felix came out holding the teacher Matthew Grant's hand because he was so shaken. He is essentially the same excitable teenager today. His sense of wonder, his sensitivity to spaces and his capacity for being utterly captivated by story are undiminished. Punchdrunk's strength derives from the power of this infectious enthusiasm and Felix's determination to make theatre that he himself would be genuinely excited to experience. It's easy for theatre companies to stray from the path of their original impulse and produce shows that are calculated to impress other people, critics, industry peers, funding bodies and the like. It's a paradoxical truth for any artist that to maximise the likelihood that your work will have as deep and broad an appeal as possible, you have to refer, above all, to your own instincts and stay true to your own sense of what is good. By making creative decisions that are surprising and thrilling to the team themselves, Punchdrunk always puts the audience first.

Drowned Man, The (2013–2014, see also: **Act 2**; **archiving**; **bar**; **cinematic**; dreams; **Dust Witch**; forests; *Searching for Stories*; touch-real; **Woyzeck, 2000**. Further reading: Harris 2017; Machon 2018; Maples 2016): With a full title of *The Drowned Man: A Hollywood Fable*, the audience were enticed to:

Step into the world of Temple Pictures where the Hollywood studio system meets a forgotten hinterland filled with dreamers who exist at the fringes of the movie industry. Here, celluloid fantasy clings to desperate realism and certainty dissolves into a hallucinatory world.

Inspired by Georg Büchner's *Woyzeck*, which already shifts between illusion and reality, the play is pulled through Nathanael West's novel *The Day of the Locust*, both re-lensed through references to David Lynch's work. *The Drowned Man* fuses characters and narratives, from all these sources, transposed to the early 1960s and the brink of the demise of the all-powerful studio system. It accentuates the cinematic, and cleverly plays with the idea of filmic doubling, merging fantasy and reality. As soon as audiences enter the world they are cast in-between audience-voyeurs, party revellers, studio visitors, 'cameras' and ghosts. Installations play with notions of fakery and manipulation; film sets, offices, executive suites, dressing rooms, seamstresses' towns, forests and trailers, situated so that boundaries blur and certainty about film-set versus 'real' setting becomes unfixed. Inhabiting spaces that are always touch-real (even where drawing attention to the touch-real-fakery of studio set), while always existing inside Temple Studios itself, invites a constant doubled reading of any events in that space from the audience. This doubling of worlds is accentuated in the space of 'Studio 3', a bar area where audience members might remove their masks, attune to the different tempo that plays out to the world outside and remain all night should they choose, enjoying the entertainment and the interactions as Kathryn McGarr describes below. This world within the wider world of Temple Studios reinvents the format first fully explored in *The Masque of the Red Death*.

The fusions of characters and plotlines from textual sources mirror, while making strange, the narratives of the original, especially in the reflected and refracted storylines of William and Mary vs Wendy and Marshall (roles devised and shared [a doubled-doubling] by, respectively, Omar Gordon/Paul Zivkovich and Laure Bachelot/Kate Jackson vs Anna Finkel/Pauline Huguet and Fion Cox-Davies/Jess Kovarsky). Some characters lived on the outside of Temple Studios, only entering when invited in as temporary staff, film extras or guests whereas mirrored counterparts, such as Mr. Stanford played by Sam Booth, or Dolores the studio Diva (shared by Sarah Dowling and Jane Leaney), inhabited Temple Studios, unable to break free. Characters in-between both realms, patrolled by 'The Gatekeeper', moved from inside to outside as permanent staff, B-list actresses, PAs or Doctors to the moguls and divas.

The ensemble who developed the material expanded to establish the largest cast, at that point, for a masked show. Formed from a combination of stalwarts, including Conor Doyle, Rob McNeill, Fernanda Prata and Vinicius Salles, it also introduced new dancers into the fold. One such novitiate, Finkel, recalls the potency of the visceral world that was established and how this inflects her dance-memory, as much as it influenced the audience experience:

I can hear the words of the first read-through of *Woyzeck*. They echo through my memory of every performance. I can still feel the rough and curiously slippery texture of the ice palace; feel myself fall from high in the trees onto the wood chips; the taste of red lemonade; hearing Mr. Stanford's voice eerily call me; desperately smearing my bloodied hands on the walls; and sitting in a pool of water with rain pouring down as the audience walked out around us. For my entire time in *The Drowned Man*, I remember feeling in awe, like I was drifting through the experience, deeply inspired by the people that surrounded me – their skill, individuality, care and ownership of the work.

Temple Studios was conceived as an interactive artistic hub. By day, it invited pupils from local schools on-site to experience *Searching for Stories*. By night, following Friday night performances, Punchdrunk hosted after-show parties in its bar. On special weekend afternoons, before the evening performances and in collaboration with BFI, the on-set, fully functioning, 1960s-styled Encino Cinema presented one-off 16mm-film screenings of *The Day of the Locust*, *Wozzeck*, *Sunset Boulevard* or *Eyes Without a Face*. The programme included an original short about Lila, a sound recordist for Temple Studios and a character in *The Drowned Man*, created by Hector Harkness and Kath Duggan. Additionally, an extensive professional development programme ran with artists invited to work on-site in response to the space and the production's sources, to produce their own original work.

Archives remain to hint at the mood and narrative of the fictional studios. The production programme and accompanying website tantalised a curious audience, hinting at closely guarded secrets around the dramatic events that led to the building being condemned. A virtual tour of the studios, designed and produced by Charles Mansfield-Osborne with the support of Stephen Dobbie and Punchdrunk, is available to experience via the Punchdrunk or Mansfield-Osborne websites. A limited-edition book, *The Drowned*

Man: A Hollywood Fable, produced in collaboration with photographer Julian Abrams, captures fleeting moments from the world of Temple Studios, published autonomously by Punchdrunk in 2015.

Duchess of Malfi, The (**2010**; see also: **Act 2**; *Apricot Orchard*; Bicât, Tina; cinematic; compromise; **costume**; **crescendo**; **design**; epic; music; **reveal**; **scenography**; touch; **visceral**): An operatic adaptation of the Jacobean play by John Webster, with an original score and libretto by Torsten Rasch. Produced in collaboration with English National Opera, in a large decommissioned pharmaceutical headquarters including a three-storey office and adjacent warehouse, at Ivax Quays, East London. This production rendered Webster's classic tragedy of murder and revenge into an epic, immersive opera. Performed by an ensemble of twenty-one singers and dancers, the production featured a sixty-nine-piece symphony orchestra, conducted by Stephen Higgins and Murray Hipkin. The search for a site for this project was particularly challenging as, along with the usual practical requirements for any large-scale masked show, the space needed to be able to accommodate an orchestra that would be scattered in various configurations across the building. Orchestra, performers and audience roamed across the 136,000 square feet of the building. The warehouse housed the finale of the performance where the full sixty-nine-piece orchestra and all the performers came together for a twenty-minute crescendo and powerful conclusion. Tickets for the entire run of performances sold out on the day of release. Tina Bicât, who collaborated for a third time with Punchdrunk on this production, vividly recalls Felix Barrett's vision for the finale:

> For days I remember people were making endless dummies out of sellotape, filling this massive space while building the set. The idea was that Ferdinand, as he's sending the Duchess to be hung, walks out, pulling the room with him, along the central walkway. The whole space was surrounded by walls of heavy, red drapes on a circular rail. Built into this was a gown that the performer put on and, because it was so heavy and strong, as he walked forward through the hellish pandemonium he pulled the 'walls' with him to reveal a huge space of hanging bodies. It was an extraordinary flight of imagination, so amazing to see it and I was very happy to be the person who worked on it with Felix. It was interesting to see how fixed he was on the picture that he wanted. The fact that it would reveal, as Ferdinand walked along, this terrible event at the end; the whole, huge space with all these hanging bodies and the orchestra whacking its heart out on the very tortured contemporary music. This vision was so clear in his mind that, for me, the actual technicalities of it faded into insignificance beside the hugeness of the picture and *really* wanting to make it happen. I remember lying on my stomach with a sewing machine and an assistant working the pedal every time I said, 'Now!' then, 'Stop!' while I was making it because the fabric was too heavy to move so the only way you could work on it was in-situ.
>
> In the tech, the orchestra was there, there were lots of crosses and a huge, great incense ball that swung across the space, the tension. It was an enormous feat of filmic imagination to put that on a stage. The audience were part of the set as were the dummies hanging and the choreography was moving towards this final moment where the Duchess is hung upside down, her delicate bleeding body – it's a very Punchdrunk image. I must have been in the central area and suddenly there was this shivering noise, and I became aware that I was really *in* the show. No longer with my techy-head looking at my work, thinking have I got this right for the audience, but I was there, watching this tragedy unfold. The shiver was the curtains just beginning to move along the track as Ferdinand began his walk forward. The curtains, the whole air, began to tremble and I didn't know what was happening, even though I made it. That reveal, this vision that all would follow Ferdinand in this great tumble of disaster, revealing bodies hanging and flaming crosses, the conductor and the orchestra, playing its heart out.

Colin Nightingale recalls how the operational experience for the team felt like 'putting a masked show together by numbers'. Punchdrunk learned how to deconstruct an opera across a vast site. It was a logistical feat despite artistic problems encountered along the way, mostly related to manoeuvring an orchestra, instruments in tow, from space to space. The production was a vital learning experience in that it pointed up new collaborative structures and strategies required for interaction and artistic development across all elements of the production process; blending costume and scenic design with dance, orchestral and operatic performance with site management. The experiences of working with an orchestra less willing to be involved showed how such practice could not work if restrictions were applied to collaboration. In this work, as Nightingale puts it, 'you can't have bolt-ons'; every element, even where a new discipline within the immersive mix, has to be embedded in the form and involved in the process. Punchdrunk's Enrichment for the first time embedded a project within the show; *The Duchess of Malfi Apricot Orchard*, created for Brittania Village Primary School.

durational (see also: **abstract/abstraction**; Act 1; *Chair*; crescendo; Exeter Experiments; *House of Oedipus, The*; *Kabeiroi*; **loops**; **mazes**; reveal; *Tempest, The*, 2003; ***Tunnel 228***): In arts practice 'durational' denotes that time is treated as an organic, experiential element of the event:

Duration is not simply 'how long it lasts', the running time of the performance from start to finish but holds a greater significance in regards to the interactive relationship established between the audience-participants and the event within the timescales set. Whether intensely concentrated to minutes or spanning days, months or beyond, the length of time spent within the work impacts on the experience of the work according to the parameters of the event. The duration of the work may be prescribed, just a few minutes with the artist as with many one-on-ones, or an event that is durational may invite the audience-participants to enter and leave the world as they choose. Each approach has consequences in relation to the interpretations placed on the experiences and narratives encountered according to the time spent engaging with the experience, dwelling in that world.

(Machon 2013a, 96)

Influenced by live art, Felix Barrett has always had a keen interest in durational work, triggered by his response to the tempo and flow of a building and encompassing the experiential quality of time in which an audience exists for the running time of the event. The audience experience of duration is accentuated by the tempo of the physical language, and the affective temporality that exists in a space and can be shaped by installation, sound and costume, where the materials and impact of those designs not only communicate (often jarring) eras and environments but hold the very sensation of time-taken, time-endured, within the very expression and motion they dictate in interaction with performer or audience member; the billow of a cape, the lightness of a silk slip that becomes heavier the more the sweat and toil of a loop takes its toll on the performer, the heavy resistance of velvet drapes that stall time as they lead the audience member

in a convoluted manner to an unexpected encounter. With a sensitivity to how to control and convey duration through space, scenography and sound, Barrett was searching for a performing style that could match this. Across his Exeter Experiments and the early Punchdrunk projects of Act 1, Barrett was striving for a gestural language with equal weight to any site or space in which it was performed. He learned this from 'failing' with *The House of Oedipus* where not only did the daylight destroy the mystery and the impact of 'the reveal', the reveal itself was lessened once encountered because many of the scenes relayed speech to deliver the narrative in the open air; 'when the audience finally came across dialogue, realistic acting, with a realistic tempo in real time, it destroyed the effect' because it was out of context and jarred ineffectively with the other elements. Additionally, this external setting and the repeated loops for the scenes proved tough for the performers, required to act 'for six hours straight'. Discomfort and reliance on speech proved incompatible with the experiential impact that Barrett was intending. In contrast, in a more controlled environment of a building with facilities, and an open-ended list of instructions for a more abstracted performance, where speech and narrative were not required, effective durational performances were possible. With *Chair*, the daily eight-hour performance required that the two performers (shared by a group of willing volunteers across the three-day run) 'live' in the space, potter about and 'just be', resulting in one performer choosing to get into his bed and sleep, another to sit and knit. For *The Tempest*, 2003, the performer playing Miranda sat alone in a room, reading and tearing pages from the bible unbearably slowly, achingly beautiful in its restraint. As Barrett summarises, 'a classic durational act'. This was sharply counterpointed by the staccato tempo and framing of the dancer playing a Sprite, moving in and out of the shadows on the periphery of the space.

As Barrett's desire to explore further a physical language that matched the expanse and expressiveness of the space advanced, and the idea of incorporating dance was seeded, a reconsideration of how duration through human performance might be explored was needed. Barrett recalls:

Up until working with Max I'd thought about the performing style as more like live art. I thought the endurance and the durational aspect of it, the toil of the performers was as much a part of the aesthetic as the installation was. It needed to be durational, it needed to be tough for the performers because that would show through the cracks in the veneer. It was stronger if the audience could experience the endurance. And then Max, rightly, said this wasn't sustainable, that the quality of the performance will go down if they're tired. Three hours is enough for the focus of the audience and the performers.

Masked shows, by their nature, need to be a certain length to allow maximum experience and exploration of the world and theatrical content. With a format that was initiated in 2000, the duration of these masked shows has been finely constructed and are now set as, approximately, fifty-minute loops, that are then replayed three times, with the final loop leading into a crescendo and finale. In masked shows, within the experiential duration of the loops across the run, an additional durational layer is established in the action of resident characters; each having distinct and repeated, concentrated loops for their narratives. In these scenarios the quality of the experience accentuates an affective temporality. Geir Hytten, an original cast member of *Sleep No More*, London, *Faust* and *The Duchess of Malfi*, notes:

Duration impacts the physical 'realness' of the world, the sense of living through an experience as a character. The lengthy investment in the performance, for audience and performer, provides an opportunity to share in exhaustion, endurance and elation. We are in this together. We get lost in the timeframe of the world, from when we started to where it ends. We are in each moment together. It facilitates a shared experience where physicality is the narrator of the moment. It is overwhelming, it is transcending, it is sublime.

Tension and a feeling of dwelling in time might be comprehended by observing someone sewing for ten minutes, lulled into a dreamlike timeframe. The choreography of the resident characters, the tempo and tracking of the most pedestrian of actions, becomes a rhythmical layer in the world and a potent holder of time, as was the case with Hector Harkness's obsessive and precise cutting of single lines from a bible with a scalpel in *Sleep No More*, London. Actions as mundane as wiping a table, as in Katy Balfour's 'Nurse' one-on-one in *The Masque of the Red Death*, or Risa Steinberg's darning of children's socks in *Sleep No More*, NYC, become an affective process where domestic actions are heightened, so rendered lyrical. Repetition of action moves beyond routine to become ritual; making the encounter meaningful, giving the moment weight and profundity. For travelling and resident characters alike, the duration of each moment in their loops is a palpable force. The speed and quality of each action and gesture can correlate to the holding of the audience's attention, so the significance of movement quality, tempo, eye contact is clear. Actions are distilled, repeated, abstracted and thereby elevated to the ritualised, or made uncanny like the gestures and language of dreams. Either way, the pedestrian becomes poetic. Correspondingly, one-on-one encounters become epic as a consequence of their concentrated narratives, with a carefully constructed crescendo and denouement, all in the span of two minutes.

In durational work the experience of absence is as vital as the attendance to presence. With *Chair*, the absence of chairs, their former presence all implied by the placement of partner furniture in the installations in each room, is apt illustration of this; a lone desk and typewriter, a reading lamp on an occasional table, with the trace of a presence suggested by marks left behind on the floor. These added to the experience of the space being ripe with temporal and physical presence formed by absence, which then influenced the subsequent impact of the reveal of chairs piled high through the exit of the event. An absence of performers in rooms, so clearly inhabited by a character as indicated by design, underscores a sensation of dwelling in time for the audience member; when might they return? How long might I have before discovered reading this letter? Similarly, an absence of action, or an implied former presence of a character, is also evoked by the durational quality of sound; beyond the tempo and beat of the composition, this relates to the *sensation* of duration communicated by the score; the unceasing crackle of vinyl denoting that, somewhere, a record has reached its end and the listener is long-gone. For Barrett:

This is why duration is so important, in action and sound. It holds an implicit threat, which comes from nothing happening because you know at some point it's going to break and something is going to shift so that event gains more power the greater the absence before it.

Barrett's and Colin Nightingale's shared interest in durational activity as live art and lived encounter was explored through *Tunnel 228*, woven together with a thematic thread inspired by Fritz Lang's *Metropolis*. The brief sent out as a casting call for performers was that the event would be:

Durational, non-text based and non-narrative. The performance language will be visual, physical and repetitive. Performers will be expected to perform for two cycles of three hours with a one-hour break. The environment is amazing but harsh – very chilly – so this project is not for the faint hearted. Performers should have a very strong presence and be able to do something very small, very well.

The six-hour performance involved a series of 'workers' climbing up walls, managing an 'epic machine' created by Ben Tyers. Performers, including Hytten and Vinicius Salles, were secondary to the art on display; any suggestion of choreography was pedestrian, mechanical, at the service of the art to which it was adjoined and with one rhythm in order to be sustainable for six hours. As Doyle puts it, 'there was no physical crescendo of the body, the crescendo was the activation of the machine'. Doyle's notes (entitled 'Cog in a wheel') for the performer working with Tyers' machine reveal the durational quality of the movement language as she saw it, drawn from the expressionist rhythm and imagery of *Metropolis*:

A single performer inhabits one of the spaces. He shifts objects / forms around the space in order that the environment changes around him. He moves with economy. He moves with an intense and determined focus. This cycle of motion is relentless . . . He follows no linear narrative. He simply completes his daily task with rigour. His body becomes a sculpture in the space. He will not interfere or interact with other bodies or objects alien to his space. His movement comes from the function of moving and organising objects – of doing his job. He displays a crescendo of exhaustion. A grey, dark, stark cycle. A cog in a wheel.

Machine and performer, framed by the dank underground tunnels and functioning alongside the other artworks and experiences programmed, persisted in partnership with time amidst the general hubbub of the club-feel environment with guests drinking and talking around the bar.

Punchdrunk remains interested in investigating the ways in which an audience's attention and tension can be held, whether for a condensed one-on-one, a fifty-minute family show, a six-hour experience across a city or a week-long journey through a rural landscape. The question of how long and how to engage and immerse an audience is a realm that Punchdrunk is eager to explore for the duration of Act 3. Gaming vernacular and the use of technology might enable Punchdrunk to consider this question. Equally abstraction, sound, the ebb and flow of temporality, journeying, eyes, senses and the synthesis of elements to control an environment will all be part of this future experimentation. Time will tell.

Dust Witch (see also: Act 2; audience; characters; *Drowned Man, The*; **ensemble**; one-on-one; **restraint**): Witches are a recurring presence across masked shows since *Sleep No More*, London. Felix Barrett has 'a total pre-occupation with witches':

It's the uncanny, the supernatural, the thing that exists on the periphery of your imagination. Witches, for all intents and purposes, are human, and you wouldn't necessarily know that they have a separate power. That's why they're so alluring.

The Dust Witch is a one-on-one unique to *The Drowned Man* which begins on the desert sands where The Dust Witch plays out activity, blind to the masked onlookers, until one becomes a supernatural presence. Performed originally in turn by Jane Leaney, Katie McGuinness or Margarita Zafrilla Olayo, the removal of sight required consent and was choreographed carefully; timing providing repeated moments for the audience-participant to bid a retreat. The Dust Witch one-on-one played with light as physical object and conveyer of heat, intensely perceived through the blindfolded audience-participant's skin, a

parcan creating the sensation of the desert's burning heat (a technique that would later be employed to heighten a comforting embrace in the final sequence of *Kabeiroi*).

Guest appearances in the role occurred as the run extended. Kathryn McGarr recalls:

Playing The Dust Witch, performing rituals in the sand, with a lone, masked audience member watching, felt like an extreme close-up, more so than in the one-on-one where that device of the mask-lens has been broken, a different kind of intimacy.

Barrett, as emergency understudy, once played the role to ensure a vital sequence occurred, where The Dust Witch delivers clothes back to a naked Dwayne. Masked by The Dust Witch veil, he provided the necessary assistance for Luke Murphy, playing Dwayne that night. Barrett recalls, 'the scrutiny from the audience was unbelievable. I realised the impulse to want to perform, to entertain them', despite knowing his own rules for restraint in performance, especially for a one-on-one. He noted first-hand:

The audience are desperate for content and you have to fight back the urge to give it to them. Key words for our performers are restraint, generosity and ensemble and I really did learn about the importance of those, particularly restraint, because you really do have to carry an audience, pass them on to other performers. I always knew it, but by doing it, I felt it. Feeling it is far more powerful. As much as I hated the experience, I can see why it's so addictive.

E

Enrichment (see also: **Act 2**; Act 3; *Against Captain's Orders*; Booth, Elizabeth; digital technologies;

Entwistle, Codie and Kyle; **Fallow Cross**; *Greenhive Green*; **Higgin, Peter**; *House Where Winter Lives, The*; **legacy**; *Lost Lending Library*; Lynch, Sharon: 'Mantle of the Expert'; Marsh, Colin; *Oracles, The*; **site-sympathetic**; *Small Tale, A*; **transportation and transformation**; *Uncommercial Traveller, The*; *Under the Eiderdown*; *Up, Up and Away*. Further reading: Cremin, Swann, Colvert and Oliver 2016; Machon and Thompson 2014; Miles 2015; Tims 2016): Punchdrunk Enrichment takes the company's innovative practice into communities and schools, creating performances with and for children, young people and participants. Integral to the creation of this work is the same commitment to exemplary design and performance that defines Punchdrunk's large-scale productions for adult audiences. Enrichment designs, as Livi Vaughan explains, 'follow exactly the same rules on a smaller scale' with the only difference, if any, that for projects 'where audience is congregated for longer moments for focused storytelling, the design is approached from a few, specific viewpoints, rather than the 360-degree, multilayered world'.

Flagship Enrichment projects include *Under the Eiderdown* and *The Lost Lending Library*. The largest-scale Enrichment project to date is *Against Captain's Orders*, a family adventure created in partnership with the National Maritime Museum. Led by Peter Higgin, Enrichment projects follow an applied theatre practice and ideology in an aim to deliver outreach aims and explore Punchdrunk's mission and aesthetic in a diversity of smaller environments. The small-scale structure of Enrichment productions offers models for performance and audience engagement that directly impact the target community and simultaneously offer strategies for managing larger-scale projects for the wider public. As Colin Nightingale puts it, Punchdrunk Enrichment is 'an incubator of ideas'.

Since its formation Enrichment has delivered twenty-two projects, several many times over, working in schools and wider communities, reaching over 100,000 participants in total. In 2016 Enrichment celebrated its achievements in a one-day symposium for teachers, artists, academics, funders and policy-makers, specifically examining Enrichment's work in schools . . .

Peter Higgin

On Enrichment, engagement and education

*U*nder the Eiderdown established a pivotal model for practice, cementing thinking around what Enrichment practice is and how it might be rolled out across schools. We owe much to two headteachers, Elizabeth Booth and Sharon Lynch, whose willingness to venture into the unknown has been vital in our journey. They, along with four partner schools, agreed to take a risk on *Under the Eiderdown* and, in doing so, inspired a new approach to Punchdrunk's work, reconfigured in a bespoke fashion, to address learning needs in educational contexts; an approach that the team has gone on to adapt in many different schools and for a diversity of community settings.

Punchdrunk Enrichment in schools uses the company's signature form to engage pupils with the most important and challenging parts of their curriculum, in imaginative ways. An important aim is to work closely with teachers to create experiences that leave pupils inspired and enriched, having a palpable impact on their attainment and personal development. Enrichment creates magical and fantastical experiences which are born out of, while fitting into, the everyday reality of school – experiences that happen to pupils, stories in which they are the heroes, stories that can't be resolved without them. Experiences designed to compel pupils to engage with skills and knowledge that help them on their educational journey. Experiences that they will never forget, that offer, to quote one pupil, the 'BEST. SCHOOL. DAY. EVER'. We also aim to inspire teachers to be more creative and bold, as it is the teachers who have the most profound impact on a child's school life.

We know there is a link between deprivation and low levels of literacy and that deprivation can link to low cultural engagement and limited access to the richest cultural experiences. We know engagement with the arts can impact attainment, engagement and personal development. Low levels of literacy impact achievement in school and can heavily dictate pupils' life chances. This is at the root of Enrichment's educational mission. All of these factors drive us to deliver our projects in the way we do and in the places we do. Over the past three years we have taken our work to deprived areas in East London, because it is in areas like this where the work is needed most. We know access to our work can inspire pupils to speak, to write, to read, to be engaged and excited by books, stories and story writing, thereby engaging with one of the most important life-skills. By embedding high-quality, artistic work within a school for an extended period of time, in a small way, we hope to help raise levels of attainment and to help pupils on their journey into a successful life. We know that measuring impact is a contentious area and that ascribing any progress solely to an arts project can be hard. Life is more complex than this. Now more than ever we must celebrate and champion the creative arts and creative approaches in education.

The impact of the work is best described through the stories of those who've experienced the work, many of which are documented in research reports that Punchdrunk Enrichment has commissioned over the last three years: a low-ability student, in the school library, frantically searching for a copy of Shakespeare's *The Tempest*. He returns to his teacher with four versions and animatedly asks which is suitable for him. He has just visited *Prospero's Island*, and is now visibly different from the student who left for the project three hours before. His teacher is overwhelmed by the change, delighted by how excited he is about this play, about Shakespeare. He immediately wants to engage with the work independently, to continue on his own voyage of discovery. This enthusiasm continued through the rest of the term. A pupil who, following a visit to *The Lost Lending Library*, is compelled to go to the class writing table; again, unusual behaviour for this pupil who usually lacks confidence at writing. This pupil uses descriptive sounds and spaces in layout for the first time. For the first time the writing is legible and can be read and understood. The pleasure for all was palpable, a giant step for a small child. An emotional account from a primary school teacher: following an experience of *Under the Eiderdown* a mute child spoke for the first time in class. Not one word but many. Expressive, excited, engaged and confident.

There are accounts of the impact beyond the classroom. In a school where parent attendance at events was low, an unprecedented number arrive at the school for a parents' sharing session. It is their children who have brought them there, talking about the project incessantly and excitedly at home. Or parents so inspired by a project that they go on to create their own installation, transforming a classroom in their children's school. Understanding the impact that this kind of work can have, they take it upon themselves to recreate it. There are many accounts from parents of children going home and writing stories freely and taking an interest in stories and libraries. Of parents reconnecting with the importance of storytelling, taking on the mantle of storyteller. This is why we do this work, because we know the profound and transformational impact it can have.

Collaborating with researchers on various Enrichment projects has helped us to better understand our work, informing future strategy and identify future areas for investigation. Across Act 3 we intend to examine the interconnected areas of 'Legacy and Impact', 'Scale and Reach' and 'Digital Engagement'.

We're investigating the forms legacy might take to ensure long-lasting impact and maximum benefit, where pupils' curiosity and enthusiasm are maintained and teachers and parents are supported in that process. We're already testing this with our pilot project *A Small Tale*. In order to build on existing impact, we have embedded a standardised evaluation structure that has allowed us to gather a body evidence on projects that we run. This helps us to hone delivery and engage critically with our practice. Partnerships with academics have ignited a reflexive approach and helped shape and mould our projects in direct response to this independent examination and analysis.

As for 'Scale and Reach', our current models work, but how can we do more, how can we share our practice further? We want to share our work in schools nationally, to invent new models for this. *A Small Tale* intends to address this. We want to link up with regional partners to tour projects as well as creating work for schools, off-site, in a permanent Punchdrunk venue. At Fallow Cross, Enrichment is already testing the ways in which digital platforms can augment and support our work in schools, with *The Oracles*. There are so many parallels with the way we structure experience and the way games are built; how you help an audience understand how they fit and function in a world; what the rules are; what the modes of game-play might be. The exploration of digital technologies in Enrichment's practice runs through all of these areas and is perhaps the most important theme in the future of our work: how it might increase the reach of projects by relying less on the transformation of physical space and instead use technologies that augment and 're-lens' the physical space and the world around us.

Enrichment Symposium

Enrichment Symposium (see also: **Act 3**; Booth, Elizabeth; digital technologies; Enrichment; **Higgin, Peter**; Lynch, Sharon. Further reading: Tims 2016): Held at Shoreditch Town Hall, 9 November 2016, the symposium came at the end of a three-year tranche of funding from Paul Hamlyn Foundation. This period had seen a development and proliferation of Enrichment's practice and a greater understanding of the impact of the work. The symposium was a day to celebrate and disseminate findings as well as to begin to talk about the future direction of Enrichment's work. It involved a mixture of keynote addresses, practical workshops, performances and discussions and marked the launch of *Doorways*, an open access review of Punchdrunk Enrichment Projects (2013–2016), commissioned by Punchdrunk Enrichment and authored by Charlie Tims. The event was produced by Punchdrunk Enrichment with organisational support from James Pidgeon and team at Shoreditch Town Hall. Keynote speeches were delivered by Peter Higgin and headteachers Sharon Lynch and Elizabeth Booth. Invited contributors included longstanding collaborators such as Norma Hewins of Jubilee Primary School, academic researchers Teresa Cremin and Angela Colvert, and invited speakers from companies working in the field of immersive, experiential and digital education. The practice shared across this day introduced delegates to Punchdrunk Enrichment's core principles . . .

On core principles

Introduction – a real-world pre-experience. Most of our projects begin in a thoroughly real-world setting, usually in a school, although a museum, a park, a school outing are all illustrative of this. The start of 'the journey' of a project will, typically, feel downbeat, everyday. Teachers don't overstate the significance and for the most part pupils are unaware; a package is delivered to the school or there is a visit from a local librarian; the appearance of an unfamiliar yet ordinary object in the playground. Theatricality is minimal to begin allowing the experience to scale up, slowly. This gives characters, and later the installation, integrity and credibility in the children's minds.

A feeling of reality. Each enrichment project is grounded in reality. This is achieved not only through the detail and realism of the installations, but also the creation and interpretation of the characters. Characters, although often heightened, are never caricatures. Children should never think that the characters they meet are actors. The fictional world of the project should be watertight. It should feel believable and stand up to logical scrutiny.

A sense of danger. Just like Punchdrunk's work for adults, Enrichment projects create involve a sense of danger, trepidation. The installations are often unusual and children are sometimes a little hesitant to enter them. The occurrence of strange things in a school setting can be unnerving or worrying for some pupils. We ensure emotions are managed carefully, that participants are protected. Trepidation heightens the senses and increases levels of perception. Children are alert and present and receiving a wealth of sensory information. Often those who were initially scared or anxious feel a sense of accomplishment and pride for overcoming initial fears. Heightened senses in the rich sensory world, coupled with an experience of high emotions, ensure that any piece lives a long time in the audience's memory. Stepping into the unknown and outside of the everyday routine can have a transformative impact on young people.

The possibility of magic. The importance of magic and adventure are integral to all Punchdrunk's work, whether that involves a magical bric-a-brac shop, a vast moving library or sneaking around a fictional film studio – each experience seeds the possibility of magic and a call to adventure. The key is to instil in young minds a curiosity and openness to the possibility of magic. The projects are imbued with this sense. It is this sensibility that we hope to bestow in pupils and teachers to take forward into their creative lives.

Installation/transformation. Enrichment projects have an installation or transformation of space at their heart. The opportunity for children to enter a fully immersive, fictional world is central to our work, for it is this experience that creates the most surprising and dramatic responses in our young audiences.

Books as starting points. We often use books as starting points. Unless permissions are given and we are completely taken by the book, we don't tell the story in its entirety; instead it may be used as a creative springboard. Pupils read the book with their teacher and then the book comes to life. Our characters will also be familiar with the book, giving a shared interest or bonding point. A book coming to life can enhance the importance of books, stories and literature in the child's mind.

Education wrapped up as a story. All of our projects are created with key curriculum-based objectives in mind, educational benefits that are packaged up within the story-world so that the children engage with learning without realising they are doing so. Coupled with the reality of the project, the pupils are given a real-world reason to engage with curriculum areas. It is this purpose that can inspire pupils to engage more fully with their learning. They are compelled to, as opposed to being instructed or told to.

Empowerment and agency. The role of the children as agents of change is central to all of our projects. In every instance the characters that deliver the project need the children in some way (although they do not always know it at first). Characters might need the children to look after their shop, awaken their creativity, write stories for a library or help them break rules. The children are entrusted with responsibility, hopefully leading to a sense of empowerment through the project and a sense that their actions have contributed to the completion of a story.

Enrichment

Gift and the importance of legacy. In large-scale Punchdrunk productions, audiences who are invited in for one-on-one performances are usually given a memento. The same is true in Enrichment projects; we like to leave participants with a gift; a letter, a permanent gold card library membership, a bottle attached to a piece of red ribbon for the owner to insert a message, a mantra, a promise to do something differently, to try something new, buttons, business cards and fabric swatches are all given away to inspire future work, a reminder of their experience and the promises they made to the characters they met. Whatever the object, it has a palpable and meaningful connection to the narrative and continues to remind the audience of the magical journey they went on.

ensemble (see also: characters; dance; design; Dust Witch; lighting; masked shows; music; one-on-one; process; restraint; soundscore): In general terms, 'ensemble' defines an approach to acting that aims for a shared imagination and process that results in a collective effect achieved by all members of a company of performers working in unison to realise a shared vision with the director or choreographer for a performance; an emphasis on performer as co-creator rather than performer as translator of a singular vision, in servitude to the director. An ensemble approach does not emphasise individual performances. 'Ensemble' also serves as the collective noun for that group of performers. Performers in Punchdrunk's work are a vital element in what Felix Barrett refers to as 'the sinuous whole' of the world of the event. In this respect the ensemble in Punchdrunk's practice includes the non-human collaborators of lighting, sound, music and scenographic design. In the build of the show it is often these technical and artistic elements within the ensemble that, for Barrett, 'pull rank', helping to find solutions for interpretative and practical challenges for performers and directors.

The signature performing style identifiable in any Punchdrunk masked show is evolved through the performers who comprise the core ensemble, formed across Act 1 and slowly augmented with each new show across Acts 2 and 3. Early performers who built this ensemble are those that volunteered as part of the band of artists mucking in to make the variety of projects that distinguish the 2000–2005 period of work, such as Katy Balfour, Sam Booth and Kathryn McGarr. *Sleep No More*, London and *The Firebird Ball* saw long-standing members including Sarah Dowling, Hector Harkness, Geir Hytten and Rob McNeill join, performers who would be invited in to build their role in response to the site and the needs of the project, as Kate Hargreaves describes below. Reminiscing on the formation of the team across Act 1 and the integration of all of the elements in a Punchdrunk

world, Stephen Dobbie notes how the shared aesthetic underpinned the mission and ethos of the company, and simultaneously resisted conventional approaches to company hierarchy:

The blurring between all of the roles in those early days; performers designing and making their own space, added to that sense of living it and to nurturing that shared sensibility. There was an amazing sense of freedom in creating those worlds that everyone embraced. Similarly, there was a blurring between role and personality for all of those performers, like Matt Blake and Kat McGarr.

Barrett notes that it is only since *Sleep No More* that performers have been cast by production. Stalwart members were added to the fold from *Faust*, including Conor Doyle, Fernanda Prata and Vinicius Salles, who shared the sensibility and became expert at Punchdrunk's unique interactive and immersive techniques, reprising roles and returning for new productions. Since *Sleep No More* in Boston, New York and Shanghai, auditions have seen to the growth of an international ensemble with a uniquely Punchdrunk style. Dancers in the Punchdrunk ensemble come from a range of backgrounds with a significant shared dance-theatre lineage:

I wanted to nurture a company of artists with a shared shorthand, that were committed to the work, that got it, with the right presence, understood the investment needed as a performer to make it work, that were great creators, choreographers in their own right. The work is better the more creators you have within it.
(Doyle 2013)

The mark of Punchdrunk performers owes as much to a distinctive presence as it does to an instinctive ability to handle the required technique, as Barrett explains:

When we audition performers, Max watches the choreography, the technique and the phrasing, whereas I watch the group who are waiting

to go on to see what their resting state is. That's how we cast. It's about not acting but being present. That brings a sense of the 'real', the authentic, to the performance, in the same way that the design of the spaces have a 'real' quality to them.

It was from *Sleep No More* that the process for the dancers in the ensemble was shifted, removing them from the build and early on-site explorations, in favour of them initiating character development in studio space outside of the building. They then rework this material once in the space, by then made safe and workable by the rest of the core Punchdrunk team, and in the final stages of the design process. Ensemble members creating non-dance material on site, the likes of Blake, Booth and McGarr, continue to evolve material in much the same way as with those original projects in the early days of Act 1. Among the ensemble for the masked shows the sensibility and skill deployed that ties the performing style together is the innate understanding of the importance of precision, detail and abstraction, an ability to explore and perform physical motifs, however grand or minimal in expression.

Assorted contributions from performers highlight the qualities required when working in Punchdrunk worlds; Dowling, Prata and Risa Steinberg draw attention to the need for detail in every moment of a movement, a gesture, in terms of its durational quality as much as its filmic close-up; Conor Doyle and Steinberg highlight the significance of the relationship with the building, Steinberg knowing she would be able to perform in this world when her body literally and figuratively met the architecture, as her leg reached the wall. Balfour, Booth and McGarr highlight the responsibilities of interactive practice in general and one-on-one scenarios in particular, all performers raising questions for the reader about immersive practice, its artistic potency and its ethical concerns. Conor Doyle, McGarr and Prata each refer to the addictive quality of performing in Punchdrunk's shows, while Barrett acknowledges this, in reference to his momentary stint as Dust Witch.

Given that performers in the ensemble are but one of the layers in the sensual material of a Punchdrunk world – responding to and resonating with the other elements of that world – any sense of hierarchy in audience appreciation should be removed in favour of experiencing this human element of the Punchdrunk world on a continuum with each other, and as a constituent of the synergetic whole. In this respect, the ensemble does not work on the premise of 'dancers' and 'actors' as binaried signifiers in the dramaturgical composition; those that move versus those that speak. Instead, Punchdrunk performers share an affinity of style in performance, related to the embodied, cinematic and abstracted needs of the world in which they work. Consequently, they may be given differing responsibilities in devising, different approaches in process, and differing functions in directorial vision and composition, resulting in divergent outcomes in performance . . .

Maxine Doyle

On masked show ensembles, dancing and acting

In the creation of the masked shows I work predominantly with the dancer-performers. Dancers have a presence, physicality and a confidence that allows them to take the building on as both lover and enemy. Dancers are at best a beautiful mix of great strength and extreme fragility. Dancers can be great actors and storytellers. Dancers push the process, saying 'yes please', rather than 'no', to our propositions. I remember the first choreographic workshop I led with Felix and a group of dancers. I had set the group a task to play with the relationship of the skin to the surface of the walls, focusing on the actions of slip and slide. There were some beautiful and immediate responses. The rehearsal room was flooded with beginnings of narratives and the space came alive. It was a moment of epiphany for Felix as he could see the potential of a detailed movement-based language to animate an epic space and charge it with atmosphere. Dancers take emotional and physical risks. For the *Faust* audition, we had asked people to bring in one-minute solos based on heaven or hell. Vinicius Salles set up his sound system, took his clothes off and performed a solo where he began to crash, slam and fly through the space like a possessed soul. Needless to say, he got the job.

The dramaturgical approach is chaotic as it flirts with words and eschews logic. A Punchdrunk actor-performer is highly imaginative and collaborative, enjoying the possibility to invent characters in response to space, sound, light and movement. They must enjoy the intricacies of non-linear narrative form and be able to embody a character through movement, action and event. Live spoken text only really appears in one-on-one experiences and, occasionally, in intimate scenes.

Hector Harkness helped to define the performing approach whilst creating the original Malcolm in the first *Sleep No More* in London, 2003. A rhythmical and specific use of small props created a particular kind of movement vocabulary. It drew the audience's eye specifically towards detail whilst playing to them on an intimate scale and directing their focus towards Punchdrunk's idea of the 'live close-up'. The subtleties of small gesture and object manipulation tend towards the cinematic, visual approach of the company. There now exists a beautiful moment in Malcolm's performance in every version of *Sleep No More*, from that first pattern set by Hector, where we watch the character cut out singular lines from a bible with a scalpel with an obsessive precision. The effect for the viewer is immediately cinematic. I often witness masked audience peering over Malcolm's shoulder straining to grasp small details.

Punchdrunk dancer-performers are highly collaborative and able to make movement from the most obscure starting point. They are resilient – happy to be left in a dark room or unfinished space for several hours working on a task. I remember Paul Zivkovich and Rob McNeill desperately trying to create a duet in the trees for *The Drowned Man* whilst battling with the cacophony of chainsaws. The forest was far from finished. The forest duet was just beginning. Previews were a few days away. It was tough.

Entwistle, Codie and Kyle (see also: **Act 1**; adrenalin; **audience**; *Drowned Man, The*; **Enrichment**; *Faust*; *Firebird Ball, The*; **Higgin, Peter**; *Masque of the Red Death, The*; *Sleep No More*, London): Codie and Kyle Entwistle are brothers and former students of Peter Higgin, at Sandown High School on the Isle of Wight. They were members of separate year groups whose combined response to *Sleep No More*, London and *The Firebird Ball* planted a seed of inspiration in Higgin, which grew to become Punchdrunk Enrichment:

Codie: I'd drifted into film and away from theatre, partly because I felt that characters were more 'real' in film. I was always conscious that I was sat in my seat in theatre, watching people on stage; even though I could get into the play and into the acting, there was the convention there that created a barrier. Punchdrunk breaking that barrier did blur a line for me between film and theatre. I remember entering *Sleep No More*, being given a mask, and feeling nervous waiting to go in. It's bizarre to go into something as the spectator where *you* are feeling nervous about it. I immediately separated myself to experience it on my own. I'm more of a traditionalist when it comes to theatre, I need to 'get' it. If have to think too much while I'm watching something I enjoy it less, so I wanted to try and follow the story but quickly realised that I wasn't going to do that. I didn't want to miss anything yet at the same time I was aware that everything was moving. I would flit back and forth between different ways of engaging; studying the rooms I was in, even where there were no performers around, to find all of those little clues, and at the same time, if I got distracted by performers I would immediately follow them. I found it hard to stick to just one method

of experiencing it; I couldn't pre-empt anything. Being up that close to the performers felt raw, powerful, physical, it was visceral. The interaction between the performers and audience was fascinating, it felt like anything could happen at any time. The nervous adrenalin would still be there, especially where I didn't know what was happening or where I was going but it quickly turned to excitement and voyeuristic pleasure.

Kyle: My first direct experience of Punchdrunk was *The Firebird Ball*, which Pete took us to as a school trip. I definitely think that having the mask emboldened me. Entering the space, wearing the mask, I immediately felt like I was part of the play. I was an actor in it as well as a spectator. You're simultaneously aware of both possibilities as it's going on around you; you could sit down at a table and play cards with someone, then be taking in the production design and thinking how incredible it is, every minute detail, while following a performer and trying to get a reaction out of them. What I found when I came out was, while everyone else was discussing, 'oh did you see that bit', and guessing which parts related to each other in the plot, the plot wasn't what interested me at all. Instead I found it was the way in which it had opened up the endless possibilities of what theatre could be that excited me. I was drunk on the sensation of a completely fresh approach to theatre. I switched off my brain in terms of trying to read plot or trying to read anything into it apart from how it felt. I just couldn't shake the amazing feeling of being in there, of what it led me to think in terms of what theatre could be of what my relationship to theatre and to audience could

be. And I couldn't shake how it made me think about how staging could affect storytelling. It was just a hundred and one different things that it offered me in terms of what I'd run with in my own work or simply in terms of how it established ideas in my head.

Codie: One thing that it did for us as students of theatre is make us feel like directors while we were in there; we could direct the version of the play that we wanted to see by having that freedom to roam where we wanted. It empowered us as an audience but also empowered me as an actor, gave me that confidence to be bold.

Kyle: *Firebird Ball* helped a great deal with my essay writing and in regard to interpreting a play by devising around it. Instead of having a conventional response it gave permission to your mind to race and be inventive. It instilled in me the importance of detail in design; the fact that a book could be open and the page could be read. It allowed for certain 'truths' and details in the text to be made present. It made me aware of not cheating the audience, because I hadn't been cheated by Punchdrunk; that had a big impact on me. It took me closer to the characters, closer to the *feeling* in the text. I was definitely influenced by that with my scripted work. With the devised project, it gave me permission to blend genres and styles. With Punchdrunk, the work felt detailed and gritty and honest, contrasted with dancing and stylised fighting. I know that it made me want to be a practitioner. I watched the film *Before Sunset* after seeing Punchdrunk and knew you could do a live performance of that, take your audience walking with you. While you're in character, you could be using the world around you as your stage. It made me *think* more and made me push myself. I feel so proud that this person who gave us so much has been so successful, amazingly so; not just because it's great because someone you know and love and respect is doing well but because they're doing something that is so different, so creative, so boundary pushing. You can see their influence in the amount of immersive theatre experiences that are going on now; there's Punchdrunk-influenced practice everywhere. It was something that informed a lot of our creativity at a point when it meant so much, where it gave us the stuff that took us on through the next ten or twenty years. It informed our appreciation of film, and that became our livelihood. It informed our love of theatre. It informed how we might look at art.

Codie: It made us smarter and it made us more critical, more analytical when it came to study in general as much as studying theatre. Theatre can so often be thought of as an easy subject. For us, Punchdrunk's work gave more weight to the subject. It's directly influenced how we've thought about things, the level of detail we notice, and the passion that we have for the arts.

epic (see also: **awe and wonder**; durational; Enrichment; experiential; masked shows; reveal; **ritual**; scale; text; transformation and transportation; visceral. Further reading: Cremin, Swann, Colvert and Oliver 2016; Miles 2015; Tims 2016): Not to be confused with Bertolt Brecht's 'Epic Theatre'. In the context of Punchdrunk's practice, epic is applied more broadly as a descriptive term. The creative team sometimes uses this term to refer to scale; comparing the concentrated and intimate to the grand and epic in design. In immersive practice it can name events that are 'both grand in execution and profound in appreciation' (Machon 2013a, 26).

Equally, the weight of carefully constructed and highly ritualised intimate encounters can still manifest a sense of the epic in theme, form and outcome. This is an attention to impressive production values that results in a potent quality of shared experience among audience members that, at its most impactful (whether on an intimate or large scale), can influence and transform individual behaviour and/ or knowledge. The event overall and/ or moments from the event in these instances transcend an evening's entertainment and potentially alter outlook on the work, on the ideas in the work, on the experience of the everyday.

If an intention is to wake up the sensory system of an audience member in a Punchdrunk world, the after-effects of this are likely to remain, perhaps to enlightening or creative ends. A measure of success is the direct impact on the creative and philosophical outlook of an individual and the way in which the experience of the show becomes part of that individual's personal folklore. The themes and narratives present within the source material are intended to shape the potency of the experience according to broad or specific philosophical ends. The themes of many of Punchdrunk's source texts have an inherent humanity at the core of the work which can inspire contemplation of human experiences, in a simultaneously immediate and layered manner within and beyond the immersive world. Profound responses are possible when the audience member feels the immediate, visceral quality of the Punchdrunk interpretation collide with the context driven, weightiness and complexity of narrative or theme. The immersive form enables a direct and multisensorial engagement with ideas as much as narratives.

ethics (see also: **caretaking**; **one-on-one**. Further reading: Frieze 2017, 135–202; LaFrance 2013; Ridout 2009; Wake 2017; White 2013; Zerihan et al. 2009): In any form of participatory performance, formal safeguarding procedures should be in place that relate to the mechanisms employed to enable shared participation in the event and ensure the safekeeping of participants

and artists alike. Experiential theatres in general require significant thought in regard to issues of ethics, safeguarding and approaches to regulation. At the time of writing this is only just beginning in regard to cultural debate between artists and audiences. Punchdrunk has been concerned with this area since inception and remains sensitive to its importance and the need to evolve appropriate methods in line with developments in the work and changing attitudes of audiences. Standard health and safety principles alongside wider company ethics are in place for any Punchdrunk project, whether large or small scale. Formal and legal procedures are followed in line with host community ethics for any Enrichment project. The detailed safeguarding procedure for one-on-ones, as detailed in the entry below, illustrate the time and attention put into caretaking and, specifically here, to the ethical implications of the practice. Examples of more general Punchdrunk safeguarding practices, beyond the creative mechanisms for establishing 'rules of conduct' in the worlds created, include information provided on publicity and at point of ticket sales regarding practical requirements for any event on comfortable shows and access needs. Lesser-known and anonymised safeguarding procedures are in place for audience members who choose to disclose a specific condition or need that may influence an ability to interact with the event, providing them with discreet, wearable tags that are a sign to performers to know not to engage in any form of interaction with that audience member during the event.

Every Good Boy Deserves Favour (**2009**, see also: Act 1; Hytner, Nicholas; **Morris, Tom**; **music**; National Theatre, The): A National Theatre production of Tom Stoppard's 1977 play, written for performers and an orchestra with an original score by Andre Previn, co-directed by Felix Barrett and Tom Morris, with choreography by Maxine Doyle. The title of the play refers to the mnemonic for the arpeggiated musical chord comprising the notes EGBDF. Although not a Punchdrunk production, this was an interesting experiment for Barrett, who took up the invitation purely because of the orchestral element. The ensemble of dancers for the production included key Punchdrunk performers Sarah Dowling, Conor Doyle, Geir Hytten, Rob McNeill, Emily Mytton, Fernanda Prata and Vinicius Salles.

exercises (see also: architecture; building: 'chairs'; characters; Enrichment Symposium; eyes; framing: Hide-and-Seek; lens; lighting; 'listening to the building'; music; one-on-one; **process**; **research**; text: Further reading: Higgin 2017): There are few 'Punchdrunk' exercises other than the trusted and repeated examples of Felix Barrett's 'Hide-and-Seek' and 'listening to the building' provided in this encyclopaedia, which are the techniques employed to initiate masked shows. Additional exercises with adults that are facilitated in Enrichment workshops, whether on-site at Fallow Cross or shared as part of teacher-training sessions, as Peter Higgin puts it, 'provide a way into thinking about working through Punchdrunk-like processes' and are included in this encyclopaedia under apposite entries, identified as just that, 'A way into . . .'. For Barrett, 'so much of the process is instinctual' and relies on a shared sensibility among the team, which is exercised by the concept and research for a project itself. Developing, and so trusting in, a sensibility that is shared among the mainstay of the core creative team, as Barrett notes, is attributable to 'exposing ourselves to the right inspiration and influences – that's crucial'. He clarifies, 'we'll always have a couple of pieces of music, we'll know a film, obviously a source text and, significantly, knowing the building. From that we respond and build the work instinctively', focusing the world through a kaleidoscopic lens. This ongoing research and shared imagining results in the core team trusting that individuals are independently 'making the right creative choices and knowing, feeling when it's right to jettison ideas'. Choosing a source text, usually a play, refocusing that through the right 'lens', intertextualising with appropriate sources, making that work in the right building, is part of the Punchdrunk process and as fundamental as any exercise that might be layered on top to,

as Higgin puts it, 'get you there. Any exercise we might use on top of that, or creative imagining through those sources in our approach, is always about building the conditions to make work'.

Exeter Experiments (see also: **Act 1**; Act 3; **Barrett, Felix**; **durational**; **failure**; Fallow Cross; 'Grandmother's Room'; *H.G.*; Higgin, Peter; **Hodge, Stephen**; **installation**; intervention; **loops**; **mask**; masked shows; Maybank, Euan; music; **one-on-one**; police; pyrotechnics; ritual; *Woyzeck*, **2000**): Felix Barrett studied drama at Exeter University, from 1997–2000, following a gap year post A Level study. Interviewed by Jane Milling, Professor in Drama at Exeter University, Barrett shared his experience of *H.G.*, using this as a springboard to discuss 'installation as a theatrical form' and his desire to use undergraduate study to investigate the question:

if *H.G.* was the theatrical starting point, what comes next? I knew you could *feel* the presence of performers in it, so what happens if you actually interrogate the presence of performers in the installation space; and if they weren't in this space what were they doing somewhere else?
(Barrett 2012)

Barrett's undergraduate years gave him a technical training, a theoretical underpinning and the time, space and resources for artistic experimentation. Learning costume, advancing lighting skills, and discovering the disappointments of directing text under traditional, naturalistic constraints were significant aspects of his three years. It was at Exeter University that Barrett tried and tested the forms that would become signature to the Punchdrunk aesthetic. It was also here that he met Peter Higgin, who would go on to become his longest-standing creative collaborator and the Director of Punchdrunk Enrichment.

The Drama Department curriculum at the time, led by Christopher McCullogh, with Stephen Hodge, Milling and Jon Primrose proving especially supportive of Barrett's work, followed an approach that, as Hodge describes below, was built

on 'a European Laboratory Theatre model'. Barrett relished the focus on 'practice and experimentation and getting things wrong'. A lesson that remains with Barrett from this was 'the "fail better" idea, better to run before you can walk'. It was like being up in the attic or building dens, 'eight hours a day of making' and testing ideas, testing the limits of the imagination to make work. Barrett recalls the effectiveness of one exercise around activating space that examined the effect of 'one performer in a room and another performer who walked from the other end of the building, outside, singing, so sound entered the space and the focus was pulled outside to in' (Barrett 2012). Throughout his own experimentation the incorporation of music and a sensitivity to the experiential impact of space became vital to his practice, not only in the aesthetic outcome but also as tools employed to prepare collaborating performers for practice.

For Barrett, it was 'all about the third year', the year where students were able to focus and structure their investigations and to specialise in a particular discipline. Barrett followed Directing, and Higgin, Applied Theatre. Barrett was keen to take risks, hungry to innovate: 'I'm in my third year at Exeter, I'm finally Directing. I'd always felt the gravitas of that; that this was the biggest, real opportunity to try some stuff out'. It was during this year that Barrett finally tested his ambition to explore installation and forms inspired by live art, specifically in regard to one-on-ones and duration. Finding his aesthetic became paramount, right down to demonstrating this with every adjunct of Barrett's practice, including the written support for his practical projects being presented as experiential documents to be read, while listening to selected music or culminating in setting off a flare.

Barrett notes that Hodge 'really got what I was doing' and provided expert feedback which encouraged Barrett to critique his practice and the original techniques he was developing (Barrett 2012). Consequently, he created a series of one-on-ones, with a pivotal piece, *La Mer*, referencing the Claude Debussy symphony used as soundscore, which took place at a swimming pool and is described in detail by Hodge below. Looking back, Barrett adds, 'the timeline of the one-on-one begins with that swimming pool encounter. That was the major one, the breakthrough'.

Barrett's Directing assessment comprised three parts: a monologue from *Faust*, a duologue that followed more conventional, studio-based rehearsal techniques and a piece created for a found space. With the monologue, Barrett extended his investigation into one-on-one encounters, framed by his interest in urban mythology, examining the murky hinterland between the real and the imagined, the seen and the invented. He was as concerned with the experiential themes at the heart of Goethe's *Faust*, and how he might create a mythology and contemporise Faust's story, as he was with the psychology and narrative of Faust's pact with Mephistopheles. It was a piece that was conceived and designed for people to see from their cars – at sixty miles per hour, for no more than a matter of seconds – on the road that led out of Exeter to Crediton with ominous forest either side. The audience were the unsuspecting passengers of the cars speeding past:

> It wasn't about the text, it wasn't about them hearing the language, it was about the narrative. I wanted it to get in the newspapers and for people to think they'd seen something they couldn't explain. It was also intended to blur art and life, making the drivers think they'd seen something real.
>
> (Barrett 2012)

The blurring of art and life also related to the manner in which Barrett worked with Joel Scott, playing Faust, employing interventions as process. From macabre parcels in the post to staged scenarios put on by friends with secret photographs that might make Scott question the real and the imagined, this was all under the auspice of a signed pact that Barrett 'would do anything for him that he wanted and would be on call twenty-four hours a day as long as

I was allowed to do anything to him in the way of rehearsal technique' (Barrett 2000). It was performed across an hour from the stroke of midnight on 'a scary, windy night, autumn term, so magic was in the air', with the dramatic crescendo of Faust's demise occurring in 'the beat of the moment'. It relied on those in their cars witnessing an image which appears out of context, flashing past, 'what you don't see rather than what you do see, with the imagination filling in the gaps' (Barrett 2012). Barrett recollects how one car slowed down, stopped, 'really very frightening'. Barrett, as director, was already hidden from view; Scott, the lone performer on the road, had time to panic and hid. A door opened and a person patrolled around and then left. This was swiftly followed by another car arriving, this time Exeter's constabulary with a warning of 'we've got dogs here'. It was this piece that marked the first visit from the police to Barrett's theatrical experiments and evidenced, somewhat, the potential to create the stuff of urban legend.

Forced back into a studio exploration with text and two performers for the duologue exercise, Barrett knew that he was being reprimanded for 'not playing by the rules' with his *Faust* experiment. The most valuable lesson this taught him was how he would not practise again. Instead, it was with the full and final production created for a found space that confirmed the approach that would become signature to Barrett: 'I was building up to that, I always knew that was where I was heading' (2012). Having located a former territorial army barracks, Georg Büchner's story of the desperate and doomed soldier, Woyzeck, was ripe for interpretation. Büchner's text, for Barrett, was 'so sumptuously succinct that it worked perfectly'. Deconstructing it further, responding to the manner in which the play was 'so sparse', enabled Barrett to begin to explore a stylised performance language with collaborating actors that corresponded to the installation in design, 'everything taken up with ritual, there's a lot of eating peas or shaving the captain, a lot of it is already gestural'. The barracks unlocked the text through form, 'I wanted to get a big, sprawling,

empty building after dark, light it with candles, dress it, installation, building into the space, so it was just as much art gallery inspired by the text as it was theatre show. Strip the text back, put it on a loop'. A nagging problem, present in Barrett's thinking since his second experience of *H.G.*, was solved, three weeks before *Woyzeck* opened:

> I knew what wasn't going to work, the audience getting in the way. I kept thinking, the audience are going to assume that fellow audience members are performers. I've had two eureka moments in my life and that was one; if we mask them they become invisible. I knew immediately it should be a neutral mask – we'd played with them throughout university – because that way an audience member could become anything.
>
> (2012)

Barrett took the edited version of Büchner's play and repeated twenty minutes of content for each performer, three times across three hours. There was no composed sound or music employed in this production; instead, in the tempo of the ritualised movement, sound was naturally created by performers as they worked. Barrett traversed the building in a mask setting off firecrackers to keep the audience on their toes, 'in a constant state of apprehension', matching the noise of the drum that he had found for the Drum Major's motif, performed by Euan Maybank: 'the crack of the snare would startle' (Barrett 2012). Barrett notes of the Punchdrunk aesthetic, 'everything was in *Woyzeck*', down to human hair collected from barbers, scents, employed around the space and taxidermy. There was a ringmaster on the gate who allowed audience members to go through individually, where they were ritually masked and entered a fairground, the portal that delineated the entering of Woyzeck's world. This production set the now classic Punchdrunk loop structure. Barrett's coursework portfolio for this project records that first loop diagram, with the structure of 'Grandmother's Room', working on its own distinct loop at its centre, the one-on-one encounter that has 'been in every show since then' (Barrett 2012) (see Figure 13). The loop was an essential discovery yet, for Barrett, 'it was the mask that was the real turning point' (Barrett 2013). *Woyzeck*, 2000 was pivotal to Punchdrunk's practice. Barrett had found the aesthetic for which he had been striving since his A Level study:

I knew it was my aesthetic. I remember at the time one of my peers telling me that she'd really enjoyed it and I saw in her eyes that it had done something to her and she said, you've got to do that again. At that point I was used to either teachers or friends saying, keep up the good work, but this was someone who was an acquaintance. It was so raw, I knew I'd found my thing.

(2012)

Higgin, who played the Captain, recollects:

I'd visited the barracks beforehand with Felix and remember climbing and crawling around derelict parts of the building. For the performance I was recovering from a peritonitis operation and probably shouldn't have been sitting in a cold, damp room, the floor of which was covered in human hair. Every half hour I was shaved by the performer playing Woyzeck. Oddly, from that moment on, I was hooked.

Barrett's three years at Exeter University had given him the space, time, resources and tutelage to enable him to realise inchoate theatrical ambitions. Despite his friends and family being in London, and a theatre scene that was beckoning to him which made it inevitable that Barrett would return, he 'made a decision to stay in Exeter another year in order to make more mistakes to try and refine the form':

The one thing I learned from university, above all else, was the best that you can do is make a mistake, learn from getting it wrong. I knew Exeter was a safe space where I could get it wrong and it wouldn't matter, that if I got to London it

would matter. With the installation module, I was given free rein, where I had twelve weeks to test my own hypothesis. I created ten miniprojects and got used to the pace of churning stuff out. I wanted to keep up that momentum, deliberately try to be as broad as possible. I wanted to carry on experimenting to see what worked what didn't. I'd got to a place where I had so many ideas I wanted to test, I had to keep that going otherwise it would burn out and the reality, the grind of the real world would slow that down. The last thing I wanted to do was spend a year speculating. I saw peers hypothesise about the type of work they'd like to make or what their company name would be, what their logo would be, and none of them ever made a show. For me it wasn't about the company or branding, I just wanted to try and explore new ways for audiences to experience.

(2013)

While volunteering as a runner in his year out, a photographer had told him, 'don't talk about it, do it'. Barrett emphasises, 'I lived by that. There's no point in talking about setting up a theatre company, just make the work. I may not have always wanted an audience to come and see it, but I knew I had to make it'. Remaining in Exeter, at the time, offered Barrett an affordable artistic environment alongside the opportunity to continue collaborating with likeminded peers who had also chosen to stay in the city. Remaining attached to the university provided practical support and resources: 'I had the backing of the university . . . access to lighting kit, space, tech capability' (2013). Equally important was the continued nurturing of the Exeter 'philosophy'; having 'a safe space' to take further risks and to learn from failing better' (2013). Barrett notes that across his three years of study, being encouraged and allowed to make work 'under the university's auspices was a crazy opportunity' and reiterates the significance of the support of his tutors directly following graduation. A fitting tribute to the work of Exeter University specifically and,

more generally, to a British university system that continues to support innovative arts programmes. It was this environment which, beyond graduation, nurtured the innovative practice of what was to become, with Barrett at its helm, a leading and internationally renowned British theatre company.

experiential (see also: immersive; **senses**; **visceral**. Further reading: Machon 2011; Welton 2011): Defining that which relates to or is derived from embodied experience, where the holistic body is the conduit for receiving and interpreting an event. Experiential performance practice is wholly aligned with immersive theatre and pertains to physical and visual practices which enable the audience to undergo an encounter with ideas, themes, narratives and situations in an embodied manner, which directly influences immediate and subsequent comprehension and interpretations of that work.

eyes (see also: audience; caretaking; **close-up**; exercises; **focus**; **one-on-one**; **restraint**): Hours of rehearsal are taken up addressing the use of the eyes in performance for the one-on-one performers. The art of a one-on-one is often expressed and understood in terms of an understanding of what proximity to eyes and communicating through eye contact invites and permits. Eye contact is vital when little or no verbal language is employed. In masked shows, there is also an art to preventing eye contact, despite being in close proximity to a lone audience member. Equally the art of directing the audience to the detail, the story, through the performer's line of vision nuances the performing style. Felix Barrett notes how Vinicius Salles is expert at manipulating audience attention 'with a flick of an eye'. Similarly, Risa Steinberg in her discussion of *Sleep No More*, NYC talks of 'eye focus' vs 'body focus', noting how the audience 'see you *seeing*' when performing in these worlds. Punchdrunk performers become adept at mastering the use of the eyes to achieve the performance objective, and to ensure an element of caretaking and control is always present for themselves as much as the audience member . . .

A way into . . . making eye contact

This exercise is intended to encourage intimacy, openness and uninhibited communication between performers. It can build confidence in making eye contact, as well as helping an ensemble to understand the power in, or problems of, breaking eye contact. It can help the performers become more skilled at working towards achieving shared or individual objectives, primarily through eye contact. It tends to work best if one person remains outside as the director, calling instruction, helping to set the tempo as required, perhaps introducing music. As with all these approaches, it can be adopted and adapted to suit the needs of the practice . . .

As a group, walk at a slow to regular pace around the space and gradually become aware of the group then individuals within it by looking at them as you pass.

Hold eye contact with someone and allow 'a moment' to pass between you.

Hold eye contact with someone and make a comment about what you see: 'You have brown hair'; 'You're smiling'. The recipient of the comment repeats, 'I have brown hair' or 'I'm smiling', then offers an observation of their own, which is in turn repeated. Thank each other and move on. These comments must be factual and not based on opinion or any sense of judgement.

At a given point spend a longer time with a partner and allow this to become a 'back and forth' series of observations.

Return to walking around, observing, holding eye contact, sharing 'a moment', without talking.

Come to a halt.

Fluidly, from one of these shared moments, choose a partner without speaking but by fixing your chosen person through eye contact alone.

In these pairs, take it in turns to explore leading and mirroring each other, only through eye contact.

Begin with the slightest, smallest actions then, gradually, allow motion, gesture and movements to become more expansive.

Experiment with pace, proximity and emotional intention.

As you become more confident, rather than taking it in turns on instruction, allow this to become a flowing 'back and forth' sharing of the leading and responding. Think of it as an 'eye contact conversation'.

Try it all again with music.

Talk about all you discover.

What could you do with this now?

F

failure (see also: **accidents**; **Act 1**; Act 3; Exeter Experiments; **process**; **R&D**): Punchdrunk acknowledges the significance of taking time and space to experiment and learn through failing. As Felix Barrett puts it, 'only when pushing beyond comfort zones and the known can you make breakthroughs'. To achieve this the core team and its collaborators need to learn from the failing. Peter Higgin adds:

Failure and learning is inherent within our practice. Punchdrunk's development has been iterative and has always adapted and responded to audience reaction. Many 'failings', which might also be opportunities, are only discovered in the process of delivering the work. Punchdrunk maintains a desire to improve the work and learn from mistakes. Increasingly these experiences have led to the team trying to foreground potential challenges and problem-solve in advance. Our motto: learn from your mistakes and try not to make the same mistake twice, in order to identify the future areas of risk and put in place measures to avoid these. It is this attention to detail and integrity that allow us to create work of this nature. Every project is unique and often needs to develop new producing and production models to enable them. The many variables associated with this work inevitably produce 'failures', and so always 'learning'. It's necessary to the process.

Fallow Cross (see also: **Act 3**; community; **digital technologies**; **Enrichment**; failure; *Kabeiroi*; **Oracles, The**; **R&D**; *Small Tale, The*; *Small Wonders*): An R&D space for Punchdrunk, based in Tottenham Hale, London. Fallow Cross is a purpose-built village (hence also referred to by the team as 'The Village'), built within a former warehouse, as Punchdrunk's first ever creative home, outside of any production space. Fallow Cross takes its name from the restorative notion of leaving agricultural land

to lie fallow for a period, without being ploughed, harrowed and sown, in order to restore its fertility, nurture its inherent components and avoid surplus production. The move to Fallow Cross marked the beginning of Act 3, establishing a nurturing space for Punchdrunk to innovate, incubate and explore its future artistic and Enrichment practice; ideas that spanned the breadth of the company's work. Felix Barrett summarises:

The village houses a series of structures – that include the church, the school room, the bric-a-brac shop and the Mayor's house – each of which hold the kernel of an idea and provide a creative space to research and develop those ideas further. It enables us to develop the use and integration of digital technologies to create a new theatrical vernacular. It allows us to fuse these experiments with our innovative enrichment projects, providing an opportunity for young audiences to help imagine and uncover the future of our work. And it is a laboratory to nurture Punchdrunk's creative team, unlocking new ideas.

Fallow Cross gave a home to projects developed with and for the local Haringey community with an aim to roll these out on a national level. It hosted a programme of workshops and professional development opportunities for artists and teachers to share Punchdrunk's established methodologies. Alex Rowse, Enrichment Producer, observes:

Fallow Cross has been a turning point, offering a unique period of R&D for Punchdrunk, where the learning is shared to every department. *The Oracles* is Punchdrunk's first videogame cross-fading into real life. Created solely for Haringey primary school children, this learning at Fallow Cross feeds a huge ambition for Punchdrunk's future international programme for adults, and demonstrates the commitment to innovation in the audience experience. The scale and quality of all of Punchdrunk's work

runs through the Enrichment programme. Our parameters may be different to the work for a wider public but the ambition and quality is the same. Because the learning or social objectives at the heart of the work are so important and certain, we can be increasingly experimental with how we take participants there. It's strange to think back to the moment when the Fallow Cross build was complete and deciding how to use it, without the pressure of a public production. Significantly, Felix and Pete reassured us that whatever projects we planned and delivered there, it was okay to fail. Now, it's busy with live, board-game experiments, sound R&D, workshops, ambitious productions for children; impossible to imagine Punchdrunk now without some kind of laboratory at its core.

Faust (**2006–2007**; see also: **Act 1**; adrenalin; **'Bad Bar'**; Bicât, Tina; cinematic; cornfield; *Firebird Ball, The*; forest; Harvey, Robin; influences; intervention; lens; **lifts**; **masks**; **music**; **'space-hunting'**; touch-real): An adaptation of Johann Wolfgang von Goethe's *Faust*, reimagined in small-town America, through the lens of Edward Hopper paintings, David Lynch's *Twin Peaks* and hints of Alan Parker's neo-noir *Angelheart*. Presented within a massive, disused warehouse on, at that time, unrenovated land, 21 Wapping Lane, East London, as Felix Barrett elaborates:

A significant part for us as a small company was that we agreed we would do a show, divided the A–Z map of London and spent the first nine months all walking the zones of London, looking for a building. It was as much part of the project as everything that followed. A lot of our collaborators helped out. We walked every street, noted every building that was empty. We then spent three months playing detective, finding out who owned them, ringing up, trying to get anyone to pick up the phone. It was a project in its own right. It felt exhilarating,

FIGURE 7 *Faust*. 2007. L–R: Fernanda Prata, Geir Hytten.

Photo credit: Stephen Dobbie

travelling obscure roads, always looking up. Ground level is full of façade and cover. If you want to know the real city you look at first, second floors and above. Hector [Harkness] found Wapping Lane. It buzzed with the sound of electricity outside, an electric fence or a broken pylon. Already that building was imbued with a crazy magic. We really believe in hiding the impact of the building by finding the most anticlimactic way in. With *Firebird*, Offley Works, you entered through a side entrance, so the size of the building was all reveal. But this was jutting like a single tooth on the horizon, awe-inspiring, domineering. We knew it broke that golden rule, so we did the opposite; made the audience question if they should enter something so domineering; made them go all the way around to appreciate its scale. Plus, it had a big danger sign at its entrance when we first visited it. We wanted our audience to discover it in that same way, have that sense of foreboding, which is why we repositioned that sign and added a 'Danger Asbestos'. It was a deliberate intervention so audience would feel wrong-footed. All conscious decisions because we knew that was where the show started.

Barrett recalls finding dark, desolate stories, underscored by beleaguered hope, when he first entered and explored the site; a Christmas tree with a handwritten note saying, 'kid zone, children only, no drink, no drugs, no dogs', written by a child; 'Tilly's Naughty Room', a long, thin dark space with just a stool at the far end, the sign in Tilly's handwriting; 'the whole space felt contaminated with a darkness'. The building was squalid, with a putrid smell caused not only by various animal faeces but by 'rotten meat' left by the previous occupants, squatters who had been evicted, possibly leftover animal food or a leaving gift, 'chucked in to leave a fetid scent explosion'. These factors alongside the overwhelming repetitive, claustrophobic feeling of the building immediately

told Barrett that this was the home for *Faust*. It required a major overhaul, which meant long days and nights cleaning, making the space safe, and reworking it to build the world. Barrett recalls how he, Stephen Dobbie, Peter Higgin and Colin Nightingale, following the form set by *Firebird*, slept on-site during the build; latterly, 'Dobbie and I would check into the Motel. It was just a given that we had to sleep in the space. It was part of the ethos of creating the world'.

With the vast size of the building, the design approach also expanded, with the support of volunteers. It was here that Beatrice Minns volunteered for the first time. Robin Harvey worked closely with Barrett to lead on the design, with Livi Vaughan now working across rooms to source and install props (rather than scavenging from the Barrett family home). At Maxine Doyle's recommendation, Tina Bicât collaborated as costume designer, to layer further the detail of the world. Bicât recalls walking into the building, 'to see all these weird things on the floor; a telephone, a skull, a mannequin head, a stuffed squirrel, all lined up. They were clearly organised, an organisation of such emotional muddle, yet I could see there was a logic to it'.

Faust also saw Punchdrunk's ensemble shift gear, with performers joining, like Conor Doyle, who instantly understood the choreographic interactions so expertly established by the likes of Sarah Dowling and Rob McNeill, alongside Vinicius Salles and Fernanda Prata, who for Maxine Doyle, 'exploded the work, brought a dangerous, visceral quality to the process':

They offered a very particular Brazilian fire. Both had already established careers as dance artists in Brazil and with Jasmin Vardimon in London. They had a real hunger to perform in such a different context. Both were fearless performers driving a more immediate connection with both cast and audience. The character of Mephistopheles was born during Vinicius's audition for *Faust*.

We had invited dancers and actors to bring a one-minute solo based on the themes of heaven and hell. I remember so clearly the moment Vinicius, stood up, very functionally took off his clothes and then began to repeatedly throw himself to the ground. This was a man in hell.

For Maxine Doyle, the performance language created for *Faust* 'really matched the building' (2013). With a cast made up of members now familiar with the form, and new additions to the cast who added to the requisite adrenalin while deft in handling the nuances of interaction, the Punchdrunk partnership between building, dance and audience immersion really came into its own. For Barrett, Salles as Mephistopheles was exemplary of such technique:

Vini was the first performer that I met whose towering presence was a match for the scale of the building. He's the ultimate master of manipulating an audience. The way he can control a crowd, without them realising, move them, direct them around the space with a flick of an eye, the turn of a hand. If he suspends his breath the whole audience will stop. It's like he's an elemental magician, deploying an audience as a force.

To match the enhancements to the performance language, technical operations also shifted up a gear; lighting was present in every room, with the cornfield solely animated through light. Stephen Dobbie's soundscore loomed, as vast and ominous as the building in which it dwelled, more complicated than before across sixteen sound zones, all needing to be worked by the technical team and cast, stage managed by Aaron Minnigin, as Prata recalls:

Nowadays, in terms of the technical elements, you just press a button and the whole show starts. With *Faust* you had different people with radios in different rooms counting in over walkie-talkies to press the button and make the sound work.

For the powerful crescendo, *Faust* employed Luigi Cherubini's Requiem in C Minor, brought in by a live rendition of the opening bars of the music, a solo soprano performed by Meline Danielewicz, encapsulating and determining the atmosphere and emotion of Faust's demise. Dobbie's composition also led the transition from this powerful sequence in the bowels of the building to the audience's decompression chamber of the bar, subtly controlling the flow of the audience, as Barrett describes:

The sound deconstructs; the orchestra breaks into this twenty-second-long, slow reverb in which it pulls you down, controlled by the sound you're led through to the bar as the lights go down behind you and then the band in the bar strikes up.

Punchdrunk was assisted by box office support and publicity from The National Theatre for the first time with this production. Barrett remembers 'going to the South Bank to see the poster and just marvelling at it. Thinking how bizarre it was that this made it look completely professional, and there we were living in the space, trying to get it on, no sleep, no food'. In a similar vein, Salles recalls of this, his first experience with Punchdrunk:

Faust was such an important moment in my life for so many reasons. It was my first contact with Max and Felix, fantastic scenes, everything was so new even the audience was different to audiences in more traditional shows. Not only for the different demographic, because the tickets were cheaper, but because they also didn't know what to expect. With *Faust*, I knew that Punchdrunk was different. It was a small company, run by friends; it felt like a family. Back then, the way in which Punchdrunk shows were made, there was only ever one performer for each character and we played all the shows. There was no sense at that point of a set language

or a formula of what worked, everything felt experimental.

For Higgin, who left teaching to assist with production management, '*Faust* felt like the moment we entered the wider theatre-going consciousness'. Nightingale describes *Faust* as 'the supersize version of *Firebird*' and took Punchdrunk 'to a place of public notoriety', which ensured 'when *The Masque of the Red Death* opened it was completely sold out'. Created and set up to run for only six weeks, the success of the production, primarily through word-of-mouth, saw it run for six months, the commitment to *Masque* bringing it to a close. Barrett concludes that the process matched the source in its epic nature, no doubt influenced by the building. Echoing Nightingale's maxim that the process of the early projects was reflected in each source:

We took three months to make it, seven-day weeks. It was a phenomenal strain, I've never been so tired, it almost broke us all. Colin would say that *Faust* is about darkness and we came very close to it. That, mixed with the heady euphoria knowing that we were being backed by The National. Same old process but now a different level of awareness.

Firebird Ball, The (**2005**; see also: accidents; **Act 1**; audience; **bar**; *Faust*; forests; Hargreaves, Kate; Hytner, Nicholas; intervention; lighting; loops; *Masque of the Red Death, The*; McDermott, Laura; Morris, Tom; **scenography**): A fusion of Shakespeare's *Romeo and Juliet* and Igor Stravinsky's ballet *The Firebird*, *The Firebird Ball* played out across a vast disused factory site, The Offley Works in Oval, South London. For Felix Barrett, this production was innovative for the team in terms of the design process, and 'significantly helped by Colin Nightingale coming fully on board. For the first time, production management came into play, working out the highest level of spatial transformation we could get for the tiny budget. Super resourceful':

Firebird was the first time we spent six weeks, seven days a week, designing into the space. It was the biggest leap up in design terms. Where *Sleep No More* completely overhauled the performance language, *Firebird* overhauled the approach to design. For the first time, we lived in the space, slept on the floor, freezing cold, working eighteen hours a day wholly on design. Sleep at four, wake at eight and go straight into it. It was punitive. With *Sleep No More*, London we'd taken just a weekend. Here we had six weeks with around thirty people on-site coming and going, with a core of six of us working every hour, every day. We had fifty rooms and designed into all of them. We knew we needed a forest, it was in the text, and we knew we wanted it to break up the space as the pine trees had in *Sleep No More*. To do that on this warehouse scale we reused the fabric from *Chair* and stylised the forest. Being limited by resource made for inventive design.

This was large-scale scenography 'rather than intervention through design'. Previously, the found spaces had each had an individual character and atmosphere that predetermined the design, which Barrett and team then sympathetically responded to with distilled installations and adjustments; minimalist interventions that accented spaces, candles highlighting the existing cracks in the wall, single objects set in the glow of a domestic lamp, furniture carefully positioned the wrong way around to skew logic. With no money and little time it had been a quick and effective approach that could be achieved over a weekend. With *The Firebird Ball*, in contrast, the design had scaled up to match a larger site with a longer get-in. As with previous projects a team of collaborators, now including Livi Vaughan, plus resident performers, such as Kate Hargreaves and Hector Harkness, were setting individual spaces (a feature that continued until *Masque*). Barrett notes, this approach remained true to the company building ethic, 'absorbing likeminded people who

△
FIGURE 8 *The Firebird Ball*. 2005.

Poster archive, designed by Stephen Dobbie

got it'. Kate Hargreaves and Vaughan had written emails directly to Barrett, articulating their response to the work in such a way that he was keen for them to join in. This was to be the last project for which this happened as so many requests were to follow that a volunteer system was put in place for *Faust*.

The Firebird Ball was also the first time that a one-on-one was worked into a masked event, in a compartmentalised manner, different to the original one-on-one styled scenes in *Woyzeck*, 2000, and to those that ran in a more improvisational and organic manner within *Woyzeck* at The Big Chill in 2004, as described by Sam Booth above. With *The Firebird Ball* the one-on-one was incorporated as an element that could be inserted and repeated to multiple individual audience members on its own loop within the wider loops of the narrative arc; with a new and vital feature being the removal of the audience-participant's mask. This structure was established to enable, and eventually ensure, that a greater number of people could experience. The one-on-one was delivered, wholly in French, by Pauline Huguet, as Juliet's Nurse. She inhabited a hospital room, adjacent to the fabric forest on the first floor of the building and took selected patients into a consultancy room, locked the door, invited the patient to lie on a couch as she removed the mask. Nightingale recalls, 'it made you feel naked, exposed, created an intensity in performance'. *The Firebird Ball* was also the first masked show to incorporate an entrance bar as portal, acclimatising guests to the world. Hargreaves and Harkness were the hosts, welcoming audience, seating them around cocktail tables surrounding the stage on which the band played, then returning to each table to invite people, by name, into the masking room before sending them into the world.

From the build to previews, the project was typically 'hand-to-mouth'; Barret, Nightingale, Pete Higgin and Stephen Dobbie living on-site with no showers, pushing on to finish the job; Barret's mother, Margaret, running the box office during her lunch hour from the family home; a manual lighting-desk borrowed from Alleyn's School via former teacher Matthew Grant. It was Barret who operated the lighting, Euan Maybank helping out on certain nights. Barret recalls:

It was euphoric. I could control the arc of the crescendo, could feel the music and push the slider in response. In both *Sleep No More* and *Firebird* we were only able to prioritise one space with lighting, for the crescendo, once each hour. I would be able to go around and see the show, just be back to cue the slider for those five minutes. It was only ever one light coming on but it was pretty high impact. I would pull down the shadowy state to nothing, total darkness, then pull up the opposing state. That shift felt monumental in a large environment, partnering the sound.

Barret's recollections of a *Firebird* preview provide an illustration of the hand-to-mouth nature of the work, yet how this itself inspired an accidental moment of awe and wonder:

The power blew, with the audience already there, so the audience lit much of the show, of their own volition, with their phones. It was a beautiful moment and they thought that was the way we'd intended them to watch it.

The Firebird Ball ran for six weeks, which allowed word-of-mouth to spread in a manner that previous shorter runs had prevented. It turned out to be pivotal in terms of public profile, the brutal work rewarded with reviews in London and national press. Laura McDermott, who volunteered as a steward, would go on to become a producer at BAC, commission *The Yellow Wallpaper* and be instrumental to the development of *The Masque of the Red Death*. *Firebird* also ignited the interest of Tom Morris, an associate director at the National Theatre who took along Nicholas Hytner, then Artistic Director, which set in motion a relationship that would support *Faust*, *Masque* and *The Drowned Man*.

flow (see also: **audience**; **building**; caretaking; found space; loops; masked shows; mazes; narrative; **queues**; tempo): Flow is both artistic device and practical preoccupation within any masked show. It is dictated by the building, the manner in which it invites a journey through the space from its emotional as much as its architectural blueprint. The way the audience and performers flow around a site is an important consideration when assessing the suitability of a building for a production. The location, quantity and width of staircases are an important factor in the audience members' overall experience as they explore across the different floors of a building. Punchdrunk continually attends to the potential frustration of dead ends and always aims to create a circular flow around a floor to minimise the need for an audience member to keep going back on themselves and to avoid performer 'loops' crossing over unless the narrative requires it.

forests (see also: *Apricot Orchard*; cornfield; *Drowned Man, The*; *Duchess of Malfi, The*; *Faust*; *Firebird Ball, The*; **long shot**; *Masque of the Red Death, The*; mass production; multiples; **nature**; Shanghai; *Sleep No More*, London, Boston, NYC, *Woyzeck*, 2004): A recurring element in the narrative and design construction in Punchdrunk work, often employed for key sequences in the narrative loop for characters, offering high-impact long-shot experiences for the audience in contrast to detailed, narrow or smaller spaces within the world. For *Woyzeck* at The Big Chill, 2004, Punchdrunk, in typical Act 1 communal spirit, constructed a vast stylised forest from fence posts. Devon's wooded countryside provided the devil's-hour embrace needed for *The Moon Slave*; *The Firebird Ball* incorporated a forest made solely from fabric, recycling material that previously shaped *Chair*'s labyrinth; *Faust* saw a whole floor reimagined as a pine-scented, fir tree forest, through which audience, witches and a crazed

found space

Valentine travelled. *The Masque of the Red Death* saw the foyer of BAC transformed into a petrified forest, trees sculpted from wood, chicken-wire, plaster and fabric by the design team with cast, crew and volunteers. For *The Duchess of Malfi*, an entire floor of trees fashioned from electrical cable became the 'Apricot Orchard', for the eponymously titled Enrichment partner project. Significant here is the metaphorical connotations, as much as the narrative settings, of the forest in the plays and stories Punchdrunk present. Forests become liminal spaces, a place of darkness and the unknown, a place where errant travellers might become lost, be transformed. This keys into the gothic and expressionist reference to forests in art and storytelling as a place of fear, terror, delight, magic and transfiguration. Every version of *Sleep No More* has incorporated multiples of Birnam Wood, as touch-real, natural environments and miniaturised abstractions, drawing nightmarish reference to Shakespeare's device for denoting subterfuge and the supernatural in the same image and perfectly serving the choreography, as much as the film noir dream aesthetic, of Punchdrunk's in-show-worlds; such as with *Sleep No More*, NYC, where a miniature wood occurs as a chessboard on the train. Forests also function as setting and metaphorical device in *Metropolis* and David Lynch's *Twin Peaks: Fire Walk With Me* and thus became an otherworldly reference and integral design construction in *Tunnel 228* and layered further Georg Büchner's already potent forest symbolism for *The Drowned Man*.

found space (see also: architecture; **building**; Exeter Experiments; **'listening to the building'**; site; **site-sympathetic**. Further reading: Schechner 1994): Found space is a term widely used in site-based practice, away from traditional theatre auditoria or studios. It refers back to the prehistoric idea that spaces, whether natural or human constructions, can inspire ritual, narrative and provide a site for the sharing of related communal experiences. In theatre discourse it is a term that can be sourced to Richard

Schechner's *Environmental Theatres*, defined as 'performance space' that 'is continuous with the terrain' and 'has available to it the past' (1994, 250–251). For Felix Barrett it is precisely these 'echoes of the past. Ghosts in the walls' and the 'resting state of atmosphere which dictates how the show plays' that serve to inspire and set the concept for a Punchdrunk event. Barrett adds, these inherent narratives and atmospheres give a 'charge and an intensity' to the worlds created within a site and across external locations. Pete Higgin illustrates:

I distinctly remember Felix showing me around 21 Wapping Lane prior to starting work on *Faust*. Inviting me to meet him there at the end of the day, as the sun was beginning to sit low in the sky. He explained the building had been occupied by squatters, handed me a golf club and told me to keep my wits about me. The building was littered with detritus and old belongings. I was completely on edge, all of my senses heightened, but realised fairly quickly, that Felix was playing with me. Even so, I still felt jittery. It was so full of stories, from the squatters, to the documents and filing systems from its time as a security building, a relic of archaic archiving in an ever-evolving digital age. There was a most amazing anomaly in one room, where a tiny hole in a window once blacked out had created a camera obscura effect of the street view below. The building had a smell which was a potent mix of decay, dust and chemical smells, of long-term industrial usage. You build up such a strong relationship to found space, especially when you work in it over time, explore it beyond the surface of its everyday comings-and-goings. That relationship is intensified if you then build a Punchdrunk world within in it. You dwell in its architectural and inhabited idiosyncrasies while creating new stories and realities within its walls and surfaces.

framing (see also: **architecture**; exercises; **Hide-and-Seek**; **lens**; 'listening to the building'; site; **space**): A term for describing and exploring the performers' responses to specific areas within a site and its spaces, and to the movement evolved within those spaces. Used within this specific context, 'framing' is not to be confused with 'lens', Punchdrunk's preferred term for the critical and contextual framing of any work through wider theoretical and artistic influences and perspectives. Exploring 'framing' within a space is an important part of the practical and artistic process for large-scale masked productions. Felix Barrett's Hide-and-Seek game, initiated when each ensemble first enters and experiences the site in which a production will run, enables the performers to be inspired by the qualities of a building and to reshape their movement language as a consequence of this. Prior to this Maxine Doyle works closely and in detail with each dancer, in the studio and then in the building, to draw out their understanding of framing as an important skill in working with the building and its features, with an established method for instigating ways of perceiving, framing and shaping composition in space . . .

Maxine Doyle

On framing

A simple exercise that is loaded with possibilities for generating stories, characters and movement as well as analysis in relation to space, site, architecture. It's a practice of both *looking at* and *composing* space. I have led this exercise with myriad different participants, from beginners to experienced professionals, with dancers, actors, designers, musicians . . .

Bring the group to one side of the space so everyone is looking in the same direction. If in a studio or rehearsal room start with the most obvious 'front' and then change orientation to include interesting frames, such as theatre seats becoming the stage, or a fire exit door.

Define the edges of your wider frame.

Person 1 neutrally enters the space and makes an image – paying attention to frames, perspective, depth. For example, a woman sits in the corner with her eyes to the ceiling . . .

Next person enters and adds to the image, trying to add to the picture and make it more interesting.

This continues one person at a time until the whole group is in the space.

Each person looks at the picture from the inside.

Each person then exits the space, one at a time, on impulse or as the director instructs.

All should notice how the frames, stories, relationships, architecture, change.

This is led by the director, observing 'outside' the experience. I often stop and start this exercise if someone makes an interesting or clumsy choice. I ask people to think about what the space needs.

There are many ways of developing this exercise:

Shrink the frame – perhaps it's now a doorway.

Change the audience perspective – move them closer or further away.

Play the frame at 360 degrees, imagining your audience all around.

Find one image and make very small changes in focus, gesture or orientation.

Ask people to interpret what they see.

Now try with a soundscore; a film soundtrack, a choral piece, the sound of dripping water. Notice how the sound changes the atmosphere and possible meanings of the images.

Practise looking at empty space with different sounds.

Go back to the very beginning of the exercise. Begin again.

G

gaming (see also: agency; *And Darkness Descended. . .*; bar; **coda**; curiosity; **digital technologies**; Fallow Cross; *Gold-bug, The*; **immersive**; in-show-world; *Kabeiroi*; *Prospero's Island*; **Oracles, The**; *Séance, The*; *Silverpoint*; visceral. Further reading: Biggin 2017; Dickinson 2011; Joho 2016; Klich 2016; Machon 2013a, 59–63): Immersive performance practice in general terms, whether tangentially or explicitly, adopts certain processes and terminology from gaming theory and there are many immersive performance companies that exploit the intersections between transmedia storytelling, gameplay and theatre. Felix Barrett has always had an interest in how the forms and aesthetics of virtual worlds, appropriating gaming techniques in physical practice, augmented by digital technologies, might be deployed within a durational experience to theatricalise 'real-world' contexts. He was drawn to the agency available to players in video games, recalling how 'the first Resident Evil was influential because it offered a world to explore with a rules-set for engagement'. Jim Bending, Punchdrunk's former Digital Development Lead, notes that Punchdrunk masked worlds specifically 'offer gaming agency; audiences decide what they want to achieve during a set time':

So much of Punchdrunk's work resonates with game-design; you enter, create your own rule-set; there's a sandbox element to it [roaming and selecting tasks at will, within the parameters of the game], so you can come out, decide whether you want to follow one particular character to the end or focus on exploring the space.

The processual nature of Punchdrunk's masked events also invites audiences to learn from one visit to another, should they choose, to build on skills and knowledge acquired in scenarios, and share this with other 'players' in the bar or online, subsequent to the in-world play. Peter Higgin explains:

We didn't set out to build work to be like first-person computer games. Instead, as our productions became more intricate and detailed it was a lens through which audiences began to view and compare the work. We recognise that the work offers fully realised realities within which audiences are immersed. Immersion of this depth is addictive and those interested in gaming feel the work offers a physical alternative to gaming. Just as games are played many times over, audiences return again and again to Punchdrunk worlds; with *Sleep No More*, NYC, an audience member who frequented the production reviewed it as one of his top ten games [see Dickinson 2011]. Work in Fallow Cross is focused on embedding game mechanics, cross-platform storytelling, extending and augmenting the physical experience with digital platforms. Projects like *Oracles* and *Kabeiroi* show there's a rich territory to explore.

This intentional fusion of gaming and theatre has been in place since *Prospero's Island*, actively investigating the potential of the visceral-virtual, as Higgin expands:

Prospero's Island examined how you employ right-brain activity in order to get left-brain reward and vice-versa. Using subject and source knowledge, analytical skills as the currency to get experiential earning and rewards. The challenge of making theatre as a game, growing the game mechanic to embrace and interrogate that deeply is where the crunchy and exciting stuff emerges. That's why we want to explore tracking technologies that interface with theatrical systems, enabling a game-world to talk to a physical space, as with *The Oracles*. We exist in a twenty-four-seven technological world culturally, so it's another tool for us to draw on, to blur real and fictional worlds, to create new experiences.

As Punchdrunk move outside of buildings and into real-world scenarios, the virtual and gaming element has taken a step up. Stephen Makin, Punchdrunk International's producer for R&D projects that blend live experiences, mobile phone and console gaming, adds:

One really exciting aspect of consciously moving into the arena of games and launching a project as a game rather than theatre means we can play with the rug-pull with people who have expectations about how a videogame works. Where once gaming mechanisms subverted theatre, now we are interested to see if theatre can subvert gaming.

Stephanie Allen, Punchdrunk International's R&D Project Manager, responsible for investigating ways to connect app-based games with real-life contexts in Punchdrunk's practice, in discussion with Makin and Bending, adds:

Stephanie: *Silverpoint* incorporated a very simple match-three game on your phone and the better you were at that and the more time you put in meant that you were closer to getting those moments of theatrical experiences as a reward. That's the opposite to a masked show, where the one-on-ones are random, you're selected from the crowd. Even though it's curated by us, for the audience member, it's slightly right-place-right-time. With *Silverpoint* we explored the opposite of that, where if you work the hardest, you could be rewarded with the most intimate scene.

Stephen: With masked shows, repeat audiences work out that it's not entirely random where the one-on-ones are. Like a game, the fans crack how to get them, crack where and how to be in right-place-right-time, and the kind of behaviour that would make a performer choose them. That's an example of how current research has evolved from seeing a pattern in a masked show, noting how audiences were responding very powerfully to one-on-ones, which made us question how we make that into a conscious search.

Jim: Games are all fundamentally about pattern matching, and pattern finding; the goldmine, the thrill of working it out.

Gardner, Lyn (see also: **Act 1**; Act 2; Act 3; *Against Captain's Orders*; **audience**; crescendo; *Drowned Man, The*; **Enrichment**; *Sleep No More*, **London**; text): Renowned and respected theatre critic and Associate Editor for *The Stage*, Gardner was an early supporter of Punchdrunk, writing the first national, broadsheet review to bring Punchdrunk's work to the attention of a wider audience. Following his move back to London from Exeter, Felix Barrett repeatedly invited reviewers to his productions, with only a smattering of interest. Core members knew the importance of being reviewed by a critic who would appreciate where Punchdrunk sat artistically. As *Sleep No More* previews approached, Barrett recollects how they would refer to that period as 'Waiting for Gardner': 'we felt she was the one critic who would understand the context for what we were trying to do' . . .

Lyn Gardner

On making demands on the audience

I saw the first production of *Sleep No More* at the Beaufoy Building, during a time in British theatre when going to a performance still, mostly, meant that you went to a purpose-built building and sat in neat rows, maybe on red velvet seats. *Sleep No More* was a complete disruption of that. We'd had those disruptions, of course, in a lot of the international work that was seen, particularly through LIFT. Nevertheless, the idea that there was home-grown, UK work that was doing something like this seemed quite remarkable. I had no idea about what it was that I was going to see so what I then experienced with *Sleep No More* was an astonishment. The very early Robert Wilson installation work was my closest point of comparison. There were very few of us there. I was possibly the only critic that saw it, I may be wrong, but there were certainly not the numbers Punchdrunk attract now. I wandered around for quite long periods of time on my own. I remember the moment the bell rang and we all went for the feast, where Banquo's ghost appears, being surprised to discover there were quite a lot of other people there. The difference then, however, was there simply wasn't the *density* of audience.

One of the things I've always really loved about Punchdrunk is that it's about all of those elements coalescing, being layered; the installation, the performance, the music, the way that things are just so beautifully lit. I very much recall the installation work in *Sleep No More*, particularly the Macbeth bedroom and how there was something about it that just so acutely defined the relationship between the characters. Punchdrunk's work has always understood that you have to take enormous care of every, tiny detail, and in so doing you take care of the audience. This is a fundamental difference to what has happened with the rise of immersive work in general, where there has come to be an idea that you can do a little bit of set dressing, you can herd an audience around and that is supposed to be 'immersive theatre'.

Punchdrunk shows require you to work at them and that is not a bad thing; to make demands upon an audience, to emphasise that you'll get as much out if it as you're prepared to put into it. The fantastic thing about it is that there are different ways that you can 'put into it' as an audience member. I'm not a great joiner-in and my idea of hell is deciding that you're absolutely going to follow a lead character and elbow other people out of the way in order to get to see everything. I like stumbling across things. I like that you can go in a room and spend ten to fifteen minutes exploring that particular room on your own and still come out with a sense of the work. With productions such as *Sleep No More*, *Faust*, *The Masque of the Red Death*, the way in which the work is very specifically based on a source that has a classic resonance helps it enormously. As an audience member you have something to hang on to. *The Drowned Man* was bigger, better, but didn't feel more layered and that may have been because there was not quite the same kernel of a great, classic story at its heart. The emotional connection was harder to get a handle on.

We shouldn't underestimate in any way that, even if you are a Punchdrunk veteran, that moment when you suddenly are plunged into this world is a moment of huge dislocation, huge excitement as well, and a trepidation about how one is going to negotiate it, 'how am I going to find my way about?'. It's a bit like suddenly being parachuted down into a city, which you don't know at all, with new landmarks to guide you and a sense that you have to get somewhere. I don't think it's Punchdrunk's fault but there's a slight element of competitiveness that has crept in among certain audiences, an attitude of 'I have to find the show'. Therefore, the more Punchdrunk do to help us find the show, arguably, the better it is. I'm not for a moment saying the company should only ever do things based on classic texts but, where it does, it makes the reference points so much easier to find. The most interesting art is often layered and references other works. It's a form of postmodernism, where one thing ricochets of another, references are a nod to other works and help you to understand the piece. Yet, because of the complicated nature of what it is that Punchdrunk do, the layering has to have a light touch. If they try too obviously to combine very different sources, it can be slightly confusing. Don't get me wrong, I'm absolutely into that kind of thing, in my own novels for children I'm constantly referencing things, like *The Duchess of Malfi* or *The Golden Bough*, but a Punchdrunk world is such a complicated experience for an audience that they need to know where they are.

There's so much that's worth celebrating about Punchdrunk's work today. I sometimes get a little irritated by the way in which, as so often happens when people become successful in British theatre, Punchdrunk is seen to have sold out in some way, or that the work is not as good as it was once. One of the things that has been truly excellent about Punchdrunk is that it could have gone down a strongly commercial route and raised a lot of money, only to put on shows that will then run clones of themselves all over the world, or big shows in London where it will get a massive audience. Yet, in many ways, its focus of attention has been on the much less visible Enrichment work; work that has been going on in schools and the smaller projects that have taken place for children, such as *Against Captain's Orders*. I think that that is something that British theatre companies need to think about, the nature of enrichment. Those kinds of projects, when they're absolutely central to a company's practice, and not just tagged on, are not just enriching for the participants but are potentially very enriching for the company itself. The move to Tottenham Hale, albeit temporarily, and the building of Fallow Cross to allow a period of taking stock and thinking about new ideas and which of those might be most valuably developed is particularly worthy of celebration. I know a lot of Punchdrunk's work has taken place in different schools and boroughs, but there's something about them being in one place, while also working internationally, that is a significant thing. I see no reason why Punchdrunk can't go on and, in doing so, go on surprising us. The only thing that audiences and commentators have to guard against is a refusal to be astonished; a 'we've been there, seen that' attitude. There are very few British theatre companies that cause great excitement when there's the slightest possibility that it might be doing a new show – yet Punchdrunk is one of those companies. There are even fewer companies where the fact that they might be doing a show causes huge excitement amongst people who would not necessarily categorise themselves as fervent theatregoers. That's a rare achievement.

Gideon Reeling

Gideon Reeling (see also: **Act 1**; Big Chill, The; **Hargreaves, Kate**; **interaction**; journeying; **'punchdrunk'**. Further reading: Haines 2017): A name that derives from its Punchdrunk roots (as in, 'punchdrunk', to be 'giddy and reeling'), Gideon Reeling is the offshoot company, founded in 2006 by Felix Barrett, Kate Hargreaves and Colin Nightingale, to take on the commercial events that Punchdrunk were increasingly being approached to create. Nightingale points out, 'we didn't want to walk away from this work as it was valuable for performers and designers for whom Punchdrunk wasn't able to provide regular work'. Barrett stepped back following establishment. Gideon Reeling produces small, medium and large-scale one-off theatrical events. Gideon Reeling, with Hargreaves as director of performances, collaborated with Punchdrunk and BAC to produce the Red Death Lates. As Hargreaves points out, at that point and since, though many Gideon Reeling and Punchdrunk collaborators overlap and an affinity exists in certain immersive and interactive techniques employed, Gideon Reeling is now a distinct and separate entity to Punchdrunk. Hargreaves summarises, at the heart of Gideon Reeling projects is a sense of 'inclusive playfulness'. In keeping with its playful approach, the website introduces Gideon Reeling as a person, a rare individual and 'a purveyor of bespoke theatrical experiences'.

Founding member Kathryn McGarr recalls, 'Gideon Reeling was born out of those early days of Punchdrunk at The Big Chill and has now found its own style', such as its 'Starty' shows, which have reappeared annually since the inaugural event in 2010. With all of Gideon Reeling's interactive projects, drawing on Hargreaves' background in museum events and McGarr's long history with Punchdrunk, there is an attention to detail in the historical research around the era and space in which the production is based. McGarr notes that this allows the performers 'to create characters that are so well thought-out that we can easily improvise, in conversation with an audience member, within the "world" that we are creating'. McGarr identifies the two leading Gideon Reeling projects as *The Great British Road Trip* and *Ahead of Time*, both of which were journeying performances, the latter being the first ever immersive aviation event of its kind, for Icelandair, as featured in 'Travel: News' of *The Telegraph*.

Gold-bug, The (2007–2008, see also: Act 1; **adrenalin**; *And Darkness Descended. . .*; **bar**; **boxes, chests and drawers**; collaboration; *Crash of the Elysium, The*; failure; flow; **gaming**; Jubb, David; *Masque of the Red Death*; *Oracles, The*. Further reading: Poe 1965, 42–70): The impetus for incorporating a treasure hunt within the world of *The Masque of the Red Death* was, as Felix Barrett summarises, because 'Edgar Allan Poe is known for the modern-day detective story, the gothic romance, the idea of the melancholic wasting away from ennui. Yet he also invented the treasure hunt with *The Gold-bug*'. Punchdrunk was keen to honour this by hiding treasure to be found inside the building as part of the construction of the Poe world. The intention was that it would slowly build as a six-month durational event, enabling plucky audience members to be rewarded for their efforts by unearthing the prize. Interactive theatre makers, Coney, took up the challenge to create this in a daring and detailed manner with, as Barrett recalls, 'incredible installations in terms of the level of content, building a bone organ and a house of tricks'.

Coney's *The Gold-bug* took Poe's short story as the stimulus and embedded a treasure-hunt within a live performance-adventure within Punchdrunk's *The Masque of the Red Death*, partnering this with an online development of clues, correspondence and action, as documented in ghoulish detail in Coney's web archives. Developed across six months, *The Gold-bug* attracted an early online audience of eighty players, and an audience of around 300 on-site at BAC, interacting physically in the Gold-bug world. For the uninitiated who, by chance, came across a mysterious hooded and masked figure playing tarot in the bar, this was the in-show route into the treasure-hunt. As it gained notoriety among those in the know, across the final three months of the adventure, players avidly shared findings and stories in the bar and online; solved puzzles and codes set by characters; and uncovered narratives, culminating in a dramatic finale, where a Bach melody played on a piano was the key to unlocking a bloody chamber and the unearthing of a box revealed the final destination of the treasure.

An outcome of the project for Punchdrunk was that the production team learned important lessons regarding different qualities of flow and tempo that can be created by audiences on a mission set up across a world *within* the wider world of an event. These audiences move at a different tempo and behave in a blinkered fashion, according to the fixed focus of the assignment, to that of the wider world that hosts said mission, shifting the dynamic that operates across audience experience. As Barrett describes:

On day one of *The Gold-bug* opening, there was an audience who were going around watching the show moving at the required rhythm and tempo manipulated by the sound and light and, counter to this, there were a few following a *Gold-bug* rhythm which impacted negatively on the wider audience's experience. They would walk straight into a scene asking, 'has anyone seen the Gold-bug'. We realised that an audience charged with a mission are an opposite entity to an audience following the mood and flow of the space and the two can't cohabit. We ended up having to limit it, with a list of instructions of things they couldn't do as it was proving detrimental to the show. What was interesting, and amazing to witness, was the wide-eyed hunger of that audience. It wasn't suitable during a masked show but it was fascinating to observe and we were keen to explore how you might build a show specifically for that audience.

The result was that a separate day was created for the *Gold-bug* audience to reach the finale to that mission and unearth the treasure. Subsequently, *And Darkness Descended. . .* came about as a consequence of these observations, with the mission-led experience further tested through *The Crash of the Elysium*. Adventure-driven projects and performances that interweave gaming techniques and digital technologies, such as *The Oracles*, will be explored by Punchdrunk on a larger scale across Act 3.

gong (see also: atmosphere; **crescendo**; influences; **pedal note**; **ritual**): The use of a gong in Punchdrunk events was initially inspired by a revival of Viennese Actionist Hermann Nitsch's durational and ritualised art event at Whitechapel Gallery, which made a deep impression on Felix Barrett. A gong punctuated the action and marked time. A gong was first used in *The Tempest*, 2003, employed as a pedal note, struck by the character of Ariel, and continues as a motif throughout masked shows. In *The Masque of the Red Death*, the gong called revellers to the ball, resonating portentously with the repeated chime of midnight that previously echoed out to reset the loops. The gong provides a cue for performers to redirect the flow of the audience, and bring everyone together, while adding to mood and atmosphere, building the sense of something looming on the journey to the finale.

'Grandmother's Room' (see also: **Act 1**; Act 2; Act 3; crescendo; **doors**; durational; Exeter Experiments; Hide-and-Seek; **one-on-one**; process; **text**; *Woyzeck*, **2000**; *Yellow Wallpaper, The*): The original rules for a one-on-one were created for this sequence, which occurred at the centre of the building within its own time frame within the wider narrative loop of *Woyzeck*, 2000. These rules relate to tempo of delivery, duration and a conclusion that continues the sense of suspense. Felix Barrett explains:

The crescendo of a one-on-one relates to proximity, you're always moving forwards in terms of proximity, touch, and tension, it's all surging, exponential. You can stay constant, but you can never go back. If the audience try to pull away, then you increase tension. The performer must remain in control unless the audience member decides to pull away from it.

As the crescendo is reached, only then can performers step back, begin to return to their own world, send the audience member away. 'Grandmother's Room' has been incorporated in every masked event since, the story itself indicating how tempo and duration are structured:

GRANDMOTHER: Once upon a time there was a poor little boy who had no father and mother; everything was dead and there was no-one left in the whole world. Everything was quite dead, so he went off, whimpering. All day and all night. And since there was no-one left on earth he decided to go up to heaven where the moon shone down so kind. But when he got to the moon it was a lump of rotten wood. Then he went to the sun, but when he got there it was a withered-up sunflower. And when he got to the stars they were little spangled midges stuck there, like the ones shrikes stick on blackthorns. So he went back to the earth, but the earth was an overturned pot. He was completely alone, and he sat down and cried. He's sitting there still, all alone.

(Büchner 1979, 83)

Grant, Matthew (see also: Act 1; **Barrett, Felix**; **design**; *H.G.*; **influences**; **lighting**; **scenography**; **Tonkin, Geoff**. Further reading: Craig 2008; Innes 2004): As teacher of Theatre Studies A Level and Head of Drama Productions at Alleyn's School, Dulwich, from 1991–2005, Grant was an early mentor to Felix Barrett. Sam Booth, in a lower school year to Barrett, notes how both Grant and Geoff Tonkin, the

Head of Drama at the time, were deeply influential in shaping their students' artistic sensibilities through numerous trips to 'all sorts of extraordinary theatre' as well as setting models of practice in their own productions. Working as a freelance theatre electrician after leaving the teaching profession in 2005, Grant was Assistant Lighting Designer for Punchdrunk's *Faust*. Now a Glass Artist, having been so since 2016, Grant recalls the significance of Barrett's A Level studies to Punchdrunk's practice . . .

Matthew Grant

On influences and inspiration

Felix was in the most charismatic and rewarding group I ever taught. The class had a very rare chemistry and a shared drive that lifted and supported everyone in the group and which, I suspect, allowed every pupil in it to perform in a higher way than they might have done if the group had been composed differently. This non-hierarchical and ensemble-like dynamic, and I include myself in that, must surely have contributed to the working practices Felix later developed in Punchdrunk. From my point of view as his teacher, the most important artistic influences on Felix were the productions, writing and drawings of Edward Gordon Craig, whom we studied as our named 'Practitioner'; the production photographs and a single newspaper interview with the Czech scenographer Josef Svoboda; and the installation *H.G.* by Robert Wilson and Hans Peter Kuhn, which we saw once only in 1995.

Craig's concept of 'the artist of the theatre' – an individual with complete artistic and practical control of every detail in a production's genesis and realisation – was clearly central to Felix's development. Craig's aesthetic tended towards the monumental in scale and was always suggestive rather than realistic, and this clearly chimed with Felix's own developing theatrical vision. Craig's belief that authentically theatrical practice and experience should have something of sacred and religious importance was irresistible to the whole group as well as Felix. A favourite passage, as quoted by Christopher Innes:

> Remember generally to seize one property . . . and round that conceive and build your scene – accompanying it always with its like a cross [*sic*: i.e. giving it the status of a symbol such as the cross, in order to make the scene] a place for PRAYER, an emblem. When you do this, you are able to help the theatre – [and it will be] full of spectators.
>
> (39)

The productions over which Craig had total control that I believe had a big effect on Felix were *Dido and Aeneas* (1901) and *Bethlehem* (1902); very significant also was the production of *Macbeth* that Craig designed for Beerbohm Tree in 1909 and his design for Stanislavski's production of *Hamlet* for the Moscow Arts Theatre in 1910. The tiny black-and-white photographs of *Macbeth* and *Bethlehem* in Innes's book, from more than a hundred years ago, still vividly communicate the intensely sculptural effect of Craig's work. Despite the almost two-dimensional flatness of the shepherds in *Bethlehem*, there is somehow at the same time an effect of almost limitless depth.

Bethlehem was performed at the Imperial Institute, in London. The way Craig got around the challenges of the space, which had terrible acoustics, and his financial limitations, displayed a practical-aesthetic inventiveness that would be used by Felix in his subsequent theatre practice. Craig solved the problems of the acoustics by lining the walls with hessian sacking. He then used the same material to make the 'sheep', which were no more than sacks of hessian stuffed with straw, each with two knots to create the ears. Craig used a black cloth stitched with glass crystals for the night sky, an effect still strikingly powerful in this ancient photograph, giving that sense of infinite depth. The transformation of a non-theatrical space in a way that enveloped the audience in the theatrical world created by the 'artist of the theatre' is clearly a central plank of the Punchdrunk aesthetic.

Another very powerful influence was the work of Josef Svoboda. This was limited almost entirely to production photographs. I had been given a black-and-white catalogue of an exhibition of Svoboda's theatrical models that had been shown in Prague in the early 1990s, but I also had a book – entirely in Czech – that had colour photographs of some of Svoboda's massive opera productions. The monumentality of Svoboda's work clearly echoed Craig's vision, and it also helped to cement the kind of aesthetic to which the class was being exposed. The massive flight of stairs that were the central feature of Svoboda's design for Verdi's *Sicilian Vespers*, for example, linked with Craig's sketches and writings for *The Steps*, a production that never saw the light of day but was crucial to his theatrical vision. Another influential image for Felix was that of the gauze used by Svoboda for the scene in Mozart's *The Magic Flute* in which Pamina and Tamino are being purified by fire and water. In class, I linked this to a production of *Titus Andronicus* by the Romanian director Silviu Purcărete. Felix's class hadn't seen this production, as it had taken place two years before they reached the sixth form, but the use of gauze in the scene in which Lavinia is raped and mutilated by Demetrius and Chiron had obviously had such an impact on me that I somehow made it important to the class – even though they hadn't seen so much as a photograph of the production itself. The important thing is that there seemed to be a thread running from Craig's use of gauze in his productions of plays like *Macbeth* (1909) and *Acis and Galatea* (1902) through the work of Svoboda to Purcărete. Although gauze itself doesn't feature so highly in Punchdrunk productions, its use to sculpt or transform stage action and design was seen by the group as an important technical tradition.

A practical workshop in the upper sixth, with the lighting designer Ian Sommerville, influenced Felix. Ian's work is characterised by a total absence of, indeed a strong contempt for, what's often called 'general cover.' A show lit by Ian will typically be quite dark, with actors lit by sidelight, and with important, while often physically insignificant, details of design picked out by very tightly shuttered light. Ian's visual references include Rembrandt, Caravaggio and Joseph Wright of Derby. I was lucky to be able to persuade the senior management of the school to let me take the class out of timetabled lessons on a Wednesday afternoon and keep them in the hall until five o'clock, not allowing anyone else into the most public room in the school so that my students could play with light. Ian had brought nine gauze drapes that he'd used in *The Turn of the Screw* with the ENO. We rigged these five-metre-high and one-and-a-half-metre-wide patterned gauzes from the nineteenth-century faux Jacobean hammer-beam roof-space. We removed the lanterns from the primitive overhead lighting rig and mounted them instead on floor stands, many set at head-height. Ian used the stands to create extremely tightly shuttered shards of light; so precise that if performers weren't on their mark they weren't lit at all. This technique has a powerfully sculptural effect and also allows performers to appear as if from nowhere. At some point during the afternoon, Ian asked if any of the students wanted to experiment with this ancient analogue desk. Felix was the first to volunteer and was immediately captivated by the process. Although he wasn't in any of the productions that Ian subsequently lit for me and Geoff Tonkin at Alleyn's, including a production of *Antigone* that Felix saw, I know that Ian's work directly influenced Felix's Punchdrunk aesthetic.

The most dramatic recollection I have of Felix was of the time I took the class to see Robert Wilson and Hans Peter Kuhn's piece *H.G.* This physical environment was designed by Wilson with sound by Kuhn, and the audience entered through a doorway into a tiny domestic room in which time appeared to have stopped in 1900. From this cramped and tiny domestic interior, you then passed into a monumental and spooky environment that you had to journey through alone and in which you encountered spaces such as a First World War hospital ward with fifty beds, or a pitch-dark vault empty except for a mummified corpse, lit by a faint dust-filled shaft of light. The auto-navigation required by this piece is obviously important to Punchdrunk's work now. There were scenes that were made deliberately difficult to see in *H.G.* but which, for that very reason, were all the more intriguing. There was a tunnel that was up-lit with massive parcans that flooded the space with purple light. It had been made intentionally difficult to see into the space by being semi-obscured by crude brickwork. When you did get down low enough to peer into it, what you saw was a flight of between fifty and a hundred arrows suspended in mid-flight in an arc that ghosted the outline of the arch of the tunnel; the fact that it was so hauntingly beautiful yet impossible to see fully amplified its powerful effect on the audience. I can think of early Punchdrunk productions, such as *The Tempest*, that had similar spaces that you couldn't fully access but which would tantalise the audience from a distance.

The effect of *H.G.* on Felix was immediately and obviously profound. The post-show arrangements were simple; after we had found our own way round the installation and exited the piece via the door into Clink Street, we would congregate at the Anchor pub and discuss the installation over a drink before heading home. As we sat talking about the extraordinary thing we had just witnessed, one of the pupils noticed that we were one short – Felix wasn't with us. Thinking he'd simply got lost, I went back to the exit and explained to the steward that I needed to go back in through the out-door to find one of my pupils who had probably just got a bit muddled and failed to find the way out. I found Felix in a room filled with what seemed like hundreds of pairs of shoes, all different styles, and all labelled with beautiful but abstract calligraphy. Felix was simply standing among the shoes, as if he had become part of the installation himself. We left and walked the short distance to the pub. Astonishing as it seems to me now, we walked the fifty metres hand-in-hand and in complete silence. When we got to the pub Felix simply sat in front of the drink that someone had bought for him. I honestly don't think he drank any of it. He had clearly gone into that installation one person and came out as someone else.

One final detail about Felix's sixth-form career that's worth mentioning is his 'Individual Skill', as one of the practical components of the final Theatre Studies A Level assessment was called. Typically, students would choose the acting option, and only a handful would choose things like costume or stage design. Felix was unique in my experience in choosing to devise a whole piece. He created a dystopian world by building a massive junk-sculpture, a giant horseshoe of discarded white goods and car components assembled in our nineteenth-century school gymnasium. This mound of discarded consumer goods, which I helped collect from local tips, had seven or eight televisions embedded in it. Felix had persuaded the Physics Department's technician to rig up the televisions so that they played repeating loops of Fritz Lang's *Metropolis*. The floor cloth was lit straight down from above and Felix's classmate, Sam Booth, who has often been in Punchdrunk shows since, played a melancholy, black-clad priest-like figure.

Craig, Purcărete, Svoboda and *H.G.* are all obvious influences on Felix's theatrical aesthetic, but what still strikes me as extraordinary is the way Felix synthesised these influences in such a way as to make the whole, which would include larger influences from his undergraduate study at Exeter and go on to define the Punchdrunk aesthetic, greater than the sum of the parts. What makes this seem even more extraordinary is the fact that a number of these early influences were not even encountered in a live context; no-one alive has witnessed a Craig production, so all this material *had* to be gleaned from written texts and photographs. I had never seen a Svoboda production and had only photographs and, to me, unintelligible Czech commentary, so my account of this scenographer's work was at one remove from its original theatrical context. Somehow Felix funnelled his sixth-form influences into his own work as a practitioner and paid homage to them at the same time.

My own theatrical relationship with Felix after he left Exeter started with the loan of equipment for the early London-based Punchdrunk productions. I scrabbled together some lanterns and cable for *The Firebird Ball*, for example, and was able to contribute in a much more meaningful way to *Faust*. Alleyn's generously granted me a sabbatical term, in which I studied lighting at Mountview Academy of Theatre Arts, where I met Matt Prentice, the Head of Lighting. Sometime after Felix asked me if I'd like to light one of the rooms in the building he had found for *Faust*. I asked Matt, by then Head of Lighting at RADA, if I could borrow a few lanterns and some cables in order to light the barn and the field of corn that was going to be built in my room on the top floor of the Wapping building. Matt asked to come and see the space and suggested that we make a proposal to light the whole thing. My own *H.G.* moment was having that proposal accepted by Punchdrunk. I ended up being Assistant Lighting Designer on *Faust*, and the incredible effect that that had on me is impossible to overstate. Working on *Faust* was the most important job of my professional life, and it's a very special thing to be able to work for a former pupil on a project as exciting as that one was.

Greenhive Green (**2016**, see also: **Act 3**; agency; Blake, Matthew; **caretaking**; **community**; **cross-fade**; **Enrichment**; **Oppong, Connie**; touch. Further reading: Tims 2016): Punchdrunk Enrichment partnered with intergenerational arts company Magic Me and Anchor Trust's Greenhive care home to create a new project for Greenhive care home's residents and staff, including those with dementia. This project, conceived as a long-form narrative experience, was part of a wider initiative by Magic Me, the Director of the organisation, Susan Langford, and Ellie Watmough providing training advice and support throughout its run, to bring innovative creative practices to residents in care homes. Punchdrunk Enrichment transformed a room in the home into a beautiful village green, complete with a florist's shop, phone box, foliage and the smell of fresh-cut grass, by freelance designer Julie Landau. A unique element for all members of the team was that they took on the role of village residents and assisted in the delivery of on-site workshop activities, rather than this primarily being the responsibility of performer-facilitators, as with projects in schools. Matthew Blake, Peter Higgin, Landau, Elin Moore Williams and Alex Rowse gathered with residents in the fictional world for weekly committee meetings that were part-soap opera, part-game and part-workshop. The participants were players within a structured storyline and could, if they chose, drive the narrative.

This became a significant pilot project for the Enrichment team and its performers, as it required that they all rethink every detail of the techniques and process as a result of working with, and learning from, residents living with dementia and their carers. Rather than aiming to create a world within the wider life of an organisation, as with the projects in schools, instead the team established an environment where the fiction created was one that participants could interact with as they chose, allowing for a scale of engagement where participants could be themselves and simply drink tea or participate in activities or choose to become characters playing within a filmic reality.

The logic of the piece was carefully constructed around the participants, many of whom had dementia, and evolved across the weeks on-site. The participants, the space and the timeframe dictated the parameters with which the Enrichment team could work; the application of the usual Punchdrunk mechanism for practice was shaped by 'the unknowns' that arose, rather than following any usual formulae. It adjusted Enrichment's approach in regard to the manner in which the duty of care increased, where a focus on small groups of participants allowed full attention to the individual needs of each participant, rather than the collective needs of a group of individuals, as is typically the case with work in schools. Tactile interaction with objects, materials and each other became a vital form of communication between Enrichment and participants. For Punchdrunk, the project culminated in a party hosted by the home and Greenhive Committee. Singer-songwriter Beatie Wolfe, who had performed for the residents during one of the workshop sessions, returned to play for the celebration, which culminated in the conclusion to the story with the arrival of Greenhive Green's Mayoress (played with due aplomb by Kathryn McGarr) who bestowed her title upon Connie Oppong, the manager of the home at the time. For the care home community, the legacy of the project involved continuing the weekly committee meetings with residents and staff, after Punchdrunk had left. It resulted in some of the Greenhive staff noting subtle shifts in the way they saw residents, which helped them in modifying caregiving needs (see Tims 2016, 39).

Oppong recalls the Enrichment team's willingness to learn from this new experience, from the expertise of her staff as much as the needs of the residents. Blake, co-director and performer for the project, noted how the experience was a learning curve in regard to interactive performance technique:

With Punchdrunk's wider work, we invite the audience-participant into our world, a world we've created. We set the pace, tempo and emotions of the action and it's up to the audience to keep up with us and find its way through. However, with Punchdrunk Enrichment, and in particular, working in a care home where many participants had dementia, the performer has to find a way into the audience-participant's world in order that we talk, perform and interact at a pace set by them. In both approaches the audience are always at the heart of the work but in very different ways.

Grey's Printing Press (**2012**, see also: Act 2; cross-fade; **Enrichment**; *Lost Toy Depository, The*; *Travelling Museum Society, The*; *Up, Up and Away*):

There was once a boy called George and girl called Gwynne. They loved nothing in the world so much as words . . . Local business Grey's Printing Press are going out of business, after years of printing the most boring black and white manuscripts and manuals around. A nearby school responds to their call for temporary storage, and as crates and boxes begin to arrive some rather peculiar things begin to happen.

Grey's Printing Press was a bespoke project for Gainsborough Primary School, created in collaboration with the Headteacher and Literacy Coordinators to inspire pupils to write stories and improve speaking and listening. Co-written and performed by Katy Balfour and Matthew Blake, the project saw everyday life become disrupted when a crate from Grey's Printing Press began to suck in items from the school's bright and colourful displays. This led to the transformation of a space in the school, where a magical world full of stories appeared, including the childhood bedroom of George and Gwynne, the printers, the

△ FIGURE 9 *Greenhive Green*. 2016. L–R: Leslie Wright, Elin Moore Williams, Edna Wharton, Julie Landau.

Photo credit: Stephen Dobbie

place they first imagined their most marvellous stories. As pupils explored this magical world, the printers asked them to become freelance writers for Grey's Printing Press. Soon the fortunes of Grey's Printing Press were turned around, and from then on, it was known as Gainsborough Printing Press. Peter Higgin clarifies:

This kind of project represented a number of one-off bespoke commissions that Enrichment undertook, responding to individual school needs and working in close contact with teachers to shape and frame work. All of these projects are whole school and tend to take around six weeks to unfold. The cross-fade began with our team flyering on the school gates a month in advance. The flyers were from a local printing company who were in the process of closing down and needed space to run a skeleton operation. Fictionally the school answer this call and open up their library to the local firm. This type of work aimed to build on the impact of smaller projects like *Under the Eiderdown* and grow the fiction and the length of time they are embedded in a school. At the end of this project pupils turn around the fortunes of Grey's Printing Press and they fictionally continue their operation in new premises with a renewed mission to publish colourful stories. We produced a couple of legacy pieces for this project; a broadsheet style compendium of all the pupils' stories and also a picture book, telling the story of the project. These one-off projects were brilliant ways in which to push the form and see how far you can take the fiction of a project.

H

Hargreaves, Kate (see also: **Act 1**; Act 2; Enrichment; **Gideon Reeling**; **Red Death Lates**): Hargreaves is Co-Founder and Artistic Director of Gideon Reeling. Erstwhile Punchdrunk

and Punchdrunk Enrichment collaborator, she worked on *The Firebird Ball*, *Marat/Sade* at The Big Chill, *Faust*, *Under the Eiderdown*, *The Lost Toy Depository*, *The Crash of the Elysium* and *The Drowned Man* as well as being a key contributor to Punchdrunk R&D projects across Act 2. Hargreaves was the Director of Performance for the infamous Red Death Lates:

My first experience of Punchdrunk was as an audience member for *Woyzeck* at The Big Chill festival in 2004. Exhausted from the festival, on the Sunday night we arrived before the performance had even opened and we stayed until they were nearly closing. The experience was so stunning, beautiful and disturbing, that I felt compelled to write to this mysterious 'Punchdrunk' the next day saying that I wanted in. It's one of the very few cold calls I have ever made on my own behalf in my working life, and definitely the most fruitful and influential. I met with Felix the following week to discuss music, theatre, museum education and how I might get involved. I was Education Officer of Gunnersbury Park Museum at the time, creating wholly immersive educative sessions for schools, families and adults. Considered unusual and quirky in our approach in the wider museum world, with costumed characters and participatory learning. Gunnersbury were later to provide training and work for a number of contributors including Peter Higgin, Becky Botten and Kathryn McGarr.

I came on board at the start of 2005, as a 'performer-without-portfolio' in *The Firebird Ball*. I was originally under the impression that I was to pull together a house band but it became immediately apparent that there were two of us engaged to do this. I sat around for a couple of days wondering what my purpose was until I grabbed Felix as he dashed by and said, 'Right two things; one, how about this wig to play The Hostess,

and two, I *have* to do something; it's okay if you don't know quite what yet but I'm here and you're paying me so give me a task'. Felix asked if I'd start at the furniture storage and see what I could find to create my character's office and to dress the bar. It turned out to be an incredibly fulfilling exercise, an amazing process to create a character through designing her space. I tore up the wallpaper and tea stained strange paperwork to create a tangled mess of a 1920s office with a linden tree growing through it. It was there that Hector Harkness would lock me, three times a night, until I broke out to sing. It was a symbiosis of space, narrative and character and consolidated a model for how I practise today.

Harvey, Robin (see also: **Act 1**; **cornfield**; *Faust*; *Firebird Ball, The*; *Marat/Sade*; McNeill, Rob): Harvey is a designer who was introduced to Punchdrunk by Rob McNeill and then volunteered during the build of *The Firebird Ball*. He went on to work as Barrett's design collaborator for Punchdrunk projects including *Marat/Sade* at The Big Chill and *Faust* before leaving to pursue other ventures in early 2007.

haze (see also: Act 1; Act 2; Act 3; **atmosphere**; **darkness**; **dreams**; Grant, Matthew; **lighting**; Maybank, Euan; *unheimlich*; vanishing): A lighting state favoured by Punchdrunk, especially within large-scale masked shows. Haze machines atomise a safe oil or mineral-based fluid in the air to create a subtle fog, establishing shards of light through which performers may materialise or sets might be perceived, such as a forest of trees. For Felix Barrett, haze is an important effect that is deployed through a careful blend of theatrical light and total darkness, to cloak a space with threat and ignite the imagination:

Haze makes seemingly empty space present, it makes it sculptural, it fills the void. Haze ensures the lighting becomes the performer. If

FIGURE 10 'Haze, forest, darkness, light'. *The Drowned Man.* 2013.

Photo credit: Julian Abrams

you have a hundred rooms and only thirty in a cast, if there's haze in the air then every room is full and alive.

The power of haze is further **explained** by Euan Maybank as 'giving life' to the space, by simultaneously creating atmosphere and animating a setting that awaits performers. When performers enter and exit a haze-filled space they appear to emerge from a dream realm and then gradually vanish. This connects with Matthew Grant's discussion of lighting that creates slithers and shafts from tightly shuttered lanterns on stands, an eerie effect that enables performers to appear and disappear in the space as if by magic. Peter Higgin observes, 'haze can create layers of light as well as obscuring the path, influencing the flow of the audience, causing them to walk slower or with a sense of unease at not knowing what might lie beyond the fog'. For Maxine Doyle:

Haze adds depth and dimension to the design whilst helping to connect spaces across sprawling buildings. It adds a thickness to the air and an eeriness to the atmosphere. Its presence contributes towards the shared space between audience and performer. It can make an ordinary object feel extra-ordinary and a simple moment feel magical. It works in tandem with sound, helping to support dramatic crescendos. Haze is a major semiotic player in the world of Punchdrunk.

H.G. (see also: audience; **Barrett, Felix**; corridors; **Grant, Matthew**; **influences**; installation; **lighting**; **masks**; tunnels): During 1995, while an A Level student, Felix Barrett experienced *H.G.* and following that 'everything changed' (2012). *H.G.* was the first commission in Britain, produced by Artangel of a work by Robert Wilson and sound and light architect Hans Peter Kuhn. Collaborating with British film production designer Michael Howells, and based on the writings of H.G. Wells, Wilson and Kuhn brought to life an encounter with time via immersive installations,

located across the interconnecting tunnels of Clink Street Vaults. Audiences entered, alone or in pairs, through a Victorian dining room where the guests had left which led to a series of scenes that similarly suggested just-missed activity; a hospital desk with a Medical Officer's notes; and an officer's boots standing to attention awaiting their owner. In addition to rooms that could be fully entered, there were also glimpses of time-forgotten lands, lush gardens and ancient ruins, through brickwork and doorways. Evocative accounts and images of the experience exist in the *H.G.* archive on the Artangel website. Barrett's A Level teacher, Matthew Grant, describes his recollections of this work, and Barrett's response to it, above. For Barrett, experiencing it for the first time, 'with very few audience members' gave him the space needed for his own imagination 'to fill in the gaps', a factor he found 'totally seductive':

It was densely atmospheric with huge, implied narrative but you *never* came across performers who were telling that story. Performers felt present but it was as though they had just left the space or they were just about to arrive.

(Machon 2013a, 164, emphasis original)

Barrett's return visit with his parents a week later proved to be a valuable reference point in regard to the evolution of the mask device in masked shows. This time 'packed with audience', the 'spell was broken . . . other people's readings and responses to it somehow dirtied the experience' and it was this that first planted a kernel of thought for Barrett:

To have an immersive experience you need to remove the rest of the audience members *being the audience* from the picture. If they're comrades with you, on the same mission, or if they're part of the scenography then they're either excluded from, or a complementary addition to, your reading of the work.

(Machon 2013a, 164, emphasis original)

Hide-and-Seek (see also: architecture; archiving; **Barrett, Felix**; **building**; **exercises**; **Exeter Experiments**; framing; journeying; **'listening to the building'**; senses; site; site-sympathetic): Felix Barrett's lead exercise in the devising of any project within a building for performers. The game is designed to provide the performers with a sense of the experience the design team had when first entering the building. Conor Doyle reflects eloquently on the significance of this game to performers in his contribution above. This exercise has been employed by Barrett for all projects occurring in architectural spaces ever since its first use during his Exeter Experiments. Performers will enter the building for the first time and engage in the designated activity (usually via a handwritten note, carefully placed, lit by a candle or natural light) in each room. There are many versions of this game, with variations on theme and activity according to the building and source material involved, **but** it is perhaps best represented by a word-for-word citation from Barrett's undergraduate written support for *Woyzeck*, 2000; detailing the first Hide-and-Seek, documenting how the textual source was interpreted through the building, charged by the performers' instinctive response to the space . . .

Felix Barrett

On Hide-and-Seek

. . . for the audience to be more absorbed they should come in one-by-one and go around alone. In this way, the cast . . . were to go around one by one and if they came across anybody else, they were to hide and try not to be seen. The tasks were as follows –

Summon up the ghosts of the past and watch them walk round the room.

Open a window and shout out where your character will be in a year's time.

Dance a jig.

(A room with twenty small candles scattered on the floor) Arrange the candles and then shout out when you are done.

Listen to the inside door creak.

(In the bar) Pour yourself a beverage of your choice and drink it, enjoying every sip.

Drunkenly look for a fight. Stumble.

In character, examine the veins in your right arm.

Lie down and listen for at least three minutes.

Perform, in character, a short monologue to all the people seated on the brown benches.

Imagine the haircut that your character has.

Think what used to happen in this room and then help the ghosts with whatever they are doing.

Have you ever been unfaithful?

Sit cross-legged in the centre of the room and whisper the name of your first kiss to yourself five times.

Touch every wall without being seen by the people who are looking in through all the windows.

Hide for thirty seconds and listen.

Watch the ghost of the past walk down the stars and come towards you.

Sing a Nina Simone tune (or another jazz classic) and fill the space with your resonance.

Who's behind the door?

(A plate of cold, cooked food in a kitchen) Dare yourself to try the food.

Tell a fairy story to the little boy in the corner. [Be gentle, as he's afraid.]

Lie on the table and imagine you are unable to move.

(A room with lots of chairs) Prepare this room for a seminar. If it is already arranged, then change the focus.

Can you smell it?

Sing –   There were two hunters from the Rhine

Rode through the woods in clothes so fine. Roaming together the wild woods free.

A hunter's life is the life for me [see Büchner 1979, 61].

A soldier's life can be . . .

(Barrett 2000)

Higgin, Peter (see also: Act 1; Act 2; Act 3; cinematic; digital technologies; **Enrichment**; Entwistle, Codie and Kyle; **Exeter Experiments**; senses; visceral): A founding member of Punchdrunk, Higgin's formal title is now Director of Enrichment and Punchdrunk Village, and he is joint CEO of Punchdrunk the charity. Higgin observed and was hugely influenced by the Participate Programme at BAC, and its mission to embed wider community projects and collaborations with theatre companies into the world of *Masque of the Red Death*. This influence, alongside his previous experience of teaching, were pivotal to the forming of Punchdrunk Enrichment. Higgin trained as a secondary school teacher of Drama, to GCSE and A Level, and held a post at Sandown High School on the Isle of Wight until 2005, following this with a short supply teaching career before starting work on *Faust*. In spring 2006 he took the decision to leave teaching and return to Punchdrunk in a professional capacity as Site Manager for *Faust*. It was while undertaking his first teaching post at a school on the Isle of Wight that he took his A Level students to see Punchdrunk's *Sleep No More*, London in 2003 and *The Firebird Ball* in 2004. Higgin was immediately impressed and excited by the manner in which Punchdrunk stimulated enthusiastic and sophisticated discussion about the work and its source material among his students on the journey home. He was further invigorated by the ways in which both works proved to be a source of inspiration and a model of practice in the group's subsequent devised exercises. These particular students, following their experience of Punchdrunk's work, went on to produce advanced durational projects themselves for their A Level productions; montaged in form and requiring multi-perspective shifts in its focus of attention. These experiences were key to Higgin's desire to explore the educational potential of the immersive form . . .

Peter Higgin

On Enrichment

My journey with Punchdrunk began eighteen years ago when I performed the role of the Captain in Felix's production of *Woyzeck*, at the University of Exeter in 2000. On a cold November evening I spent much of my time in a room, in an ex-army barracks, on the outskirts of the city. The room was covered in human hair and dimly lit by candles. Audiences wandered through this space over three hours, sometimes encountering me, alone in my room of hair, mostly in character, almost certainly freezing my butt off. Despite this chilly start, I was hooked. I loved the ambition of the work, the sense of danger and the radical rethinking of what a night at the theatre could mean. It was exciting, and I knew it had potential. I wanted in, wanted more, infected by a Punchdrunk spirit.

Alongside my passion for Punchdrunk I am also passionate about education and the practical application of drama in educational and community settings. This passion comes from an innate understanding of how exposure to the arts can be transformational – because it was for me, from an early age. I specialised in Applied Drama at Exeter, exploring practical applications across a number of settings. After graduating I spent a lot of time delivering workshops and performing in educational work across the country. This led me to teaching, and, in 2003, I stepped back from Punchdrunk and embarked on a teacher-training course. I wanted to gain my qualification and to use this to help support my own practice, to have a career to fall back on if Punchdrunk didn't work out. I trained on the Isle of Wight, teaching Drama to GCSE and A Level at secondary school, continuing to work on Punchdrunk's Big Chill projects in the holidays. Later I brought my students to see *The Firebird Ball* and *Sleep No More* in London. My students' responses to Punchdrunk's work would prove pivotal on my journey.

These A Level students were captivated and infected by a Punchdrunk spirit, as Codie and Kyle Entwistle illustrate in their contribution to this encyclopaedia. Journeys home were full of discussion about the productions; discussions that were unlike any post-show conversations we'd shared following other, more conventional productions. Usually talk of anything other than the theatre trip would dominate. After these Punchdrunk shows, stories of their experiences and encounters filled the train carriage or coach, and it didn't end there. It impacted their practice and their engagement with Drama. They wanted to recreate these experiences and were more engaged and enthusiastic about the possibilities of their work. It was at this point that I realised Punchdrunk's practice could reach and impact new audiences and the kernel of a possibility for the work was formed.

Fast-forward, through *Sleep No More* and *Faust*, the latter production being that which drew me back fully to the Punchdrunk family, and to *The Masque of the Red Death*. It was this collaboration with BAC that would sow these seeds, informed and inspired by BAC's Participate Programme, which embedded community projects and collaborations with theatre companies into the world of *Masque*. A trip to Camber Sands, during the run of *Masque*, was the first time the core team gave itself space to take stock and think strategically, imagine what the future of Punchdrunk might look like, honing the idea of a Punchdrunk Lab, a place to generate and test out ideas. We began talking seriously about an education and outreach programme, creating opportunities for this within the worlds of our large-scale events. It wasn't until Punchdrunk secured Arts Council England Regularly Funded Organisation Status and a Paul Hamlyn Breakthrough Grant that Felix and Colin Marsh approached me to take on the role of developing what would become Enrichment with an open brief to realise these ambitions.

An ideal was to embed Enrichment projects within our large-scale worlds, piloted with *The Apricot Orchard* yet only fully tested with *The Drowned Man*. In the interim years we came up with different models to create a Punchdrunk approach to engagement, with an array of communities. Now, in Act 3, Fallow Cross has been pivotal in terms of how Punchdrunk gives space and time to investigating and discovering future ideas. Recent developments, as with those nomadic projects of Act 1, are strategically proactive rather than reactive and responsive. Punchdrunk has a playful yet hardworking and uncompromising approach to pushing boundaries and we want to continue to embody this spirit as the company grows and ages.

Hodge, Stephen (see also: **Act 1**; adrenalin; **Exeter Experiments**; **immersive**; **installation**; **one-on-one**; pyrotechnics. Further reading: Jubb and Tompkins 2011): Artist and core member of Wrights & Sites, Hodge is Associate Professor in Live Art and Spatial Practices at the University of Exeter. Hodge was a significant mentor to Barrett during his undergraduate years, helping to nurture his interests and skills in creating installations and one-on-one events. Hodge's own practice with Wrights & Sites, a collective of four artist-researchers, including Simon Persighetti, Phil Smith and Cathy Turner, explores people's relationships to places, cities and walking; employing disrupted walking tactics as tools for playful debate, collaboration, intervention and spatial meaning-making. Inspired by these and other theories and techniques introduced to him, Barrett made a number of pieces during his third year at Exeter University, one of which was an encounter made solely for Hodge . . .

Stephen Hodge

On installation, one-on-ones and the Exeter Experiments

Founded by John Rudlin in 1968, the Drama Department at the University of Exeter was built on more of a European Laboratory Theatre model than a literary one. That was still apparent in the course from 1997 to 2000, when Felix was in Exeter. Students would focus intensively on a particular area of performance practice for a five-week 'project', sometimes for up to sixty hours a week, before moving on to the next 'project', which would usually have a completely different focus. In Felix's third year he elected to take a module I convened titled 'Technical Specialisation', which was designed as an extension of the second-year 'Stagecraft' module. Students were required to undertake an external placement relating to a particular technical area they already had explored in the second year, before moving on to produce more advanced practical demonstrations accompanied by a critical narrative. In his second year, Felix had studied costume, but I remember agreeing that he could explore a broader area of installation instead. In the first term of his third year he'd studied directing with Lesley Soule. The module demanded that he direct a work in a found space, something that was clearly important to his future practice, and something that he wanted to push further in the 'Technical Specialisation' module. Much to the Technical Manager's horror, rather than creating the expected one or two demonstrations, Felix produced approximately ten pieces of work, a series of very ambitious and fairly wild experiments. One was a performance piece he made just for me. I remember turning up at the university swimming pool, as instructed, then being ushered into the changing room, where I found some swimming trunks and a towel on a bench. Daunted, but committed at that point, I exchanged my clothes for the swimwear, after which I was ushered into the main swimming pool space. A masked figure sat at the top of the lifeguard's ladder. A number of other figures stood around and about the dimly lit room. Claude Debussy's *La Mer* filled my ears. I was accompanied into the room by a young woman, who welcomed me warmly and led me to the water's edge. She didn't talk to me. Communication was conducted through facial expression and touch. She blindfolded me, span me round several times on the spot, and kissed me for a very long time. Then, much to my surprise, she pushed me into the pool, still blindfolded. It was truly shocking. I was mentally and physically disorientated, first by the unexpected kiss, then by the unexpected envelopment in chlorinated water. That was immersive theatre for sure. Somehow, I managed to resist the urge to rip off my blindfold. I suppose I knew that the other figures in the space (masked I think) were there for safety reasons. I lay on my back in the water for some time, in darkness, trying to process my recent experience. It's rare to be the only audience member to experience a piece, and I felt particularly privileged this time, despite the shocks.

Another one of Felix's module outputs was a sleep deprivation experiment, in which a small invited audience spent the night sleeping in a large studio, only to be woken periodically and forced to perform a series of tasks in a semi-conscious state. Even handing in his portfolio at the end of the module became a spatial performance. I was tasked with tracking a number of clues around the city centre, a treasure hunt of sorts. The last-but-one node on my journey was an old medal shop, where I was given a key by the aged proprietor and directed towards the bus station. Once there, I located and opened a left-luggage locker, only to watch 100 or so ping-pong balls fall out onto the public thoroughfare. After scrabbling to pick them up and drawing significant attention to myself, I located a big suitcase in the locker, containing his portfolio. With it was an emergency flare and an instruction to go to the bottom of a nearby valley, let off the flare and, by that light, read the portfolio. I have to admit that I didn't carry out that part as it was pretty close to a fire station and would have almost certainly caused me a lot of trouble.

Although my memories of Felix's time at university are largely half-remembered and anecdotal, what is certain to me is that Felix was really pushing at the boundaries of each of his third-year modules in order to conduct a programme of experimentation focused on testing models of immersive theatre. Felix was also a keen musician and worked with a lecturer and saxophonist called Steve Cockett; music was important in much of Felix's work. It was surprising that he opted to study costume in the second year, rather than set design. Felix was often surprising, and often pushing himself into new territories. After he graduated, Felix worked alongside me on a site and journey-based module, part of which comprised a fire installation along two miles of the Exeter Canal for an audience aboard a boat. I experienced the early Punchdrunk work, *The Tempest*, at Poltimore House, on the outskirts of Exeter, *The House of Oedipus*, and then *Sleep No More* and *The Masque of the Red*

Death in London; a number of works in which I was required to wear a mask. Secretly, part of me wanted the formula to break after a while. It works, of course, but I had become truly inspired by the Felix who was always shifting, always trying something new.

I've rarely met anyone who won't ever take no for an answer. I remember many years ago now, Felix told me about his plans to secure H.M.S. Belfast for a project, and I may have laughed a little. His level of ambition is operatic. Somehow he manages to construct and hold these gigantic visions, and then to realise them; to pull it all together with, it must be acknowledged, the help of an awful lot of people. I have to admit that, watching the Punchdrunk model develop, with its dependence on large spaces and armies of people, I thought this is pure start-up ambition and energy, this is not economically sustainable. But, somehow, Felix and his early collaborators managed to persuade enough people to commit to the vision for long enough to build the momentum and catch the attention of the big players. That's determination. His energy and vision are infectious. That Felix and the team managed to persuade David Jubb at BAC to give over the whole building, including their offices, for so many months for *The Masque of the Red Death* is quite extraordinary.

Nowadays, most of the students who come to Exeter will have seen or heard of Punchdrunk, and their emerging student work often chimes with the company's practice. Of all the student work I've seen in over twenty years in academia, Felix's *La Mer*, in the swimming pool, is the most memorable. In 2011, I experienced Helen Cole's *We See Fireworks*, an aural installation she created over several years, which comprises curated audience responses to live work. One at a time, audience members listen to a series of voices talk about performances that had a significant impact on them, before recording their own, which then becomes part of the collection. It was my memory of Felix's *La Mer* that I added to Helen's collection, and now I've added it to yours too.

House of Oedipus, The (2000, see also: **Act 1**; **Exeter Experiments**; journeying; masked shows; **Tempest, The, 2001**): Across thirteen acres of wild Victorian garden, two of Sophocles' tragedies played out in tandem, *Oedipus the King* and *Antigone*. Performances took place in secret groves and under the cover of ancient oak trees, all in the shadow of the ivy-covered skeleton of Poltimore House, Devon. *The House of Oedipus* provided a crucial learning point in relation to masked shows for Barrett, his second 'eureka moment':

Outdoors, daytime six-hour durational, masks. Didn't work. Because of the natural light. It didn't work for the audience. For me Punchdrunk is about curiosity, exploration and discovery of those beats of wonder. If **you** can see in the distance what you're going to discover in five minutes time once you actually get there, it invalidates it; there's no reveal. You need the reveal. The reveal is crucial.

(Barrett in Machon 2015, 260)

For Barrett there have been two eureka moments: 'the first was the mask and the second this. I remember them because the adrenalin is so incredible and then the euphoria you get from it all clicking into place'. It was also as a consequence of lessons learned in *The Tempest* and fully realised with *The House of Oedipus* that Barrett knew once and for all that he wanted to find an alternative, more physical language to work with and rethink the manner in which speech was to be included in adaptations of textual sources.

House Where Winter Lives, The (2013–2014, see also: Act 2; boxes, chests and drawers; Enrichment; forests; tunnels):

Mr and Mrs Winter invite you to join them in their warm and welcoming cottage, as they prepare for a winter feast. Unfortunately, they've mislaid the key to their larder. Wrap up warm and join them on their journey through a secret forest to find the missing key.

Punchdrunk Enrichment transformed the Story Studio of Discover Children's Story Centre in Stratford, East London, into a magical, frozen forest. Children aged three to six years old, with their families, explored the wonder of winter in an interactive storytelling adventure, baking biscuits, speaking with woodland animals via burrow-hidden telephones, and travelling through a wooded tunnel to an enchanting storytelling conclusion, told via a papercut world, discovered in a box. The project was a development of the learning from projects in primary schools, as well as drawing on the form and techniques established during the run of *The Crash of the Elysium*. The project successfully took the company's work into a more traditional studio space, ensuring that the immersive form was both intimate and more readily transferable. Peter Higgin recalls:

Sally Goldsworthy, then Executive of Discover, approached me about creating a piece for their story den. I was familiar with the venue and admired its approach to child-led learning and the way they used the space to engage pupils. Although we'd created many school projects and *The Crash of the Elysium* had been a success with families, this was Enrichment's first chance to make work for a paying audience. It was a good-sized studio, but incredibly small in Punchdrunk show terms. I relished this challenge and was interested in creating a project that tapped into the trope of adventuring into the woods, to take children on a wintry adventure. The idea of bringing the outdoors in was exciting. We gathered seven van-loads of foliage, installed it in the studio to create a magical forest that covered most of the studio.

A replica of the production toured to the Perth International Arts Festival in 2014.

Hytner, Nicholas (see also: *Drowned Man, The*; *Every Good Boy Deserves Favour*; *Faust*; *Firebird Ball, The*; **mask**; **masked shows**; *Masque of the Red Death, The*; Morris, Tom; *Sleep No More*, NYC): Director of the National Theatre, 2003–2015, Hytner is a self-proclaimed Punchdrunk 'superfan'. The National Theatre (NT) is based on London's South Bank, set up to produce a classical repertoire alongside commissioning and supporting new work. Its extensive history and remit can be sourced via its online archive. Hytner's directing legacy for the National includes *One Man Two Guvnors* and *The History Boys* and he introduced 'National Theatre Live' cinema broadcasts, worldwide. He also directed the anniversary gala *Live from the National Theatre: 50 Years on Stage*, blending live and archive performance on stage with live broadcast on BBC2 and in cinemas around the world. Together with Nick Starr, Hytner is a founding partner of London Theatre Company, an independent producing company, and founder and director of The Bridge Theatre, London. Under Hytner's Artistic Directorship, NT offered in-kind support to Punchdrunk for *Faust*, *The Masque of the Red Death* and *The Drowned Man*, bringing Punchdrunk to the attention of a wider audience. In 2009 Hytner invited Barrett to co-direct, with Tom Morris, a production of *Every Good Boy Deserves Favour . . .*

Nicholas Hytner

On masks, narrative and audience

I remember going to *Firebird*, Tom Morris took me, and I had no idea what I was going to or what to expect. I do remember feeling the mask was a little bit of an imposition, but then being liberated by it; that element I realised pretty immediately. I've never looked for narrative coherence in a Punchdrunk show, that's not how I enjoy them, so I had no problem at all with not knowing what was going on in *The Firebird Ball*. I took it entirely as a sensory, visceral experience. I was absolutely fascinated by it and fascinated at the end to discover that there was a massive fight I saw that nobody else in my party had seen. I remember finding it viscerally really exciting. I don't look for story, in fact I didn't know that that was what I was being asked to do. If I'm being honest, the only one where I actually got some sense of narrative coherence was *Sleep No More* in New York, maybe because I locked into an order of events or maybe because I'm so familiar with the source material. Every single one of them that I've seen I've had a good time. I've found myself stirred and excited. I come back to the word, visceral. I find them, on a sensory level, extraordinary, always. The proximity of the action; finding myself with Faust and Gretchen in a small room, just me, I found quite extraordinarily disturbing and an experience that would have been unbearable without the mask. At the end of *The Masque of the Red Death*, I remember being in the main hall for the final ball, being grabbed by some boy and being whisked around the room, something that I found quite exciting and transgressive and would simply not have been prepared to do had I not been wearing the mask. But even with *The Masque of the Red Death*, I didn't get a story.

I thought *The Firebird Ball* was great and with Tom, who knew Felix and had all the connections with Punchdrunk, offering to do what we could to make life easier was not very hard. Punchdrunk has a huge audience of a particular type; they have their audience, the National Theatre has its audience, let's try and get both audiences to find out what the other one enjoys. It wasn't a difficult or heroic decision. It was a case of: what can we do for you, can we sell your tickets, can we give you some kind of infrastructure, is there help you need? It felt really straightforward, win/win. It expanded the National's audience in that people booked for Punchdrunk who wouldn't have otherwise booked. I don't think it meant that necessarily they came to other stuff and it doesn't matter. I managed to get Felix to come and work on a stage and it was great having him around. *Every Good Boy Deserves Favour* was one of those things that briefly happened, thrilled that it did, but was obviously not a road that Felix wanted to travel down because otherwise he would have done more shows in theatres, where people sit in rows and watch the stage. But the combination of the orchestra and Punchdrunk performers, and he and Maxine bringing some of that slightly secretive, slightly transgressive, charged atmosphere, to the Olivier stage was great.

As for the mark Punchdrunk has made on British theatre, it would be a tremendous mistake to try and build a policy around Felix and his collaborators; the mark they've made is *who they are*. They plough their own furrow. Felix has a particularly clear, particularly individual, vision of what an evening in Punchdrunk's company should be. To me the British theatre is, at any time, to the extent that it is *anything*, or can be defined as anything, the sum total of the interesting people that are working within it. The impact Punchdrunk's had is precisely that lots of people have responded to the way Punchdrunk makes events. It's worth remarking that as you stand in a queue to be admitted into one of Punchdrunk's shows, you're looking at people who don't very often come to see plays at the [Royal Court's] Theatre Upstairs. I say that, I don't know that, but it doesn't feel like there's an overlap and it doesn't matter whether there is or not. We can get terribly lost, bound up in a pointless campaign to get people who like one thing to like another. It doesn't matter. The mirage that there should be some perfect theatrical event where a perfect cross-section of the entire community comes together to watch, say, *Three Sisters*, I don't think that matters at all. Not at all.

If Punchdrunk is to be studied, it would be better to encourage those who study them to make their own events. I would have thought it would be extremely productive to ask people to think about why and how Punchdrunk's work is different to other forms of theatre and other ways of experiencing live performance; to think about why it's different and in what ways it's exciting, at the same time as considering in which ways other forms of theatre are exciting.

I

immersive (see also: epic; **experiential**; **in-show-world**; installation; senses; synchronicity; visceral. Further reading: Alston 2017; Biggin 2017; Frieze 2017; Machon 2013a): A water analogy of being submerged in another medium can help to describe and define immersive performance practice, while 'immersion', defining deep involvement in an activity, indicates the experience once inside an immersive event. Additionally, adopted from computing terminology, immersive performance usually provides stimulation for multiple senses, not only sight and sound. An alternative analogy for describing the form, for Maxine Doyle, is 'the metaphor of an immersion heater, its association with intense heat and pressure'.

Since the mid-2000s, with Punchdrunk playing a significant part in bringing the term into performance discourse, immersive has been freely used across marketing publicity, theatre criticism and in academic study, as a shorthand for a particular type of experiential practice, evolved from a broader, interdisciplinary and participatory arts inheritance. Immersive aesthetics are usually multisensory and move audience appreciation into a whole-body interpretation, incorporating the smell, touch and feel of the work, typically involving some kind of direct interaction within the piece. In this way, the audience-participant is directly implicated in the aesthetics of immersive work, from concept through to production. Immersive performance encompasses minimalist, one-on-one encounters through to large-scale spectacles. Typical features that distinguish immersive performance from traditional stage/auditorium productions include the audience-participant always having direct, practical contact with the work, as individuals or a collective. The audience will be able to detect, immediately or as the piece progresses, an 'in-its-own-world-ness', to the event, which usually involves interdisciplinary aesthetics. Consequently, the design, performing style (if, indeed, performers are present) and activity within these worlds will offer a more complex layering to the ways in which central ideas and themes emerge.

With Punchdrunk worlds, there is a synchronicity among the immersive ingredients, with each and any element holding its own weight and validity in the experiential moment. With the masked shows, if any one of the elements 'pulls rank' then this will be carefully designed within the show; the 'magic' occurs for Felix Barrett when the relationship between each element is 'imperceptible'. The audience experience of the shift between performers space, light, sound, design and installation should be fluid, with all of the elements working together 'as a sinuous whole'. Audience is integral to any Punchdrunk world, in concept, content and form. The audience-participant's direct insertion in, and interaction with, the world shapes and transforms potential outcomes of the event, in narrative, theme or form. For Barrett, Punchdrunk's work can be defined as immersive specifically in relation to:

the empowerment of the audience in the sense that they're put at the centre of the action; they're the pivot from which everything else spins. It's the creation of parallel theatrical universes within which audiences forget that they're an audience, and thus their status within the work shifts . . . [I]t's the fusion of all the disciplines and the belief that no one discipline is more important than another; the light is as important as the sound, which is as important as the action, which is as important as the space. Also, what's crucially important is the detail in the work; the implication that you can always dig deeper and find something of merit. It's implied in the spatial detail, there are always secrets to find, but also in the work as a whole; to know there are other rooms, other scenes, more backstory to a certain character; a perfect angle to see a lighting transition from or to capture a little *son et lumière*. There's always the promise of more to discover.

(in Machon 2013a, 159)

influences (see also: **Act 1**; abstract/abstraction; aesthetics; **Barrett, Felix**; Barrett, Margaret and Simon; **cinematic; corridors**; Exeter Experiments; Grant, Matthew; **H.G.**; lens; **mazes**; **music; research**; Reverse Dolly Zoom; ritual; Tonkin, Geoff): 'Influences' is included as an entry in this encyclopaedia to identify those inspirations that have occurred along the way and unlocked an approach or aesthetic for Felix Barrett and other members of the core creative team. In addition to his parents, Margaret and Simon, who were a major influencers and supporters of his artistic pursuits from an early age, Barrett also remains loyal to the significance of his Drama teachers, Matthew Grant and Geoff Tonkin, in shaping his theatrical tastes. Influences that are, arguably, deeply embedded in an approach that has been forged by Barrett from an early age include the practice of Edward Gordon Craig, Silviu Purcărete and Josef Svoboda. Following university Barrett cites Marina Abramović and acknowledges 'the *principle*' of 'Deborah Warner's St. Pancras project' as 'hugely impressionable', as was the work of Geraldine Pilgrim (Machon 2013a, 164–165, emphasis original).

Looking back across formative works that inspired him, whether directly or in a more oblique fashion, Barrett acknowledges specific productions that he 'immediately rebooked to see again'. In chronological order: Bob Carlton's *Return to the Forbidden Planet*, Robert Wilson and Hans Peter Kuhn's *H.G.*, Wilson's *Woyzeck* and Baz Luhrmann's *Moulin Rouge*. Barrett vividly recalls Wilson's interpretation of Georg Büchner's *Woyzeck*, toured to the Barbican, London, in 2002, and its expressionist use of light and stylised performance, noting, 'I periodically check to see if that's on anywhere else in the world. I'd jump on a plane to see it again'. Where *H.G.* is a vital and repeated reference for Barrett, included as a separate entry in this encyclopaedia, other works help to illustrate the inchoate and evolving aesthetic in Barrett's practice. More generally, they offer texture and insight to how broader, indirect influences persist and have tangential impact on Punchdrunk's work. In reflecting on early influences and memorable events, the formative influence for Barrett lies at a visceral level in terms of a forceful reaction to the form of the work, which warranted repeated viewing in his earlier years. As Barrett puts it, 'because the impact was so great and so potent, I just wanted to feel it again'. The significance of the specific works cited as impactful, at whatever point in history they were encountered (and acknowledging the diversity of forms), relates to 'the intensity of the experience' they evoked which proved consequential to Barrett's emergent practice, as he elucidates:

With H.G. and *Forbidden Planet* it was about the sensation of presence, having direct contact with space, light and soundtrack or feeling alive in the space because of the performers. Every synapse was firing and I felt like time and space had come to a halt and I was at the centre of it all. With Wilson's *Woyzeck* and *Moulin Rouge* it was about the pace of the production and the variety of the images with which my head was saturated; I couldn't take it all in so had to go back to see it again.

Barrett also notes, in terms of inspiring a mode of practice, 'there's a lot about being singled out in my early formative experiences of *Cats, Return to the Forbidden Planet*, De La Guarda. That singling out from the audience makes you feel special, even though it's all inside, all artifice'. For Barrett this difference between feeling special as opposed to exposed when singled out, as with *The Rocky Horror Show*, 'is the intention that the performer brings. If it supports the work and is enticing and mysterious' it can be effective, 'whereas that *Rocky Horror* experience was just aggressive', which encouraged the audience to be similarly hostile.

Beyond these formative experiences that have impacted Barrett's practice in various ways, it is shared influences among the core creatives that underpin Punchdrunk's unique approach and aesthetic. Film is of great significance in terms of its impact on form and shared vocabulary as well as cinematic genres becoming the lens through which many a Punchdrunk world is refocused. Individual films and practitioners feed into a storehouse of reference points from which the core creatives draw. *Metropolis*, an iconic work of German expressionist cinema, released in 1927, and directed by Fritz Lang and written by Thea von Harbou and Lang (a wife and husband creative team), reappears from Barrett's A Level examination piece through to *Tunnel 228* and it continues to influence ideas for the future. *Metropolis*'s art direction, juxtaposing light and shade to dramatic effect, provides a strong example of how expressionist film influenced the chiaroscuro effects of film noir, for which Alfred Hitchcock is renowned. A film noir aesthetic permeates *Sleep No More* in London, Boston, New York and Shanghai and the nuances of movement qualities in Hitchcock's films influenced Maxine Doyle's choreography, as an extract from her notebook for *Sleep No More*, Boston reveals:

As with Hitchcock, our key protagonists hover on an edge of tempestuous instability. Screen dialogues become intense physical duets between characters and the body becomes the site of debate. Similarly to Hitchcock, Punchdrunk characters are dwarfed by grand, architectural sites and suffocated by confined spaces . . . Shades of Hitchcock films permeate the world wandering through Macbeth's story. We see Duncan's wife, like the young Mrs De Winter from *Rebecca*, her fragility like a rare light in the thick night. She is searching for her lost husband – and is bullied by Macbeth's cruel housekeeper – Danvers. In *Rebecca* Mrs Danvers has a supernatural function. Hitchcock never films her walking – she always appears out of thin air peering over her charge's shoulder. In our world, Danvers is all seeing. She is aligned with the three witches and tends malevolently to Lady Macduff's pregnancy paranoia.

Significantly, the vertiginous effect of Hitchcock's Reverse Dolly Zoom helps to describe the sensation that Punchdrunk strives to reproduce in audience members during moments of high visceral impact. The tempo and aesthetic of more recent films have also played their part in Punchdrunk's aesthetic. Stanley Kubrick's 1980 film *The Shining*, adapted from the novel by Stephen King, remains an oblique reference for Barrett, highlighted when discussing the significance of mazes and corridors in Punchdrunk work. Barrett recollects, from watching a video of this film with a friend at a too-young age, appreciating the visceral quality of the pacing of a narrative, the embodied recall of the illicit and the recurring motif of corridors and mazes:

The rhythm and tempo and that Kubrickian pacing was so alien, dangerous, scary. We knew we were too young to be watching it. It felt illicit, but the rhythm made us stick with it, drawn to the mystery of it. It culminates in a maze but throughout, the hotel itself is maze-like, with corridors that don't make logical sense.

David Lynch's back-catalogue partnered by Angelo Badalamenti's scores is a shared influence across the team and homage to Lynch's work is discernible in many of Punchdrunk's large-scale masked production, as reiterated in various entries in this encyclopaedia. It is possible to draw a sideways connection to *Moulin Rouge*, with its sensuously bawdy aesthetic that conveys the *fin-de-siècle* bohemian Paris of its narrative and the painterly satirical expressionist style of Henri de Toulouse-Lautrec (of whom an interpretation appears as a character in the film), and the Music Hall world within *The Masque of the Red Death* and the Red Death Lates. Barrett adds 'that film was doing something that blew my mind'. Similarly, Barrett notes repeat viewing is required for Lynch's work, to take in its complex visual and narrative signifiers:

I had to watch the first episode of the new *Twin Peaks* [2017] three times because it's so dense with material. Every scene is so measured you just want to absorb it properly.

Visual references and influences that capture qualities of the cinematic and the framed are also relevant to the research for both design and choreographic practice. These include the discernible traits of Edward Hopper's oil paintings of urban scenes of mid-twentieth-century Americana, identifiable in *Faust* and *The Drowned Man*. Equally the work of the American photographer Gregory Crewdson, who creates evocative, while otherworldly, images of contemporary American homes and neighbourhoods, is a visual influence on the work of Barrett, Beatrice Minns and Livi Vaughan. Barrett notes how Crewdson's 'use of light, composition and clarity of vision', supports the undercurrent of 'the *unheimlich*' which runs through his work. Crewdson's stark imagery also provides recurrent stimuli for Maxine Doyle's choreographic practice. In terms of 'framing', the late Parisian artist, Charles Matton, who produced a series of 'Boîtes' ('Boxes'), miniature installations displaying otherworldly dwellings and interiors, suggestive of the abodes of dreams as much as models of actual inhabited rooms, is an influence on the work of Vaughan.

Music influences are fundamental to Barrett's approach, driving a concept, setting the mood and era of an interpretation, unlocking the means for a finale. Often significant works or composers return as inspiration, as is the case with Igor Stravinsky's *Firebird Suite*, Claude Debussy's *La Mer*, Benjamin Britten's *Peter Grimes* or the crooning of The Ink Spots. Just as with Badalamenti's scores for Lynch's works, Bernard Hermann's compositions for Hitchcock's films hold equal influential weight. It was the influence of Hermann's score for *Vertigo* that inspired Barrett's concept for *Sleep No More* back in 2003. Stephen Dobbie notes of Hermann's scoring that it provides 'a quintessential modern take on classical music. It isn't overly flowery or decorative'. More significantly it hints at the liminal and time-suspended in his interludes. Dobbie explains that they employ 'only two or three chord changes yet they might last a minute and a half'.

As these examples indicate, shared influences among the team from across arts practice – in form, theme and philosophy – have proven to be arbiters of style and illustrate the ease with which a collective aesthetic has evolved. Repeated reference points abound and indicate shared interests, passions and approaches. Literary sources, such as Hermann Hesse's *Steppenwolf* or John Fowles's *The Magus*, are inspirational, as detailed in the entry for 'text' below; each having also served as stimulus for a concept, as Colin Nightingale illustrates with *Clod & Pebble* and Peter Higgin notes in terms of the blurring of life and fiction in regard to Punchdrunk Travel. Illustrating how shared interests serve to orient practice and connect stylistic approaches, Maxine Doyle recollects: 'Badalamenti and Lynch were great talking points at my first meeting with Felix and a good establisher of taste'. Important to note is that the collage of influences that exist within and across the core creative team are too many to mention, but when intertwined they create the unique Punchdrunk stamp that, for a likeminded audience, demonstrates artistic affinities or working processes; Doyle cites Pina Bausch and Anne Theresa De Keersmaeker; Vaughan includes Robert Lepage where Minns cites a wealth of literary and folkloric inspirations, with constant inspiration drawn from James George Frazer's compendium *The Golden Bough*; Higgin flags educational thought-leaders Dorothy Heathcote and Ken Robinson, while Dobbie and Colin Nightingale share a background in 'music archaeology' and DJing.

Certain shared references might be discernible across masked shows while other influences may only appear fleetingly, a consequence of specific research for one production in particular.

An important point to note is that Punchdrunk's process has evolved from a history of being curious about how to blur the lines between live performance, real-world contexts and its practice. Each and every Punchdrunk project is critically underpinned by extensive research that draws from a range of sources and influences. These influences, drawn together in note form, whether individual works or practitioners, lend insight into the manner in which Barrett's approach to practice has evolved and been layered by the core creative collaborators to produce the signature Punchdrunk aesthetic. In this regard, Barrett is adamant that the more abstract influences and recurring motifs that appear in concept and form across different projects and productions have equivalent importance to Punchdrunk's practice as the practitioners and artworks cited. These include such entries as 'corridors' and 'mazes', and other conceptual, imagistic or tangential allusions. For Barrett these should be noted as essentials that 'inspire and make up who each of the core team are as artists and practitioners'.

in-show-world (see also: **aesthetics**; **design**; dreams; **immersive**; installation; **nature**; 'Norman the Eel'; Pluto: 'Rebecca the Bird'; 'Specials'; **touch-real**): For Punchdrunk, the logic of everything within the aesthetics of any production, whatever its scale, has to stack up so that it creates its own unity, even where this logic plays with the illogical, the imaginary and otherworldly. Punchdrunk create a dense world within a chosen site that interprets its intertextualised source material in forensic detail in order to shut out the 'everyday' world so that the audience might leave this behind for the duration of the event. The aim is to establish, in a multidimensional and multisensory manner, a whole-world, authentic environment that 'lives' and functions according to its own rules, regulations and logic. This world is set through the building, its spaces, the design and the atmosphere established by music and lighting. Only then is it populated by performers; those who have established their characters in the studio and also those who create characters in response to the on-site world emerging through the build and installation, finding and fixing the character that is invoked by the rooms within the world. Felix Barrett clarifies:

The 'universe' comes first in its set, you have a space, you build the world, over the course of that you may have an idea of some of the characters but not necessarily all of them. Once you've created the world within that universe, only then do you know how to inhabit it.

A shared intention and accepted rules-set in process among the core Punchdrunk team is that, in the creation of these worlds, no one area is considered to be more important in conveying theme, narrative or finding a form for the ideas within a project. In this respect there is no desire to establish a hierarchy of performance elements within the world created. As Barrett elucidates, 'in *Chair*, the fabric walls, the typewriter and the fish-tank, the performer sleeping in the bed, the flickering smart candle, all had equal weight'. With this in mind it is notable that audience members may share this understanding and respond sympathetically to that intention once inside the world of a masked show, allowing any single element to take precedence or be experienced alongside the montage of other elements, in piecing together the wholeness of the universe, as much as its themes and narratives. Equally they may be drawn to or led by the element or discipline in which they are most interested; installation, sound or performance. Conversely, audience members may choose to create a hierarchy in piecing together the world, taking a more conventional approach where they prioritise the stories the performers tell, over and above the stories told by the rooms, objects and sound with which the performers are in league. For Barrett:

The purpose is not to try and find the performers, that is not the gauge in how far you've succeeded in

having a great night. The purpose of any project is that you're listening to your gut and being led by your instinct and whatever piques your interest, drives your curiosity, that's what you follow. That's going to be different things for different people.

Punchdrunk's approach to the aesthetic realisation of any world relates to the more general definition of the 'in-its-own-world-ness' of immersive practice (see Machon 2013a, 93).

installation (see also: **abstract/abstraction**; **accidents**; Barrett, Felix; **dens**; **design**; *H.G.*; influences; **Minns, Beatrice**; nature; **research**; scenography: 'Specials'; taxidermy; touch-real; **Vaughan, Livi**. Further reading: Bishop 2010): Installation loosely refers to any artwork or design experience into which audiences enter and are surrounded by the sensual, often interactive, materials of the work. Felix Barrett, evolved from his den-building days, was interested in installation as an art form from an early age and followed through with such a design approach from his A Level work onwards. In addition to being influenced by Robert Wilson and Hans Peter Kuhn's *H.G.*, Barrett was also inspired by the installations of Geraldine Pilgrim. His Exeter installations, alongside the early London productions, were sparser than the detailed installations since *Faust*: 'That's how we used to do it, we'd appropriate and refocus what was available or found on-site. A lot of that was because we had no budget, so you had to otherwise there would be no show'. Prior to *Faust*, Barrett's family home provided most of the objects for early Punchdrunk installations, 'no-one else had the sheer quantity of ephemera'. Barrett adds, 'back then we were, not quite magpies but hunter-gatherers of design'. With the original *Woyzeck*, 2000, Barrett made use of everything lain to waste in the barracks, including medical slips and mess invitations discovered on-site. In this was there was an expediency to the way in which he built his installations and also an element of inspiration that came from those found objects, ripe for artistic

reinvention in the worlds he was creating. In the design entry above, Barrett highlights how mood-driven installations can be achieved with minimalist precision as long as the space – the floor and ceiling in particular – support the mood and narrative.

Barrett invited collaborators and ensemble members to take on the responsibility for installing the design in certain rooms, with *Sleep No More*, London and *The Firebird Ball*. Since *The Masque of the Red Death*, Beatrice Minns and Livi Vaughan have led on Punchdrunk's installations, meticulously creating touch-real worlds, realised through intensive research and attention to the tiniest of details. Minns' first title, 'Head of Detail', demonstrates the significance of installation in creating Punchdrunk worlds. Adam Curtis recalls of *It Felt Like a Kiss*, an entirely installation-led experience:

It benefitted immensely from Beatrice Minns, who is a total genius. She understands mood. I would find her, late in the evening, adjusting things. She's an artist. You could tell she had a clear idea of what she wanted and that was so impressive. It's that attention to detail that makes Punchdrunk different to other immersive theatre, there was something substantial in what Bea did. I would talk to Livi and Bea about, for example, the history of intelligence agencies, and it would come out in this incredibly imaginative way.

Regardless of whether it is a single room or a vast set across a building, any Punchdrunk installation establishes a 360-degree world that is as authentic, while otherworldly, as possible. The audience has access to that space via the full human sensorium; touch and smell as much as vision and sound. The interaction invited in that space holds up to the situation and stories that the space holds.

Installation in any immersive performance requires an innate understanding of how to design for three-dimensional interactive space, as opposed to designing with the same materials on a stage; the impact of fir trees in an installed environment through which the audience walks is very different to the visual presence of those same trees on a stage in an end-on auditorium set-up for the audience. As Barrett puts it, 'the ingredients that thicken space in an environment aren't the same ones that thicken space on stage'. Installation makes ideas that exist within the source material tangible and three-dimensional. It can be especially resonant when subtextual elements, through abstraction, like the dance vocabulary with which it is partnered, encourage the audience to experience expressionistic undercurrents, themes and ideas; to interpret the work in a non-linear way.

interaction (see also: **access**; **agency**; **audience**; **caretaking**; curiosity; gaming; **immersive**; masked shows; **touch-real**. Further reading: Oddey and White 2009; White 2013): This relates to any audience participation within an event and involves interaction with space as much as performers. It implies that the audience has agency within the world, although this **will** be carefully controlled. A feeling of liberation may be present in masked shows in the freedom granted to construct narratives and experiences. Punchdrunk's immersive events ensure any interaction has been designed and, even where multiple outcomes might be possible, these have still been controlled by the company, similar to the processual rules of gaming. For Peter Higgin the invitation to interact is opened up, primarily through the creative environments where 'you can touch and move items'. With any interaction that invites creative agency in Punchdrunk worlds, the audience can, subtly or in dynamic ways dependent on the intentions of the project, change the course of action:

There are very few instances, if any, where the audience can or has changed the course of a show; you can't change the narrative, you can't change the ending. You may be able to have multiple experiences,

all unique, but you can't radically change the outcomes of the piece. All of the company's work is highly crafted to drive towards a definitive ending. The interaction creates a sense that you are impacting the work but, in its current form, the audience doesn't have the power to change narratives nor experiential plot of any show. We don't yet have the resource to facilitate multiple endings, contingent on different decisions and choices. It's interesting territory, but for this work to come to fruition the boundary between audience and performer would need to be blurred much further.

Higgin is adamant that the active nature of the immersive form is part of the success of Enrichment's practice:

Moving around makes people present, alive and alert. It forces them to be so. This active, exploratory nature in concept and form is also a big reason why the Enrichment work is often such a big hit with pupils, often boys, who tend to remove themselves from learning activities in the classroom and have difficulty engaging with academic work. These pupils love the sense of adventure, love that the project is otherworldly and not part of a traditional, more sedentary school life.

Kathryn McGarr has performed with Punchdrunk since *Woyzeck*, 2004, straddling Enrichment, R&D and mainstream practice, and so honed a range of methods of interaction with audiences. Applying these techniques in her wider work with Gideon Reeling, alongside her performance partnership with Matthew Blake, she attributes her aptitude for this work to those early Punchdrunk projects, into which she dived and immersed herself while still a student . . .

Kathryn McGarr

On immersion and interaction

The first Punchdrunk production I experienced was *Sleep No More* while an undergraduate. I had never seen anything like this before – it was a total experience and it was addictive. The excitement of running free in a derelict building that had been transformed into a living world, with *Macbeth* layered within it, was magical. I felt so many emotions simultaneously – fear, excitement, anger, elation. I could *feel* that I'd been inserted into a fantasy and was living within it. I was totally hooked and I went back to that production many times. I volunteered, assembling masks and helping out in any way in order to be part of the experience and to relive that feeling.

During summer 2004, I volunteered as a performer, alongside twenty or so others, to create *Woyzeck* at The Big Chill, building it as a collective over the course of the week. I stapled fabric and became skilled in ruching to make the sideshow circus. It was like epic arts and crafts. Once our playground was made, by the weekend of the festival, we were able to set our characters free. Assisting with the design ensured we knew and understood the world so well that we had an innate sense of the tone and type of play required – even though we hadn't spent that much time devising the performance. Everything was active, the three-dimensional sets, the audience, plus we were interacting with nature, lit by the moonlight and climbing trees. During this project I learnt to guide an audience into playing; at a level that was make-believe yet real. I was a vagabond and became a dab hand at pick-pocketing people. I would steal someone's wallet, walk past and say 'have you lost something', waving it, invitingly. They were 'in the game' then. I returned it, obviously, but it certainly blurred boundaries between reality and make-believe. It was intoxicating. If I think of *Sleep No More* as my introduction to the ocean of practice in which I'm now immersed, *Woyzeck* was like walking the plank from the student boat to the unchartered professional waters; scary and exciting, enticing me in further.

By *Faust* I was joyfully floating through it and learning new strokes. As Diner Girl, I performed my first one-on-one which was exhilarating. Building on lessons learned during *Woyzeck* and *Marat/Sade*, it created a new intimacy in performance, an authentic moment between two people, albeit in a fictional world. Although I was playing a character, and audience members a version of themselves in those encounters, the nature of the interaction liberated them to enter into the fantasy with me; aided by the installations, the narrative and, most importantly, the sense of play. *Faust* was the first time I performed in a masked show with the surrounding audience zoning-in. That really helps performers to focus in on their world. I liken it to being on a film set with the masks as multiple cameras coming from all directions, prickling the skin on your back.

The Crash of the Elysium sent me swimming in a slightly different direction, helping develop my ability to gain audience trust. Directing them, like an extended one-on-one across an hour's action in a game-like encounter, established a play between the real and not-real. You're looking them in the eye, saying 'I've got your back so dive into this with me'. It was a good lesson in working out what was necessary to hold onto in the plotline and what can be jettisoned or replaced in terms of interaction and audience involvement; stating story and set-up early on so that they understood their role. *Under the Eiderdown* was the first Enrichment project I worked on and I realised it to be at the heart of immersive work. As an adult, it helps you understand childlike play and the way in which you need *to be* in the world created; a world in which you know somewhere that it's a game, but you embrace an overriding commitment to utter belief. That quality of belief displayed by the pupils was, and is, inspiring to see. They aren't held back by judgement or fear, their reactions are uninhibited, and that acceptance helps the world fully exist, enriching the magic of it.

Dive years ahead to *The Drowned Man*. The performance world that had been opened up to me as a student had evolved to be so much greater in every respect. *The Drowned Man* brought together lessons learned from those Big Chill projects, alongside a style I had developed with Gideon Reeling and as Kat and Matt; encouraging or enticing people to play, interact with you as a character within the world. Creating Studio 3 within the wider world of *The Drowned Man* was about understanding what that moment needed to be for people within their wider experience of the show. It was a space that grew as the show went on, because it could only be realised with an audience. Set in the bar area where audience members could de-mask, get a drink and verbally interact required different ways of communicating to make audiences aware of setting and the role that they could now play, while also keeping the tone and atmosphere of the world from which they'd emerged and to which they might shortly return. Shifting between entertainment – live band, songs – to light-touch interactions, moving from table to table regaling and inventing tales of Temple Studios, hinting at a deeper adventure, which led a select few in for a two-on-one with Matt and I. This allowed the atmosphere to change and the dark undertones of Temple Studios and the world outside Studio 3 to seep in. These interactions required us to place roles upon the audience as they entered; from the starlet to the Hollywood producer to the director, and the 'has-been'. Each relied upon willing audience members with a necessary twinkle in the eye and a heavy dose of fun and quick-wittedness. The scenarios we created in Studio 3 were partly scripted and partly improvised, allowing audience members to enter into a different mode of play and to influence the shape of the experience. This necessitated an inherent charm and wit that comes closer to improvised comedy in order to guide the experience, so that the audience willingly accept the role given them. This then sent them back into the masked show with a more informed focus or mission, to 'have a consultation with the doctor' or 'go downstairs for a party with the studio boss'. Audience walked away from that interaction being 'contractually signed into the studio'.

Punchdrunk's total attention to detail in all areas is where the magic lies. It ensures that audience members can truly lose themselves in the world. The same goes for a cast member, devising and performing in that level of detail. Significantly, it is the space in which you lose yourself that you find your character so authentically.

intervention (see also: adrenalin; *Borough, The*; *Cherry Orchard, The*; *Clod & Pebble*; coda; corner; cross-fade; *Kabeiroi*; multiples; *Moon Slave, The*; *unheimlich*): A device employed by Punchdrunk, intended to change the way the audience views the 'everyday' world, or the in-show-world of an event. Interventions can happen in any form through any theatrical tool; light, sound, performer, architecture. As Felix Barrett puts it, 'every single facet can be used to destabilise'. Performed interventions, as Felix Barrett describes, create 'punctuation, beats of the uncanny. Peculiarity. The suggestion that there's something not quite right'. These may be brief moments of interaction with another human being where the audience member is unsure whether that individual is part of the experience or an unusual interlocution in the everyday world. It immediately establishes a sense for the audience member that they exist within a strangely liminal space between the 'real' and the imagined. If employed as part of the cross-fade performance, interventions may establish a sense of anticipation or trepidation, as with their early experimental interaction employed with *The Cherry Orchard*. They might involve glances in the street, or uncanny lip-synching to the audio in your headphones, as with those designed in *The Borough*. When employed and reiterated throughout an event in this way, as was also the case with *Kabeiroi* – strangers passing on the street slapping portents into your hand or catching your eye, warning you, by name, that you are being watched – they immediately trigger adrenalin and adventure, making the experience immediately become more visceral.

Interventions are also established through architecture, design and sound; moments are at odds with a sense of surety one might have settled into within the Punchdrunk world. Instantly unsettling. The unexpected turn of a corner that reveals a corridor of statues; a lone telephone in an otherwise empty, darkened room, illuminated by a single shard of light; the constant crackle of a stuck gramophone or the pulse of intoxicating club-music intervening in an otherwise otherworldly tempo of 1930s melodies. For Barrett, interventions, whether outside in the everyday world, or within the building that houses an event, are staccato in rhythm and tempo, with the intention to 'keep an audience present', via the rug-pull, the subversion of expectation.

If a space is too predictable it can be overturned through clever interventionist devices. For the generic space of *Faust*, Barrett and team considered 'blocking corridors so the audience wouldn't trust the logic of the space, but we couldn't afford that, so instead we obtained thirty-six Blessed Virgin Mary statues, by the sculptor Susan Shaw, managed to get them for free for a credit in the programme'. Rather than making the generic spaces architecturally different, this played with overturning expectation by breaking the logic of the footprint of the space, intentionally ensuring that generic space 'looked exactly the same', removing signs that located floor level and installed these replicated Virgin Marys at every entry point so that audiences 'wouldn't necessarily tell if they'd been on the floor before or not, could get lost in the expanse of space'. In this way object and architecture intervened to destabilise expectation and keep the audience, physically and imaginatively, on its toes.

In the lead-up to masked shows, interventions might also be used as tantalising tasters of the world to come, a means by which the audience, unsuspecting or otherwise, can gain first entry to the realm and be drawn into its delights. These might take the shape of mini-performances in designed spaces, such as with was the case with *The Drowned Man* pre-show fortune-telling one-on-ones that, tangentially, served as word-of-mouth publicity vehicles, or curious letters sent to keyholders with clues embedded in the sparse text. The overriding intention is that these initiate the point at which the world begins, influence presence and participation once wholly within the world and inflect appreciation of the event, before, during and subsequent to leaving that world.

It Felt Like a Kiss (**2009**; see also: Act 2; **adrenalin**; **chainsaw**; **corridors**; **Curtis, Adam**; **Poots, Alex**; *unheimlich*): Commissioned by Alex Poots for MIF 2009, *It Felt Like a Kiss* was created in collaboration with documentary filmmaker Adam Curtis and musician Damon Albarn, with the original score performed by the Kronos Quartet. The Punchdrunk world was an immersive installation, meticulously created by Beatrice Minns with Livi Vaughan in response to the visual imagery of Curtis's film of the same title. For Curtis,

> The question was, how do you take what Felix does, which is about the individual creating their own story, and put it together with my film, which has a clear, narrative structure. It benefitted both of us, fitting together two forms which really shouldn't have worked together.

Installed in a deserted office block in Manchester, the production occurred in three phases. The audience entered through the clown's mouth of a 1950s Fun House and, in groups, took a lift up three floors alighting on 1950s Americana, complete with a domestic home, and gradually moving through the decade and the physical manifestation of scenes within Curtis's film; passing from the American dream through abandoned CIA offices, Detroit ghettos, ancient monitors revealing the assassination of John Kennedy, the Vietnam war and into a medical research centre which set up the transition to the central phase. Initiated by a quarantine exercise, the audience then entered, in the same group or perhaps with different people according to how long individuals chose to remain in the previous installations, for a showing of Curtis's film. Audience members could stay for one or more showings of the film before being evacuated into the final series of ransacked rooms, prison cells, around every corner a hint of hidden threat that descended into theatricalised terror as groups were chased by a man with a chainsaw, separating them to ensure they exited alone, along a dark

FIGURE 11 *It Felt Like a Kiss.* 2009.

Photo credit: Stephen Dobbie

corridor, as Colin Nightingale puts it, 'to face the ultimate terror, one's own fears'.

Curtis's documentary examines America's global rise to power during the golden age of pop and Hollywood, on the cusp of the late 1950s and through the 1960s. It tells a story of the telling of stories by America; stories that are 'enchanting' or 'frightening' that 'make sense of that world' but that fall apart, leaving only fragments which 'haunt like half-forgotten dreams' (see Curtis 2009). His film exposes the lies that bind one decade to the next and the nightmares that returned to haunt the world at the turn of the millennium. The title is taken from The Crystals' 1962 Phil Spector-produced song, *He Hit Me (It Felt Like a Kiss)*, written by Carole King about the domestic abuse of her then babysitter Eva, who became the popstar Little Eva. Like this song, which immediately forces the listener to recoil at the disturbing juxtaposition of disposable-pop music and disconcerting lyric-content – the disjuncture between the dream and the truth of the situation – Curtis weaves together hidden narratives of this era. Combining the political with the personal, he links across domestic abuse, political conspiracy theories, coups, corruption, gun ownership, the rise of individualism, advertising that sells the dream and personal finance and credit consumerism that buys into it. Drawing narrative connections across pop-music, cinema and politics, from Carole King to Little Eva to Phil Spector to Doris Day to Rock Hudson to Enos the chimp to the Congo to the CIA to Saddam Hussein to James Bond and on, showing 'cause' while allowing the viewer to comprehend for themselves the prescient 'effect', Curtis uncovers how horror stories of the recent past set in motion the terror of the present:

I wanted to do a film about what it actually felt like to live through that time . . . Where you could see the roots of the uncertainties we feel today, the things they did out

on the dark fringes of the world that they didn't really notice at the time, which would then come back to haunt us.

(Curtis in Brooker 2009)

Punchdrunk tapped into this idea of the fear and terror, connecting the politics of the past to the mechanics of America's 1950s terror rides. Felix Barrett recalls, 'we did so much research, in Japan, visiting haunted houses and dark rides, to examine every mechanism they use. It needed to be hyper self-aware' in order to lay bare the mechanics of the horror that, literally, catches up with the audience at its end. Colin Nightingale describes this project as 'a politicised Walk of Terror', the horror tropes and mechanisms serving to theatricalise, destabilise and underscore the themes at the root of the film. For Barrett this project was an illustration of how 'adrenalin' can function in Punchdrunk work: 'when someone says, wow I really felt alive or equally, they experience themselves kicking into survival mode'. In terms of heightening this sense of trepidation and simulated, theatricalised fear to tap into Curtis's themes, Barrett explains that the entrance to the event:

imitated the signs of 1950s American dark rides and declared, in that manner, what we were going to do to them. The chainsaw was a device that was used in those scare attractions. We brought in the deliberately naff clichés of haunted houses to prove that they worked, got the adrenalin pulsing.

These were more threatening, given greater weight when paralleled with the constructed narrative of Curtis's documentary. As Barrett notes, 'Adam would say that America is haunted by itself, constantly looks back on its past, makes it a source for its own fear'. In this respect there were 'rock-solid, valid artistic reasons for doing what we were doing with *It Felt Like a Kiss*. Those historical dark-ride devices illustrated America's past catching up on itself. Like an ouroboros'.

Curtis details in his entry above how the 'hybrid' form produced was an interesting experiment. Yet it also proved to him that immersive practice is a product of its time, 'like a three-dimensional rendition of the Internet. You can go anywhere and make your own story' which ultimately prevents collective comprehension of the same political narrative (in Curtis and Buxton 2017). A landmark production in that it made the front-page news of *The Guardian*, Curtis, above, and Poots, below, describe the process and outcome of *It Felt Like a Kiss*, highlighting the intention and impact of the adrenalin-fuelled finale and, for Poots, how the project addressed 'artistic and structural issues that were fundamental across the performing and visual arts' in addition to the deeply political issues it exposed'.

J

Jonny Formidable: Mystery at the Pink Flamingo (**2001**, see also: **Act 1**; failure; journeying; synchronicity): Produced for Roborough Studio, Exeter, this was a three-dimensional noir 'flickbook' set to a jazz soundtrack. An interactive lip-synched show, tailor-made to engage the audience as they travel as a group throughout the world of Jonny Formidable, drinking in dive bars and eventually dancing the night away; audio-journey meets club-night. Barrett recalls of this Act 1 experiment:

> We took the principle of the head-set and we put it in a theatre space, and it didn't work because it was for multiple audience and you were reading it as a theatrical experience rather than reading it as something that had invaded your real life.
>
> (Barrett 2013)

Looking back, Barrett adds, 'it wasn't perfect but we learnt from it', elements of which were then redeployed in *The Borough* with lip-synched moments performed by members of the Aldeburgh community, 'the impact of synchronicity. I've always been fascinated by that':

> The beauty of *Jonny Formidable* and *The Moon Slave* was the taking of orchestral scores that prompted an emotional response, cutting them together, laying narration over the top. Almost like investigating how you take the intimacy of a radio-play and theatricalise that.

journeying (see also: **flow**; immersive; **loops**; **masked shows**; ***Moon Slave, The***; Punchdrunk Travel; site-sympathetic): In Punchdrunk productions there is always a sense of journey embedded in the themes and forms of the work and each event is designed in such a manner that the audience has some degree of ownership of that journey. When in a conventional theatre set-up, where auditorium and stage are configured as end on, thrust or in the round, with the audience largely static (whether seated or standing), it is the performance that moves and travels in front of the auditorium for the audience to observe. In Punchdrunk work the audience travels with the performance and takes decisions about which characters, narratives or aspects of said performance it wishes to accompany on the journey. This is a vital aspect of the Punchdrunk experience in masked shows, where the journeying occurs within and across a building, perhaps even its surrounding locale. Punchdrunk has a history of exploring journeying in outside locations, blurring the boundaries between the 'real' and imagined world. In early works such as *The Tempest*, 2001 or *A Midsummer Night's Dream*, this occurred on foot through the gardens and landscaped vicinity of the site. Walking to and around The Big Chill projects, *Woyzeck* and *Marat/Sade*, was in keeping with the festival environment and a significant aspect of each production's aesthetic and experience.

The Moon Slave was the first Punchdrunk work to experiment with journeying in a layered manner; from the invitation to find and reach the location where the piece begins, to the disquieting journey in the car, transported by a silent, masked driver to the destination, the grounds of a house through which the audience member then continues on foot, guided by a narration through headphones to reach the crescendo of the piece, following which the audience member is then directed back to the car with the same driver who returns you as the denouement plays out over the car stereo system, to the start point. Across the last eighteen years Punchdrunk has experimented with the journeying in a range of works including *The Uncommercial Traveller*, and its partner projects, *Living Cities*, *The Borough* and *Kabeiroi*. The majority of Punchdrunk's R&D work has incorporated journeying within the form and narrative. Journeying is pivotal to the ambition and future plans for Punchdrunk Travel.

Jubb, David (see also: accidents; **Act 2**; **architecture**; **building**: Cake Friday; collaboration; community; **Enrichment**; *Gold-Bug, The*; **in-show-world**; legacy; *Masque of the Red Death, The*; mass production; **McDermott, Laura**; one-on-one; **Pluto**; *Quest of a Wave, The*; touch-real; volunteers; *Yellow Wallpaper, The*. Further reading: Jubb and Tompkins 2011): Artistic Director of Battersea Arts Centre (BAC) since 2004 and CEO since 2008. A leading London arts venue, housed in a former Victorian town hall, BAC is equally renowned for its community work and its support for innovative performance practice. It established 'Scratch' events, where artists share and develop work with an audience. At Laura McDermott's recommendation, Jubb was responsible for commissioning *The Yellow Wallpaper*, *The Quest of a Wave* and *The Masque of the Red Death*. Jubb, with David Micklem, founded BAC's One-on-One Festival, inspired partly by collaborations with Punchdrunk from *The Yellow Wallpaper* onwards, while *Masque* contributed to the rebirth of the BAC building . . .

David Jubb

On BAC, buildings, community
and Punchdrunk

B AC is based on the idea of Scratch, people testing ideas out, and on the idea of developing artists; that's the *raison d'être* of the organisation. At the heart of that, over the last fifteen years, has been the role of the producer. We have a producing team here who are multi-skilled and able to run workshops in schools, programme festivals, develop artists. Back in 2005 I had three junior producers who I'd appointed and by 2006 they'd graduated to being full producers; Laura McDermott, Harun Morrison and Shelley Hastings. Laura McDermott was a big fan of Punchdrunk and had seen *Sleep No More* and been involved in *The Firebird Ball*. She described the work to me and on the back of that I got excited in terms of the nature of the experience. At the time, our mission as an organisation was to invent the future of theatre, it remained that mission for ten years, from 2005 to 2015. It felt like Punchdrunk's work, in terms of inventing the future of theatre, had a different relationship with the audience, a different relationship with story, and particularly interesting to me was a different relationship to space; exploring the role of a building as a character in the story, a character in a production. I always think wherever you put a show, whatever the show is, it's different according to that space – we all know that in the audience but sometimes there's an assumption, professionally, that it doesn't make a difference, or at least there was then. Now, partly down to Punchdrunk, there's a much greater appreciation of the impact that a space has on work, even when you just show it there – let alone if you create it in that space – if you just show it in that space, the context and the way that the audience relates to the work shifts and that's really important.

Laura got me super excited about the company, and I can't remember exactly the order of events but we started to talk to Punchdrunk about a building-wide project around the same time we invited the company to take part in two festivals with *The Yellow Wallpaper*, for Octoberfest 2005, and then for Burst 2006, a festival of sound and music, they created a piece called *The Quest of a Wave*, another one-on-one experience. *The Yellow Wallpaper* was the very first Punchdrunk show I ever saw and, in a way, I feel that I had a very pure experience of Punchdrunk because of that. At the heart of the excitement about the work is that illicit opportunity for an audience member to take off their mask and, in doing so, walk, metaphorically and actually, into the fiction, into the drama, to become a character; to stop being an observer and to be *in it*. With *The Yellow Wallpaper* we got a very true experience of a Punchdrunk world. By the time I experienced that we were already on a journey to a bigger event. I seem to remember we were going to stick *The Yellow Wallpaper* on for three days but we ran it for the rest of the festival for three or four weeks and lots of people came to see it. It was one of those great festival pieces where people end up coming from across town to see this something special.

Felix and I, with Laura, Colin Marsh and Colin Nightingale, began to have meetings to discuss an idea Felix and I had; how you could create an arts centre *inside* the world of a show. So often, in fact pretty much always, shows live inside the world of the venue; they exist in a space, you go in to watch a fiction and you come back out and you're back in the venue. We wanted to flip that. We had this thought about how the show could be the entire building and the arts centre could exist within the world of the show. That was the first creative provocation in terms of working with each other. What was maybe not unique but potentially quite problematic for Punchdrunk at that time was that this was a living, breathing, operating building. Rightly and understandably, the company tends to work in spaces where it has total control, total ownership, as much as possible because it enables them to have the kind of control they need in order to create the worlds they create. This was a more complicated, potentially traumatic, combination of how you encompass our arts centre living inside a Punchdrunk world. My office was above the Scratch Bar, about fifteen of us worked in there, and if you wanted to get out after seven o'clock in the evening you had to put a mask and a cape on, tap to check there was nothing going on in the next room with the storyteller and then you would go out into the little library space; literally, a bookshelf would open, you'd come out with your suitcase and your mask on and you'd walk through the world of the show in order to leave, to go home. It meant that the team here developed such an intimate relationship with *Masque of the Red Death* because we literally lived and worked inside the world of that show.

Felix gave us the opportunity to create two commission spaces, a rarity in Punchdrunk's work, which was not without its challenges for the company and for us. What we wanted to do was recognise that BAC had for a long time developed and supported artists. If this show was going to take over, we didn't want it to become a complete cuckoo and throw everything out during that period of time. Two spaces were designed in order for Punchdrunk and BAC to work together to commission new work. It's amazing to look back and see the artists who produced commissions, Paper Cinema who created *King Pest* along with others like Lundahl & Seitl, Kneehigh, Suzanne Andrade, Mel Wilson and our young people's theatre. There was one on the ground floor which was more of a full-on immersive space like Punchdrunk's one-on-one model except several people would go in at once and you would take your mask off and have this experience inside it, like you were on the periphery of the world of *Masque*. There was also a storytelling commission space in the library where we invited artists to come in and tell a story based on Poe. All the commissions, in fact, drew inspiration from Poe or Gothic-styled narratives.

Additionally, working with Coney and Tassos Stevens, *The Gold-bug* adventure ran concurrently through the world of the show. This experience ended up taking on its own life and had a midnight building takeover where a load of people came, and in the very hatch we're sitting next to [in what is now the waiting room of BAC], discovered treasure. Again, not uncomplicated because it created a different world and set of rules within, but adjacent to, the world of *Masque of the Red Death*. There was a different agenda at work for the *Gold-bug* audience among the wider audience. From my perspective, all of these things, whilst challenging, created a real depth and richness to the total narrative, the total experience, of the show.

Another element was that we still maintained a working studio theatre, formerly Studio 1 and now The Bee's Knees, during *Masque of the Red Death*. My tech team went in and covered it with egg boxes to soundproof it, with its own separate entrance on 66 Theatre Street, so we called it 'Studio 66'. If you exit by the box office and turn right onto Theatre Street you can still see it, all the lettering of Studio 66 is still there, somewhat broken up. Studio 66 operated as an independent studio theatre that our producers programmed. It hosted artists like Nic Green, Will Adamsdale and 1927. Audiences would visit it separately to see a show. It had its own bar and if you wanted to go to the toilet as an audience member you had to put a mask and a cape on, exit and return through its internal double door; you'd have audiences who'd gone to see Nic Green, coming out into this strange world with trees, crazy haze and reverberating clock chimes. I remember very occasionally the reverse happened, which was obviously a mistake, particularly during Nic Green's show, *Cloud Piece*; a live artist, performing a beautiful production about clouds and her relationship with the environment but, somehow, the double door hadn't been locked and a couple of Punchdrunk audience members came in with their masks on to find this show with its own audience. In any other context in an arts centre you'd go, 'Whoops, sorry wrong show' but of course, they went, 'Whoa! We've found the most incredible, secret part of *Masque*, there's a whole audience here and they're all watching us!' – until the point where they were made aware, politely directed out and Nic carried on the show.

There were several different elements – the commissioned spaces, the Coney show, Studio 66, our offices – which meant that the show became this organism which we were all part of. It meant that the staff team here held the production and everyone who made it with huge affection. It became this incredible family endeavour, as I'm sure all Punchdrunk shows do, where everybody is working together. The wider Battersea volunteer community were equally involved, especially Pete and Joan, who are an institution in the organisation. They live across the street and have volunteered here for many, many years. Pete would look after the fire upstairs. Felix and I chose a cat from Battersea Cats and Dogs, Pluto, who still lives here very happily, has got a bit fat in his old age to be honest. Pluto used to, every night, go into the fireplace room of his own volition and lie in front of the fire. Pete would light the fire, the cat would lie there, audiences would come in looking around, look at what they thought was an animatronic cat, go up to it and Pluto would turn around, clock them to great surprise, 'oh my god it's a real cat!'. It's made him a terrible show-off in general. It's like sending a child to stage school for the first ten years of their life. Pluto's never quite recovered from every night 250 masked audience-members walking into his room, staring lovingly and amazed at him. Ever since he's carried an air of slight dismissiveness of large groups of people.

As well as create exceptional experiences for audiences, Punchdrunk also creates history and memory for a space, and we're very lucky that those memories from *Masque* have been absorbed by the walls of a cultural space like BAC. Some of my favourite moments were related to the fact that once a week, during the creation of the show, we threw a big picnic in the Grand Hall with bags of food from the local supermarket. It was one of the final spaces that we attended to because the front of building, with all the warren of spaces and the split level of the building, was where the huge people-commitment and volunteer effort was; the collective making of the cloaks, wine bottle making and loads of multiple-make activities, which involved hundreds of people. We would get food from the local supermarket and just lay it out on the floor in the Grand Hall and we'd all sit and have lunch together; literally 150, sometimes 200, people sitting on the floor of the beautiful old Hall, having lunch together, from volunteers to Punchdrunk to artists working in the commission spaces to all the staff here. There was something old fashioned and community driven about it in terms of a production company coming together, creating a community and making work.

Since 2000, we've developed lots of shows using the Scratch process and we 'scratched' aspects of *Masque*. I remember we had a mass adventure across the building one evening with about 250 young people on a treasure hunt, to test how that many people worked in terms of circulation around the building. About a year before *Masque of the Red Death* we started to recognise and question why we weren't using Scratch for more of what we do. We'd used Scratch for the creative process of making shows and learning from making mistakes, listening to feedback and getting responses but we didn't run the organisation like that. We had a departmental model, like a car manufacturer, just as lots of arts organisations have; you're doing incredibly creative things, but you run the organisation itself in an uncreative way. We wanted to apply Scratch to more of what we do and one of those things was our approach to the way we developed the building. In partnership with Steve Tompkins, of the company Haworth Tompkins, a Stirling Prize-winning, visionary architect who designs lots of theatres, we decided together to work with an improvisatory method of architecture; we wanted to test ideas out before we invested loads of resources. The linear approach in architecture – someone having an idea, doing a bit of consultation, developing the idea, followed by all of those stages of design – means that mistakes that are made early on in the process tend to get baked into the design. If you look at Lottery-funded arts buildings built in the last twenty years you'll find that some of them weren't very well loved, weren't successful, some of them were even closed because they weren't fit for purpose. That demonstrates and highlights a problem in how design works within the sector. Steve was thinking about how improvisation can play a role in architecture, so we started talking about a building project in Battersea that would test or Scratch ideas before fully developing them. That approach then fed in to our entire methodology for the whole renovation project and *Masque of the Red Death* played a hugely formative role in helping us think about how that methodology would work.

Felix, Steve and I went on several walks around the building together talking about ideas for the show. The simplest example to describe is what is now called 'The Fireplace Room'. Felix was describing how fire was an important symbol in Poe and how ash and fire were significant in the storytelling. Steve suggested that we open up the chimney in that room which ultimately led to that being a significant space in the world of the show but also to BAC having a convivial, sustainable, carbon-neutral approach to heating some spaces. It was a perfect confluence of art, organisation and architecture.

Masque was so important in terms of how it offered a new approach to testing out ideas for the building with artists and is something we always root back to. It provided a template and mould for that process and led to what we called the Playground Projects; a coming together of architecture, the building and artists. A core philosophy of our work is that magnolia is not neutral; what rooms feel like is vital to an experience, as is the sense of a building showing its history. Punchdrunk's legacy at BAC relates to how the company has contributed to attitudes to the building and its spaces. The process for re-imagining BAC is bound up in *Masque of the Red Death* – for me it was a legendary show because of that. My memories of walking the building, the music, the sound, that repeated chime of midnight to reset the narrative loop, all really remain with me, because there was a perfect match between Poe and the building, that sense of faded grandeur.

It was a creatively fertile time for the building and the organisation and would not have been possible without the exceptional vision, generosity, flexibility, rigour and kindness of Felix, Max, Colin Nightingale, Pete, Colin Marsh and the wider Punchdrunk community of artists, performers, makers and volunteers. There are few companies, in history, I think, who you can say have changed theatre forever. These are often companies of artists who bring together a series of approaches to something that becomes a definitive version. Punchdrunk has defined immersive theatre in the twenty-first century and has become the single most important reference point for all other immersive performance. Like one of Felix's breathtakingly beautiful rooms in *Masque*, in which he created a delicate palimpsest on the walls, so too the company's work has become the layer beneath the layer beneath the layer of the work of others.

As someone working in the building during *Masque*, walking the corridors during the show, it so often felt like a dream within a dream, a heady cocktail of theatre, everyday life and community. The imaginative potential of the worlds that Punchdrunk create is one of the reasons why Punchdrunk Enrichment is now showing us the way in terms of creative pedagogy. The potential of that story has only just begun and I hope it will prove to have an even more profound impact on our approach to learning than Punchdrunk has had on theatre.

K

Kabeiroi (2017, see also: adrenalin; compromise; cross-fade; digital technologies; failure; journeying; Punchdrunk Travel; scalability; soundscore):

But I do not treat you as an omen of my journey . . .

Inspired by the ancient Greek myth of the women of Lemnos, *Kabeiroi* was an adventure for paired audiences, played across London for a duration of four to six hours. Beginning, seemingly, as a straightforward sightseeing tour of Bloomsbury, it merged into an ominous game where participants became embroiled in a mission to unlock the narrative, which led to each pair being separated with one having to save the other before entering a high-octane crescendo together, with a beautifully serene conclusion. Billed on publicity material as 'different to what's come before', this was an early Act 3 exercise in trialling new work with a limited audience. It was reliant on smartphone and audio technology, first as the conduit of the audio-narration, then as the means by which messages might be relayed via texts with an unseen, while deitylike, all-seeing, games-master (in reality, a Punchdrunk control team overseeing the experience through this text interaction and satellite navigation). As the piece progressed, audiences became increasingly unsure whether members of the public were plants and performers or simply merging with the invented world as one's imagination ran with the story.

For Felix Barrett, the fundamental purpose of the project was blurring the liminal space between the imagined and everyday worlds joined by the narrative journey. It proved the effectiveness of the melt between the narration, which began as a straightforward sightseeing tour of Bloomsbury (some following a literary route, other pairs led around squares and streets by sculpture) into an atmospheric soundscore, most charged at the eventual destination of this first phase of the experience, the British Museum,

while apprehending statues of Greek goddesses. Here in a simple yet electric cross-fade, a silent, open-faced woman passed you the envelope with the next phase of the mission. However, he is also quick to point out the problems that arose:

The theatrical shape of *Kabeiroi* ended up being completely skewed, almost the opposite to what we wanted because we were trying to achieve some semblance of economic stability as much as a narrative coherence. We've done tests with only two people across a day and it's been the most powerful thing, because we could totally control the experiential arc. *Kabeiroi* ended up being so far out of our control – even at times in the control room itself – because the piece is so finely tuned. If a couple of audience members get lost, it initially would cause pandemonium, with operators shouting, 'Tier Two, let's operate Tier Two', which meant that the control room had to work in a half-hour delay because of that one couple that had got lost. Observing that, I queried what that might feel like for the audience. Punchdrunk is built on what the event is supposed to *feel* like, not what you think or process necessarily, and it was that bit that was being dropped because of logistics. That's kind of crushing but it's also the perfect example of why we need to fail because now I know how to make it work the way I wanted; to stabilise it. Now I know what to do with the second attempt, to get it to a scale and a level of importance theatrically and to fix the right final destination to make that form-breaking. The whole reason we began *Kabeiroi* was because we found this amazing space in Beckenham – and for us, everything is germinated from the space. That site would have given the most incredible finale. You begin in Central London and then you end up in the countryside, from the urban to the rural with a loss of control that comes with that sense of expectation, and once at that

site, only then would you all come together as a group of twenty-four, all wearing a disguise not knowing who was a performer and who wasn't, nor who your partner was, with half an hour of a Punchdrunk event in this country-house and its crumbling surroundings, which nature has engulfed. We spent ages building the relationship and then we lost the space. In the spirit of doing something rather than not doing it, not experimenting, we forged ahead with a Plan B, but it was a shame having to stay in one palette, solely the city and the game. With *Kabeiroi* I was adamant that we had do something, even if it didn't work, so that we could test it and move on from there.

As many of the reviews outline, it resulted in a mixed experience, many loving all or some of it, most guessing that this was the pilot for future experiences. The lottery for tickets was simultaneously not well received by critics, while equally causing a stir of excitement among fans, and there were some that felt that tickets were overpriced (although many acknowledged that the staffing required to oversee the experience explained the cost). In fact, the ticket prices were heavily subsidised by Punchdrunk. Barrett summarises: 'the only way we would push the form was by trialling it, for it to prove a need that projects like that require great resourcing and staffing. To be human and ethical you have to prioritise audience, cast and crew comfort and experience'; necessary factors of work of this nature but that had a detrimental impact on Barrett's artistic ambitions. The learning from *Kabeiroi* is now being implemented in a forthcoming Punchdrunk Travel project, as Barrett summarises:

All I can see is the potential for it down the road. We had the right ingredients in there – if it had been the correct arc of the experience it could have worked. It's the promise of what's to come and I'm completely confident that it will work, in the same way with *House of Oedipus* I knew what wasn't right and what was interesting about what didn't work, but I could see where it was going.

keyholders (see also: **Abloy**; **Bow**; boxes, chests and drawers; **community**; **doors**; funding; producing; R&D; **Valet**; **Zeiss**): The support scheme run by Punchdrunk to help fund projects. Annual keyholders are able to unlock access to Punchdrunk experiences and receive regular news of Punchdrunk events. At the time of writing, there are four different keys available, Bow, Valet, Zeiss and Abloy, each of which unlock different levels of engagement with Punchdrunk experiences. As Act 3 progresses, a new Cross Key level will be introduced. Sarah Davies, Punchdrunk's Head of Development, expands:

Our keyholders represent some of Punchdrunk's most committed stakeholders and provide the company with vital charitable support in the form of annual donations. The group, born out of a traditional 'Friends' Scheme' much like that of many arts and community organisations, evolved into a multi-tiered patronage system engaging supporters at different levels with corresponding means of access to Punchdrunk news, unfolding plans, projects and project-related events. Each of the four groups is named after a special type of key: the Valet Key; Bow Key; Zeiss Key; and Abloy Key – each metaphorically unlocking the company's secrets. For the higher-level supporters who are bestowed with physical keys, these *literally* unlock doors, boxes and objects in specially devised events. Since its inception the keyholder scheme has enabled members to be involved in one-off, live action experiences, games, project previews, supper clubs, all of which incorporate performance elements and live theatrical 'teaser' experiences prior to major project launches, alongside a more conventional programme of drinks events, previews and talks. The company's supporter engagement activities reflect the innovative approach and distinctive aesthetic of Punchdrunk's work – appealing to the company's keenest fans and long-standing supporters, offering them an enhanced, layered and more personal connection with the company. In turn, the collective charitable contribution of the keyholders helps to enable the continuation of all Punchdrunk's UK work. A passionate and dynamic group, a large contingent of the keyholders are part of an active community of international immersive theatregoers who engage in an enthusiastic online dialogue via Facebook groups, blogs and other social media platforms, forming a rich and lively community of their own.

L

Lambeth Walk, The (**2011**, see also: Act 2; community; Enrichment; **intervention**; **journeying**; R&D; research): *The Lambeth Walk* was a bespoke project created for seven primary schools in Streatham, with the aim of inspiring pupils with the heritage of their borough. Pupils in each school received an old map, sent to them by Lambeth's Archivist-in-Chief Albert Letemps. Albert asked the pupils to find out what they could about the map and the places marked on it, so it could be added to Lambeth's archive. Following the route to several heritage sites around the borough, the pupils encountered people, members of the public and Punchdrunk performers, along the way on their own Lambeth adventure. Pupils ended their journey at the archivist's office, added their stories to the archive and discovered new stories in the interactive environment. Peter Higgin expands:

This project aimed to widen the horizons of pupils living in Streatham, getting them out of their postcode, showing them the rich history of their borough. Artistically, it was a chance to take pupils on a fantastical journey born out of a very simple and everyday map. It also allowed us to play with intervention. One of the most exciting moments was when pupils who made a journey to Kennington Park piqued the interest of a random passer-by. The children were looking for a park, but it didn't seem to exist. The passer-by coincidently knew the whereabouts of the park and the fact that it was now known by another name and agreed to take the pupils there and thus their journey took on a new energy; a seemingly chance encounter changing their fortunes and the direction of their morning's investigations.

lampshades (see also: **collaboration**; community; design; lighting; *Masque of the Red Death, The*; **mass production**; **multiples**; Red Death Lates; **reveal**; **synchronicity**; vanishing): The lampshades in BAC's Grand Hall, for the final scene of *The Masque of the Red Death*, according to Colin Nightingale, offer insight into the Punchdrunk process:

Understanding the story behind how 150 lampshades ended up hanging from the ceiling of the Grand Hall of BAC during *The Masque of the Red Death* can help to explain a lot about our creative process, especially during the preview period where we adjust everything to ensure the best experience for the audience. The Grand Hall was used for the finale of the show and we knew from the initial planning that were going to need to use a significant amount of our production budget transforming it by draping the walls and ceiling in dark material to avoid light-bounce off the ornate white walls. The room was also an impressive height so felt a little too cavernous; draping the ceiling while also providing a lighting rig would require the installation of a lighting truss and so we took this as an opportunity to lower the ceiling height and bring some intimacy to the vast space. It was the largest room that the company had tackled design-wise and there were many ideas that we were struggling to achieve with the limited budget we had available.

The point at which the show opened for two weeks of previews we all knew instantly that the finale wasn't working. The audiences were hurriedly 'evacuated' en masse from the main part of the BAC building that they had been exploring for two and a half hours. They were held in groups in claustrophobic fabric chambers around the perimeter of the hall before being released into the main room. We had struggled to make an impactful transition from these chambers and we needed to find a way to shift the energy in the room as the audience first entered. We really wanted the reveal of this grand space to offer the crescendo we had always imagined, as it would then be the perfect set up for the balletic choreography that would follow before 'Death' would enter the space and ultimately vanish with the twist of his black cloak. Despite having lowered the ceiling, the room was still too cavernous so a plan was hatched to lower the truss further. With a new lighting design in process, Stephen set about making changes to the sound design.

Livi and Felix started discussing ideas for an installation that could fill the void in a more abstract fashion. It needed to be cheap and quickly executed as the clock to press night was ticking. We asked all staff at BAC to come in to work the following day via their local charity shops and buy up any old lampshades they could find. Consequently, the next day we were surrounded by piles and piles of lampshades and a design was conceived that would see them hung at various heights from a nylon rope grid rigged on the truss. During this period, we were still running the show each night so scheduling work in the room, while simultaneously giving Maxine time

to rehearse new elements for the finale, had to be carefully planned. We identified a single night by which we would be ready to install and focus the new lighting design and also rig the lampshades. An overnight crew was assembled and we set about the transformation, to be ready for a show the following evening. Thankfully everything went smoothly but we were still busily tweaking things while that evening's audience was exploring the rest of the building.

As we approached 9.40pm and the start of the finale, the core of the creative team assembled in the shadows at the back of the Grand Hall. The music started and there was a rush of adrenalin as, for the first time, performers invited audience members into the centre of the room to join a flamboyant new party sequence that had been devised in those last-minute rehearsals. I can remember the hairs standing up on my neck as I realised that all the lampshades that I'd hung over night at various heights now beautifully, albeit accidentally, created a 'mirror' effect with the new choreography that involved certain performers standing on wooden boxes (the latter also hurriedly constructed that day). The heads of the crowd were at different heights, as were the performers on boxes, and this mirrored the random heights at which the lamp shades fell. It was a perfect, unplanned Punchdrunk moment where all the elements just seamlessly come together.

The changes to sound and lighting amplified the energy in the room. As the audience was theatrically ushered to all sides of the room for the finale sequence we all knew that we had cracked the problem. With some refinement over the remaining preview nights and the introduction of cannons to fire red confetti, an effect that Felix and Maxine had wanted that had been delayed due to technical challenges, it all came together.

As the confetti whirled around the space on Press Night we knew we were ready. None of us had realised that the confetti would also give as a bonus effect after it had settled. As the ominous presence of 'Death' crossed the room dragging his long, black cloak along the floor behind him, it would discreetly pick up pieces of this fine red paper which would then be swirled into a little cyclone as the cloak was whipped away by another performer, punctuating perfectly that Death had vanished just as we faded to black. Cue drum-roll. Cue after-party. Cue Red Death Lates.

Last Will (**2008**, see also: Act 1; collaboration; corridors; **digital technologies**; **gaming**; mazes; R&D. Further reading: Reid et al. 2010; Sharp 2008): An R&D exercise for Punchdrunk, in collaboration with Hide & Seek, HPLab and Seeper which led to a prototype 'Multiplatform Immersive Theatrical Experience' (MITE). Paired players, one who remained in the physical world (installed at Cordy House, Shoreditch) and the other taken to a screen showing its virtual equivalent, had to work together to unlock a narrative crescendo. Rob Sharp provides a useful account (2008), and an archive of the project exists on Seeper's website. The ideas explored in this project were later developed further in *The Séance*.

legacy (see also: **awe and wonder**; Booth, Elizabeth; Enrichment; *Greenhive Green*; *Lost Lending Library, The*; Lynch, Sharon; *Masque of the Red Death, The*; Moonjuice; Oppong, Connie; **Small Tale, A**; *Under the Eiderdown*; *Up, Up and Away*): There are various ways of approaching and acknowledging legacy in Punchdrunk's practice, whether that be, as Peter Higgin notes, 'on a building, on an area, on the perception of the theatre world or in relation to creating legacy projects to continue the impact of Enrichment works'. Higgin continues:

A legacy of sorts spans all work, the thing that binds them all is the shared or individual experience and memory of work. I clearly remember

△ FIGURE 12 'Lampshades'. *The Masque of the Red Death*. 2008. Performers: Fernanda Prata and Vinicius Salles.

Photo credit: Stephen Dobbie

during *Faust*, our costume assistant, Natasha Brain, recounting that the woman who managed the local launderette had broken down and cried when Natasha told her that the show was closing. It had brought much-needed income to the launderette, as well as friendship. It's interesting to note how our work, and much that has followed across the sector, has played an important role in regeneration of local communities and towns, especially in regard to the role of artists and companies in occupying space and positively changing an area in advance of redevelopment and regeneration. In the last few years Punchdrunk Enrichment has begun a formal process of developing legacy projects for teachers to use as the follow-up to the in-school delivery of *Lost Lending Library*. Props and materials; a world map and postcards, an official rubber stamp from the library, alongside the opportunity to use our teacher-led project, *A Small Tale*. These tools allow the teacher to maintain the magic and the reality of the project, and to commit to the 'reality' of the experience, sustaining the myth of the event within the school community. Importantly it does so without the need for our continued input and the teachers take on the creative and storytelling mantle. Increasingly the Enrichment team wants to explore ways to help support teacher creativity, in the support of projects like *Lost Lending Library* as well as more generally in championing an immersive pedagogical approach to teaching.

Punchdrunk Enrichment's projects in schools are driven by approaches to sustaining best practice and celebrating outcomes through legacy . . .

Elizabeth Booth and Sharon Lynch

On legacy, impact and 'awe and wonder'

Elizabeth Booth: The relationship with Punchdrunk Enrichment and our collective of schools started years ago. It started with the impact the work had on me. I first experienced Punchdrunk's work when I went to see my son, Sam, perform in *The Firebird's Ball*. Later I visited *Faust*. In both instances I felt a very strong sensation of being personally involved; I seemed to be in charge of the narrative. I felt much more engaged with what I was witnessing than I ever had in a proscenium arch theatre production. All my senses were heightened and activated. This feeling persisted for a long time afterwards. I could recall the sights, sounds and how deeply I had become affected by the experience. I remember thinking at the time how wonderful it would be if equivalent experiences could be made available for school children. In passing, I mentioned to Felix how much I would love this same type of experience in my school. Years later, in 2008, I met with Peter Higgin, Punchdrunk's newly appointed Enrichment Director and the first idea for an Enrichment project in a school was formed, with an aim to harness that experience of awe and wonder.

Sharon Lynch: Our schools, Dalmain Primary and St. William of York, worked in partnership, with four others, Stillness Infant School, Stillness Junior School, Rathfern Primary and Holbeach Primary, to develop *Under the Eiderdown* as a means of enriching our curriculum. The focus was on raising standards in 'Writing' and 'Speaking and Listening' and the inspiration was *Who Are You Stripy Horse?*. Starting with a simple workshop based on the storybook with a creative facilitator, introduced to us as either Agatha or Algernon, the Punchdrunk Enrichment design team sat in the background, quietly collecting ideas from the children, busily scribbling in their notebooks, collecting snippets, anecdotes and capturing the workings of the children's imagination. Over the course of a weekend, a team of designers and carpenters wove its magic and created and installed The Weevil's Bric-a-Brac shop in a corner of our school.

Liz: Bringing their incredible production values in design, Punchdrunk Enrichment created absolute copies of all of the objects in the book. Jim Helmore, the author and the illustrator, Karen Wall, came and talked with the pupils about the book. They witnessed *Under the Eiderdown* themselves and absolutely loved it. Translating the experience of awe and wonder to a learning environment enables children to be stimulated in such a way that they want to express themselves, in speaking, listening and writing. The outcomes are many and varied. The joy of the experience is that it's holistic, and that's not always the case when you're working with a stimulus to encourage speaking or writing. As was the case in my own response to a Punchdrunk world, our pupils have had direct experience of worlds in which they cannot be wrong and anything is possible to imagine. Their imaginations had been sparked, the teachers needed only to fan the flames. The desire to keep the bric-a-brac shop open, or to keep the story balloonists afloat with enough stories to go around the world, gave the children a clear purpose and an audience for their writing.

Sharon: However, the impact went far beyond any academic measurements, the experience developed children's confidence in sharing their own stories resulting in exciting dialogues within families.

Liz: At Dalmain we set up arrangements for the parents to go through the bric-a-brac shop. The teachers, cleaners, cooks, governors and other interested Heads from Lewisham all came to sample the experience. Our Premises Officer, who had never been to the theatre, was so inspired that he brought in an antique camera and gave it to the Punchdrunk team to place in the shop. It had a profound effect on my staff, all of whom talk about the project still. On top of the impact on our children, these projects have also had a significant impact on our teaching teams. We now know that we're not averse to risk-taking. We can see how our teachers have been inspired to think differently and creatively when planning lessons. For example, Mr. Roberts, at Dalmain, still makes a magic elixir of 'Moonjuice' to stimulate the children's imaginations when story writing. Mrs. Rose built her own installation within a dark room, so she could demonstrate the night sky when the children were studying the topic 'Light and Dark'. Teachers are performers and delight in finding different ways to impart knowledge and skills. Punchdrunk Enrichment projects have shown them how to do this in new and unusual ways.

Sharon: Collaboration underpins all of Punchdrunk's work and it's key to Enrichment's relationship with schools. It's a solid partnership; we share ideas, skills and knowledge, cooperate fully to achieve amazing experiences for our pupils.

legacy

Liz: It's very different from other theatre companies who come in with a fixed idea, well thought through maybe, but with an aim to impose that fixed idea on the school. Punchdrunk has a growth mind-set; the team wants to learn and doesn't mind making changes, as part of that learning, to get a project to its full potential. Punchdrunk makes it easy for us to say if an element isn't going to work; constant dialogue, always productive, always professional. We are the experts in teaching and learning, Punchdrunk is the expert in creating unique immersive worlds. The synergy between those two areas of expertise in Enrichment projects is what establishes exciting collaborations and produces such fantastic outcomes.

Sharon: I took my staff for training at Fallow Cross; an exercise that immediately established the understanding and sense that everybody has something to contribute. Teaching Assistants can sometimes get a second-hand deal because the teachers get the training, which is then passed on to them. It was really powerful to take the session all together and gave a voice and status to what the Teaching Assistants had to contribute. Punchdrunk creates that whole team approach; everybody buys into a commitment to make that pedagogic approach, and the eventual project that will play out, a positive experience for the children and the school. Teachers tend to be ready to be more inventive, creative and daring and to take risks when given that ownership.

Liz: Enrichment's work is wholly inclusive, modelled on equal access. *The Lost Lending Library* was tailored and adapted to be accessible for our children who have autism. Equal opportunities are put in place to ensure that every child gets the maximum from the experience. Sometimes adaptations are as small as being able to hold someone's hand as the child enters, sometimes it's writing down the social story of what they can expect before they go in, or showing a photograph of what they will see and talking through each stage before they go in.

Sharon: With Enrichment projects the set-up for any child can feel like they're going into 'daunting' situations. The willingness to take that step into the unknown, which is the same for staff as well, is part of the process of learning. Children realise that the act of taking that step is an incredibly positive experience. We explain that it's okay to be scared, because when we're scared, it allows us to be brave. These projects create memories, and I don't just mean warm, fuzzy memories that relate to positive experience, but those memories that give us the skills to tackle the next event that's a little bit difficult. The projects link to wellbeing, in relation to staff as well as pupils. Standard testing pressures are onerous and quite negative but working with Punchdrunk gives us the opportunity to focus on what teaching and learning *is actually* about; inspiring children and giving them the skills-set to look for inspiration in unknown places. It's important to note the psychology of this learning approach, the firing-off of positive neurones to make creative connections. It's really important to establish learning situations where you're forming those neurological pathways that have a long-term impact; an impact that establishes an ability to learn in a particular way, that involves risk-taking and curiosity, as much as an impact from those pathways exercising and implanting a personal attitude to situations. Nothing works in isolation, it all has to be put into a context. You can use Punchdrunk's imaginative worlds to apply that learning in the everyday world. And the everyday world, for most kids, is quite challenging. We know that children in ten years' time are not going to remember their KS2 SATs but they'll remember a Punchdrunk experience.

Liz: As Headteachers, we have the privilege to have a profound and beneficial effect on the lives of children within our schools. It is our job to help develop successful learners, children with a work ethic, a growth mindset, children who will become confident individuals and responsible citizens of the future. It is important that we stimulate and engage all children through moments of 'awe and wonder', helping them to use their imaginations and develop their creativity. In turn, we know that this can improve the quality of their speaking, listening and writing. Of course we should ensure children are taught to reach and exceed national expectations in tests but never at the expense of their growth as thinking, feeling and caring individuals who are able to thrive and survive equally well both in and out of school. Children taught in systems that are formulaic, dull, repetitive and assessment driven are more likely to become stressed, demotivated underachievers who behave badly. They will not find school enjoyable, which in turn will impair their performance in tests both in and outside of the classroom. Happy, emotionally healthy pupils with high self-esteem and self-confidence will invariably be better placed to achieve and attain high standards. Across the last eight years, five imaginative and creative projects have had a profound impact on our schools and our communities and have formed models of practice for Punchdrunk Enrichment.

Sharon: The impact of these projects is not finite; it's long-lasting and remains part of our schools' histories as the most memorable learning experience for a generation of our community. If you are a Headteacher willing to take a risk, open doors, tiptoe through the darkness and use your curiosity to try new things, Punchdrunk will lead you down a new path which will inspire and motivate you, your pupils, your parents and staff and enrich their learning forever.

lens (see also: **abstract/abstraction**; **aesthetics**; **cinematic**; dreams; **epic**; **multiples**; **music**; **research**; **text**; *unheimlich*): Punchdrunk's shorthand for the interpretation of a textual source through the lens of other works and contexts. Barrett's interpretation will force sources together that create a kinetic energy and new way of reading the original text in the fusion, such as Shakespeare's *Macbeth* re-lensed through film noir. Re-lensing one work through others establishes a layered world. The collision (and collusion) resulting from the combination adds an uncanny undercurrent to the ideas and narrative of the original source.

letters (see also: **design**; **Enrichment**; in-show-world; one-on-one; *Small Tale, A*): A recurring device used in assorted ways within and across all Punchdrunk projects. A letter hidden in the breast pocket of a jacket, packed up in a suitcase, formed the very first encounter that anyone had with *Sleep No More*. When the suitcase was unpacked and the letter discovered by Colin Marsh, it resulted in Felix Barrett's award of Indepen*dance* producing support and set Punchdrunk on the journey towards national recognition. In Enrichment projects, letters are often the device that triggers the participants' engagement with the immersive world created, as with *Under the Eiderdown*, which used letters as the central motif. The use of letters is a simple yet effective device to create an air of mystery around the world into which an Enrichment audience is being invited, while simultaneously providing the instructions and clues as the means by which that audience might **understand** what is expected in terms of its response to the invitation. Letters as an invitation to an organisation within another world are authentically achieved with headed paper and business cards, as were those received by the school children inviting them to Temple Studios for *Searching for Stories*. Extending this idea, certain Enrichment projects and *Tunnel 228* have deployed fake websites to make worlds appear real.

For masked events, letters are concealed within scenography, shared between characters or may be passed on to an audience member. These reveal narrative clues and provide insight into character psychology. Letters, scribbled notes or small souvenirs might be divested during one-on-ones. Curious messages by email, or letters through the post, might also be sent from Punchdrunk to interested parties, keyholders or audience members in advance of an event as a tantalising taster, a means to divulge necessary information or subsequently as a reminder of that experience or simply as an acknowledgement of thanks . . .

Katy Balfour

A letter to my one-on-one

I do not know your name, I never will and I suppose that you will never know mine, but this evening we shared something beautiful. I know you felt it and I wanted to write to let you know that I felt it too.

I had been aware of you for some time, in my peripheral vision. You had been so patient and kind, watching me arrange the bottles on the shelf. I could sense your generosity, but also your apprehension. I was glad that you stayed with me, watching me while the others came and went. You gave me space, and I appreciated that. I could tell that the other people wanted me to see them. I could tell by the way that they positioned themselves in my path, into my eyeline, but they quickly got bored when they stayed invisible. I wanted to share it with you. So I made you aware that I saw you. Really saw you, no longer out of the corner of my eye but looking directly at you. Do you remember? Do you see that moment still? Can you still that moment to see . . .

I see your body tense. I clamp a rag to my mouth and throw disinfectant at you – the red death is everywhere, I need to know it's safe to approach you. You start. Gasp. I notice your impulse to move to the door. And your exhalation as I lock it. I do not take my eyes off you for a second. We are alone.

I am scared. Terrified that perhaps you have infected this place with the plague. As I slowly move towards you I ask you if you have brought it here. You shake your head and move back to the wall. I repeat my question. Closer now. There is perhaps a metre between us. You stand your ground. 'Show me', I say, 'show me', as I place my hands firmly upon the mask you wear. Never breaking eye contact. You raise your hands to stop me and place them on top of my own. I understand that you are scared too. Slowly, I soften. I realise that you are a friend. We're in this together. Any vehemence on my part is gone. My eyes prickle with tears. I whisper, pleading now, 'Show me. I want to see your face'. Your hands drop. Our bodies are close. I can feel your heart pounding. Slowly I remove your mask, as though peeling off a layer of your skin. And now I see you. Really see you. And you are beautiful. I take in your face. You seem exposed, vulnerable – but you needn't be. You are exquisite. Your eyes moisten. Has it really been such a long time since someone looked at you with such wonder?

I confide in you. I want to help you. We are surrounded by death, by a vicious plague. We must be clean. I take your hand and lead you to a washbowl filled with water, resting on the bed. Still holding your hands, the bed now between us, I plunge our hands together into the ice-cold water. As I wash your hands, my eyes fix upon yours, 'It starts with a sharp pain. There is sudden dizziness. And then each and every pore begins to weep blood'. Your eyes have not left mine. I look down at our hands. Your eyes follow mine. We see it together. The basin is filled with blood.

I compose myself and dry your hands. I tell you that I have something that will protect you. Do you want it? Can I trust you? You nod your head. I lead you to the shelf of bottles and find a small vial. We're facing each other again. Eyes fixed upon each other. I take the vial to my nose and I inhale it quickly, one nostril at a time. Camphorous and cleansing. I can see you are nervous once more. I hold the vial towards you – asking your permission with my eyes. Will you take it? You nod and inhale twice, deeply.

I take the vial and tip a drop onto my thumb tip. Holding your gaze, I reach one hand behind your head and lift my thumb up to your forehead. I slowly make the sign of the cross upon it and whisper that it won't last long. My thumb now traces a path down the side of your face so that I'm gently cupping it between my hands. I tell you that you must find your way into the castle. I want you to find your way to the castle. It is the only hope that we have left. My hands now at the nape of your neck, gripping firmer and firmer. 'Everything else will soon be darkness'. I am devastated. I know you want to comfort me. I feel your hands upon my waist. I search your face, your eyes for reassurance and hope. I pull you closer. 'Promise me', I say, 'promise me you will meet me at the castle?' My hands are clasped around your face, my face an inch from your own. I need to know that you will be there. I need to know that this will not be the end. I am urgent. Insistent. You nod. I smile, basking in your beauty once more. 'And will we dance?' I say. 'Will we dance?' You nod again. 'Thank you', I say, unable to stop my tears. 'Thank you'. I kiss your cheek and we throw our arms around each other. I feel you give into it. You seem to need the embrace as much as I do, maybe more.

I finally pull away. I look at your face once more, committing it to memory. With great sorrow I replace your mask. It is time for us to part. 'Beware the air', I whisper. I take your hand and lead you towards the door. Not taking my eyes from yours, I unlock the door and open it. With a final squeeze of your hand I remind you, 'Until the castle', then drop my gaze as I close the door behind you.

I will remember you, although we will never get to dance. Perhaps that is for the best. Those few minutes were perfect and complete.

Thank you.

lifts (see also: Act 1; Act 2; Act 3; audience; **cross-fade**; *Faust*; loops; narrative; portals): Elevators in US English, these are a device used in masked shows, partly as a cross-fade, partly to disorientate and partly as a practicality, to transport audience members, literally and figuratively, from the everyday world into the world and narrative of an event. Lifts were incorporated into the 'real-world' plots of *Kabeiroi*, increasing the sense of expectancy and trepidation in the physical and narrative journey of both as a consequence. Colin Nightingale recalls how Punchdrunk learned a great deal about using lifts to disperse the audience during the run of *Faust*:

> For the first time we had a building with a working lift that reached every floor. As a bonus it was a goods lift so could hold twenty people at time. We originally conceived that we'd send groups to the top floor in the lift and release them together to find their own way down through the building. The space had been designed and dressed to reflect Faust's descent to Hell from an idyllic cornfield, sunshine streaming through a wooden barn on the fifth floor, to the caged underworld in the basement. During previews, we observed that groups tended to stay together and not explore on their own. We started to experiment with letting smaller groups out at each floor as a way to scatter the audience, reinforce that its best to find your own path rather than following others. The lift experience was honed and theatricalised further during *Faust*'s run. It's now our preferred method of audience entry into the masked shows.

As this illustrates, lifts are often used in a similar vein to the fabric maze constructs of early projects, such as *Lost Persons* or *The Tempest*, 2001, to cause audiences to lose their sense of orientation and give the impression that a distance has been travelled. While the physical distance is in actuality very little, the imaginative journey taken can be as epic as the audience member allows.

lighting (see also: **atmosphere**; audience; awe and wonder; **Barrett, Felix**; blackout; **cinematic**; coda; cornfield; crescendo; dance; **darkness**; **design**; durational; exercises; Exeter Experiments; flow; Grant, Matthew; *H.G.*; **haze**; Maybank, Euan; **music**; **pyrotechnics**; *Quest of a Wave*; reveal; **site**; smart candles; **soundscore**; synchronicity; *Tempest, The*, 2003; **tempo**): Lighting is crucial to the Punchdrunk aesthetic. Felix Barrett's interest in lighting is bound up with the primal and mythical potency of light and flames:

> I'm obsessed with light, obsessed with fire and candlelight. It's the intimacy that comes with it, pulls you in, it's got such a focus. It's dangerous as well, the closer you get the warmer it gets but if you come too close it'll burn you. It's the magic and the threat in one.

Lighting has been a critical performance element for Barrett since his school days, influenced by his teacher, Matthew Grant, who introduced him to theories and techniques of theatrical lighting design through stories and images of the work of Edward Gordon Craig, Silviu Purcărete and Josef Svoboda. These further enhanced Barrett's understanding of the innate potential of the flicker and crackle of the flame as a theatrical language as much as it introduced him to the possibilities of 'sculpting' light in space:

> There were many moments at school where I realised, wow, this is allowed to be art, this is professional. It was often related to light. Prior to these experiences I'd always assumed that candles would be thought of as trivial, so when Matthew Grant gave us permission to whisper a text, under a chair, lit only by candlelight, it changed all that. It proved that a candle can be a theatrical light source, can be theatre.

Forearmed with these influences and with practical skills acquired during workshops, in his gap year between A Levels and university, he worked as a lighting technician at Alleyn's School. Following graduation, having further advanced his technical know-how, inflected by cinematography in theory and vocabulary, Barrett proactively explored the experiential potency of light across Act 1. Barrett and design technicians continue with R&D around the affective qualities of old and new lighting equipment, analysing not only its aesthetic qualities but also the point at which it is present and perceptible through temperature as much as volume of light.

Lighting is a multifaceted player in a Punchdrunk world; it establishes setting, creates atmosphere and is 'a character in its own right'. The lighting for masked shows is typically designed by Barrett in collaboration with technicians and designers, with final localised touches added by Beatrice Minns and Livi Vaughan. For Barrett:

> Light creates the ecosystem. If it's too bright it's too easy for the audience, there's no tension, the light dissipates the atmosphere. It's not simply light as ambient light but as sculptural character. That's why haze is a deal-breaker. If a fire alarm system were to prevent the use of haze then that would jeopardise the whole show. The haze solidifies the space.

Barrett uses the term 'volumetric' to describe the three-dimensional quality that lighting establishes in a space, a cinematic term inherited from Grant, who used it to describe the work of Craig, Svoboda and Hans Peter Kuhn's light installations with *H.G.* Volumetric lighting defines beams of light perceptible through an environment that create depth and mood that can give the impression of the wider, unseen canopy that might be creating those shafts. When manipulated in these ways, the sculptural quality of light captures dream-states and suggests the void behind the light, the spaces between, as much as the presence of the light itself. Barrett notes that much of the character and action of the lighting is created through 'fade times' that operate 'between nought to ten percent' which 'creates that magic, the burning ember of the filament glowing, like a firefly', which can be imbued with personality. Whereas the moment the lighting 'goes over ten percent it becomes light that's illuminating other stuff', so no longer its own character, instead at the service of another entity. In this way, in Punchdrunk worlds, lighting is artfully designed both to defer to, and animate, total darkness, ultimately setting the mood and tempo of the audience journey. There is always just enough light to draw the audience in and invite curiosity, allow for discovery. For Barrett, the skill in lighting Punchdrunk worlds lies in the play between light and darkness to create, 'the unseen, the shadows, the space between light. That's where your imagination is invited in'.

Barrett recalls working with a lighting designer and watching him looking at the throw of light on a part of the set and thinking, 'why's he doing that, it's not about the object the light is illuminating, it's about the shard of light itself'. Building Punchdrunk worlds through collaborations with other designers has been for Barrett a careful balance of sharing the process with those that instinctually understood that same approach and aesthetic and those that had technical expertise and access to equipment to realise the vision. For Barrett, in technical terms, the lighting of a Punchdrunk world relies on an innate understanding of 'looking into the lighting source rather than looking at what the light is hitting':

Looking at the filament itself. Noticing the way that filament can introduce itself, arrive slowly, the curve, the arc of its announcement in the space. That's like a performer coming into the room. In fact, in spaces that won't have a performer I'll incorporate a lighting change, because it will fill the space and imply more action. That

introduction of the light has to be fluid and has to have the same fluidity of gesture that a performer has. The reason we work with dancers is because they have that control of their body, and light does the same thing. I really see light like a tall, spindly man walking around the space, with tendrils of light hooking around door frames, pulling in this creature that's quite solid in composition when he arrives but imperceptible when he leaves. Light has to be functioning on a subconscious level, creating the uncanny, creating the sense that there's a presence that you cannot quite fathom, a sense that it's haunting the space. That's why I spend so much time doing it, smoothing out corners so that the only staccato beats in lighting are intentional, beats of counter and shock, while the rest of it is fluid, to achieve that dream-state. We can't work with light sources that have no alternative but to snap on, that are staccato. If you walk into a space and see the source snap on then that's going to wake you from the dream, break the flow of the experience. Anything that breaks that flow reminds you that you're in a theatrical conceit and lessens its power. It's the difference between slowly creeping through the doorway and jumping in. In a liquid, dream world where everything is slightly under tempo, the light needs to be able to play the same way, to control the audience, to hold the performers or the crowd back or guide it through. If the light's out of control the whole thing is destabilised, the ecosystem breaks down.

Qualities of light, shadow or total darkness created by a single light from domestic sources establish a sense of narrative when set within an installation. By casting a localised pool of light which is then absorbed by the darkness around it, they inspire curiosity, enticing the audience towards the details of the design that fall in its light. Flickering smart candles placed at the edges of contiguous spaces set

pathways that beckon the audience towards installations and sequences of action. Correspondingly, theatrical lighting that is layered over this relates directly to its compositional and choreographic influence on audience flow, slowing down the tempo of the space and the audience journey through it, while simultaneously setting an aesthetic state. Barrett explains:

We don't tend to use fresnels, we use profiles, because they have a crisp edge which defines the shape of the light, with clarity, giving it persona. Lights with a different lens that don't have the softness and spill don't work for us because it doesn't create a character through the light. Half of the conventional theatre lighting equipment and palette doesn't work for our worlds, because they're primarily designed for lighting performers and we actively don't light performers; we deliberately light the space and sound so that the installation is as weighty as any action. If we think of light as a performer, the duet with sound and light is as satisfying as any duet between human performers. We consciously know where we'll include a scene for light and we'll build the sound composition around this.

Lighting draws together the feeling of synchronicity among the immersive ingredients of a masked show. For Barrett, it is vital that design collaborators understand the non-hierarchical approach in process and outcome and, where necessary, that it is light that pulls rank over the performers rather than the other way around:

We have scenes where a performer duets with another performer, but we consciously give as much weight to a scene where light duets with sound; the light is choreographed as a performer would be. With *Faust* we had a whole floor, the cornfield and scarecrows, where the active duet was light choreographed to sound. If we've only got the ability to change the lighting states in a few rooms, we prioritise those in rooms where the performers will never go. There's domestic lighting everywhere but the theatrical lighting is more important in a space devoid of performers.

As this suggests, rooms are lit so they have their own affective energy. They are never static, but always shifting in the balance. Lighting, sound, design and dance are interlinked, bound together by the artistic embrace of the building which holds the themes and narratives, the Punchdrunk world, in its architectural arms. Given that the localised lighting of domestic lamps and smart candles create their own ambience and entice the audience into the narratives, psychologies and themes that the rooms reveal, lighting is crucial to Minns and Vaughan's practice. As Minns explains:

When we create the design plans we mark out where we want the domestic lighting, the lamps in the room. We then know where we want to focus the detail in the space. Once the lighting is in, always, it's much darker than we ever anticipate so we end up putting more smart candles in to highlight an element that we want to be seen.

Vaughan expands, describing the difference between the lighting that nuances the installation and that which is choreographed in the space:

There's levels of lighting for us. The lighting that ends up illuminating the performance. Then there's more traditional stage lighting that's programmed and animates our world and our rooms, so when a performer leaves a room the lighting is still on a track that changes which means the room feels like it has an energy of its own, working with the soundtrack, highlighting wall texture and the physicality of the space. Then there's the domestic lights. Finally, our signature device is the smart candles. Once we're in tech, Bea will go around with a bag of them, highlighting points

that we want to make the audience aware of and to draw audience through the space – a candle in the far corner – testing how far you can make the audience journey solely through light. Even in abstracted spaces, smart candles will be there to encourage the audience to explore. They're our crafting tool.

When lighting space that will be inhabited by performers, the three-dimensional quality of the light remains significant. Barrett elucidates:

We use a lot of back lighting. We never do top or front lighting because it flattens the picture. If you light from behind it implies there's more to discover and suggests 'the unseen'. Because you're always entering a space and looking into sources it's almost like you experience the lens flare.

The use of the term 'lens flare' here, again from cinematography, describes the experience of bright light at which a lens gazes, scattering, becoming flared, which impacts the image beheld. This illustrates how light is a significant factor in placing the audience member as camera, capturing and piecing together the experience. What this lighting effect demands is that the audience 'imagine, fill in the gaps. There's the darkness through which you can't see yet where there is a light, it obstructs your view rather than illuminates'. Referring back to the notion of looking into the filament, comprehending the tangibility of light as an entity, rather than at the object which may be illuminated, Barrett acknowledges, 'it's probably the opposite of what most lighting designers would normally do, against their better judgement. We don't allow lighting designers to look at performers and scenes in the rehearsal room for that reason, because otherwise we'd have to unpick the design'.

In masked shows when the technical run is first set and then modified through the previews, the theatrical lights are always set to the soundscore and the space and not the performers

so that later on in the process once the world is designed and installed, the performers have to find their light, to learn to duet with the light as it is set and exists in the space. Punchdrunk performers are trained in knowing how to work the light in tandem with darkness, as two powerful forces in the world of the event. Whether they have a dancing or non-dancing role, they become adept in their duets with light, shadow and the dark. Barrett explains:

All performers have to learn to use the light. The dancers choreograph the lighting cues into their performance. The lighting is set to the soundscore not the performers, so the cast have to work that into their action, not the other way around. It's a case of repetition, learning that it can take six weeks to bed in, but it's pure magic when the performers know the sound and light cue so well that it looks as though the performer is creating the cue rather than the other way around. It relies on the sensitivity of the performers to understand and respond to those elements.

The performers in the ensemble are trained to understand the importance of finding their light once on-site. Maxine Doyle recalls of *Sleep No More*, London, and *The Firebird Ball*, one might 'find a little solo underneath an exit sign because there was no light anywhere else'. Euan Maybank, below, draws contrasts in comparisons between lighting in a theatre and his learning from working in Punchdrunk environments, especially the difference between working with dancers in a space that draws attention to its architectural features, as opposed to working with those same dancers on a stage.

Light in Punchdrunk worlds is a durational entity, choreographed and timed carefully, in turn inflecting the *feel* of temporality once inside the world. Where natural or organic light defines the composition – daylight into twilight into the darkness of night, or a wax candle that has its own built-in ephemerality, that will eventually gutter and extinguish – this becomes a palpable force in the audience experience of the fictional world they inhabit. Light in this respect drives the compositional score of the world, accentuates and punctuates. Music will inspire the concept and drive the narrative and immediately dictate how lighting will work in an event, 'unlocking what the lighting will do, where the surge is, the rhythm and tempo of the scene'. From knowing how to light a scene Barrett consequently knows 'what the performer will do'. Light accentuates the power of moment, creates crescendo, underscores the awe and wonder. As Barrett illustrates:

> The importance of the car headlights or the flare in *The Moon Slave* is critical; light as punctuation, light as the lead beat in a show. The music triggers emotion, and you accentuate that through light. Shoot a marine flare into the sky to turn the clouds pink, to such an extent that you need to warn the coast guard because its visible for fifteen miles; it's a lighting cue that requires a synchronous precision point. In *The Tempest* [2001], just as Miranda gently touches the glass of the window and in the distance, five miles away, a single firework goes off, which only the audience member standing close to her would witness and experience the sound in the room with her; with *La Mer* one-on-one, the lighting change when the audience member is pushed in the swimming pool, the point at which Debussy's score surges. It's so critical.

Barrett remains intrigued by experiences built on the same principle as *Quest of a Wave*, where light and sound are the only performers present, 'light taking your hand and leading you':

> I can imagine that for a lot of people light is an afterthought, where the production is worked out on stage and then lighting designers come in and apply their ideas on top. For us, it's the opposite, the lighting comes first. In Punchdrunk worlds light is a character, a spectre, the unseen, the bogeyman hiding under the bed, or the friend, the guide that embraces you, an ally, a performer that holds you close and asks you to follow it into the darkness, to guide you through that darkness. It can reach out an arm to you and show you where to go. In equal parts it's like a playful child, a supportive parent and a wise grandmother. It knows everything yet is seeing things for the first time with you.

A way into . . . playing with light

In a Punchdrunk world there are different languages and qualities that define the possible ways of thinking around and employing light. Each has equal weight and significance according to the needs of the encounter it will embrace and support. Each can be thought of as a way to nuance the feel of the encounter as much as underpinning a technique by which that quality might be achieved. Play with these – as ideas, as qualities, as technical outcomes – as you compose light in any space . . .

Darkness – magic
> **Twilight** – the space between, the liminal, the uncanny, either or and neither nor
>> **Sculpture** – haze – warmth – cold
>>> **Filament** – looking into the source, the element, the wick, the burning embers
>>>> **Crescendo**

Always question – how will the audience respond to this?

Think about a candle as a durational and storytelling device, as much as how it influences an atmosphere – hold onto the *feel* of the flicker of the flame, the crackle of magic, the ghost stories it tells.

Try this:

Take a scene, from any play.

With the working light source on – most likely a ceiling's fluorescent-tube light – ensuring the space is functional and sterile, read the scene aloud, as a group, sat around a table.

Then . . .

Take the same scene to a space where you can get it as close to blackout as possible.

Individually, find a shelter, under a table, a chair, in a corner, a space that is as enclosed as possible.

Lighting only a single candle, an organic light source to emphasise the ephemerality of the light – it may burn out at any point – from wherever you are positioned, look into the light source.

Now whisper the same scene . . .

'listening to the building' (see also: **architecture**; **building**; dens; design; **exercises**; found space; **Hide-and-Seek**; lighting; masked shows; senses; **site-sympathetic**; **visceral**. Further reading: Bachelard 1994; Pallasmaa 2005): A phrase that captures Felix Barrett's approach to initiating a project and entitles an exercise he leads in which all members of the creative team and cast participate, on their first entrance to the building. For Barrett the exercise is to inspire curiosity, to nurture an instinctive response to the site and the world that it might engender, encouraging collaborators to enter like artistic archaeologists 'on an emotional excavation, spatially *feeling* the footprint and floor-plan of the building'. This exercise precedes the tasks set in Hide-and-Seek, themselves developed by Barrett in light of his first response. Listening to the building involves the whole creative team tapping into its visceral blueprint and finding, individually, the most threatening part of the building and its safest part. The exercise permeates the core team's subsequent response to that site. Later, when the performers enter the building, they transpose their first encounter through Hide-and-Seek into their studio-based research on their characters and narrative, allowing the space to reinforce, alter, texture and abstract their existing choreography. For Livi Vaughan and Beatrice Minns, their experience of listening to the building permeates the design of the world for each event:

Livi: Our first response to the space, with Felix and Colin, is really important. We all take note of our reactions, what feels welcoming, where we feel scared, comfortable, where temperature changes. We tune into qualities that the building has without any design in it and at the point before it's been made safe. That walk-around is a physical response, reacting to the stories it's telling on a sensual and emotional level. Colin will also be looking at the building on a more practical level, fire-escapes, stairwells. We explore on our own then come back together and take time to share our responses. Responding to the architecture rather than the history of the space.

Bea: *The Masque of the Red Death* has been the only production so far where we were deeply responding to the historical living world and the history of the building, as much as that more immediate reaction.

Livi: That's why Felix doesn't use the term site-specific, but site-sympathetic. The work is never about designing a show that's wholly about that building and its history; instead the work evolves within it. Over the years, the more buildings we've looked at, the more we have a sense of what show will work in that space, especially when we're looking to remount a back-catalogue of work. Once we've responded to what's physically there and how it feels we then become quite practical. Once we've worked out the practicalities we work out if we have to build anything additional in that space –

Bea: and ensure that it works organically, make sure that it feels shapely and unusual.

Livi: I'll draft a design and we'll return to the building and re-walk it, imagining those walls, editing and reworking the layers until we've got something that works for us. The physical reaction definitely comes first, identifying where the wildernesses are, where the heart of the building is, where we feel people will want to gravitate, which staircases are appealing. We always get a sense of whether or not a building is welcoming us to come and make something and that does have an effect on whether we feel we can work there or not . . .

Felix Barrett

On 'listening to the building'

Uncover the emotional footprint of a building by responding to it instinctively.

Discover a building for the first time by letting yourself be led by the architecture of the space. Your goal is to locate the safest room within the building, and then also the most threatening. Allow yourself to be pulled along the transitions of the space and, at every step, let your instinct lead you:

Where does my gut want me to go? Where on the barometer of safety am I? At this crossroads am I seduced by the stairs to the floor above, pulled into a room in front of me, or rushed down the corridor to my left to escape the ominous, dark void?

This game can only be played once. It can only be played on your, and the group's, first exploration of a building. Following this, from the second walk-around onwards, a preconception will exist in your mind; your head will lead the exercise, rendering it invalid.

long shot (see also: **cinematic**; **close-up**; dance; **design**; **framing**; haze; lighting; **tracking shot**): A further example of how film terminology is employed by Punchdrunk to describe the making and experience of the work. In cinema, long shots are synonymous with wide or full visuals. They establish setting, and provide a perspective on the surroundings of the subject in question with a full view of setting, in relation to any characters placed within it. 'Long shot', for Punchdrunk, indicates the view taken in the approach to responding to larger spaces within a building; to designing for those spaces and the choreography that might be created within that space. Performers are highly trained in understanding how to enter, have presence and pull focus when 'in long shot'. Maxine Doyle refers to this skill, below, as an 'interesting alchemy'. Long shot, in turn, pertains to the manner in which the audience will experience the space when they enter the world.

loops (see also: **characters**; **crescendo**; **dance**; **durational**; **Exeter Experiments**; **masked shows**; **narrative**; *Sleep No More*, **London**; *Woyzeck*, **2000**): A device that is unique to Punchdrunk's large-scale masked shows, first designed and implemented by Felix Barrett in his undergraduate production of *Woyzeck*, 2000. A 'loop' defines the unit of time that completes one full narrative cycle to the penultimate sequence before the crescendo. Sarah Dowling, above, and Fernanda Prata, below, illustrate how loops are composed collaboratively between Barrett, Maxine Doyle and the performers. The loop itself is broken down into twelve scenes for each character, which plot each stage of that character's narrative, fluidly resetting itself from scene twelve back to scene one as the cycle plays out. Sam Booth, above, identifies a palpable 'sense of fatalism' that can be felt through this looping repetition of narrative. Multiple loops for all characters will repeat, many intersect, before the final crescendo of the third loop, which leads to the finale and audience being led to the bar by performers. The duration is typically a fifty-minute loop repeated three times before the finale, creating a three-hour run. Doyle illustrates through *Sleep No More*, London:

Felix and I were in the Beaufoy building, having gone through the process of working out Macbeth's and other character scenes, one to twelve, and I suggested bringing everyone together for the banquet. That was the beginning of a shift in the formula that supports the work; you have individual journeys and then you have a shared experience in one space. It's a formula, a process of working out from the main characters, those that we have more information about in the text, plotting their journey through the space; writing treatments for their scenes, and then gradually filling out a grid. As the grid gets further away to the characters that live on the edge of the space, their stories are much lighter. When we begin the rehearsals on site we give characters loads of information, resources, stimuli and a sheet of paper with scenes one to twelve on and a location and a starting point for the scene. Some characters, like Macbeth, would have all twelve, and other characters, like Miss Danvers, probably had just three or four beginnings and a journey. Often the journey is mapped but the content isn't. Then we do lots of work in the studio to create a language, an atmosphere, a working ethos and a frame, so that dancers understand the edges of the frame and know that running into a space and doing an arabesque and three pirouettes isn't right for this work. The fun bit is when everyone goes into the building and just goes off and start creating. Felix, rehearsal directors and I, then jump around the building in a process of editing. Performers come up with a lot of their own material. That's why it's a really collaborative process and why you have to empower people to have ownership because otherwise they won't have the skills or the confidence to create that solo or write that letter or whatever. It

grows really organically. Often, the first time we run the loops it's absolute chaos because people are late or early, characters running into an ensemble scene when the ensemble is leaving, or people coming in three minutes early for the ensemble scene so they'll find a light and create something underneath the light.

Lost Lending Library, The (2013–present; see also: Act 2; Act 3; Booth, Elizabeth; Enrichment; installation; Lynch, Sharon; **text**. Further reading: Machon and Thompson 2014; Miles 2015; Thompson 1998; Tims 2016): *The Lost Lending Library* was created in 2013 and has become Punchdrunk Enrichment's flagship primary school project, visiting schools across boroughs of East London. It aims to raise standards in literacy, speaking and listening. A freelance librarian, Petra or Peter, visits pupils at a primary school, where, together with the pupils in each class of the school, they discuss their favourite books and stories. A shared love of the book *How to Live Forever* by Colin Thompson and the discovery of an antiquated, locked book leads to the mysterious arrival of 'The Lost Lending Library', staffed by an enigmatic librarian, Peabody. At 814 floors high and with 402 spiral side departments, it is the largest collection of books in the world. The Library leaps from school to school, arriving where it believes it will uncover the most precious books of all; new stories written by young apprentices of the library. Headteacher Sharon Lynch summarises:

It starts with a book and it started with a book. It started with a discussion around Colin Thompson's, *How to Live Forever*. The illustrations opened up a plethora of ideas for the setting. And so it was that *The Lost Lending Library* was created. An ancient and special book was found in each classroom. The book became the magic key which opened the door and let the children into the cramped, dense world of the Library. Here they met Mr Peabody, who commissioned them

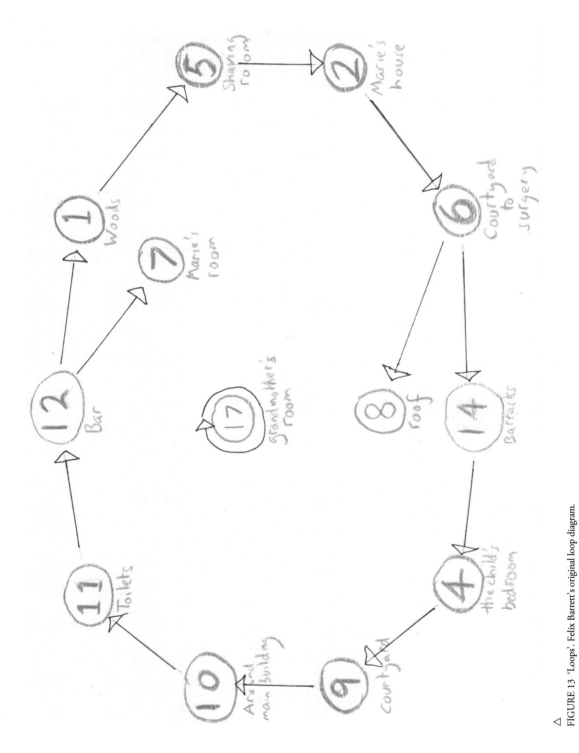

△ FIGURE 13 'Loops'. Felix Barrett's original loop diagram.
Archives (Barrett 2000)

as 'writers' to perpetuate the gift of stories and the chance to earn their 'Golden Librarian Card'. The books that were created by our children are their pride and joy and take pride of place in our school library to this day. Although the library 'disappears' over a weekend, the wonderful experience seeps into the children, the staff and the parents so that it is deeply embedded in their creative minds.

Peter Higgin highlights that the Enrichment team has 'made a conscious decision to focus on *The Lost Lending Library* as a core project, as opposed to continually creating and delivering new projects':

It was created with long-term delivery in mind. The installations are very tourable and more sustainable than previous projects. We've compiled a large body of data to evidence the value of the project. It's also allowed us to raise the profile of Enrichment's practice.

Lost Persons (see also: **Act 1**; **bar**; **building**; failure; installation; **mazes**; **Nightingale, Colin**; *Woyzeck*, 2004): The name of club nights produced by Colin Nightingale and the title of the first collaboration with Felix Barrett in autumn 2003. It was hosted by 291 Gallery, a deconsecrated church and arts venue located at 291 Hackney Road, London. Nightingale's unorthodox approach to flyering for these club-nights, leaving a trail to the venue as a code with arrows pointing to the location of where the party itself took place, illustrated for Barrett how they shared 'the same ideology, an attitude and a belief in adventure' (see Figure 14):

I'd been so used to just banging things out with what was available to me. I knew I had reams of fabric to reuse from *Chair*, and now had found a likeminded collaborator in Colin. Let's just use it again and make something else. We thought it would be great to test an audience's curiosity, sense of adventure, to create a maze with installations that led you to the party at its centre. You'd arrive having worked out the puzzle and deserving your drink and entertainment.

Nightingale adds, 'though from different artistic worlds, we were both looking to create the same thing, almost with the same format. We were exploring the transformative effect on the audience's mood by disorientating them in the maze before entering the party. The maze also served as a space to play or chill out'. Having planned for a bar at the centre of the maze, under the night sky framed by the gallery's open-air atrium, the venue was unable to licence this for health and safety reasons. Furthermore, the system for the soundscore through the maze failed to work as intended. 'Failings' that the audience were undeterred by, as Hector Harkness reveals, recalling this, his first introduction to Punchdrunk worlds:

My recollection is, appropriately, pretty hazy like a dream – a church on Hackney Road buzzing with the promise of something strange inside, then a glowing, white maze of billowing fabric, lit only by candle-glow. I remember getting entirely lost in it, finding my way through by identifying little pockets of detail; a tiny bed, a chair with a letter on it. There was a light wind that made the fabric bulge and contort, like it was shapeshifting around you. I know for sure there was a bar afterwards, and a sense of excitement that I'd found something very special.

Barrett adds, 'in those days we were doing it for the sake of doing it. You'd get as far as you could with a build and you'd have to open the doors. It was just the two of us, a scaffolder and a few mates'. For Nightingale, it illustrates how the early projects '*felt* so powerful' because the company and the type of practice 'was so unknown'. *Lost Persons* led to Punchdrunk taking *Woyzeck* to The Big Chill Festival the following year.

Lost Toy Depository (**2014**, see also: Act 2; Booth, Elizabeth; boxes, chests and drawers; Enrichment; *Up, Up and Away*): This was one of two bespoke projects created for Dalmain Primary School, the other being *Up, Up and Away*. 'The project was born out of a desire to create a project that explored the importance of play and playfulness in education', recalls Peter Higgin. A package of toys is misdelivered to Dalmain Primary School. Edna and Elsie, recent inheritors of the depository, and fastidious collectors and recorders, arrive at Dalmain to collect the toys. Finding the pupils playing with them surprises the collectors, for whom toys should be boxed and stored on shelves. Awakening a spirit of play inside them, in response the *Lost Toy Depository* magically appears for three weeks, creating a space where pupils' stories could be brought to life.

Lynch, Sharon (see also: Act 2; Act 3; **Booth, Elizabeth**; curiosity; Enrichment; Fallow Cross; *Lost Lending Library, The*; *Miniature Museum*; *Oracles, The*; **Under the Eiderdown**): Headteacher of St William of York Catholic Primary School, Lynch worked alongside Elizabeth Booth to lead the collaboration with partner schools and Enrichment for its first project for primary schools, *Under the Eiderdown*. Her school has since hosted *The Lost Lending Library* and was among the first to test *Miniature Museum*.

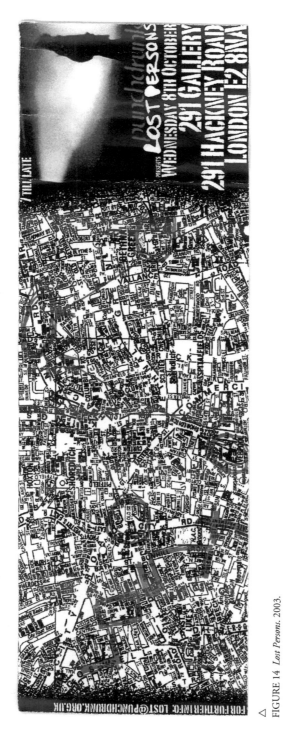

△

FIGURE 14 *Lost Persons*. 2003.

Flyer archive, designed by Stephen Dobbie

M

'Mantle of the Expert' (see also: **cross-fade**; **Enrichment**; **objects**. Further reading: Heathcote and Bolton 1995): A learning technique coined by Dorothy Heathcote, a leading figure in the field of education. Heathcote's approach creates a context that elicits and enables students to take responsibility in their learning rather than enforcing directives by a teacher. Heathcote identified the ways in which such dramatic-inquiry serves teacher and student alike. Peter Higgin adds, 'Heathcote's approach to working with young people chimes with my beliefs. She had an undying commitment and belief in the power of *the imagined* and *the possible*'. Punchdrunk Enrichment naturally employ this technique in a variety of community contexts. Enrichment's performer-facilitators are highly skilled at putting participants in role as expert, claiming the role of ignorance (teachers are also put in this role as they know only as much as the pupils of the world) so that the pupils are the participants who hold all the knowledge in this realm. Enrichment projects often employ objects that travel between the world of the event and the edges of that world where project activity blurs with daily activity, tantalisingly establishing the cross-fade between the everyday world of the host site and the magical world of the project. In schools, performers deftly elicit rather than force responses: 'I'm just wondering what the connection is between . . .' muses Petra, a Visiting Librarian to the school, as she talks with the class while pulling books and objects from her carpet bag:

[T]he palpable excitement of the Nursery year group in regard to Petra's presence (an unusual character in their midst, with a Mary Poppins-esque carpet bag full of strange and delightful books) but especially when they share her knowledge; Petra's favourite book is one they recognise (gasps of recognition, pleasure that they have something to contribute), their knowledge matches hers. This in itself bridged a gap and shifted the traditional hierarchy of learning; where before the role of librarian/adult/teacher was familiar to them, now they become the consultants/experts too.

(Machon and Thompson 2014, 12)

Marat/Sade (**2005**; see also: **Act 1**; **The Big Chill**): A festival adaptation of Peter Weiss' play for The Big Chill. Following the success of *Woyzeck*, 2004, the organisers were keen to include Punchdrunk and so paid for reams of fabric required for its build, that was then reused for *The Firebird Ball*. *Marat/Sade* was built on similar principles to *Woyzeck*; however, for Felix Barrett, 'it didn't work as well', partly due to positioning by the organisers, 'close to the Dance Music tent, because they wanted us to be at the heart of the festival'. Colin Nightingale elaborates:

On a shoestring budget, we had to transport eighty people to the site, feed them for a week, build a massive set and then run the show for three nights. We relied heavily on friends and collaborators coming to play with us on the promise that we'd look after them as best we could. Day one, we had a crisis meeting. In the run up to the event I'd been focused on my day job at Greenwich & Docklands Festival. Pete had taken time off and come up to help from the Isle of Wight. He found himself spending two days on the phone with a credit card ordering everything we needed to be shipped to the site. I'd managed to arrange for heavy-duty equipment to punch holes in the ground to plant a forest, so something that had taken us a week in 2004 only took us a day. However, we hadn't thought of getting any cooking equipment. Becky Botten and Kate Hargreaves had to go to the nearby town to buy a stove and food and we all took turns on cooking duty. I often talk about how the creation of many of our early shows reflect the source material and there was something fitting about how the crazy approach that we'd taken to planning the project matched the madness at the heart of the text.

Seven-hour durational and interactive performances occurred across the site each night, as Phin Foster summarises, with 'fairground masters, jazz singers, doctors and ballroom dancers . . . bewitching and bewildering. It proved a major talking point of the weekend' (2005).

Marsh, Colin (see also: **Act 1**; Barrett, Felix; Doyle, Maxine; **Enrichment**; **producing**): Marsh was Punchdrunk's first Producer, holding the title from 2003 and later taking on the mantle of Executive Director until June 2011. He met Felix Barrett in 2002, following Barrett's application to Indepen*dance* for producing support. Marsh produced and developed all of Punchdrunk's major works from 2003–2010, including the original London production of *Sleep No More*, *The Firebird Ball*, *Faust*, *The Masque of the Red Death*, *Tunnel 228*, *It Felt Like a Kiss*, *The Duchess of Malfi* and the mounting of *Sleep No More*, NYC. Marsh played a vital role in the professionalisation of the company and initiated early management, marketing and audience development strategies. In partnership with Barrett, Marsh was one of the first recipients of a Paul Hamlyn Foundation Breakthrough Award (2008–2011), launched to support exceptional arts practitioners to achieve their vision. Subsequently, Marsh led Punchdrunk to its Arts Council England National Portfolio Organisation status (now Regular Funded Status). Peter Higgin adds:

When Colin Marsh arrived Punchdrunk was a collective of hardworking practitioners, each committed to the company as a personal creative project, with very little money in the bank. When he departed, it was a professional company with National Portfolio status and fast becoming a major player in global theatre. He secured Punchdrunk's first major funding grants and helped to establish its charitable status. Colin must also be credited with coining the term 'Enrichment' and for helping to set the Enrichment agenda. We were clear from the outset that the department should be unique and not pigeon hole itself as the education arm of the 'company proper'. Significantly, the aim was always for Enrichment to be a force to nurture the whole company, to develop its workforce, rather than the other way around. Enrichment made sense and stood apart from any term employed by other theatre companies. To this day people still remark on how apt this title is; one of many things for which we are indebted to Colin.

mask (see also: accidents; **Act 1**; **audience**; **cross-fade**; **Exeter Experiments**; failure; **masked shows**; stewards. Further reading: White 2009): A critical mechanism for participation and presence the audience to enable a sense of anonymous immersion. The mask is now generally regarded as a signature aesthetic and device in large-scale Punchdrunk work. It allows for anonymity, prevents communication between audience members and makes a clear distinction between audience and performers. Masks are not employed for projects where the audience is charged with a mission and thus cast in a role within the work, examples being *The Moon Slave*, *Woyzeck*, 2004, *The Borough*, *The Crash of the Elysium* and *Kabeiroi*. In this same vein, with Enrichment productions, masks are never used as alternative strategies enable participants to enter and engage with the constructs of the worlds:

With different concepts and different performance structures it varies. The mask is a critical device – it can remove the audience from the picture, shifting their status and making them ghostlike. They're empowered because they have the ability to define and choose their evening without being judged for those decisions. They are also removed from the traditional role of the passive, hidden audience, as they become part of the scenography and sometimes actually create walls to frame the action, providing a more intimate environment. The impact of the mask differs for each audience member – for some wearing the mask gives them a sense of character, enabling them to come out of their shell and adapt their behaviour accordingly. This is empowering because it means they have the freedom to act differently from who they are in day-to-day life. Since first using the mask in *Woyzeck* twelve years ago this change was immediately apparent. People apologised afterwards because they felt they had acted out of their own control. The use of the mask divides opinion. It seems to affect people in very different ways depending on the individual's nature.

(Felix Barrett in Machon 2013a, 160–161)

The evolution of Punchdrunk's masks provides evidence of Barrett's vision, tenacity and initiative, from their first use in 2000 within his undergraduate experiments, through each subsequent iteration across Act 1:

Mask One: *Woyzeck*, 2000. Barrett borrowed a neutral mask from Exeter Drama Department, took a cast of it along with the correct plastic sheets to the University of Plymouth Art School and vacuformed multiple versions himself. The white colour was purely practical, the cheapest available. Barrett drilled holes into the eyes in order that that mould would work effectively: 'I probably got my flatmates to help me cut them out, couldn't be more hand-to-mouth'. These masks were reused for *The Cherry Orchard*, which was when the fact that they were highly uncomfortable came to light; the homemade neutral mask meant that the mouth was blocked, and the eye-holes were 'hacked out'. Despite its discomfort, as a theatrical device for audience engagement, Barrett was reassured by his mother's response, recalling, 'if it could work on Mum, who's usually so timid and apologetic, I knew it could be effective'. Margaret Barrett herself acknowledges:

For a rather shy, little mum who would have felt diffident about poking around in dusty places with performers in, would have felt unsure that I was allowed to go into certain rooms, the mask was really important. With a mask on I became brave. I'm usually anxious to do the right thing, don't want to be embarrassed, or to be an embarrassment. Without the mask on, even if I'd been told that I could poke around, I wouldn't have done that, but with the mask on I could do everything.

Mask Two: *The House of Oedipus*, 2000. Barrett designed a mask from a Greek chorus mould. With an intention of alleviating discomfort, particularly for spectacle wearers, the mask was designed to be oversized with a fabric back. However, the large size resulted in the mask flopping forward. Barrett recalls 'it was a disaster. Also, because the Greek chorus form gave the mask a personality, it gave the audience too much authority, it didn't remove their presence but accentuated the fact that they were in the space'.

Mask Three: *The Tempest*, 2001. Barrett returned to the neutral design but this time with the mouth to chin section cut out to make them breathable. It used the same construction process as the original (by now second nature to Barrett who had regularly been buying plastic sheets and borrowing vacuforming equipment), with Punchdrunk collaborators assisting with the cutting and elastic threading: 'because we had a larger audience across three nights of performances, there were even more complaints about them being uncomfortable and impossible for glasses wearers. Also, the mouth cut out didn't work as it meant that the audience would talk'.

The production of *Chair*, 2002 saw the return of Mask One, quite simply as Barrett puts it, 'because *Chair* was a shorter duration it wasn't so much of a

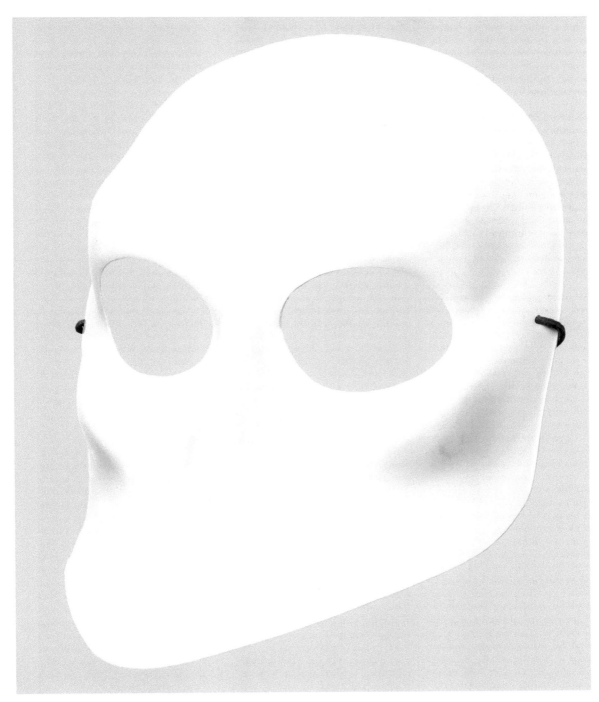

△
FIGURE 15 'Mask 8'.

Photo credit: Stephen Dobbie

problem for them to be less breathable. We kept all of the versions and would reuse them for years; this box of masks being rolled in and out, was part of the stock gear. We'd sterilise them each time with antiseptic wipes – we were still using wipes even in *Faust* days'.

Mask Four: *The Tempest*, 2003 saw to the fourth reinvention. Barrett took the original mask cast and used a moistened fabric that would take the shape of the cast as it dried which created a neutral mask that was breathable. However, again, this iteration failed. Over the course of the run the repeated wear, and thus repeated breathing through the mask, caused them to perish. By the run's end, half of the fabric masks had been replaced by the original plastic versions.

Mask Five: *Sleep No More*, 2003. Barrett again worked to ameliorate the recurring problem with the neutral mask, its breathability and discomfort around the eyes, especially for those who wore spectacles. With the help of Simon Davies, who was also assisting with the installation on site, Barrett redesigned the mask, building out the mouth, nose and eye area so that it protruded from the face, 'like a monster, a duck-faced alien. It was a clear jump, looking closer to those we use now, and it worked; people kept them on'.

Mask Six: *The Firebird Ball*, 2005. Similar to the *Sleep No More* mask but with small adjustments for comfort, such as larger eyeholes. Aesthetically, however, for Barrett, they were still problematic.

Mask Seven: *Faust*, 2006. Punchdrunk initially, for the audience journey through the event, was playing around with the concept of heaven and hell, with Faust's damnation mirroring the biblical fall from grace. An idea was hatched to have two masks to denote angels and devils, with half of the audience wearing 'angel' masks following one journey, while the 'devils' would follow another. Both designs turned out problematic in terms of aesthetic and comfort so were rejected

and previous masks from *Firebird Ball* were redeployed. In deciding against the angel and devil idea, a practical outcome of the test was that the angel design, made from the black plastic to distinguish from the audience, was used for Punchdrunk's stewards for the first time.

Mask Eight: *The Masque of the Red Death*, 2008. Coming close to Barrett's vision of making different iterations of the mask, unique to the form and theme of each show, Punchdrunk designed and created a Venetian ball-styled Plague Doctor mask: 'we finally had a new mask that worked, but, as with *Faust*, daily cleaning and weekly pressing of new masks was still required as they'd eventually break with wear, plus they were being stolen in large numbers on a nightly basis. It was such a huge job and everyone and anyone who was around would help out. With those masks, because the nose was arched higher and was longer it meant that you got fewer out of one sheet of plastic. It ended up being more problematic to keep making them so in the end we put the original ones back into circulation. By the end of the run we were using half new and half the original batch'.

Following this eighth version, for *The Drowned Man* Punchdrunk used the *Sleep No More*, NYC design, an improved and refined version of its London predecessor and finally mass-produced by a factory. This potted history of the mask illustrates Punchdrunk's approach to creating a bespoke aesthetic with an attention to detail in execution, in order to strive for and implement the best while most practical techniques possible for ensuring a particular quality of experience. Reflecting back, Barrett matter-of-factly summarises:

So much of the Punchdrunk process, which is now seen as signature, occurred because it was the only thing we could do. My original plan was the mask should change for each different production because, in my mind's eye, we

weren't creating a generic mask for every show but instead ones that were bespoke to the narrative and the world. Every time I tried they either failed or we didn't have the time or the budget to do it.

Punchdrunk settled with the original white mask, albeit in its 'organically evolved' form. For Barrett, the original neutral mask gave the audience a greater sense of threat, cast them as faceless ghosts haunting the space. In contrast, the carnivalesque *bauta* and plague doctor models added to the sense of mystery, secrecy and accentuated a sculptural aesthetic that the mask bestowed upon the audience. Barrett points out, 'everyone thinks the look of them now is intentional but so much of that early Punchdrunk approach and aesthetic was set for purely practical reasons, because it was the only way we could manage the effect for the least amount of money, just as it was making the best of the building which was the only one that we could get, we were used to working with tight parameters'. Given the hard work and history attached to the masks, Barrett was recently astounded to discover:

Rehearsal directors of *Sleep No More*, Shanghai, long-standing cast members who have been working in New York for five years and are now teaching the next generation of performers, had assumed that the masks, from day one, were a job lot bought from a factory in China and that there's only ever been one Punchdrunk mask. The amount of hours and cut fingers and bleeding fingertips and broken scissors that have gone into those masks. The weekly pressing of them in those long running shows. I remember, when a man threw his mask at us during *Faust* shouting, 'this is not theatre', we were more gutted that the mask broke than at his response being one of distaste.

masked shows (see also: Act 1; Act 2; Act 3; **audience**; **Barrett, Felix**; building; *Chair*; *Cherry Orchard*, *The*;

Drowned Man, The; Duchess of Malfi, The; Exeter Experiments; *Faust; Firebird Ball, The;* **flow;** found space; *House of Oedipus, The;* **immersive; masks;** *Masque of the Red Death, The;* Morris, Tom; **queues;** *Sleep No More,* London, Boston, NYC, Shanghai; *Tempest, The,* 2001, 2003; ***Woyzeck, 2000***): Developed from Felix Barrett's original concept for performances that deconstruct sources on loops across a found space, first piloted with *Woyzeck,* 2000, in his final year of university. 'Masked shows' is Punchdrunk's shorthand for these large-scale events. Always located in vast buildings, the audience is required to wear a mask as they enter the space and engage with its world. Maxine Doyle sums up:

I remember Tom Morris saying years ago at a Board Meeting, 'well you will go and create a new form of theatre' and that sits with me. There's loads of other exciting work that Punchdrunk's developing but the masked shows, that's one of our forms. I feel like there's so many shows within that form and it's not that we're just doing the same thing but that it's become our form of theatre, one of the ways that we like to tell stories, to offer the audience an experience of discovering the stories in that way. There's lots more stories to tell in that form.

(2013)

Masque of the Red Death, The (**2007–2008,** see also **Act 1;** Act 2; **bar;** Bicât, Tina; building; collaboration; community; **costume;** crescendo; **dance; design; Enrichment;** forests; ***Gold-bug, The;* Jubb, David; lampshades;** legacy; masks; mass production; **one-on-one;** Pluto; production management; **Red Death Lates;** research; reveal; touch; vanishing; visceral): An adaptation of Edgar Allen Poe's tales, co-produced with The National Theatre and BAC. Conjuring Poe's themes and obsessions, through the Victorian origins of Battersea Old Town Hall, *The Masque of the Red Death* lured audiences into a macabre world of mystery and the supernatural.

Sorting through Felix Barrett's archives uncovered the opening preface quote to Poe's short story, *The Masque of the Red Death,* ripped out and inserted in his *Faust* journal from 2005. Barrett realised, 'I must have been connecting the two sources and certainly thinking of the next project while working on *Faust.* Clearly *Masque* was percolating at that time'. The percolation of this idea is pertinent to the significance of the building as the key to the eventual unlocking of a source. Barrett remembers that his fascination with masked balls was a constant, illustrated by *The Firebird Ball* and this fragment of text, but it took the BAC building to find a home and architectural stimulus that met this interest.

The overhaul of the building in design terms was vast although, for the first time, it felt wholly achievable because there was now a wealth of support in place. That said, Barrett, Stephen Dobbie, Peter Higgin and Colin Nightingale continued to work nineteen-hour shifts, into the early hours, in order to deliver the show on time and achieve the ambition; as Nightingale puts it below, like nocturnal, problem-solving 'elves'. The wider support of BAC also resulted in the design process feeling 'significantly less dangerous' for Barrett, not only in terms of practicalities but also atmosphere, 'because BAC was a lived-in space'. How to inject a functioning organisation with that sense of preternatural peril that had existed in the previous found spaces became a question the team asked of every room. To address the needs of each room, *Masque* brought together Beatrice Minns and Livi Vaughan for the first time, to set the forensic level of detail in each installation and foreground what would become a signature design aesthetic of Punchdrunk's touch-real installations. Tina Bicât once more collaborated on costume, and by chance, Kate Rigby would end up helping out and joining the wider design team. A graduate of Central St Martins where she had befriended Vaughan, having offered to lend a hand, Rigby recollects:

I found myself in the foyer of BAC, with Livi's parents' chaise longue, a pile of cloth and a staple gun. While I was there I wandered along the corridor and was absolutely fascinated by the amount of costumes being made; it was a hive of activity and I really wanted to be a part of the team. I met Tina Bicât mid-costume-fitting. She was asking a performer to walk up and down the corridor while she checked the hem of one of the many cloaks they'd made for the show. I remember thinking how beautiful the performers looked in the space. I must have been standing there for ages because as soon as the fitting was over, Tina handed it to me to alter. It really made laugh, I hadn't even introduced myself properly but had somehow managed to get a job. From that moment I worked on *Masque of the Red Death* in the wardrobe department throughout the run. I managed the cast change and the costume remake and ran the wardrobe daily working closely with Tina. I remember seeing Liv in the corridor every now and then and she'd say, 'Oh are you still here? Great!'.

Punchdrunk's ensemble continued to grow with longtime collaborators Matthew Blake and Kath Duggan joining the fold. A new inclusion to Punchdrunk's format was the show-within-the-show, of The Palais Royale Musical Hall, set within the bar. Though toyed with in previous productions, such as the waiting bar area of *Firebird Ball,* The Palais Royale established a space that audience members could choose to while away the whole night and experience a fully rounded, discrete performance within the wider world of the event. With its own tempo and performance language, audience members could remove their masks, enjoy the series of acts and be party to encounters set solely within this realm. The Palais Royale's proscenium arch stage presented its own hour-long series of acts during the wider three-hour loop. Blake played one of the characters, interacting with the audience in a series of scenarios: 'I remember once talking to Marc Almond, taking him to a seat, and sitting him down next to Sting, quite by accident'.

The one-on-ones scattered around the world of *Masque* really came into their own. As Katy Balfour eloquently illustrates through a 'Letter to my one-on-one' above and her reflections on the technique required for these intimate sequences below, these scenarios were as intricately constructed as the rooms in which they occurred. Advances with sound within the one-on-ones were made, with investigations in terms of the tactile quality of the audio experience being carried out through Rob McNeill's one-on-one, also described further below. An elaborated one-on-one format of a Victorian séance for eight people was performed by Meline Danielewicz, who learned to cold read especially for it; deceptive artistry employed by fortune tellers and mediums. This is illustrative of the many carefully researched historical forms interspersed throughout *Masque* that tapped into the Poe-inspired, laudanum-soaked aesthetic. In designated rooms around the periphery of the building, other companies and artists were commissioned to produce work for the world. These heightened further the sense of cluttered Victoriana and stained-at-the-edges sepia; *fin-de-siècle* sideshows that framed the lurid landscape. *The Gold-bug*, devised and presented by Coney, added a further layer to the Masque world, running as a separate treasure hunt through it, setting its own (sometimes incongruent, as examined above) tone and tempo across the world of *Masque*. The overall composition in form thus mirrored and met the source; shows-within-a-show-within-a-show which presented a collection of short stories rather than one overarching, protagonist-led narrative. For Barrett, these assorted theatrical flavours were 'crucial to the success of *Masque*'.

In response to the vast scale of the project and to ensure the successful run of the loops within this complex network, across the build and run of *Masque*, Nightingale worked with Aaron Minnigin to produce an important, albeit loose, system for notation and stage management. The outcome would later be finessed during *Sleep No More*, Boston. Additionally, Elgiva Field, now Associate Director with Punchdrunk International, joined the production team during *Masque* and brought a can-do attitude to the evolving tiered approach to assistant-directing and production. Barrett adds:

Elgiva's a perfect collaborator, in turns both director and producer, whether as a steady pair of hands on a show or when we're trying to break a new idea. Above all, her calm tone reassures everyone in the room, even when the maelstrom swirls outside.

The major innovation for Punchdrunk was the fixed finale, with the ultimate reveal of a previously unseen finale space. This ensured that whatever stories audience members had followed or spaces they had frequented, everyone was drawn together for the first time for a ten-minute, collective experience combining the impact of the largest space in the building, this being BAC's opulent Grand Hall, with a concluding narrative spectacle. This is a feature that has continued with every masked show since. The crescendo of the production was an intoxicating ball scene where the ensemble whirled in multicolours red-lit by hundreds of assorted lampshades above, with a crescendo that peaked with a cannon firing red confetti and a vanishing act. Friday and Saturday night performances were quickly to be followed by 'Red Death Lates'; party nights involving live music, programmed by Joana Seguro, with interactions and cabaret acts, shaped by Kate Hargreaves and Gideon Reeling.

David Jubb highlights above how succeeding in such an ambitious aim – to reinvent a building, continue running its organisation and put on a multilayered show – was the major innovation and achievement. The architectural refurbishment of spaces in the building, as a consequence of Barrett's concept for the production, for Jubb established an approach to renovation that was a 'perfect confluence of art, organisation and architecture'. As well as reawakening parts of the building that had been lying dormant for years, as Jubb chronicles above, an important part of the remit for the collaboration with BAC was to embed the 'life' of the arts centre – its mission and programming – into both the working organisation and artistic structures of the event; an organisational feat achieved by Barrett, Nightingale and Higgin with the BAC team. Additional companies and artists, including Blind Summit, Nic Green, Paper Cinema, WildWorks and BAC's youth theatre, were programmed, as described, symbiotically with Punchdrunk's world. BAC's local community continued to engage with the arts centre, a number involving themselves actively within the creation and operation of the world for the length of its run. *The Masque of the Red Death* played for a seven-month sold-out run and was seen by over 40,000 people. It marked a point at which mainstream theatre wholly embraced immersive practice, with Punchdrunk's practice heralded at the forefront of this. In addition to the turning point in regard to finale and stage management, the legacy of this production was significant for BAC and, crucially, for Punchdrunk Enrichment. The extensive outreach programming across a Punchdrunk world led to the imagining of what Enrichment would become during a creative trip, away from the busy-ness of the run, for Punchdrunk's core team. For Barrett, *Masque* marked the end of Act 1, not only for the repositioning of Punchdrunk within British practice, but also bitter-sweetly, 'because from *Masque* it all became easier. It put an end to those impossible and unsustainable design builds and it became about professionalising'.

mass production (see also: **community**: 'company building'; **cornfield**; design; *Faust*; forests; lampshades; *Masque of the Red Death, The*; multiples;

volunteers): Designing the world for a masked show always requires some element of mass production by the core creative team and volunteers. Prior to *Faust* much of the mass production for shows was single-handedly taken on, or led and manufactured, by Felix Barrett, as the creation of the masks for each event or the sewing together of fabric sail material into a maze to fill a large former distillery in Deptford for *Chair* illustrates. Spurred by this attitude, from *Faust* onwards the core team members have repeatedly galvanised forces to produce those properties that are required in vast amounts, calling upon the design team, technical crew, wider production staff, volunteers and any other willing parties to get involved. Peter Higgin recalls:

For *The Masque of the Red Death* we created a petrified forest in the foyer. The trees were sculpted out of wood, chicken wire, plaster and fabric. We had a small team working on these daily, but it was clear without an injection of people power we couldn't make the amount of trees we needed. As with the cornfield for *Faust*, we broke down the process and worked intensively over a weekend to complete our forest. In those early productions, this type of moment was immensely satisfying and also demonstrated the power of pulling together as a team, what can be achieved with good planning and organisation. For those involved we made these days as fun as possible and we also made sure as many senior staff who were vested in the company also chipped in.

Nightingale notes how this all-hands-on-deck, collective approach is indicative of the core ethos of the creative team, to make the work happen:

I would really push this type of activity whenever I was production managing as they really were unifying moments in the production process that helped make the wider team believe that the scale and ambition of the design was possible if we all worked together.

In addition to the cornfield in *Faust* and the forest in *The Masque of the Red Death*, for *The Duchess of Malfi*, we created an entire floor of trees from electrical cable, which involved the purchase of two industrial skips of old cable from a local scrap-metal merchant, and an army of people to create the trees. At the end of the project we had to strip all the cable off the trees to sell it back to the dealer. We had similar intensive making sessions on *Sleep No More*, NYC, building a wall-garden and the Speakeasy. We had one of the producers, Jonathan Hochwald, chipping old mortar off bricks on a Sunday; that was a significant moment in terms of making everyone understand we were all in it together to get the project open. Nowadays we have assigned roles and responsibilities but it's important to remember, as the company evolves, that the blurring of roles and working collaboratively was always at the core of how we made work.

Maybank, Euan (see also: **Act 1**; Act 2; *Against Captain's Orders*; *Borough, The*; *Bunker, The*; *Cherry Orchard, The*; *Duchess of Malfi, The*; **Exeter Experiments**; *Faust*; *Firebird Ball, The*; **haze**; *House Where Winter Lives, The*; *It Felt Like a Kiss*; **lighting**; *Marat/Sade*; *Masque of the Red Death, The*; **Moon Slave, The**; *Sleep No More*, London, NYC; *Tempest, The*, 2001; *Tunnel 228*; **Woyzeck, 2000**): Freelance Lighting Designer and Technical Director Maybank was a collaborator on many of the early Punchdrunk projects. As well as assisting Felix Barrett with lighting, his duties in the Exeter Experiments sometimes extended to non-verbal roles in productions. Technical Associate on large-scale masked events through to *Sleep No More*, NYC, Maybank also worked with Colin Nightingale on *The Borough* and Peter Higgin on *Against Captain's Orders* . . .

Euan Maybank

On lighting Punchdrunk worlds

One of the things I've learned in the work that I've done outside of Punchdrunk is there's a truly radical difference between those people who've been taught a specific skill in theatre – directors, actors, technicians – to what we were taught at Exeter. What I feel we were taught at Exeter was how to make theatre, which I feel is very different to a professional, technical training. There's a huge range of disciplines required to make theatre, not least theatre that's new and inventive. To create that you need a good level of practical research, you need the knowledge not just of what different equipment can do, but of what different disciplines in theatre can offer.

In the early years of Punchdrunk we worked very well as a team to create the work and were always willing to strip bits apart and make it work better. We took quite a scientific, investigative approach, forensically examining elements. The approach early on was to strip out the majority of the intrusive and modern world in these environments and to take them back to something more basic and raw, more instinctive. Early on in the process we did a lot of technical research and we experimented a lot with lighting in a controlled environment to test what could be achieved with one piece of equipment. We spent hours working through different scenarios and capturing the essence of what makes a lighting fade exciting. We had long fades, which was all about the environment, drawing out those transitions. You don't want snap transitions because they break the spell, they tear the environment away from you too radically.

Our approach had to be sparse; if you rent theatre space you rent the equipment, perhaps get access to a technician. If you walk into a bare building you get absolutely nothing. The economics of that is a massive influence on what you can do. You begin where you can afford to begin – five borrowed floodlights, a borrowed dimmer and some table lamps. I remember begging and borrowing the right period table lamps only to find they threw too much light so had to modify them all. We developed a three-layered approach to the space. You might have smart candles in a certain part of the room, then you'd have a layer of 'practicals', domestic lighting, and then over the top of that you'd have a layer of theatrical lighting. The lengths I've gone to to disguise lighting fixtures; recessing them into ceiling spaces, hiding them with a natural covering, while also managing not to set fire to the building. What we're doing in any one of the dressed spaces in a building is creating a miniature theatre.

To me the light is key to leading the audience through the space, helping them make informed decisions about what they might do and where they might go. If you're in a space, you've witnessed a scene and a scene is about to start in another space, then it's very important that the light that is part of that scene is caught within the adjacent space, the influence of that space creeping into your room and drawing you out. You might have a desk in the corner, pictures on a mantelpiece, lit by a lamp, allowing people to see that set-up so that once they get over there they can see what's next to it, the details and clues. There's a practical reason for it as well. If you over-light a space people move through it too quickly, they think they see everything and want to move on and they lose elements of the story. In practical terms you're slowing people down, giving them time to pace themselves to explore the space, find a book, sit down and read it. If you hadn't picked it out within a darker space, they would have missed it. What you can do with a very dark space and specific pool of light is say, 'read this book' so they find the essence of the story that you're trying to tell with that space. In a dormant space you want to explore the space slowly.

In a performance state there are two elements to it involving many of the principles of lighting for dance performance; lots of top, back and side light and as little front light as possible. Within that there are lots of practical considerations as well. If people are moving quickly through a space, they need to see where they are. The biggest challenge is to create a space that feels enigmatic but isn't under or over lit. The key questions become about the blocking of the scene: Where do we want to see the performers? What are the images that will stay with us? Where do we need to signal, 'here's a bath that you don't want to trip over'?

There's a lot to be said for the physicality of the performers in the space. Throw performers into a great big dark space and you want to light them as structures; it's necessary to throw the light across the space, to fill it out. You want to see the physical form of the performers breaking the light beams, animating the space. The use of haze has become absolutely critical to lighting these performances. It gives structure to the environment. Even without the performers, if you have haze and a tree, there's a huge amount you can do to animate the space. The challenge in a building is creating pictures within an already dynamic environment, where anywhere that the audience chooses to stand will be exciting. If you're working end-on or even if you're working in thrust, there are ways you can achieve that but where you don't have that control over audience, the use of haze and the use of hard-edged lighting is really key to giving that space life. There's something uniquely exciting about somebody emerging through the haze that just isn't there when they emerge from the dark alone.

The building tells you what it needs to do to be the exciting space you want it to be – whatever the themes of the show are. It tells you where you need to put the fixtures. As a lighting technician, I have to question what the perspective is that audience members will take on this space, where they will go, what they'll want or need to look at. Lighting will inform that, point them in the right direction. The technician has got to make it look exciting from as many angles as possible. The audience is always the driving force.

Maynard, Arne

Maynard, Arne (see also: **Act 1**; collaboration; dreams; mazes; *Midsummer Night's Dream, A*; site-sympathetic; *Tempest, The*, **2001**; *Woyzeck*, 2004): British garden and landscape designer and early admirer and advocate of Punchdrunk's work, central to Maynard's work is his ability to identify and draw out the essence of a place, giving his gardens a quality of harmony, responding to its surrounding landscape, history and the buildings within and around its confines, as well as to the needs of its owners. With these values underpinning his work it is no surprise that there was a happy collaboration to be had with Punchdrunk early on in its history. Maynard first encountered Punchdrunk while staying in Dartmoor with his assistant, Kristy Ramage . . .

Arne Maynard

On dreams and the magic of Punchdrunk

It was October, so dark in the evening. The Bed & Breakfast proprietor said, 'there's some sort of play on at the Abbey, you could go along'. We walked up to Buckland Abbey, bought a ticket for *The Tempest* and, following that, it all became rather bizarre and wonderful. Kristy and I were separated, let in one at a time through suspended white sheets. I remember entering and thinking, 'Oh goodness, I'm on the stage, I've gone through the wrong door', not knowing anything about what was going to happen. I noticed Kristy across the space and she looked equally terrified. All of a sudden, the cast ran off and the audience followed them; despite thinking it weird, Kristy and I followed them and entered the most magical experience. We moved to the bottom of a staircase with torn-up love letters being thrown down through the air, falling around at our feet. Then to the old kitchen with food laid out, people preparing food. At that point we realised that we were seeing different scenes from different angles in the building. We pieced the whole thing together. It was really exciting to be thrown into this world, having to learn and discover how the play worked; just magical.

This was at a time where I was trying to work out what to do for my fortieth. I got in touch with Felix, which resulted in *A Midsummer Night's Dream* at my house, Guanock, in Lincolnshire. We sent out invitations to friends and clients quoting Oberon's speech, 'I know a bank where the wild thyme grows', told them no more than that. We found a rehearsal space for Punchdrunk in London at my brother's hotel and then they came up to Guanock House and had about a week rehearsing in the garden. It was delightful; I was gardening, they were rehearsing and we'd have barbeques every night. It was an intimate group of performers, so nice to get to know all the actors really well through those dinners and time together beforehand while they were camping in the field.

None of the guests knew that there would be a performance. We had the tables set out with white tablecloths under the lime trees. The performers were there as if guests, and all our friends who hadn't met them before were asking how they knew us, so the cast were making up funny stories. The guests sat down and after the main course an argument broke out at the table. It was the beginning of the play but all of our friends and clients were embarrassed wondering what was happening with this huge row erupting. Once they realised it was a play it just clicked.

I think that clicking is the magic, where you realise that you have to be proactive in it. People were running from scene to scene. We cut a path in the cornfield with a great big tent there and they ended up dancing on the lawn at the end of the play. Our birthday cake was the wedding cake. It was all so atmospheric. They responded to the spaces and places in the garden and landscape, and that became their stage. They went out into the meadow and reacted to the buildings and the house. There's a direct correlation in their work with the environment, it wholly influenced how they performed the play. That's the very clever thing about what Felix does; it's the spaces themselves that help him to put together a new way of doing things.

I received lovely letters from guests saying it was the best party they'd ever been to. It was one of those events that friends still talk about now. It introduced a lot of people to Punchdrunk. Many of them tell me how they often go to Punchdrunk productions as a consequence of our event, which is rewarding because I'm aware that it was very early on in the company's career. I took my office for our Christmas party to *The Drowned Man*. Everybody loved it, nobody knew what to expect. Punchdrunk has the ability to create pure magic. It's a more intelligent way of doing a play; you're not spoon-fed, you've got to work it out, piece it together and by doing that, everybody sees things differently. From the dialogue and discussions, it was like we'd each experienced a different play. I know that some went back again and again because they'd missed things that others had talked about. Punchdrunk experiences are clever and more thought-provoking than just going to the theatre, following it from A to B and then the production's finished. You become more involved and absorb much more of it because you have to make the effort to piece it together. It sits more closely with you, within you, than just watching a standard performance.

mazes (see also: abstract/abstraction; aesthetics; corner; **corridors**; curiosity; dens; influences; journeying; masked shows; multiples; portals; queues): A recurring motif in Punchdrunk's work. Corridors, corners and mazes are involved in some manner in the concept for most projects. They are always integral to the build and design of any masked event. Mazes ignite curiosity and require exploration. A maze mystifies and needs to be puzzled out. A maze is underpinned by a principle of travelling in order to achieve a goal or reveal a secret at its centre. Mazes are mythic and offer an allegory for human experience, from their recurrence in ancient stories to the more abstracted journey, rhythm and duration implied in a Greek *meandros* (Μαίανδρος) mosaic pattern, which is at once symbolic of the Meandros River and the meandering of mortals. In art and design meandros is also referred to as a Greek 'key' motif. Correspondingly, mazes in folklore, once puzzled out, represent a key that unlocks a mystery; in many tales the prize at its centre becomes a literal or figurative portal to an alternative place. In Punchdrunk productions mazelike grids are regularly used as the first decompression stage from the outside world, to channel audience to the threshold of the Punchdrunk world, such as the maze of suspended pages of the text for *Chair*. In *Chair* and *The Tempest*, 2003, labyrinthine structures were further used to compartmentalise the space, to create a sense of journey and disorientation, to delineate rooms and reveal abstracted narratives. The cheapest way to achieve this was through large-scale fabric mazes, single-handedly sewn by Felix Barrett. Similarly, in current works, built structures lead the audience on a meandros-styled path, through to the entrance of the world for *Sleep No More*, NYC or Shanghai.

The function of a maze pertains more to methods of sensory deprivation – modulating light, sound, scent – in order to acclimatise to a new medium; decompression from the everyday world being left, rather than a memorable space in-and-of-itself; as Barrett

describes, 'a segue more than a focused beat'. Similar to the entrance space of *The Tempest*, 2003 – devoid of natural light and defining features but full of atmosphere and candlelight that beckoned onward – entrance mazes are often designed to be non-descript for this reason. Labyrinthine spaces are also often created within rooms within the world, sometimes leading to one-on-one experiences, such as the maze of heavy, red velvet drapes in the Seamstress Store of *The Drowned Man*. Mazes are a visceral aesthetic and work as potent imagery when inside the world, as well as establishing curious and playful, or threatening and disorientating, journeys contained in the geography of a building or a landscape, and thus within the world of the event, as was the case with the prison-like maze of walls in the high-octane chase for the penultimate sequence of *Kabeiroi*.

McDermott, Laura (see also: Act 1; **Jubb, David**; volunteers): McDermott volunteered as a steward on *The Firebird Ball*. As an appreciator of Punchdrunk's work, McDermott was instrumental in the company's history. After taking up a junior producing position at BAC, it was McDermott who was responsible for Punchdrunk being invited to make *Quest of a Wave* and *The Yellow Wallpaper* for two BAC festivals, Octoberfest 2005 and Burst 2006. McDermott was the lead producer on *The Masque of the Red Death* for BAC. She left BAC to be the Joint-artistic Director of the Fierce Festival and is now Creative Director of the Attenborough Centre for Creative Arts at the University of Sussex.

Midsummer Night's Dream, A (**2002**, see also: Act 1; curiosity; cross-fade; intervention; **Maynard, Arne**; Punchdrunk Travel; *Tempest, The*, 2001; *Woyzeck*, 2004): With a full title of *A Midsummer Night's Dream: 'The Garden Party'*, this was a one-off event created for garden and landscape designer Arne Maynard. It was an interactive reworking of Shakespeare's play in Maynard's private house and

garden, Guanock House, Norfolk. Maynard had bought tickets for *The Tempest* at the suggestion of the proprietor of the guest house at which he was staying, having no clue what he and his colleague were getting themselves into. As Peter Higgin puts it, 'the best way for any audience member to experience it; with no expectations, so they're captured, swept away'. As a consequence, Maynard contacted Punchdrunk to see if the company might stage an event for his fortieth birthday party in his garden. Having learned from *House of Oedipus*, *The Moon Slave* and *The Tempest*, 2001, Felix Barrett knew how to work with the parameters of the event (durational, open-air, daylight to darkness, access to a beautiful landscape) and was excited by the opportunity to test the potential of the crossover between 'real-world' contexts and 'the world of the play', blurring reality with a dreamlike world.

Invitations indicated Shakespeare's *A Midsummer Night's Dream* was the theme, quoting Oberon's speech from Act 2, Scene 1 of the play, 'I know a bank where the wild thyme blows . . .'. Party guests, while appreciating the reference to wildlife and nature, were entirely unaware of the experience that was to ensue. Sitting at the table for dinner al fresco, 'Hippolyta' and 'Theseus', ensconced among the guests as Maynard's friends, triggered the cross-fade, striking up the first act of the play while guests ate by initiating a full-blown row. As the audience realised that they were within a performance, rather than embarrassed witnesses to a public break-up between this couple, they quickly delighted in being incorporated into the world of the play and encouraged to wander the garden, following the activities of the Rude Mechanicals, who entertained them after dinner. Punchdrunk doubled up as cast and crew for the event. A string quartet were part of the ensemble and provided live music. As the party rolled on and the piece played out, the children at the party were given fairy-wings, so becoming Titania's fairies. This illustrates

◁

FIGURE 16 *A Midsummer Night's Dream*. Fairy-wings, interaction, transportation and transformation. 2002. Guanock House.

Photo credit: Rosie Atkins

for Peter Higgin (as Snuff, The Joiner and technical production) how 'lots of nice touches' emerged as mechanisms for interactive practice, adding: 'it was important for us at that stage to grasp any opportunity to explore the fictional in a real-world context' as well as testing how far they 'could embed immersive work in a party setting'. For Barrett, *Midsummer Night's Dream* provided a model for The Big Chill projects, where 'you're yourself but in an emerging, fictional narrative':

The audience were at one with the characters, in their world and gaining their trust. The more performers let you in, the more narrative you discovered. It was dreamy, hazy, ripe for the source material. It's in the same canon as the festival projects and directly connects to the principles of Punchdrunk Travel. It was a raw attempt at a new form.

Miniature Museum, The (**2018**, see also: **Act 3**; boxes, chests and drawers; community; curiosity; discovery; Enrichment; legacy; **objects**; scalability; **Small Tale, A**):

The pùca: a strange creature that moves objects in the night and has a unique obsession with lost treasure. Sometimes invisible, this little sprite often takes the form of a magpie.

A venerable history society lends a primary school an old educational 'Miniature Museum', laden with curiosities in an effort to inspire them to interrogate their local history. Seven artefacts are exhibited but when Year 6 pupils open a pùca box displayed in the Folklore section of the Museum, a pùca escapes on the hunt for lost treasures. This magical creature makes bells ring when it listens, leaves intricate nests where it has slept and muddy bird prints where it has hidden. The only way to get it safely back into the box is to place a trove of lost treasure inside that it cannot resist. But where will the school find such a trove of lost treasure? They might discover more than they ever imagined about the lost stories and histories of their local area,

but time is against them and the pùca is in danger . . .

Miniature Museum gives teachers and pupils alike the platform to build a narrative around their local area, its history and geography, while placing teachers as facilitators of creativity and magic. Found objects become the tool to spark imagination in order that pupils are led to think creatively about how history develops. Scaling up from Enrichment's first teacher-led adventure, *A Small Tale*, designed for one teacher and their class, this model is designed for a whole school within a long-form narrative across three weeks. The challenge for Enrichment lay in augmenting a whole school's reality, where the difference between what a nursery child and a pupil on the brink of secondary school might imagine is vast. Project creator and Enrichment Associate Director Tara Boland explains:

Finding something that would be magical, intriguing but with a hint of mystery was the biggest nut to crack. Basing the project around the Irish pùca offered pre-existing mythical tales that would support the children's belief that these creatures weren't made up by the teachers. However, how it manifested in the school needed to be convincing in order to really get the older children on board. The idea was born of a cabinet of curiosities, that could house hidden creative technologies so that wireless controllers could be worked by the slightest touch of the teacher's hand on a remote-control hidden in their pocket. Having piloted this project in two schools, we've discovered how exciting and stimulating it is for teachers and pupils. Teachers took the project on with great enthusiasm and made it their own, allowing it to bleed into every area of the curriculum and giving their class free rein for discussion. I witnessed a Year 6 teacher allow her class to engage in lively discussion about the physics and science of what they had just seen in the

sequence where they trapped the pùca, involving a box closing, seemingly on its own. The discussion lasted an hour, was articulate and passionate, and ended with one child taking the teacher's place so that he could outline the space-time continuum as a theory to explain events.

Minnigin, Aaron (see also: **Act 1**; Boyd, Carrie; **notation**; production management; stage management; volunteers): Minnigin was significant to Punchdrunk's development of an approach to stage management that met the needs of a masked show. He was a volunteer on *Faust*, where he took on stage management responsibilities, and was Punchdrunk's first formally titled 'stage manager' for *Masque of the Red Death*, having demonstrated his capability and credentials as a volunteer on *Faust*. Colin Nightingale summarises:

before *Faust*, projects had no stage managers; instead responsibilities had been divided among the team. Aaron wasn't a trained stage manager, but became a presence during *Faust* and *Masque*, whilst also pursuing his own theatre-making with his company, Tin Horse.

Minns, Beatrice (see also: **Act 1**; **characters**; **design**; in-show-world; installation; narrative; **research**; **senses**; text; touch-real; **Vaughan, Livi**; **volunteers**. Further reading: Frazer 1950): Ceramic Artist, Designer and long-standing Punchdrunk collaborator, Minns takes the Punchdrunk titles of Design Associate and Head of Detail. Minns and Livi Vaughan together, working closely with Felix Barrett, were responsible for establishing the signature Punchdrunk in-show-world aesthetic:

I got to know Punchdrunk when I volunteered on the build of *Faust* for a summer as a maker and installer. The scent of the huge empty warehouse has always stayed with me, even now, over ten years on. When I find myself smelling that specific mix of paint, damp, sawdust and mustiness I'm immediately hit with the sense of wonder I felt at the time, at what was being created, the excitement at the unknown and the possibilities of that building and the people in it.

Minns, in collaboration with Vaughan, is painstaking in her research for masked shows. In addition to photographic sources, she lists various texts and writers as crucial influences in her practice, the constant being James George Frazer's *The Golden Bough: A Study of Magic and Religion*. First published in 1890, it is a comparative study of mythology, religion and science and thought scandalous at the time of publication in Britain as it cross-referenced Christian stories with myths and magic. This text is important to Minns due to the manner in which it documents intriguing links across images and natural phenomena, providing definitions and references for each entry across religious, folkloric and scientific derivations:

If you turn to the index and look up 'seed-corn' it will give you ten different pages to refer to showing the reasoning behind the anthropological customs from different countries. If you turn to 'Scotland', it gives you references and assorted descriptions: 'magical images in/ witches raise wind in/ iron as a safeguard against fairies in/ witch burnt in/ harvest customs in/ saying as to the wren in/ witchcraft in/ worship of Grannus in/ Beltane fires in/ few traces of midsummer fires in/ halloween fires in'.

Minns receives a different edition annually as a Christmas gift from her mother.

Moonjuice (see also: **cross-fade**; objects; **portals**; **ritual**; senses; **transportation and transformation**; *Under the Eiderdown*): A transportation device: the drink by which, upon imbibing, participants in Punchdrunk Enrichment's *Under the Eiderdown* are able to unlock their imaginations and thus invent, tell and write powerful stories. Peter Higgin elucidates:

When creating *Under the Eiderdown* we thought carefully about the use of the senses, and decided we wanted to give all pupils who visited the bric-a-brac shop a drink. The owners, Mr and Mrs Weevil, reveal that Moonjuice is a creative elixir made from the story waters of the moon. These waters unlock even the most stubborn imaginations to inspire great stories. The ritual of drinking the elixir has been picked up by a number of teachers who continue to use it in their class, as a tool to unlock the imagination. Symbols and objects as take-away gifts are important in Enrichment projects, serving as a souvenir that can transport audiences back to the moment they visited that world.

Moon Slave, The (**2000**, see also: **Act 1**; atmosphere; awe and wonder; **coda**; costume; crescendo; darkness; forests; influences; **intervention**; journeying; **lighting**; **music**; **one-on-one**; **pyrotechnics**; **reveal**; **soundscore**. Further reading: Pain 2014): A one-on-one, performed four times over one night, in Exeter. There were only ever four audience members who experienced this piece; Jane Milling, Felix Barrett's former tutor at Exeter, being one. *The Moon Slave* is the model to which the company returns and aspires and Barrett references it to explain the Punchdrunk approach to potential stakeholders. Speaking at an event in Montreal in December 2017 Barrett, 'beat-for-beat', retold *The Moon Slave* as 'a perfect illustration' of pure atmosphere, crescendo, reveal, awe and wonder in a distilled form.

Instructed to come to an old village hall, alone, you enter and see that it appears to be set up for a conventional performance; classic proscenium arch, programmes on every seat, a naturalistic drawing-room set on the stage. You notice a package on the table centre-stage. It rings. Keeps ringing. You step up onto the stage and open it. Inside is a mobile phone. You answer and are instructed to go outside and get in an awaiting car. The silent masked, gloved chauffeur, head-to-toe in white,

provides an alarm to hit if you want the performance to stop at any point. Safely positioned on the back seat, he drives you into the crepuscular countryside. A soundscore begins via the car stereo-system; Igor Stravinsky's *Firebird Suite* overlaid with a prologue, narrating the tale of Princess Viola who, from birth, was forbidden to dance. The car turns onto a dirt track, pulls up at a ruined mansion, one lit window at its very top. Your chauffeur opens your door, puts your headset on, returns to the car and speeds off. Alone again. The soundtrack continues, intimately, just for you via the headphones. Tonight, Viola has fled the palace, and is following a path into the forest. A burning torch lights your path. As Viola reaches a gate in the story, so do you and you realise *you* are Viola. The moon beckons you to dance in its light in a clearing. You're missing your betrothal party to do so. You turn a corner and see a banqueting table laid out for twenty people, coffee steaming, cigarettes smouldering. You journey on through installations that layer and illustrate the narrative playing out through your headset. The night before the wedding day, dusk falls, Viola has burst from the palace, cutting her feet in her haste to reach the clearing. You see a flash of white petticoat far ahead. She calls to the moon, hears its music playing more powerfully than ever before. But it is the night of the lunar eclipse. As you feel the music surge, the eclipse occurs and '*she was no longer dancing alone*' (Pain 2014, 57). Alone for thirty minutes, firelight ensuring you cannot see beyond your immediate vicinity, 'at the point of that italicised sentence the music swells', a marine flare shoots into the sky, turning everything for fifteen miles bright red and revealing 200 scarecrows: 'the biggest reveal achievable on £200', to suggest those that have danced with the devil before (Barrett 2013). Milling's recall of this point in the experience was, 'oh how marvellous, that's what I needed to see now, dramaturgically and scenographically' (Machon 2015, 271). A second flare fills the sky and reveals a figure, your chauffeur, walking towards you, through the scarecrows. He takes your hand, leads you back along the path, removes your headset and returns you to the backseat of the car. As he drives away, over the car stereo the epilogue plays. Viola's fiancé, Hugo, found the blood-trail leading to the clearing, discovered her footprints in the sand alongside another set, with a cloven hoof. At this crescendo, driving through nocturnal country lanes, Joel Scott is lurking in the shadows, as Hugo, waiting for you. If you happened to glance from your window you would see the flash of his face looking intently at you, a chilling coda, as you return to where it all began:

Out of the four audience members, two of them were sitting on the wrong side of the car; he was out there for hours for a total of twelve seconds of performance . . . it's all about the moment, the punctuation.

(Barrett 2013)

The Moon Slave, for those involved, was and remains 'the ultimate Punchdrunk experience' (Higgin 2013). Euan Maybank, who played the chauffeur, recalls how it created an 'intensity of experience for the audience', the 'raw concept' being 'absolutely what the one-on-one experience is all about. Incredibly decadent to create an immense performance for one person at a time'. As Barratt puts it, '*Moon Slave* set the rules for *The Borough* and *Kabeiroi*'. Audience members were pivotal and progressively aware, from the moment they chose to step onto the stage, that they were performers; simultaneously voyeur and protagonist. Sensual installations took them through each stage of the story. The location and journeying were integral to narrative, theme and orientation into another world, blurring boundaries between the real and imagined. The use of gothic fairy-tale heightened and layered the experience. The final reveal, a spine-tingling crescendo, visually, aurally and conceptually, was underscored by its subsequent coda. The influence of *H.G.* is clear, yet here the silent, unreachable presence of performers accentuates the point that audience *becomes* protagonist.

Milling 'was glad there were no people in it . . . there was nothing to disrupt the game that you were having with your imagination, with the narrative and with the excellent acting that the environment was doing' (Machon 2015, 272).

Morris, Tom (see also: **Act 1**; *Every Good Boy Deserves Favour*; *Firebird Ball, The*; Hytner, Nicholas): Morris is Artistic Director of Bristol Old Vic, an Associate Director of The National Theatre since 2004, and was Artistic Director of BAC, 1995–2004. His extensive credits include programming BAC's 1998 Playing in the Dark Season, directing *Jerry Springer: The Opera*, 2001 and, for The National, co-directing *War Horse* with Marianne Elliott. It was Morris who took Nicholas Hytner to *The Firebird Ball*, thereby setting in motion Punchdrunk's backing by The National Theatre. Morris served on Punchdrunk's first Board of Trustees and co-directed, with Felix Barrett, *Every Good Boy Deserves Favour* . . .

Tom Morris

On extraordinary ideas

M y first memory of Punchdrunk is of various people telling me that I had to see *Sleep No More*. I missed it, but I'll never forget the people who told me about it. Those early Punchdrunk fans ranged from a complete stranger on a bus in Lavender Hill, who recognised me as the guy running BAC, to my assistant at the time, Sally Gibson, who had collaborated with Felix at Exeter University, and Bill Bankes-Jones, who at that time was a staff director at ENO, now founder and Artistic Director of Tête à Tête. When people from a wide variety of backgrounds tell you that something is really extraordinary you take notice. I went to see the next show, *The Firebird Ball*, in an old factory in Kennington and was blown away by it, despite the fact that I spent the first two hours of the show thinking there were no performers in it. When I eventually found some, I was even more impressed. By then I was working at The National and took Nick Hytner to see it, who also loved it and agreed that The National would support Punchdrunk's next show, *Faust*. We could see that what Felix and his collaborators were attempting was astonishing in terms of its impact and its complexity and, under Nick Hytner and Nick Starr, The National Theatre saw it as part of its role to promote work which challenged the rules of theatre to create new forms.

There were two extraordinary things about *The Firebird Ball* and *Faust*. First, the audience was completely engaged with the world from the moment they entered the space, and second (and this is the truly radical and truly simple aspect of the work), everyone in the audience was in control of their own point of view. If you wanted to move to watch something from a different angle, or leave it to find something else to watch, the form invited you to do that. From the moment they discovered Punchdrunk, audiences felt deeply involved in the shows they were watching because they were making choices about how and where they watched, which view they would focus on, which sequence they would watch on repeat, which character they would follow. The permission to explore, combined with the care that was taken in creating the world in design and music, performance and choreography, was really rich and, in my experience, completely new.

My early support of the company resulted in me being on Punchdrunk's first board at a time when the company was trying to professionalise. Up till then, the shows had been produced for next to nothing by a very small number of people. Employing people on a fair basis and professionalising from a legal and contractual point of view is very demanding for a company at that stage in its career. The fact that they managed to do that over about a five-year period, with the support of The National and others, was in itself an achievement. Those of us lucky enough to be on the board were able to learn from the way Punchdrunk had set itself up and made work. For instance, when we looked at the list of jobs from the early shows, there was a design group within which was a 'Head of Detail', not a job that any of us had seen before and the thinking behind this, prioritising the creation of a world, has influenced a whole generation of artists since. One of the responsibilities of my job at The National was to bring unusual voices and artists into the programme. Nick Hytner suggested we invite Felix to work on a production in one of the theatres at The National, which prompted one of a series of conversations with Felix about what that show might be. He had consciously turned his back on theatres because he wanted to explore alternative spaces, so why would he do that? The route in was through music and we considered various projects that might fulfil that interest. In the end Nick Hytner suggested *Every Good Boy Deserves Favour* and we agreed early on that we should work on it together.

I came away from that project thinking that Felix was a genius who would almost certainly end up making films. A key collaboration in its development was between Felix and the designer, Bob Crowley. I witnessed how Felix's visual imagination worked in its complexity and scale and Bob was very inspired by the things that Felix would throw at him. In terms of the rhythm and punctuation of the piece, Felix also seemed to think like a film-maker, imagining the whole show as a sort of visual score containing, but not defined by, the wonderful performances of Toby Jones and Joe Millson in the central roles. Felix was also a natural and remarkably flexible collaborator and made the production a truly joyful experience.

The impact of Punchdrunk's work has been immense. I have done things in theatre that I wouldn't have imagined had I not experienced Punchdrunk shows. The company has changed the toolkit that is available to live storytellers and theatre makers. In other words, Punchdrunk has caused a paradigm shift in what is possible in theatre-making. Felix is a groundbreaking artist and, as such, the most important thing is that he and his collaborators are given the resource to take the next leap of experimentation that they want to take in whatever art form they choose. Punchdrunk's job is partly to give Felix the freedom he needs to ensure that his extraordinary creativity can flourish. He is the kind of artist who can turn the brains of a generation inside out and we as a society will be enriched according to how successful we are in supporting him.

multiples (see also: **abstract/abstraction**; adrenalin; close-up; **curiosity**; **decay**; deception; dreams; **intervention**; lampshades; long shot; **mass production**; objects; **scale**; **'Specials'**; *unheimlich*): Repetition of objects is key to the exaggeration or heightening of subtextual elements that exist within an original source, and its intertextualisation with other references, to expose character psychologies and themes, enabling audience to piece these together in an effective manner. 'Multiples' refers to objects repeated in installations and also duplicated environments built within the site from miniature to vast scale. In *Faust* replica statues of the Virgin Mary were set to deceive and disorientate while the cornfield, intricately made of pages of scientific formula for growing corn, surreally repeated the scientific papers and formulae in Faust's laboratory. In *Sleep No More*, NYC, the performance begins in The Manderley Bar, which is replicated later, exactly the same in scale and design but aged, decayed, by forty years. In the pristine nursery of the Macduff house, a two-way mirror stands, which reveals an identically matched chamber showing the room after the children have been killed, fusing time, exposing the narrative. An intention with replication is to encourage the audience to become alert, to question, to sharpen and refocus attention to these spaces and the narrative or thematic ideas they hold. In this way, they add to the sensation of the *unheimlich*. Carefully constructed by the design team, multiples underscore the art of the in-show-world, while accentuating its dreamlike quality. Multiples can encourage an audience to explore and understand the world, through the design alone, curating a journey through the space. As with the Macduff nursery, there may be a broad long shot but it is the rug-pull of the close-up, a detailed layer created for the curious, that twists it and sets the adrenalin running.

music (see also: **aesthetics**; **afterbeat**; atmosphere; **Barrett, Felix**; **corner**; crescendo; Dobbie, Stephen; flow; influences; **lens**; lighting; loops; **soundscore**; **tempo**): Music, distinct songs and orchestration, is crucial to any Punchdrunk world. Music unlocks, flavours and defines the entire aesthetic and atmosphere of a production. Felix Barrett 'cannot create a project without music':

> I experience euphoria when I unlock how to do a scene through music. Music unlocks the idea, unlocks what the lighting will do, where the surge is, the rhythm and tempo of the scene. Once you've got that, it's easy to slot in the performer.

Claude Debussy's impressionistic *La Mer* drove the first one-on-one Barrett created for Stephen Hodge and was woven into crescendo moments for both Punchdrunk iterations of *The Tempest*. Igor Stravinsky's *Firebird Suite* unlocked and underscored *The Moon Slave* and returned to be interwoven with Sergei Prokofiev's *Romeo & Juliet* for Punchdrunk's *The Firebird Ball*. In contrast, it was the recordings of The Ink Spots, played to Stephen Dobbie, with their immediately identifiable introductory chord sequence that counted in each song that ensured doo-wop-styled music became a constant presence in the composition of Dobbie's soundscores for masked shows. For Barrett, this musical style impacts the body in a visceral manner: 'though saccharine sweet you can hear the darkness behind it'. As these examples illustrate, music inspires the initial concept for any project once the building has brought it to being and becomes stimulus, equally, for designing and devising.

Music is the central device, closely followed by the installation and costume, that sets the era in a masked show. The overriding era of any show is researched by Barrett and Dobbie, resulting in them, together and separately, listening to a range of music of that period. Although not all of the music employed in a production will have originated directly from that era, Dobbie and Barrett will have found music that is highly evocative of the period, which has been re-filtered through a contemporary lens:

Felix: There's always a key musical reference for each show that establishes the aesthetic; provides a sound bed and an atmosphere we aspire to. Sometimes it's classical, sometimes blues, country, 1940s pop music. The final combination of a range of musical styles in the soundscore is influenced by that initial musical reference.

Stephen: We might find a song, which may only exist for four minutes within the show, so there is a world of sound around it that needs filling, inspired by that song, mixed with a palette of sound we have archived.

Felix: There's a difference between the atmosphere and the melody and tonal strongholds within the music. The syncopation, rhythm and punctuation that music offers, the silence in between tracks, all propel the narrative forward. We work out the major scenes, how they culminate, that's the corner. That corner is normally marked with a piece of music or silence, a breath, as a punctuation mark. When the music breaks, set sequences happen, there's an almost euphoric release manipulated and accentuated by the emotional pull of the music.

Examples of current musical sources which take a pre-existing style to rework it in evocative ways include Nick Cave and Warren Ellis' *Burnin' Hell* or Ramsay Midwood's *Chicago*, both of which inspired the aesthetic of the cowboy bar in *The Drowned Man*. The blurring of time periods through music arises out of (and feeds into) the lens that establishes the world of each event. Sometimes, the jarring of eras through music is a clever device to subvert expectation, accent the otherworldliness of the space and reorder the dream logic of the experience, as is the case with the incorporation of contemporary club music in an otherwise 1930s film noir world in *Sleep No More*. In form and theme these musical references connote era, evoke atmosphere and establish aesthetic. Barrett elucidates:

> When I listen to music of any kind, pop or opera, I don't hear or listen to the lyrics or libretto. I feel the emotional wash of the sound. My ear hears the melody. Music cuts to the quick and it's that immediacy and impact that fascinates me. It can transport you in a way that text can't. Where textual sources might create a block in processing, music can fast-track you, take you where you need to be, subconsciously. It's the rug-pull. I like it when something gets you before you've had time to prepare yourself for it. We might push against time period because you always need that friction that creates the sparks. The music choice provides the colour. It becomes the anchor point to which we return. Often, we won't know where the lead song will occur in the show but knowing what it is provides the pivotal point from which the soundscore evolves.

Music is vital to the choreographic language, in masked shows, inspiring the work in the studio as much as setting the dance on-site. During a masked event music is used within set sequences of choreography, sometimes pre-recorded, sometimes performed live. Orchestrated interludes will be woven into Dobbie's soundscores for transitional journeys and installations. Within these it is a musical refrain that crafts the crescendo of each loop and leads to the finale. Whatever its style or format, music is a vital presence and an embodied experience for performers and audience members alike . . .

△ FIGURE 17 'Music', *The Duchess of Malfi*. 2010.

Photo credit: Stephen Cummiskey

A way into . . . embodied imagining through music

A simple and straightforward exercise to ignite the imagination and instil a cinematic vision through the body:

Lie down.

Switch the lights out.

Play your chosen music as loud as possible.

Open yourself up to *feeling* that piece of music. Let it wash over you and, only then, following your instinctive response, allow yourself to visualise the music internally.

Let your mind's eye travel across an imaginary landscape.

Feel the journey become cinematic. This may be abstract or representational, or a combination of the two.

Let the music become the soundtrack to this imagined film.

You are protagonist or camera or both.

Allow the music to help you navigate the imagined terrain, to set the atmosphere, to create pictures, to tell narrative, to colour emotion, to find its crescendo.

Allow the exercise to reach its natural conclusion as the musical score ends.

This exercise can be reworked according to a project's needs in order to initiate a response to the materials to be explored, so the musical choice may well fit the concept and sources.

Different musical choices, of course, lead to alternative imaginative responses. Interludes are good for this. Anything with lyrics is likely to be too prescriptive, unless it gives an underlying impression of mood, era or otherworldliness. Try Benjamin Britten's 'Dawn Interlude' from *Peter Grimes*.

The exercise can be translated to reworking that imagined terrain in the physical space through movement or design. It can serve as a springboard for discussion and practice and, as such, can be reworked and applied in form through any given discipline, such as writing, costume or lighting design, or installation. The music could be taken and played loudly through your found space, combining the imagined terrain, atmosphere and narrative with a physical location and its architectural or landscaped features.

Use the exercise to think beyond the exercise and into the world to be created.

N

narrative (see also: afterbeat; **bar**; building; **characters**; cinematic; communal; corner; Curtis, Adam; dance; design; dreams; durational; experiential; flow; Gardner, Lyn; Hytner, Nicholas; **lens**; **loops**; Maynard, Arne; Morris, Tom; Oshodi, Maria; pedal note; Poots, Alex; **research**; **text**. Further reading: Biggin 2017; Flaherty 2014; Ritter 2016; Worthen 2012): Punchdrunk's work is always rooted in a textual source. Whatever the form, narratives are always fragmented and layered. They usually follow a dream logic, prioritising the physical and experiential in construction and composition. Narrative in masked shows is abstracted to get closer to the ludic lucidity of dreams, constructed from intertwined, looped, abstracted narratives rather than a single, linear storyline. The interweaving of narratives is always embedded in the dramatic logic of the textual source yet always reinvented through that dream-logic and filmic lens. The experience may take on narrative coherence for audience members who choose to follow the loop of one or two main characters throughout the event. It becomes relational when multiple characters are followed or if the space, installations or any other performance element is prioritised during the course of the event.

Punchdrunk's non-hierarchical approach to performance signifiers means that, unlike conventional drama where performers are primarily responsible for telling the story, here they are but one element. In Punchdrunk worlds, the building becomes the text, a room becomes a character and the physical performance language conveys the nuances and details of interwoven textual and visual sources. To acclimatise to Punchdrunk worlds, audiences need to enter with curiosity, willing to find experiences and to collate theme and story led by instincts and interests. Building on theories and approaches learned from his A Level studies onwards, a primary concern for Felix Barrett is how 'a space devoid of live performers can be loaded with narrative, with a threat of what's to come'. It is the space that drives the concept and decides what experiences, sensations and stories will unfold within. For Barrett it is antithetical to the Punchdrunk process to decide narrative, character and outcome before visiting and attuning to the building and the sensation of its spaces. Colin Nightingale adds:

I had a very pure way of working with Felix when first creating the masked events. I'd get him to walk me around the building and tell me the key bits and I'd get really excited about it. I didn't read *Faust* and I've since, actively, not read the sources in advance because, if it doesn't make sense to me, and I'm part of the production team, then how the hell is it going to make sense to an audience, how are they going to penetrate it? I knew that there was more cerebral work going on around those sources but for what I was going to deliver, I just needed to know the crescendos, the touchpoints, the moments of engagement, because that's where the energy needs to go, how the audience needs to flow.

In constructing narrative in response to the space through design, Barrett adds:

At any given point, depending on what's happening in the narrative, there will be a different element prioritised. Sometimes it will be sound, or pitch-black space; the feeling of *absence* of any element is as important as the presence of another. Sometimes the lead will be the spectacle in the distance, sometimes it will be the brush of a hand against your hand. The constant focus is the sensation for the audience. If we were driven by the logical, a narrative choice might be to get fake ivy to suggest setting on a narrative level, but it would all look a bit theme-park. Instead, if we have only purple water bottles at our disposal then we can only create poplar trees out of them, because it's the cheap way of doing it and, better still, it will look amazing. We'll then retrofit the story to go with the installation; a character makes water bottles or works for a plastic plant. Consequently, when the audience come in, they can't automatically pre-empt narrative because it's a dream logic in construction. Wikis that have worked it out and constructed those complex narratives, because a community of people have made those connections, then that's a win. It's the pleasure of solving the riddle of it. It requires a particular attitude and logic, which is usually opposite to coherent, conventional theatrical thought.

Dramatic coherence is always interpreted through a multilayered dramaturgical approach that, as Maxine Doyle puts it, 'is chaotic' in the manner that it 'flirts with words and eschews logic', or as Sarah Dowling describes, is 'anchored and wild at once'. This form enables audience members to *feel* the interior and exterior worlds of the characters and their narratives simultaneously. It demands a collaging in interpretation from these stories and sensations, which inevitably leads to a questioning of the implications and outcomes of form in a Punchdrunk event and can create a tension between enjoying choice but wanting greater guidance.

Punchdrunk's work is elliptical and sensual. Its dream-logic works differently to speech-led, argument-driven narratives. The cryptic nature of the work can leave the audiences frustrated and feeling as though they have missed important sections, or that it necessitates repeat visits in order to even begin to piece together a total experience. Adam Curtis highlights the problems of a fragmentary schema for narrative, where the individual is given freedom to draw their own threads through a world, at the expense of social commentary. He argues this as a limitation of the immersive form, itself a product of a climate that prioritises individualism and rejects institutional or ideological narratives. Although classical source material may provide a narrative spine, for Curtis, this is at the loss of telling new, specifically political, stories. The deconstructed and sensory play with source material allows for an intertextual and sensual interpretation of themes. For some this is at the expense of plot, character and dramatic cohesion, denying interpretative resolution on the audience member's part. While criticism levelled at Punchdrunk's work in regard to the lack of obvious coherence is understandable, it also works against the intention of the form. For many the interpretative freedom is a joy and the affective memory of the work a pleasurable conundrum to work through in an ongoing appreciation. Elizabeth Booth, Codie and Kyle Entwistle, Lyn Gardner, Nicholas Hytner, Arne Maynard, Tom Morris, Maria Osohdi and Alex Poots, in their contributions to this encyclopaedia, all highlight the pleasures of piecing together narrative through experience in these worlds. All illustrate how Punchdrunk's experiential narratives can make people think and feel; think through feeling.

Whatever the critique of Punchdrunk's practice, it underscores the need for an interpretative approach that meets the form, rather than battles with it by measuring it with the same yardstick employed for linear and hierarchical theatrical genres. From *The Masque of the Red Death* onwards additional performance mechanisms were put in place, involving a pedal-note prompt and performers drawing audience members through to bring everyone together to experience the crescendo and conclusion. An afterbeat, led by music and performers, then ushers audience through to decompress, share experiences and narratives gleaned in the bar. The practice of piecing-together respects the involvement of the audience in the construction of narrative. It accentuates how Punchdrunk's deconstruction of a classical story highlights the repercussions of grand narratives on individuals, elaborated by B-characters being given equal space and time within a show to protagonists. Given this, and in

response to the problems of prioritising individual – at the expense of collective – experience, Barrett argues the bar is vital, designed as a communal space for shared comprehension of stories:

The intention is to fuel a grand conversation. Everyone is at the same event within the same scenario, but because they're seeing it from different angles, in a different order, and they're seeing it through a personal lens, each individual interpretation is different. It's only through conversation at the end of the show that it becomes a communal experience. Our focus on the individual journey is only intended as half the experience, and, yes, that can be frustrating. The other half is intended to be communal. It's utterly critical that you get to share others' experiences and that your context is added to by other interpretations. This is why a communal space is so crucial.

Discussion struck up between friends or among strangers in the bar, alongside fan-blogs and wikis, prove this collective conversation is desired and exists. It points towards Punchdrunk's practice acknowledging the importance, and fact, of differing perspectives and different ways of being in the world. It encourages individual interpretation while simultaneously inviting a collective and communal building of narrative; a narrative which is indebted to the weight, concerns and issues that lie at the heart of the source material through which any Punchdrunk world is rooted, which might resonate with social situations at work in the wider world.

nature (see also: *Chair*; **decay**; **durational**; Fallow Cross; *Faust*; **forests**; immersive; **in-show-world**; **installation**; loops; masked shows; **multiples**; 'Norman the Eel'; Pluto; 'Rebecca the Bird'; **touch-real**): Natural elements such as trees, plants or moss, in various stages of growth or decay, employed and repeated within the design and overall installation of a large-scale masked show, emphasise the sense of

time passing, time on a loop. They underline the organic 'wholeness' of the world while, conversely, highlighting the art of the installation within a building, blurring the lines between the theatrical and otherworldly and the touch-real. Natural elements implicitly create an aesthetic that suggests the world is alive or in a state of decay, that it has its own energy and forests, in particular, are repeated across productions. Animals have made an appearance, carefully looked after on-site, the first being Rover the fish, in *Chair*, to Pluto who lives on, much-loved, at BAC.

Night Chauffeur, The (**2010**, see also: Balfour, Katy; *Black Diamond*; **cinematic**; intervention; **journeying**; **lens**; narrative; soundscore; transportation and transformation): Scripted and co-directed by Hector Harkness with Katy Balfour, this project tested immersive performance mechanisms while journeying in cars through London in the composition of the narrative. A soundtrack played in vintage Citroen cars, moodily established a French, film noir atmosphere. As individual audience members were driven through London, attention was refocused through this soundscore, heightening the everyday world as viewed through the double lens of the windscreen and the film noir aesthetic. Performers were placed at key points *en route*, such as Parisian paperboys at work, so audiences could be pulled further into this world. The blurring of the real and the imagined ultimately tested the ways in which grouped, yet separated, audience members might become characters for each other as the narrative played out. Harkness elaborates:

The creative agency, Mother, came to us with a richly evocatively world already worked up for this project, so we treated it much like we'd take a film or literary source and began to translate it into an experience. The interesting theatrical proposition was that the central playing spaces would be vintage cars. We researched how best to use the cars to accentuate ideas around transportation, figuratively and literally. The interesting line to tread was the difference between the controlled atmosphere inside a car, kitted out with lighting and a beefy sound system, and the world outside the car, which was unpredictable, uncontrollable, and therefore felt ultra-real when you stepped outside onto the street. We used four cars that departed regularly from a series of pubs around London. Each car had a different route and story, with each story contributing to the overarching narrative. Written as four loops, the intention was that no audience member would see the whole story but later come together in a bar and discover they had all been part of the same narrative; vital that each story had echoes and intersections with the others. In some ways, the car and its windscreen were like a mask, allowing the audience a defined viewpoint and frame on the world outside. A fight breaking out in front of one of the cars could frame the action, light it with the headlamps in a filmic style, all synchronising with the noir aesthetic of the piece. Rhythmically the piece was very different to how we'd normally structure an experience. One of the strongest moments was when the audience stepped out of an intense, soundscored scenario in the car and were left alone on the pavement, to then meet a character, walk back along the quiet streets with them, sharing a simple conversation that was undramatic yet touching in its feel of understated authenticity. A gentle decompression after the heightened theatricality of the car journey.

Nightingale, Colin (see also: **Act 1**; **Act 2**; **Act 3**; Area 10; bar; Big Chill, The; building; *Chair*; *Clod & Pebble*; *Faust*; Gideon Reeling; *It Felt Like a Kiss*; **Lost Persons**; *Marat/Sade*; **production management**; *Sleep No More*, Boston, NYC, Shanghai; *Tunnel 228*; *Vescovo & Co*; *Woyzeck*, 2004): Creative Producer for Punchdrunk, Nightingale

leads on managing and evolving operational structures for creative projects, especially large-scale or complex experimental events. Nightingale first discovered Punchdrunk at a period in his life when he was 'hungry for art and culture' and 'using music as a vehicle to connect with people'. He recalls how he 'carved out a period of time to explore' and find what he wanted to create, find an arts practice that was meaningful to him:

If someone invited me to the pub I would've said no, because I knew what the evening would be, but if someone invited me to Peckham when Area 10 was just beginning, I was there. I was hungry to be at the birth of an idea and see it explode. What was so refreshing with *Chair* was that my expectation was so low but it just kept giving; the pay-off was so great. I was trying to find work that could alter your state, be transformational, without the need for drink or drugs. Part of that was tied up with the fact that my DJ partner was a Muslim. If we were going to carry on working together long-term, we'd have to establish a different approach to mind-altering environments for music, unlike other club settings. In getting to know Felix and working with Punchdrunk it became much more than that.

Felix Barrett adds, 'There were only three people who were cold approaches to me that I followed up on; Colin Nightingale, Livi Vaughan and Kate Hargreaves. I put Colin's number in my phone as "Colin the DJ" and he's still in there as that' . . .

Colin Nightingale

On creative producing, artistic ambitions and practical constraints

My role has been multi-focused and very fluid over the years. It has generally been characterised by a need to plug various gaps to help facilitate the creation of projects and the general growth of the company, initially filling the missing role of Production Manager. Since then I've held the titles of Director of Operations and then Senior Producer until we settled on the title of Creative Producer in 2016 to better explain my role. I see my main function as one that's trying to bridge the gap between the artistic ambitions and the many practical constraints we face in making groundbreaking unconventional productions. In addition, I try to develop and maintain relationships with current and potential partners. On certain occasions I'm the initial catalyst to create projects such as *Vescovo*, a collaboration with Jack White and XL Recordings, and *Tunnel 228*, our collaboration with The Old Vic in 2008. I also activate ancillary activities within show spaces, such as the first aftershow bar entertainment in *Faust* and *Sleep No More*, NYC, to film screenings with the BFI during *The Drowned Man*. I generally keep an eye on what's going and spot potential new avenues for us to investigate.

In the early 2000s I was busy exploring the fringes of London's art and nightlife culture for inspiration for my own projects. Not from any formal arts background, my creative output at the time was as a DJ, running a series of parties called *Lost Persons*, housed in unusual locations with invitations sharing minimal information; clues on the street or hand drawn maps that were, intentionally, slightly wrong. I was exploring how the audience's journey might ultimately affect the atmosphere of the party. On my hunt for inspiration and to feed my growing interest in site-specific and installation art, I attended Deptford X Arts Festival in summer 2002. I witnessed a badly executed sound installation and then a poorly curated exhibition of prints in different parts of the old buildings. I was about to leave when someone stopped me and asked if I'd been into Punchdrunk. I walked up some steps, was handed a mask and entered what I can best describe as an embryonic version of the Punchdrunk masked show. It played around with disorientation, taking the audience out of their comfort zone; elements that resonated with me. The unexpected nature of what I discovered – my heightened senses, desire to explore and the feeling of excitement and general elation that I experienced – has stuck with me ever since. I try to channel these emotions into all elements of my work at Punchdrunk regardless of how practical the task might be.

After about a year of meeting up and chatting through ideas with Felix we finally decided that we should work on something together. In autumn 2003, we mounted a one-night-only version of *Lost Persons*, in the 291 Gallery, a deconsecrated church. We filled the old nave with scaffolding, draped in white fabric to create a giant labyrinth. We were purposefully vague with publicity, totally undersold what it was, leaving clues on the street to mark the route to the entrance. On arrival, audiences were released into the maze and at the end of their journey they discovered a party in a bar where they could hang out or return to the maze to continue their evening exploring. The whole project was pulled together with limited time, resources and budget and we didn't have time to curate the music or the content of the evening properly. However, audiences were suitably impressed by the experience we'd created. Of the seventy people that attended, one was a good friend of the organisers of The Big Chill Festival. Subsequent conversations I had with them led to the invitation to create *Woyzeck* at the festival in 2004.

While I no longer define myself as a DJ and music archaeologist, or 'crate digger', I still hold the true values of this artform close to my heart. Elements of this culture have been lost in the digital age with instant access to every sound imaginable, rendering the skills and hard-earned knowledge required to be a music archivist virtually obsolete. However, my desire to share sounds and to take audiences on a specially crafted musical journey, fused with my fifteen years of experience working on Punchdrunk projects, informs my outlook on life and my work. I also draw on four years as the Senior Project Manager at Greenwich & Docklands Festivals (GDF) where I worked on a wide range of large-scale outdoor spectacles and events with many of the leading international outdoor theatre-makers and designers in a range of unconventional locations. This period of work with GDF ran alongside the early development of Punchdrunk. The scale and volume of GDF projects gave me numerous transferable skills to help deliver the ever-ambitious Punchdrunk productions like *Faust* and *Masque* and informed the operational blueprint and approach to audience management that I helped shape for the company.

Nightingale, Colin

Punchdrunk is at a major stage of development and it does feel like it's entering a new chapter of its evolution. We're taking stock of processes, both creative and practical, that we've been honing over the years to help us be more efficient at training other people, especially when mounting masked shows in the future. We're sharing knowledge more widely across the teams and support systems are being put in place to build a company that will be suitably resourced to enable us to work on multiple large-scale projects simultaneously. The move to Fallow Cross has allowed us to develop a focused approach to R&D that will result in new theatrical forms and ideas becoming integrated in the output of the company. The future of Punchdrunk is full of potential.

'**Norman the Eel**' (see also: Act 2; **in-show-world**; **nature**; Pluto; 'Rebecca the Bird'; *Sleep No More*, **Boston**): A brackish water eel, Norman lived in a bathtub in a ward of the King James Sanatorium in the Boston version of *Sleep No More*. Colin Nightingale recollects, 'the impact on audiences who unexpectedly discovered him tended to be pretty intense so it was no surprise to us when he ended up being referred to in the opening sentence of one of the early reviews of the show'. As with all live animals used in productions, Punchdrunk had a detailed care plan for his well-being and at the end of the run he was safely returned to the pet shop from which he had originally been bought.

notation (see also: Act 1; archiving; **Boyd, Carrie**; masked shows; Minnigin, Aaron; Production Managing; **Stage Managing**): A legacy of *The Masque of the Red Death*, prior to which working processes and organisational structures had never been recorded. During *Masque*, Punchdrunk unlocked what a system of notation for masked shows might be. This framework was developed during the rehearsals and run of *Sleep No More*, Boston, by Carrie Boyd. Boyd was responsible for providing the prototype for 'the book', or prompt copy, recording all the information required to run the loops of a production across a night. This notation system has been replicated for every masked show since.

O

objects (see also: abstract/abstraction; **cross-fade**; **design**; installation; *Lost Lending Library, The*; **multiples**; portals; **ritual**; touch-real; *Under the Eiderdown*): Also referred to as props in theatre. Objects in Punchdrunk Enrichment worlds serve as portal and storytelling device, such as the locked book that becomes the key to open 'The Lost Lending Library'. They are a mobile element of the scenographic installation, charging the classroom with the magic of the installation and directly related to topics that year groups are investigating. Equally, the tactile presence of artefacts and books from classrooms, or invented objects from pupils' imaginations, when installed within the design of the Library or Weevils' Bric-a-Brac shop, 'reinforces ownership, blurs the lines between the school world and the immersive world':

In a preliminary workshop with a Reception year group there is total silence and striking focus as soon as Petra's 'bag of books' is introduced; a palpable shift in focus so that observers can *feel* the curiosity in that moment ... In this short workshop the Punchdrunk approach is clear; it's the particular handling of the objects, the innate understanding by the performer of how the project will build, that facilitates that 'moment'. The objects, alongside Petra's tone, draw them in. The room crackles with the pupils' attention and interest, especially in regard to 'the book that won't open'.

(Machon and Thompson 2014, 11–13, emphasis original)

Where offered as a reward or gift to Enrichment participants, objects often bestow status on participants to whom they are given, such as Gold Membership of The Lost Lending Library.

In Punchdrunk's wider worlds, especially in masked shows, objects are touch-real and dress rooms to set era and denote character. They take on a symbolic potency when abstracted and repeated across rooms and spaces. In these installations, nothing is casually placed; everything is bound up with meaning and layered with thematic and narrative import. Objects within installations invite the audience to interact with them, work out the clues they hold. When incorporated into a character's narrative, objects become heightened signifiers, providing an obsessive focus, the means through which durational activity can play out. As Maxine Doyle illustrates:

The possibilities of small objects to develop narrative and offer a complex rhythmical layer is tenfold. Often in a Punchdrunk show you will witness a character's detailed prop sequences. In *The Drowned Man* we see Mr Stanford, played by Sam Booth, grating a small horse made from sugar in the preparation of a ritual libation. In *Sleep No More* we witness the taxidermist grating bones or Hecate collecting a vial of tears from Mrs De Winter. These actions are strange and do not have an immediate narrative correlation. They exist in a dream-like logic, to conjure up mystery and provoke curiosity.

one-on-one (see also: Act 1; Act 2; Act 3; adrenalin; afterbeat; Balfour, Katy; Barrett, Felix; *Borough, The*; caretaking; characters; *Clod & Pebble*; coda; crescendo; durational; Dust Witch; ethics; exercises; Exeter Experiments; 'Grandmother's Room'; Hodge, Stephen; letters; loops; masked show; *Masque of the Red Death, The; Moon Slave, The*; objects; restraint; ritual; soundscore; *Uncommercial Traveller, The; Yellow Wallpaper, The*. Further reading: Heddon, Iball and Zerihan 2012; LaFrance 2013; Schulze 2017; Wake 2017; White 2013; Zerihan et al. 2009): The one-on-one is a prototypical Punchdrunk form that has been an essential component of the practice and vocabulary of Felix Barrett's vision since his undergraduate experiments with the format: 'the timeline of the one-on-one begins with the Exeter experiment, *La Mer*, that was the major one, the breakthrough'. Barrett's development of the practice, and first use of the self-coined term between 1999 and 2000, runs concurrently with the form being tried and tested more widely in live art circles, directly in the wake of 1960s arts practice, such as that of Yoko Ono and Marina Abramović. 'One-on-one' performance (also referred to as 'one-to-one'), defines any work that is designed for one audience member, as *participant* in the work. It explores the direct connection between performer, audience and space. At its purest, it often establishes a sense of shared ritual between artist and audience-participant. In theatre practice it may open out to 'ones'-on-one, involving any number of performers facilitating a single audience-participant's experience.

Punchdrunk's *The Yellow Wallpaper* cemented the term as vocabulary among the team to define the format and, in so doing, it named and blazed a trail for a host of future work and festivals at BAC. Barrett had invented the phrase during his Exeter Experiments and consequently it had become a shorthand among the Punchdrunk team and ensemble when working on projects. It was the producing team at BAC that took the term for its 'One-on-One Festival', off the back of Punchdrunk's *The Yellow Wallpaper* and *The Masque of the Red Death*. The inaugural BAC One-on-One Festival was initiated, in part, to acknowledge the legacy of *The Masque of the Red Death*. Barrett recalls, 'they asked me to co-curate the festival as they associated one-on-ones with Punchdrunk, and I didn't do it. A big regret'. Although Barrett and Punchdrunk were not the only practitioners working with the form, given BAC's contribution to the naming and rise of this intimate practice in mainstream and fringe arts events nationally, acknowledgement is partly due to Barrett and Punchdrunk.

In addition to *The Yellow Wallpaper* and *Clod & Pebble*, since *The Moon Slave*, Punchdrunk has continued to test the impact of journeying in one-on-one experiences. *The Borough*, though for one person at a time, required large-scale artistic and operational structures. The procedures developed fed into subsequent projects created for paired audiences, such as *The Night Chauffeur*, *Kabeiroi* and pilot tests for Punchdrunk Travel. Punchdrunk remains committed to investigating ways in which the principles of a one-on-one can be deployed for individuals, each having separate encounters but as part of a bigger performance occurring across a building or location, who eventually come together with other audience members within that world.

Though one-on-one techniques are employed across many Enrichment projects, albeit for larger groups rather than individuals, it was *The Uncommercial Traveller* in 2011 that was Punchdrunk's first project to facilitate and explore the handling of one-on-ones by amateur performers, to empowering ends for the ensemble.

One-on-one experiences in Punchdrunk's practice include carefully designed, clandestine moments created for one member of the crowd, that occur at specific times within the masked shows; assorted embedded sequences within the wider, three-hour loop structure, that run on their own repeated cycles. These scenarios are composed of pre-planned, carefully scored action, designed by a performer trained in the Punchdrunk approach to one-on-ones. For these precisely timed sequences, the performer chooses an audience-participant to be enticed behind a closed door, away from the rest of the action. Here the audience member's mask is removed, and the audience-participant is spoken to directly, as a brief scenario is played out, usually lasting no more than five minutes, after which time the audience member is sent on her way. As Conor Doyle describes in his entry above, they can be powerful encounters that may be profoundly transformative for the performer and audience member alike. Equally they may be exhilarating, playful or disquieting moments of interaction that influence the experience of the world, for its duration and in any subsequent interpretation, from then on.

The form of one-on-ones in masked shows has evolved along with the shows themselves, and as a consequence of the learning undergone from the different formats of the worlds created, and the diverse audiences who were involved with them. Using the original *Woyzeck* 'Grandmother's Room' sequence as a model, the first one-on-one introduced within a masked show was for *The Firebird Ball*, using the same Grandmother's tale, although delivered in French. For French speakers, the story added a poignant edge;

for others it textured the heightened-otherworldliness of the encounter. *Faust* was the first masked show to employ its own individual soundscore, original music composed by Stephen Dobbie. Performed by Sam Booth as the preacher, he worked a button under his table to trigger the sonic crescendo to accentuate the shape and damascene tale of his one-on-one. *The Masque of the Red Death* was the first time a one-on-one incorporated soundscore with narration, replacing live dialogue. Performed by Rob McNeill, climbing across a net above the audience-participant lain in a hammock in the dark, it tested the tactile quality of sound and perceived movement. The soundscore interwove the narration of Poe's story *A Descent Into the Maelstrom*, and was switched on by McNeill before inviting his audience in. Individual soundscores continue to be employed for certain one-on-ones in masked shows, involving their own discrete crescendo and afterbeat to match the composition of the narrative that unfolds.

Katy Balfour, erstwhile creator of one-on-ones and expert in the Punchdrunk technique, explains how these offer a concentrated theatrical adventure within the wider journey of the event:

The one-on-one is fundamental to Punchdrunk's practice: it's a moment that can often *appear* fleeting, impromptu, perhaps even improvised. It is a mini-show in itself that should take the audience on a journey. There are many types of one-on-ones in many forms; from stand-alone, 'pop-up' encounters such as *Clod & Pebble*, to fully realised shows such as *The Borough*. In general, the principles, techniques and considerations of the one-on-ones in a masked show apply to the stand-alone variations of the form. In masked shows it is only during the previews that one-on-ones are set. Until that point it is an idea, maybe fragments of text, a smell or sensation. The starting points for one-on-ones are varied; for some it will be the sole purpose of their character, others might have a gap in their loop that needs filling. Often this distinction will depend upon whether a character is 'travelling' or 'resident'. If a travelling character has a one-on-one, this will have a specific function within their loop; a moment of confession or realisation that's central to the rest of their narrative. A resident character on the other hand has a less defined role and narrative. Resident one-on-ones are repeated throughout the loop and may be performed up to fifteen times per show. Travelling or resident aside, the one-on-one is a moment where the character 'sees' the audience, which, as a general rule, only happens if characters are magical, in a state of madness or ghosts. The creation of a one-on-one can be led by narrative, character, design or sensation but a successful one will utilise all of these elements providing the audience with an intimate, sensory experience that enhances their overall understanding of the world of the show.

Sam Booth points out how early projects, such as *Woyzeck* at The Big Chill in 2004, played a crucial role in shaping the skills and techniques required to handle one-on-ones. Conor Doyle notes how any one-on-one will require the performer to adjust the tone and feel of the notated score as she or he interacts with the chosen audience member, intuiting how that individual is responding in the moment. Balfour highlights how a one-on-one requires a blend of discipline and empathy from the performer: 'it can't be ego-driven, all about the character. A one-on-one should never feel like someone is performing *at* you and not taking your response into consideration'. One-on-ones require a control that allows the performer to be simultaneously inside and outside of the character, responding instinctively in role while always mindful of the audience member's uncertainty in the scenario. Balfour continues:

A one-on-one, like all of Punchdrunk's work, remains only

half-conceived until it has an audience. As creators we position ourselves in the role of audience, consider it from that first-person experience. It is this skill, this ability to place yourself in the position of audience which is central to creating and performing a one-on-one. Considerations are: Who is the audience? Why have they been bought here? What do I want them to think/feel/experience at any given moment? What sensation do I want to leave them with? In the wider world of the show, the characters' intentions are towards other characters; in a one-on-one your intentions are to the audience-participant.

Within masked shows, the performers devising one-on-ones are required to find the nuances that operate across the world of the event, intensifying these in their one-off encounters. Here, the performers' original response to the building and to the specific room of the encounter inspire and shape what these become. The performance that results is then nuanced further according to each unique interaction with individual audience-participants. In turn, the audience-participant is likely to have a marked awareness of her or his ability to influence the performance. Audience becomes both canvas and catalyst in the scene, modulated by the performer. The necessary and slow accumulation of ways to engage in the scenario adds to the sense that the masked show is alive, establishing an immediacy that is bristling. The intuitive shifts required cause performers to dwell in the moment, find new perspectives on their characters, enjoying the ongoing subtle modifications to the portrayal of that role while always remaining in control of the situation. Balfour elucidates:

Though the audience becomes a playing partner in one sense, the one-on-one in a Punchdrunk production is not an equally weighted dialogue between two people. It is not equally interactive; they are not required to perform in order

to affect or alter the course of the scene. The performer is always in charge, always leading, showing the audience where to go and what to do. That is not to say that the performer dominates, bulldozing the audience into submission. Care and nurture are paramount. A skilled performer asks for permission, she gives space to allow the audience to digest information, she makes sure that her transitions through each section and moment of the sequence are clear. I've performed the same one-on-one hundreds of times and each time it is different because each audience member is different. There are always similarities; people are prone to move in similar ways, gasp, perhaps weep, in similar places. And my performance remains consistent; the same text, the same blocking, the same timing. So what changes? It's the emotional tone and content. My intensity, approach, motivation for action, is all altered by what I perceive that audience member's needs to be.

Balfour emphasises, when choosing audience-participants, performers are encouraged to pick the cautiously curious individuals in a crowd, the lone and unassuming observer left behind:

The most exciting times for the performer occur when audience members don't know what's going on, what's about to happen; there's an equality there in choosing. I rarely pick the pushy people. The idea of surprise is fundamental to the success of the work in general and the one-on-one especially. If people are waiting for a one-on-one outside your room we tend to walk past them in order to reach out and draw in the unsuspecting person, or the one who's quietly, patiently been observing you for a long while.

Where one-on-ones within masked events are sought out by experienced (and often repeat) Punchdrunk audience members, Balfour argues that this is not

FIGURE 18 'One-on-ones', *Clod & Pebble*. 2008. Hector Harkness playing the ghost of Robert Blake.

Photo credit: Stephen Dobbie

necessarily in an urgent need to 'win' or beat everyone else to them, but because they are 'drawn to that search for meaning' in the work. The deliberate seeking out of a one-on-one is usually related to a desire to piece together all the hidden moments and secrets that exist within the world of the event. In this respect, Punchdrunk one-on-ones serve as a microcosm of the wider world of the masked shows. They operate on various levels, all concerned with transporting the audience member's imagination and sense of being within the world of that event, which can lead to a ritualised connection with the space, the performers and the stories and secrets they reveal together. Irrespective of the concentrated, duration and sparse content of these one-on-one encounters, they can uphold the epic stature of the wider world, intensifying it by offering the audience member a shared moment that is potentially profound. Balfour has witnessed one-on-ones liberating people and recalls holding people as they quietly sob, willingly giving in to her. She highlights the importance of Punchdrunk's ethical approach to one-on-ones, the caretaking procedures in place and the skills of the performer to manage these expertly. Balfour argues that with the one-on-ones of *Faust*, *The Masque of the Red Death*, *The Duchess of Malfi* and *The Drowned Man*, a sense of danger, intrigue, 'needs to be lurking in the subconscious'; the trepidation charges the theatrical moment, layers the thematic underpinnings of the works, adds to the state of being in those worlds. Yet great control and safeguarding is required to enable this to operate effectively.

The alluring, potentially disquieting, nature of one-on-ones points up the need for caretaking and strict (even where tacit) codes of conduct and consent in these worlds, that must be respected by performer and audience alike. Recent debate around this has intensified Punchdrunk's attention to caretaking. It has pointed out the importance of self-regulation through codes of practice for artists alongside issues of consent and audience responsibility during immersive

and experiential theatre events (see Ahmed 2018; Gardner 2018b; Solokis 2018). This process of regulating a Punchdrunk one-on-one, whether for masked events or stand-alone projects, involves a scrupulous procedure. The performer develops the material, showing this to a director or associate director who, when satisfied that it meets the artistic and ethical standards required, will sign it off. The standards relate to the material being theatrically interesting and also involve a safeguarding of performer and audience alike. In simple terms, the performer will have scripted exactly when and how action and emotional content arise ('I place my hands on the audience member's shoulders here . . . I whisper in the ear . . . at this point, my distress becomes clear'), timed and scored perfectly with the unique sound composition of the sequence. This provides a documented composition, on paper and in performance-demonstration, of intricate and specific detail about any moments of physical or emotional contact and content. Once signed off, on a Punchdrunk form that is filed, the performer cannot deviate from those specific actions and that content.

The codes of conduct that are set, and the signing off of the one-on-one, always involve an understanding of action and attitude that respect behavioural norms, while allowing for a feeling of being outside of those norms within the encounter. A delicate balance of trust and tacit codes of consent, moment by moment, is communicated, to be accepted or rejected by audience and performer alike as the sequence plays out. Given that one-on-ones shift and morph according to the responses of individual audience-participants, any improvisational or intuitive reworkings permitted relate to the modulation of emotional tone and objective. As Balfour notes, 'you can take actions away, but you can't embellish'. Where new members of the ensemble are being trained up for these roles, they will work closely with a director, and the experienced performer if handing on the role. This ensures a passing on

of expertise not only in the skills and techniques for how to deliver the scene safely, but also in methods for ways of generating material.

One-on-ones are always designed to take the audience-participant and the performer to what Balfour calls the 'just missing of the moment'; the possibility of what might have been, plotting the charged point to create a concentrated crescendo. While it is not an equally weighted dialogue that is on offer, the sequence is carefully choreographed, with a dexterity on the performer's part in defining and physically articulating every thought process, as if in close-up and frame by frame, to ensure that the audience member is never taken by surprise, is able to give consent on a beat-by-beat basis, and invited into that thought process to see, read and comprehend every detail therein. Balfour notes that the incidence of people rejecting one-on-one in masked shows is less common in comparison with earlier productions. Where an element of surprise may exist, this will be a component of the choreography in which the audience member is complicit. Balfour provides illustration of this in her 'Letter to my one-on-one', in the entry above.

Where sound is incorporated in the composition of a one-on-one, to set atmospheric tone, narrative arc and duration, it adds a cinematic quality, heightening the experience, accentuating the otherworldliness of the moment. Soundscores will usually be composed in collaboration with the performer as she or he generates the material for the sequence. Balfour sets the scores for her one-on-ones, initially with a voice recording of action and content, for the benefit of all involved with its sign-off ('I close the door, I move away from the audience member'), to which Stephen Dobbie responds (this shared process between Balfour and Dobbie became key to the development of the material and score for *The Borough*). This is a means by which duration, crescendo and afterbeat are plotted; the climax of this individual drama always followed by the character's return to her former state, the audience member released, the return to routine business and obliviousness to audience, until the next allotted time. Balfour summarises:

> The classic one-on-one formula, set by the music, involves exposition; a distance between myself and the audience member; a couple of minutes of physical proximity and perhaps first contact, including the removal of the mask; the peak of the crescendo will incorporate the maximum moment of contact, involving emotional intensity, physical proximity and a peak in the music, both content and volume; followed by the dénouement and the audience member's exit.

For masked shows, on leaving the one-on-one an intention is that the audience member will have moved from a voyeur to feeling that they have been charged with an active role in the world of that event, even where that is simply about perception of action, for instance, '**you** need to find the castle where we'll dance'.

A way into . . . a Punchdrunk one-on-one

Develop your material from the source text and your designed space. Your starting point can be character, theme, spatial reveal, a trick, an emotional gap in the work (for example, is there a need for more tenderness in your narrative or in this world?). The generation of your scenario will depend on the wider world and the forces that drive it. A layered, more complex one-on-one will involve a bit of all of those things.

If the wider world involves a narrative structure, where does your one-on-one come in that arc and is it to be repeated on a loop? If so, are you a travelling character or resident character in that loop? If you are a resident character, your one-on-one needs to be something you can repeat over and over again without tiring of it. At its root it has to be something with which your character is preoccupied, an obsession, that enslaves you in repetitive compulsive, actions.

Is your character dead, in an extreme mental state, or magical? This will influence the timing, shape and feel of your moments of lucidity and presence. The point at which your story involves an episode of intense lucidity is the point at which you will be able to see the audience, invisible to all other characters in your world.

Choose that audience member wisely. It must be instinctive. Choose someone who is attentive and interested in what you're doing – invite them into the one-on-one – giving them the opportunity to refuse – a non-verbal gesture, extending your hand, checking consent is given through that – a tentative game . . .

You cannot improvise a one-on-one. It is unsafe for both parties for this to be an entirely spontaneous act. Within the careful construction of a one-on-one, intuitive and improvisational responses should arise naturally and subtly. Within the discipline comes the control and thus the freedom.

Removing the mask may require persuasion. Audience members may put their hands to the mask to prevent you. This is always the first point of inviting the audience in to each transition in process, of thought, emotion, gesture and action to enable them to be consensual and complicit in the proceeding scenario. It may be the first point at which you plead or use your skills in these situations to set them at their ease. Nothing happens without the opportunity for the audience member to say no.

The one-on-one will involve a constant process of negotiation and reassurance. Trust on both sides is paramount.

Set a get-out clause for your audience-participant at every stage of your sequence. This will relate to the content and actions of your one-on-one. If you encounter a 'let me out', a 'no', a 'stop', you must try to put your participant at their ease; only then can you offer another invitation to engage, 'will you stay?', but if they respond in the negative then you must let them leave.

Oppong, Connie

Oppong, Connie (see also: **Act 3**; *Against Captain's Orders*; **Enrichment**; *Greenhive Green*; **legacy**): Connie Oppong MBE was the manager at Anchor Trust's Greenhive care home in Peckham, London since the home opened in 2002 until her retirement in 2017. In 2015, under Oppong's leadership, Greenhive became the first care home in London to be rated 'outstanding' by The Care Quality Commission and the whole staff won Best Team Award for London in the Great Britain Care Awards 2016. Punchdrunk Enrichment's *Greenhive Green* project, produced in collaboration with Magic Me and the Anchor Trust in 2016, was a crucial learning experience for the Enrichment team and an example of its willingness and ability to adapt techniques and process for a host organisation and its participants . . .

Connie Oppong

On *Greenhive Green*

The conversation started with Magic Me where we were informed of the funding to deliver these projects. We then had a meeting with Punchdrunk. At the time they had nothing concrete to present so I couldn't be sure how it was going to be suitable for our residents. I was conscious that most of the work they had done had been in schools and this was their first attempt to do something in a residential home, so I wasn't confident about what it could bring to the residents. I had the opportunity to go with Magic Me to see *Against Captain's Orders* in Greenwich, which was impressive. I came out thinking my kids and my grandchildren would love it, but I don't know about the residents! So, in some respects, that left me more confused. I like to give everything a chance, so we, Punchdrunk and Magic Me continued to bounce ideas together at the meetings. I saw the drawings and thought it sounded more suitable and the discussion became about rooms they could use. We were very involved in all of those discussions, right from the beginning, they needed a lot of input from us.

The way Punchdrunk converted the room into the village was so impressive. The speed with which they built it was like magic. The magic of the whole thing, I've never seen anything like it, how the lights came on, when the train ran, the smell of grass and flowers in the room. The room itself became a little haven to us. The project itself happened every Tuesday each week, but the rest of the week the room was there for us to use. We could go and sit in there and enjoy the smells, the sensory feel of the room, the lighting. I would work in there, we held meetings there and had several people who came just to visit the room. As part of the early discussions we had a meeting with the families of the residents; it wasn't well attended but, of the few that came, I remember two sisters who were adamant that their dad wouldn't be interested, as he preferred to stay in his room. They couldn't see how it would benefit him. But the dad went to every session and really enjoyed it and the sisters themselves appreciated the opportunity to see the room. I've worked in care for many, many years and it was something fresh, very different, that I'd never seen anywhere before.

Punchdrunk learned a lot. I remember in the first session I thought, 'mm-mm, no, you have a lot to learn here' because they were working with people who were living with dementia. The pace was too fast, for instance, so they learned quickly to slow that right down. After every session we would have an evaluation and even seemingly small things like some of the language that was being used would be noted. For example, calling the room, 'the space'. I remember how the residents who attended the first Greenhive Green Committee meeting, when Punchdrunk performers mentioned 'space', all of them looked up as if to the sky. Punchdrunk only referred to it as 'the room' from then on. Matt [Blake], who is very tall, quickly realised that he'd have to come to the level of the residents so where in the first session he'd stood up, from the second session onwards he remained on a stool. I observed a lot of that, Punchdrunk changing things to meet the needs of the residents. Every week there would be something that would be picked up at the review and you could see how they constantly adjusted things, right up to the end.

We had a signpost, which was displayed on the hallways so that residents were aware that Greenhive Green activities were taking place. Where Punchdrunk had originally planned to run a session in the morning and have drop-in sessions in the afternoon, so many residents were interested in what was going on that Punchdrunk had to run two sessions a day, one in the morning and one in the afternoon. Sometimes residents who'd attended in the morning still wanted to push in on sessions in the afternoon. Typical of the Greenhive staff, they embraced the project; they embrace anything that would be of benefit to the residents. We had two Activity Coordinators who were very keen and worked so well with the Punchdrunk team. The size of the room meant we had to limit the number of staff in each session. An important part of the project was that after Punchdrunk had left, the project continued and staff took over similar activities with the residents. It was crucial that the Activity Coordinators would be the main Greenhive staff in each session so there could only ever be one or two other staff members in addition to that. I made the point to Punchdrunk afterwards that some staff were feeling left out so Punchdrunk immediately held a session for them, which I thought was really nice. The final celebration saw the Greenhive 'Mayoress' turn up. We had pictures taken and there was a large screen showing the activities that had taken place across the project; it was a lovely party.

After Punchdrunk left we continued to use the room for 'Greenhive Green Committee' meetings with the residents, every Tuesday. At the final party with Punchdrunk the role of Greenhive Green Mayoress was handed over to me, and I kept all the regalia in the office, so every Tuesday, I would go in wearing it. Although the rest of the design had to be removed, the noticeboard that had displayed the daily activity was left to remind us. We ran activity sessions exactly the same way that Punchdrunk did, including a High Tea. We'd bring the prompts in that they'd left, the post box, the telephone box, and put the board out stating that the Greenhive Green Committee Meeting was taking place. The residents enjoyed it so much and it gave them so much stimulation. It worked as a memory jog for a number of residents to continue the activities.

What Punchdrunk offered that we hadn't experienced before was art mixed up with magic within a live show. Although we'd had performances in before, we hadn't had anything of that nature. The room made a big impression on people; the sounds, the lighting, all was so different and new, for me, the staff, as well as the residents. The residents remembered Greenhive Green and all the different activities, the badges that were made for participants were kept and handed out at each meeting that followed. The relatives, the staff, all the visitors who came to experience it, everyone was ecstatic about it. It was money well spent because it made a lot of the residents come alive again. Everybody was happy to see Punchdrunk arrive each week. Punchdrunk gelled with the team and made friends with the residents. Since they left I've let Pete and his team know when residents have died and they've always sent messages of condolence and stayed in touch, and that cannot be taken for granted.

Oracles, The (2017–present, see also: **Act 3**; **adrenalin**; awe and wonder; design; digital technologies; discovery; Enrichment; *Fallow Cross*; gaming; **objects**; **transportation and transformation**): A cross-platform storytelling project developed for KS2 primary school pupils in Haringey. *The Oracles* takes place at the village of Fallow Cross and within an online game developed for the project. Loosely based on Hercules and the twelve labours, the premise of both worlds is that the village of Fallow Cross is in danger and its villagers need help. It tests the boundaries of where the walls of Fallow Cross end and the world of game begins, investigating the fusion of physical and virtual landscapes where the village exists in both realms, one mirroring the other. Enrichment Producer Alex Rowse explains:

> We partnered with Google's Creative Lab to develop the technology to lend a magical quality to the audience's movements within the physical space. This technology helped us to animate physical props in a manner that made the audience-participants feel magical themselves when inside the physical space by augmenting a visceral relationship with the digital game. A physical object placed by audience-participants in a range of possible positions in the village of Fallow Cross would then appear in an identical place in the virtual equivalent in the game when they returned to the classroom. We're interested in the feedback loop and the audience's 'player' relationship between the worlds. The learning from this process has fed into research on future Punchdrunk forms.

The audience first encounters Fallow Cross while playing a maths game in groups on a tablet in class, unlocking an invitation to the village. Pupils arrive at the schoolroom and the physical adventure unfolds. Designer Kate Rigby describes:

There's a moment in *The Oracles* when the real village of Fallow Cross is revealed to them. It had never occurred to me that during the reveal the children would assume it was just a projection of what they'd seen in the game. When they discover that the village is actually a real place that they can step into and explore, they're just blown away and so overwhelmed; it's really magical to watch.

The piece takes place over seven episodes across the physical and digital world as pupils help characters from Fallow Cross save their village from the evil sorceress, Circe. The performance in the physical space employs locked-room challenges, aligned to KS2 maths curricula. Pupils must work in teams, and unlock clues and codes, in order to collect objects from various locations in the physical village to help complete their mission. On returning to the classroom and the online world, pupils discover those same items now manifest in the virtual village.

The Oracles is an example of Enrichment taking an area of interest for Punchdrunk and piloting a project to explore the territory with a young, inquisitive and exacting audience, before rolling the ideas and techniques out to a wider public audience. It explores the relationship between visceral and virtual forms of storytelling to create a cohesive piece, while directly applying mathematical skills and logic. In design terms, it experiments with installations that are equipped with sensors, allowing the physical space to match the intuition of a game engine. A body of advanced technological research was undertaken by Punchdrunk, around connecting sensors to game servers and theatrical cueing systems, creating responsive stage technologies. For Rigby, it's an example of an Enrichment project 'igniting the village with real purpose'. Peter Higgin elucidates:

> *The Oracles* not only serves a need of the KS2 curriculum, it explores the

idea of cross-platform storytelling and game play mechanics, using new technologies to augment the live experience. When Enrichment was initially set up we discussed this mode of operation as a way of enriching audience experiences, while simultaneously enriching Punchdrunk's practice. I would say *The Oracles* is the first time we have done this in such a conscious way and on such a large scale.

Felix Barrett's approach to any Punchdrunk design process – imagining the world from above like a tracking shot, taking in a bird's-eye view of the whole landscape, then focusing in on the specifics of the structures of the town and then in through the open doorway of a house, into a bedroom and finally zooming in on a letter in that room – has been made both digitally and physically manifest in *The Oracles*. The virtual world, designed by Jim Bending, does exactly that in digital form; 3D-imaging of bird's-eye views of landscapes and starry nights that zoom into a digital animation of the village of Fallow Cross, all of which is accessed initially by the participants off-site, playing the game in the classroom. As Rowse describes above, the awe that is then palpable when pupils witness the reveal and physically enter Fallow Cross to play out the game on-site is a wonder for all observers to behold. The participants themselves zoom in, wholly experientially, stepping through the screen into the multidimensional world.

Oshodi, Maria (see also: **access**; digital technologies; *Faust*; lifts; *Masque of the Red Death, The*; senses; **soundscore**; **touch**; *Uncommercial Traveller, The*): Oshodi is a freelance writer and Artistic Director and CEO of Extant, the UK's leading company of visually impaired theatre artists. Since its formation in 1997, Extant has pioneered theatre practice with the express inclusion of visually impaired performers and audiences, touring these internationally. In addition to designing site-specific, multi-sensory

FIGURE 19 *The Oracles* at Fallow Cross. 2017.

Photo credit: Paul Cochrane

productions, Extant lead arts consultancies, seminars and research in access and technology and deliver training in education, business and the arts. Oshodi's expertise in inclusive practice and Extant's interest in the use of sensory technologies in theatre experiences have resulted in a mutual sharing of experience and advice between Oshodi and Punchdrunk . . .

Maria Oshodi

On access and inventiveness

I remember, around 2006, there was a buzz in the air about Punchdrunk. It was at a time that Extant were being earmarked to receive RFO funding and we'd attended a meeting for others in the same position, which is where I first met with Colin Marsh and Colin Nightingale and heard about *Faust*. As a consequence of my work with The National Theatre, consulting on its audio description, colleagues there contacted Punchdrunk to fix a visit. An access worker who worked with me at the time was also a dancer with a friend in the production so we went together. I met both Colins in the bar afterwards as they were keen to hear my feedback as a blind audience member.

The whole thing blew my mind from the very beginning. For a start, it felt like it was in the middle of nowhere. We had a long walk around an industrial estate to get to the site itself followed by this strange experience of being herded into the lift with a loud, American lift-operator, only allowing a certain number of people to get out at each level. That was so palpably terrifying, I definitely hadn't experienced anything like it before.

What stands out for me in terms of my journey through the space was the up-close and personal, one-on-one nature of the work coupled with wandering around in vast, empty spaces within the building. Those two experiences juxtaposed with each other were memorable. Upstairs there was a bar, separate to the main bar where the wider entertainment was going on; this was more like a cowboy joint. We leant against the bar and I remember a hand coming out and touching me. Being blind, a hand reaching out and giving me a shot of something was surreal, sensual and unexpected. I also remember being with Old Faust upstairs in his laboratory, him focused on these repetitive actions and movements around his equipment. I was very close to him, extremely committed to his internal process and performance; locked into his internal monologue, moving about between these items in the laboratory, and equally locked into the chemical procedures he was carrying out. You could stand right next to him without him interrupting his continual muttered dialogue, get in his path without him being perturbed by that. I was standing so close to him but at the same time feeling separate as an audience, more like an entity hidden behind my mask. You had the feeling of being detached while you were right in it. I remember everything being very close yet there was also a sense of space and distance as well. You were able to move around freely and then also have this very tight, physical experience.

The fact that I could touch everything was important. A formal touch-tour as part of an accessible performance always feels very organised, like a staged performance in itself. I don't really like touch-tours. I feel like I'm a recipient of this othered gesture that's being made especially for me as a visually impaired audience member and feel self-conscious, like I have to behave myself. This was totally different, it was part of the landscape of the production that everyone was involved with and felt marvellous, like a release. It was wonderful to feel the boundary between being an observer and being in the performance itself being broken down because of that ability to touch and be at liberty in the space.

With *The Uncommercial Traveller*, Punchdrunk were exploring different ways of evolving access to the work and had attached a touch-tour to the piece, which I was happy to go along with. It smacked a bit of the traditional preamble that you might have on a touch-tour, although the piece was a totally different experience to *Faust* because the ambulant part had been prior to reaching the soup kitchen. When we arrived there, the audience were led in and sat down in groups at tables with different performers. The thing that I most remember being pointed out to me on the touch-tour were the mugs that were hung in the soup kitchen; those I really took in and that stays with me. They were the mugs that we were then handed with soup in when the performance began. The most enriching element of that experience for me was the sound. It's a significant element of Punchdrunk's work and is something that the company do phenomenally well. In *The Uncommercial Traveller*, the soundbed provided an underlying score. I'm very sensitised to sound atmospherics and the fidelity of the sound was very pure; it held the atmosphere and tension. It was particularly marked in that confined space and so the experience was made deeper by the soundscore.

With *The Masque of The Red Death*, Punchdrunk gave BAC my name to consult with me on exploring how the production could be made more accessible to a visually impaired audience within the authenticity of the production. I attended the production and was guided by one of the team through it. Consequently, they extended that process into this terrific idea of travelling guides, characters that might be found in Edwardian Paris, to accompany each visually impaired audience member. They guided us, one-on-one, through the twists and turns of the experience, describing in character as they went. To this day visually impaired people who went to the show still remember and comment on it, agreeing wholeheartedly that it worked absolutely brilliantly and was a stand-out theatrical access experience. It has to be acknowledged because it was Punchdrunk proving that its inventiveness worked in absolutely the right way.

pedal note

P

pedal note (see also: **adrenalin; gong**; music; **soundscore; visceral**): The lowest, fundamental note of a harmonic series or the note sustained in one part (usually the bass) through successive harmonies. A pedal note for Punchdrunk is, as Felix Barrett puts it, 'the tone that roots a building'. Looped within Stephen Dobbie's soundscores, the pedal note is a deep bass, sustained note that is vibrational and repetitive, felt and retained in the body. Through this, an intention is that the audience is *present within* the music rather than *listening to* it. It underscores a sense of threat, implies that something is going to happen, keeping the audience on edge. Dobbie clarifies, 'the music list and sound palette that we use, throw a rhythm or melody into the pedal note, creating an expectation or anticipation that something will happen, exercised by that constant state of tension'. Barrett adds, 'when music breaks happen, full scores or songs, there's an almost euphoric release from the pedal note. A release that's accentuated by the emotional pull of the music'. The shimmer of a gong has been employed in various productions including *The Tempest*, 2003 and *The Masque of the Red Death* to create a pedal note, drawing the audience together as a collective for a finale.

'Peru' (see also: aardvark; Act 2; Big Chill Festival, The; **caretaking; *Marat/Sade*; 'Peruvian Michael'**; 'safe-words'; *Woyzeck*, 2004): The safe-word used during *Woyzeck*, 2004, between performers and the wider crew. The term Peru derives from Peruvian Michael.

'Peruvian Michael' (see also: Act 2; adrenalin; **Big Chill Festival, The**; masks: 'Peru'; *Woyzeck*, **2004**): Peruvian Michael was a Peruvian ceremonial knitted mask that was acquired by Punchdrunk. The name derived from 'Michael mask', an earlier moniker given to a latex, full-head mask, which made all who wore it look like Michael Myers from the *Halloween* films. 'Peruvian Michael'

was worn by a character who hid within a maze during *Woyzeck* at The Big Chill, who would jump out at unsuspecting audience members, causing them to exit the maze in fright at speed. The safe-word 'Peru' derives from this character, used during *Woyzeck*, 2004.

Piggott, Greg (see also: **Cake Friday**; *It Felt Like a Kiss*; *Masque of the Red Death, The*; Production Managing; *Quest of a Wave*): Piggott was the Production Manager at BAC when Punchdrunk created *The Yellow Wallpaper* and *Quest of A Wave* and he collaborated closely with the team during the build of *The Masque of the Red Death*. He was a staunch advocate of the project and his support was key to helping Punchdrunk reinvent how the arts centre would operate within the show. Piggott was instrumental in establishing 'Cake Friday' as an important communal activity. He went on to work with Punchdrunk on *It Felt Like a Kiss*, 2009 before his untimely death in 2011. BAC held a memorial event for Piggott at which Peter Higgin and Colin Nightingale devised a 'Memory Palace' for attendees to visit and quietly reflect on Piggott's life. Housed in the space that had been used in 2006 for *Quest of a Wave*, guests were invited to bring an object that was related to or reminded them of Greg to place in the room as a tribute to him.

Pluto (see also: Bicât, Tina; community; **in-show-world**; Jubb, David; *Masque of the Red Death, The*: 'Norman the Eel; 'Rebecca the Bird'. Further reading: Poe 1965, 223–230): BAC's resident theatre-cat, named after the eponymous Edgar Allan Poe short story, 'The Black Cat': 'Pluto – this was the cat's name' (Poe 1965, 224). Chosen by Felix Barrett and David Jubb from Battersea Dog and Cat Home, Pluto helped realise Barrett's dream of having a black cat asleep at the fireplace in the library, as a living part of the in-show-world of *The Masque of the Red Death* and a reference to the Poe story. At the time of writing, Pluto remains in residence at

BAC and a significant member of the Battersea community.

police (see also: **accidents**; Act 1; Act 2; **building**; Exeter Experiments; *Faust*; forests; **taxidermy**): During many early productions, the police were called out by suspicious members of the general public, unwittingly observing the strange goings-on of Punchdrunk worlds. During the Boston run of *Sleep No More*, Felix Barrett and Euan Maybank stayed late in the building working on the lighting and thought a banging resulting from air-locked pipes was an intruder. A police officer who answered their call, while exploring the building, ended up drawing his pistol on a taxidermy wolf that had been hidden to startle audiences in a room of hanging sheets. Colin Nightingale adds:

The unusual nature of our projects, especially in the early days, had a tendency to raise the suspicions of local residents given that we were inhabiting disused buildings previously perceived as being empty. This led to local constabularies attending the sites at least once during the run, despite us informing them of our activities. One memorable night was in the final stages of the build of *Faust*, working late into the evening. The security company remotely monitoring the site's CCTV were concerned about an individual in a baseball cap hanging around outside an adjacent storage warehouse and had asked the police to check the site. The three officers were escorted by one of the set-builders to our workshop on the second floor to discuss the issue. We ascertained that the individual in question was, in fact, one of our team, everyone was assured that nothing unusual was going on, when the police received an emergency call. Needing the quickest way out of the site, we hurried them to the nearest staircase to the ground floor. This led them into an unexpected forest of pine trees that they hadn't seen on the way into the building. The bewilderment

△

FIGURE 20 Pluto. *The Masque of the Red Death*. 2008.

Photo credit: Stephen Dobbie

on their faces as they ran through the indoor forest only served to reinforce to us, in the final days of the build, the power of the design we were creating across that abandoned building.

These predicaments provide illustration of Punchdrunk's willingness and capacity to handle unexpected occurrences pragmatically and with diplomacy, while relishing the anecdotal pleasures they may bring.

Poots, Alex (see also: Act 2; **chainsaw**; *Crash of the Elysium, The*; curiosity; **Curtis, Adam**; *It Felt Like a Kiss*; narrative): Founding Artistic Director of Manchester International Festival (MIF) from 2005–2015 and now Founding Artistic Director and CEO of The Shed in New York. Conceived to be an artist-led festival to present new works from across the performing and visual arts and from mainstream and popular culture, MIF quickly became a leading commissioning, biennial event for a diverse audience. Poots produced *It Felt Like a Kiss* for MIF 2009 and subsequently commissioned Punchdrunk to create *The Crash of the Elysium* in 2010. Poots collaborated closely with Felix Barrett and Adam Curtis from 2007 to 2009 in the development of *It Felt Like a Kiss* . . .

Alex Poots

On *It Felt Like a Kiss* and 'curiosity machines'

I've always been interested in how artistic formats evolve and how they can be reinvigorated. There's room for the preservation of form, a respect for the treasures of the past, and to support forms and genres evolving. Punchdrunk's *The Masque of the Red Death* felt like I was witnessing something new happening, beyond what I had understood as theatre and the production of a play. There didn't seem to be a structured narrative running through it and for good reason. Part of the delight of the format of Punchdrunk is the liberated feeling you have as an audience member. It merges gallery engagement with theatrical experience. It was like some of my senses were heightened, while others were diminished. It fascinated me and also revealed an opportunity that would return in a subsequent discussion with Adam Curtis.

I first met Adam around a talk he gave at the MIF launch in 2007. Adam is, and was, extremely interested in telling emotional stories using the medium of television and 'found' recordings. By that point he had already made *The Power of Nightmares*. In our early discussions, Adam wanted to explore ways of sharing important stories of our time in a live, theatrical and more physical, embodied way. When Adam and I discussed how to make his documentary style more emotional, more live, I intuitively felt that layering a Curtis narrative into a Punchdrunk world could answer that. That conversation pointed up how a collaboration between Adam and Punchdrunk might offer the audience a certain amount of freedom to walk around and piece together an experience while still finding a shared narrative through it; a sense of the whole being greater than the sum of its parts, with an evolution to the experience. That fuelled Adam's interest and so we brought him and Felix together.

One of Felix's many talents is that he is open to trying new ideas. This project was messing a bit with the toolkit that is the magic of Punchdrunk, but it felt like an exciting experiment. The freedom that Punchdrunk was giving the audience to lean in, rather than be spoken to, the power of that, aligns itself more with a gallery or museum experience. That sense of, 'I'm an individual, I go this way, I go that way, I can choose what I want to be interested in and make up my own narrative, my own journey', Punchdrunk was creating that at a high level for its audience. Adding a layer of fixed narrative to that could have created an oil and water situation, because it was potentially robbing Felix of some of the devices that allows his toolkit to fly. The opportunity we had related to finding a third way.

A week before we opened, there was still a gear change in the show that wasn't working, which Felix and Adam worked at, on their feet, to fix. The transition was between the more ambient way of discovering information, where audience members didn't necessarily have to follow the same route as each other, and the second part of the show, which was more structured through time. That transition jarred enough to take you out of the theatrical spell. The solution was a quarantine zone where, suddenly, individuals were being questioned and having to complete a form, which allowed the required gear change but in a manner that kept audience members in a heightened state.

The show lasted ninety minutes but, if people lingered in the first part of the show, the overall time could be around two hours. Depending on which, you may end up in a group of around eight, with your friends, or you might have ended up with no one you know. Either way, towards the very end of the show and irrespective of the total duration, at that point you suddenly heard the sound of a chainsaw behind you. By that time, you were in such an altered state that you pushed people out of the way to get out, whoever they were. The audience were scared and had lost a certain sense of decorum, I guess. Someone came up to me after the show and said, 'How could you do this? I pushed my friend out of the way, I was so scared'. Adam and Felix inserted fear into the event. It wasn't a case of 'here we can see that King Lear is fearful', but rather that you, the audience, *felt* it. Your whole body was set alight in this state of heightened observation and self-defence. In terms of form, a number of people didn't like *It Felt Like a Kiss*. I suspect they felt it had crossed a line of involvement; they got involved to the point that they were *in* it with a loss of control rather than observing it, which is quite fascinating.

It Felt Like a Kiss was a really exciting experiment. Nowadays for audiences there can be a tussle between wanting the freedom of the gallery experience yet with the focus and concentration of a seated theatre event. How can we have both? That's part of what I was trying to figure out with *It Felt Like a Kiss* and still am with other shows that we're developing now at The Shed. The arts are so wide-ranging, you can't really say that a focus on one form means that you're missing out on another. Exploring possible fusions can provide an interesting evolution to the artistic format. Similarly, I felt that there was an opportunity not to diminish or augment the track that Felix had already been on, but to identify how the Punchdrunk approach, combined with a narrative junkie like Adam, could yield some interesting conclusions; conclusions that may end up populating some other art form – you never know how these things will migrate and be appropriated.

Felix has a very rare gift – strong in artistic vision but also kind and collaborative. That's a powerful combination. Some of the things he excels at are less visible. The fact that he's generous provides a lot of the oil in the machine that gets things moving and keeps things happening. If he was more the authority figure, the traditional idea of what the artist is, then I don't know if he would have got to where he is. Adam is different; he has an incredible gift for storytelling and is very focused on getting that idea across the line and nailed down. Felix was a little more, 'let's find a way to make it work'. If they'd both been alike, it wouldn't have worked. My desire to get them together was a deliberate intention to make one plus one equal eleven in terms of what I'd experienced of Punchdrunk's work and what Adam could bring to the table. I doubt if *It Felt Like a Kiss* would have achieved what it did without Felix's temperament and talent and Adam's skills and determination. In turn, there were a lot of people around Felix who helped realise his and Adam's ideas. Livi Vaughan and Bea Minns were two key players, as was the Festival's Producer, Christine Gettins, who worked wonders to move the production through to its premiere. Livi and Bea were reactive in a way that was really impressive, evolving their craft as the vision was being developed. They worked in tandem, echoing or counterpointing what Felix and Adam were conceptualising. Not easy.

Damon Albarn, although he came in later on in the creation process, once the show structure was clearer, had been invited to collaborate early on. Damon has an incredible musical gift to compose in the moment and so, when needed, can compose relatively quickly. Some questioned why we invited someone of Damon's stature to write the music for this project, but I felt he was the right composer with a genuine curiosity. Also, I'd promised myself and the city an international festival, one that would offer Manchester audiences the most ambitious work our artists could create – something out of the ordinary that was worthy of festive celebration.

It Felt Like a Kiss was one of those shows which the arts world, the general arts audience and practitioners, found interesting, whether they liked it or not. It was addressing artistic and structural issues that were fundamental across the performing and visual arts. It was also addressing things that people cared about – the story was relevant and of our time and the format was new and hadn't been done before. Added to that, people who really didn't participate in the arts calendar as a regular audience were signing up to come in their droves. We were widening our base of interest and generating curiosity, creating a curiosity machine. Because *It Felt Like a Kiss* was produced in the early years of MIF, it didn't get the attention it would have got had it been a show in London. If I'd done exactly the same show, at one of my previous places of work, such as the Tate, the Barbican or Somerset House, it would have had a different reach from before it opened through to the end of the run. I think that's something that continually needs to be thought about in the UK, but that's a separate story. So how was it received? From ecstatic to mediocre, but it was one of the first ever arts reviews to run on *The Guardian*'s front page and not because they particularly liked it but, presumably, because they thought it was a significant enough show to be national front-page news.

portals (see also: *Clod & Pebble*; **cross-fade**; curiosity; discovery; **doors**; intervention; **lifts**; mazes; **transportation and transformation**; tunnels; **wardrobes**): A key point of transportation, the threshold into the Punchdrunk world; sometimes obviously through a door, sometimes via other means. The portal is the mechanism that triggers the cross-fade from reality to the fictional world. In *The Lost Lending Library*, a hardback book is employed as the magical key for a concealed portal, a door disguised as a bookshelf. The express intention of this is to play on the idea of books as gateways to possible worlds, fostering a love of literature among pupils and a belief that books are magical in their capacity to transport the reader. With wider Punchdrunk work the portal might be a journey from A to B, on foot or in a car, or a descent in a lift. It may be marked by the crescendo in a soundscore via headphones, the point from which the everyday is perceived anew. A portal may be opened up by an unexpected intervention, momentarily defamiliarising the world, a passer-by thrusting a secret note in your hand. Portals may allow a cross-fade to be slow and subtle, or relatively swift, but it will always open up an entry point where the audience-participant unmistakably commits herself to another world. Where the portal is physically marked by a door through which the audience member passes, these will vary in form; a wardrobe, the cantilevered clatter of an industrial lift. These entrance points may be easy or difficult to find; you may be directed there, or you may discover it as a consequence of your own curiosity. It might entice you by the use of an inconspicuous sign: 'Magic. Theatre. Enter. **Come** in. If you dare'.

process (see also: Barrett, Felix; **building**; 'company building'; dance; design; Enrichment Symposium; ensemble; **exercises**; influences; lens; 'listening to the building'; research; site-sympathetic; **space**; text. Further reading: Higgin 2017; Machon 2011, 89–99): Punchdrunk has a shifting process underpinned by fundamental principles and a rules-set that supports the ability to evolve according to the ambitions and needs of a project. For Felix Barrett, people 'who get Punchdrunk' are those that understand that any perceived 'hierarchy' of performance elements, including lighting, sound, duration, dance, speech, text and scenography, is broken down. Where any rank is pulled, it is often lighting or sound, closely followed by installation, that would be granted permission to dominate, as opposed to the performer. The general rule is that space leads; it is the decision maker in whether a project goes ahead. Music, specifically a musical refrain, is the key that unlocks and drives the manner in which any source material will then be interpreted across that space.

An important part of Punchdrunk's process in the early days related to a commitment to the drudgery of clearing and cleaning buildings, transporting material and props, as much as to any artistic invention. Barrett's natural ability to inspire a collective to contribute to hard work alongside creative ideas proved to be infectious among original core team members. Colin Nightingale believes the Punchdrunk process relies on that shared sensibility and shorthand forged through the early work:

> We're a project-led company; we lose ourselves in a project, that's what our process *is*. We've created a landscape for ourselves where the core team is now trying to work across multiple projects, with a new task force. That's shifted the process. It's difficult to dip in and out because people need answers to be able to work, yet we no longer always have the space to work out those answers organically from deep within the project.

This embedded approach to project-driven practice, set during the industrious years of Act 1, is now being returned to in Act 3. An overview of Punchdrunk's approach to making theatre was recently added to the British Library online archives. Enrichment work is driven by this same approach, made bespoke to each community for which projects are produced, as the core principles shared at the Enrichment Symposium lay out above.

The devising process for any project, masked or otherwise, is tempered by Barrett's idiosyncratic approach to a destabilising turn as it evolves; the only hard and fast rule is to break the rules. Barrett explains, across the spatial and aural design and performance devising, the team agree a rules-set, for example 'everything is 1930s' only to create a moment, detail or character that intentionally breaks those rules in order to subvert expectation, 'because otherwise the audience would quickly get everything, become too comfortable'. As for a production process, the nature of working site-sympathetically, whether building, city or countryside, requires a very different approach to traditional conventions of technical and dress runs. With masked shows, the diversity of spaces, the loops and checks required for all elements of performance, require teams of people to be in a range of spaces to ensure the smooth realisation and delivery of the production, all of which has to be refined during previews once a public audience enters. Although the process shifts according to the format and foci of investigation for any project, Barrett agrees there is now a standardised approach established for masked shows that can be summarised as follows:

1. **Mining the text**. Close-reading of the original source, page-by-page to identify and colour-code; setting; character; narrative; design for narrative; design for atmosphere; sound. This may be done months or years in advance of any production as it relies on a building to unlock the final interpretation. Any initial mining will be returned to and reinforced in light of the response to the building.

2. **Building, site, space**. Finding and securing space is the most crucial part of the process for any

Punchdrunk production. A site that inspires Barrett becomes the key to unlocking the source that will be interpreted, where all that work on text can explored and made manifest. The building is always the driving purpose for any project. Where a building is found but eventually not secured then a project will be halted or become a different beast, as was the case with *Kabeiroi*. For Barrett, 'moment one of the production process is when you have the key in your hand and agree the date to return it, knowing the show will finish the day before the key's returned. Those keys set the amount of time we have to make and present the show'.

3. **Listening to the building**. The most significant part of the process for Barrett:

I don't know what the show will be until I listen to the building. I have a circling pool of sources, a pool that's probably quite limited, but they're each treading water or lying dormant until the building sparks it and I know which it will be. It wasn't a case of me saying, 'Oh I'd love to do *Faust*' but instead that text lay dormant for me and it was only when I entered the building and felt that it was claustrophobic, felt there was evil residing there, that I knew it was right for *Faust*.

Barrett, Nightingale and Livi Vaughan then walk the building together and work out its emotional footprint, allowing the building itself to unlock the way in which the source text will be interpreted.

4. **Devising, detail and rehearsal**. For masked shows this involves a threefold approach:

   i. Build and installation of the world of the event in the building. For other projects where the world of the event may involve journeying through specific locations, as with *The Borough* or *Kabeiroi*, the devising, detailing and narrative build of the show occur

according to those same principles but are tested and rehearsed in the external locations, with existing sites chosen for aesthetic and/or practicality along the route of that journey. Any additional design layered in these spaces will be minimal.
   ii. Studio devising – Maxine Doyle and ensemble, with Barrett and Stephen Dobbie at regular intervals, developing narrative arcs, building character, individual and collective multilayered research, alongside the development of the choreography.
   iii. Fine tuning and rehearsal on-site, including the development of one-on-one material in given rooms.

5. **Reworking the world with the flow of the audience . . .**

In terms of sharing the practical, creative approach taken by Punchdrunk in workshops or offering suggestions for exercises that might provide a way into the more instinctive strategies that the core team members have deployed since first coming together, Peter Higgin notes:

What is most consistent about Punchdrunk is that it's forever changing and striving to reinvent itself. To operate in this mode of working means to continually reformulate approaches so it's hard to define practice in a way that is convenient for those studying or wanting to gain further insight into the work. There are only a handful of what you might call 'Punchdrunk exercises', developed over the years primarily by Felix and Maxine, most of which are included within this encyclopaedia. The work develops in an instinctive, organic and iterative way and steps for rehearsal are reactive, responding to space, design, cast and emerging ideas. Like much theatre practice, there is no simple way of creating and certainly no one Punchdrunk method. Over the history of the

company we have facilitated many workshops and residences and have collated a range of exercises that can best be described as 'ways into' Punchdrunk's practice. We have incorporated these within this encyclopaedia at relevant entries, identifying them as such. They are in no way intended to reflect the company's rehearsal process, nor do they represent stock exercises. In many cases they are exercises acquired elsewhere and repurposed for our needs, so may already be familiar to the reader. We hope they will form the beginnings of thinking about Punchdrunk's practice, through practice. Ultimately, especially if you are reading as someone interested in devising work in the style of Punchdrunk, you may want to use these as a springboard for your own exercises and approaches.

producing (see also: Act 1; Act 2; Act 3; building; keyholders; Marsh, Colin; production management; Thomas, Jen): For the early projects of Act 1, Felix Barrett produced his own shows. Resourcing the early projects owed much to Barrett's ability to inspire people with his vision to lend him what he needed; from items of taxidermy to country houses. Barrett also attempted the difficult task of applying for funding himself, recalling leveraging the *promise* of space against a fruitless funding application to BAC. It was with his successful application to Independ*ance* that he was awarded producing support and from then, with Colin Marsh taking on the role, professionalising Punchdrunk's approach to producing projects was given impetus and would eventually find a producing approach that met the mission and practice of the company. Despina Tsatsas notes, 'a level of collectivism is required to produce a Punchdrunk show':

In traditional production companies the producing function might only be spread across dedicated producing staff, such as Colin Marsh, Griselda Yorke, Rebecca Dawson or myself. However, in Punchdrunk these roles are very closely integrated with creative, operational and production staff, in particular Colin Nightingale, and production manager roles. In addition, past major works required close engagement with co-producers from partner venues, including MIF, BAC, ENO or Aldeburgh. In the Punchdrunk context, the producing function also includes the building dimension, sourcing it, leasing it for the correct use, existing in it appropriately during the life of the show, returning it appropriately. In Acts 1 and 2 the funding for productions was sourced from charitable streams, but *The Drowned Man* engaged third-party investors along with co-producers like The National Theatre. The Act 3 structure offers the flexibility to place projects into either side of Punchdrunk, financing cutting-edge works of adventure and innovation from subsidised sources in the charity, and larger-scale works requiring greater financial risk in the commercial production company, where funding can be sourced on different terms . . .

Rebecca Dawson and Despina Tsatsas

On producing for Punchdrunk

Despina: A traditional way of describing the role of a theatre producer is threefold; banker, cheerleader and fire-fighter. That can apply to the role of someone working within a company or on a specific production. An Executive Producer occupies those three responsibilities in relation to the wellbeing of all the elements of a production; the overview of the production budget, the overview of the people and processes involved, and the trouble-shooting element. That's scaled up on a more macro level when you have a company of people coming to work every day whose ultimate goal is to make those productions and, in Punchdrunk, invent new forms of entertainment.

Rebecca: I would add to that the air-traffic-control analogy; bringing lots of craft in to land.

Despina: It's dealing with the strategic requirements of the business and how they can support, rather than obstruct, the creative processes within it. There's a lot in the air-traffic-control analogy about guidance. The skill set requires persuasion and influence, whether that's with internal teams or external stakeholders who are potentially giving you money or leasing you a building or co-producing with you. Rebecca's very elegant at the soft power approach, which ultimately relates to influencing the outcomes of the process of how works are made and supporting the team to move in the direction that will best serve the objective, whether that's a production or Enrichment work or a new home for the company.

Rebecca: What is unique about the role at Punchdrunk are the layers of complexity in producing a show. Where I've worked previously, while there are hurdles to get over, I understood the heart of the form we were trying to get into the world, which means there are certain paths you follow and 'knowns' about how to achieve your aims from what you've done before. At Punchdrunk there are very few paths and many unknowns. There are many, many layers. It's a 360-degree process, like a Rubik's Cube – very complex.

Despina: There are many differences between building a Punchdrunk work compared to a traditional piece of theatre. A Punchdrunk masked show, for example, combines a site-specific location that provides a building with its own character and characteristics, which in turn informs Felix's and Maxine's practice; it has no singular pre-existing text but rather combines multiple source materials; it also requires an intense devising process with little ability to rehearse the show unless you're actually in the building using a set that has already been built to enable performers to devise from and work with as a canvas; alongside the inability to say in advance what *any* of that looks like in order to raise money or to persuade a landlord to give you the building. That complexity presents a lot of challenges for a producer. As we look forward to the future, wherein both Pete and Felix have a huge desire to invent new forms and formats for entertainment, there is even less to hold on to from a producing perspective. There are no budget or schedule templates because you're trying to create a new approach to the form – there's not a lot that is recyclable. On any project, systems, documents and processes are built from scratch all the time.

Rebecca: That building from scratch each time is significant. It really feels like sea level start for every project, and the production requires forging a path for the full climb from base to top.

Despina: The reinvention of the form is necessarily mirrored in the business function and producing approach that the company has to fulfil collectively. Rebecca and I are doing our best to mirror that goal to reinvent by running the company within a new type of business model. Given that, the baseline approach that we take when initiating those discussions with external stakeholders is to communicate the mythology of the company and the artists at its heart.

Rebecca: A lot of people have the sense of Punchdrunk's mythology and profile. The initial hook in, getting people on board, is usually straightforward because we have a huge number of people who want to work with us, to leverage with a range of partners. It's what happens after that initial hook-in that's more difficult, ensuring that everyone's on the same page and understands what it is we're trying to achieve; which includes how much it costs, and how much it might then take to recoup or fundraise. There's a breadth of people that we might work with yet a very small percentage will actually best fit a given project. The artist-led vision of Punchdrunk provides the decision-making framework for ensuring we have the right partners and structures in place.

Despina: It's important to find people or companies who embody the characteristics that we need from those partnerships. Initial partner meetings are often about diagnosing levels of comfort with the unknowns and the uncertainly principle. Everyone in the organisation is open to existing in an environment where nothing is fixed or certain. Trying to find partners who are willing to commit a building or fund a project while also living in that place of uncertainty can be more tricky.

Rebecca: The differences between producing for the two different arms of the company, Punchdrunk the charity, incorporating Enrichment, and Punchdrunk International, relate to the reason for the division of the business in the first place, which is on the basis of scale. The large, international productions need equivalent international finance and operate on a commercial basis. The small/mid-scale, UK-focused projects are financed via a subsidised charitable model; the relationship with partners and audiences, as well as the scale of operation, is therefore necessarily different. In the charity we seek a mix of projects and partners that support UK-wide engagement and allow us to test and push the boundaries of Punchdrunk's practice.

Despina: Yes, it relates to purpose and to risk. Within the charity, projects explore opportunities that take on a manageable level of risk for the company on the basis that, ultimately, Punchdrunk might have reinvented a new type of creative practice. With Punchdrunk International productions, we begin from a place of understanding that there will be a significant element of financial risk and everyone is bought into that. If it works, it works very effectively and if it doesn't work it will be extremely risky. In a commercial theatrical model, that risk exists there too, but the variables are more known and identifiable than those buffeting a Punchdrunk work. You can identify a suitable theatre and raise money on the basis of a title or a star actor; where budgets are large, they'll resemble budgets for comparable work of the same scale. In contrast, the parameters of producing work in a building that has never been used for a theatrical purpose is far from straightforward. The building may require capital works to make it viable for that theatrical purpose, which means that you might begin by approaching the landlords from a point of assuring them that they will want to lease the building to you on the basis it will have a positive impact on the local area, will create certain localised job opportunities or attract a certain type of business to the local economy. We can't necessarily evidence it beyond the anecdotal and small amounts of empirical data from previous shows. Instead we're asking them to buy into the legitimacy of Punchdrunk as a company that's been running successfully for so many years. We come with some proof and we ask them to meet us at a financial and operational level with a belief that we can deliver that. In the West End model, theatre owners use other more established forms of evidence to diagnose the question of whether a show will perform well and run for a long time alongside whether they believe the producer has the ability to pay the rent and bear the costs of mounting the production.

Rebecca: The charity has a mixed-income profile. Following the creation of two entities, sustaining National Portfolio funding from ACE for the charity is redoubled in importance. It was vital to the growth of the company in the early days and it now supports the next phase of development, providing core security to the heart of the operation and allowing us to build from there. It also acknowledges the continued quality of Punchdrunk's work and ongoing commitment to serving interesting and diverse audiences.

Despina: By being an RFO the charity can take risks that have a purity of artistic purpose at their core, or a purity of applied theatrical benefit, whether that's an impact on young people or literacy levels in Hackney. It's specifically to fund work that is pressing at the vanguard of practice and will be extraordinary if it succeeds but if it doesn't, the company is protected from risk by this subsidy. The goal is that Punchdrunk and Punchdrunk International develop in alignment and the more successful we are at innovating, the more we'll have a place from which Punchdrunk's practice can be amplified internationally with a capacity for continuing to take that type of creative risk alongside a corporate structure that can further support that risk.

Rebecca: Ultimately, the success of Punchdrunk International supports the success of the charity and this supports a strong culture of collaboration between the two. However, it's not all commercially sewn up. Both companies must work hard to build income profiles and the work requires significant cost. People make a lot of assumptions about what might be happening on the inside of an organisation from the type of practice that it's producing outside. We're not funded 100 per cent. RFO funding is roughly twenty per cent of our turnover per year. That's a healthy way to use public investment; to shore up and provide a core level of stability to a company that is then able to think ambitiously about innovation and how it engages audiences in different places. It's leveraging the company and enabling Punchdrunk to go much further in those contexts, which is exactly how public funding should be used.

Despina: It also offers trusts and foundations and other sources of charitable finance the quality 'stamp of approval' that asserts that Punchdrunk represents the best of British work. The investment that goes into Punchdrunk, the charity, from the DCMS via ACE in some respects is even more valuable than anything else. The artistic vision and mission at Punchdrunk, led by Felix, is genuinely trying to evolve new forms of work. Given that goal, in terms of a return on investment to the country and to the creative industries, Punchdrunk is providing a lot for that percentage of funding. In terms of working with Felix and how the structure reflects that, there's a very clear relationship between the shape of the organisation and its working practice and the influence of Felix as a person and an artist. Punchdrunk Enrichment and Punchdrunk International both have an artistic stamp that is deeply connected to who he is and the work he's compelled to make.

Rebecca: What Pete brings to that vision and mission is his great commitment to and knowledge of how you work in different spaces and with different communities. The 'teacher head' working with the 'theatre head' gives a very clear focus to his approach. He has a very close relationship with Felix that has lasted over many years so naturally, the mirror exists, and reflects that relationship but Pete also builds in all the other crucial stuff that has to happen in order to make Enrichment what it is, which means that, for example, school children receive the specificity of experience that makes a project profound in impact. Understanding the needs and culture of the communities in which we work is vital to success.

Despina: That's amplified through the core creative team as well. Punchdrunk is made from its wider pool of practitioners whose characteristics as artists imbue the company's work at a day-to-day level. Even if Felix is setting the vision, Punchdrunk's work couldn't happen without that collective approach to realise it. There's the dream, the feeder vision, that gets funnelled through the Punchdrunk vial of magic and comes out the other end as the experience. Felix's vision is nothing if it can't be lived, experienced and enjoyed. Everyone in the creative team is an integral piece of helping that vision through the process that brings it to life in the real world. The people that are part of the company and succeed within its organisational culture are those who are necessarily curious, flexible and devoted.

Rebecca: It's interesting the idea of a 'shorthand' shared among the creative team. There's such a strong feeling of history and, among core members who've been together a long time, an immediate understanding of when something is *not* 'Punchdrunk'. They're often not able to articulate fully what that is but it's accepted and that immediate response is quite common, and it's shared. With new people that come in, it's noticeable how they respond to that aesthetic, to the intrigue and the uncertainty. Those that are open to it immediately settle in, but you do have to pick a lot of it up intuitively, by osmosis.

Despina: It's iterative, the Punchdrunk process, to the extent that, when we're forecasting budget or schedule we have to make space for that iteration if you want to be assured of having a product at the end of it that's uniquely Punchdrunk. The opportunity to experiment, see the results, change course, experiment again, change course is a reasonably time-consuming and expensive way of doing things but it also creates a very instinctual, experiential and visceral thing for an audience.

Rebecca: The starting point is often with Felix's vision and desire for a particular idea to be realised. You begin to put all the pieces together around that; however, as the experiential context for the original idea emerges and is explored, so much shifts. I've often been surprised by the fact that the kernel of the idea feels fixed and then it becomes massively iterative and changes completely around the context, whether that's architectural or social, for instance. It's really interesting watching how that happens. Once you move beyond the confines of walls, into a world where anything can happen and the audience experience becomes the vital ingredient and marker, you can't control completely where the original idea will end up. It's exciting, but it adds to the risk assessment.

Despina: It speaks to an energy and appetite for scale and ambition that's untempered. You can see the passage of that view in the trajectory of productions, from a building to a larger building to a six-storey building to a city, in *Silverpoint* and *Kabeiroi*, for example. It makes logical sense and it's wonderful to be living in a time where we have the technology at our disposal to enable us to walk around London, using a mobile phone within a game that reskins your surroundings in a strangely believable way.

Rebecca: The drive for the real-world experience is that it feels properly new and we're learning every day. Going through the *Kabeiroi* process reveals that it's massively different to being in a building or controlled environment. Some stuff we've got very right, other stuff we haven't. The role of audience action and agency at the heart of a project has been forever in Punchdrunk's work but if you change the context radically, for example to the streets of London, it's a whole different ball game of how you animate that agency and sustain the energy of the work.

Despina: On a granular level, the documentation around every aspect of *Kabeiroi* was extraordinary and the active learning was meticulous across the six hours of the show, noting what was and wasn't working and changing it accordingly on the spot. Everything is captured on a minute-by-minute basis inside very detailed show reports and debriefs that occur at the end of every performance between the teams that are running the show. That evaluation and live audience feedback in terms of agency, action and outcome is very immediate.

Rebecca: Indeed – feedback in general is very forthcoming from Punchdrunk audiences, emails, social media, phone calls. We also have structured evaluation frameworks – especially in Enrichment where input from our partners is so important. We use this to assess ways in which we can learn and continue to innovate in applied contexts, and in order to reflect on how we communicate with audiences. Looking at *Kabeiroi*, as a public iteration of Punchdrunk's work, it's clear that there were fans that were hungry for a new show and it wasn't what they were expecting it to be; some have totally embraced it and others have not. It's shown that it's important for us to think about the messages that we want to give out about our creative direction, being clear and confident about that, while recognising that it's not going to be for everyone so finding ways to build trust with fans that want us to repeat the same form over and over again.

Despina: Alongside the reviving and re-imagining of existing work, we're allowing for supporting and financing changing practice so that the creative team are able to work on things that are new as much as capitalising on things that have gone before. It creates an interesting tension with how we respect and allow for the response of fans of Punchdrunk who love the masked shows, and how we support the artists in a company wherein the key creative voices rightly maintain a desire to innovate their practice.

production management (see also: Act 1; Act 2; Act 3; Boyd, Carrie; Minnigin, Aaron; **Nightingale, Colin**; **stage management**; volunteers): Punchdrunk's approach to the management of individual productions has developed organically, evolving alongside operational structures as much as the ambitions of each new project since Act 1. Early productions involved a small ensemble, a handful of dedicated crew and a nightly team of volunteer stewards. Now long-running masked shows employ over 120 people on a daily basis; cleaning, maintaining, managing, resetting, running, performing and stewarding; supporting every aspect of the production. Colin Nightingale recalls:

Early production management was unconventional. We were working with limited budgets and few personnel, trying to build ridiculously ambitious projects in very short periods of time. I would joke about the pointlessness of costing and scheduling the design install as it would eat into precious time and only show that we didn't have enough days, crew or money. It would have constrained the ideas. So many design ideas were generated concurrent to the build, so we didn't have plans to cost. It felt futile to build a schedule around a volunteer workforce as we never knew how many people or what skills we'd have on any given day. Instead, the core team would throw a huge amount of energy at the projects and try to make everyone around us believe in the dream. Without a set plan to follow or a clear endpoint for the design my early role as Production Manager was to problem-solve and assess our progress, focusing the daily resources to achieve the next required task that would keep the design developing and the rehearsals on track. Communication was kept fluid and efficient. In terms of 'meetings', I remember many an occasion during *Faust* or *Masque* where, at the end of the day, Peter Higgin and I would pick a task

from the 'to do list' and, while completing that task, discuss the priorities for the following day. Often, this would lead to Pete and I undertaking impromptu work overnight in order to solve an issue. To others it must have felt like elves had been in and created some magic to ensure all kept moving forward.

Where stage management, across the evening's run of a masked show, and production management, across the months of the full run, were once conjoined, nowadays stage management is closely connected to but no longer interchangeable with this role. Nightingale explains, prior to *Faust*, given that the performance loops set duration, performers and crew alike relied on these 'to cue everything':

Any resetting and maintenance would be shared by the whole company including the performers. I can remember furious last-minute glass washing for the bar in *The Firebird Ball* with performers, halfway through completing their hair and make-up, joining in. The runs were short and we would muddle through with non-performing members of the company covering the functions of stage management, steward management and Front of House, along with anything else that needed doing. By the opening night of *Faust*, the performing ensemble had grown and, as we were hoping for an extended run, we knew that we needed to initiate some structure to ensure the run was sustainable for everyone concerned.

A vital area of production management is the supervision and stewarding of the audience in a manner that has little detrimental impact on the artistic aims of a project, while deferring to regulations required by the host site. Nightingale clarifies:

The safety of the audience and performers is of utmost importance and a key concern of the authorities, who

ultimately give final permissions for productions to go ahead. As we create shows in different territories around the world we have often made subtle changes to meet the needs of local legislation or cultural differences. We prefer stewards to be in the shadows as their presence is to ensure safety, not to guide the audience. It's important for the work that people try to find their own path and our stewards attend inductions to understand their role in the world. With early productions, stage management and stewarding were interlinked as they were both concerned with managing the audience. Core team members would coordinate the stewards while simultaneously running and supporting the show. Following the approach developed during *Sleep No More*, Boston, stage managers now oversee more complex scenes as they have knowledge of the choreography and can subtly ensure the audience is safely positioned; vital now audience size has increased.

There are clear rules for the behaviour of all crew, stage managers, stewards, technicians working in the world of the show as their presence and speed of movement can have an impact on the audience's experience. During early shows, staff would wear the same masks as the audience to blend in. We experimented with stewards being identified by discreet armbands. As audiences grew and the responsibilities of the stewards developed, we accepted there was a need for them to have a stronger presence, so a different colour mask was trialled. We realised it was important that the stewards had the ability to speak. A black half-mask, that had failed as an audience mask for *Faust*, lent itself perfectly to the needs of the stewarding team. Adopted from the outset for *The Masque of the Red Death*, from that point on these masks have been worn by stewards, stage managers and other operational staff required to interact with audiences. Wearers have to remember that the mask doesn't make them invisible; in fact, it does the exact opposite. If staff need to blend in, such as rehearsal directors noting performers, they wear the general audience mask.

The Drowned Man and *Sleep No More*, NYC and Shanghai saw major operational developments as run lengths and frequency of weekly performances increased. The size of the ensemble and the use of understudies, or swing performers, has grown to accommodate illness and holidays. Regular access to physiotherapists and injury prevention is now provided due to the physical intensity of durational performance. Wardrobe, props reset, maintenance and stage management departments have all expanded. Nightingale concludes, 'resourceful Production Associates, like Andrea Salazar and Ben Hosford, have brought new ideas that have helped refine our production management during builds and running of the shows':

The nature of site-based work and the ever-expanding artistic ambition of the company mean that every production has its unique set of operational needs. Years of development and progress have seen to us being able to implement sensible operational systems from the start for masked shows. This has made it easier to train and integrate new staff and has taken the pressure off core Punchdrunk members once shows are up and running, ensuring they can move on to develop new projects. Many operational systems and learning from the masked shows have been transferable to other non-traditional theatrical forms that Punchdrunk has developed and continues to explore.

Prospero's Island (**2014**, see also: **Act 3**; cross-fade; Enrichment; text; transformation. Further reading: Cremin, Swann, Colvert and Oliver 2016; Tims 2016):

Hidden in the darkness, somewhere in the shadows, is the story of a storm, an island, and a man with unfathomable powers . . . An invitation from the Games' Master and the appearance of a mysterious key is the beginning of a voyage of discovery for secondary school students and their teachers. Inside the hub and around the school, the completion of each challenge draws them deeper into the world of Shakespeare's The Tempest.

Prospero's Island was a project developed with the support of The Hackney Learning Trust and the Petchey Academy, designed to engage KS3 students with Shakespeare. Learning objectives include increasing pupil engagement with literacy, improving standards in writing, speaking and listening, and improving social learning. A creative space known as the hub was transformed into the Games' Master's control centre hosting performers Katy Balfour, Matthew Blake and Kathryn McGarr, initially in role as the Master's minions. The students were set team-based challenges to unlock further levels, and thus installations across their school. As the game unfolded, the characters of each performer ultimately transfigured, becoming characters from the text.

Prospero's Island, unlike previous work delivered in primary schools, required a different ruse to enable engagement for an older, demonstrably more sceptical age group. It was also designed to ensure different year groups entered at higher levels of the same activity. Students undertaking the activities would be inspired by the manner in which spaces in the school, such as the reading room, had been radically transformed. The Enrichment team noted that the students involved were willing to go along with this as an interactive game, rather than a world in which they were immersed; willing to be swept along by the narrative and to share in creating the adventure. In terms of modulating the mechanisms for immersion, this age range responded to a different type of cross-fade to those typically used with primary pupils. It shifted away from facilitating an investment of belief in a magical world, to an investment in the skills of technical and imaginative play required to function in the Punchdrunk world. Casting the students as gamers in a compelling, live quest enabled an immediate cross-fade. Like Shakespeare's characters on-board ship, caught in Prospero's tempest, the participants at Petchey Academy were hurled into a real-world reinvention of Prospero's imaginative and potentially dangerous games. Spanning two school terms in full, *Prospero's Island* was carefully planned around the school curriculum and timetable. In addition to the immersive experience designed for the students, this pilot project incorporated a 'Teaching and Learning Day' and eight twilight CPD sessions on immersive learning techniques for Petchey Academy staff and other teachers across the borough. The autumn term delivery saw a return to the installation for the Year 7 and 8 students in a session facilitated by teachers rather than performers. During the subsequent spring term Punchdrunk supported those same teachers in the development of immersive learning techniques within English lessons.

'punch-drunk' (see also: **Act 1**; **awe and wonder**; Exeter Experiments; Gideon Reeling): A term that more generally names a characteristic of the behaviour of a person who has suffered repeated blows to the head; synonymic with dazed, stupefied, giddy, reeling. 'Punchdrunk', coined by Felix Barrett as a name for the company, denotes the sensation its work intends to induce through the experience of an event.

Punchdrunk Travel (see also: **Act 3**; adrenalin; *Borough, The*; failure; in-show-world; intervention; **journeying**; *Kabeiroi*; keyholders; lens; *Moon Slave, The*; ritual; scale): For Felix Barrett, Punchdrunk Travel is 'a pure, distilled form. It couldn't be more potent. We're in the throes of exploring it, we know what we're trying to do but we just have to work out what it requires to get there'. The concept and practice tests how Punchdrunk might 'create a theatrical veneer and a story across the exploration of a city, a town, or countryside'. The premise, as ever, is to put the audience at the heart of the experience in concept and form, with the aim to 'change the lens through which the real world is viewed':

Moon Slave, The Borough, Kabeiroi all explored audience in the 'real world', audience as character. Unlike with the masked shows where the audience are cast as spectres, in the real world they're cast as the lead character and need to feel contextualised. Where we swear by being able to control the environment in a building, in the real world all manner of things can happen; how do you theatricalise random events that might occur, the weather and the like? It's about changing the lens through which the audience view the world, that's the unifying concept. *The Moon Slave* and *The Borough* were fairly easy to make because we were only worrying about one audience member. *Kabeiroi* was tricky because we were trying to scale it, roll it out, in order to make it financially viable and available to a wider audience. *The Borough* would have been sixty pounds a ticket if it hadn't been subsidised. I really believe in this form but it's fiercely expensive when you've got a team of forty people behind the scenes but only one or two audience members. In terms of the lineage, from *Moon Slave* to *Kabeiroi*, it's less about developing creative principles and more about developing the logistics behind it. *Kabeiroi* could have been creatively far more exciting if we were only doing it for one couple, but as soon as you start creating a one-on-one experience for multiples then limitation after limitation – fewer of this, less of that, breaks needed here – come in and of course we were also trying to make it cost neutral. We're learning and its exhilarating, in the same way that we learned through a process of testing and getting it wrong with the masked shows.

When questioned as to how Punchdrunk Travel would compare to the more commercial Murder Mystery Weekends, or how it might shake off the cinematic overtones of the 1998 Peter Weir film *The Truman Show*, Barrett responds:

We're trying to break the confines of the building and investigating what happens if you take the content of three hours' worth of a masked show, and scatter it across a county, the journey of which takes three days to walk. It's long-form, durational narrative, spreading the story across three days with seventy-two hours of storytelling. Audience arrive at a place they've never been to before knowing that anybody they meet could be a performer but might not. It's hung on journeying, it's the essence of that Punchdrunk principle; it's not just what you get when you arrive but, more importantly, what happens on the way to getting there. It's theatricalising the travelling. It comes closer to Robert Wilson's seven-day pilgrimage [*KA MOUNTAIN AND GUARDenia TERRACE*]. There's an element of ritual, durational, live art to it, but there's always that element of adrenalin, beats of wonder, of the heart racing along the way.

For Barrett, the audience are always 'in on it', which denies the *Truman Show* idea of being fed a lie. The audience is aware that 'it's a fictional conceit' into which they are invited yet the manner of the immersion will ensure that they can 'feel life becoming a work of art', enabling the audience member to frame their world as such. In terms of creative agency, the willing audience member would experience the safety net of source material; be able to feel the manner in which their life is resonating with that artwork and the narrative and thematic conceits of the fiction. As was the case with *The Borough* and *Kabeiroi*, any source material involved would resonate with the location, the landscapes, architectures, histories or folklores that linger in these places. With *Kabeiroi*, titles

and preparatory communications, hints and clues, in the spirit of the world, that also served as preliminary, basic safeguarding devices, indicated which sources might be plundered further for guidance before embarking on the journey. As Barrett clarifies:

This real-world work doesn't always need a textual anchor point but for scale it certainly helps. When it's just one or two people, who have our undivided attention, then there's a degree to which we can create the narrative, but when it's at scale and we don't have the people to guide them continually then we need the safety net of familiar material to support them. We've conducted a few studies on this and it's fascinating to note what works and doesn't.

In the steps to find an effective methodology for Punchdrunk Travel, Barrett and the team are only able to learn what works by consistently 'trying it live', putting the concept and the content into practice with a series of test audiences. This directly corresponds to the spirit of experimentation, trying through failing, and putting on work whatever the budget, deadline and limitations impacting a project. As the journey to the masked shows demonstrates, it is only through repeated endeavour, finding what works and refining that, exposing the problems and addressing the pitfalls with the next iteration, that the ambition of the original vision is achieved. As Barrett notes in regard to how the lessons of early projects feed into the testing of new approaches, 'without having done *The House of Oedipus*, we might never have known we need to plan for loo breaks'; it is these small elements and adjustments that need to be in place in order for the fictional world to remain (pun unintentional) 'watertight':

Kabeiroi was exactly the same, as soon as you're required to put a break in for the audience the structure collapses and half the interactions we wanted to put in became impossible. Doing anything that's outside of a three-hour show on a stage is complicated. Even though it doesn't appear to be part of 'the art' it's crucial, because if the logistics don't stack up the world breaks. The logistics are the base for the narrative arc. In *Kabeiroi*, if an audience member, not a performer, needed to go for a wee it broke the conventions of the world. Every time we try something new, we only learn if it works by putting an audience through the world.

pyrotechnics (see also: Act 1; awe and wonder; **crescendo**; Hodge, Stephen; intervention; *Moon Slave, The*; synchronicity; *Tempest, The,* **2001**): Fireworks, cannon shots and flares. For Punchdrunk's early productions, pyrotechnics were a cheap way of achieving a powerful reveal, as illustrated by *The Moon Slave*, underscoring a brief moment with majestic ephemerality. For Felix Barrett, pyrotechnics can create the ultimate intervention or a poignant crescendo, creating moments of excitement and danger; a touch of the uncontrollable and the elemental. The stillness of a night sky can be transformed by such effects. A flare will momentarily turn an entire canopy of clouds bright red then, in a matter of seconds, its effects are gone. Pyrotechnics are only ever employed for a limited audience, to focus attention and create profound moments of awe and wonder. With *The Tempest*, 2001, pyrotechnics were employed as the beat of a crescendo for an intimate audience with Miranda, providing a synchronous moment where the work came together, thematically, narratively, theatrically and experientially.

Q

Quest of a Wave (**2006**, see also: **Act 1**; installation; Jubb, David; McDermott, Laura; *Moon Slave, The*; music; one-on-ones; R&D): Presented at BAC as part of its Burst 2006 programme, *Quest of a Wave* experimented with

audio-journeying techniques, first tested with *The Moon Slave*, as *son et lumière*, where sound and light alone animate the space and guide the audience member, making the environment active and imaginative without the presence of a performer. For Felix Barrett, 'it was basically like a five-minute, interior *Moon Slave*, more of an investigative exercise than a show'. Barrett adds that Punchdrunk now has the time and resource at Fallow Cross to approach this type of exploratory exercise again: 'trying stuff out to see how it works and feels, finding different ways of manipulating the audience, different ways to tell the story'.

queues (see also: audience; **bars**; corridors; **cross-fade**; **flow**; masked shows; **mazes**; production management): In early projects, audiences entered through labyrinthine constructions, made from lengths of fabric sewn together by Felix Barrett, or pages from books. Nowadays, similar maze-like systems operate as a practical necessity and an equally important mechanism in the cross-fade or antechamber experience prior to entering the world of the event. Colin Nightingale elaborates:

Planning masked productions includes a lot of consideration around minimising queuing for audiences. We issue different arrival times, spread out over an hour to avoid everyone turning up at once, working on the assumption that a third will be early, a third on time and a third late. This means we generally create a steady flow of people arriving and entering the building. Once through box office and coat-check, we often create an 'entry bar' that serves as a waiting area before being dispersed into the world of the show in small groups. These bars are fully designed and charged with atmosphere, so waiting audiences feels like they're already in the show.

Inside the world a lot of consideration is given to the type of scenes that are created in relation to the size and the capacity of a room or corridor.

We aim to avoid audiences having to queue to get in or out of a room. A general principle is if a room is small then we'll keep performers who use the room during their loop to a minimum, so audiences arriving with them is then manageable for the space. During open dress rehearsals and previews we spend a lot of time looking at the flow and behaviour of audiences and if we notice regular points of congestion, we adapt performer loops or design.

R

R&D or 'Research and development' (see also: **Act 2**; **Act 3**; **digital technologies**; Enrichment; **Fallow Cross**; **gaming**; research; scalability): An arts industry term for the development of work, often via small-scale projects through which mechanisms for practice are tested, piloted and refined. R&D also refers to the research and development for particular productions in relation to source material, studio development of the choreography with performers, and design-driven research into the forms and themes of any given production.

'Rebecca the Bird' (see also: Act 2; Boyd, Carrie; **in-show-world**; **multiples**; Pluto; **nature**; 'Norman the Eel'; *Sleep No More,* **Boston**): Birds are a key motif for the character of Malcolm in all productions of *Sleep No More*. Rebecca is real Cockatiel that inhabited Malcolm's Office in the Boston version. A lively bird during the day, she had an unfortunate habit of deciding to sit motionless on her perch during the show and so the majority of the audience thought she was just another piece of taxidermy. As with all live animals used in productions, Punchdrunk had a detailed care plan in place for her well-being and at the end of the run, Rebecca was adopted by the show's stage manager, Carrie Boyd.

Red Death Lates (see also: Gideon Reeling; in-show-world; Jubb, David;

Reekie, Jonathan

Masque of the Red Death, The; **Seguro, Joana**): Live bands, cabaret and magic shows extended the experience of *The Masque of the Red Death*, blurring the boundaries between the end of the whirling finale of the show and the beginning of a Poe-drenched club night. Performances were overseen by Kate Hargreaves, by then Artistic Director of Gideon Reeling. Kate Rigby, who had begun volunteering and ended up as part of the Punchdrunk costume team, recalls:

> Working late one evening I met Kate Hargreaves, she was bundling the strangest costumes into the dressing room and I offered to help. She turned on her heels saying, 'Actually, darling, I'm looking for someone to costume some performers, can you do it?'. During the day I'd work with Tina Bicât on *Masque* and then I'd work on the *Red Death Lates* with Kate on a Friday, getting home at about 2am.

Honouring the costuming standards within the world of *Masque*, audience members for the show would dress in the manner of cloaked, Poe characters, and remain through the night as Red Death revellers. Surprise entertainment included Basement Jaxx, Rob da Bank, The Correspondents, Katie Melua, Dani Siciliano, Shingai Shoniwa, Luke Vibert and Jonny Woo. Colin Nightingale recounts the final Red Death Late, as vivid illustration:

> Felix and I often discussed how powerful it could be to take a 'Punchdrunked' audience, disoriented and purposefully confounded for three hours, and to mix their energy with people coming for a party. Our intention was that a show audience, having fully surrendered to the experience, would be so engaged and hungry for it to continue that it would fuel the energy of the event. We'd previously experimented with this during the final months of *Faust*, programming live bands to play after the house band. One particularly memorable night, I'd booked a twelve-piece

ska-punk-hip-hop band called Imperial Leisure. They couldn't all fit on the tiny stage yet still managed to transform the energy of the post-*Faust* bar, with the audience bouncing around dancing. In the corner of the room were a group of middle-aged, well-to-do National Theatre types standing watching with wide eyes and equally wide smiles on their faces. Situations like this gave us the confidence to push these ideas further.

At the core of the development of *Masque of the Red Death* was the incorporation of a decadent aftershow party for weekend runs. As the finale concluded in the Grand Hall, we seamlessly segued into an upbeat, swinging house band and bars opening around the audience. Every Friday and Saturday, we injected additional audience and extra performers from Gideon Reeling into the space to add energy. These performances, guest bands and DJ sets provided another three hours of entertainment. Running those parties was a lot of work and expense and it was a challenge to realise the ambition. We decided that during the two-month extension of the run we would focus on creating a series of one-off themed parties.

The very last of these was held after April Fools' Day on Saturday 5 April 2008, entitled 'Fools' Gold'. We took all the best bits of everything we'd learned over the previous months and set about creating the best party we could. At the finale of *Masque* the house band, now with an extra brass section, struck up an extended set with numbers performed by guest singers, one of whom was Matt Blake who'd honed a wonderful swing version of Madonna's *Material Girl*. The party filled up with extra guests and performers from Gideon Reeling, who'd been schooled by Kate Hargreaves over the previous Lates, weaving their magic, mingling with the crowd, all of whom had been

encouraged to attend in fancy dress. It was hard to distinguish between performers and audience.

As the band finished an eccentric compere with a bizarre German accent, played by Sam Booth, switched the audience's attention to another part of the room and The Correspondents, resident DJs for a number of months, took over and energised the crowd still further with their hybrid swing-drum'n'bass mash-up, coupled with the live MC-ing from 'Mr Bruce', the flamboyant frontman of the duo in colourful tights and a dinner jacket. Attention returned to the stage with The Correspondents handing over to an incredible rhythm tap dancer called Junior. He performed a fifteen-minute call-and-response routine with a live drummer, where each took turns to create faster, more complex rhythm patterns. Putting Junior on in this setting was a risk as I'd never seen him perform other than in a tiny club, but he rose to the challenge and captivated the 600-strong audience with his extraordinary skill and athleticism. As he finished the baton was passed to the surprise guests, Basement Jaxx and a high-energy set which culminated in one of their biggest hits, *Where's Your Head At?*. This had the entire crowd dancing wildly and was a fitting end to the seven-month run of Red Death Lates.

Reekie, Jonathan (see also: Act 2; ***Borough, The***; *Bunker, The*; music; Seguro, Joana): Director of Somerset House Trust since April 2014, Reekie began his career at Glyndebourne Opera and then went to be General Manager at the Almeida Theatre, founding Almeida Opera. He is an Honorary Fellow of the Royal Academy of Music and in 2013 was awarded a CBE for services to music. In 1997 Reekie took over as CEO of Aldeburgh Music where he remained until 2014. Aldeburgh Festival was founded by composer Benjamin Britten and singer Peter Pears in 1948.

{234}

Held annually in June, it has grown from a modest, local event to become an internationally renowned classical music festival, comprising concerts, dance, community activities and encompassing opera, orchestral recitals, lectures and exhibitions. Produced by Aldeburgh Music, the festival takes place in various locations and assorted venues across Aldeburgh, including local churches and town halls that were used during the early years by Britten and Pears, to the Snape Maltings Concert Hall, a converted nineteenth-century industrial building. For the 2013 Aldeburgh festival, a significant year in Aldeburgh's history as it commemorated the centenary of Benjamin Britten, Punchdrunk was commissioned by Reekie to create a piece, which resulted in *The Borough* . . .

Jonathan Reekie

On awakening the senses

The first time I experienced Punchdrunk's work was *Faust* in 2006. Later, in 2008, I was working with the producer, Joana Seguro, on *Faster Than Sound*, an experimental music series as part of the Aldeburgh Festival, located at an abandoned airbase in Suffolk, Bentwaters. That became my first direct contact with the company, when it created, with collaborators Seaming To and Semay Wu, a one-night piece called *The Bunker*. Audience members, a handful at a time, were abducted and taken to a bunker where they experienced an unexpected sound installation. With both events, *Faust* and *The Bunker*, I responded like many seeing Punchdrunk for the first time; an awareness of an awakening of the senses in a way I'd rarely experienced before. *The Bunker* was very different to *Faust* but both were enlivening and new and they seemed to break lots of rules, or challenge adopted thinking about what theatre should be and how stories should be told. I was really excited by how it turned theatre-going from a physically passive experience into an active one. It felt like an approach that chimed with lots of other things that were happening in contemporary culture more broadly; it took theatre into the realm of other forms such as computer games, IMAX cinemas or theme parks.

Much of the work that I did at Aldeburgh and that I now do at Somerset House is about supporting artists on whatever creative journey they're taking. *The Borough*'s development began from meeting Punchdrunk and discovering artists who were creatively restless and continually interested in trying out new things, developing new ideas. There's a mistaken idea about Punchdrunk that it's come up with a formula for immersive theatre-making and that that's all it does. If you've only seen two or three of the big shows, you might be excused for thinking that but what interests me about Punchdrunk is that curiosity to pursue other paths.

A key theme in the conversations I've had with Felix over the years is his deep love of music. We've spent a lot of time talking about music, his approach to theatre and how they might combine. We both love opera, so we've talked at length about how the techniques he has developed in theatre would work in opera, or rather, how they *wouldn't* work in opera, and therefore how one might address that. Punchdrunk's only staged opera, so far, with ENO, *The Duchess of Malfi*, was a brilliant experiment, which worked at certain levels, and didn't quite at others, because of the challenges of the operatic form. The principal problem relates to how you move live music around a space when it involves making an orchestra mobile. We talked about the ways in which one could deal with that, for example by recording music or deconstructing live music in certain ways. It's perhaps a shame that Punchdrunk's first exploration of opera wasn't of either an existing piece that is familiar to audiences, so it could be successfully deconstructed, or an original piece specially written for a Punchdrunk experience. It's brilliant that they experimented and I really hope that Punchdrunk come back to opera and music as a form. Felix is so profoundly musical that it would be a real shame if he didn't.

In those conversations, Felix repeatedly mentioned that *Peter Grimes* was very important to him. Approaching the Britten Centenary in 2013, I was particularly interested in how, 100 years after his birth, Britten's influenced a huge number of artists in different ways, not just from music but across many different art forms. One of the themes of our year of celebration was to commission artists from other disciplines to create works that were in some way linked to or inspired by Britten's music or Britten himself. Felix and I discussed *Peter Grimes* and the different ways he might respond to it. It was very clear from the start that it wouldn't involve staging the opera. Talking about the location and themes of *Grimes*, and about the original poem on which it's based, led to the creation of *The Borough*.

Most exciting for me was, not only was this an artist responding to Britten for the first time, but the challenge was pushing Felix to do something that he hadn't done before. He's since mentioned that *Kabeiroi* is a piece that evolved out of Punchdrunk's experimentation with *The Borough*. In the bigger productions you're used to a lack of boundaries in the storytelling, in the sense that you are taking yourself on your own journey. *The Borough* is the opposite of that because it was a predetermined journey that the audience takes, on a timetable determined by a headphone-soundtrack, in this case the 1958 recording of *Peter Grimes* that Britten made, with narration written by Jack Thorne. It blurred the boundaries between the real and imagined by creating a space that contains the performer, audience and general public who unknowingly become part of the action, all framed by the location itself. This blurring plays with your perception in very interesting and unsettling ways, heightening the central theme of a community turning against an individual. It was also unusual for Punchdrunk because, in addition to the recorded soundtrack the narrated text was a key element of the piece. In other words, it was a drama driven by text and music. It had a really positive response from the local Aldeburgh community, not least because one of the central venues for the piece was a working bar in the town through which the audience moved. I don't think the people in that bar would normally have had anything to do with the Aldeburgh Festival and vice versa. It got the town engaged with the Britten Centenary in a way that they probably wouldn't have otherwise.

In celebrating the Britten Centenary in his home Aldeburgh, the sense of place was very important and no piece that Britten wrote embodies that sense of place more than *Peter Grimes*. For those audience members lucky enough to experience it, the piece created something new, unexpected, extraordinarily vivid and powerful, particularly the startling and shocking ending. It brought a new audience to the festival, to Britten and to George Crabbe, and the festival brought a new audience to Punchdrunk.

research (see also: abstract/abstraction; **boxes, chests and drawers**; building; **characters**; curiosity; dance; **design**; discovery; exercises; **influences**; **installation**; **lens**; 'listening to the building'; music; **process**; R&D; soundscore: 'Specials'; text): Contextual, critical and creative research is fundamental to all areas of Punchdrunk, to any project and to all of the performance languages employed. Enrichment projects are underpinned by research in education and policy as much as by the bespoke learning required for each individual host community. Colin Nightingale draws attention to the years of research in practice that set learning through doing, in terms of operational and production management strategies. Rigorous research is undertaken for any performance project in terms of artistic and theoretical underpinnings and its practical application. The overview of Punchdrunk's process above provides greater detail, beginning with Felix Barrett's initial 'mining' of the textual source, which serves as inspiration as much as offering a blueprint for narrative composition and atmosphere. The concept is underpinned and driven by extensive and creative research. From her first experience on *Faust*, costume designer Tina Bicât observed the detailed research driving the process:

There was a room with stuff pinned up, stuff everywhere for reference, piles and piles of books, music, CDs, loads of bits of paper and very clear reference to films and to Edward Hopper. As soon as Felix started talking about the framing through film and Hopper, which is *so* framed, I started imagining quite quickly. The Americana aesthetic was clear and the idea of Old Faust living in this room of memories; oh, the richness of that idea. Because the vision is so clear for Felix, but more importantly because everyone does the research and it's very clear what the research is – it's not just reading, it's looking and listening – that research is very secure, very widely artistic and wide disciplined.

This intertextualisation of literary, cinematic and visual materials creates the lens through which the original source is refocused; multilayered research which is then applied and expanded through practice across all performance elements. Performers respond to the play-text, work individually and collectively to mine it for narrative, psychologies, gestural qualities and fragments of dialogue to underpin character work, as articulated by Sam Booth, Conor Doyle, Sarah Dowling, Rob McNeill, Kathryn McGarr and Fernanda Prata. In terms of choreographic research in practice, Maxine Doyle adds:

During creation I often ask the cast to 'put on their movement research hat'. If an improvisation is dying I might say, 'Don't be interesting, be interested'. It's the performer's job to be curious about the process of creating and curious about the process of performing. One of my main jobs is to provoke, support and channel the results of such curious investigation.

Beatrice Minns and Livi Vaughan undertake and apply meticulous theoretical and practical research to create the many layers of the design and installation for any project, especially in relation to masked shows. Working from Barrett's original concept and vision of the world – its themes and narratives alongside characters and scenes – a list of elements that need to be delivered is drawn up. This provides the backbone for the overriding narrative loops which is set by the building and early design work. This is then layered and nuanced by the detail of the installation, alongside the performance language evolving in the studio and eventually reworked on site. Barrett pinpoints that design-research really took off with *Sleep No More*, Boston. Minns and Vaughan have since refined a rigorous approach to research in curating theme and character via scenography and installation . . .

Beatrice Minns and Livi Vaughan

On research and realisation

Livi: Felix will come to us with a brief. He'll know 'the story world', as we call it; the year, the location, references for the kind of world he wants to create and a rough layout of key scenes and information plus the key text, for example *Macbeth*, and supporting sources, as told through the lens of a film noir aesthetic; the conceptual starting point. Practical research with Felix revolves around building layout, talking through scenes and the world. Bea and I then approach researching and designing in a lateral, non-linear way. Our references range across photographers, artists, films; it's such a broad spectrum in order to create a layered world that interacts with real life.

Bea: We begin with our historical, social and religious interiors as a fundamental level of research into what the 'real' life of that world, those characters, would be and then we layer our interpretations and narratives on top of that. The things that make it interesting are the clues that we get from the source text that invite us to refer to *The Golden Bough* or certain photographers or artworks that capture a feeling of the time.

Livi: Our photographic research is interesting as we always spend a lot of time sourcing documentary photography, whether China in the 1930s or Russia in the 1900s; you don't want what is fabricated or *presented* as what a culture was like, you want the gritty authenticity of that time and place. Those sources are hard to find. It's a case of collecting unusual books and images that interest us; going to Foyles and finding an obscure book documenting everyday life to influence the pedestrian feel of the world. It's easier to imagine the glamorous side but the day to day, the minutiae, less so. Those details we find by spending hours rifling through bookstores. It's a process of discovery. Those sources can't be looked up in library catalogue, searching for a specific title, because you won't know that it is until you discover it. We also do a lot of research online.

Bea: We used to go to a bookshop off Hampstead High Street, a labyrinthine, old shop that's now closed down. The owner would have every book; you could ask him for, say, a 1917 scientific journal and he'd have it. It's now become an antique, junk shop, which is also very good. In terms of prop research, when we first started working together on *The Masque of the Red Death*, we found an amazing lady who did house clearances and she would welcome us in to these caves under the arches in Bermondsey to choose masses of props.

Livi: Objects with a history as they were from someone's home; whole drawers that had been chucked into a bag so they already came with a sense of narrative and detail. You wouldn't necessarily have bought them individually as props, but together they became special. You need those associations to support the world created; all the trinkets and drawers full of sewing thread, letters and books. When creating the handwriting of characters, it becomes so much easier if you have actual letters from the 1930s to draw from. Bea and I have a really clear vision of the characters and their world, we have to be able to imagine the full character and the world in order to be able to deliver their environments.

Bea: We clarify with each other the grit of the story, what needs to be in the world and what needs to be in each space. We pull out the things that we find intriguing and unusual. We both have a good sense of the surreal, of things that aren't as they seem.

Livi: – the elements we want to exaggerate. We have to set a full world, a base to return to, to make decisions together. For example, if there's a character who's married to someone that the audience will never meet, we still want to know when they married, what their life was like, when they moved into their house, the supporting world behind the story. Once we understand that story we then have freedom to go into the surreal and the abstract but it has to have a foundation that we understand, even if we can't ever present that to our audience in its entirety. We spend a lot of time talking through and understanding the world. From that we can pull out key components – a ring being a repeated symbol, or horses – together we understand what it's rooted in. That's important because of the amount of design there is to do and how that relates to performance, character and the history and detail of the space. You need that base. We flesh out that world beyond what is seen. That wider work allows us to go into the details and the psychological narratives of the characters in the space.

Bea: Aesthetically we play with all the relevant images, pare them down, home in on the bits that we want to replicate. That process takes a really long time. We have folders and folders of image research that we pore over and edit, edit, edit to get it down to the key images to work from for each space.

research

Livi: We have a practical answer for each space, a lead image, a colour palette, an important piece of furniture and then for many of the spaces we'll also have a more abstract, emotional response.

Bea: We create a document, inputting all of the information for walls, floors, ceilings, furniture, small props, detail.

Livi: It allows you to work in layers to the experience. Our first layer is the logical, the colour palette for the walls, the texture on the floor. Once that's in then the installations and abstractions come as the conceptual layer from that more logical foundation. Often the abstractions apply to what's in the space anyway; if we know it's a bedroom and we know what the feeling is that permeates, that allows us to imagine where we want to take it; if it's a room that merits abstraction or needs to be more practical.

Bea: It's also a juggling act because a lot of it is waiting for information from the performers or Felix. Sometimes we go ahead with an idea which isn't quite right so we have to edit when a key idea comes very late. They might be a combination of psychological narratives evolved by the performers or practical requirements for the choreography.

Livi: Maxine's working with the performers developing the characters in a studio rehearsal space initially and there is often little crossover until the performers enter the site. This can mean that the performers eventually come into that space and feel that it's not right for them. We've learnt that there needs to be a greater crossover earlier on because, although we're all coming from the same place and working from the same source material, we're creating detailed information and subtextual abstraction that might not correspond to the equivalent detailed and abstracted work that the performers are doing.

Bea: Or Max might need a wider viewing-point so we have to incorporate an elevated area in a larger room. A lot of the details can come later because the performers are devising right up until the last minute; things will come up that we'll need to include in the set or clear from it.

Livi: Sometimes it works the other way. We might have ideas that we love but they'll move around the set until after the previews. For example, the horse in *The Drowned Man* was going to start off in Mr. Stanford's office, on a stage that was needed for one scene only and was drawing attention with nothing happening on it, sapping energy. The horse fitted perfectly on it and established a beautiful moment where a performer danced around it, interacted with it. It worked perfectly because it had storytelling and symbolic weight when the performers weren't there. However, because it was fake, although it was beautiful and made by the team who make *War Horse* horses, it wasn't touch-real. If you prodded it you would feel its fakeness. We battled with that. Eventually it moved to The Clown's one-on-one in the basement, which was an incredible space and a really strong punctuation point and ending for that scene. There's a balance between where something will look good for us and where it's important for the performers and audience. It definitely had to journey around until it found its home. We had to deal with the problem of the stage another way, with curtains and floor-paint. There's a lot of challenges which feel like building blocks and have to be repeatedly moved in order to make it all – in terms of themes and narratives – fit. We always say we never have enough time but what I love and wouldn't want to change is the fact that the design process is dynamic during the build and the run. There are large- and small-scale experiences to the creation of the design process, long shots and close-ups, working between creating a space that's massive to the rooms that are small and simple. With our 'specials' we have to curate where they go, on the go as we see where performances are moving and how rooms are being used. We might end up with a room that feels really dead if the performance is taken out of there, so we have to work out how to exaggerate it, to give it the weight it needs – or to agree that we're happy with it feeling dead, to encourage that.

Bea: We take regular walk-arounds together, working out which spaces need a boost or a lift or a change. At a certain point we separate with me taking on greater responsibility for the detail, creating individual character's worlds. The detail is incredibly important, it's the intricacies that make the world rich and real. Picking out the things from the text that give the character a three-dimensional quality; the everyday things that a character might do that you can turn into something that makes them unique in that world. If you're creating someone's bedroom, it's the attention to how that person gets out of bed and puts on their shoes, what's in their wardrobe, those really small observations of human character, that's important.

Livi: We would make the performers get into the bed and mess them up on purpose so it *feels* like it's actually been done by a person rather than 'set' by a designer.

Bea: All of that has to be authentic otherwise it breaks the spell immediately. When you're creating someone's space there are so many clues that you can leave for the audience to pick up on about a character – if they have an obsession, if they're hiding something, if they have lots of stuff pinned to the walls, if they've got empty drawers – you can saturate a simple space with someone's essence.

Livi: When we talk about the balance, it's because that side of the world is so real and considered and detailed, that we can shift into the abstract. It wouldn't work to have the one without the other. They balance and ground each other.

Bea: I'm really interested in the slightly banal reality of a space; what book is by their bed and if they have clean sheets; everything that builds the profile of a whole person.

Livi: While Bea's attending to that minute detail, I'll take on greater responsibility with the big build, working with the carpentry department. Bea and I have worked out the layout together but I've usually drafted it, figuring out where walls go, the details of the windows and doorways, anything that we need to have made, like the horse, or the gates to Temple Studios, designing what we need and making sure it's installed in the correct way. It's constant practical research; continually listening to the building, making sure we have the right flow, the right number of doorways or conversations with Felix and Max, about what's needed, where performers need elevation. Bea and I come back together to find the solutions but I'm more hands-on with the team figuring out what's achievable. We share a shorthand, know not to reveal a whole room as you open a door; question the journey within that room. Felix likes us to get to the stage where we've got walls, floors, ceilings, furniture and we're starting to put some detail in. He enjoys responding to that space and he'll then identify that we need to put a secret in a corner or suchlike. An example is the Macduff's nursery, in NYC. We discovered two adjacent rooms with a two-way mirror on the adjoining wall. We dressed both rooms identically, except the one the audience is able to enter is perfect and the other, behind a locked door, reveals the room after the children have been murdered. Unless you look closely through the glass, an audience member might miss that it's not a true reflection, that it's a replica room but with a blood-stained bed. We elaborate on that idea of the repeat, reacting to objects found in the space, building the design around that. Equally we work the other way and decide it would be great to have a double mirror here or how can we focus the audience around this table; tweaking what we've arrived at and re-lensing it.

Bea: Problem-solving things that Max has requested that fit in with the narrative. Things that Felix identifies that need further investigation. Felix's involvement becomes like an editing process from then on.

restraint (see also: 'chairs'; cinematic; close-up: ensemble; **eyes**; process; *Sleep No More*, London): A defining requirement of the Punchdrunk performing style is restraint. Felix Barrett explains his advice to any cast members:

If you feel obliged to tell the story with your face in these worlds, it becomes melodramatic. The choreography is big, the space is vast, so facial expression will become over the top to match it. Always do less than you think you need. Always remember the restraint. The cinematic close-up will click in and it will work. The intimacy, the filmic, is all.

Sarah Dowling provides strong illustration of this below, as does Risa Steinberg in reference to Punchdrunk's guidelines for 'keeping it simple'.

reveal (see also: Act 1; **awe and wonder**; **corner**; **crescendo**; discovery; *Duchess of Malfi, The*; *House of Oedipus, The*; **Moon Slave, The**): The reveal defines the point that makes an audience gasp, the foreshadowing or culmination of the crescendo. Felix Barrett explains:

When Livi and I are developing the design, we imagine we're steady cameras tracking through a space. When you turn a corner into a room and frame that space perfectly, at the optimum viewing point for the room, that's where you provide the reveal of the world beyond. It's like door five in [Béla] Bartók's *Bluebeard's Castle*, which reveals the bloodstained kingdom. Musically that's the crescendo of the entire opera.

A reveal is usually layered in advance by a series of corners that build experiential moments, and provide literal and figurative turns in the narrative. This is perfectly illustrated by *The Moon Slave*, where a series of installations led to the final reveal and crescendo or the final sequence of *The Duchess of Malfi*, where inventive scenographic

practice established a powerful reveal. It was lessons learned during *The House of Oedipus* that reinforced the significance of this moment:

Punchdrunk is about curiosity, exploration and discovery of those beats of wonder. If you can see in the distance what you're going to discover in five minutes' time, once you actually get there, it invalidates it; there's no reveal. You need the reveal. The reveal is crucial.
(Barrett in Machon 2016, 260)

Reverse Dolly Zoom aka Hitchcock's Zoom or 'Vertigo effect' (see also: **adrenalin**; awe and wonder; **cinematic**; **influences**; senses; tracking shot): The dolly zoom is a cinematic effect that distorts visual perception. The effect is achieved by adjusting the focus and view of a zoom lens while the camera is pulled away from the main subject on a dolly track (the 'dolly' being the cart on which the camera rests and the 'track', the rails on which it is smoothly pulled along), resulting in a distortion of visual perception so that the background appears to change size relative to the subject. In the classic Hitchcock example, the effect created is of a sensation of vertigo, causing an unsettling and emotionally charged response. The sensation of a Reverse Dolly Zoom is an effect that Punchdrunk strives to reproduce in live performances but so far it has proven difficult to stage.

Reynoso, David Israel (see also: abstract/abstraction; Act 2; Act 3; adrenalin; **costume**; scenography; *unheimlich*): Costume designer for *Sleep No More*, Boston, NYC and Shanghai, Reynoso's work was a powerful addition to the nightmarish feel of Punchdrunk's scenography. He met Punchdrunk's aesthetic, enabling costume to be a trigger for a theatricalised adrenalin-rush, epitomised as much by the tiny, otherworldly details sewn into dress-suit pockets as the more outlandish Goat's Head of the Witches' Rave scene.

ritual (see also: **awe and wonder**; Club Shelter; cross-fade; dreams; **durational**; epic; exercises; experiential; influences;

journeying; lighting; objects; one-on-ones; synchronicity; transportation and transformation. Further reading: Mitchell and Bull 2015; Schechner 1995): Much of the experience of Punchdrunk's work is ritualised, where the term is used to define carefully designed activity or attention to space within the event so that it becomes heightened; to borrow from Richard Schechner, 'by means of condensation, exaggeration, repetition, and rhythm' (1995, 228). Ritualised experiences in performance become meaningful and involve degrees of investment from performer and audience alike. A ritualised moment in Punchdrunk experiences may involve an encounter with space, installation, a performer or all of these which evokes a purity and distillation of form – where form *becomes* content. In the beat of a moment, or across an extended duration, a ritualised encounter moves the audience beyond any esoteric knowledge and towards an ineffable and sensate understanding of the power of that image, action, gesture, or journey and what it reveals to the receiver within and about the wider context in which it occurs. Ritualised encounters with space, design, music and performer in Punchdrunk works are crafted with a poetry and potency. They are imbued with the themes of the source material for which they are inspired yet equally owe as much to the meanings and responses that any audience member brings to that moment. For Felix Barrett an experience of ritual owes as much to an audience member's openness to that possibility as it does to the crafting of that 'magic':

Ritual involves endurance, time and respect, pacing and quality. You can easily walk down the street at a regular or speedy pace and think nothing of it, or you could walk along the street slowly, knowing that with each step you're getting closer and closer to something at which you'll arrive and *acknowledge* all those beats of time and effort. The ritual of it creates the event.

Like pilgrimage, with such journeying, each step or stage matters. Any sense of action or repetition in Punchdrunk projects moves beyond the routine and mundane and is elevated to a sense of ritual precisely because the individual invests in that encounter, brings a heightened sense of awareness and respect to the detail of that moment. There may be a blurring between experiences for audience members who unexpectedly, through the crafting of the work, become aware and *attend to* their awareness in that moment with those who bring that intention and attention to that moment. The pre-performance techniques employed by Punchdrunk, whether antechamber sequences, through mazes or in lifts in masked events, or part of the initial journeying before and during events produced for 'real-world' contexts, such as *The Borough*, *The Night Chauffeur* or *Kabeiroi*, also tap into a sense of ritual in action and tempo in establishing a heightened state of encounter within the world of the event. As Barrett explains:

Slowing an audience down so they're watching and receiving in a different rhythm to the outside world. It's similar to the way in which you might enter a church; you slow down, tune into the sense that you have to be more respectful because it achieves a reverence which means that you're more focused and your senses are heightened, you become more aware.

Punchdrunk deliberately draws on these devices of tempo and duration, in partnership with atmosphere and aesthetic, which instil a sense of ritual and reverence.

Barrett was inspired by the idea of ritualised theatre when an A Level student, introduced to the theories of Edward Gordon Craig and Silviu Purcărete. Barrett understood and responded to the manner in which Craig sought to accentuate the quality of ritual in theatre by imbuing objects and materials with a symbolic potency in design. Barrett was particularly taken by Craig's idea of taking one property and reinventing it, ascribing it a

significance beyond the mundane: 'making the everyday magical but through the power of abstraction'. This idea for Barrett comes back to the practical and pragmatic that underpinned the artistry of the work created in his early years of experimentation and continues to the present in design terms: 'we always take one material', as commonplace as reams of cheap fabric or plastic bottles, 'and in any given space that becomes a lead, driving impetus in terms of a property'. Barrett also draws on Craig's principles regarding the ritualised delivery of text:

We still use this technique now in rehearsal; for Hamlet's long speeches where his mind is becoming unfixed, Craig's notes instructed that his performers not worry about the meaning of the text, instead see how the pattern and the shape and the rhythm of the words affected their breathing; concentrate on how the breathing affects the body. The idea that we don't need to be able to hear the words we just need to see what it does to you as an individual – words and meaning imbued with breathing; that quality of *felt* experience.

For Barrett, a sense of ritual is shaped in a Punchdrunk event through 'ambiguity and mystery, where we don't want to spell everything out for our audience, instead we want them to solve the experience for themselves. Working out our dream logic they understand the narrative of the show'. In this respect, the audience member has to give into that dream logic, think laterally rather than literally, respond instinctively. Barrett continues, 'ritual defines the solemnity, respect and gravitas' with which a gesture, an object, a space 'can be imbued'. One of the few exercises that Barrett facilities for performers uncovers this ability to imbue an object in this way. Performers are required to take an everyday object – a wooden spoon, a clay jug, a glass bowl – and reimagine it as a domestic deity. 'It establishes a gestural language', literally becoming the object of the ritual, which is worked through and repeated,

'to keep your god happy'. This exercise is 'always durational', where the time taken is loaded with the weight of the action, whether fifteen minutes or longer. Barrett acknowledges that for it to be done 'absolutely properly' he would choose to follow Purcărete's approach, where the performer would accentuate the sense of ritual performing this repeated action in a given space with a candle for the duration of the night. The aim of this is to establish a duet, a gestural and durational dialogue between performer and inanimate object in such a manner that the sense of ritual produces two characters within the space, irrespective of the fact that one of these began as a wooden spoon. A sequence that began as one character with a functional prop becomes two characters and is invested with meaning beyond the functional. By the end of the ritual the duet will have traversed (and so be loaded with) emotion and nuance; pain, anguish, tenderness. For Barrett this exercise is crucial in developing performers who are able to generate a performing style that understands the potency of object, space, time, as equivalent, if not greater, signifiers in the world of the event. It conveys the significance of duration as *experience*, of temporality in action, rather than action alone. For Barrett, this exercise is 'a crucial building block for all the shows', whether masked events or one-on-ones: 'When you only have twenty-five performers in a space with a hundred rooms you have to give them the skills to enable their presence to spill out into the space. That can all be created through ritualised behaviour'. By building a relationship with objects and finding a way to make their presence a palpable entity in the space, the skills worked through in this exercise support the manner in which the performer is also trained in engaging with audience members in masked shows, themselves cast as an 'unseen' presence and object in the space.

Punchdrunk one-on-ones are imbued with this sense of ritual. They are designed to be heightened encounters where any action or dialogue shared between performer and participant is heightened, even if a seemingly frivolous act of nail painting. The sense of ritual is accentuated by the highly charged atmosphere established from the enclosed space in which they occur, the removal of the mask, the story shared. Each encounter is carefully structured and sparse in narrative. The pace of the encounter is deliberately mapped and ceremonial, employing repetition of action, distillation of content, and intensification of emotion. One-on-ones play on the idea that the audience-participant has been a confidante, a secret has been divulged. In this way there is often an implication that they audience-participant has encountered the forbidden, has been singled out and chosen. One-on-ones can generate a sense of transgression in this way and, potentially, of transcendence dependent on the secret shared and the willingness of the audience-participant to play along and be present within that encounter. As Katy Balfour recounts in the one-on-one entry above, the condensed duration and the story shared can often inspire a feeling of transportation from one state to another for the audience-participant, a rite of passage within the world of the event. An aim is for these heightened encounters to charge any subsequent experience for that audience-participant within the world; a refocusing of the lens through which they view and engage with it, offering an added layer of understanding of the world. It is not uncommon for the audience-participant to be given a token, a trinket, as an outcome, a memento of that encounter and a marker of moving on or into another stage within the world. For the audience member, a sense of ritual in one-on-ones may come from this heightened presence and from the feeling that they have been seen and chosen with an intensification of the magical and otherworldly.

S

'safe-words' (see also: **caretaking**; **ethics**; **one-on-one**; **'Peru'**): During any

Punchdrunk project code words are used by cast and crew to alert the team to situations in which they are feeling unsafe or compromised in their ability to perform as required. Once the word is uttered, as the performance plays out, the team has strategies to ensure that member of the cast is made safe, without impacting the flow and feel of the event. It is a simple and standard caretaking device to protect performers, while ensuring the performance continues without, as far as possible, compromising the experience or safety of other audience members.

sampling (see also: corner; design; Dobbie, Stephen; music; **soundscore**): Stephen Dobbie's soundscores are composed from collages of sound effects, musical refrains and references to establish the atmosphere and era of the world. This editing and manipulation of material from a range of sources owes much to Dobbie's background in 'sample-based music-making' where 'sampling establishes a palette from which you build the composition'. It is the new context in which these samples are mixed together and the spatial and designed context in which they are then played that shifts the narratives and atmospheric themes of the original excerpts into an entirely new score for the Punchdrunk world. For Dobbie, sampling creates a musical environment that is 'defamiliarised' because 'the audience sort of knows it but it's reworked, a blending of upbeat, downbeat, orchestral' snatches of era-defining, 1930s pop music, creating, as Barrett puts it, 'an emotional immediacy'. Dobbie's sampling, whatever the musical style, combines the 'well known but obscure' to establish a feeling of 'nostalgia and familiarity'. In Punchdrunk worlds this form establishes 'trigger points that are evocative of the era' and 'roots the audience in time and place'. Felix Barrett adds that sampling of sounds that feel well known while being obscure provides a 'sense of dusty familiarity' that also retains a level of disquiet. The sampling technique itself can subvert expectation, creating an aural rug-pull when it suddenly mixes in a jarring musical

style, to turn an emotional or narrative corner or to disorientate and defamiliarise at moments of high impact, as illustrated by the 'Witches' Rave' in *Sleep No More*, Boston and NYC.

scalability (see also: journeying; **R&D**): A term that describes the process of using small-scale, R&D and pilot projects to test forms, technologies and mechanisms for audience engagement and interaction which can then be up-scaled for Enrichment work and masked shows or journeying and one-on-one shows. *The Oracles* and *Kabeiroi* are early Act 3 projects, developed at Fallow Cross, that have investigated new models and techniques that have the potential to be expanded for a wider public audience.

scale (see also: **abstract/abstraction**: 'chairs'; **cinematic**; **close-up**; decay; **design**; dreams; exercises; **long shot**; **multiples**; 'Rebecca the Bird'; scalability; taxidermy; *unheimlich*): In design, this refers to the 'micro to macro' nature of the Punchdrunk world created. Scale in design is different to 'scalability' in regard to the research and development phase of any project. Livi Vaughan clarifies:

We have the detail down to what's written on a hidden piece of paper in a book on a shelf compared to a huge installation of an exterior high street. There is also a scale of abstraction, which involves a repetition of objects to defamiliarise the space. If everything remains realistic, the audience will stop being surprised by the world, so we play with scale and what we put in the world in order that it heightens it or jars against that realism.

Scale layers the levels of interpretation available to the audience. In *Sleep No More*, a cascade of salt ran through the dining room while on shelves, repeated cutlery crucifixes were planted in salt mounds. For *The Masque of the Red Death*, those who discovered the attic would find a puppet, ill in bed, with repeat medical prescriptions nailed to the wall indicating an illness that pervades for a long, long time. This abstracted repetition of objects and images, from the micro to macro, accentuates the *unheimlich* dream-logic of the world. Abstraction of ideas through scale becomes expressionistic; a physical and symbolic manifestation of character psychologies and textual themes. *The Drowned Man* created an opportunity to experiment with this in a new way as the installation intentionally accentuated scale to expose the 'authentic' and the fake, the long shot and the close-up, in the shift between 'real' location and film set within the world of Temple Studios; the icy settings and the sand suggested emotional states of characters while also implying studio set and location; the move from grand to minute scale within these spaces accentuated the blurring of realties and played on the ontologies of film worlds.

Vaughan and Beatrice Minns' approach to scale in design resonates with a practical exercise devised by Maxine Doyle entitled 'chairs', which adapts Jacques Lecoq's ideas around scale and levels of tension. Playing with states as design components that can be scaled up or down, stretched, softened or deleted underscores the approach to making a room inviting, threatening, curious. This has come to inform the design workshops that Vaughan teaches related to the level of tension in a room and how that can be expanded or decreased.

scenography (see also: Barrett, Felix; Bicât, Tina; building; **design**; *Firebird Ball, The*; **installation**; intervention; Minns, Beatrice; objects; Reynoso, David Israel; ritual; Vaughan, Livi): 'Design' is an umbrella term for Punchdrunk for all of the layers and techniques of the design process from the large-scale overhaul and architectural shifts that might be put in place on vast, open-plan sites, to the minute detailing within touch-real installations within a room, to minimalist design interventions. For Felix Barrett, scenography involves large-scale vision, 'takes an empty space and turns it on its head through dressing'; painting the space, bringing in materials

and design plans to alter the shape and feel of the environment. Aligned with Punchdrunk's philosophical and practical approach to the interrelatedness of all elements of theatre, 'scenography' defines the sensual and technical design elements – space, materials, properties, light, sound, technologies – and relationship between each other as much as with any performers and the audience in the experience of the production. Scenographic practice was a major influence on Barrett at school in the work of Edward Gordon Craig. It was Craig's ideas around the artist of theatre who should have a coherent vision that shaped the whole environment of the world to be presented to an audience, alongside the majesty of his stage designs recorded in photographic plates that first proved significant to Barrett:

It was the principle that the abstract can be as credible as the hyperreal. Scenography was a primary signifier. The broad visual sweep of Craig's designs for *Hamlet*; Hamlet and the full court, King and Queen wearing a full cloak that spreads across the whole stage, courtiers' heads just popping through.

Silviu Purcărete and Josef Svoboda, two artists of theatre, also greatly influenced Barrett's theatrical vision. Pioneer of advanced technologies in lighting and multimedia in his designs for the stage, it is Svoboda who is renowned for having given currency to the term 'scenography' to highlight the significance of design and its equal place and co-creation within a theatre production, matching any directorial vision. Svoboda's productions were radical for his early interplay of live and filmed sequences, relayed via projections and television monitors and dreamlike architectural elements and exaggerated features, such as sweeping stairs or enormous mirrors that distorted the stage floor. Barrett's scenographic practice now holds its own weight in contemporary stagecraft. Tina Bicât describes how the challenging technicalities of his vision, 'faded into insignificance beside the hugeness of

the picture and *really* wanting to make it happen', while Tom Morris, above, refers to Bob Crowley being inspired by the 'complexity and scale' of Barrett's scenographic imagination.

Séance, The (**2011**, see also: **Act 2**; crescendo; **digital technologies**; **dreams**; portals; **R&D**; *Sleep No More, NYC*; *unheimlich*. Further reading: Dixon, Rogers and Egglestone 2013; Higgin 2012): Supported by an ACE and Nesta Digital R&D fund, Punchdrunk worked in collaboration with MIT Media Lab, the research arm of Massachusetts Institute of Technology, working with students in Tod Machover's 'Opera of the Future' group, to test the immersive possibilities of remote connectivity within a live experience. The project was installed within the pre-existing, functioning production of *Sleep No More*. On-site audience members at The McKittrick Hotel were partnered with online counterparts, in the US and UK, to solve the mysterious disappearance of Agnes Naismith. Those online, with a signature soundscore relayed through headphones, accompanied by atmospheric virtual locations on the screen, would respond to real-time questions and clues related to the characters and setting. A number of portal moments were created, that connected the two audiences, such as a Ouija board sequence, where some online audience members were able to hear questions asked by the live performer and responded by typing their answers. These responses from the virtual player instructed the automated planchette to move across the Ouija board; in the physical space, as if by sorcery or spirit. Other online players could type messages to their real-world counterpart that would appear, written in 'dust' on a mirror, which was in actuality a disguised flat-screen monitor. In The Lawyer's office, those online could hear real-world conversation, while typed responses from their computer keyboard would be relayed, uncannily, via a vintage typewriter in the office. For those engaging via headphones, keyboard and screen across the Atlantic, this meant staying up until 3.30am for

△ FIGURE 21 *Searching for Stories*, on set at Temple Studios. *The Drowned Man*. 2013. L–R: Katy Balfour, Kathryn McGarr.

Photo credit: Paul Cochrane

the experience, which culminated in an unexpected and somewhat unnerving, yet delightfully worth it as far as crescendos go, live phone call from Agnes.

Peter Higgin recalls how the digital R&D was a useful experiment yet the outcome of both 'sides' of the experience proved 'tricky'. The aim was that the online experience would offer the audience 'player' an experience bespoke to the digital realm that would be beyond that available to those audience members participating in the physical space in terms of narrative and crescendo. It also hoped to accentuate a sense of the uncanny via the liminal engagement offered by online connectivity. For Higgin, 'it was great working this experiment into *Sleep No More* but, in truth, it would have been better to create a brand-new piece that tested the technologies'.

Searching for Stories (2014, see also: **Act 3**; **Drowned Man, The**; Enrichment; legacy; **letters**): An adventure begins in the classroom and leads pupils on a clandestine visit to the legendary Temple Studios. There they help Temple Studio's 'Creatives' to generate new ideas for the next film, 'The Mystery of San Bernadino'. *Searching for Stories* was a literacy project, developed and performed by Katy Balfour and Kathryn McGarr, created for seven primary schools in the borough of Westminster, as part of the Enrichment programme for *The Drowned Man*, reimagining the set as stimulus for a creative adventure. While delivering *Searching for Stories*, Enrichment also ran a project in St Mary's Hospital, which neighboured Temple Studios, combining aspects of this and *Up, Up and Away* to bring storytelling to children in the hospital school. Additionally, it worked with secondary schools to develop approaches to immersive practice in the classroom. Peter Higgin adds:

> Ever since *Masque*, Enrichment has approached any major site-based projects with a desire to ensure that the production runs a comprehensive outreach programme. In a climate where art and placemaking drives regeneration and gentrification we ensure that, beyond the positive impact on the local economy, we involve and work with the communities in that area. *The Drowned Man* provided great opportunity for this.

Seguro, Joana (see also: **Act 2**; ***Bunker, The***; collaboration; durational; *Faust*; found space; **immersive**; Jubb, David; music; **Red Death Lates**; Reekie, Jonathan; **synchronicity**; *Vescovo & Co*): While on a Clore Fellowship, a leadership programme for the cultural and creative sector in the UK, Seguro collaborated with Punchdrunk on *The Masque of the Red Death*, programming the music acts for the Red Death Lates. An interdisciplinary creative producer, Seguro also commissioned Punchdrunk to create *The Bunker*, a project for the 2008 Faster than Sound Festival. Launched in 2006 and co-produced by Aldeburgh Music and Seguro, Faster than Sound began life as a partner festival to the annual Aldeburgh Festival, based at Bentwaters Airbase, later evolving into an arts programme that connects musical genres and digital art forms . . .

Joana Seguro

On synchronicity, immersivity and club culture

My first experience of Punchdrunk involved a lot of synchronicity and a lot of shared interests coming together. I'm from a music background with a strong focus on electronic music; always drawn to the experimental, using gallery spaces for events, the work that I was involved with was immersive and very much about club culture. Additionally, I've always had a keen passion for theatre. During the Clore Fellowship I was introduced to people from different disciplines involved in the Cultural Sector in the UK. Across a period of about a year, around 2006, when I told people from different organisations what I did, including David Jubb at BAC, they would say, 'so you've met Felix, right?'. They'd be surprised that I hadn't and encourage me to do so. Finally, at a point when BAC was in the process of collaborating with Punchdrunk on *The Masque of the Red Death*, and while *Faust* was on, David suggested that I go and see it before I met with Felix. I was blown away by it; the level of detail plus I'm a huge *Twin Peaks* fan, a huge contemporary dance fan. Afterwards I sat down with Felix and he said, 'in the last few months everyone has been asking me if I've met you . . .'. The synchronicity of that is interesting, in terms of our worlds coming together.

As *Masque of the Red Death* developed we got support from the Jerwood Foundation for me to work on the production. I was given the title of 'Line Sound Producer' and for the first few weeks I was wandering around as the sets were built and rehearsals were taking place, soaking it in but a little bit confused about how I was going to contribute to this world. Colin Nightingale and I connected over our club culture backgrounds, how it's inherently immersive. I do a lot of work with classical musicians and visual arts practice, presenting both disciplines within environments and as experiences. The club scene is one of the best examples of that happening automatically. You go to the Barbican and it can offer a fantastic experience but you're still sitting on a chair and the 'talent' is on the stage so it creates this relationship of 'us' and 'them'. In theatre or concerts, very often, the stage holds the performance a prisoner. In club and DJ culture, it's not even a case of breaking down walls and seeing the process, the action happens on the dance floor, the crowd is part of it, that's the dynamic of the experience, right down to the point at which you choose to go to the bar and who you encounter there. DJ culture is interactive; the DJ is reading the audience, making the audience dance and creating a soundtrack to the environment. Obviously, DJs perform for an audience, especially at large-scale festivals, but I'm thinking particularly of the roots of club culture. If you look at the history of Paradise Garage or The Loft in New York, it is very much a melting-pot. It's about worlds coming together, artists mixing with regulars; it's about the characters, the dance floor, the space. It's not about watching a performance, it's about being part of the performance.

Colin and I talked about the non-linearity of the club experience and party nights and how that related to what Punchdrunk had done previously, so an idea developed about doing a series of events every Friday and Saturday night. These were planned to emerge out of the performance and to incorporate a performed musical element. By that time there were lots of musical celebrities coming to Punchdrunk shows and saying that they wanted to get involved but there was no structure for how that could happen. Consequently, that became my role; programming the Red Death Lates and finding ways to make it work with the non-linear *Masque* world that ends in a ballroom sequence. Specifically, how you capture the energy and richness of that world and make that transition into a party, with live music performances. We had all these performers and dancers so, rather than just putting a band on and leaving it at that, we knew that we needed the interactive element. That's when Kate Hargreaves got involved with Gideon Reeling. In a way the Red Death Lates were all those worlds colliding; the *Masque* world meeting a party environment which itself incorporated a structured and distinct Red Death performance.

When you collaborate on such an intense experience it's bonding and results in you wanting to explore and develop those themes and reactions that emerge in different formats. At the same time, I was developing Faster than Sound with Jonathan Reekie in Aldeburgh with an aim to take classical musicians away from the concert hall and stage, while equally taking electronic musicians away from the club world, so that no one is in their safe area and artists are encouraged to be experimental. It was located in a disused, Cold War airbase, which in itself inspired the musicians to experiment because it was such a surreal space. It also supported our desire to incorporate other elements alongside musical performance.

Punchdrunk's *The Bunker* was part of the third Faster than Sound that I'd produced at the airbase. In the first two years of Faster than Sound we had multiple stages in one particular area of the airbase but in its third year we wanted to give the audience a greater sense of that space. *The Bunker* came about as a consequence of Felix and Colin Nightingale visiting the airbase in 2008, discovering all the crazy spaces in it, which is one of their favourite things to do. Again, that's illustrative of the synchronicity between us. I like unusual spaces, audiences will be stimulated by the space the performance occurs in. I don't like that sense of linearity or knowing what to expect from a performance, which you get from concert hall events.

We partnered Punchdrunk up with the musicians Seaming To and Semay Wu with the idea that Punchdrunk would create the journey to Wu and To's performance. There was a degree to which it was a practical necessity because you had to travel there, given where the setting was in the wider airbase, but we played on that theme even more to turn that journey into an adventure, a treasure hunt. It referred to rave culture; that idea that you ring a number to find out about the meeting point for a secret party, which turns out to be a petrol station from which you all find out where the venue is and travel together to get there. *The Bunker* was a one-night event that took place in a bunker on the airbase, fitted with surround sound. The audience began at the Hush House, a massive space which had been previously used to test jet engines; the metal mesh all around it created amazing acoustics. Much of the music line-up was programmed there. Following certain performances, the audience would be invited to queue at a 'Stop' sign from which a select few were chosen to be taken in a jeep to the decontamination bunker on the airbase. That occurred on a loop, because the space could only take a limited number at a time and it kept it intimate. Once at the bunker, each small audience was then led in through a door and had to make its way through a corridor in a way that suggested that each group was going through a decontamination process. You could then engage with it the way you wanted; you could follow the spotlights and find the performance area or you could look for clues and follow the narrative if you were more of a 'treasure hunter'. You had to navigate your way through the bunker until you would arrive in a room that felt very much like the *Twin Peaks* Red Lodge, very Lynchian, where Seaming and Semay were performing a duet between live cello and electronics and voice. Finally, the audience had to crawl out through a hole in the wall to exit. I remember they all came out a little bit like, 'what just happened?!'. The overwhelming sensation was that we'd all been through this decontamination process and come out into this beautiful experience, almost like a parallel universe from what was happening in the main space. Seaming performed for something like six hours non-stop because there was this steady flow of people coming through the experience.

What makes Punchdrunk exciting is that sense of secrecy and possibility around what they create which helps people reconnect with expectation and adventure. When you grow older you lose that sense of wonder, you know what to expect and Punchdrunk returns audiences to that feeling of excitement, of not know what's going to happen, while creating a strong sense of shared intimacy. The work is about you and how you navigate it through the choices that you make. It's about being in that moment. I know that people are so against any sense of exclusivity that goes alongside that. Access is an important issue but that doesn't mean work that has limited access, in terms of time or reach, is not a valid form. I don't see why you have to be everything to everyone. Some Punchdrunk projects play with secrecy and limiting access to that experience, but that's not the case with projects like *The Drowned Man*, *Faust* or *Masque of the Red Death*.

When people who are not used to this kind of work are exposed to it, the response is so exciting, so the fact that it's limited, the fact that it's secret makes it even more powerful. That's a strength of it. I live in Berlin and there's a constant discussion here about underground culture and keeping it underground. It's similar to those arguments that *Saturday Night Fever* killed disco; the idea that something that begins with only a small, secret crew doing it and then when it becomes huge it's ruined. That feeling of what it is *because* of that secrecy, that's part of it. There's something in there about the importance of holding on to the mystique. That process of having to go through certain stipulations, having to crack the code before you're allowed in, or before you can get that tickets, that's what makes the form and the experience powerful. I understand the 'exclusive' criticism, but I don't agree with it.

Punchdrunk's work is special because it works with all these ideas. The non-linearity and complexity that each world provides, with different entry points for diverse personalities and minds, plus the manner in which it equips you for ways of engaging with that world, is totally unique. In theatrical experiences and musical performances audiences are usually fed a story, which they can interpret in different ways perhaps, but the experience overall is not unique as everyone gets fed the same thing in the same way. Punchdrunk's immersive environments, having such range and complexity within those worlds, allow people to behave in different ways within them; if I want to be a voyeur, I can just be a voyeur; if I want to go up close and follow someone, I can do that. Those different entry points can give a certain power to an audience. It works the same way as a club; if I want to be by the bar and chatting with people I don't yet know I can; if I want to be by the DJ, or on the dance floor in my own world, or standing to the side and observing the dynamics, or just be catching up with my friends because I haven't seen them in ages, I can choose to do all or any of those things. Normally, in the arts, there isn't so much freedom, everything is curated and structured and people are told to behave a certain way. Punchdrunk breaks that, and that's its power.

senses (see also: abstract/abstraction; **adrenalin; aesthetics; arsenic; audience;** close-up; dance; darkness; experiential; long shot; narrative; space; soundscore; **touch;** touch-real; **visceral**. Further reading: Banes and Lepecki 2007; Di Benedetto 2011; Machon 2011; Welton 2011): Crucial to the experience and interpretation of any Punchdrunk production, especially masked events, where the whole human sensorium is manipulated in a 360-degree environment. In Punchdrunk worlds, smell, sound and touch are vital and often prioritised above the visual where darkness and shadows are employed. A whole-body engagement occurs via the act of journeying across external landscapes or traversing the many spaces installed across a building. Here haptic awareness comes to the fore, emphasising the tactile perceptual experience of the body as a whole and foregrounding kinaesthetic awareness as a constant (but often ignored) mode of human perception. This involves attention to the body's locomotion in space incorporating proprioception (stimulation produced and perceived *within* the body relating to position and movement *of* the body). In this way, haptic perception relates to an audience member's awareness of her own interactive body, alongside her perception of the moving bodies of others; performers and audience. Olfactory manipulation is crucial to any installation within the world created. Specific smells denote environment, communicate character narratives and hint on a more abstract level at underlying themes, as with the scent of almonds employed across rooms for *The Duchess of Malfi*. The choreography and proximity of athletic, progressively sweating, bodies telling stories and conveying emotional and psychological states through dance, intensifies the sensuality of the world. The senses contribute to the logic and unity of the in-show-world and are often a key element in any audience recall of a Punchdrunk event.

Silverpoint (**2015**, see also: **digital technology;** gaming; intervention; journeying; *Kabeiroi;* **R&D**; scalability): A collaboration between Punchdrunk, Absolut and Somethin' Else, *Silverpoint* began in a game-world, spilling out across various London bars, to culminate in a gaming experience in the real world, with a narrative layered across the city, according to the locations participants playing the game, culminating in leading the audience to a specific location to complete the storytelling. Felix Barrett explains:

The project was testing the liminal space between the real and the fictional, where the narrative is forced to leave the confines of the building and spills out onto the street. If you're leaving the building and scattering across the city, where does the story go? How do you carry the story? On your phone. If you're stretching a journey, and stretching time within that world, you need to be drip-feeding the story as you go. A mobile game felt like a good way to do that. It's episodic, you uncover story along the way.

The tying together of the everyday world experience with the *Silverpoint* world occurred through digital-gaming and storytelling. A smartphone served as the tool and receptacle through which episodes of the story and information about the protagonist, Chloe, were unlocked and revealed. *Silverpoint* highlighted some potentials and pitfalls of using basic rules of gaming in a theatrical context. Hector Harkness, director for the project, summarises:

We were experimenting with how game interaction could pull you into and through a story. The biggest challenge was creating a game that was compelling, addictive, but didn't become meaningless once the theatrical elements started to emerge. We tackled that by creating a story that could be unlocked in written chapters only by playing the game.

Andy Warhol's sketches, as used in Absolut's campaign, became a reference in the work. Sketches and notes from Chloe's journal entries followed Warhol's style and shaped the narrative as the player unlocked more of the story, gaining rewards as they played; from emails with the promise of additional clues to cocktails at playing bars, to chances of heading to the right place at the right time for fleeting interventions or one-on-one encounters. The narrative and any related encounters framed the *Silverpoint* world within a pop-art, pulp-fiction-styled narrative. Warhol's work triggered a backstory inspired by the sketches, and tapping into themes of surface and lies, being led into an underground, fantastical world; an otherworldliness that was accentuated by the celestial bodies connecting, cross-fertilising and exploding at the player's will in the planetary candy-crush-like game. Barrett summarises, 'the theory behind it was the game would go live; players would realise they had moved from the voyeuristic play on a smartphone to suddenly becoming the live-action players in the real world'. However, ultimately the project proved that unlocking narrative via a matching game was problematic, positioning the audience outside of the narrative rather than letting them merge with it. For Harkness:

Silverpoint offered a plethora of interesting experimental moments, but not a failsafe cohesive experience for every audience member. The most exciting theatrical moments were the ones that *felt* real, immediate, and seemed to emerge from the everyday; a hair salon where a consultation becomes strange; a guy in the street who asks for a light, then slips you a significant note.

Harkness adds, what 'face-down', smartphone engagement did point up was the potential of 'eyes being lifted to see the real world afresh', establishing 'two very different frames through which to experience the same story at the same time'.

Silverpoint was also partly an exercise in how digital engagement might lead to a live, immersive crescendo. For

Barrett, despite the crescendo falling short, being 'retrofitted to the space' rather than inspired by the location, the project was an example of:

Doing it for the sake of breaking new ground and trying something. It wasn't about artistic perfection. It was a forerunner to Act 3. *Silverpoint* was linked to *Kabeiroi*, *Kabeiroi* is linked to Punchdrunk Travel. It may even be what will become our signature work, where you first enter the world via technology in your home and then eventually travel through the real world to 'the show'.

site (see also: **architecture; building; found space;** journeying; legacy; **site-sympathetic; space; 'space-hunting'.** Further reading: Massey 2010): Site in Punchdrunk's practices covers all types of location in which the company works and creates imaginative worlds. When used as an equivalent to 'space', the term encompasses the landscapes and cityscapes that support any outside journeying, and equally the dimensions and details of rooms, corridors and internal structures within any building. Used synonymously with 'building', it acknowledges the internal and external architectural features of that site.

Punchdrunk Enrichment's response to site also responds to its purpose and history; the living, working organisation and politics of that space. In schools or residential homes, this includes working with timetables, behavioural protocols, administrative procedures, as much as the environmental parameters of the site. The specific rules of engagement for host audiences in Enrichment works incorporates these limitations and restrictions creatively, which can extend to the home-life of the participants. In any Punchdrunk project where a host organisation is housed within a working site, such as BAC or the National Maritime Museum, a shared vision for the project between the hosts and the creative team becomes as vital to the development of the concept and aesthetic of the project

as the building. With Punchdrunk masked shows, housed in vacant buildings, these aims tend to relate to the needs and protocols of the wider community neighbouring the site, beyond any immediate creative collaboration and legacy this extends to respect for the local environment, such as queue management or noise pollution.

site-sympathetic (see also: architecture; building; **design; found space;** framing; **immersive; 'listening to the building'; site; transportation and transformation.** Further reading: Bachelard 1994; Kaye 2008; Pearson 2011): Punchdrunk prefer to employ site-sympathetic as it defines the activity of responding to the *feeling* as much as the aesthetic of an uninhabited found space. As Barrett puts it:

Site-specific, to me, was about having to fit the work to the building and its history. If it was a former tyre factory, then it would need to be about that, to present the literal echoes of that building. Site-sympathetic is an impressionistic response; drawing on similar impulses but creating a dream world within the space rather than a practical, literal retelling of the building.

This sensory response gives as much weight to the temperature of a room and the cracks in its wall as to the walls themselves: 'building a story around a broken pane of glass'. In masked shows the design is led by a building and the creative team's immediate response to it. Dancers may create a concentrate of the choreographic language in a studio-space, but it is only when on-site that the movement vocabulary is opened up, nuanced and further inspired through a sympathetic duet with the surfaces, textures and temperatures of the site. Where creating projects within a working organisation, such as BAC with *The Masque of the Red Death*, or travelling through it, as with The British Museum for *Kabeiroi*, Punchdrunk responds sympathetically to the sensual overtones, structures and (hi)stories of those spaces, building narrative, theme and atmosphere from

there. With Enrichment's work, site-sympathetic extends to incorporating organisational structures within the concept and composition of a project ensuring that the imaginative 'place participants are taken to "sympathises" with the place they have left' (Tims 2016, 47); so a library can magically materialise in the hidden walls of the school hall, recasting that space as magical, rather than the hall casting the library as mundane; the Greenhive Committee Room is a peaceful meeting room in the care home while simultaneously recreating the scents and sights of a village green.

Sleep No More, Boston (**2009–2010**; see also: **abstract/abstraction; Act 2;** Boyd, Carrie; design; installation; 'Norman the Eel'; **notation;** 'Rebecca the Bird'; **research;** *Sleep No More*, London; *Sleep No More*, NYC. Further reading: Opie and Tatum 2009): A reinvented and expanded version of the original production presented in London in 2003, produced in association with American Repertory Theatre (ART). Based in Cambridge, Massachusetts at Harvard University, ART while under Diane Paulus's tenure as Artistic Director in 2008, *Sleep No More* was programmed as part of her inaugural season, 'Shakespeare Exploded'.

For Felix Barrett this production was vital in terms of reinventing the content of *Sleep No More* for a US audience. Characters with little colour, definition and narrative, such as the Witches, were imbued with greater detail plus one-on-ones were incorporated. Given the success of the choreography with *Sleep No More*, London, finessed through *Firebird*, *Faust* and *Masque*, for Barrett, Beatrice Minns and Livi Vaughan, this remounting – reinvigorated by a different school building – provided an opportunity for an intense refocusing on design language with this production:

We had two months of development, pre-rehearsals, providing the headspace for design research for the first time. Where increased budgets meant that design improved,

△

FIGURE 22 *Sleep No More*. Banquet scene. Top: Boston, 2009. L–R: Geir Hytten, Alli Ross, Luke Murphy, Stephanie Nightingale (née Eaton), Robert Najarian, Phil Aitkins, Kelly Bartnik, Vinicius Salles, Conor Doyle, Sarah Dowling. Bottom: London, 2003, L–R: Geir Hytten, Robert McNeill, Elizabeth Barker, Hector Harkness, Gerard Bell, Dagmara Billon, Mark Fadoula, Andreas Constantinou, Sarah Dowling.

Photo credit: Top: Stephen Dobbie and Lindsay Nolin. Bottom: Stephen Dobbie show-by-show, resulting in a heightened naturalism with *Masque*, we wanted to ensure now that raw, abstracted detail was there. The breakthrough was, for the first time we had source material solely for that detail. We took *The Oxford Dictionary of Superstition* and similar texts, read them cover-to-cover, then placed one superstition in each room, to ward off evil, protect, tempt or endanger the characters who frequented it. It was a new way of doing a show, to see if the audience would discover the superstition; a layering in of abstraction. During *Faust* I was fascinated by the plane on which Bea was working, intricate, high impact. This was where Bea came into her own in terms of detail. We'd tested detail with *Masque*, referencing images given in the Poe stories, yet it was still an extension of the overall design. Here, where top-level scenography referenced film noir and *Macbeth*, the detail referenced superstitions. Through the reading we distilled, whittled down superstitions, very collaborative that process of sifting. Where before, I'd have done my one crunch through the central source material and relied on imagination to do the rest, here there was time for a depth of research at the heart of the process. As a result, I think Livi and Bea loved it; it felt really thick and structured. It was because we were reinventing a show we'd done before, had ideas to build on and completely reinvent. That's why, in turn, NYC and Shanghai are so very layered.

In terms of wider breakthroughs, this production saw to the expansion of Punchdrunk's international ensemble. The run began with seven established UK-based Punchdrunk performers; Conor Doyle, Fernanda Prata and Vinicius Salles, plus Sarah Dowling, Hector Harkness, Geir Hytten and Rob NcNeill who reprised the roles they created for the original London production. New members of the ensemble, cast in Boston, included Ali Ross, Tori Sparks, Stephanie Nightingale (née Eaton), Phil Atkins and Rob Najarian. The wave of performers that came in to take over the roles as the production ran included Kelly Bartnik, Hope T. Davis, Eric Jackson-Bradley and Luke Murphy, many of whom went on to open the NYC version. Sparks, who originated the role of Mrs Danvers and took over the role of Lady Macbeth from Dowling (later she would originate the character of Agnes Naismith for NYC), instantly attuned to the performing style, appreciating the interplay between performer and audience, between 'theatre, dance, site and its cinematic perspective':

As a performer it offers a unique sense of play with boundaries, rules, tension and timing. You're supported by a densely informed space to create the most real and intimate of experiences for audiences. They are so close they can hear your eyelashes flutter.

Murphy who took over the role of Macduff from McNeill, remembers watching a preview after his first day of rehearsal:

I spent the three hours just shaking, I couldn't believe the scope of what was around me or how real, yet not real, this world was. Later on, Hecate, took me in for a one-on-one, at the end of which, she backed me into hallway where the ceiling got lower and walls narrowed the deeper we went. Despite the fact I knew without a doubt that this was theatre, I'll never forget thinking 'No, it's a ruse, this whole thing is a front, they're vampires, she's going to kill me and I'll never be found'. I was sent out of a hidden door back into the main performance and didn't know what to do with myself. While I was still recovering, Rob McNeill jumped off a table and went flying over my head. It was amazing.

Another significant impact of *Sleep No More*, Boston in terms of its legacy on Punchdrunk's practice and process is that this was the first production for which a trained stage manager, Carrie Boyd, was employed. Consequently, Boyd went on to help the company create a notation system and template for large-scale masked shows. Though the production was planned to run from October 2009 to January 2010, the run was extended through February 2010, and immediately sold out.

***Sleep No More*, London** (**2003**; see also: **Act 1**; Barrett, Margaret and Simon; *Cherry Orchard, The*; cinematic; **contact improvisation**; dance; doors; ensemble; Gardner, Lyn; restraint; *Sleep No More*, Boston; *Sleep No More*, NYC; *Sleep No More*, Shanghai): *Sleep No More* tells Shakespeare's tragedy *Macbeth* through the shadowy cinematic lens of film noir. This was the first of the now renowned large-scale masked shows which incorporated Felix Barrett's singular vision and design aesthetic with Maxine Doyle's choreography and the ominous soundscapes composed by Stephen Dobbie. Sam Booth and Kathryn McGarr both experienced Punchdrunk's work for the first time through this production, recording their responses above. Colin Marsh, having garnered Arts Council project funding, enabled the core team to take the first steps to embracing professionalism. With funds now to pay performers, but very little money for the design, the installations were similar to previous shows. Responding to the Beaufoy Institute Building, a former Victorian school in London, Barrett let the hauntingly chilling space work its own magic, accented by standard Punchdrunk lighting and items from Barrett's parents' house, 'stylised by their positioning in the room, abstracted by the sparse nature of the layout and the context, objects out of place'. For Barrett, this production was pivotal in Punchdrunk's history:

The innovation was the choreographic language, without a doubt. That process and discovery was revelatory; finally, there was a performance language that matched the impact of the building. When you stumbled across a scene, instead of diluting the experience, it accentuated it. In terms of the loops, the lead narrative was so strong, fervent, clear and driving, providing a backbone in a way that it hadn't before. It was strong because we had a much longer process to work on it. Beforehand, the performance was thrown together in a week, now we had longer with Max and I working together on it. We shared a similar approach to deconstructing text, bleeding the source dry. It was also the nature of dancers, the presence they brought to the process. Actors would disappear between scenes whereas this introduced me to the thing that I was trying to get out of actors, confidence of body in space, being in tune with every single fibre of your being, alert and ready to move. With that first audition process, Max observed choreography and I, the resting state. I realised from this process that actors approached it from the head, had to understand it, analyse cerebrally. Actors ask why or how, before doing, whereas dancers approach from the body. That suddenly clicked in a profound way. It had a natural affinity with the way I wanted the audience to read it; not right-hand brain processing intellectually but the body absorbing it, an instinctual emotional impact that happens before your head's had a chance to catch up. That synergy, that's the way dancers make stuff. Through contact improvisation I realised these were masterful performers whose technique was about immediate response; fold in, release, absorb, respond, melt, bounce, lead, unmediated physical response. Contact improvisation as a form and process was mind-blowing for me. Max was insistent that I should participate – I'm no dancer but for my own process, to understand it, I went along with it. It's such a generous, open, democratic form, all about response, doesn't matter if you have no technique whatsoever because it's supportive, you're literally supporting your partners' bodies. That translates to how they would then support the audience. It all made sense, the nature of it,

constantly evolving. It also meant that they were incredibly inventive and would have that same response to physical objects.

This production thus established a troupe of dynamic performers, all expert at generating material from the body. Of this original cast of dancers, Sarah Dowling, Geir Hytten and Rob McNeill, all of whom originated lead character portrayals, remain regulars in the ensemble to this day. For Barrett, the dancers became 'superhuman, extraordinarily other':

Rob McNeill was particularly inventive, playing with architectural partners; a wall, a staircase or bannister. He found a door and started duetting with it. It was extraordinary, I remember studying at university the idea of imbuing an object with power, but never witnessed it. It became completely emotional, how he could manipulate this object, give it character, drive, purpose. Rob's a master of finding the humanity in an object, being able to displace his body in space and perform the impossible.

McNeill, who created the role of Macduff, clearly remembers this duet, recalling it as a partnership between the building, its natural light, its walls and that door:

I remember exploring the space, walking through messy rooms in complete disarray, and coming across an old wooden door detached against a wall. I was fascinated by the shadows it created, how it allured me, suggesting a hidden world behind the wall. It was the shadow of the door that was alluring, its ability to morph and shift the poetic nature of dark and light, presence and absence; how it worked metaphorically, held a multiplicity of meanings. It was with these ideas, and that massive door, that I went to Felix. His enthusiastic response meant I spent the next weeks improvising and working with a block of wood,

a partner much bigger and heavier than myself. This door became both my liberator and burden during the process. It opened up for me an approach to physical exploration into the nature of states of being, specifically in relation to how they unfold from space and architecture. My interaction with that door became the foundation for my first loop in *Sleep No More*. Each loop since has created different challenges, questions and explorations whilst always referring back, somehow, to that early experience.

Barrett also recalls the simultaneous restraint and openness of Geir Hytten and Sarah Dowling, who played Macbeth and Lady Macbeth respectively:

Geir's face was almost neutral, but his body was laden with narrative. The intention and focus in every single gesture. It was all there but through restraint, which made you ten times more engaged; it felt forceful, ambiguous, laced with mystery. It made you want to interrogate it further, so invited the audience in. Sarah Dowling, contrastingly, could act as well as she could move. The physicality came first but she was able to layer in beats of text, sound, word, anguish. Over the course of her loop, it was the most extraordinarily open descent into madness. Sarah is expert at close-up, intimacy and restraint.

The non-dancing performers equally set an idiosyncratic approach and intense physicality to the performing style. Maxine Doyle notes how Hector Harkness helped define this approach as he developed the role of Malcolm with 'a rhythmical and specific use of small props' that focused in on the detail, defining the notion of the close-up and restraint. In terms of the material generated across the rehearsal period Barrett notes how, for the first time, the narrative backbone became much stronger, because it was developed with the cast and choreographed:

The main narrative was pretty much set, only the Witches improvised. What we learned from that was, because performers went rogue and were difficult to control, the quality barometer was wobbling because they were at the beck and call of audience, or the flights and fancies of those performers in the moment. We realised that everything needs to be choreographed. It can *feel* improvised but can't be improvised because you can't guarantee the experiential arc. Those improvised performances were slightly out of control, with an audience watching, and *The Cherry Orchard* flooded back to me, that need for control in the performance. If it wasn't a narrative driven, experientially probing scene then it just distracted from the overall intention.

This first iteration provided a basic template for the loop structure of future productions reinvented in Boston, NYC and Shanghai. In this respect, where certain characters, narrative loops and choreography bear similarity to this original production, the design, dance, one-on-ones, and newly imagined counter-narratives are bespoke to each new audience in response to the buildings that give a home to each new project and the cultural influences that come to bear upon the retelling of the story in those specific locations.

Sleep No More, London galvanised the team, an ensemble, a spirit and style, pulled together by the force of Barrett's original concept, all of which was instrumental in helping the work to be acknowledged as credible theatre. Lyn Gardner proved vital in Punchdrunk's history. She visited this production and wrote the first national, broadsheet review to bring Punchdrunk's work to the attention of a wider audience.

Sleep No More, NYC (**2011–present**; see also: **Act 2**; **Act 3**; caretaking; characters; durational; mazes; restraint; *Sleep No More*, London; **Sleep No More, Boston**. Further reading: Kozusko et al. 2013; Ritter 2016; Worthen 2012): A completely reimagined version of the original 2003 London production, produced by Emursive, a partnership formed by Jonathan Hochwald, Arthur Karpati and Randy Weiner with the express intention of bringing *Sleep No More* to a New York audience. Felix Barrett and Colin Nightingale met with Weiner in NYC when first trying to find financing for an NYC *Faust*. Weiner then visited London to see *The Masque of the Red Death*. After experiencing *Sleep No More* in Boston with Hochwald, both were keen to join forces with Karpati to find a Manhattan site for a Punchdrunk collaboration. Emursive's interest in *Sleep No More* marked the first point at which a business partnership had been keen to produce a commercial enterprise from a Punchdrunk show. Nightingale emphasises:

Emursive had incredible vision to see the potential in the project. They successfully secured a site in Manhattan, which has been an important factor in the show's long-running appeal. We worked with them to turn this into the fictitious McKittrick Hotel.

The McKittrick Hotel inhabits what were once disused warehouse buildings, converted into famous nightclubs (Twilo then Bed) in Manhattan. Barrett recalls of the mounting of the show, Emursive 'let us get on with it', cleverly publicising the build-up to the event by blurring the space between real and fictional, suggesting it was an actual refurbishment and reopening of a 1939 hotel:

During Boston we talked about setting it in a hotel because we had the character of the porter and there were entrance lockers which felt a bit like a hotel lobby, we'd been interested in blurring the school/hotel worlds, creating an ambiguous space. So that seed had been planted. When we visited the building in NYC, literally flew in and out of Manhattan to see it, that was enough to know that the space was perfect. In equal parts it was anonymous and had loads of character, because of its history; places we could design into and spaces where the design was almost done for us. Immediately it felt like a hotel, so we could bring that earlier idea to fruition. The design became more detailed. We lost a little of the abstraction, that live art element we had in Boston, like single rooms that were completely black with just a spotlight on a telephone.

Building on the lessons learned from Boston regarding reinventing an existing production for a new audience and location, this version of *Sleep No More* also refined content and choreography. Nightingale adds, 'Emursive encouraged us to make the best show possible and created a working environment that avoided commercial pressures stifling creative ambitions and ensured that our core artistic values were upheld'. Elizabeth Romanski, who took over the roles of Hecate and Matron, having first witnessed it as an audience member, notes from both positions how working with an audience 'in such close proximity never ceases to be thrilling. The audience is the wonderful moving target each night'; she adds:

What makes Punchdrunk's work special is if you are willing to imagine, play along, follow a character down this hallway or into that room, there are worlds within worlds for you to find, every single time. The settings change but inside these spaces every cylinder is fired, every sense is engaged, and kinetic, unexpected moments are free to unfold.

Punchdrunk's *Sleep No More* has been highly influential in terms of immersive practice and New York theatre. As the company's first commercially produced project it allowed Punchdrunk to achieve design and technical ambitions while transforming its operational structures and public perception on an international scale. It is the longest running of Punchdrunk's productions and, while wholly managed by Emursive's team, continues to be overseen by Punchdrunk. Nightingale emphasises:

Emursive has worked tirelessly to keep The McKittrick Hotel a vibrant location, hosting special events, opening a roof-garden called Gallow Green and a restaurant-performance space called The Heath; both of which were designed in conjunction with Punchdrunk to ensure they feel part of the world of *Sleep No More*, while operating alongside it as separate ventures.

Sleep No More, NYC has grown Punchdrunk's international pool of performers, a number of whom went on to establish the original cast of *Sleep No More*, Shanghai. It has attracted to its fold new members of the New York dance scene, including Risa Steinberg. Internationally renowned as a solo artist, teacher, as well as partnering with artists such as Rudolph Nureyev, Steinberg is also a former student, and now director of the works of, José Limón. With her extensive background in the field of contemporary dance, she offers a particular insight into the contribution of *Sleep No More*, NYC to the dance world . . .

Risa Steinberg and Maxine Doyle

On *Sleep No More*, NYC

Maxine Doyle: Can you make any connections to your lineage, from Martha Graham, through the Limon Company to your training as a soloist with Annabelle Gamson, and how that experience was rediscovered when you came into *Sleep No More*, NYC?

Risa Steinberg: All of the work of these creators of modern dance, they were all speaking, they weren't demonstrating they were really *speaking*, that's the connection. José [Limón] was a huge humanitarian, nothing was just for 'show's sake', everything had a reason for being and you had to defend that reason. That makes much more sense to me than, say, making sure that the line my body makes is really perfect; instead I really care that my line is *saying* something. I've always been trusting of my gut instinct, so when you emailed, 'Do you still perform, do you want to be in *Sleep No More*?' I remember this total calm – and I'm not a calm person, I'm neurotic and very dramatic – but calm came over me and I just replied, 'Yes. Yes'. And even though I knew I might be too old, and too small, I never got nervous about it. I went to work with Erik [Abbott-Main] who was my student and I didn't have any ego and I said, 'this may or may not work and I trust that you'll tell me the truth'. I jumped on the table and my feet reached the wall, which was like, 'ok, check!'.

Max: Could you talk technically about your experience as a dancer in this very specific performance context?

Risa: It's so different to proscenium. I'm not sure I'd be interested in doing a proscenium production any more. With this, you're living – you're functioning and living as this person. Yes, there are lots of people around you, immersed in your life and they are very free with their boundaries, to extreme degrees, but the world that you walk around in, when I'm really, really there, then all of the other things are background to me. They become, even if they're really close and I can feel them, blurred in a way. The world is so demanding, captivating, fulfilling, challenging, physically challenging. I look at some of the other performers and I'm totally blown away by what they're doing physically. There's this magical balance between knowing you're performing and not performing; that you're just living that moment in that day. That's remarkable and that's not proscenium. I loved proscenium, did it for a very long time but it always had an element of 'show' and, therefore, evaluation; I can evaluate whether you're good or not because I'm watching you via this flat screen. I go upstairs to become The Nurse a half-hour early. I walk into that floor and I can be depressed, sad, tired, hungry and I walk onto that floor and every detail about every floor and every room feeds you information that supports all of your questions, all of your concerns, all of your answers, that then change. I'll walk into one of the rooms that I don't have a relationship with, like the dentist's chair, and I'll just be in it, and you become whatever it is you choose to become within the frame of this character.

Max: It sounds like you're saying the space, the design, transforms you into a vessel, you absorb the information.

Risa: Oh you are. I'm in no way *not* present, I am me; a crazy New Yorker that's incredibly intense. But we're not limited, we have so much potential for stretching and becoming and finding variation in the form. Sometimes I want you there because I want to make sure that I'm not stretching it too far. In the guidelines Punchdrunk gives us, one of the things that you write is, 'stay simple'. Staying simple is very hard in such a complex environment and always my challenge because I'm not a simple performer, I'm always having to make sure that I'm making decisions based on that moment in time; just there, just you – and *then* there's all of a sudden these people.

Max: So how does audience shift it then?

Risa: It shifts enormously on so many levels. My favourite thing is when you look across the room and then everybody looks because they see you *seeing*. You don't have to be 'seeing' anything, but they see you see so they look to see. That has such a power in it. When I do that and they don't follow I know I haven't done something well, something is missing in it, I haven't let go of me, I haven't brought them with me.

Max: There's a specific rhythm and part of the job as a resident is to guide the audience, guide their focus and attention, whether that's to the action or to the space or the detail.

Risa: Absolutely. And they come with their own terror; it's dark and they don't know when someone's going to turn a corner. There's no control. People are jumping and yelping all the time and you have to work with that. In the scene where I'm cutting mazes, a woman slammed her hand down and I jumped. I had to figure out what to do with that. I just gently held her hand for a moment, let it go and moved on. It caught my attention and then I had to question if it was okay that it caught my attention. I'm constantly in the process of evaluating those moments. In the window solo a woman grabbed my legs – now, the building is full of unforgiving surfaces, one slip and a whole bunch of bad things could happen. She was grabbing my legs so hard that I had to, in a split second that felt like four hours, stay in character and yet release her from my legs. There are people who come there to jab you and test you, and there are people who come there and just observe you, and I'll be doing this big dramatic thing and they'll just walk by, so I have to calm my ego.

Max: It is interesting the way you have to manage your ego as a performer in this work. I remember with *Sleep No More*, London, watching Lady Macbeth's solo in the boudoir and being very inspired by what I was watching, witnessing audience disengaging and walking away. I remember in the beginning I felt angry about that. I felt angry for me because they weren't appreciating my work and I felt sad for the dancer because they were ignoring her. I came to realise you just have to let that go and the audience will follow their intuition. Then I noticed that, generally, the mass stay. Some go and that's right too, we offer them that opportunity.

Risa: It's something to contend with, to organise. I didn't understand fully who The Nurse was until now, doing Danvers. Now I have a clearer understanding of characters that circle and those that intersect. The Nurse circles and Danvers intersects. The responsibilities are different. My timing with Danvers is dependent on having to be some place for someone else's storyline, whereas with The Nurse that's rare. Danvers has more mutable walls. Danvers is creating a lot of the story in a very quiet way and The Nurse is cleaning up the story, supporting the story.

Max: That's a nice way of thinking about it. Danvers wasn't created as a travelling character, was conceived initially as a resident, but she ended up guiding people through the space and her role became fuller. How is it to be followed by audience?

Risa: I was nervous, I'm so small but what I'm finding is that focus does so much of the work. Focus is my passion, I teach it all the time. So my body language is secondary to my focus, especially in [the sequence] Curse Two; there are so many people, because Lady Macduff has brought them in and I have to navigate them and clear the space, not just for me but for her, she's falling and climbing all over the place. I'm finding it excitingly challenging. I have to be careful as we're moving quickly and she is really thrusting her weight but I don't want to become a pusher of the audience, but to navigate the Nurse's gentility with authority. I'm loving that focus – be it eye focus or body focus – it's really aiding my doing that.

Max: I wonder if there's something about your age and maturity that offers, and demands, respect. I feel that having mature performers in the work gives it such gravitas. Even though you say it's challenging for you to be simple, actually you do very little and can be so captivating because of that presence, that experience, because of that weight that's in the space. Similarly, we have a little person in the cast, Colin Buckingham, and it's interesting watching the way the audience navigate his height. He doesn't disappear, he pulls focus. It's interesting how this work can challenge our preconceptions. I've seen big, tall people disappear because they don't have the skill to control, or to navigate or draw; they don't have the skill and charisma that you have. It's an interesting alchemy.

Risa: I find with the Nurse, perhaps because it's also on the spookiest floor, the fifth floor, they'll all walk by. In the beginning I thought, 'oh, I'm just not as sexy as those other women, they're looking for the glamorous women in sequence'. You're there for three hours and it's hard especially with the durationals, the writing durational, it's hard to be that empty, to have that much emptiness; or folding clothes.

Max: When I watch that loop it feels full now. When we first created it there was nothing. It was Stephanie Eaton [since, Nightingale] in her Nurse's dress with a couple of things to do. Lots of these resident roles weren't ready when we first opened, it was just these performers with a role, with these ideas in a space, allowing the space to tell a story. Gradually over time those roles became fleshed out. There's something really important about the rhythm of those characters that you need in the bigger picture of the world to balance out the chaos. You need those places of stillness. I'm happy when I see audience find a resident character, engage a little bit and go away, then come back. I also understand the need to impress and to perform and present and those resident roles have less obvious opportunity for that.

Risa: They don't impress and stun in a traditional performance way, but they surely do in a human way. The mirroring for example, the simplest thing is so beautiful; to discover the shadow of that woman in the window. Speaking as an audience member before I was in it, if you're calm enough to be open to receive that simplicity, it's so stunning. I love how, when I'm hanging clothes, the simplicity of just connecting two pieces of clothing together; the awareness of these two hands coming together at that moment. One of the things that I am so consistently moved by is the kindness of the ensemble, the people in the building. I've been in this field for over forty years and I have never experienced such generosity, support, transparency, in a group of people. And it's a large ensemble.

Max: I'd like us to finish thinking about dance as a form, as a language and why it has been so successful in the work. What is it about dancing that allows a building to breathe in a particular way? And, secondly, given your history and background, what do you see as the impact that *Sleep No More* has had on the dance and theatre community?

Risa: Dance to me is only about communication. With this work, nothing is for show's sake, nothing is to impress unless *the goal* is to impress you; I am here to impress you so that I then captivate you. One of *Sleep No More*'s impacts with the dance community is the breadth of ages in the building. For the younger dancers, to be responsible for defending what they're doing physically, communicating something through it, that makes for artistry. All of the dancers and actors in the building are beautiful movers, but to take ownership of *why* you're performing that gesture versus just making a pretty line, that has impacted the community in a very quiet way. It asks a young dancer to make sense of *why* they use their bodies to communicate.

Max: There's an empowerment in that isn't there, that's what I witness, even just at audition level. When I do workshops with your students, I witness that epiphany; my body isn't just about technique, what I can do. I can think, and I can feel, and I can own and understand. And if I can harness all that, I can offer something transformative to an audience.

Risa: And, therefore, I have the responsibility of owning what I'm communicating. I'm not just doing your steps. There are different ways to get better at being what you are. If our job as dancers is to get better at being physical communicators, there's lots of different ways of achieving this. You can take class or do supplemental training but you can also get there wanting your body to communicate something. If you know what you're trying to say then your leg will get there, and all of a sudden you don't have to worry about technique because it's coming from an intention.

Max: In creation some things are driven, come from a clear intention but lots of things come from a very abstract place; a movement research or task. Ultimately it all has to come back to intention but often I will let the dancer's work that out, their back story. I do trust the artists to work it out because I can't know everything.

Risa: I've watched the dancers that I know really well become artists that are able to make decisions. I don't think we always make the right decisions but being an artist means that you get to acknowledge that and make another one tomorrow. Not to evaluate as right or wrong but to note what was interesting and then try something different.

Max: On a more pragmatic level, how has it impacted the community?

Risa: Firstly, it's employing a huge amount of people. The employment it serves, in this community is amazing, huge. Yes, it's hard, physically challenging but on the other side of that we have support, physical training every day. It's one of the most sought-after jobs. Secondly, the cast changes and even if you're not leaving you're swapping roles. It's not the same show every night, like on Broadway, same cast. Everything is switching. We walk in and won't know who's on that night so it's always evolving and changing. Everybody's different enough that it makes it fascinating.

Max: When I started this work years ago, I couldn't imagine how you would have anything other than fixed roles. I thought it would be a weakness to keep changing. But as we've gone on through the years I realise it can be a strength of the work, keeps it alive.

Sleep No More, Shanghai (2017–present; see also: **Act 3**; cross-fade; portals; *Sleep No More*, NYC. Further reading: Shepherd and Zhang 2016): The first production produced by Punchdrunk International with SMG Live, taking Punchdrunk's work to China, Shanghai's Jing'An District, for the first time. *Sleep No More*, Shanghai is a full-scale reimagining of the original production. Each different iteration is 'rebuilt from the ground up', as Felix Barrett clarifies: 'they may have the same score, some of the same characters, but the inflection and detail is very different'. Keen to understand what would resonate for the Shanghai audience, Barrett knew from the outset that the references to superstitions would need to be overhauled in order to make sense:

It wasn't simply us barrelling in and doing it in a new territory. It was a long, detailed process with our Chinese counterparts, working closely with Chinese designers to make it feel like it was created and owned by the city.

Transposing the world from 1930s Scotland to 1930s Shanghai naturally shifted its aesthetic. While the setting, seeded in Boston, of the colonial hotel remains, new stories traverse six storeys of The McKinnon Hotel. An entirely new sub-plot, the Chinese legend of 'The White Snake', now serves as the narrative anchor. Once through box office and coat-check, audiences head up one floor where, through a darkened maze that prioritises hearing and touch, loud film noiresque soundscore runs through matt-black, felt flats that absorb the limited light. This serves as the cross-fade, a transportation device between the present and Shanghai 1937. It takes its audience to The Manderley Bar, a halfway-house, where performers talk to you, drinks can be ordered, the band might have a contemporary edge, yet the dressing is of this other time. As Barrett explains:

It further plunges into the world of the narrative as you leave Manderley and move into the masking ritual.

The whole entrance, approximately twenty minutes before you're pushed out of the elevator, is all decompression from the everyday world, acclimatising you to the dream-world, easing you into it to wash away the outside world. It has to be a gradual plunge, not a staccato fall, into the world to enable the audience to acclimatise.

The Manderley Bar later serves as the portal back to the present, following the finale. Looking back across each iteration of *Sleep No More*, from the first to this most recent, Barrett notes, 'with *Sleep No More*, London we didn't even think about phones. By Boston smart phones were around but not a problem', yet like a gauge of societal shifts and 'pronounced addiction to screens, with this version we've had to enforce a ban on mobile phones in order to guarantee they won't be used and spoil the show':

It's interesting to mark those developments in technology and attitude through those audiences. In comparison with the *Firebird* preview where the lighting failed and the audience lit the show with their mobiles – so beautiful, intimate, pure lighting direct from source, focused – whereas now we have to physically deny an audience their screens because they'd rather look at them than at live performers. Rather than wholly resist it, we're going to try and build work that utilises it.

Small Tale, A (see also: **Act 3**; discovery; Enrichment; **Enrichment Symposium**; *Miniature Museum*): With the full title of *A Small Tale: A Teacher-Led Adventure*, this is a Punchdrunk Enrichment project for primary schools designed by Associate Enrichment Director, Tara Boland and project-managed by Elin Moore-Williams, to be led by the teacher in the classroom. Launched at the Punchdrunk Enrichment Symposium in November 2016 and tested by volunteer teachers, it aims to inspire and develop imaginative pedagogic practices for literacy. Teachers are given the tools to lead a creative-learning project which aims to ignite and inspire a passion for writing, raise standards in reading, speaking and listening while, tangentially, providing opportunities to discuss life in the 'big world'.

Teacher and class together read a mysterious old picture book about tiny, mischievous and messy Abe and Alba, who love stories. When the class returns to the book the following day the pages are blank, except for two sets of tiny footprints. The characters have escaped, and the pupils have only a short time to get them back to safety. Luckily, they discover a letter from the book's previous keeper, Orla Hennessy. Using the help and guidance scribed in the letter, by being curious and looking closely in unusual locations around the school, pupils discover sock-sleeping-bags and tiny tee-pees in trees where Abe and Alba have camped out. The only way to return the characters to the safety of the book's pages is to write them a story. Time is pressing, and they are in danger out in the world of big people. Boland expands:

A Small Tale was born from a desire to allow teachers to be seen as magical by the class, to support a teacher in delivering curriculum creatively and placing them squarely at the centre of that creative delivery. We also wanted to reach more teachers, further afield. The premise was a whole project in a box, that could be posted or carried away easily by a teacher, delivered with minimum installation. This was an excellent creative restriction. It led to a project where the emphasis would be on allowing children to imagine that the world of their school had become magical, rather than us physically augmenting the environment with an installation. You can do something very powerful by making children *believe* that their environment has changed. That was a massive moment of learning for me. The nature of immersive work is that you're surrounded by

△

FIGURE 23 *A Small Tale: A Teacher-Led Adventure.* 2017. 'Curiosity and discovery'.

Photo credit: Stephen Dobbie

a world. If you take away the walls of an installation but allow another world to leak into the everyday, a child will imagine that their whole world has changed. The augmentation has no limit because children will imagine far more than we could ever create. That felt really exciting; to make the children and their teachers re-imagine their school as a whole new world, in this case, one where two tiny people were running around at night and setting up camp on the head teacher's shelves. We hear many stories of children seeing evidence of Abe and Alba's escape far beyond the designed elements we have created; cracks in skirting-boards as a means for them to hide under the floor; holes in the ceiling enable Abe and Alba to listen in on the class. Children bring biscuits in from home to leave out and about for Abe and Alba to nibble on.

In this way, children notice their world afresh through the imagined world of *A Small Tale*. Felix Barrett takes pleasure in noting how the packs created and sent out to each school for this project resonate with his very early application for Indepen*dance* support, back in Act 1, where a suitcase full of mystery, imagination and portent – a life story and a proposal – was left to be opened and unpacked, in order for its imaginative discoveries to be revealed. For Barrett, the thought and activity that has gone into the manner in which the package arrives, as much as the contents enclosed, 'work on the same principle as that suitcase' on how it might 'invade someone's space and allow the magic to percolate out from within'.

Small Wonders (**2018**, see also: **Act 3**; **boxes, chests and drawers**; community; Enrichment): Commissioned by Punchdrunk, LIFT and Bernie Grant Arts Centre, this miniature-installation-led family project explores the power of collective, intergenerational imagination; and the importance of the little things in life. Peter Higgin with Alex Rowse, Tara Boland and Kate Rigby

originated a Punchdrunk approach to using Charles Matton-like boxed installations as three-dimensional photographs; to capture time and tell stories. With a focus on installation as interactive exercise, storytelling stimulus and scenographic design, the work produced with Tottenham's UpLIFTers (a partnership between Duke's Aldridge Academy School, The Vale School, LIFT and LIFT commission, that enables young students to create arts events with and for their local communities) led to the creation of *Small Wonders*:

Inside Nanny Lacey's flat are her collection of miniatures, home-made creations that capture the adventures she's shared with her daughter, Bella, over the years. With age, Nanny Lacey has started to forget things. Change is on the horizon and she'll soon move into a care home. Before she goes, there is one final miniature to share, and story to be told.

Conceived and realised by Punchdrunk, *Small Wonders* is written by Nessah Muthy, inspired by the stories and dreams of the Tottenham UpLIFTers. It premiered at Tottenham's Bernie Grant Arts Centre, with the support of the *Small Wonders* Giving Circle and the Ellis Campbell Charitable Foundation.

smart candles (see also: design; **lighting**): Also referred to as 'flameless candles', these are LED alternatives to organic candles or tea lights. The illumination occurs through a small bulb, which imitates a flame, so they comply with theatrical health and safety regulations and do not lose their form as a result of melting. They have the aesthetic of a candle or tea light although lose the durational qualities that were once so inspirational to Felix Barrett. The emotional nuances evoked and the quality of the storytelling that arises from these lighting states are signature to the Punchdrunk aesthetic. This, alongside their effectiveness as apparatus to ignite curiosity in the audience member, encouraging individuals to explore installations, is crucial to Livi Vaughan and Beatrice Minns' designs,

hence Vaughan's reference to them as a 'crafting tool'.

soundscore (see also: abstract/abstraction; **atmosphere**; caretaking; cinematic; corner; Dobbie, Stephen; **durational**; flow; *Moon Slave, The*; **music**; **pedal note**; **process**; **sampling**; *Sleep No More*, London, NYC, Shanghai; *unheimlich*; visceral): 'Soundscore' names the full aural composition for any Punchdrunk project whatever its format and composite elements, such as music, abstract sound or narration. Sound has been a vital element of Punchdrunk projects from *The Moon Slave* onwards, where the technicalities of delivering a bespoke, audio experience through headphones, synchronous with action, was a remarkable achievement for Felix Barrett and collaborators. For the early masked events across 2000–2002, sound compositions were incorporated sparingly. They served as the beat of duration or built crescendo and were mitigated by sparsity of equipment and no single person taking responsibility for sound design, for example; the persistent snare drum-drill and regular snap of firecrackers in *Woyzeck*, 2000; or the repeated gong-shimmer pedal note, contrasting with the crescendo of Debussy's *La Mer* in a single room, for *The Tempest*, 2003. For Stephen Dobbie, the sparsity of *The Tempest*'s sound composition was effective as it matched the reverberations 'of the freezing, concrete building'. Barrett adds, it was the 'point at which Debussy came in and the music suddenly filled the echoey cavern' that the team realised the power of surround-sound. Consequently, from *Sleep No More*, 2003 onwards, soundscores for masked shows have been designed and installed across all zones of a building rather than localised in one space, partly, to serve that 'cinematic experience' for an audience (Dobbie 2013). Barrett recalls,

it was a vast leap from one piece of music playing at one point during an event, to soundscore on a fifty-five-minute loop with a final crescendo. It felt radical at the time to put speakers everywhere and have that soundscore playing around the building.

Nowadays, for masked shows, the sound is composed in partnership with the space, led by theme rather than narrative. It constantly evolves alongside the design-build, and partly through liaison with choreography in the studio or, latterly, in the building. The layering of the soundscore is threefold. Pop-songs or music evoke historical period and geographical setting. Abstract sounds establish an expressionist undercurrent, eliciting an imagining beyond the touch-real installations to evoke a *feeling* rather than a hearing or seeing of the wider world. These indicate the edges of the world, as with *The Drowned Man* where indecipherable ambient sounds in the mix suggested the haze of deserts and the rhythmic toil of derricks. Thirdly, orchestrated interludes are plundered and used to punctuate and manipulate emotional threads, as well as serving as audio citations from soundtracks. An important part of the composition is the added effects that overlay the sampled material to create a montage of sound. It involves drawing through, expanding or slowing down musical refrains, composing new bars of music inspired by the era or atmosphere of the world; a to-and-fro between discovering atmosphere in existing sound samples versus manipulating a mix in order to instil that atmosphere in the composition. Any melodious swells in the composition serve as reset signals, eventually functioning as a cue for performers to return fluidly to the beginning of their loop. In this way, it is soundscore that controls the loop structure. In a duet with the sound, each character reaches their own mini-crescendo, the threshold of a denouement, which returns them to their starting point. These resets deliberately incorporate the repetition of a melodic theme that, for the audience, hints at the climactic yet always pulls back from this until the final and momentous crescendo of the show. Barrett clarifies, the moment of reset within the soundscore is often 'an "Ethics Special"' and is 'huge, crucial',

involving 'a piece of music' that, when mixed, 'becomes far more than the sum of its parts'.

To illustrate, the palette of the first *Sleep No More* soundscore was a fusion of assorted orchestrated interludes, pulled through and around themselves so no longer recognisable in their original form. Across the loop these fused with the crackle of a record player, a ticking clock, ambient atmosphere and a deep, bass pedal note. Dobbie adds, 'everything that happened in the sound in the first *Sleep No More*, we're still doing now, albeit on an expanded scale'. With the original *Sleep No More* composition, what felt 'revolutionary' for Barrett was the reverb effects that Dobbie employed that 'slowed time' and took on an organic quality within the world:

It wasn't soundtrack as background accompaniment but as the overt manipulator of audience. Despite it being abstracted the sound held them back, stifled them, made them nervous, or run to something. What was impactful was the sheer control that came from the sound.

The incessant and omnipresent crackle of a gramophone was a key element in evoking the durational concept of the *Sleep No More* world, suggesting time left unattended. It established a palpable otherworldliness and a constant presence of foreboding from that state of suspension; a sensation of both time and breath being held. Barrett elaborates:

It was the sense of the uncanny, something was already always wrong, the record has finished but been forgotten, so where has the listener gone? It was so sparse and empty, seven minutes of crackle. This is why duration is so important, in action and sound. It holds an implicit threat, which comes from nothing happening because you know at some point it's going to break, and something is going to shift. The event the follows gains more power the greater the absence before it.

For set sequences in *Sleep No More*, London, where the ensemble came together for the Banquo's ghost scene, Dobbie's soundscore beckoned audience members towards this and created a fluid movement between the building's spaces, the audience journey and the performer's needs which ensured the transitions in the composition retained the atmosphere of the world in which that sequence occurred and accentuated the dreamlike haunting of the moment. Barrett recalls, 'we knew we wanted to have a tea dance, so Maxine and I found a piece of music that would work, got a tea dance specialist in, and then Dobbie put a dreamy bit in before and after'. Dobbie elucidates:

It involved a playlist of sounds that complemented the music, reverby. With the Boston version we took that same soundscore and injected more menace into it, so this rather quaint, romantic tea dance became consumed by that feeling of threat.

Barrett adds, the injection of menace came from 'Dobbie's instinctual impulse to build the track before and after'. The manner in which Dobbie was responding to the evolving narratives and themes of the world on-site generated a 'creative baton passing' where the directors and dancers then responded to the new soundscore. As this suggests, for masked events, 'a lot of the show is developed from the cast responding to the sound in the space'. Dobbie continues:

We strive for the transitions between scenes to be smooth or imperceptible. With that tea dance sequence, we had to make sense of a song appearing out of nothing. Those transitions are simply about easing the audience in and then holding their hand on the way out. They experience this powerful, harrowing scene that creeps up on them and crescendos, but they're not then left bereft, swimming around in a sea of confusion, the sound guides them out. Those transitions are a principle that has carried through from that original *Sleep No More*.

Here, then, soundscore becomes an indirect caretaking device. Evolved through Boston and into New York and Shanghai, the *Sleep No More* soundscore still interweaves multifarious samples, blurring and jarring musical styles and eras. The compositional attitude in this regard relates to a typical aspect of the Punchdrunk process, what Barrett describes as stipulating 'a rules-set, "everything is 1930s", and then intentionally breaking it' to subvert expectation, 'because otherwise the audience would immediately get everything, become too comfortable'. Dobbie explains, 'the contrasts in sound worlds in *Sleep No More*, NYC, are so opposite, from scratchy Ink Spots-styled music, 1930s melodies, with lush orchestral scores and crackly vinyl in the background'. This establishes a time-blurred mix of music and sound that allows the Witches' Rave sequence to create an adrenalin-fuelled vertigo effect, shifting the stability of the world. As Dobbie describes, bursting out of an ominous dance-music pulse, a monotonous swell that creates a sense of 'the hypnotic, gets under the audience's skin so, without them realising, they get carried toward this crescendo'.

In terms of interweaving music within any soundscore for the masked shows, this tends to be sourced from interludes in classical or film scores, as opposed to any well-known melodic sequences. Dobbie clarifies, interludes are 'less prescriptive':

A lot of the soundscores I create are inspired by those interludes, the sections in-between because they're so atmospheric and deeply evocative of the mood and feel of the world. In initially trying to create something incidental, nondescript, only supporting of the atmosphere, that works subconsciously as opposed to driving narrative, we've created something instead which is lasting in people's memories.

Here sound works in much the same way as the choreography, allowing a fluidity of experience and a piecing together of narrative, rather than enforcing linearity. For Barrett the effectiveness of interludes is that they indicate 'transition' and support continuous movement; they flow into the punctuation, the corners and crescendos provided by any corresponding samples of melody:

All the corners, the key tracks are chosen for their emotional resonance, to manipulate the audience to feel a certain way, much like film soundscores. We deliberately then pull back from that and give an opposing sound from elsewhere in the soundscore. There will always be an individual compositional experience of sound for each audience member according to the journey that they take through the building. If the audience are constantly moving it's important that the score is not narrative. If they arrive at a big melodious piece then that will be a scene, but that happens rarely. Often samples of melody will be used as a reset point, sometimes it might recur as a theme, but we deliberately don't use famous bits of soundtrack because it will have clear connotations and make that moment solely about 'that bit in the film' so take you out of the world we've created.

In Punchdrunk worlds soundscores manipulate how audiences feel *within*, as much as how they feel *about*, the world created. The composition of soundscore is generated, first and foremost, on creating an atmosphere and adding a durational quality that influences the tempo and flow of the audience, as much as any emotional response to the narratives played out within the world. Responding to the atmosphere and era of that world, rather than the specifics of the narrative, enables the sound to take on a lateral inventiveness, establishing what Barrett calls an 'instinctual and dreamy' tone. Where working literally, the installation as much as the composition of the sound works on tandem to impact experientially on the audience. For example, songs that play out through specific scenes through a transistor in a single bedroom, providing emotional resonance, tapping into nostalgia; the sound will then expand to fill the rest of space, reverberate against the walls as much as through the body, envelop the audience in time and, seemingly, travel with it to locations beyond that room. The sonic collage from space to space, expertly crafted and installed to play across the zones of the building, establishes a dreamlike blurring and blending, as opposed to a clashing, of audio that meets the fluid experience of the design and the dance. It is only where the sound has been designed as a rug-pull, as with the *Sleep No More* Witches' Rave, breaking the rules of tempo and era intentionally to subvert audience expectation, that it creates a space to attend to the turning of a corner in narrative or experience.

The masked show soundscores are only one of the formats employed to establish the world of the event. Journeying, one-on-one and Enrichment projects all have different requirements. *The Moon Slave* entry provides a strong illustration of how soundscore led to the creation of atmosphere and delivered the narrative of the world. *The Borough* and *Kabeiroi* developed this approach, serving to blur the real and imagined through sound. Where soundscore in masked shows heightens the atmosphere of the building and installations, through headphones they heighten an individual's imagination and re-lens the view on the outside world, proving the power of sound as the driver of experience.

space (see also: architecture; atmosphere; **building**; corridors; exercises; found space; framing; **'listening to the building'**; process; **site**; site-sympathetic; tunnels): A generic term that encompasses the generalised and more abstract parameters, qualities and properties of the area in which a full event occurs. In more recent works this incorporates the virtual as much as physical realms of any world created and, as with the physical and imaginative journey between the two realms in *The Oracles*, embraces the lacuna between the two. As a practical term it incorporates the broad range of spaces in and across which work may be devised or set and through which the world of the event is imagined. It equally corresponds to a single room or the wealth of connected but different rooms, contiguous hallways, corridors, tunnels across a site. More broadly it can extend to the different kinds of space that become interconnected within any journeying event, stretching to pavements, streets, different buildings and rooms, lifts, or transport. Although a shorthand among the creative and production teams, when working with the residents of Greenhive, the Enrichment team quickly had to take on board how the term does not always translate to everyday environments, as Connie Oppong explains above.

For Felix Barrett the concept for any project is driven by his initial response to space, to the 'emotional wash', elicited on first 'meeting'. Correspondingly, the creative team are required to attend to the nuances and details of atmosphere and experience of each different phase of a space when designing the event, in order to attune to the manner in which the audience are likely to apprehend, then comprehend, the whole experience. This is why, for Barrett, it is retrogressive to attempt to plan and fix any project in advance of knowing and spending time within the site, journey or building across which the event will occur because 'the cerebral, hypothetical work away from the site often doesn't work, and you can only realise that when you get into the space'. It is the space that modifies and inspires the choreographic language. For Maxine Doyle, space 'offers an immediate context to work within', which is 'liberating' (2013). The choreography collaborates with the architectural features and existing qualities or impressions provided by the space, deferring to the manner in which it tells stories and offering emotional and narrative possibilities for an audience and performer . . .

A way into . . . considering space

Punchdrunk has used all sorts of space over its history. Making work in space and *making space* requires an acute awareness of space, place and your presence within it.

Exploring a space – any space, inside or outside – is vital when thinking about how an audience might eventually respond to it, as much as how it might be used to generate work. Reading that space and the stories its tells, attuning to its tempo and atmosphere, are important starting points before thinking about the placement of performance or activity in appropriate locations within the space, or imagining how you might go about staging work across that space.

Punchdrunk aims to heighten an individual's senses and levels of perception in a space – audience and practitioner alike. Marks scuffed on floors or etched into walls tell a story. Changes in temperature, light levels, ceiling height, fixtures and furniture, smell, all tell us about a space and its history. Using the following exercises can help tune into a space in order to unlock its creative potential while also awakening the senses of a performers and designers to its creative possibilities.

The following can be applied to any space, working in groups or individually. If in a building its best to begin, first and foremost, by 'listening to the building'. Participants can respond to questions openly or they can internalise thoughts. This list of instructions is by no means exhaustive, so you should adapt them to your needs and to your space.

Walk around the space. What do you see? Shout to all the things that you can see in this space. Create a list in your mind.

How would you describe this space to someone who had never been here before?

Where do you feel strong, playful or weak, exposed? Where in the room feels sad, scary, secret? Move to that space. Absorb and reflect on its surfaces and sensations. Sketch it, write it, make a note of its ambient sounds, move in it – respond as appropriate to your needs.

Where would you hide a secret note? A murder weapon? A love letter?

Find a detail in the space that you like, that interests you: A scratch on the table, a loose thread in the curtain, a mark upon the wall. Create a story that explains its existence. How did it come to be? Who put it there? Why?

Imagine all of the actions that may have happened here. All of the people who must have walked on the floor. Start from the literal, the likely – the cleaner mopping the floor, the electrician mending the light fitting, the playgroup that meets on a Saturday to the imagined, the possible – the lovers meeting for a tryst, the woman who eats her last meal here alone, the mother who has lost her child, the grandmother waiting to tell her story. Where do you position these characters within the space? Where in the room *feels* like the best location for these actions to take place?

A shorter version of this would work as follows . . .

'Find a place where . . .'

As the group walk around, the facilitator instructs them to 'find a place in the room where . . .'

Shift those 'places' from physical aspects – corners, light, dark – to emotional states – comfortable, safe, lonely, powerful, scared, brave.

This simple exercise builds on Felix Barrett's 'listening to the building' exercise and can help an ensemble respond to space and the stories a space tells, while also picking up on any core or implicit atmosphere or feelings generated by the space.

'space-hunting' (see also: building; *Faust*; found space; process; site; site-sympathetic; space): The search for a suitable building for performance projects is a never-ending obsession. For all of the early projects Felix Barrett independently hunted out inspirational buildings and secured their loan for projects. *Faust* was a turning point in terms of the times spent and project-like rigour and exhilaration involved in the hunt for a site. The approach to sourcing space, tramping the streets, looking up and around the city rather than at ground and surface level, went on to influence the approach to creating work across a cityscape for *Silverpoint* and *Kabeiroi*. Nowadays Punchdrunk has designated 'space hunters' who regularly explore locations with the sole intention of finding sites for potential projects. Without a confirmed site, there is no show. Colin Nightingale adds, 'there is nothing more exciting than visiting a site for the first time and imagining the possibilities it offers':

There is no set method to space hunting and we've employed various techniques over the years that have all, in equal measure, borne fruit or failed miserably; from walking the streets to find empty buildings, nurturing relationships with local councils, contacting space hunting agencies, employing our own specialist property-searcher, forging relationships with developers or organisations with empty buildings. It's become more challenging to find sites in London over recent years as many other businesses, creative and commercial, are now looking to repurpose disused buildings, plus, the scale and ambition of our work has grown and the duration of time required to run a show has increased. Up until *The Drowned Man*, in 2013, we'd essentially accessed spaces in the UK for free. On this occasion we needed a massive site in central London and paying rent was the only way to secure it. Our approach to hunting for and securing a site, which no

doubt will continue to morph, is a factor alongside creative curiosity, that's driving us to see what's possible in the virtual realm.

Space Invaders Agency (**2011**, see also: **Act 2**; community; **Enrichment**; **installation**; legacy; *Small Wonders*; **tunnels**): The Space Invaders Agency, global experts in transforming space, enlisted pupils from ten London schools to help them with a special mission: to discover London's Olympic Voice. Agents helped pupils to transform spaces within their schools, before inviting them to Agency HQ where pupils learned Agency Skills and explored their creative ideas. Punchdrunk Enrichment harnessed the excitement around the London Olympics to engage pupils' creative energy, channelling this into their design of interactive installations bespoke to an arch under Waterloo, which has since become part of The Vaults. A further sixteen London schools visited the final installed environment, responding to it in written form. This was the largest-scale Enrichment project undertaken at this point and the first time the team had collaborated as part of a wider programme of work. Entitled 'The Biggest Learning Opportunity on Earth' (BigLop), led by ACE-funded Bridge organisation, A New Direction, it brought together various arts organisations, including Nimble Fish and MakeBelieve Arts, a year before London 2012 to explore what the Olympics meant for young people in schools across London. For Punchdrunk, the chosen focus on installation as the method and outcome for participatory arts practice developed ideas that had been initiated by *Brixton Market* and would be refined, in miniature scale, for *Small Wonders*, 2018.

'Specials' (see also: **abstract/abstraction**; curiosity; **design**; discovery; in-show-world; installation; multiples; **research**; scale; visceral): A significant and sometimes expensive design feature that is custom-built or carefully sourced for a production, whether a singular object or series of objects. The intention is that it will have a powerful

impact on the audience; where there is expense, these features have to have great significance to justify that investment. 'Specials' are clues to the world of an event and the manifold interpretations it offers. These are often abstract and installation-based and of great significance to the in-show-world interpretation of one or more of the source texts. Centred around an image that interconnects the narratives and themes of the world across floors, they will work on a narrative level but are also deeply symbolic. In *The Drowned Man*, the life-size, lifelike-yet-dead fake horse was such a 'special' to work alongside reiterated statues of horses and Stanford's menacing sugar-sculpting of a horse, all of which serve to underscore the references, simultaneously pedestrian and thematic, that underscore Nathanael West's *The Day of the Locust* while foregrounding Büchner's 'astronomical horse' which 'puts human society to shame' (1979, 15). Similarly, the production's Red Moon Motel sign and the postcard of the Red Moon Motel in a glass dome jar found on a plinth in the basement are further examples of 'specials' that fuse imagery and the worlds of the sources.

stage management (see also: Act 2; Act 3; **Boyd, Carrie**; Minnigin, Aaron; **notation**; **production management**; stewards): Vital to any process of performance production, Punchdrunk has evolved unique operational strategies and practitioner skills for this role. Skills related to stage managing a Punchdrunk masked shows are reinvented as required for different projects, whether audio-narrated travelling experiences, Punchdrunk Enrichment projects in schools or Punchdrunk Travel; the needs of *The Borough* or *Kabeiroi*, for example, being wholly different to a masked show. For masked shows, stage manager responsibilities share some similarities with traditional theatre practice; resetting props, looking after performers, producing call sheets, running rehearsals, 'calling' sections of the production and writing show reports. Colin Nightingale points out that requirements of the role extend beyond this, connected to, although not interchangeable with, production management:

The stage manager role for us is much more reactive than conventional theatre, closer to Event Management. The stage manager, in traditional contexts, controls everything to ensure shows run as rehearsed, but our audience bring in an element that can be random and throw up challenges that have to be dealt with in real time. Increasingly we're meeting stage managers who are excited by this challenge. Peter Higgin built up a good working relationship with Aaron Minnigin during *Faust*. Aaron had been volunteering on the build, so we asked if he'd like regular work as the stage manager. His main job was to wrangle the performers and make sure the show went up on time, rather than calling cues, given that the performers were well trained in doing this themselves from the soundtrack. With *Faust*, the technical elements of the show were run in a fairly simple and crude manner due to budget limitations. We had five or six sound zones without a central source. To ensure they were synchronised we had to station people, performers or technical support, to press play on CD-players on different floors of the building at the same time. Aaron was able to coordinate this via radio mics – once he'd convinced members of the team to help him.

For *The Masque of the Red Death* there was a little more resource. Euan Maybank pushed for a centralised control point for most of the sound zones, so starting the show was a bit more straightforward. It also allowed for lighting cues to be automatically triggered from the audio timeline, which enabled a greater number of locations in the building to shift through different lighting states during the loops. Up until this point, we mainly had static states across the building

because lighting had to be manually operated. Along with the show evolving technically for *Masque*, the set design also made a big leap forward, which included a lot of detail and performer props. Many of these props needed replenishing on a daily basis so stage managers, Aaron and Georgina Bottomley, would work tirelessly during the day to ensure everything was reset before the performance. The set would have maintenance on a weekly basis by Livi Vaughan and Bea Minns, which managed to keep at bay the impact of the stealing and general wear-and-tear on the set. Everything was reliant on core team members as the knowledge about what needed to be done each day was in their heads because we hadn't mastered how to notate the show nor had time and resource to dedicate to documenting process.

The unconventional nature of the work and the lack of paperwork made us slightly nervous about working with traditional stage managers; an apprehension that was completely overcome when we started planning *Sleep No More* with ART. In early conversations, Chris De Camillis, ART's Artistic Coordinator and resident stage manager, would continually ask to see our scripts, preset lists and information on team structure. Despite devising a framework for documenting and cueing the master loop during *The Masque of the Red Death*, the lack of resource meant that we hadn't spent energy reinforcing it. Chris identified a recent stage management graduate, Carrie Boyd, whom he thought would be perfect to work with us. I spent time with Carrie prior to rehearsals on site, explaining the intricate nature of the work and how it would evolve in situ. I stressed the need for a reactionary, as opposed to 'controlling', approach, akin to event management, during the performances. Carrie willingly used her knowledge and training to take the basic framework we provided

and populated these documents with detailed information and timings. She also assembled and trained a team of assistant stage managers and resetters.

With previous productions, the first few nights of the shows we were always a leap into the unknown for the team as it would be the first time we'd have a chance to understand what we had created once all the elements were put together. Sometimes there would be major revelations about scenes or performer loops clashing but as we have refined our creation process and ability to notate the content, there are fewer surprises now as many issues are resolved in rehearsal. However, we can never replicate the impact of the audience. Dress rehearsals with invited audiences and previews always throw up unexpected issues that we have to address creatively either through changes to performance, design or audience management.

stewards (see also: audience; **caretaking**; flow; masked shows; masks; **production management**; **stage management**; volunteers): The team of people who are in place as a silent presence to maintain audience safety, support technical areas and ensure the smooth flow of audience through the masked shows. Where, in very early productions, stewards were a combination of the Punchdrunk team who were stage managing across the building alongside volunteers who wore the white masks with an arm band to indicate their role, nowadays stewards are dressed entirely in black, distinguishable by black masks.

synchronicity (see also: **accidents**; Act 1; **awe and wonder**; 'company building'; crescendo; flow; lighting; pyrotechnics; soundscore): The term that defines the simultaneous occurrence of events which appear significantly related but have no discernible causal connection. Synchronicity relates to the coming together of all elements to create the organic whole of a Punchdrunk world.

In masked shows this incorporates, at a fundamental level, the elements of space, light, sound, installation and performers, working together as a holistic, malleable formation, each with its own distinct character, tempo, rhythm and palpable quality. As Felix Barrett puts it, the synchronicity of elements creates the 'magic' of the world when 'everything's working together, the audience might *feel* shifts in the balance, but they won't necessarily know what's changed'. For Barrett, in masked shows, light and sound are the supportive 'glue' in any combination of elements.

Synchronicity also refers to the manner in which Punchdrunk events are designed to enable an audience to undergo moments of intense experience. The crafting of a moment, for an individual or collective, is expertly shaped so that the audience arrives at the experience, as if by chance, as if it has *not* been crafted to be so. As Peter Higgin notes, with small- or large-scale projects for the audience the experience of synchronicity can be a mixture of the designed in the world and the coincidental in terms of the audience journey through it: 'being in the right place at the right time, when the stagecraft comes together'. The Miranda moment in *The Tempest*, 2001, the intervention of 'Hugo' on the roadside as the finale of *The Moon Slave*, the final crescendo of *Faust*, are all perfect illustration. For Barrett, the synchronicity of the crafted with the serendipitous is 'so key' to Punchdrunk's mission and practice: 'those moments where, in one beat, everything comes together and then separates'.

Synchronicity also relates to the manner in which the core creative team came together across Act 1, as much as how the early projects came about throughout this period.

T

taxidermy (see also: **Act 1**; Act 2; Act 3; design; dreams; **installation**; masked show; nature; police; *Sleep No More*, NYC; **visceral**; *Woyzeck*, **2000**): The art of cleaning, preserving, stuffing with specialist materials, and mounting the skins of animals and birds so that they appear lifelike. Taxidermy is a signature detail in masked show installations. It has been present from the first *Woyzeck*, a means to populate empty space with the suggestion of a living form. In this respect, the use of taxidermy resonates with the statues in *Firebird Ball*, the Virgin Mary statues in *Faust*, Mark Jenkin's sellotape effigies in *Tunnel 228*, the hanging bodies in *Malfi* or the straw congregation in *The Drowned Man*. Taxidermy also has an intrinsically *unheimlich* quality; always lifelike, seemingly animated yet no longer of this world. For *Sleep No More*, NYC, Felix Barrett with Beatrice Minns and Livi Vaughan bought the entire stock of a taxidermy menagerie that was closing down. As if referencing this key feature, a character named The Taxidermist resides in his shop 'Bargarran Taxidermy', ensconced in the world of The McKittrick Hotel. Taxidermy for Barrett, is not solely about the sinister quality of dead animals staring at the onlooker, but its effectiveness as an alternative 'performer':

Taxidermy is not inanimate, it's got the illusion of motion. So much of Act 1 was about filling the space with non-human performers via various means, taxidermy, statues, otherwise it would simply have been empty space.

Margaret Barrett recalls of *Woyzeck*, 2000, 'There was a stuffed dog in one of the rooms of the barracks. For some reason the police were called and I overheard them go into a room and, seeing this dead dog, gasp in horror, saying to each other "I don't want to be in here mate, let's go"'. Barrett expands, 'it was lying down, looking up at you as if it might attack you, really authentic. Coincidentally, taxidermy dogs on their haunches are now in *Sleep No More*, Shanghai'.

Taylor, Jennifer (see also: **Act 1**; Act 2; Act 3; Bicât, Tina; community; 'company building'; digital technology; doors; epic; failure; *Faust*; research; visceral; volunteers): Taylor first experienced Punchdrunk as an audience member at *The Firebird Ball* while a Physical Theatre student at St. Mary's College, London. She went on to volunteer on *Faust*, working with her then costume tutor, Tina Bicât. In 2008 Taylor became Punchdrunk's first employee, Administrative Assistant to Colin Marsh. She was quickly promoted to Company Administrator and then General Manager, before eventually leaving in 2017 after nearly a decade in the Punchdrunk family, having made a significant contribution to its history:

As a volunteer on *Faust*, I recall being awestruck by the incredible reveal upon entering the building. The grey exterior in a silent street hiding such a rich experience behind its doors. The attack on my senses as the show was being built remains vivid in my mind. From the repulsive remains of a pigeon-infested warehouse to the resplendent design that masked its cold, bare walls. I'll never forget the smell of that building. Sometimes I'm reminded of it and transported right back there for the briefest of moments. That's the power of a visceral memory, a moment never forgotten by your body.

I often find myself referring to the 'Punchdrunk magic' – a phrase that now rolls off the tongue, because it's true that there's something about Punchdrunk that is completely spellbinding. That magic comes from the strength and clarity of Felix's vision, and the imagination and investment of the team with which he works. There's something very special about Punchdrunk's artistic process; the space that is protected for play and true exploration; the space to experiment and the permission to fail; the open ears and doors to collaborators; and the breadth of research that informs the work. The process is epic and extraordinary, and

△
FIGURE 24 *The Tempest*. 2003. Old Seager Distillery, Deptford.

Poster archive, designed by Stephen Dobbie

that depth is reflected in the work. Looking ahead, the sky is the limit for Punchdrunk. It's constantly maturing, but that youthful energy and experimentation remains stronger than ever. It's growing in its strength and resilience to deliver work at an extraordinary scale. With the right partners, nothing is impossible. As digital technology continues to be rapidly evolving, so too is our understanding of what it is to experience storytelling, or to live and breathe a fictional adventure. Punchdrunk is shaping a new generation of storytellers, artists, cultural leaders, teachers, practitioners and policy-makers, and those seeds of magic are being sown not only in the cultural sector, but in educational settings, special care facilities, international travel, science and technology, dining and leisure, to name but a few. I for one can't wait to see those buds flowering, with unique forms.

Tempest, The (**2001**, see also: **Act 1**; **awe and wonder**; **darkness**; *House of Oedipus, The*; Maynard, Arne; mazes; *Midsummer Night's Dream, A*; **pyrotechnics**; **restraint**; reveal; ritual; synchronicity; *Tempest, The,* 2003): Punchdrunk was commissioned by the National Trust to bring a new audience to Buckland Abbey, Dartmoor, an historic property in the South-West of England. The company reimagined the building and its grounds as Prospero's island, sympathetic to the interior and exterior spaces of the site. Where *House of Oedipus* had proven that daylight destroyed a reveal, the use of external environments in this production was effective as they were under cover of darkness. Valuable lessons were also learned in relation to the ritualised nature of an understated gesture, matched by a precise detail of pyrotechnic spectacle, to establish the epic in the intimate, as set by one profound moment from this production:

A beat, where we were playing Debussy's *La Mer* and Miranda looks out of the window. We lit one firework in the distance to punctuate the crescendo. It only ever worked twice but for those moments it was magic. Poor old Pete was the person who was out there lighting the firework. It was a loose science in timing so chance if it hit precisely the right note.

(Barrett 2013)

This was the final masked show presented in Exeter. Landscape designer Arne Maynard who happened to experience the production, also by chance, describes his recollections of the event, from first entrance through the fabric maze to the magic of the experience overall. It resulted in Maynard commissioning *Midsummer Night's Dream,* which would become a pilot model for The Big Chill projects.

Tempest, The (**2003**; see also: abstract/abstraction; **Act 1**; Barrett, Margaret and Simon; *Chair*; **darkness**; **durational**; **gong**; installation; lighting; masks; mazes; **pedal note**; ritual; **touch-real**; visceral): Responding to the Old Seager Distillery, London, Felix Barrett and his collaborators reinvented the space as Prospero's Island. Individuals entered a vast antechamber devoid of natural light with suspended bags of dripping water hanging up (a technical effect later revived for *Kabeiroi*), candle glow beckoning towards the different floors of the world. As Barrett describes, this entrance was full 'of atmosphere but no visuals; a cavernous nothingness. You could only go up or down from there'. The installations above or below, divided by fabric hangings, sewn by Barrett and suspended from scaffolding, established the assorted dwellings of each character across the space and employed artefacts scavenged from Barrett's family home. The minimalist aesthetic, lit only by domestic sources and smart candles, necessitated by the limited access to props, established 'a purity of design', in the enormous environment, evoking an abstracted dreamlike world. A job-lot of antiquated books bought from a closing bookshop lined Prospero's shelves, while fresh pheasant and fish in Caliban's lair rotted over the duration of the run, the reek of which blended with the distillery's musty dampness and permeated the building. Having noticed with its predecessor at Buckland Abbey that the naturalistic delivery of Shakespeare's text was a problem, with this reworking Barrett became acutely aware that the incorporation of speech was anticlimactic and had to be resolved. Where the historical embrace of Buckland Abbey had been sympathetic to Shakespeare's speeches, in the echoes of this cold, cavernous distillery they were entirely at odds with the space.

Building on the potency of the Miranda moment at the window in Buckland Abbey, steps toward remedying performing style versus site were put in place, with erstwhile collaborator, Joel Scott, assisting with movement direction for a solo sequence for Miranda, played by Boo Pearce. Barrett noticed how the magnitude of each gesture 'matched the space', while the movement quality met the threat created by darkness and flickering light:

It played with liquid time, not real time, it slowed the pace of everything. She was reading a bible, steadily ripping pages out, classic durational activity that now exists in every show. It was ritualised, stylised, far from realistic.

This abstracted movement proved entirely absorbing, bordering on hypnotic, and met the abstracted atmosphere generated by all other elements within the space. Furthermore, and in contrast, Prospero's Sprite danced around the perimeter of the building, flitting in and out of the shadows, appearing and vanishing at whim, duetting with the chiaroscuro light to influence the tempo of the space as much as play within the narrative. This was underscored by a lone gong pedal note, struck by Ariel, reinvented as an austere and taciturn butler played by Tom Mallerburn, who ushered in the swell of Debussy's *La Mer* as a looped crescendo in the cavernous space. Noting the impact of these performing styles, Barrett resolved to employ only a physicalised language from then on in order to match the experiential qualities established by space and installation, darkness and light. Punchdrunk's first London-wide review in *Time Out* identified the power of this work (pre an 'immersive' definition, notable too is its unfixed classification of form) and the fact that it was the performance language that, at times, fell short in contrast to the other experiential languages at work:

This isle is certainly full of noises. And of strange, white-masked apparitions moving uncertainly around its cells and stairwells. Ah, yes: that'll be the audience. Punchdrunk Theatrical Experiences unquestionably have ambition, and application. They have commandeered a disused warehouse overlooking Deptford Creek and spread across its five storeys this impressive promenade production/ art installation . . . edited down to a dozen or so key scenes, which play out in a series of intricate loops . . . while you are watching washed up Trinculo ply Caliban with wine on the first floor, Ferdinand is (most likely) fetching and carrying wood with Miranda upstairs . . . [T]he random factor can detract from – as well as add to – the magic, and some of the acting is a little underwhelming . . . but in the end the acting is almost beside the point. The play just can't compete with the beautiful lighting, soundscape and design. Theatre comes second to art.

(Gibbs 2003, 144)

Stephen Dobbie, who developed his collaborative relationship with Barrett by creating the flyer for the event and designing the bar area, recalls the unforgiving freezing atmosphere and the hard, concrete aesthetic of the building with its 'rancid stench of rotting meat' emanating from Caliban's lair. For Dobbie this harshness was matched by 'moments of intimacy', not only through the compartmentalised installations, but through the more stylised, hushed delivery of speech, 'in huge, epic spaces; Ferdinand and Miranda on

the bed in her room' drawing the audience towards them to hear, while the adrenalin was kept pulsing by 'a crazed Sprite running around' the room's perimeter. In the cavernous space, darkness denied sight of its edges, 'and all you could hear was the echoes of someone running around. That was enough to keep you on your toes'. Barrett embellishes, 'this is why darkness is so important. There was one lightbulb above a four-poster bed, in a giant room. Just the gloom, the threat, generated by that which you can't see'. Darkness, shadows, ritualised performances in flickering light, all working together, setting a style, enabling that sense of foreboding to become as vast as the space and the audience member's imagination.

tempo (see also: atmosphere; audience; building; dance; design; flow; lighting; music; soundscore): Any site chosen holds its own temporality which influences the feel and footfall of a journey through a Punchdrunk event. The stairs, enclosed rooms, corridors and expanses of a building set a tempo which sets the flow of a production. Audience directly impacts the tempo of the performance once it enters the site, conversely influenced itself by the crafting of all the elements of the world of the event. In terms of soundscore, tempo is often determined by music, while abstracted compositions drive the temporal feel of whole floors of a building. Tempo is a key factor in the choreographic score across the three-hour loop. The manner in which the space and installations are lit sets the tempo of the world, inviting the audience to dwell in the surroundings or move on quickly, influencing the experience and comprehension of that world.

text (see also: atmosphere; characters; Enrichment; **influences**; **lens**; **narrative**; **process**; **research**. Further reading: Fowles 1983; Hesse 1969; Thompson 1998): 'Text' is a shorthand for any written source that provides the critical and creative stimulus for large-scale masked shows, as identified in production entries. A written source always provides the backbone

and forms the narrative arc of a masked show and is the key stimulus from which the world is evolved. Chosen classic texts are usually interwoven with, and interpreted through, additional sources from film, art, music, as well as wider literary texts. Written sources originate the overriding theme and narrative and interwoven references offer sub-plots and themes. These references, explored in relation to the written text, may well be an influence on the world created *prior* to finding the written source text but they are developed as an intertextual experience only in relation to that written source. Where there is an equivalent non-literary source that becomes central to the narratives and themes of the world created, this is referred to as the 'lens' by the core team, through which the textual stimulus is refocused and interpreted. Punchdrunk's *Faust* was based on Johann Wolfgang von Goethe's eighteenth-century, two-part classic play, unpacked through a range of classical interpretations of that work, reinvented through the cinematic lens of David Lynch's *Twin Peaks: Fire Walk With Me*, further framed by Edward Hopper's artworks. Peter Higgin notes how, with masked shows:

Classic texts as the bedrock of the production help to root audiences in a narrative they might be familiar with already, which is important when in an unfamiliar environment and an unfamiliar form. These provide a secure and solid source and strong narrative base to return to for creative decisions.

For Felix Barrett, 'sources are critical because they're the anchor point, a safeguard for the audience. An event might be experientially challenging in its non-linear form so the source becomes a navigational tool', the baseline from which the space can be triangulated in order to 'pinpoint yourself on the map' of that world. Through that text, the audience is more likely not to 'be befuddled, but instead begin to solve the riddle of what the world is'. In this respect the source text might also be seen as a cryptograph that both enciphers then deciphers the puzzles and narratives of the Punchdrunk world. Barrett and Peter Higgin expand:

Pete: If you take a classic text like *Macbeth* or *The Tempest* then your audience is familiar with that text, that narrative. Arriving with that knowledge often means that the world can make more sense to the audience.

Felix: That's critical. We deliberately did that back in Act 1 because the form was so new. If people had knowledge of the source then they had a route in. With *Sleep No More*, Shanghai, we've interwoven Chinese sources so that the audience has that hook to pull them through the world. With future work that we're planning, testing new forms and formats, the company is going back to familiar texts to assist the audience's passage. Textual interpretations are always exciting for us and it also meets our manifesto of empowering the audience. How can you empower them if they don't know what's going on?

Pete: It would never preclude the audience piecing together their own story as they journey through their individual experiences of the world. The success of the work is that audiences are being given opportunities to experience classics reinvented, in unexpected contexts. Germanic *Faust* in 1950s Americana provides a contrast, the familiar becomes unfamiliar and invites a new reading of the work.

Felix: It's the sparks that fly between the friction of two seemingly opposing texts that create a Punchdrunk show.

Since Act 1, Barrett has been inspired by and returned to the same texts as stimulus, primarily because of the 'humanity at their core', instilling a desire in him to translate that same connection with the situations represented to an audience. Another crucial aspect of the textual choices that have inspired the large-scale events is that they are driven by:

A sense of 'the other', an inherent magic or ambiguity. If it's not overly there then we'll fuse it with a text that does have that, the uncanny, *unheimlich*, the sense that you can't quite put your finger on what's going on, a sense of disorientation, is implicit within the narratives.

In this respect, there is an intuitive connection with the way in which the classical, gothic and expressionistic tendency, in form and narrative, that is embedded in these sources expose and explore aspects of the human condition; connecting emotional and psychological states with the manner in which wider society impacts (for good or ill) on individual and collective experience.

All of the texts that Punchdrunk has adapted have been edited for practical reasons and to accentuate this essential otherworldliness. Recalling his production of *The Cherry Orchard*, Barrett notes:

[Anton] Chekhov's text is sparse and dreamy. We cut the text to stylise it further. It worked *because* the writing permitted it, in the same way that Georg Büchner's *Woyzeck* works because there's an innate poetry to it, an abstraction and economy within the writing.

In contrast, Barrett recalls how his first production of Shakespeare's *The Tempest* 'didn't work', because the inclusion of long passages of the text was 'too dense', resulting in the audience's experience of the speech requiring one's 'head to translate it for you'. It was a lesson that proved to Barrett that he needed to find a physical language to translate Shakespeare's more complex poetry and narratives and those epic themes. Recalling his adaptation of Chekhov's text, Barrett adds, 'we could do *The Cherry Orchard* again, employ speech in the same way, and the form would still work'.

For Barrett, a vital element in interpreting text to foreground the imaginative and subtextual landscapes that exist within them is:

the dream logic that's enabled when you aren't bound by the laws of the rational. Suddenly, when you have something that you can't articulate, you can shift, you can turn on a pinhead, things can evolve and make no sense, you can open a door and be transported to a completely different world.

All of which establishes its own, strange logic. Barrett posits, to come from a perspective of 'rationalising' sources, through design, soundscore, and performing style, denies any sense of 'magic', makes it 'functional' and 'predictable' which is the antithesis of the Punchdrunk approach: 'we're trying to do the opposite, make the world as unpredictable as possible, where you don't know what you're going to get in each new space. It's about us being unreliable with the source'.

With the express intention of deliberately undercutting the sensation of security and coherence, of knowing exactly where you are with the text, the rigour applied in avoiding the predictable is a mainstay of the Punchdrunk's rules-set for interpreting a textual source. This includes *breaking* the rules to undercut any sure stability in that world, much as occurs in dreams. Barrett explains:

If we were to take a play like *Journey's End*, a play that's rooted in fact and history, it relies on the head leading, everything can be rationalised. But when you're dealing with a text that is beyond that, which speaks to a world that we don't quite understand, your head isn't able to solve it initially, so you have to trust your gut. It relies on instinct and returns to that fundamental building block of Punchdrunk; this is theatre to be experienced by our bodies before our minds. Better still, if it can be something that is considered a classic, so that as many as possible have a working knowledge of it, then that's what also provides the safety-net of the text, which we can then subvert to get to that instinctual essence.

Lyn Gardner, in her contribution above, echoes this sentiment identifying that, given Punchdrunk worlds are 'such a complicated experience for an audience . . . they need to know where they are' through the source. For Gardner *The Drowned Man* with the already fragmented *Woyzeck* and *The Day of the Locust* as the central sources, lacked the 'kernel of a great, classic story at its heart', which resulted in vast complexity of the piece being 'harder to get a handle on'. Barrett partially agrees:

I knew that myself, not to undermine the production because we created an amazingly detailed work, but I was aware we were cutting out that security of as many people as possible being able to grasp the source on their first visit. Only so many of those texts exists, where anyone – from eighteen to eighty – has a received knowledge and a shared vocabulary around that text.

Adam Curtis, above, acknowledges how received narratives create this security for an audience, but he suggests that a reliance on myths as a shared reference point means that it is a challenge for Punchdrunk to originate new stories, especially ones with a political dimension, as was the aim with *It Felt Like a Kiss*. For Barrett, experiments with forms other than the masked shows, such as *It Felt Like a Kiss* or *Tunnel 228*, benefit from a narrative and thematic source to connect the episodic and experiential structures at work, whether Curtis' film or *Metropolis*, as in these examples, in the same way that a classic text supports the world of a masked show:

Because we interpret so much content through installation, deconstruct our sources across a space, it needs to have a really strong

bedrock. That's why Punchdrunk, different to Enrichment, is wary about writing our own material. The truth is, it would feel too unstable, too top-heavy.

Higgin explains:

With Enrichment projects it's a key challenge, issue or question that provides that bedrock, to which every artistic decision returns. With *Against Captain's Orders* or *A Small Tale* we've written the text, made up that world. Where we do use a picture-book for primary literacy projects, we rarely tell that story, but use it as a springboard to create the world. It's important for us that, as pupils see a book come to life, they understand the potential and power of fiction.

Books chosen by Enrichment tend to be visually rich, with an aesthetic that is sympathetic to Punchdrunk's approach. A good example of this is Colin Thompson's *How to Live Forever*. Replete with intricate detail and labyrinthine puzzles to unlock in the illustrations, and an otherworldly poetry to the storytelling, this serves as design stimulus and central device in the narrative construction of *The Lost Lending Library*. Whatever the project, Punchdrunk's interpretation of text always intends to invite audiences into a world that interprets those sources anew, to experience a source from the inside, establishing an exploratory access to that source.

Beyond those texts chosen as the source and lynchpin for the world of Punchdrunk productions there are also two texts that remain inspirational to the philosophy as much as the form of Punchdrunk's practice. One is the novel by John Fowles, *The Magus*, set in Greece, with a narrative that blurs the lines between the 'real' and the imagined. Maze-like in structure and theme, it reads like a puzzle to be worked out for its characters and reader alike. It narrates the enigmatic events that permeate the life of one character, consuming him in a fiction and making

it difficult to work out where fantasy begins and reality ends. *The Magus* has been a reference for Barrett and Higgin since university, as has the second inspirational text, Hermann Hesse's *Steppenwolf*. For Higgin, *The Magus* 'reads like a Punchdrunk Travel show' whereas *Steppenwolf* 'offers insight to the psyche of Punchdrunk and a quality of experience to which the company strives'. *Steppenwolf*, with its focus on the senses and its use of visceral and hallucinatory images, is steeped in a dream-world aesthetic. Presented as the found records of Harry Haller, the book-within-a-book format provides a first-person narration of Haller's disturbing, self-revelatory and ultimately redemptive experiences subsequent to his entrance through a portal to another world:

I was amazed to see a small and pretty doorway with a Gothic arch in the middle of the wall, for I could not make up my mind whether this doorway had always been there or whether it had just been made . . . Probably I had seen it a hundred times and simply not noticed it . . . over the door I saw a stain showing up faintly on the grey-green of the wall, and over the stain bright letters dancing and then disappearing, returning and vanishing once more . . . at last I succeeded in catching several words on end. They were:

MAGIC THEATER

ENTRANCE NOT FOR
EVERYBODY
(Hesse 1969)

The *Steppenwolf* ideal influenced a series of Exeter installations Barrett and Higgin created post-graduation along a disused railway line with no particular audience in mind:

It felt like real-world interventions; it was less us doing a production in a building, more occupying a space, making it theatrical then leaving it before anyone caught us. Creating that plaque to be noticed, something that somehow you managed to miss previously.

For Barrett, the aim to tease curiosity, reward with discovery and inspire with a magical world on the other side of a portal continues to the present: '"magic theatre, not for everyone" that's key to what we're trying to do. *Steppenwolf* is the ultimate source; it houses the imagination'. Higgin expands:

Steppenwolf is perhaps the best example in literature of how we would, ideally, like an audience member to stumble across a show. Opening your eyes to the possibility of the world is particularly important to Enrichment work – opening up to the potential of magic, being curious. By noticing that door, everything else becomes heightened. Switching that on, re-lensing the world, taking them away from the humdrum so that they attend to the imagination. The important point about those Exeter installations is that it didn't matter if an audience didn't see it. It was slightly guerrilla and created as much for us as it was for an audience.

Or, as Barrett concludes, 'it was more about just knowing it was **there** and that there was always the possibility of someone discovering it by chance'.

Thomas, Jen (see also: **access**; Act 2; *Believe Your Eyes*; *Brixton Market*; **Enrichment**; producing: 'scalability'; *Silverpoint*; *Uncommercial Traveller, The*; ***Under the Eiderdown***. Further reading: Punchdrunk Enrichment 2012): Thomas joined the Enrichment team at Punchdrunk in 2009, as Enrichment Officer. She was promoted to Enrichment Producer in 2012 and continued in the post until 2014, when she left to pursue freelance projects. Thomas was key to the development of important Enrichment projects, including *The Uncommercial Traveller*. She continues to collaborate with Punchdrunk as a freelance producer and has worked on various projects, including *Silverpoint* and *Believe Your Eyes*:

My first experience at the company was Punchdrunk Enrichment's pilot school project, *Under the Eiderdown*. I had just started as Enrichment Officer and so to get up to speed, I visited the project when it was already live in a school in Merton. Because no adults can visit the performance with the pupils, I entered in and experienced it on my own. I hadn't yet met Katy Balfour, who was playing Mrs Weevil, nor had I seen the space in advance. It was truly profound: I was captivated by the story that unfolded all around me. It was like being a child again, caught in a spell. It's something I held with me through all of the projects I worked on and tried to emulate for audiences to come. One of the first projects where I got my hands dirty in the creative development was a small experience created in the Brixton Market Village. We worked with a group of local teenagers to transform a shop unit into a standalone immersive experience, which told the story of an old collector. The space was designed by the young creatives who worked with our team to produce something whole, design and sound telling a perfect story for the audience to explore one by one. The audience were a mixture of people who knew about the experience and booked, and those who simply stumbled across this magical world in the middle of their shopping trip. It taught me a lot about how we can create meaningful experiences at different scale, how to inspire young creative thinkers, and how to wallpaper a ceiling without getting too covered in paste.

Since then, I've worked on Punchdrunk projects in tiny school rooms, listed buildings, bars, parks, libraries, abandoned carparks, shops, and rooftops. I've produced experiences that unfold across a whole city, through a building, in headphones, via a mobile app and in virtual reality. What makes Punchdrunk special is that the work isn't limited by space, or form. An experience isn't approached differently depending on whether the audience is five years old or fifty years old, whether they're sitting in their own house, or roaming the streets during the experience. What drives the creative process is simply the question 'what will make the experience unique, powerful, emotive, exciting?' To get to the answer takes an incredible collaboration between the diverse creative teams that build each experience. They meet that question with ideas, inspiration and innovation, and it's been a huge privilege to be part of that.

Tonkin, Geoff (see also: **Barrett, Felix**; Exeter Experiments; **Grant, Matthew**; **influences**): Head of Drama at Alleyn's School from 1988–2010, Tonkin was influential in Felix Barrett's early academic career. Sam Booth, also Alleyn's alumni, refers to Tonkin as 'beloved' by his students. It was Tonkin who advised Barrett to take up a place at Exeter University. Matthew Grant worked under Tonkin's leadership and recalls how 'he was an incredible sixth-form tutor. Pupils in his tutor group all knew how lucky they were to have him in charge of their university applications'. On his retirement Alleyn's School established the Tonkin Academic Drama Prize for high-achieving Year 13 students.

touch (see also: contact improvisation; **design**; exercises; experiential; installation; one-on-one; **senses**; **touch-real**; visceral): For Felix Barrett, 'touch is arguably the most pure and potent sense' in Punchdrunk worlds (Machon 2013a, 162). Touch is fundamental to the design, to the performance, to the experience of one-on-ones. Touch grounds experience in the visceral and so makes the dreams imagined plausible. Touch makes the world of each event sensually and physically real. Touch is vital to all Punchdrunk's work . . .

Maxine Doyle

On touch

. . . Touch
Skin
Muscle
Bone

Touch is a fundamental aspect of Punchdrunk's practice. It manifests itself in multiple strands of the work. As a primary source of communication in a rehearsal process between performers, touch is a way of developing trust and the commitment of an ensemble. It can open up the rehearsal studio as a place of risk. As dancers, actors, movers, performers we listen through the skin shifting between anatomy and psychology. In a rehearsal process we train ourselves to question the intention of touch – a light, soft touch can tickle and tease or it can ignite and irritate. Intention leads us to physical storytelling – an abstract gesture of touch suddenly becomes meaningful when driven with intention. It gives us a way to interpret and abstract a source – play, movie, art work.

Touch becomes a connective fabric of the choreographic language between body, bodies and site. The skills experienced in the studio which draw on a sophisticated relationship between the anatomy of touch – of skin, muscle and bone – translate to the way a dancer /performer / character moves in relation to the scenography – walls, chairs, a pool table, a floor covered in sand. We practise moving from light touch – skin – to deeper touch – muscle – through to bone and the architecture of the skeleton.

We translate the process of body to body, to body and site.

In a Punchdrunk show the set becomes your partner. We investigate the moving body in terms of its implicit architecture – edges, surfaces and ledges. We roll, slide, push and slip through doorways and forests, across beds and bar tops. Some of our spaces / rooms / installations are tactile playgrounds of fabric, feathers, earth and water.

We often invite the audience to enter into an intimate dialogue of touch. A character may offer a hand, meeting his audience at a place of skin. He or she may embrace the audience gradually moving through skin to muscle and then to the bones of the skeleton.

Try standing opposite a partner and very slowly, moment to moment going through the process of an embrace. Take your time to listen to the breath, heart beat and skin, then journey a little deeper to discover the thicker tissues of the muscle, gradually and ever so slowly meeting your partner at a place of bone. Try not to have an intention here. Just explore the anatomy of an embrace and pay attention to what you experience both physically and emotionally.

Take two / five / ten minutes to play this and try with very different music. Don't worry about what you look like.

Touch offers a shared language between performer and audience and obliterates the 'fourth' wall. In a performance context, touch can trigger an intense connection to our humanity and can be both nurturing and terrifying.

touch-real (see also: abstract/abstraction; audience; cinematic; **design**; immersive; **in-show-world**; **installation**; masked shows; **multiples**; **nature**; 'Norman the Eel'; Pluto; 'Rebecca the Bird'; research: 'Specials'; **touch**): The term used by Felix Barrett, Beatrice Minns and Livi Vaughan to describe the attention to detail in research and installation. Touch-real defines the attitude to realising a design concept and its subsequent impact, and effect on the audience. Installations are as close to 'real' as possible; offering authenticity in the sensual reality of rooms and contiguous spaces. Touch-real installations invite the audience to interact with the world and enjoy dwelling within the narratives that these intricate spaces are telling. Lyn Gardner, Tom Morris and Alex Poots each make reference, in their entries above, to the effectiveness of the touch-real installations, to Beatrice Minns and Livi Vaughan's skills, and to the way in which Punchdrunk prioritise detail in the design. This is clearly identifiable in Beatrice Minns' first job title on *The Masque of the Red Death*, 'Head of Detail'. As the worlds Punchdrunk create have grown in scale, the level of detail in installation has become ever more layered and intricate.

This commitment to touch-real settings and a forensic level of detail in each room has been present since the very early productions and in Barrett's aesthetic arguably since his den-building days when a child. Barrett's *Woyzeck* in 2000 made use of found objects in the army barracks that housed the project, adding opportune textures of authenticity, alongside borrowed taxidermy and piles of human hair collected from local barbers. Barrett illustrates further:

Those early designs involved real soil, real trees, real food. For *The Tempest*, 2003, Caliban's lair had real pheasant and fish, that rotted over the duration. It got infested and the performer [Adam Shipway] couldn't go in there without gagging. A bookshop was closing so we'd also bought all of the books with our tiny budget, and we went through

each spine trying to find books that were relevant to the various scenes. We knew that even if only one person got those references then it was worth it. Colin Nightingale got it. It illustrates that, when you have really little money, choose to spend it on crisp, pinpoint detail.

Nightingale adds, 'I was standing in Prospero's study and looking at the bookshelf when the exact name of the book was uttered by Prospero close by. It blew my mind'. The experiential accuracy established by the touch-real in the design co-exists perfectly with abstraction in Punchdrunk's dreamworlds. As Vaughan explains,

we'd rather spend money on building a real shed out of wood and leaving it lit but empty, with a single note pinned to its wall to give it weight, than having an obviously fake, vacuformed shed stuffed with loads of naturalistic detail, which would destroy its authenticity in close-up.

Vaughan continues, 'we'd board up a brick wall that is the actual exterior of the building we're in, in order to disorientate the audience, so that they don't realise where they are in the building' in order to 'support both the experience of the world and the narrative of that world'. Barrett adds, it is this blending of the touch-real and the abstracted that enables the 'audience to stay inside the dream world'. This fusion of the real, the possible, and the imaginative or impossible establishes an illogical-logic within the world.

The Drowned Man provided a useful experiment for the company in terms of exploring how, by setting the world in and on the borders of a movie studio, how the blurring of the stronger walls of the outside world could contrast to the less solid walls of the intentionally fake sets. This not only enabled this vast project to be more affordable, it also offered a twisted thematic logic to the world where everything and nothing was as it seemed, everything and everyone was a

potential fake; all was entirely manipulated and everything was a construct of a world within a world.

tracking shot (see also: **agency**; audience; **cinematic**; **close-up**; **long shot**; **journeying**; Reverse Dolly Zoom): Another example of how film terminology is employed by Punchdrunk when creating a project. In film discourse, a tracking shot is produced by the camera following the subject of the frame in a manner that the audience feels that they are travelling alongside, moving in advance, or above, or on a curve to said subject. The effect is created by the camera being mounted on a dolly track (the camera is on wheels, on rails) and pulled alongside the subject of the frame so the sensation created is one of constant motion. In a masked show, the audience become like a living camera, as if filming its own tracking shot, moving through floors, tracking the performers capturing how the sequence plays out. Moving through an enclosed space into an open space as the lighting cue triggers and the soundtrack soars can stimulate the effect of moving from close-up to long shot; audience members can feel that they are directing a cinematic world. By re-treading space and stories, refocusing the manner in which rooms or spaces are explored, audiences may feel that they are editing themes and narrative together from alternative viewpoints.

transportation and transformation (see also: **awe and wonder**; **cross-fade**; **dreams**; **epic**; legacy; lens; **portals**; **ritual**; site-sympathetic): Critical aims and outcomes within the creation of a Punchdrunk immersive world. Transportation describes the effect created by the use of portals and cross-fades, carrying the audience member figuratively into an imaginative world that is fully supported by the touch-real, highly inventive production design and performing style. In Enrichment work, the plausibility of the cross-fade is carefully constructed, ensuring the space of the imagined world sympathises with the space of the everyday; from a games designer's visit to test a game with pupils in class, unbeknownst to pupils inducting them to the world of *The Oracles*, to the subsequent reveal where Fallow Cross transforms from a digital display to a physical 'reality' is a moment of pure awe and wonder. Correspondingly, transformation relates on this level to the manner in which the imaginative world of the event can re-lens the audience member's experience. For wider Punchdrunk work, where set in the everyday world, it can have an exciting impact, elevating the everyday to an imaginative plane, as with *Kabeiroi*. In more profound contexts, transformation can also describe the impact on an audience member in response to the work that has deep and lasting positive effects. Enrichment evaluations record instances of such occurrences for individual pupils with interpersonal as much as academic skills. More broadly, as Elizabeth Booth, Sharon Lynch and Connie Oppong attest, this can relate to attainment in schools or day-to-day experiences with community groups.

Travelling Museum Society, The (**2013**, see also: Act 2; Enrichment; objects):

> *RULE NUMBER 1: Don't touch the objects.*

A team from the Travelling Museum Society arrive at St Mary's School tasked with creating an exhibition with the school. The theme is 'Female Explorers' and will be curated by two junior curators – but they are in hot water. A couple of recent blunders mean this is their last chance to impress their boss, Professor Coldheart. They must take heed not to break any of the society's archaic rules, especially 'Rule Number 1: Don't touch the objects'. While installing the exhibition late at night, the team discover something rather magical. A story of two ex-pupils, brave in their own ways, encourages the curators and the school to consider the importance of taking risks. In a grand finale, the school curate a series of experiential exhibitions in their classrooms that bring history to life. Co-written and

performed by Matthew Blake and Kathryn McGarr, Peter Higgin elaborates on this bespoke project:

> Enrichment's brief from the Headteacher was to create a project that made the pupils step outside of their comfort zone, take risks and learn to fail. Pupils were scared of getting things wrong and were therefore often unwilling to try them in the first place. The classes studied strong female explorers, such as Diane Fossie. As the project developed, pupils became aware that the museum, its staff and especially its junior curators went on a parallel journey with them, discovering the benefits of breaking the rules. *The Travelling Museum Society* was one of the few times where we've directly explored with pupils the benefits of presenting as much as investigating ideas in a more interactive and immersive way. One class recreated a Crimean war field hospital as a way of exploring the life of Florence Nightingale.

Tunnel 228 (**2008**; see also: Act 1; characters; collaboration; corridors; **durational**; **installation**; **tunnels**): A collaboration with The Old Vic, London in the abandoned tunnels beneath Waterloo Station. With a production deadline of six weeks, *Tunnel 228* was a defining project during Act 1 for Punchdrunk. It explored the interests of Felix Barrett and Colin Nightingale in particular, to create an event that fused the visual arts with performance installation, where the artworks were the lead 'characters' in the event. As Nightingale elaborates:

> *Tunnel 228* developed from a desire to curate an art exhibition, which had been an avenue that I thought could be explored ever since discovering the world Felix had created for *Chair*. The opportunity was made possible following *The Masque of the Red Death*. The Old Vic approached us about doing a project, but we didn't really want to create another masked show at that point.

Barrett continues, 'we deliberately didn't want to create a project with dancers and a gloriously designed, cinematic set'; instead the aim was 'to do something very different from what we were becoming known for'. Punchdrunk were given access to an empty tunnel complex, under Waterloo Station, across the road from those that are now home to The Vaults, Waterloo. Nightingale recalls of the location that it:

> had recently hosted Kans Festiva, set up by the street artist Banksy, which had inadvertently led to the creation of a legal graffiti area along the Leake Street tunnel. In response to this we proposed to create a durational performance art installation incorporating the work of a range of contemporary new and established visual artists along with street artists.

During initial visits to the site Nightingale and Barrett discovered a further set of abandoned interconnecting tunnels and arches that had been dormant for twenty years. The Old Vic successfully negotiated access with the owners of the tunnels, though as Nightingale notes, 'before we could inhabit the space they had to be cleared of asbestos'. Barrett embellishes, the space itself consisted of 'five different archways, 30,000 square feet, dripping damp, already hugely evocative, we didn't need or want to do anything to the space, no spatial transformation as we'd done with *Faust* and *Masque of the Red Death*. We wanted to play with reinventing the white cube style of art gallery and instead, put artworks in a place of atmosphere'. In terms of logistics Nightingale remembers:

> We had a tight window of time to fit in the project as we were committed to creating *It Felt Like a Kiss* in the summer. It meant that when we were finally given the green light we had less than two months to pull off the project which included bringing in a new power supply; we spent the first couple of weeks using head torches to navigate the space.

Barrett emphasises:

The curation of *Tunnel 228* was driven by Colin Nightingale from the contacts he'd created over the years. In the same way that he followed the spilt white paint line, that turned out to be Banksy street-art, or the bits of text to *Chair*, he discovered Slinkachu's miniature installations embedded in the real world. Colin appreciated the link between what they were doing and what we were doing. He got Vhils over from Portugal because he knew that it was the same attitude and ideology in the work; art created for an audience to stumble across in a public place, in the same way that an audience member might discover one of our shows. That's what Colin aimed to condense and curate with *Tunnel 228*.

Barrett acknowledges, Punchdrunk was able to collaborate with significant artists, 'because we were ballsy, with a great passion for contemporary art, plus the backing of The Old Vic helped'. Using Nightingale's contacts and knowledge of the street-art scene, Punchdrunk, with Hamish Jenkinson of The Old Vic, set about inviting contemporary artists who shared an affinity in approach, aesthetic and ideology, to loan or create pieces for the space. For Nightingale and Barrett, the driving force for the project was their composition of the artworks in response to space and to light in the space. Barrett recollects:

where Colin was quite happy for it to have no specific narrative shape, I felt it needed a coherent backbone. Fritz Lang's *Metropolis* has long been a fascination and became the reference for us for the pieces that were remounted or commissioned.

The artworks provided the setting, character, narrative and theme, with *Metropolis* as the starting point to bind the artists and their work together. The collaboration saw Nightingale and Barrett working on-site with commissioned artists building the world of the

event. Barrett describes how the setting suggested 'the workers beneath, the elite above, the forest they play in, a factory, a machine, a god. We curated it by finding works that fitted within that frame and commissioned new work where needed'. Nightingale elaborates:

After conversations with Maxine, developing the performance element of the project with Felix, the first artist that we started working with in the space was a Cambridge engineering graduate called Ben Tyers. We commissioned him to create a giant, Rube Goldberg contraption that would traverse the tunnels, representing 'The Heart Machine' from the movie.

Incorporating shelves of cascading books, giant cogs and a full-size railway track and cart that circumnavigated the space, echoing its underground surroundings, and referencing the workaday train station above, Tyers' machine provided, as Nightingale notes, 'a way to link many of the artworks together'. It led audiences 'to retrace their steps around the "gallery" and discover links between these items that at first might not have initially been obvious'. This included commissioned work from street artists such as, Vhils, who created a giant, imposing carved face at the far end of one of the tunnels, ceiling murals from Xenz & Busk, a wall of workers by French-born and London-based street artist, ATMA, plus hidden miniature installations by Slinkachu. Lightning & Kinglyface were invited to reimagine their existing paper forest idea on an epic scale, filling one half of a tunnel, and referencing the forest in Lang's film. Mark Jenkin was invited to contribute and made the trip from America to create his signature bodies, as Barrett elucidates:

We flooded part of the space and Jenkin, who made bodies out of sellotape, clothed them in hoodies and drowned them, so they were floating in the space. Those bodies implied the presence of performers.

These implied performers fuelled an interest for Barrett in how live performers might be integrated within the event:

Having got the artworks on board, we thought it would also be interesting to have some one-on-ones in the empty space. It was a return to the Exeter ideal of filling the void and delivering the unexpected. Some of the art was two-dimensional, painted onto walls or etched into surfaces, so we were exploring how we might make the experience of that three-dimensional.

Instead of the usual approach to one-on-ones, Barrett now reimagined the performers as part of the machine, adding a live scenographic quality to the space. In response to the two-dimensional artwork, performers would be set in motion walking up walls, pulling the audience's gaze along the two-dimensional vertical and up to the ceiling, bringing a three-dimensional perspective to the curation itself, as much as to the artworks. For Barrett every element was actively working differently, 'trying not to be' what Punchdrunk had become known for; that is, lavishly designed and choreographed masked events. Performers were cast for their willingness to work under durational constraints within the space. The actions they were given were deliberately durational and repetitive, deliberately devoid of narrative, composed as pure function, through which thematic connections with the film source could be interpreted. As Barrett puts it:

It was about the physical demands of that action, the endurance of the repetition. We wanted the performers to be viewed as a live art work more than a story. We were using them to question further how you reinvent the gallery experience, how you shift the manner in which a curated exhibition is received. It was a shifting of the relevance that a live performer has in a Punchdrunk world. In a masked show, if you come across a performer playing

FIGURE 25 *Tunnel 228.* 2009. Machine.

Photo credit: Stephen Dobbie

Macbeth, for example, he's holding the narrative and is a driving force in telling that story. You might feel that he's the zenith of that show and want to follow him.

In contrast, with *Tunnel 228*, the performers were characterless material, solely facilitating the audience experience of the machine. The machine itself 'was the epicentre of the show' and in this respect performers and visual art pieces were all servicing the experience of the machine, communicating the world of *Metropolis* as sensation, presence, without narrative or psychology, automated. Performers were purely cogs in the machine, an individual's repetitive movement being one cog in the machine and equivalent to the next, which may be an installation of books, set with its own action and function. Put together, whether artwork or performer, the effect was to create the equivalent of 'a Rube Goldberg machine on its hour-long loop', servicing the automated artwork created by Tyers. As Barrett illustrates:

One of the cogs was made up of books that fell over, domino style, another was a performer that walked up a wall and back down again. The performer was deliberately understated, pure function, durational material, so that in some instances a visual artwork had more presence than the performer. The performance overall was the kinetic energy flowing around the space that came from all of these different elements creating the machine. Where in a masked show the hour-long loop belongs to, and is driven by, the performers, in *Tunnel 228* it was a machine, a seemingly automated object, driving that loop.

In this way, the performers were deployed as human artwork, exposing the body as pure labour, directly tapping into the themes at the heart of Lang's *Metropolis*.

Performers were 'deliberately generic, costumed for androgyny, sex, gender, class, everything was stripped back so they were bodies doing actions, servicing the machine'.

As this suggests, much of the movement choreographed in the space came from installations and art pieces, rather than performers; the train that repeatedly looped around the space, the books installed to perform their domino function within the system to set off the next sequence. In this way it was the artworks that were choreographed, curated to pull focus. For Barrett, the performers became a background detail within the whole event with artworks 'cast' within, around and as the machine and so the lead characters: 'Janet Cardiff and George Bures Millers' *The Killing Machine* was remounted as a protagonist whereas the live performers were scenography supporting that artwork'. Nightingale embellishes, Cardiff and Bures Millers' *The Killing Machine* was a 'chilling sound and kinetic masterpiece' which tapped into the dystopian themes of the exhibition. He adds that additional existing artworks were selected were from established visual artists:

Paul Fryer, Alastair Mackie, Doug Foster, Hugo Wilson, Susanna Hertrich, Philip Cath and Khloe Sjogren, Olympia Scarry, Petroc Sesti and Luke Montgomery and Anthony Micallef, all spread throughout the underworld. Taxidermy pieces from Polly Morgan and Kate McGwire were displayed in the fading grandeur of the wealthy bourgeois quarters. The majority of the projects costs were covered by a generous donation from Bloomberg that allowed us to make 15,000 tickets available for free, all of which disappeared in a day when the project was announced.

When *Tunnel 228* launched it made page three of *The Evening Standard* and was generally well reviewed, acknowledging, as Barrett puts it, 'the glamour and mystery of it; the reinvention of the art show'. Lyn Gardner was one of those who grasped how *Tunnel 228* evidenced Punchdrunk's desire to experiment and push its own boundaries, fusing theatre and visual art. *The Guardian* was quick to create an online archive of images, following Gardner's review:

It's a sure sign that a company is firing on all cylinders creatively when it doesn't just keep repeating the same formula but tries something different . . . This wormhole experience is like stumbling into the strangest gallery in the world; it's a dark, underground place that is miles away from the white-walled, antiseptic experience of most galleries.

(2009)

The underground venue went on to become known as The Old Vic Tunnels until 2013 when it was taken over by the footwear company Vans, who now operate an indoor skate park in the tunnels, known as the House of Vans.

tunnels (see also: *Beneath the Streets I*; *Bunker, The*; **corridors**; *Crash of the Elysium, The*; found space; *House Where Winter Lives, The*; **mazes**; site; Space Invaders Agency; *Tunnel 228*; *Under the Eiderdown*; **Woyzeck, 2004**): Like corridors and mazes, tunnels are a recurring motif in Punchdrunk's work. Several Punchdrunk productions have been sited within tunnels, exploiting the dank and eerie underworlds they offer. *Tunnel 228* and *And Darkness Descended. . .*, set in underground locations, used networks of connected corridors to good effect. Punchdrunk designs employ tunnels, whether part of the site or manufactured by the design team from fabric, as entrances, portals and decompression chambers, serving as a simultaneous preparatory and disorientation technique, to take the audience away from the 'real world' and into the world of the event, as was the case with *Woyzeck*, 2004. Equally tunnels and corridors were employed within the storytelling and mission of *The Crash of the Elysium*. In Punchdrunk Enrichment projects, such as *Under the Eiderdown* or *The Lost Lending Library*, exiting the installation (the bric-a-brac shop and the library) occurs via a short tunnel whereas with *The House Where Winter Lives*, a short, woodland tunnel was travelled through as part of the story-telling, in the journey from 'Badgers' Burrows' to the forest.

U

Uncommercial Traveller, The (**2011**, see also: **Act 2**; **community**; **Enrichment**; journeying; **one-on-one**; Oshodi, Maria. Further reading: Machon 2013a, 214–228): Running concurrently with the more high-profile, Punchdrunk, BBC and MIF collaboration, *The Crash of the Elysium*, Enrichment teamed up with Arcola's 50+ theatre group, at that time Hackney neighbours, to create a unique theatrical experience in the heart of Dalston, London. Owen Calvert Lyons, then Arcola's Head of Participation, responded to Peter Higgin's request:

Enrichment wanted to create a piece of work that was born out of our home borough with an older generation. Research about the area led us to Charles Dickens, specifically his lesser-known collection of journalistic writing, *The Uncommercial Traveller*.

Dickens wandered through Victorian London, documenting life by capturing the city's everyday joys and tragedies in this socio-realist work. With Enrichment, Arcola's 50+ participants researched their local history, creating characters based around stories they discovered alongside those of Dickens' characters. A series of workshops developed the material into an audio experience that culminated in an intimate performance in a disused shop. Following the audio-journey, audience members arrived at a Dickensian 'Self-Supporting Cooking Depot', were led in and sat around a booth with a character, to take a cup of soup and experience a haunting tale. Lyn Gardner reviewed this project, affording it the same status as national, large-scale Punchdrunk shows:

The few minutes after a Punchdrunk show are often as thrilling as the piece itself, as the audience comes together again to share stories of what occurred and discover that they have all experienced different versions of the same show. So it proves in this latest piece . . . a little bit of a beautiful thing happening in east London . . . there is something about the way you can hear the murmur of other stories being told that helps to create a sense of a patchwork of 19th-century London life, conjuring a complete world where Miss Havisham-style brides are jilted, the ayahs of the British Raj abandoned, babies murdered, and William Blake whispers of immortality offer comfort to a man with a gnawing conscience.

(Gardner 2011)

Uncommercial Traveller: Living Cities, The (**2012–2014**, see also: **Act 2**; *Borough, The*; community; **digital technology**; **journeying**; *Uncommercial Traveller, The*): *A walk for the incurably curious* . . . Evolving the collaboration with Arcola and drawing further on Charles Dickens' non-fiction account of his wanderings around London, Enrichment with Arcola worked with participants globally to develop audio tours of their local area. Dickens documented life in a rapidly developing London and this project sought a twenty-first-century resonance around the world; celebrating communities and their relationship to the city in which they lived. The British Council brokered many of the relationships with local communities in Cape Town, Karachi, Melbourne, Penang, Portsmouth, Singapore and Valletta. Much of the learning in regard to audio-journeying that guides a walker, synchronising with geography and its local community while telling a story, went on to inform *The Borough* and *Kabeiroi*.

Under the Eiderdown (**2009**, see also: **Act 2**; **awe and wonder**; **Booth, Elizabeth**; doors; **Enrichment**; **legacy**; **Lynch, Sharon**; **Moonjuice**; **objects**. Further reading: Punchdrunk Enrichment 2012): *Enter the world of Weevil's Bric-a-Brac shop, a magical place where every object is straight out of a child's imagination, a place where every object tells a thousand stories* . . . Inspired by the book *Who Are You, Stripy Horse?*, *Under the Eiderdown* was a primary school project designed to develop children's speech, language and communication skills through engagement with a story in an extraordinary environment. It was the first project piloted in schools by Enrichment and has proven to be paradigmatic in approach, providing the template from which all future Enrichment projects were evolved. It was as a result of *Under the Eiderdown* that Enrichment first understood and acted on the aims, spirit and needs of the host organisation as the backbone of the event, making projects bespoke to a community, an organisation and its inherent audience, as much as to the needs of a building. It was instigated by a conversation between Peter Higgin and Elizabeth Booth that involved a shared thinking around how Punchdrunk could translate the effect of awe and wonder generated in the masked events into a primary school setting. Early on both Higgin and Booth agreed that it needed to be around a literary text, a storybook which becomes the vehicle for the project – a piece of literature that comes to life. Booth managed to galvanise the partner schools, known as the West B collaborative, which comprised Rathbone, Dalmain Primary, Holbeach Primary, Stillness Infant and Junior School, St William of York Primary. All decided to spend the money budgeted for Speaking and Listening curricula on an Enrichment Project. As this was a pilot the Enrichment team focused on specific year groups across the collective schools rather than on whole-school delivery. Higgin spent weeks working with literacy coordinators across the schools to identify the needs of the project, finally agreeing on *Who Are You, Stripy Horse?*. Matthew Blake and Katy Balfour collaborated as the original co-writers and performers who played 'The Weevils', the owners of the magical bric-a-brac shop that

△ FIGURE 26 *The Uncommercial Traveller*. 2011.

Photo credit: Marco Pineal

became the inspirational setting. This bric-a-brac environment celebrated the storytelling potential of objects while allowing for the limitations in space, time allocated to transformation of that space, and budget. The design team was led by Livi Vaughan, working alongside Dan Richards, who had worked on *The Masque of the Red Death* as a designer-maker-carpenter. The first installation formed the template that was then reinvented within assorted rooms in the many different schools that went on to host the project. The transformation of a small, often overlooked space, including storage cupboards in some locations, in each school created the Weevil's Bric-a-Brac shop. As Vaughan recalls, there was expedience regarding the setting:

You could make anything work in a bric-a-brac shop, we could use what we already had in the store. The key point is that we weren't dumbing down or changing the level of delivery. It was also challenging because of the limitations on time and money. Important Punchdrunk elements were involved in the design; not getting a full view of a room on entrance, instead access involving a winding journey; a magical device to get you into the space. We added the element of leaving the space via a different, unusual exit and a central setting that involved a number of different stories providing stimulus and inspiration to the children. We knew the children would want to speak about the experience in the playground at lunchtime, much like in the bar at a masked show, so we needed to make sure they wouldn't spoil it for each other by providing different stories. It was a twofold design process. As with large-scale work there was the building of the structure of the room, the bric-a-brac shop, but instead of layering in the narratives and psychologies of characters, this time we were layering in the ideas and stories that the children had provided related to objects they believed might be in there. I would be present at the preliminary workshop, silently sitting

in the corner logging everything they came up with that might be in the bric-a-brac shop; we found everything and put in the shop. It resulted in an intense two days of market-buying and making but it was incredible because the children genuinely saw their ideas come to life. They would be given extra time to go back into the shop after their first experience, could look around more and relish it.

Enrichment's evaluation report records how pupils embraced this event, which, in turn, inspired and ignited their imaginations. Following its first iteration in 2009, and its pilot run with the Lewisham collective, the project visited schools across London boroughs, reaching over 10,000 pupils and 600 teachers.

unheimlich (see also: abstract/abstraction; adrenalin; atmosphere; **design**; **dreams**; haze; installation; intervention; loops; multiples; soundscore; touch-real; visceral. Further reading: Freud 2003; Jentsch 1995): The German word for 'uncanny', the literal translation being 'unhomely'. In his 1906 essay, 'A Psychology of the Uncanny', Ernst Jentsch defined *unheimlich* as a thing that is 'novel' or unknown, so often first perceived as negative. Sigmund Freud repositioned the term in his 1919 essay '*Das Unheimliche*', arguing that *unheimlich* was in direct opposition to *heimlich* (meaning homely, familiar and additionally, secret, concealed or private). For Freud, 'unheimlich' moved beyond fear around the new or unknown to bring to the surface that which was hidden, repressed, or unnerving at a subconscious level (see Freud 2003, 121–159). Consequently, *unheimlich* describes a perceived object, image or experience, where something is seemingly familiar, yet alien at the same time, resulting in uneasiness, a sense of disquiet without quite being able to identify or reason this out. Where a situation feels uncomfortably strange yet strangely familiar, it can create threat or be pleasurably exhilarating. Dreams, doubles and perceived repetitions

which feel familiar and yet unusual, like déjà vu, are full of the *unheimlich*.

This sensation permeates the atmosphere of Punchdrunk's work. It is set in the design of the masked shows through installations that play with repetition and abstraction, heightened by the soundscore and accentuated by the loops and performance languages from which the performance is built. Equally, Punchdrunk's project set in real-world environments and contexts play with defamiliarising the familiar, employ interventions which set an audience on edge, causing everything to be framed as unusual in the imagined world; cleverly layering the ordinary so that it falls out of the ordinary. This establishes an alternative logic within the world, which invites the audience to experience and interpret its sources afresh, via lateral and multisensory modes of perception.

Up, Up and Away (2012–2013, see also: **Act 2**; **Booth, Elizabeth**; **Enrichment**; **legacy**): *Up, Up and Away* brought to life the tale of Marianne Montgolfier, Vincent Lunardi and Bernard Blanchard. As balloonists they travel the world, letting the wind carry them from place to place, collecting, gathering and telling stories. Eager to spread and find the art of story-telling, they decide they can only visit places that they know will provide them with brilliant new tales. *Up, Up and Away* was originally created for Dalmain Primary School. Elizabeth Booth vividly recalls Dalmain Primary School's experience of the project:

I had a conversation with the Enrichment team and suggested a project based on balloons. Why? Because I've always felt there's something strangely magical about a balloon. I had one main idea at that time and it was that at the end of the project the whole school should release balloons full of stories into the atmosphere. The planning of the rest of the project I left to Punchdrunk and Dalmain staff. This resulted in the children arriving at school one morning to see a gigantic red balloon attached to the roof. During

△
FIGURE 27 *Under the Eiderdown*. 2009.

Photo credit: Daniel Richards

morning assembly questions were asked about it. One suggestion is offered, that it's someone's birthday – but nobody claims it. The staff room window looks onto the roof where the balloon rests, so two members of staff gesture animatedly to the children that they can see attached to the balloon is some sort of package. Then, timed to create maximum impact, while children line up after lunch, the premises officer appears carrying a ladder, climbs onto the roof. Children watch as he retrieves the balloon and shows the children the package tied to it.

I call an emergency assembly where the mystery package is opened. Revealed is a letter, presented on sepia-tinted paper with beautifully designed letter heading. It's from three story-balloonists, a history of their exploits, travelling across the world collecting stories. The children are sent away to research the history of balloonists. Imagine the excitement when nine children working in the computer suite find a YouTube clip from the story balloonists who are planning to visit Dalmain, within a fortnight, arriving by balloon in order to collect stories from the children. The balloonists arrive over the weekend and children enter a magical experience discovering what it's like to travel in the basket of the balloon, surrounded by the balloon itself; stories that inspire new stories. As the balloonists prepare to leave every child in the school takes out a fully blown-up balloon. Together they release the balloons into the atmosphere, some of which have memory sticks attached to them containing all the children's stories. As the balloons float away, we realise that we have taken on the mantle of story balloonist. We have made our mark in story ballooning history. Utterly magical, utterly memorable and transformative.

From Dalmain the project travelled to Holy Trinity Primary School and then to Land of Kids in May 2013.

V

Valet (see also: Abloy; Bow; journeying; **keyholders**; Zeiss): A Valet Key, historically, names the car key that would open the driver or passenger door and start the ignition yet would prevent a Valet from gaining access to the trunk of the car or its glove box, where valuables may be stored. 'Valet' here means one who holds the key to journeying and knows of valuable secrets and potential rewards to be discovered behind hidden doors. Punchdrunk is extremely grateful for the support of all its Valet keyholders.

vanishing (see also: awe and wonder; deception; *Masque of the Red Death, The*; Zeus): Conjuring tricks were used in *The Masque of the Red Death* and played a significant role in the climax and finale of its crescendo in the ballroom. Kath Duggan, who began as a performer on this production and has since gone on to become Creative Associate, recollects:

Learning how to vanish. I loved that. As a performer you're often required to be as present and visible as possible. Performing in *Masque* was the first time I needed to disappear from audience members. I loved discovering how to vanish and playing with a sliding scale of presence.

Vanishing is an effect employed illusorily in all of Punchdrunk's productions from the manner in which performers seem to disappear from sight along corridors when followed by audience members, to The Lost Lending Library, which magically appears in schools, only to eventually disappear when its work is done.

Vaughan, Livi (see also: **collaboration**; compromise; **design**; **Minns, Beatrice**; **volunteers**): Senior Designer at Punchdrunk, Vaughan is a longstanding member of the core creative team:

My first experience of Punchdrunk was volunteering on *The Firebird Ball* while still studying for my BA at Central St Martins. As I was full time at college I would go to Kennington in the evenings and work through the night with the team, it was so exciting to be allowed the opportunity to create freely. I was grateful that the team were so trusting and allowed me and my friend, Alicia Farrow, to design a whole room ourselves. There was such energy in the building, a feeling of expression and collaboration that I was totally drawn to.

The Masque of the Red Death was my first time working with Bea, and the beginning of our long and important collaboration. Our roles were Head of Dressing (me) and Head of Detail (Bea) and we realised quickly how important collaboration and communication were within the work and team, it formed the basis of our working practice.

I'm inspired by the creation of worlds in art. I have influences from all over the place; Robert Lepage's *Far Side of the Moon*, storytelling with objects in an abstract space; Gregory Crewdson's photographs create set scenes that feel familiar, yet something is slightly off-kilter so they become otherworldly, dangerous; Charles Matton's boxes, tiny worlds where you're focusing the audience's viewpoint, and at the same time revealing secrets to them.

Punchdrunk places equal weight on all aspects of production. This allows us all to tell stories through our own mediums. We're creating worlds in which audiences can get lost, crafting that world to our highest ability, without compromising on the intention, even if we have to compromise on the budget!

Vescovo & Co (**2014**; see also: Act 2; Seguro, Joana): A fictional medical research company and project title created for a one-off, secret gig project with XL Recordings and Jack White, musician and former member of The White Stripes, with space provided by Joana Seguro and The Vinyl Factory. Taking inspiration from White's second solo album entitled *Lazaretto*, referring to the isolated islands used as quarantine stations for maritime travellers, 'Vescovo' named one of the first of these islands, found off the coast of Italy in the middle ages. Colin Nightingale elucidates:

The project came about after a series of conversations that I had with the team at XL Recordings in the years immediately preceding the opening of *Sleep No More*, NYC. We discovered that many of the team at this record label had seen a number of shows including *Masque*. There was a shared desire to work on a project together in the future which eventually resulted in their Managing Director, Ben Beardsworth, contacting me about Jack White's forthcoming album. He thought the ideas behind the album might be interesting for us to play around with. On hearing the music for the first time, Felix and I were clear that its raw energy meant a live performance by Jack had to be at the heart of anything we would want to make. This led us to create a special one-off gig that took place on Wednesday 2 July 2014, three weeks after we posted a fake 1949 infomercial about the Vescovo & Co medical research company on a Jack White Fan forum. Curious fans then found themselves entering into a type of Alternative Reality Game in which they signed up for a free medical screening from the modern-day incarnation of Vescovo company. After a series of email, text and phone conversations, the lucky few were offered an appointment at an after-hours clinic which, following several individual medical tests, saw them ushered into a decontamination chamber before the sudden reveal of Jack and his band in a wash of blue light. The whole project was conceived and executed in about two months. The first time

we ever met Jack was about thirty minutes before the gig.

Joana Seguro notes that the experience that Punchdrunk created before the audience were rewarded with 'this high-profile artist really played on that excitement of the unknown, not knowing what you're getting at the end of it but being up for the adventure'. Two weeks after the event Punchdrunk received this email:

dear sirs,

sorry, it took me a while to be by myself enough
that i could write to you and thank you so much
for such an incredible creative work we did together.
your whole team were so incredible, and inspiring
and most impressively, interested in the small details
which made it so much more enthralling. i always
think it's the small parts that are most important
and can make or break an idea like you had. we
pulled it off, and even better, we did it without
rehearsing it! that's something to be proud of,
that's the way i love doing things and you seem
to be floating in the same sea. thank you kindly
for all the hard work, and please thank all
the actors and behind the scenes workers for me
that i didn't get to meet.
i hope we get to meet sometime and discuss, but if
we don't, that has a beauty to it as well!

jack white III

visceral (see also: **adrenalin; awe and wonder;** epic; **experiential;** ritual; senses; synchronicity; *unheimlich*. Further reading: Machon 2011): Visceral relates to the internal organs, and also names deep feelings and emotional reactions that are instinctive

and embodied rather than reasoned and cerebral (hence, 'gut instinct', wholly visceral). A visceral concept and aesthetic drives and describes a Punchdrunk world and the intention is that the audience member's experience and recall of an event is embodied and sensational; as Felix Barrett puts it, 'a series of flashes of memory, right-brain first, left-brain second'. Barrett here refers to the theory, based on neuroscientific research, that the left side of the human brain is literal, processes logical and mathematical thinking, dealing in linear sequencing and facts, while right-brain activity works laterally, related to intuition, imagination, feelings, responding to non-verbal forms. It is the fragments of sensual memory described by Barrett that are pieced together when recalling the overall experience and impact subsequent 'left-brain' analysis and interpretation of the event, its narratives and themes. Furthermore, affective memory can create its own logic from the lateral and sensual and understand the work on an embodied level without necessarily being able to explain this; the felt *is* the understood. It is this sensory human intelligence that Punchdrunk is keen to tap into, especially in regard to the triggering of theatricalised adrenalin. The instinctive response naturally synchronises with the visceral aesthetic and dream logic – blurring the lines between the real and the imaginary – of Punchdrunk's worlds.

volunteers (see also: access; Act 1; collaboration; community; masked shows; mass production; stewards): Punchdrunk was formed in a spirit of volunteering, of making the work happen through commitment, drive and passion for the idea and practice, with no one being paid. Where there were funds, these were minimal and spent on production costs. With the early large-scale London masked shows, *Sleep No More*, *The Firebird Ball* and *Faust*, volunteers provided a vital workforce, often made up of friends, friends of friends, interested individuals and fans of the previous show. As the professional structures for the company were put in place the approach to volunteering followed suit. Colin Nightingale recalls, 'we created volunteering opportunities among the arts community in NYC as *Sleep No More* was built to make sure this group was aware that the show was opening and those who wanted to be involved could be'. For *The Drowned Man* the profile and practice of the company shifted from a reliance on volunteers to deliver any project to a need to create waiting lists for those keen to have the experience of helping with the build or with stewarding. By this time Punchdrunk had systems in place to communicate early on in the process that any voluntary opportunities on offer could only be for a finite number of people, to observe and experience how large-scale immersive work was created, ensuring that it was understood as an opportunity for those individuals to learn. Speaking in the April before *The Drowned Man* opened, Griselda Yorke, Punchdrunk Executive Producer at the time, mused:

It's become very political the issue of volunteering. It's interesting, it's okay for people to volunteer on the Olympics, it's not okay for people . . . to volunteer on *You Me Bum Bum Train*. Volunteers are not there simply to paint so many walls black but there because they have a desire to experience how Punchdrunk makes things work.

(Yorke 2013)

Providing opportunities for volunteers is a practice that continues to this day, publicised by call-outs and word-of-mouth for Punchdrunk's large-scale masked shows. The educational internships and learning opportunities on offer are evolving and increasing with the success of Enrichment. Peter Higgin expands:

We recognise that the use of volunteers is rightly a contentious issue in the creative industries, with companies exploiting volunteers as unpaid labour in roles that should be a paid position. Alongside this, many can't afford

to volunteer, which means it denies a whole swathe of individuals the possibility of access to these opportunities. Punchdrunk's early use of volunteers was never intended to be exploitative, but was a means-to-an-end of getting work on in an environment where very few people were drawing down a wage. Punchdrunk would approach university courses and seek out undergraduates who were looking for design and making experience. I remember we found some really talented people through this process. We found the process enriching and core to our practice at the time, using large-scale worlds as a shared creative endeavour, open to all. We continue to offer similar volunteer places on projects and see this as a great way of opening up our practice. Although the public-facing nature of Punchdrunk's work is fiercely protected, it's always been possible to get involved in practice behind the scenes. That collaborative nature fed into much of my thinking around inclusivity and open access that led to Enrichment's work.

The opportunities Punchdrunk offered to certain volunteers across Act 1 in turn created opportunity for the company through the relationships developed. Notably, not least from the contributions to this encyclopaedia, across the years Punchdrunk has employed a number of key people as a consequence; Katy Balfour, Matthew Blake, Sam Booth, Kate Hargreaves, Kathryn McGarr, Beatrice Minns, Kate Rigby, Jennifer Taylor and Livi Vaughan all started out as volunteers, willingly taking on assorted roles and responsibilities. Laura McDermott volunteered as a steward on *The Firebird Ball*, and proved instrumental in Punchdrunk's history, commissioning projects for BAC when she joined its producing team. Volunteer networks were also vital in spreading the word about early projects, generating new and receptive audiences as much as producing like-minded collaborators.

W

wardrobes (see also: abstraction; **boxes, chests and drawers**; **characters**; **corner**; **costume**; **curiosity**; dens; **design**; **discovery**; **doors**; installation; masked shows; one-on-one; portals; senses. Further reading: Bachelard 1994, 74–89; Lewis 2009): Left open or there to be opened. Scents, clues, stories and psychologies dwell inside. A wardrobe was the portal to *Woyzeck*, 2004 while, in *The Drowned Man*, a labyrinth of heavy red velvet curtains and clothes in Mary Dove's The Seamstress Repairs Shop (est. 1959) led the curious audience member in a Narnia-like fashion around clue-filled corners to Temple Studios working wardrobe, and, for the chosen few who entered there **alone**, to an elusive one-on-one.

Woyzeck (**2000**; see also: **Act 1**; *Drowned Man, The*; Exeter Experiments; found space; **loops**; **mask**; **portals**; **ritual**; taxidermy; text; *Woyzeck*, 2004): Based on Georg Büchner's incomplete play, *Woyzeck* was Felix Barrett's final undergraduate project at Exeter University, for which he collaborated with fellow students, including Peter Higgin, who played the Captain, and Euan Maybank, who played the Drum Major. This directorial and design concept became the prototype for Punchdrunk's future shows involving the first use of masking the audience and the now classic loop construction for the staging, which emerged from editing the play to a twenty-minute version, which was then played on repeat for three hours. This edited version of what was an already deconstructed play, due to its unfinished form, blurred the boundaries between installation and theatre. Scenes were scattered across an abandoned army barracks in Exeter and the masked audience found their own paths through the story. Everything that has followed in Punchdrunk's history can be traced back to this point. In an interview in 2013, while *The Drowned Man* was in the 'space-hunting' stage, Barrett recalled:

Returning to *Woyzeck* again, I know the source inside out. It's so inherent within Punchdrunk's practice that actually it allows me to think about the other stuff; the audience experience and how we can start to push that. In the original *Woyzeck* there were performers delivering speeches from the text installed in separate spaces across the barracks, rather than bodies dancing. The text is so sumptuously succinct that that worked perfectly. The next *Woyzeck* will include speech. Originally it was so sparse, everything else involved was taken up with ritual, there's a lot of eating peas or shaving the captain, a lot of it is gestural anyway. There was no composed sound because we didn't have the budget for it, the sound was naturally created by performers. I was going around in a mask with firecrackers, lighting them on the floor to keep the audience on their toes and in a constant state of apprehension. I'd found a drum, so it became the drum major's motif, the crack of the snare would startle. We had The Ringmaster on the gate and a fairground outside, allowing audience members to go through individually, where they were ritually masked. The entering of the fairground ride, already an otherworldly event, marked the entering of Woyzeck's world. I knew it was my aesthetic. I remember at the time one of my peers telling me that she'd really enjoyed it and I saw in her eyes that it had done something to her and she urged me to do something like it again. At that point I was used to either teachers or friends saying keep up the good work, but this was an acquaintance. It was so raw, I knew I'd found my thing.

(2013)

Woyzeck (2004, see also: **Big Chill, The**; **'company building'**; **durational**; **forests**; **'Grandmother's Room'**; *Lost Persons*; *Midsummer Night's Dream, A*; one-on-one; tunnels; **wardrobes**; *Woyzeck*, **2000**): A reinvention of Felix Barrett's original undergraduate concept as an interactive adaptation of Georg Büchner's play for The Big Chill

Festival's Arts Trail, Eastnor Castle, Herefordshire. Staying true in content to Büchner's enigmatic tale of soldier Woyzeck, the play was deconstructed across the furthest reach of the field. The camouflaged world, fronted by an inexplicable wardrobe, lured curious audiences into a surreal maze of intrigue and sideshow thrills. The ensemble included first-time (now long-time) collaborator-performers, Katy Balfour and Kathryn McGarr. It was the point at which Kate Hargreaves discovered Punchdrunk's work and immediately, as she puts it, 'wanted in'. Peter Higgin recollects:

Core Punchdrunkers and a community of friends and artists convened to create *Woyzeck*, in commune-like conditions for a week. The lines between performer, designer, deviser and crew were beautifully blurred with everybody mucking in to make a shared vision come to life. We were left to our own devices in the far corner of the Art Zone. When word travelled about what we were doing we were quickly inundated with festival-goers, desperate to enter the wardrobe that led to Woyzeck's world. We performed across three days, five hours each night of the festival, immediately followed by a gruelling get-out and a long van journey back to London. It helped us all understand how to make and maintain a world, performing on repeat, being in character for hours on end. Improvising and thinking quickly on our feet was excellent training. Many collaborators from this project continue to work with Punchdrunk or in immersive practice. You had to love it to be there; we weren't being paid and it was hard work. There was no better way of galvanising a likeminded bunch of individuals.

In terms of the development of process and practice, a fundamental question for Barrett and Colin Nightingale was how long it would take for word-of-mouth to spread across the festival site; an ongoing preoccupation with ways

to entice an audience to be curious, and so find and adventure through an event, first tested by the two with *Lost Persons*. The festival environment enabled scrutiny of this on a much larger scale in an already out-of-the-ordinary environment. For Barrett, the experimentation partly worked because the Arts District of the festival meant that much of the audience 'was made up of individuals looking for playful, artistic experiences'. Nightingale elaborates:

We spent a big proportion of the production budget on camouflaging the exterior fence. Open from 10pm–3am, across the Friday night, around 200 people stumbled upon the wardrobe entrance. By the Sunday night there was a queue of about 300 people waiting to get in before we'd opened the doors. It reinforced a key ideal for Punchdrunk at that time; if you managed people's expectations by underplaying the event in publicity and then over-delivered on the experience, your audience would do the marketing of the project for you. This philosophy served Punchdrunk well during its growth across Act 1 and Act 2. Now the concept of immersive theatre has reached a mass audience it's harder to manage an audience's expectations purely through limiting information in advance, as many have preconceived ideas of what a project should be.

For Barrett this project tested several core mechanics for creating a world within a 'real-world' context: 'the budget spent on Herras Fencing and camouflaging' not only created a secrecy about the world but also protected 'the reveal'. It set a model for mechanisms by which audience members could be given currency within the world, affording them direct interaction and connecting them with each other, not by the wearing of a mask but, by the role they play within the world:

We picked the furthest point from the centre stage of the festival and put a wardrobe in the middle of

△ FIGURE 28 *Woyzeck*. 2004. The Big Chill.

Photo credit: Euan Maybank

the space with a candle by it. If you happened to stumble across this wardrobe, by candlelight, and were curious enough to open the door and go inside, you'd discover a twenty-metre tunnel. If you got down on your hands and knees and crawled through it, at the end you'd come out into this abstracted forest made of fence poles. Again, we'd spent half our time putting those up just so that there was a sense of discovery and disorientation on arrival, sensory bombardment. You arrive, are given six coins as a reward, and find yourself on the outskirts of the town. We'd built a military encampment, a hamlet in the fields in the distance, a fairground, all of which you were free to roam through. It was quite a long walk with the fairground twinkling yonder, so felt life-like in scale. You could use your coins to go to the fairground, visit stalls to earn tokens to go on the rides. Equally you had to be careful because there were performers playing vagabonds who might rob you. If you ran out of money, which is where the narrative kicked in, the only way you could earn it back was by doing jobs for the military or be tested on by The Doctor. You end up in the position of *Woyzeck*. You didn't need a mask because you were given a role, which gradually became apparent. Curiosity earned your way into the more exciting parts of the world, which meant going through the military experiences to do that. Or, you could remain a bystander, watching this all play out.

The currency, literal and figurative, thus enabled interaction and requital of the audience member's choosing. Barrett notes how the impact of much of this learning is only now being redeployed in forthcoming projects:

Woyzeck at The Big Chill really broke new ground. Of the body of work to be explored across Act 3, five or six are in that same vein, where audience members are contextualised by the community they're part of.

Y

Yellow Wallpaper, The (**2005**; see also: **Act 1**; Exeter Experiments; *Firebird Ball, The*; **'Grandmother's Room'**; **installation**; Jubb, David; McDermott, Laura; **one-on-one**; R&D; **site-sympathetic**): Laura McDermott, having stewarded at *The Firebird Ball* and while Junior Producer at BAC, drew David Jubb's attention to Punchdrunk. Conversations ensued, and *The Yellow Wallpaper* was created as Punchdrunk's first collaboration with BAC, commissioned for Octoberfest 2005. A ten-minute piece in total – from the first step of the stairs to the final exit and return downstairs to the bustle of BAC's cafe and lobby – conceived for a tiny, hidden space in the eaves of the building. Lone audience members ascended the creaking, wooden stairway to the attic, to encounter a nameless woman confined to her room. As an experimental project it reworked well-formed material, interweaving the disquieting storytelling and action of Felix Barrett's original Grandmother's one-on-one, from Georg Büchner's *Woyzeck*, with Charlotte Perkins Gilman's 1892 short story, *The Yellow Wallpaper*, in narrative and theme. Barrett reflects on the significance of this small-scale R&D piece:

It told Grandmother's story from *Woyzeck*, the definitive one-on-one. The directions for the performer are always the same; increasing proximity, increasing volume of touch, playing against the language, telling the story like it's a bedtime-story, the most beautiful tale in the world. It establishes a feeling of a loss of control for the audience, because the delivery doesn't equate with the language. It's a constant crescendo, its exponential, the performer's always moving closer, the grip is tightening, the closest they can get to you is their lips touching your ear, becoming quieter and quieter. It's raw, distilled Punchdrunk philosophy in three minutes. Pure crescendo, tactile, sensory, not making logical sense so it jars, audience member trying to catch

up with it. For this version all we did was put a bit more shape on the original one-on-one, rework a beginning and end to it.

The design of the space was inspired by the short story in response to the BAC attics. Matthew Blake who, as a Duty Manager at BAC at the time, had to lock the building on his own at night ('an already nerve-fraying experience'), illustrates the eeriness of the intimate installation. He recalls how Punchdrunk 'would occasionally leave the creepy, soundscore playing by mistake along with the strong smell of mothballs and the beady-eyed Victorian dolls sat on the clinical bed'. In terms of the performance, before entering this room, audience members, as they ascended the stairs to the lofts, were given a cup of tea, which they were asked to take to her. The audience member would enter and approach her, sat in her own world on the bed. With a subtle turn of her head, she became aware of you, and invited you to sit by her, as you hand her the cup of tea. The scene then played out as Barrett describes above. On completion of the tale, having reached the crescendo and withdrawn from you, drawn back to pulling at a piece of wallpaper by the bed which indicates that your time in her world is at its end. Barrett continues:

As you left, you exited through an installation of hundreds upon hundreds of discarded cups of tea, a realisation that this has been going on obsessively, like a mania, for a long time. The reveal was all in the cups; I'm not the only one who's left her here, alone.

As much as Perkins Gilman's *The Yellow Wallpaper* served as source material, the piece was also inspired by a childhood memory of Barrett's:

An old lady, whom I now realise must have had Alzheimer's, would appear on the street corner, approach you and say, 'Excuse me, can you help me? I think there's someone in my house'. I was too scared but if an adult came past, they would offer to help, take her back. There'd be no one in the house, they'd calm her down and she'd go back in. As I got older, she got worse and worse and more distressed, and when you'd accompany her back, you *would* find someone in the house; it was the people that she'd brought in who'd gone in to help before.

In terms of the learning for Punchdrunk this project was the first time, since Barrett's swimming-pool experiment created for Stephen Hodge, that a one-on-one had been created to exist by itself as a stand-alone piece of work, 'where someone might have left their house simply for a five-minute piece of theatre. That felt huge at the time'. *The Yellow Wallpaper* proved equally important for Matthew Blake, being his first experience of Punchdrunk's work.

Z

Zeiss (see also: Abloy; Bow; **keyholders**; Valet): Zeiss is an antiquated and uncommon form of lock and key combination, also known as a Cruciform keyway ('cruciform' meaning literally 'having the shape of a cross'). It is sometimes, although seldom nowadays, found on safes. Because of their rare usage, they have a mystique and magic about them. Zeiss is the name given to higher-level patrons of Punchdrunk. At time of writing, these are:

Shareen Chua • Alexander Claremont • Victoria Davison • Ben Fenby • Sandra Flatt • James Goolnik • Elizabeth and Reade Griffith • Paul Groombridge • Sarah Heenan • Nadia Higson • Craig Mawdsley • Marina Mello • Karen Myers • Jordon Nardino • Ari Omar • Rohani Omar • Chris Schleicher • Michael Sparkes • Simon Tesler • Chris Trevor • Melisa Tupou • Simon Tuttle

Zeus (see also: Act 1; Act 2; **Act 3**; **audience**; **awe and wonder**; *House of Oedipus, The*; soundscore; vanishing): The god of sky and thunder, king of the gods of Mount Olympus and chief deity in Greek mythology. In Sophocles' tragedy, *Oedipus at Colonus*, a thunderstorm sent by Zeus signals Oedipus' imminent death. As Zeus' storm crashes around him, Oedipus delivers his final speech to his daughters, Antigone and Ismene, and to Theseus, King of Athens. In this speech, his dying words, he reminds Theseus to keep his burial place a secret, so that Oedipus's presence there can serve as a powerful defence for Colonus and the city of Athens. Oedipus insists that, despite his blindness, he will find this secret place alone and it will remain a mystery to all others who seek it out. He leads Theseus, his daughters, and their attendants away as the Chorus chimes up amidst the ominous soundscore. The storm quiets and a messenger returns, to recount Oedipus' death; after his daughters mourned him and received his blessing, Oedipus told everyone but Theseus to leave. When Antigone and Ismene looked back, a final gesture of lamentation, Oedipus had vanished. Oedipus' story, with its omnipresent soundscore provided by Zeus, underscores the awe and wonder that is at the centre of Punchdrunk's mission. It is the source of a quotation that Felix Barrett first cited in the critical commentary to his final undergraduate projects and now acts as the portal to Punchdrunk's website. Barrett explains:

Audiences have to discover these moments, those beats of awe and wonder, for themselves. If we told them where they can be found, it would remove that feeling. The quote that we were inspired by in Act 1 that we come back to now in Act 3, having removed it in Act 2, appears as you first enter our website: 'These things are mysteries, not to be explained; but you will understand when you get there, alone'. It's from **Oedipus at Colonus**. If we were to spoon-feed, to tell the audience everything explicitly, the awe and wonder would be dilute. If it's left for individuals to work it out for themselves then the experience, potentially, becomes richer; the audience will *feel* it.

PUNCHDRUNK PERSONNEL

Felix Barrett Artistic Director

Tara Boland Associate Enrichment Director

Sarah Davies Head of Development

Rebecca Dawson Executive Director

Maxine Doyle Associate Director and Choreographer

Francesca Duncan Enrichment Assistant

Sarah Elghady Development Assistant

Judith Glynne Finance Manager

Peter Higgin Director of Enrichment and Punchdrunk Village

Anna Jones Administrator

Elin Moore Williams Enrichment Projects Manager

Rory O'Brien Production Assistant

Polly Pearson Senior Individual Giving Associate

Alex Rowse Enrichment Producer

Andrea Salazar Head of Production

JoJo Tyhurst Communications Manager

Punchdrunk International

Stephanie Allen Research and Development Projects Manager

Jessica Banting Designer

Felix Barrett Artistic Director

Gareth Collins Creative Partnerships Lab Producer

Stephen Dobbie Creative Director

Maxine Doyle Associate Director and Choreographer

Adam Driscoll Managing Director

Maïto Jobbé Duval Senior Designer (Maternity Cover)

Elgiva Field Associate Director

Judith Glynne Finance Manager

Ben Hosford Production Associate

Stephen Makin Producer

Punchdrunk personnel

Sandy McKay Creative Partnerships Lead

Andrew Morgan International General Manager, *Sleep No More*, Shanghai

Colin Nightingale Creative Producer

Charley Sargant Executive Assistant

JoJo Tyhurst Communications Manager

Livi Vaughan Senior Designer

Lucy Whitby Producer

Lauren van Zyl Finance Director

REFERENCES AND FURTHER READING

ABTT (Association of British Theatre Technicians). (2016) *Non-Conventional Theatre Spaces: A Guide to Providing Safe Performance Spaces and Venues.* London: ABTT.

Ahmed, Samira (Presenter). (2018) 'Immersive Theatre', *Front Row.* With Maureen Beattie, Sarah Hemming, Alexander Wright [online]. Thursday 15 March. Available at: www.bbc.co.uk/programmes/b09tyzt3/segments (Accessed March 2018).

Alston, A. (2017) *Beyond Immersive Theatre.* London: Palgrave Macmillan.

Alston, Adam and Welton, Martin (Eds). (2017) *Theatre in the Dark: Shadow, Gloom and Blackout in Contemporary Theatre.* London: Bloomsbury.

Artaud, Antonin. (1993) *The Theatre and Its Double.* Transl. Victor Corti. London: Calder and Boyars.

Bachelard, Gaston. (1994) *The Poetics of Space.* Transl. Maria Jolas. Foreword, John R. Stilgoe. Boston, MA: Beacon Press.

Banes, Sally and Lepecki, André (Eds). (2007) *The Senses in Performance.* London and New York: Routledge.

Barrett, Felix. (2000) Unpublished written documentation of Directing projects. University of Exeter Drama Department, Exeter. January.

Barrett, Felix. (2012) Unpublished interview with Josephine Machon. National Theatre Studios, London. 18 September.

Barrett, Felix. (2013) Unpublished interview with Josephine Machon. Young Vic, London. 5 February.

Barrett, Felix and Machon, Josephine. (2007) 'Felix Barrett in Conversation with Josephine Machon', *Body, Space and Technology Journal*, Vol. 7. Issue 1 [online]. Available at: http://people.brunel.ac.uk/bst/vol0701/home.html (Accessed June 2017).

Bending, Jim and McKay, Sandy. (2017) 'Punchdrunk: A Case Study – Exploring the Limits of Performance', *Medium* (Creative Economy Interview), 23 March [online]. Available at: https://medium.com/intersections-arts-and-digital-culture-in-the-uk/case-study-punchdrunk-a8eba629f3c7 (Accessed January 2018).

Bennett, Susan. (2003) *Theatre Audiences: A Theory of Production and Reception.* Second edition. London and New York: Routledge.

Bennett, Susan. (2012) *Theatre and Museums.* London and New York: Palgrave Macmillan.

Biggin, Rose. (2017) *Immersive Theatre and Audience Experience: Space, Game and Story in the Work of Punchdrunk.* London: Palgrave Macmillan.

Billington, Michael. (2009) 'It Felt Like a Kiss', *The Guardian.* 3 July [online]. Available at: www.theguardian.com/culture/2009/jul/03/manchester-international-festival (Accessed April 2018).

Bishop, Claire. (2010) *Installation Art.* London: Tate Publishing.

Boal, Augusto. (1996) *Games for Actors and Non-Actors.* Transl. Adrian Jackson. London and New York: Routledge.

Brooker, Charlie. (2009) 'The Untied States of America', *The Guardian.* 20 June [online]. Available at: www.theguardian.com/culture/2009/jun/20/it-felt-like-a-kiss (Accessed April 2018).

Büchner, Georg. (1979) *Woyzeck.* Transl. John Mackendrick. London: A and C Black Publishers.

Bulman, James C. (Ed.). (2017) *The Oxford Handbook of Shakespeare and Performance.* Oxford: Oxford University Press.

Butterworth, Jo. (2011) *Dance Studies: The Basics.* London: Routledge.

Calleja, Gordon. (2011) *In-Game: From Immersion to Incorporation.* London and Cambridge, MA: MIT Press.

Carlson, Marvin. (2012) 'Immersive Theatre and the Reception Process', *Forum Modernes Theater; Tübingen.* Vol. 27. Issue 1–2, pp. 17–25, 127.

Cavendish, Dominic. (2009) 'It Felt Like a Kiss in Manchester Review', *The Telegraph.* 6 July [online]. Available at: www.telegraph.co.uk/journalists/dominic-cavendish/5760122/It-Felt-Like-a-Kiss-in-Manchester-review.html (Accessed May 2018).

Cavendish, Dominic. (2011) 'How Poe and Persuasion Fought Off Death', *The Telegraph.* 12 January [online]. Available at: www.telegraph.co.uk/culture/theatre/3670434/Battersea-Arts-Centre-How-Poe-and-persuasion-fought-off-death.html (Accessed April 2018).

Chatzichristodoulou, Maria and Zerihan, Rachel (Eds). (2011) *Intimacy: Across Visceral and Virtual Performance.* Basingstoke and New York: Palgrave Macmillan.

Copeland, Roger. (2004) *Merce Cunningham: The Modernizing of Modern Dance.* London: Routledge.

Craig, Edward Gordon. (1913) *Towards A New Theatre.* London and Toronto: J. M. Dent and Sons.

Craig, Edward Gordon. (2008) *On the Art of Theatre.* Ed. and Intro. Franc Chamberlain. London and New York: Routledge.

Cremin, Teresa, Swann, Joan, Colvert, Angela and Oliver, Lucy. (2016) *Evaluation Report of Prospero's Island: An Immersive Approach to Literacy at Key Stage 3.* London: Hackney Learning Trust, Open University and Punchdrunk Enrichment.

Cunningham, Merce. (1985) *The Dancer and the Dance: In Conversation with Jacqueline Lesschaeve.* New York: Marion Boyars.

Curtis, Adam and Buxton, Adam. (2017) *The Adam Buxton Podcast: Episode 44.* 18 May. Available at: https://soundcloud.com/adam-buxton/podcast-ep44-adam-curtis (Accessed May 2018).

Di Benedetto, Stephen. (2011) *The Provocation of the Senses in Contemporary Theatre.* London and New York: Routledge.

Dickinson, Dan. (2011) 'Games of 2011: *Sleep No More*', *Dan Dickinson: The Primary Vivid Weblog*, 25 December [online]. Available at: http://vjarmy.com/archives/2011/12/games-of-2011-sleep-no-more.php (Accessed December 2017).

Dixon, Dan, Rogers, Jon and Egglestone, Paul. (2013) *Digital R&D Fund for the Arts: Between Worlds Report for Nesta On Mit/Punchdrunk Theatre Sleep No More Digital R&D Project.* Available at: www.researchgate.net/publication/256855723_Digital_RD_Fund_for_the_Arts_BETWEEN_WORLDS_REPORT_FOR_NESTA_

References and further reading

ON_MITPUNCHDRUNK_
THEATRE_SLEEP_NO_MORE_
DIGITAL_RD_PROJECT (Accessed
May 2018).

Dobbie, Stephen. (2013) Unpublished
interview with Josephine Machon.
London, 22 April.

Doyle, Maxine. (2013) Unpublished
interview with Josephine Machon. 9
April.

Doyle, Maxine and Machon, Josephine.
(2007) 'Maxine Doyle in Conversation
with Josephine Machon', *Body, Space
and Technology Journal*, Vol. 7. Issue
1 [online]. Available at: http://people.
brunel.ac.uk/bst/vol0701/home.html
(Accessed July 2017).

Flaherty, Jennifer. (2014) 'Dreamers
and Insomniacs: Audiences in Sleep
No More and The Night Circus',
Comparative Drama. Vol. 48. Issue
1/2, Spring, pp. 135–154, 187.

Foster, Phin. (2005) 'The Big Chill,
Eastnor Castle, Herefordshire', *FT.
com*, 9 August [online]. Available at:
www.ft.com/cms/s/0/34ca9d12-0872-
11da-97a6-00000e2511c8.html?ft_
site=falconanddesktop=true (Accessed
June 2017).

Fowles, John. (1983) *The Magus*. (Revised,
with a foreword by the author.)
London: Granada.

Frazer, James. (1950) *The Golden Bough: A
Study in Magic and Religion*. Abridged
edition. London: Macmillan and Co.

Freshwater, Helen. (2009) *Theatre and
Audience*. Basingstoke and New York:
Palgrave Macmillan.

Frieze, James (Ed.). (2017) *Reframing
Immersive Theatre*. London and New
York: Palgrave Macmillan.

Freud, Sigmund. (2003) *The Uncanny*.
Transl. David McLintock. Intro. Hugh
Haughton. London and New York:
Penguin.

Gardner, Lyn. (2003) '*Sleep No More*',
The Guardian, 17 December [online].
Available at: www.theguardian.com/
stage/2003/dec/17/theatre2 (Accessed
August 2017).

Gardner, Lyn. (2009) 'Tunnel 228', *The
Guardian*, 12 May. Available at: www.
theguardian.com/stage/2009/may/12/
theatre-review-tunnel-228 (Accessed
February 2018).

Gardner, Lyn. (2011) '*The Uncommercial
Traveller* – Review', *The Guardian*,
12 July [online]. Available at: www.
theguardian.com/stage/2011/jul/12/
uncommercial-traveller-review
(Accessed March 2018).

Gardner, Lyn. (2018a) 'Is Immersive
Theatre Growing Up or Growing Too
Big, Too Quickly?', *The Stage*, 11 April
[online]. Available at: www.thestage.
co.uk/features/2018/immersive-theatre-
growing-growing-big-quickly (Accessed
April 2018).

Gardner, Lyn. (2018b) 'Lyn Gardner: It's
Time to Discuss Protecting Performers
in Immersive Shows', *The Stage*, 5
March [online]. Available at: www.
thestage.co.uk/opinion/2018/lyn-
gardner-its-time-to-discuss-protecting-
performers-in-immersive-shows
(Accessed March 2018).

Gibbs, Jonathan. (2003) 'The Tempest',
Time Out London. 29 January to 5
February, p. 144.

Gorey, Edward. (1998) *The Gashlycrumb
Tinies*. London: Bloomsbury.

Hagan, Joe. (2003) 'Elephant in the Room:
White Stripes Hit New York', *Observer*,
24 February [online]. Available at:
http://observer.com/2003/02/elephant-
in-the-room-white-stripes-hit-new-york
(Accessed December 2017).

Haines, Gavin. (2017) 'First-Class Fun
or Aviation Disaster? Our Take on
Icelandair's In-Flight Theatre', *The
Telegraph*, 9 September [online].
Available at: www.telegraph.co.uk/
travel/news/first-class-fun-or-aviation-
disaster-icelandairs-in-flight-theatre
(Accessed December 2017).

Harris, Geraldine. (2017) 'Differences
in Degree or Kind? Ockham's
Razor's *Not Until We Are Lost* and
Punchdrunk's *The Drowned Man: A
Hollywood Fable*', *Reframing Immersive
Theatre: The Politics and Pragmatics
of Participatory Performance*, Frieze,
James (Ed.). London and New York:
Palgrave Macmillan, pp. 265–288.

Harrison, Connie. (2013) Unpublished
interview with Josephine Machon.
London, 9 April.

Harvie, Jen. (2013) *Fair Play: Art,
Performance and Neoliberalism*.
Basingstoke and New York: Palgrave
Macmillan.

Hayes, Kevon. J. (Ed.). (2007) *The
Cambridge Companion to Edgar Allan
Poe*. Cambridge: Cambridge University
Press.

Heathcote, Dorothy and Bolton, G.M.
(1995) *Drama for Learning: Dorothy
Heathcote's Mantle of the Expert
Approach to Education*. London:
Heinemann.

Heddon, Diedre, Iball, Helen and
Zerihan, Rachel. (2012) 'Come Closer:
Confessions of Intimate Spectators
in One to One Performance',
Contemporary Theatre Review. Vol. 22.
Issue 1, pp. 121–134.

Hesse, Hermann. (1969) *Steppenwolf*.
Transl. Basil Creighton. Update,
Joseph Mileck. New York: Bantam.

Higgin, Peter. (2012) 'Innovation in Arts
and Culture #4: Punchdrunk – Sleep
No More', *The Guardian*, Friday 25
May. Available at: www.theguardian.
com/culture-professionals-network/
culture-professionals-blog/2012/
may/25/punchdrunk-digital-
innovation-sleep-no-more (Accessed
March 2018).

Higgin, Peter. (2013) Unpublished
interview with Josephine Machon.
London, 11 April.

Higgin, Peter. (2017) *A Punchdrunk
Approach to Making Theatre*. British
Library Catalogue. 7 September
[online]. Available at: www.
bl.uk/20th-century-literature/articles/
a-punchdrunk-approach-to-making-
theatre#authorBlock1 (Accessed
March 2018).

Innes, Christopher. (2004) *Edward Gordon
Craig: A Vision of Theatre*. Second
edition. London and New York:
Routledge.

Jentsch, Ernst. (1995) 'Zur Psychologie
des Unheimlichen' ('The Psychology
of the Unheimlich'), trans. Roy
Sellars. *Angelaki*. Vol. 2. Issue 1,
pp. 179–196.

Joho, Jess. (2016) 'Are Videogames
Ruining *Sleep No More*?', *Kill Screen*,
29 August [online]. Available at:
https://killscreen.com/articles/
videogames-ruining-sleep-no (Accessed
December 2017).

Jubb, David and Tompkins, Stephen.
(2011) 'Presentation to Theatres
Trust Conference by Steve Tompkins
and David Jubb', *Battersea Arts
Centre Blog* [online]. Available at:
https://batterseaartscentreblog.
com/2011/06/06/presentation-to-
theatres-trust-conference-by-steve-
tompkins-and-david-jubb (Accessed
August 2017).

Katz, Helena. (1997) 'O Coreografo
como DJ [The Choreographer as
DJ]', *Lições de Dança 1 [Dance Lessons
1]*, Pereira, Roberto and Soter, Silvia
(Eds). Brazil: UniverCidade,
pp. 11–24.

Kaye, Nick. (2008) *Site-Specific Art*.
London and New York: Routledge.

Klich, Rosemary. (2016) 'Playing a
Punchdrunk Game: Immersive
Theatre and Videogaming', *Reframing
Immersive Theatre*, Frieze, James (Ed.).
London: Palgrave Macmillan.

Kloetzel, Melanie and Pavlik,
Caroline (Eds). (2009) *Site Dance:*

Choreographers and the Lure of Alternative Spaces. Gainesville, FL: University Press of Florida.

Kozusko, Matt et al. (Eds). (2013) 'Site, Space, and Intimacy: *Sleep No More*'s Immersive Intertext', *Borrowers and Lenders: The Journal of Shakespeare and Appropriation*. Christy Desmet and Sujata Iyengar. (General Eds.) 7(2) [online]. Available at: www.borrowers. uga.edu (Accessed May 2018).

LaFrance, Mary. (2013) 'The Disappearing Fourth Wall: Law, Ethics, and Experiential Theatre', *Scholarly Works*. Paper 772. Available at: http://scholars. law.unlv.edu/cgi/viewcontent.cgi?artic le=1794andcontext=facpub (Accessed April 2018).

Lecoq, Jacques. (2002) *The Moving Body (Le Corps Poétique) Teaching Creative Theatre*. London: Methuen.

Lewis, C.S. (2009) *The Lion, The Witch and the Wardrobe: The Chronicles of Narnia*. London: Harper Collins.

Lynch, David. (2007) *Catching the Big Fish: Meditation, Consciousness, and Creativity*. London and New York: Tarcher/Penguin.

Machon, Josephine. (2011) *(Syn)aesthetics Redefining Visceral Performance*. Basingstoke and New York: Palgrave Macmillan.

Machon, Josephine. (2013a) *Immersive Theatres: Intimacy and Immediacy in Contemporary Performance*. Basingstoke: Palgrave Macmillan.

Machon, Josephine. (2013b) 'Punchdrunk's *The Borough*: Stand Curious in a Dream and Hear Those Voices That Will Not Be Drowned', *Sixty-Sixth Aldeburgh Festival of Music and the Arts: 7–23 June 2013 Programme*. Aldeburgh: Aldeburgh Music.

Machon, Josephine. (2015) 'Punchdrunk', *British Theatre Companies: 1995–2014*, Tomlin, L. (Ed.). London and New York: Bloomsbury, pp. 255–282.

Machon, Josephine. (2016) 'Watching, Attending, *Sense*-Making: Spectatorship in Immersive Theatres', *Journal of Contemporary Drama in English*. Vol. 4. Issue 1, pp. 1–15.

Machon, Josephine. (2018) 'The Aesthetics of Immersion in Punchdrunk's *The Drowned Man: A Hollywood Fable*', *Live Cinema Cultures, Economics, Aesthetics*, Atkinson, Sarah and Kennedy, Helen W. (Eds). London: Bloomsbury.

Machon, Josephine and Thompson, Charlotte. (2014) *Punchdrunk Enrichment Preliminary Report*.

London: Middlesex University and Punchdrunk Enrichment.

Maples, Holly. (2016) 'The Erotic Voyeur: Sensorial Spectatorship in Punchdrunk's The Drowned Man', *Journal of Contemporary Drama in English*. Vol. 4. Issue 1, pp. 119–133.

Massey, Doreen. (2010) *For Space*. London: SAGE Publications.

Miles, Emma. (2015) *The Lost Lending Library: A Case Study of Punchdrunk Enrichment's Practice and Impact: A Creativeworks Researcher-in-Residence Report*. London: Creativeworks, Punchdrunk and Royal Holloway, University of London.

Mitchell, Jon P. and Bull, Michael (Eds). (2015) *Ritual, Performance and the Senses*. London: Bloomsbury.

Montagu, Ty. (2013) *True Story: How to Combine Story and Action to Transform Your Business*. Boston, MA: Harvard Business School Publishing.

Montola, Markus, Stenros, Jaako and Waern, Annika. (2009) *Pervasive Games: Theory and Design*. Burlington, MA: Morgan Kaufmann Game Design Books.

Morgenstern, Erin. (2012) *The Night Circus*. London: Vintage.

Nield, Sophie. (2006) 'There Is Another World: Space, Theatre and Global Anti-Capitalism', *Contemporary Theatre Review*. Vol. 16. Issue 1, pp. 51–61.

Nield, Sophie. (2008) 'The Rise of the Character Named Spectator', *Contemporary Theatre Review*. Vol. 18. Issue 4, pp. 531–544.

Oddey, Alison and White, Christine (Eds). (2006) *The Potentials of Spaces: The Theory and Practice of Scenography and Performance*. Bristol: Intellect.

Oddey, Alison and White, Christine (Eds). (2009) *Modes of Spectating*. Bristol: Intellect.

Opie, Iona and Tatum, Moira (Eds). (2009) *The Oxford Dictionary of Superstition*. Oxford: Oxford University Press.

Pain, Parry. (2014) *Stories in the Dark*. London: Black Heath Editions.

Pallant, Cheryl. (2006) *Contact Improvisation: An Introduction to a Vitalizing Dance Form*. Jefferson, NC: McFarland and Co.

Pallasmaa, Juhani. (2005) *The Eyes of the Skin: Architecture and the Senses*. Chichester: John Wiley and Sons Ltd.

Pearson, Mike. (2011) *Site-Specific Performance*. Basingstoke and New York: Palgrave Macmillan.

Pine, Joseph and Gilmore, James. (2011) *The Experience Economy: Updated Edition*. Boston, MA: Harvard Business Review Press.

Pitches, Jonathan and Popat, Sita (Eds). (2011) *Performance Perspectives: A Critical Introduction*. Basingstoke and New York: Palgrave Macmillan.

Poe, Edgar Allan. (1965) *The Complete Tales and Poems of Edgar Allan Poe*. London and New York: Penguin Books.

Punchdrunk and Abrams, Julian. (2015) *The Drowned Man: A Hollywood Fable*. London: Punchdrunk Theatrical Experiences Ltd.

Punchdrunk Enrichment. (2012) *Under the Eiderdown Evaluation Report 2009–2012*. London: Punchdrunk.

Reid, Josephine, Hull, Richard, Clayton, Ben, Porter, Gary and Stenton, Phil. (2010) 'Priming, Sense-Making and Help: Analysis of Player Behaviour in an Immersive Theatrical Experience', *Pervasive and Mobile Computing: Human Behavior in Ubiquitous Environments: Experience and Interaction Design*. Vol. 6. Issue 5, October, pp. 499–511.

Ridout, Nicholas. (2009) *Theatre and Ethics*. Basingstoke and New York: Palgrave Macmillan.

Ritter, Julia M. (2016) 'In the Body of the Beholder: Insider Dynamics and Extended Audiencing Transform Dance Spectatorship in *Sleep No More*', *Reframing Immersive Theatre*, Frieze, James (Ed.). London and New York: Palgrave Macmillan, pp. 43–62.

Schama, Simon (Writer, Presenter). (2018). 'Second Moment of Creation', *Civilisations*. Dir. Tim Neal. Series Producer Melanaie Fall. Nutopia and BBC. 1 March [online]. Available at: www.bbc.co.uk/iplayer/episode/ p05xxsmp/civilisations-series-1-1- second-moment-of-creation# (Accessed April 2018).

Schechner, Richard. (1994) *Environmental Theatre*. London and New York: Applause Theatre Book Publishers.

Schechner, Richard. (1995) *The Future of Ritual: Writings on Culture and Performance*. London and New York: Routledge.

Schulze, Daniel. (2017) *Authenticity in Contemporary Theatre and Performance: Make It Real*. London: Bloomsbury.

Sharp, Rob. (2008) 'Online Theatre: All the Web's a Stage', *The Independent*, 12 November [online]. Available at: www. independent.co.uk/life-style/gadgets-and- tech/features/online-theatre-all-the-websa-stage-1011927.html (Accessed March 2018).

Shepherd, Aaron and Zhang, Song Nan. (2016) *Lady White Snake: A Tale from Chinese Opera*. Bilingual edition. Union City, CA: Pan Asian Publications.

Slade, Hollie. (2014) 'Meet Emursive, the Company Behind *Sleep No More*, the Off-Broadway Production That's Been Sold Out for Three Years', *Forbes.com*, 19 March [online]. Available at: www.forbes.com/sites/hollieslade/2014/03/19/meet-emursive-the-company-behind-sleep-no-more-the-off-broadway-production-thats-been-sold-out-for-three-years/2/#1d80368a3573 (Accessed December 2017).

Solokis, Alexis. (2018) 'The Problem with Immersive Theatre: Why Actors Need Extra Protection from Sexual Assault', *The Guardian*. Monday 12 February [online]. Available at: www.theguardian.com/stage/2018/feb/12/immersive-theatre-punchdrunk-sleep-no-more?CMP=twt_a-stage_b-gdnstage (Accessed March 2018).

Thompson, Colin. (1998) *How to Live Forever*. London: Red Fox Books.

Tims, Charlie. (2016) *Doorways: A Review of Punchdrunk Enrichment Projects 2013–2016*. London: Punchdrunk Enrichment.

Tufnell, Miranda and Crickmay, Chris. (2001) *Body Space Image: Notes Towards Improvisation and Performance*. London: Dance Books.

Tufnell, Miranda and Crickmay, Chris. (2004) *A Widening Field: Journeys in Body and Imagination*. London: Dance Books.

Yorke, Griselda. (2013) Unpublished interview with Josephine Machon. London, 10 April.

Wake, Caroline. (2017) 'The Ambivalent Politics of One-to-One Performance', *Performance Paradigm*. Vol. 13. Available at: www.performanceparadigm.net/index.php/journal/issue/view/22 (Accessed May 2018).

Welton, Martin. (2011) *Feeling Theatre*. Basingstoke and New York: Palgrave Macmillan.

White, Gareth. (2009) 'Odd Anonymized Needs: Punchdrunk's Masked Spectator', *Modes of Spectating*, Oddey, Alison and White, Christine (Eds). Bristol: Intellect, pp. 219–229.

White, Gareth. (2013) *Audience Participation in Theatre: Aesthetics of the Invitation*. Basingstoke: Palgrave Macmillan.

Worthen, W.B. (2012) '"The Written Troubles of the Brain": *Sleep No More* and the Space of Character', *Theatre Journal*. Vol. 64. Issue 1, pp. 79–97.

Zerihan, Rachel et al. (2009) *Live Art Development Agency Study Room Guide on One to One Performance* [online]. London: Live Art Development Agency. Available at: www.thisisliveart.co.uk/resources/Study_Room/guides/Rachel_Zerihan.html (Accessed February 2018).

Useful and cited web references (alphabetised by first name or title)

Punchdrunk

Black Diamond: https://vimeo.com/86714034 and www.motherlondon.com/creative/post/60

Last Will: www.seeper.com/work/last-will

Lila: www.youtube.com/watch?v=8cfY46ZnDMk

The McKinnon Hotel: www.sleepnomore.cn/sleepnomore/index.htm

The McKittrick Hotel: https://mckittrickhotel.com

Punchdrunk and Punchdrunk International: www.punchdrunk.com

Temple Studios Virtual Tour: https://streetvisit.com/temple-studios-virtual-tour or http://tour.templestudioslondon.com

Vescovo and Co: http://vescovoandco.com and http://jackwhiteiii.com/the-truth-about-vescovo-a-message-from-nurse-hopper

Punchdrunk Enrichment

Against Captain's Orders: www.youtube.com/watch?v=YymSj_-PB3g

Enrichment Symposium: www.youtube.com/watch?v=GB8sx4N0Rjg

Lost Lending Library: www.youtube.com/watch?v=Tmehxk37fgs

The Oracles: www.youtube.com/watch?v=GWGPUCuIGd4

The Séance: www.youtube.com/watch?v=9SuJ-3XPjUE

The Uncommercial Traveller Projects with Arcola: www.arcolatheatre.com/projects/uct

Under the Eiderdown: www.youtube.com/watch?v=OJwbXCjOYKY

Individuals and individual works

Adam Curtis, *It Felt Like a Kiss*: www.bbc.co.uk/programmes/p003x62n

Adam Curtis, *The Power of Nightmares* (BBC, 2004), Part 1: www.youtube.com/watch?v=dTg4qnyUGxg; Part 2: www.youtube.com/watch?v=7QTaJ_ZVn-4; Part 3: www.youtube.com/watch?v=WD1BRE-DBsA

Alastair Mackie: www.alastairmackie.com

Antony Micallef: http://antonymicallef.com

Arne Maynard: www.arnemaynard.com

ATMA: www.atma-art.com

Banksy: www.banksy.co.uk

Beatie Wolfe: www.beatiewolfe.com

Ben Tyers: www.allvisualarts.org/artists/ben-tyers.aspx

Coney's *The Gold-bug*: http://coneyhq.org/2011/11/02/the-gold-bug

Dani Siciliano: www.dani-siciliano.com

Doug Foster: www.dougfoster.net

Geraldine Pilgrim: www.geraldinepilgrim.com

Helen Cole's *We See Fireworks*: http://weseefireworks.blogspot.co.uk

Hermann Nitsch: www.nitsch.org/index-en.html

Hugo Wilson: www.hugowilson.com

Janet Cardiff and George Bures Millers' *The Killing Machine*: www.cardiffmiller.com/artworks/inst/killing_machine.html

Joana Seguro: www.lumin.org

Jonny Woo: www.facebook.com/jonnywoopage

Josef Svoboda: www.svoboda-scenograf.cz

Journey to the End of the Night: http://ichaseyou.com/about

Julian Abrams Photography: www.julianabrams.co.uk

Junior (Ademola Junior Laniyan): www.juniorlaniyan.com

Kate McGwire: http://katemccgwire.com

Katie Melua: http://katiemelua.com

Last Will: www.seeper.com/work/last-will

Lightning and Kinglyface: www.lightningandkinglyface.co.uk

Luke Vibert: https://en.wikipedia.org/wiki/Luke_Vibert

Mark Jenkins: www.xmarkjenkinsx.com

Nic Green: www.artsadmin.co.uk/artists/nic-green

Olympia Scarry: http://olympiascarry.com

Paul Fryer: www.paulfryer.net

Petroc Sesti: www.petrocsesti.com

Philip Cath and Khloe Sjogren: http://mrandmrsphilipcath.com

Polly Morgan: http://pollymorgan.co.uk

Rob da Bank: www.facebook.com/robdabankworld

Robert Wilson: www.robertwilson.com

Robert Wilson's *KA MOUNTAIN*: www.robertwilson.com/ka-mountain-and-guardenia-terrace and https://vimeo.com/4608926

Robert Wilson and Hans Peter Kuhns' *H.G.*, produced by Artangel: www.artangel.org.uk/project/hg
Seaming To: http://seaming.co.uk
Semay Wu: https://semaywu.wordpress.com/about
Shingai Shoniwa: www.instagram.com/shingai
Slinkachu: https://slinkachu.com
Susanna Hertrich: www.susannahertrich.com
Susan Shaw, 'Virgin Mary Archive': www.susanshaw.net/faust
Thomas Heatherwick: www.heatherwick.com
Vhils: http://vhils.com
Will Adamsdale: www.willadamsdale.com
Xenz and Busk: http://ldngraffiti.co.uk/streetart/streetartists/Xenz/index.html and http://ldngraffiti.co.uk/graffiti/writers/Busk/index.html

Arts companies, organisations, historical sites and festivals

1927: www.19-27.co.uk
Aldeburgh Festival: https://snapemaltings.co.uk/season/aldeburgh-festival
Aldeburgh Festival Britten Centenary: www.brittenaldeburgh.co.uk
American Repertory Theater: https://americanrepertorytheater.org
Arcola: www.arcolatheatre.com
Arcola 50+: www.arcolatheatre.com/projects/50plus
Artangel: www.artangel.org.uk
Basement Jaxx: www.basementjaxx.com
Battersea Arts Centre: www.bac.org.uk
Bernie Grants Arts Centre: www.berniegrantcentre.co.uk
BigLop (A New Direction's 'Biggest Learning Opportunity on Earth'): www.anewdirection.org.uk/knowledge/case-studies/biggest-learning-opportunity-on-earth
Blind Summit: www.blindsummit.com
Buckland Abbey, Dartmoor: www.nationaltrust.org.uk/buckland-abbey
Coney: http://coneyhq.org
Creativity, Culture and Education: www.creativitycultureeducation.org
Emursive: https://mckittrickhotel.com
English National Opera: www.eno.org
English Touring Opera: http://englishtouringopera.org.uk
Extant: http://extant.org.uk
Extant's collaboration, *Flatland*: http://flatland.org.uk
Faster Than Sound: www.fasterthansound.com
Gideon Reeling: http://gideonreeling.co.uk
Goat and Monkey: www.goatandmonkey.co.uk
Hide&Seek: http://hideandseek.net / www.hideandseekfest.co.uk
Hijinx Academy: www.hijinx.org.uk/the-academy
Hijinx Theatre: www.hijinx.org.uk
Imperial Leisure: www.imperial-leisure.co.uk
Kneehigh: www.kneehigh.co.uk
LIFT: www.liftfestival.com/about-us
Lundahl & Seitl: www.lundahl-seitl.com
Magic Me: https://magicme.co.uk
Make Believe Arts: www.makebelievearts.co.uk
Manchester International Festival: http://mif.co.uk
National Theatre: www.nationaltheatre.org.uk
Nimble Fish: http://nimble-fish.co.uk
Old Vic Theatre: www.oldvictheatre.com
Paper Cinema: http://thepapercinema.com
Poltimore House, Devon: www.poltimore.org
Seeper: www.seeper.com
SMG Live: www.smg.cn
Spacemakers: www.spacemakers.info
The Correspondents: www.thecorrespondents.co.uk
Tin Horse: www.tinhorse.com
UpLIFTers: www.liftfestival.com/meet-the-uplifters
Vaults, Waterloo: www.thevaults.london
WildWorks: https://wildworks.biz
Wrights & Sites: www.mis-guide.com

Funding and research bodies

Arts Council England: http://artscouncil.org.uk
Bloomberg: www.bloomberg.org
Clore Fellowship: www.cloreleadership.org
Esmee Fairburn: www.esmeefairbairn.org.uk
Google Creative Lab: www.creativelab5.com
Jerwood Foundation: https://jerwood.org
HPLab: www.labs.hpe.com
MIT Media Lab: www.media.mit.edu/research/?filter=groups
MIT's Opera of the Future Group: www.media.mit.edu/groups/opera-of-the-future/overview
Nesta: www.nesta.org.uk
Paul Hamlyn Foundation: www.phf.org.uk

Other web sources

British Library Resources – Gothic: www.bl.uk/romantics-and-victorians/themes/the-gothic
Mantle of the Expert: www.mantleoftheexpert.com

INDEX

Entries in *italics* refer to figures. Emboldened page references denote entries in full in the main body of the encyclopaedia or where direct and detailed reference to the relevant person/topic exists within another related entry.

Index

Index

Index

Index